D1591391

CUSHING AT ZUNI

Cushing in Full Dress as Zuni War Chief. (*Century Illustrated Monthly Magazine* 24 (1882).)

Cushing at Zuni

The Correspondence and Journals of Frank Hamilton Cushing

1879–1884

Edited by Jesse Green

University of New Mexico Press
Albuquerque

Library of Congress Cataloging-in-Publication Data

Cushing, Frank Hamilton, 1857–1900.
Cushing at Zuni : the correspondence and journals of Frank Hamilton Cushing, 1879–1884 / edited and annotated by Jesse Green. — 1st ed.
p. cm.
Includes bibliographical references.
ISBN 0-8263-1172-5
1. Cushing, Frank Hamilton, 1857–1900—Correspondence. 2. Zuni Indians—Social life and customs. 3. Ethnologists—New Mexico—Zuni—Biography. 4. Zuni (N.M.)—Social life and customs.
I. Green, Jesse, 1928– . II. Title.
E99.Z9C88 1990
978.9′83—dc20
89–70751
CIP

First edition

Design by Milenda Nan Ok Lee

Contents

Preface and Acknowledgments

When Frank Hamilton Cushing set out on the venture that would make him the world's first live-in anthropologist, he was instructed by his supervisor in Washington to "write frequently." Fortunately, he did; and, better still, a great many of both his letters and those of his correspondents have survived, with the happy result that his four-and-a-half year stay among the Zuni Indians of New Mexico from September 1879 through late April 1884 stands not only as an important pioneer experience in anthropological field work but as one of the better documented of such experiences. In addition to this prolific correspondence, moreover, it turns out—contrary to the generally accepted view of Cushing as a poor record-keeper—that he kept a meticulous day-by-day journal. Hitherto buried from view and unsuspected of existing at all, six notebooks filled with daily entries from the Zuni period have recently come to light in the papers of a family member, along with forty-three other minute vestpocket diaries of later date—quite evidently a tiny, fortuitous sample from a two-decade collection, now mainly lost.[1]

In these diaries and in the letters he wrote to associates and friends Cushing recorded his activities, experiences, observations, thoughts, and discoveries—and also the needs, frustrations, and troubles—encountered in his experiment of living with the Zunis. Written as circumstances allowed, many of the letters and journal entries were produced in haste and under pressure. Never intended for publication, they are not polished compositions, but as such writings sometimes do (Malinowski's 1914–15 field diary being a famous case in point), they reveal aspects of character or situation which might not otherwise come to light. They also carry the sense of immediacy that comes of being close to the events described—at least if one is a natural storyteller, as Cushing was. The Zuni letters and journals, in short, are often of considerable interest not only as sources of biographical, historical, and ethnological information but also as literature—with the risk that implies, to be sure, of blurring conventional distinctions between fact and fiction.

Various other surviving letters and accounts written by, to, or about Cushing provide additional perspectives—as, for example, letters Cushing wrote as a spokesman for the Zunis, letters he received from figures in the locality, and reports by visitors to the pueblo such as fellow investigators John G. Bourke, Adolph Bandelier, and Herman ten Kate. Unfortunately, there are no writings by the Indians themselves, who, in the nature of the case, must speak only within the quotation marks provided by their white interlocutors or translators and thus are heard only as the latter understood them, or thought they understood them.[2] Granted this limitation, the papers that do exist, together with Cushing's published accounts of his "adventures in Zuni," comprise a rich and many-sided documentary history of what was involved in being a pioneer anthropologist in the Southwest in the 1880s—or at any rate what was involved in being *Cushing* as he pursued his unprecedented method of fieldwork in the particular pueblo of Zuni.

This book, then, is a collection of Cushing letters and diaries and a variety of other relevant papers dating from the period of his stay in Zuni, almost all of which are seeing publication for the first time. Along with letters actually mailed, a number of unmailed drafts of letters have been included as well, in cases where the mailed versions have not been found or where the draft contains material of interest that has been omitted from the final copy. The aim throughout is to convey, insofar as it may be through such documents, and with as much immediacy as possible, a sense of the day-to-day experience in its unfolding. Hence, with a few exceptions, the arrangement is chronological rather than generic or topical, diary entries being interspersed with letters and other dated materials in the order of their composition. So far as possible, the documents are left to speak for themselves. Apart from the general introduction and needed bits of background provided along the way, editorial comment is mainly confined to the interrogatory mode, leaving conclusions, if any, to be drawn by the reader.

It should also be understood that some of these century-old materials—many of them written rather lightly in pencil to begin with—present serious problems of legibility. Where these were insuperable, the gaps have been indicated by elision marks or connecting words inserted in brackets. Elision marks not contained in brackets indicate editorial selectivity, sometimes fairly severe in order to avoid redundancy or excessive diffusion. There are also problems both in translation and in the mere reproduction of words written in the Zuni owing to Cushing's sometimes uncertain command of the language and to changes in usage and in orthographic conventions as well as to the irregularities in Cushing's own renditions (sometimes he used italics, sometimes not; sometimes he divided between syllables and inserted hyphens, sometimes not). For the sake of clarity, my practice with respect to Cushing's text has been to italicize all Zuni words except the names of persons and places and, where the words are divided by him, to insert hyphens between syllables. Where appropriate, modern orthography and/or translation is given in parentheses. Modern usage is followed in the notes—or rather, modern usages, since consistency, while aimed at, has not been altogether achieved. In other respects, except for occasional minor adjustments of syntax or punctuation in the interest of clarity, the materials are printed as written.

Members of my family have sometimes accused me of lacking the good sense to ask for help when I need it. This book will prove them wrong. There is hardly a page in it that doesn't depend on somebody for something. To the Smithsonian Institution, the Southwest Museum in Los Angeles, the Huntington Library in San Marino, California, General Edwin V. Sutherland and the U.S. Military Academy Library at West Point, the Harvard University Library, the Wheelwright Museum of the American Indian in Santa Fe, the New Mexico State Archives, the Museum of New Mexico, the New York State Library, the Philadelphia Art Museum, the Thomas Gilcrease Institute of American History and Art, Tulsa, Oklahoma, the University of New Mexico Press, the Westerners' Los Angeles Corral, and Anne E. Smullen, I am grateful respectively for permission to print the letters, diaries, photographs and other items collected here. A list giving the source of each item included will be found at the end of the book. For assistance in tracking down these items and in the research involved in the project generally, I owe much to a host of librarians and archivists at the above repositories and others, including the National Archives—Denver Branch, the Library of Congress, the Heye Foundation Museum of the American Indian, the Newberry Library, the University of California's Bancroft Library, Northwestern University Library, the University of Pennsylvania Library, the Boston Public Library, the American Philosophical Society, the Nebraska State Historical Society, and the Massachusetts Historical Society. I am particularly indebted to James R. Glenn of the National Anthropological Archives, Daniela Moneta and Ruth M. Christensen of the Southwest Museum, William A. Deiss of the Smithsonian Institution Archives. Marie T. Capps of the U.S. Military Academy Library at West Point, Larry Jochims of the Kansas State Historical Society, Katherine Spencer Halpern and Susan McGreevy at the Wheelwright Museum, Lois Entrekin of the Lee-Whedon Memorial Library in Medina, New York, and Elizabeth de Veer of Northfield, Massachusetts, all of whom went to considerable lengths to accommodate when confronted by my repeated raids on their domains and/or mailed entreaties for burrowing on my behalf. For having saved her mother's little hoard of Cushing diaries and letters and for having made these hitherto unknown documents available for study and publication, Anne E. Smullen deserves not only my thanks but those of all other Cushing students as well. Then there were the needs resulting from the presumption of a middlewestern English teacher in taking on such a project as this book in the first place—an idea, incidentally, for which Fred Eggan may be held responsible. As will be seen, I have been entirely shameless in my ignorance, taking my questions to those, whether living or dead, who could speak to them and printing their responses more or less verbatim in the notes. Aside from publications on Zuni history and culture, I have drawn heavily on experts who were willing to write to me—repeatedly and painstakingly—and who are hereby acknowledged, to the degree of my exploitation of their respective letters, and with humble gratitude, as co-authors: Keith W. Kintigh, E. Richard Hart, T. J. Ferguson, Emory Sekaquaptewa, Jerrold E. Levy, Madeleine T. Rodack, Nancy J. Parezo, Richard B. Woodbury, Lea S. McChesney, Louis A. Hieb, Theodore R. Frisbie, and Triloki Nath Pandey. To the latter I owe special thanks for many additional kindly deeds, including the arranging of a several day joint visit to Zuni during which, through the erudition, ingenuity, and patient good nature of several of his friends, nearly all of Cushing's approximations in the Zuni language achieved, more or less, translation into English. Owing to these friends—chiefly Mrs. Vera Eustace, Mr. Wilfred Eriacho, Mr. and Mrs. Chester Mahooty, and Mr. and Mrs. Chester Gasper—I also now know from first-hand experience why it is that Zuni is famous for its warm and generous hospitality. For final editing of the translations and application of her linguistic wizardry to the last intractable puzzles (as well as for her good cheer in carrying through a much larger assignment than she had bargained for), I am very greatly indebted to Jane Young. I also owe thanks to John Smith of Chicago State University for assistance with the photographic work and to Brian Twardosz, Mark Wiljanen, and the Chicago State University Department of Geography respectively for drafting and for providing the facilities for drafting the maps. For a year-long fellowship providing time for work on this project and for a supporting grant for travel and research, I give thanks to the National Endowment for the Humanities and the American Philosophical Society, and for providing me with a sabbatical leave, I give thanks to Chicago State University. Finally, I am grateful to Loki Pandey, Peter D'A Jones, Jan Pinkerton, Nancy Green, Juliet Wilson, and Curtis M. Hinsley, Jr., for making their way through all or parts of a mountainous and rugged manuscript and doing their best to help straighten the path. The last named of these is really in a category by himself. Indeed, whatever intelligibility the book may have is due in no small measure to this friend, whose persistence in fingering weak spots and offering provocative suggestions seemed proof against any amount of abuse. I can't thank him enough. For whatever intelligibility or other good quality it lacks, I hasten to add, only I am accountable.

Introduction

Cushing at Zuni: Beginnings of American Anthropology

Throughout the period of westward expansion, the frontier army post served also as a hostel for travelers from the East, and in the spring of 1881 a fort near the western boundary of New Mexico was the scene of a memorable encounter recorded by a Boston journalist named Sylvester Baxter who was touring the Southwest in search of stories:

> At Fort Wingate, . . . sitting in the officers clubroom one warm afternoon, we saw a striking figure walking across the parade ground: a slender young man in a picturesque costume; a high-crowned and broad-brimmed felt hat above long blond hair and prominent features; face, figure, and general aspect looked as if he might have stepped out of the frame of a cavalier's portrait of the time of King Charles.[1]

Thus in Baxter's account, published in the June 1882 issue of *Harper's New Monthly Magazine,* complete with illustrations, readers across the nation were introduced to Frank Hamilton Cushing, young genius of the government Bureau of Ethnology, junior "chief" of the Zuni Indians, and author-to-be of most of the writing collected in this book. Having been sent out to study the pueblo dwellers of the Southwest, Cushing was making anthropological history as the first in his profession to pursue his investigations by actually living among the native people he hoped to understand. In an age that worshiped science and also thirsted for romance, Cushing was to become a legendary figure, the original "anthropologist as hero." His career epitomized that mythic American initiation into the wilderness of the West, a quest from which in this case the adventurer returned to civilization steeped not only in the wiles and wisdom of the "savages" but in the wealth of their ancient culture. Writer of a number of brilliantly idiosyncratic works on the Zunis and other anthropological subjects, a dazzling talker and personality, eccentric, controversial, and doubly famous, first as "the man who became an Indian" and then as the discoverer who unearthed the ruins of a series of ancient aboriginal American cities, he acquired the aura of a sort of combination Heinrich Schliemann and native shaman. Among his peers in the new science of anthropology, according to one contemporary admirer, he was like a "sun, . . . illuminating all of them [and setting] them on new trails."[2] Then abruptly in April 1900, three months short of his forty-third birthday, he died and was quickly put aside with the other relics of the nineteenth century, as anthropology moved on into the twentieth.

Largely ignored over the years, though not altogether forgotten as a colorful figure from the past, Cushing has been gradually reclaiming in the last few decades some of the attention he deserves as one of the founding fathers of modern anthropology—initiator of what is now known as participant observation, pioneer of ethnological and archaeological research in the American Southwest, and an original theorist whose ideas have influenced the practices and thinking of anthropologists on both sides of the Atlantic. Indeed, it was a Frenchman, Claude Levi-Strauss, who reminded his American colleagues of Cushing's importance, along with Lewis Henry Morgan, as "one of the great forerunners of social structure studies" and a source of inspiration to his own precursors in that tradition, Durkheim and Mauss.[3] Another recent study points out that it was Cushing too who originated the modern use of the term "culture" in the plural and the concept of cultural patterns made famous by Ruth Benedict.[4] Moreover, Cushing was a gifted writer whose engaging accounts of life among the Pueblos belong to the same genre as Parkman's *Oregon Trail* and Melville's *Typee.*[5]

From Washington to Zuni

How a twenty-two-year-old assistant curator in the National Museum got his start toward life as an Indian in the Southwest is told in the opening lines of the most autobiographical—and most popular—of Cushing's writings, "My Adventures in Zuni":

> One hot summer day in 1879, as I was sitting in my office in the ivy-mantled old South Tower of the Smithsonian Institution, a messenger boy tapped at my door, and said:
>
> "Professor Baird wishes to see you, sir."[6]
>
> The professor, picking up his umbrella and papers, came toward the door as I entered.

"Haven't I heard you say you would like to go to New Mexico to study the cliff-houses and Pueblo Indians?"

"Yes, sir."

"Would you still like to go?"

"Yes, sir."

"Very well then, be ready to accompany Colonel Stevenson's collecting party, as ethnologist, within four days. I want you to find out all you can about some typical tribe of Pueblo Indians. Make your own choice of field, and use your own methods; only, get the information. You will probably be gone three months. Write me frequently. I'm in a hurry this evening. Look to Major Powell, of the Bureau of Ethnology, if you want further directions. Good-day."[7]

We cannot be entirely certain that these few abrupt remarks were the only—or the exact—ones uttered by the Secretary of the Smithsonian in handing his young protégé the most important assignment of his life, but no matter. There is verisimilitude in this image of how some of the business of science was conducted in the Washington of Rutherford B. Hayes and in the peremptory assurance with which this particular Victorian scientist and bureaucrat set forth the task and the time he expected it to take. Three months should suffice for an intelligent young man to bring back the essential facts about a tribe of Indians.

In any event, for Cushing this was quite literally a dreamed-of opportunity,[8] and he lost no time in collecting a suitable outfit, including plenty of notebooks and sketchpads. In keeping with the occasion, he even fit in a session with a studio photographer. Among the prints left with his bride-to-be, Emily Magill, is one showing him in a poetic pose against a woodland backdrop, the picture of innocent youth decked out as a sort of gentleman Leatherstocking, complete with gaiters, belted hunting knife, reclining rifle, folded gloves, and pen and pad in hand. One senses in this photograph a cultural point of departure, faintly adumbrating the picturesque figure soon to be cut in real life (as well as portraits to come), but at the same time conveying, through its pale and Eastern manner, what a distance there was yet to be traversed.

The objective of the expedition to which Cushing was assigned was to tour the Pueblo settlements in the New Mexico and Arizona territories, gathering artifacts and information and making "as careful a study as circumstances [would] permit of the Pueblo ruins and caves in that district of country." In the march of national progress, what the Anglo Americans called civilization had by this time forced its way from coast to coast. Pockets of resistance remained (Geronimo's surrender and the massacre at Wounded Knee were still to come), but the "Indian frontier" had "virtually disappeared" according to an announcement the year before by the Secretary of the Interior,[9] and in the grand white empire of the West the systematic mapping and surveying of the land and its exploitable animal, vegetable, and mineral resources had been proceeding for two decades. The time had come when this great surveying enterprise was to be extended to what remained of the human societies whose dwelling place that land had been and whose cultural heritage, now that it was seemingly programmed for extinction, had become another kind of national treasure. To study, while it was still possible, "our North American Indians in their primitive conditions," to record their customs and oral traditions, and to salvage as much information and material evidence as possible relating to their cultural development, the Bureau of Ethnology had just been established as a branch of the Smithsonian Institution under the directorship of the premier Western surveyor of the day, Major John Wesley Powell.[10] Under its aegis in the years between 1879 and the end of the century (Powell died in 1902), American anthropology would take shape as an organized discipline.

The "collecting party," led by an old associate of Powell's in the U.S. Geological Survey, Col. James Stevenson, was the first expedition mounted by the new Bureau. Having visited a number of Pueblo communities a decade earlier in the course of his famous explorations of the Colorado River, Powell had been impressed by the degree to which these hitherto isolated tribes had maintained their ancient customs despite a subjection to European rule which dated back to the sixteenth century. He had also noted the wealth of hitherto unmolested ruins of stone and adobe towns scattered widely through the area. It was, as Cushing would exclaim in a letter, a "paradise of ethnography"—from which, it was hoped, much would be learned about the evolution of the great Indian empires of Central America and of human society generally.[11] American settlement of the area had meanwhile been progressing apace, however, and the isolation was soon to be ended by the arrival of a new transcontinental railroad. Moreover, popular as well as scientific interest in the relics of past or vanishing cultures had made the collecting of artifacts a competitive affair. Hence the high priority of the Southwest for the Bureau of Ethnology.

The expedition's first major destination was the pueblo of Zuni, situated on a mesa- and butte-rimmed plateau on the western edge of New Mexico some thirty miles south of Fort Wingate. Here, on the plain outside the pueblo, the group set up its tents on September 19, 1879, having journeyed across the territory on mule-back from Las Vegas, the farthest point then reached by the Atchison, Topeka, and Santa Fe Railroad on its way westward. And here, Cushing commenced his task of learning all he could about a typical tribe of Pueblo Indians. The Zunis, however, had no desire for strangers to pry into their affairs. Soon realizing how much hostility and mistrust his activities were arousing and how little he could learn under those circumstances, Cushing took the unprecedented step of leaving his tent and moving in with the Indians. This was a distinct departure from conventional behavior; while many respectable people, including Powell himself, had "gone among" the natives to negotiate with them, trade with them, educate them, convert them, or even study them, no scientist hitherto had actually crossed over to live with them.[12] It was a move evidently greeted without enthusiasm either by Cushing's colleagues or by his new hosts, whom he had neglected to consult beforehand. "How long will it be before you go back to Washington?" the Zuni governor, or secular chief, wanted to know, upon discovering the unwanted guest in his home, and was dismayed when Cushing answered, "Two months."

Cushing began to realize how much more than anticipated there was to learn about this small tribe of "savages," however, as he gradually won acceptance and gained proficiency in their language. His stay, which stretched past one projected departure date after another, had not yet reached the midpoint two years later when he caught Sylvester Baxter's eye on the Fort Wingate parade ground. By that time, he had entered so fully into Pueblo life that he had not only been adopted into the Zuni governor's family but had taken on a role of leadership in the tribe and was within a few months of initiation into the prestigious warrior society, the Priesthood of the Bow. Using his own methods, as Professor Baird had given him liberty to do, and indeed quite consciously regarding his actions in the Zuni community as a method he had originated to get the kind of information he was after, Cushing thus set an example of participant observation more than thirty years ahead of Malinowski, who is generally given the credit for having "invented modern anthropological field work in 1915, when he set up his tent in the village of Omarakana in the Trobriand Islands."[13]

Cushing's four-and-a-half years of residence in Zuni, from September 1879 to April 1884, had much the same kind of importance in his career as that early sojourn in the Trobriand Islands was to have in Malinowski's, the Samoan experience in Margaret Mead's, and the Brazilian excursions in Levi-Strauss's—to mention only three illustrious instances of what has become a commonplace pattern among anthropologists. Flooded with new experiences; subjected to unanticipated demands and tests, serious illnesses, and attacks of uncertainty, severe depression or sheer longing for "civilized" company; rewarded by the satisfactions of successful adaptation, the warmth of newly-formed relationships, the dawning light of comprehension, and—at one culminating point described in a letter—the sense that he was living "the grandest, most interesting, weird and terrible days" of his life and that "the sublimest depths of meaning to [his] researches" were opening before him, Cushing, through this extended immersion in the strange world of the Zunis, was undergoing his dual initiation as an Indian and as an anthropologist. From the standpoint of those who followed, he was also establishing a model of conduct, both inspiring and cautionary, in what was long to remain the typical fieldwork situation—that of the investigating visitor from the world of power and his intricate interaction with the native population subject to his intrusion.

Admittedly, Cushing's is a special case. Not until

quite recently has any collector of ethnology included in the report of his observations so much of the story of the personal involvement on which those observations were based. None has revealed so openly (to the peril of his professional standing) the imaginative nature of that involvement; nor is any likely to carry it to the lengths that Cushing did, acquiring a title like "1st War Chief" and making, as he had to, his own collection of scalps for that privilege. He was not only first in the field; he was unique. Or perhaps one should say rather, of the role awaiting him at Zuni, that *it* was unique and that among the fortuities involved was his peculiar readiness to discover and enter into it.

AN ANTHROPOLOGIST IN THE MAKING

However Olympian Professor Baird's manner may have been in bestowing Cushing's appointment, there was nothing offhand in his choice of the man to represent him on the Bureau expedition to the Southwest. At twenty-two, Cushing was very respectably qualified in his profession. In the course of some four years of experience with the Smithsonian he had conducted several archaeological digs, and he was already beginning to attract attention through his impressive finds and the several papers he had presented before the newly founded Anthropological Society of Washington, which had elected him its first curator.[14] Though he lacked university training, except for a few months at Cornell, Cushing was nevertheless well grounded in the contemporary literature of anthropology (he had long been familiar, for example, with such writers as Morgan, Tylor, and Lubbock).[15] His practical experience included a summer just concluded working on Cheyenne ethnology with a young informant named Titskematse, who was later to rejoin him as an assistant in the Southwest. For his method of fieldwork in Zuni, however, there was another kind of preparation, entirely personal.

Brought up in a rural area of western New York, the frail third son of an independent-spirited small-town doctor who scorned conventionality (and shoes), Cushing evidently eluded some of the normalizing rigors of contemporary childhood, such as regular attendance at the district school, and was left much to himself to roam the countryside at will.[16] His first discovery of Indians came, we are told, at about the age of eight, in the form of a flint arrowhead picked up and tossed to him by his father's hired hand. Though already familiar with the people who went about in the summertime selling handwoven baskets, he was struck with wonder by the sudden realization that the ground all about him had once been *theirs* and that it held the relics of their history from time immemorial.[17]

As time went on, he became an indefatigable and skillful explorer for Indian remains, ranging for days at a time in the neighboring counties and eventually into central New York as well. As he learned to sense telltale peculiarities of terrain, vegetation, and soil, he became adept at spotting sites of former Indian encampments. His gatherings of excavated weapons, utensils, and ornaments grew to a large hoard, eventually deposited at the Smithsonian.

His interest, moreover, was not merely in collecting. Wanting to know how the objects he found had actually been made and used by their originators, he tried to reproduce them himself. To this labor of love, pursued in a series of woodland workshops, he seems to have devoted endless patience. In his essay "The Arrow" (1895), he describes one memorable evening when, having produced but crude results during months of experimentation, he discovered accidentally how to make a proper arrowhead. Chipping at the bone handle of his toothbrush with a piece of flint in an attempt to replicate a bone harpoon he had unearthed, he momentarily reversed the two objects—and found himself flaking the flint with the bone. "I never finished that harpoon," he wrote. Turning about, he "used it as an arrow-flaker [and] made arrow after arrow in the joy of new discovery, until [his] hands were blistered and lacerated."[18]

The discovery he had made in this way, through his own experimental efforts, was actually a *re*-discovery; it was later confirmed that the technique he had found was one employed quite generally by Stone Age craftsmen. Using the same approach, he subsequently discovered other techniques used for working flint; and as he became proficient in other crafts as well, both in these early years and later on, he made further remarkable discoveries about primitive methods of workmanship.

Thus Cushing's childhood efforts to recreate in his own experience the life of the early Indians resulted not only in the growth of the handcraft skills and powers of observation for which he was to become famous among his peers but in a "new method of research by experimental reproduction" which became one of his major contributions to archaeology.[19] A "significant aspect of modern archaeological research," as one contemporary expert puts it, the experimental method pioneered by Cushing is, according to another, "more highly regarded today than ever before and the basis of much serious work in Europe and America both."[20]

What particularly strikes one about this early experimental method of studying Indians is how much of a piece it was with the participant method of observation Cushing was to use in his work in Zuni with living Indians. Clearly, they came to be identified in his own mind, at least retrospectively. Writing of the former in an often quoted passage, he speaks of its "profoundly personal" nature:

> If I would study any old, lost art, I must make myself the artisan of it—must, by examining its products, learn both to see and to feel as much as may be the conditions under which they were produced and the needs they supplied or satisfied; then, rigidly adhering to those conditions and constrained by their resources alone, as ignorantly and anxiously strive with my own hands to reproduce, not to imitate, these things as ever strove primitive man to produce them. . . .[21]

Similarly, looking back on his experience with the Zunis in a passage in one of the late autobiographical notes, he speaks of following "the method he had initiated of ethnologic and archaeologic study by means of actual experience and experimentation, endeavoring always to place himself as much as possible in their position, not only physically but intellectually and morally as well, [to] gain insight into their inner life and institutions."[22] Compared with this early expression of what George Stocking has called "the modern anthropological viewpoint," Malinowski's famous credo of striving to "grasp the native's point of view, his relation to life, to realize his vision of the world," reads almost like a paraphrase.[23]

Cushing's way of approaching the archaeological past, then, prefigured and paralleled his way of approaching the ethnological present. Both were equally the expression of a "personal equation," both equally participatory, manifesting alike, in the manual dimension and in the social, their common origin in the "unconscious sympathy," the gift for entering imaginatively into other identities, which his friend Alice Fletcher was to call "the keynote" of his personality.[24]

Initiation into Zuni

In one of his articles on Cushing, Sylvester Baxter sums up what he calls Cushing's "reciprocal method" in a list of qualities typifying his friend's approach to ethnological investigation, and necessary to it—qualities such as "sympathy and adaptability to the ways of others" and being on a footing of "thorough equality with his subjects."[25] As Joan Mark observed in her perceptive study of Cushing, his ways of reciprocating eventually came to include the exchange of European for Zuni folk tales and of Eastern for Zuni hospitality.[26] Reciprocation in a sense was the pattern of Cushing's relations with the Zunis from the outset, when, as a blond young stranger—and one incapable as yet of communicating in Zuni or even in Spanish, which some Zunis could use—he took up his task of "getting the information" about them. The character of the reciprocation seems largely to have emerged, unanticipated, from the events, however. The very nature of much of the information he would get, let alone what he would do to get it, remained to be discovered.

As the story is told in "My Adventures," Cushing's introduction to life as a Pueblo Indian began with a lucky encounter on his descent toward the pueblo from the Zuni Mountains on the last leg of his long journey from Las Vegas. Riding alone some way ahead of the rest of his party, he had met a Zuni herder, who, when Cushing shook hands with him, "breathed reverentially on [Cushing's] hand and from his own." Applying this lesson in Zuni courtesy when he was confronted in the pueblo shortly afterward with forty or fifty excited men motioning him away (he had arrived in the middle of a sacred dance), Cushing grasped the hand of one of them and breathed on it, thereby winning a cordial welcome.

This episode illustrates nicely the dynamics of reciprocity and the mix of luck, aptitude, and design which characteristically went into what Cushing called his "method." Given the chance appearance of the herder, what one notes are the quick intuitive grasp of meanings conveyed symbolically, the deft adaptability to a strange set of manners, and the knack, even under stress, for turning situations to advantage.[27]

This was the merest preliminary, of course. Recognizing at once that if he were going to learn anything much about the Zunis he would have to learn their language, he was soon "hard at work securing the dialect," as Colonel Stevenson reported in an early letter. Meanwhile, he set himself to the kind of ethnological tasks he *could* do—going about with his notebook and sketch pad, taking the measurements he had been instructed to obtain for a scale model of the pueblo, and recording what he saw of costumes, dances, and other externally observable phenomena of Pueblo life.[28]

Unfortunately, from the Zuni standpoint the notebook and sketch pad represented a particularly objectionable form of intrusion. With a kind of prophetic wisdom, they feared that copying things down and taking them away in a book was a way of stealing the spirit out of those things. They grew increasingly distressed and angry, even though Cushing had been succeeding in his efforts to ingratiate himself personally by the exercise of his considerable charms and by tending to the wounds and sores of the Zuni children as well as bestowing candy on them. His move into the pueblo was evidently a further strategem to penetrate Zuni defenses, by the gesture of giving up his status as an official visitor for that of fellow "insider," though he certainly presumed blithely enough on his superior position in proceeding without invitation, simply hanging his hammock in a room of his choice and settling in. In any case, it was a step into deeper water than he seems quite to have appreciated at the time.

To begin with, there was the reaction of his white associates. "From most of my party," he writes in "My Adventures," "I received little sympathy in my self-imposed undertaking" (MAZ 204, *Zuni* 68). "Most" of his party consisted, in fact, of Colonel Stevenson and his wife,[29] the only other members being the expedition photographer, John K. Hillers.[30] Brought over to the new Bureau from the U.S. Geological Survey, Stevenson and Hillers were old cronies of Powell's, fellow veterans of earlier western expeditions as well as of the Civil War. In this weathered company, as the youngest member and also as Baird's man rather than Powell's, Cushing seems to have been something of an odd number, though he evidently hit it off with the genial Hillers, his tent mate.

With the Stevensons, on the other hand, relations had been strained from the beginning. Unlike Hillers, whose position as official photographer was clearly staked out, Cushing was one of three members of the group with claims to the role of ethnologist, and he soon found himself in competition with the Stevensons—or, to be more exact, with the already formidable Mrs. Stevenson, who would be his lifelong rival as an expert on Zuni—over questions of turf and relative status.[31] She in particular seems to have taken offense at Cushing's move into the pueblo. With her in mind, he refers, in a letter to Baird, to "a presence in our party" who "from the beginning, has been incapable of recognizing in my self-inflicted degradation to the daily life of savages any motives other than [ones of a] rather low character." Like a malign spirit, she haunts the pages of his correspondence. The Colonel himself, an innocuous enough figure, maddeningly mild-mannered and obtuse, as he comes through in Cushing's accounts, seems chiefly to have been guilty of sins of omission—failing to treat Cushing or his ethnological venture seriously and neglecting time and again to come through with the support that Cushing relied on him to provide. This was a failure with important consequences for Cushing at the very outset of his adventure with the Zunis.

On October 8, not long after Cushing's move into the pueblo, the rest of the expedition set out for the next objective on its itinerary, the great cliff ruins of Canyon de Chelly and the villages of the Hopi Indians.[32] With no one left to talk to in English except the Presbyterian missionary, with whom at this point he "was by no means intimate,"

Cushing found himself much lonelier than he had expected. Worse, Stevenson had left him without the provisions he had counted on. Seemingly alienated from his own compatriots, Cushing was thus totally dependent upon those on whom he had been intruding—and in no position, certainly, to reciprocate on his own terms. "Little brother," the Zuni governor remarked, "you may be a Washington man, but it seems you are very poor" (MAZ 204, *Zuni* 68).[33]

As first in the field, Cushing could not know that much of what he experienced would also be experienced by other anthropologists in similar situations, until they eventually recognized in themselves the pattern of the initiation process they so often observed among the natives. In an essay that applies to the field experience the classical terms introduced by Arnold van Gennep in *The Rites of Passage,* Rosemary Firth sees the process undergone by the field worker as one of *separation, transition,* and *incorporation*: "The necessity to cut one's ties with one's own background and throw oneself on the social mercies of the local people is that which epitomizes for me the nature of the anthropologist's task."[34]

In his "time of transition after separation and before incorporation," Cushing was lucky in what looked at first like misfortune, for his was an instance in which, as Firth would put it, "the feeling of helplessness which may make the field worker miserable, [did] elicit the help he need[ed]."[35] But he had to relinquish something in return. He would have "mothers and fathers, brothers and sisters, and the best food in the world," the governor said, *if* he did as they told him (MAZ 204, *Zuni* 68).

A rhythm of such exchanges seems to have marked Cushing's "time of transition" generally. The Zunis, if Cushing was to remain with them, were determined to make a Zuni of him by feeding him Zuni food, dressing him in Zuni clothes (they eventually hid his own), and "hardening his meat" by taking away his comfortable hammock and warm underclothes and generally subjecting him to their own rigorous regimen. On his side, Cushing won the hearts of the Indians by what Kant would have called his "affirmation of the obligatory" despite the cost to his dignity, and, more seriously, to his health, which deteriorated progressively, and permanently, in the course of his stay. However much he may have complained of his miseries in the letters he wrote,[36] he willingly endured them, and it is clear that by the end of October he was very much enjoying the success of his "method." Writing to Baird of his discoveries to date, he explained:

> Because I will unhesitatingly plunge my hand in common with their dusty ones and dirtier children's into a great kind of hot, miscellaneous food; will sit close to [those] having neither vermin nor disease; will fondle and talk sweet Indian to their bright eyed little babies; will wear the blanket and tie the *pania* around my long hair; will look with unfeigned reverence on their beautiful and ancient ceremonies, never laughing at any absurd observance, they love me, and I learn.

As Cushing relates in *Zuni Breadstuff,* his polite use of a spoon he was considerately offered at his first meal "out" won him the sobriquet "He-Who-Eats-From-One-Dish-With-Us-With-One-Spoon" and a flood of dinner invitations from all over the pueblo. In the meantime he had made a place for himself in the household of the governor and had been instructed to regard that worthy as his "elder brother."

For all the apparent cordiality, however, there was still a serious unresolved conflict between Cushing's interests as a collector of ethnography and the Zuni fear that the power of their ceremonies could be taken away by being copied down. The governor, whose inseparable companionship served to keep Cushing under constant guard, seems to have warned him repeatedly to put away his writing stick. In a letter of November 7, Cushing reports having been "compelled to brave all Zuni for the chance of sketching their sacred dance, the *Ka-k'ok-shi* ['Good Kachinas']"—an episode also described in "My Adventures," where he represents himself as pulling out a knife and threatening to cut to pieces anyone tampering with his notebooks or drawing pads (MAZ 205, *Zuni* 70).[37]

As related in "My Adventures," this conflict came to a head shortly thereafter when, in a performance of the "*Ho-mah-tchi*" ("Knife Dance") called for the purpose, two of the performers, brandishing huge stone knives and shouting "Kill him! Kill him!," started climbing up to where Cushing sat sketching on a roof of the pueblo. According to his account, he was saved by his cool show of fearlessness, flashing his own knife in the sunlight and smiling down on his attackers, who forthwith decided they had made a mistake—he was not a Navajo, after all, but a *ki-he,* or spiritual friend to the Zunis—whereupon they killed a dog instead. As a result of this dramatic event, Cushing states, he was "never afterwards molested to any serious extent in attempting to make notes and sketches." He had also completely won over the governor, "and by doing so had decided the fate of [his] mission among the Zuni Indians" (MAZ 207, *Zuni* 74).

As it happens, one of Cushing's surviving journals is almost entirely taken up with an entry for October 20, 1879, describing this "*Ho-mah-tchi*" dance. It was indeed a fascinating and dramatic performance, and one which, considering what a newcomer to Zuni he was, Cushing recorded with impressive thoroughness and insight. A special harvest ceremonial featuring a good deal of ritual violence, it did in fact culminate in the killing of a "Navajo," and for a few tense moments attention clearly seems to have been focused on Cushing as a possible candidate. Whether it was for the purpose of intimidating or disposing of him that the whole performance was gotten up is another question—and one that evidently occurred to Cushing only later, since nothing is said of it in his diary. Perhaps the Zunis had not yet explained, or perhaps when he wrote "My Adventures" he added this claim as an improvement to the story—as when he adjusted the chronology to place the more exciting *Homachi* episode *after* the *Kak'okshi* confrontation mentioned above, when in fact it had occurred about two weeks earlier.

As for his victory in the matter of sketching and note-taking, that too was somewhat less clear-cut in real life than in the literary account, but his problems did diminish (probably more due to his generally agreeable behavior than to any bravado he may have shown). As they did so, another cycle in the induction process began when, later in November, he received permission from Washington to extend his stay in Zuni beyond the planned three months. The Zunis now began to press him to "dress entirely in the native costume and have [his] ears pierced," for "that would make a complete Zuni" of him (MAZ 509, *Zuni* 91). According to the account in "My Adventures," he strongly opposed these suggestions, but in a letter dated December 24 he reported his best progress to date:

> With the partial acquisition of the Zuni language, and the entire adoption of their native costume and habits of life, I have not only opened an easy way to their more obscure relations but also have overcome that superstitious prejudice [i.e., against curious strangers?] with which all observers of savage life have most to contend.

The ear-piercing turned out to be an essential part of the ceremony in which he was formally adopted and given his Indian name, Tenatsali (Medicine Flower, the Zuni name for datura or jimson weed, revered for its magical powers of healing). After this, the next step in the Zuni schedule for Cushing's adoption was to get him married into the tribe. Throughout the two years remaining until he could bring back a bride from the East, it required all the ingenuity and tact he could muster to evade without undue offense the logic of this expectation and the efforts to promote its fulfillment.

What can be seen in this initial period, then, is as much the evolution as it is the application of a method of fieldwork. As he acquiesced in each step of his assimilation, Cushing the ethnologist made the most of the opportunities afforded by the insider's position—to increasing effect, as he gained, along with the Zunis' confidence, an improved command of their language ("the two necessities," as he puts it in one letter).

A glimpse of the young anthropologist at work—as he appeared to his fond, and sorely tried, Zuni hosts—is afforded by Cushing's recollection of one of their names for him: Hets-ithl-to, or Cricket, "since I was forever 'whistling and singing, moving and jumping about, running hither and thither over the housetops and up and down ladders, without every staying myself to behave seemly or with dignity,' so they said."[38] Generally welcomed as "our *ki-he*," well-meaning and eager to please, if ignorant, always full of questions, and frequently in the way (as his own narratives delightfully illustrate), Cushing was in fact all over the pueblo, looking in on the household activities, trying to sort out kinship relations and the Zuni system of land and house ownership, learning Zuni etiquette, and generally saturating himself in the kind of lore of Zuni daily life that would find its way into publications such as *Zuni Breadstuff.* He learned about cookery, pottery-making, and metal work. He went on hunting trips with the governor, in the course of which, among other things, he learned the Zuni technique for pulling rabbits and wood-rats out of their holes with a stick and for grinding the latter (bones, viscera, and all) into an aromatic soup known as "rat-brine."[39] At home with the governor and his wife, plus nine other assorted relatives, he learned a good deal at close range about Zuni domestic life and family relations (as well as what it was like to live in the total absence of privacy). He was in on the winter story-telling sessions in the darkness around the coals of the council-room fireplace, some of the products of which would be collected eventually in his *Zuni Folk Tales* (including a Zuni version, much improved, of a European tale contributed by Cushing). As the year turned, he witnessed the gambling games and foot-races of early springtime and the rites and labors attending the planting, nurturing, and harvesting of the corn crop—the cycle of ceremonial dances, fasts, and feasts that mark the Zuni calendar.

Slowly, as the months passed, he grew more comprehending of what was going on about him. At the same time, new dimensions were opening to his view—most notably that represented by the network of esoteric sacred societies which he would come to see as having so fundamental a role in Zuni life. According to the account in "My Adventures," the existence of this hidden world was initially disclosed to him during the celebration of the great November *Shalak'o* (or "Coming of the Gods") festival of 1879 when he followed a group of costumed dancers to their meeting house and gained momentary admission. His glimpse of their secret rites revealed a "mysterious life by which [he] had little dreamed [he] was surrounded."[40]

After that, he seems to have danced, intrigued, or pushed his way into other such meetings, including one all-night initiation ceremony of the "Rattlesnakes and Fire-eaters." When he pretended not to understand members' requests for him to leave, he was allowed to stay—on condition that he spend the whole time making and smoking corn-husk cigarettes.[41] Thus he was introduced in one night both to the rites of the societies and (after his initial nausea) to the "dreamy pleasures of the smoker" (MAZ 31, *Zuni* 101). Such experiences as these initiated a two-year-long effort on Cushing's part to win actual membership in one particular secret society, the Priesthood of the Bow, acceptance in which would guarantee his entry into the meetings of all the others.

He was also making important discoveries about Pueblo—and Spanish—history. "As gradually their language dawns upon my intellect," he wrote to Baird in late October 1879,

> not the significance alone of [the ceremonial dances] but many other dark things are lighted up by its morning. They are the People who built the ruins of Cañon Bonita in De Chelly.[42] In their language is told the strange history of these heretofore mysterious cities, each one of which has its definite name and story in their lore.

Subsequently, having heard the Zuni names for several other less ancient ruins in the local vicinity, he came across some excerpts from the sixteenth-century chroniclers of Coronado's conquest of New Mexico and found that the Spanish names for the famous Cities of Cibola closely approximated the Zuni names for these long-abandoned pueblos. This discovery, which clarified an identity grown dim and uncertain over the centuries (from the European standpoint), was dramatically reinforced when he learned that an episode in the old Spanish accounts—the murder by the Indians of a North African Black named Estevanico—had its counterpart in a Zuni tale about the killing of a "Black Mexican" in "the days of our ancients."[43]

Other evidence of Zuni history appeared in the myths and stories Cushing learned, in the local ruins and pictographs he ran across, in the archaic regalia and usages he found featured in the ceremonies, and in the memorized "formulas" or "ancient talks" he found people following in such arts as the decoration of pottery and the design of clothes.

Through observation and questioning he likewise began to form an idea of the elaborate system of clans and orders comprising the Zuni social organization and to get inklings of the "world view" which mirrored that system—leads that would eventuate in his famous theory of the sevenfold division of the Zuni universe.[44]

How protracted a learning process this was is suggested by a letter of March 12, 1881. "Familiar as I am with their language, and one of them by adoption," he writes, having just spoken of the hardships he was suffering, "I have not until within a week secured anything like a complete vocabulary of their consanguinity terms, or any conception of their *true* belief in immortality and its conditions. Notwithstanding that this has been one of the facts I have constantly searched for during a year and a half."[45] In the pattern of numerous other letters in which he writes of his physical suffering and loneliness, Cushing's expressions here of weariness and discouragement are a sort of circumference to the enthusiasm and excitement at the center: "I am making more rapid progress in the study of the *inner life* of these wonderful savages during the past few days than ever before." The announcement is typical, as well as expressive of the true focus of all his studies; as new dimensions of the mysterious inner world of the Zunis opened to his vision, he saw ever-lengthening vistas of work to be done and time needed for doing it.

It should be added that success in this quest carried its own particular challenge for Cushing (as it would for later participant observers), for some of what he came to witness among "these wonderful savages" was in gross violation of his own culturally engrained standards—and not merely in matters of taste. In a letter of July 1880 he writes:

> The matter of superstition, . . . while very interesting and all that, [is] not very pleasant. The Zunis have, within the past ten days, killed one of their own men from its dictates. His trial, on the absurd ground of sorcery, I attended personally and as in every other public debate of the tribe, had more or less to say—of course, so far as possible, for the defense. His death took place in the night [and] was horribly violent—although partaking more of the character of a sacrifice than of an execution.

Cushing omits to mention here how he responded to this situation, other than as an advocate for the accused. Later in the same letter, however, in a different context and without explanation, he makes the extraordinary statement that he had "pounded the War Captain the other day in a crowd of opposers [and] settled in the same way the Governor, who attempted to interfere."

Years later in a newspaper interview Cushing seems to provide the link missing in the letter, when he recalls the occasion on which he had "first witnessed the trial of a sorcerer [and] in a most foolhardy manner attempted, even by violent means, to protect him." The execution of the sorcerer was clearly an event which overtaxed Cushing's capacity for cultural adaptation or detachment. Not for long, however. Fractured as it was, even that initial account was part of a general stock-taking which must have been prompted by the execution; elsewhere in this same letter he summed up the results of his stay in Zuni with the interesting remark that it had brought him to a "more practical and cosmopolitan view of humanity and its institutions." It was this latter view that he expressed twelve years later in the newspaper interview, where he discussed the Zuni treatment of accused "sorcerers" as in fact a scrupulous and legitimate form of criminal justice with which it was unwise for outsiders to interfere.[46]

There were other ramifications to this episode. In trying to prevent the execution "by violent means" Cushing had himself violated a strong taboo in a culture which viewed shows of anger and physical aggression within the community as unacceptable. A diary note made a few days later indicates one way in which the breach was healed; he records a "sacred rite" he had been obliged to perform to relieve "a little girl who had been scared at me on the day I struck the war captain."

"Chief Councilor" of the Zunis

Meanwhile, there were other developments and further intricacies of mutual compensation. By the end of 1880, according to the Bureau of Ethnology *Annual Report* for that year, Cushing had "so far acquired knowledge of the Zuni language as to take an important position in councils and [had been] made chief councilor of the nation."[47] Cushing's gratification at this elevation of his status is expressed in the draft of a letter. Having described the "tyranny" exercised over him by the well-meaning Zunis in forcing him to conform to their usages, he writes happily:

> By policy and patience I won in long months their confidence, respect and esteem, gained authority over them, and with the acquisition of their language, became their chief councilor, so that at present the table is turned and I am *their master.* Perhaps no young man of my age ever had such grand opportunities, such chances of distinguishing himself as are now in my grasp [the italics are his].

Whatever reluctance Cushing may have felt at first about assuming an Indian costume, he obviously had no such qualms about becoming a chief. Indeed, this euphoric announcement and other scattered allusions to "my Indians" or to his "command" over them betray a tendency in their author, once established in Zuni, to confuse ambition for his fieldwork with dreams of empire. No doubt this was accountable in part to his youth (he was, after all, only twenty-three) as well as to a side of his character and self-image. But in his imperialist and romantic age Cushing was hardly the only one to imagine becoming ruler of a tribe of savages. It was a notion played out, among other places, in Conrad's *Heart of Darkness* just eighteen years later, and, to the chagrin of many, it turned up again in the diary kept by that other pioneer of modern anthropology, Bronislaw Malinowski, during his stay among the natives of the western Pacfic.[48] In the scientific circles of 1880 there was nothing in the idea of an ethnologist seeking "mastery" over his subjects to elicit any reaction other than complacent approval.

Exactly what Zuni concept it was that Cushing translated as "head councilorship" we do not know. For that matter, it is not entirely clear what Zuni meaning lay behind the title "first war chief" which he acquired or assumed a year later, since the position seems not to have been a traditional one in the tribal structure.[49] Titles aside, however, it does seem clear that Cushing's penchant for gaining mastery over the Indians carried him well beyond mere fantasy. By the fall of 1880, he appears to have been exercising some degree of actual administrative power as a sort of surrogate for the governor. In a journal entry for October 6, for example, he reports having that day, in the governor's name, "shot two hogs which were in the corn. Had some high old councils and about one third of the Pueblo [were] ready to eat me up for it. I told them to shut up. *Muy seguro,* I am boss here just now."

Entries over the next several weeks continue in a similar vein. We hear, for example, of Cushing's ambitious but mercifully short-lived "experiment" at organizing the Indians into work squads for the mass production of adobe bricks—and of his resorting to "force and violence" to press one of the head priests into this labor. He even seems to have given orders to the governor himself. For example, in a note concerning his efforts to halt Navajo use of Zuni land for grazing purposes, he reports having fired some warning shots and then "commanded the Governor to drive the herd into Zuni"—an act prompting a young Navajo to call on the Zunis to dismiss their governor "for carrying out the instructions of *Americans*." The governor must have fretted more than once about things getting out of hand.[50]

It would seem, then, that in dealing with his native brothers Cushing, too, was capable of the kind of domineering behavior for which his successor in Zuni, Matilda Stevenson, would gain such a reputation. For that matter, such behavior seems to have been characteristic of anthropologists generally in those simpler days before the intrusive and power-laden aspects of fieldwork had to be taken into account. Between Cushing and others of his class, however, there was the notable difference that his degree of "mastery" over the Indians in question derived not merely from his colonial standing as a "Washington man" (important as that undoubtedly was) but from his standing within the tribal structure itself.[51] Cushing can be criticized for enjoying his power, exaggerating it, misusing it, or—more pertinent from a modern anthropological standpoint—having it at all. But at any rate he used it, with rare exceptions, not to extort secrets or favors from the Indians but to carry out his perceived responsibilities to the tribe—in expectation, to be sure, of ultimate ethnological returns on the investment. Controversial as some of his services may have been, moreover, the Zuni leaders seem clearly to have had use for someone like him at that point, and whatever the title given him may have been, by late 1880 he was playing an increasingly prominent role in the community.

SPOKESMAN FOR THE ZUNIS AND FIRST WAR CHIEF

One of Cushing's first inspirations in his effort to ingratiate himself in the pueblo (as may be seen in two early notes he wrote to the governor and his father) had been his offer to "plead the cause" of the Zuni nation. He had come among the Zunis at a particularly crucial juncture in their history. Following "two hundred and fifty years of Spanish rule and thirty years of American fraud and aggression," as he put it in one of his later lectures (*Zuni* 175), the Americans were now consolidating their hold and flooding into their new possessions in growing numbers.

As a small, sedentary tribe located on generally unappealing land, the Zunis had escaped armed conflict with their new rulers, and indeed were even benefited by the pacification of their hereditary enemies, the Navajos and Apaches (though sporadic outbreaks among the latter continued through and beyond Cushing's tenure in Zuni). But they were subject to new rules and constraints in their still uncertain relations with these old enemies, with the Mexicans, and with the incoming settlers from further east. Like other Indian groups, the Zunis were now under the charge of a U.S. government agent (located in Santa Fe), as well as under the surveillance of the local military garrison at Fort Wingate. Like the others, they were having to adjust to a narrowly boundaried reservation, theirs having been established just two years earlier, in 1877—with a serious omission, as it turned out. No longer having free access to a number of their customary grazing areas, religious sites, and other places traditionally identified as Zuni, some of which were now occupied by neighboring ranchers or farmers, they had instead to contend with violations of their new boundaries by some of these same neighbors, including local Navajos used to grazing their animals on what were now exclusively Zuni lands. Other, newer neighbors were the proselytizing and land-eager Mormons, who had been moving into the area since 1876, when their first two missionaries had arrived in Zuni. Then there was the Presbyterian mission, just recently established in the pueblo. And additional traders, miners, cattlemen, lumbermen, missionaries, homesteaders, and others—including a host of roving ne'er-do-wells—continued to arrive, the influx accelerated after 1881 by the completion of the railroad through nearby Fort Wingate. Unsurprisingly, in this general rush to exploit, convert, displace, absorb, and civilize the Indians while studying them in their primitive state, the various instrumentalities of the new American rule were somewhat at odds with one another.

It was, in short, an opportune time for the arrival among the Zunis of someone who could mediate for them in the complicated world impinging upon the pueblo. As the Zuni caciques came to trust Cushing and caught on to his possibilities as such a mediator, he began to take on a portfolio of functions that expanded into a kind of joint ministry for foreign affairs, defense, and public information. In this further complex of reciprocations, the ethnologist became a busy man of affairs as well. Among other things, he smoothed over quarrels with local ranchers; negotiated with the local sheriff and helped in dealings with local traders; dealt with Indian school officials in quest of Zuni pupils; briefed a succession of Pueblo Indian agents and a U.S. government teacher in Zuni; represented Zuni interests to agents for other Indian groups; policed the reservation against encroachment by neighboring Mormons, Mexicans, and Navajos; defended the authority of Zuni headmen against the subversive efforts of missionaries (including an abrasive Presbyterian who apparently threatened to "knock the stuffin'" out of any Indian who didn't obey his orders); and, when famine threatened, sought help for the Zunis from Washington.

As "First War Chief"—a position to which, by his account, he was named in the fall of 1881—he led the Zunis more than once in pursuit of horse thieves (generally American). Indeed, his prestige was greatly heightened when, on at least one occasion, the culprits were actually caught and two of them killed in the assault, though the Zunis were "mostly unarmed."[52] Also as war chief, he was authorized by the governor of New Mexico to organize the Zuni war society into a troop of militia for more effective defense both against horse thieves and against settlers attempting to take up land inside the reservation boundaries. To what extent this latter project actually materialized is not clear, but his efforts in protecting the reservation against such invasions did produce one well-known item of Cushing lore. When he shot some trespassing Navajo horses and signed his reply to the Navajo agent's complaint with his title of "1st War Chief," the agent wrote back with lofty asperity: "I have ever counseled a departure from the Indians' former practice of reprisal, believing that it was our policy to bring the Indian *up* to our standard, rather than going *down* to his—which you appear to have retrograded to." The ranchers were less refined. One of them wrote, for example:

> Now Mr. Cushing, please to tell Mr. Injin that the next one of them I catch riding a horse of mine is going to get hurt sure as hell. Besides this, some of them killed a cow of mine a short time ago. I will give $25 cash to find out what Indian done it.

Above any other service was the help Cushing provided in the closing period of his stay in Zuni when a group of local army officers, aided by a powerful U.S. senator, tried to take advantage of a mistake in the 1877 drawing of the Zuni boundaries and entered claims to a large section of vital Zuni farmlands. To defend his adoptive people against this depradation, Cushing quietly mobilized his friend Baxter and other influential journalist acquaintances in the East as well as the Pueblo agent in Santa Fe—with such effective result that the enraged senator threatened to destroy the Bureau unless Cushing was removed from the scene. He was.

On account of the disputes in which Cushing became entangled as a Zuni tribal spokesman, it has been argued that his activities in that role were incompatible with the requirements of his role as ethnologist.[53] One could hardly disagree. Cushing became so partisan to the cause of his adoptive people that he took on their view even of their *Indian* enemies, once referring to the Navajos, for example, as "wandering coyotes"—definitely an eyebrow-raising remark coming from an anthropologist.[54] There is likewise no question that a great deal of the time and energy that might otherwise have gone into his professional work were spent instead on the business of being a tribal leader and front man. But however true all of this may be, the point is in a sense academic, since in Cushing's case the two roles, if incompatible, were also inseparable.

How inseparable they were may be inferred from the fact that when he was put on trial at one point on suspicion of sorcery, a crime for which he could have been put to death, he defended himself and shamed his accusers by calling attention to such good deeds as his having helped evict Mexican and Mormon poachers from the reservation. Inversely, when he was unable to take direct action against the army officers who were trying to take over part of the reservation, his standing in the tribe fell so low, according to his account, that an attempt was made on his wife's life. As a personally appealing young American who worked his way into the Zuni community and claimed to be a Zuni but refused to take a Zuni wife and continued to pursue much business of his own (including the sketching of sacred ceremonies), and, on the other hand, as a young "Washington man" claiming to have an important government appointment but treated with condescension or worse by other members of his expedition, Cushing seems to have inspired, among at least some of the Zunis, an ambivalence and mistrust recurrently verging on outright hostility. According to his account, this mistrust was so widely shared at the time of this trial for sorcery (probably sometime in 1880) that he had at its outset only two firm supporters—his adoptive father and his "elder brother," the governor.[55] And despite the successful outcome on that occasion, the fact is that, for all the successes of his adaptation, he remained on trial throughout his tenure in Zuni, needing again and again to prove himself. From a latter perspective, one might well wish he had been of a somewhat less ardent and assertive temperament, but his active partisanship and leadership became in effect conditions of his existence in Zuni, of a piece with the other forms of participation upon which his observations and insights as an ethnologist depended.[56]

FROM COLLECTOR OF MATERIAL CULTURE TO PRIEST OF THE BOW

Perhaps less incompatible but comparably demanding, another function which Cushing was called upon to fill, as an agent of the National Museum, was that of collector of Pueblo material culture. From his repeated (often frustrated) requests for trading materials and transport facilities, as well as from reports of his activities and other references in the letters, it is clear that a considerable portion of Cushing's time throughout his stay in the Southwest was devoted to the acquisition of artifacts of all descriptions through barter, purchase, and excavation and to the labeling, packing, and hauling of these by the wagonload to Fort Wingate or some other depot for shipment.[57] (Toward the end, indeed, he seems not only to have been supplying the Smithsonian but to have ventured into private enterprise, contracting through his friend Adolph Bandelier with the Berlin Museum, and perhaps with others as well.) He spent much time, moreover, away from Zuni on long, arduous, and frequently hazardous excursions over a wide radius of New Mexico and Arizona exploring Pueblo ruins, sacred caves, mines, and other sites he had heard of from the Indians. On occasion he visited other Pueblo tribes, adding to the collections and at the same time seeking traces of prehistoric migrations referred to in the Zuni myths, evidences of Zuni cultural evolution, and comparative data relating Zuni to Pueblo culture generally.

On one such venture, in the first winter of his stay in the Southwest, he went in search of an ancient turquoise mine the Zunis had told him about (without divulging its exact location), found it, lost his mule because a traveling companion stole the lariat with which it was picketed, and spent two days finding his way on foot out of the Zuni Mountains in a snowstorm. On another expedition he "lost by thirst three animals and nearly an Indian" crossing the desert on his way from Oraibi to the village of Havasupai, hidden away in an "almost inaccessible box canyon of the Colorado River" and visited only once by white men. Among the journals included in this collection are those Cushing kept during these two expeditions.

It was on his return from the latter of these ventures, in September 1881, that the break came which he needed to win his admission into the Bow Priesthood. Passing through a region of eastern Arizona which was just then the scene of Apache hostilities, he had the good fortune to witness a skirmish between some "ranchieros" and an Apache raiding party and managed to possess himself (without ever explaining exactly how) of an Apache scalp. With this and two others he had obtained, less adventurously, from the East, he was able to persuade the Zuni caciques of his eligibility—a success owing in part to the fact that most of the tribal scalp collection had been swept away in a recent flood and was in need of replenishment.[58]

Vividly described in several of his letters and other writings, the ordeals and ceremonies of Cushing's initiation into the Bow Priesthood were the high point of his entire Zuni experience. The view that was opened into the "inner meaning" of the phenomena he had been observing changed entirely his sense of the work before him. In his two years in Zuni he had become aware of a whole interior world of secret cults and of an immense body of unwritten and largely esoteric sacred lore, including an epic origin myth requiring some six hours to recite. With his initiation he would be admitted to the meetings of all these secret fraternities. With respect to the rich body of rituals, songs, and prayers proper to the Bow Priesthood itself, he would not only witness—struggling to record what he could make out in the rapid flow of performance—but would actually be instructed in this material and expected to memorize it. Until this point he had been revising from letter to letter his expectations about how long it would take to finish his work in Zuni, never projecting a stay of more than an additional few months; now he could see that a lifetime was too short to exhaust the field.

Ethnological advantages aside, the initiation itself was clearly a powerful experience. "Weird and impressive," as he put it in one letter, and "grand beyond power to describe," it went on for sixteen days, including the initial period of purification—four days spent in motionless, silent meditation (one of them sitting bareheaded in the hot sun on a sandhill filled with ants), with nightly instructions, prayers, and endurance dancing in the estufa followed in the early morning by massive doses of an emetic. Every detail in the ceremony as a whole, he wrote, was "symbolic, poetic, intensely interesting, and its results on the mind of the man who passes through it more amazing than anything else I could relate to you."[59]

Without trying to trace any specific or elaborate consequences of this experience, one may surmise that as a culmination of two years' immersion in Zuni communal, family, and ceremonial life, this rite of passage must have generated a potent sense of expanded consciousness, a sense of entry to a depth hitherto undreamed of, into truly *Zuni* consciousness. Such experiences lay in the background for the man who later, in the deliriums of fever, would deliver harangues in the Zuni tongue and who was famous for an uncanny power to "think like the Indians" and to draw forth from "the crude ceremony, the archaic thought, the mnemonic symbol," as Alice Fletcher put it, "the secret meaning which through them was struggling for expression."[60]

An Eastern Tour, an Eastern Wife, and the Last Years at Zuni

With admission to the Bow Priesthood, Cushing was pressed more insistently to confirm his solidarity with the tribe by marrying into it, the latest candidate being a relative of the governor's. The alternative he proposed at this point was to take a group of Zuni leaders on a journey east, to visit the President in Washington and to bring back for their rain-summoning ceremonies some of the water of the Ocean of Sunrise. Such a pilgrimage having long been a Zuni ambition, the idea won immediate favor in the pueblo, as it did likewise with Sylvester Baxter and other new friends in the East, who began to arrange speaking engagements. With the grudging approval of the Bureau and free passes provided by the railroads as a promotional venture, the group set out in February 1882.[61]

The tour was an inspiration, not least because Cushing came back from it with a wife. It was also a way of repaying the Zunis for their hospitality to him—and of heightening his prestige among them. Satisfied too was Cushing's not altogether repressed desire for recognition in his own part of the world. Wherever they went, the group made front-page news, and Cushing's audiences in Washington and Boston were dazzled by his costume, his companions, and his tales of life in Zuni. According to a recollection of an appearance at Harvard late in March:

> the great Hemenway Gymnasium was jammed. . . . Cushing, indeed, was epidemic in the culture-circles of New England. . . . His personal magnetism, his witchcraft of speech, his ardor, his wisdom in the unknowabilities, the undoubted romance of his life of research among "wild Indians of the frontier" . . . all were contagious."[62]

The visit to the Boston area was a crucial one so far as the Zunis were concerned, since the site chosen for the ceremonial gathering of water from the Atlantic was Deer Island, outside Boston Harbor. It was also crucial from Cushing's standpoint, since it brought him into contact with a host of admirers, some of whom would provide important support for his work in the future. Among these was the philanthropist Mary Hemenway, who would sponsor his famous Hemenway Southwestern Archaeological Expedition. The crowded schedule included several talks by Cushing, three receptions at the Old South Meeting House, a special tour of the Peabody Museum at Harvard, and an evening at the Paint and Clay Club, where Cushing met such luminaries as Francis Parkman and William Dean Howells. There were also visits to Wellesley College, the State House, City Hall, a minstrel show, and the village of Salem, where one of the Zunis made a little speech of gratitude to the townspeople for their efforts in eradicating witchcraft. The water-gathering ceremony, also a well-attended event, seems to have had particular significance for Cushing, since according to the news accounts it included a rite beginning his induction into the Kachina Society.[63]

Other appearances followed in Washington, including talks before the Anthropological Society and the National Academy of Sciences. Meanwhile, at the Bureau Cushing was under pressure to get his notes into readable form before returning west and to complete at least one article for the next *Annual Report*. In the course of the spring and summer he filled the second assignment by completing his essay "Zuni Fetiches." In off-duty hours, he wrote for a more popular audience. "The Nation of the Willows," his account of the Havasupai expedition, appeared that fall in the *Atlantic,* and in December the *Century Magazine* carried the first of three installments of "My Adventures in Zuni."[64] This venture into magazine writing revealed Cushing's talents in a genre made popular by writers like Melville, Dana, and Parkman—"non-fiction" accounts in which literary young men reported their romantic and perilous adventures among strange peoples in far-off places. According to Charles Lummis, himself a popular writer of the day, "My Adventures" "made a sensation throughout the country."[65]

Among the other events of this crowded season was Cushing's marriage to Emily Tennison Magill, the fiancée he had left behind in Washington. To his relief, the Zuni caciques (according, at least to one contemporary account) took an instant liking to Emily and gave their hearty approval despite their earlier plans for him.[66] Hence the group which set out at the end of August on the return trip to Zuni was augmented by the new Mrs. Cushing and (answer to another prayer) a cook—this Eastern contingent to be increased a few weeks later by the arrival of Emily's younger sister Margaret, who would remain with the new household for the duration. Pausing en route for a visit to the Tonawanda Indian Reservation in western New York, where there was much comparing of notes between Pueblo and Senecan clan mates and where Cushing was much impressed with the degree to which the old Indian ways persisted beneath appearances to the contrary, the party reached Zuni in mid-September.

When Cushing's friend Washington Matthews heard about the wife that Cushing intended to bring back to Zuni from the East, he wrote a characteristically blunt letter expressing, along with good wishes, his doubts about the wisdom of this move. Admitting that "you need someone to care for your stomach, your work, your time and your money—in short, that you need a wife badly," he questioned whether Cushing had fully considered the hardships she would encounter or, more seriously, the effects of the marriage on his own relations with the Indians, who would no longer be able to monopolize his attention or enter his room when and how they wished. "Your wife will have to be a woman of rare tact and rare liberality of mind," Matthews predicted, "if she does not rather hinder your work than aid it."

Matthews had a point, though when he met the new Mrs. Cushing he evidently thought better of it. While not the enthusiast that her sister Maggie was for life in the field, she seems to have taken on its challenges with a sturdy determination and to have been accepted by the Zunis as well as by Cushing's American friends.[67] Changes there certainly were, however. Baxter, visiting Zuni in November 1882, reports finding the new entourage settled in the same house that Cushing had lived in as a bachelor:

> but how changed it was. . . . Where before he had slept on the floor exposed to sundry crawling things and had eaten from primitive dishes set on a blanket spread on the same, there were now beds, tables and chairs, with an abundance of nice crockery and cooking utensils. . . . The refining touch of a woman's hand was everywhere manifest.

Mrs. Cushing did also amend the rules of accessibility. According to another visitor, she had "forbidden (the Indians) to intrude into her apartments without permission, and [had made such] frightful examples of some of them [that] they adopted the civilized mode of knocking at the door and awaiting a welcome."[68]

As well as showing a woman's hand, this transformation in life-style was symbolic of Cushing's altered position in Zuni. The trip east had demonstrated decisively—at least for the moment—the strength of his credentials as a "Washington man" and an American of importance who was able to follow through on his promises. He had returned a famous man, his value to the Zunis thereby considerably enhanced—and their expectations of him correspondingly heightened.

That all of this was not an unmixed blessing soon became evident. For one thing, Cushing—and the Zunis—had to contend with the tourists who were attracted by the news of the "man who had become an Indian" and wanted to be entertained in like manner. One briskly businesslike letter, for instance, states of the bearer and other ladies and gentlemen of his party: "They all desire to become members of the Zuni Tribe, and, not being acquainted with any others, I am forced to call upon you to have them initiated. Please put them through in good shape and draw upon me for the amount of their initiation fees."

Noticeable generally about the year and a half remaining of Cushing's residence in Zuni is the extent to which—when he was not simply ill, as he was much of the time—his attention was taken up with matters outside his ethnological and archaeological studies. He had hardly arrived back, for example, when a crisis arose owing to the murder of a Zuni man by a gang of American horse thieves. In his "proper sphere as war chief," Cushing was called upon (or considered himself called upon) to take action. For the first time, he actually assembled and led a war party in pursuit of the murderers.[69] Back from that apparently unsuccessful venture in time to receive a visit by Major Powell, he was given instructions by the latter which soon took him off on a collecting expedition to Oraibi. With time out for a brief return to Zuni in November to observe the *Shalak'o* festival, this assignment took up the remaining months of 1882 and January 1883.

Once more in Zuni at the beginning of February, he suffered a relapse of the "pulmonary and dyspeptic troubles" which had prostrated him during his first winter in the Southwest. Again he was disabled through much of the winter and spring, though during periods of convalescence, according to his reports to the Bureau, he was able to add substantially to his notes on the Zuni "sociological system" and folklore. In May he spent two weeks exploring ruins in Arizona that were identified in Zuni tradition with the route of their early migrations. By June, however, his illness had returned, and he continued to suffer more or less serious attacks throughout the remainder of his stay—indeed, through the remainder of his life.

Meanwhile, he had been embroiled since the end of 1882 in the famous controversy over the outlying Zuni spring and farmlands at Nutria to which three enterprising officers at Fort Wingate—one of them a son-in-law of the senior senator from Illinois, General John A. "Black Jack" Logan—had laid claim. Whether or not the senator was ultimately responsible for Cushing's removal from the pueblo, this was an affair with ramifications which would plague him through the rest of his time in Zuni, both undermining his standing among the Zunis, who apparently believed he could solve their problem if he only chose to do so, and subjecting him to a systematic campaign of vilification outside the pueblo.[70]

Nor was Logan the only source of trouble for Cushing during this second period of his assignment in Zuni—merely the most serious. His feuds with the Presbyterian missionary in Zuni and with the U.S. Indian agent for the Navajos also resulted in agitation for Cushing's removal in the form of letters to Washington—one from the Presbyterian Board of Home Missions in Albuquerque, the other from the U.S. Indian Service. As might perhaps be expected from these two charitable bodies, while their specific complaints differ (the one concerning Cushing's alleged subversive influence against the mission schoolteachers in Zuni, the other against his "reckless and lawless" shooting of several Navajo horses), the common target of their attacks is the same as that of Senator Logan—the personal character of a man who would lower himself to the life of a savage. According to the Presbyterian, he had "pandered to the lowest passions of the people," while the Indian Service official alluded to his widespread "reputation for licentiousness."[71] Living among the Indians may have gained admiration for Cushing in some quarters, but it clearly won no credit for him among the agencies of church, state, and private enterprise that were interested in manipulating those "savages" for their own ends. To be sure, what the hard eye of the competitor may have seen in Cushing—not without some justice—was a fellow manipulator, for he too, of course, had ends of his own.

Last Days at Zuni

In view of the tribulations and distractions which fill the record of Cushing's last year and a half at Zuni, it might seem that he would have anticipated, even welcomed, his recall. With his standing in the pueblo restored by the seeming Nutria victory in May 1883 and a successful campaign against horse thieves in August, however, he commenced the optimistic project of building a house—a major project since, by his own account, he did "all the carpenter work etc. with [his] own hands." The Cushings had just moved into this new house in January 1884 when the letter came ordering his return to Washington. Characteristically, he was in considerable debt for building expenses. Honor bound to pay his debts in the area before leaving, he proposed staying on in Zuni through the spring—a proposal which seems to have won at least tacit approval, since that was what he did.

While the effect of the recall notice was, in Cushing's phrase, to "put a period to his field work in Zuni," these last salvaged months in the pueblo were far from wasted. In addition to witnessing various ceremonials, including a Kachina society initiation during which he listened, for the second time, to a ritual recitation of the epic-length Zuni origin myth, he undertook a series of local explorations of Zuni votive shrines, sacrificial grottoes, and burial places.

The major activity of this final period in Zuni, however, was writing—for money. As a writer, Cushing was by now in considerable demand from various quarters. Following the success of his earlier pieces in the *Atlantic* and *Century,* he was sought after by both these and other popular journals for further contributions. On the other hand, there was also the pressure created by his success in the field to publish the scholarly papers bearing the fruits of his research. The pattern with the latter was one of struggle and delay, as it would be, with fortunate remissions, throughout his life. While in Washington, he had been provided by the Bureau with a stenographer, on Professor Baird's suggestion that this kind of assistance might help to speed the process. As Baird probably understood, having received some very long letters from him as well as an apology once for not having time to write a shorter one, Cushing's problem was not with words but with the constraints involved in reducing his ever-dilating experience and knowledge to systematic form. Back in the field, Cushing found one obstacle after another (all real enough, to be sure) in the way of completing the desired assignment. When he was not ill, there were other pressing demands. Now, however, perhaps inspired by the bills to be paid on his new house and by the handsome contract he had been offered as well as by the suggestion of a peculiarly happy plan of composition, he set to work on another project altogether—a series of articles for an Indianapolis-based trade journal called *The Millstone.*

Focused on the Zuni use of cereal foods (principally corn), these articles, which began to appear in January and which he worked on through the winter and spring of 1884 and beyond, would reappear, posthumously, in book form as *Zuni Breadstuff,* the work generally regarded as Cushing's masterpiece.[72] Despite its dryly narrow title, *Breadstuff* is a wide-ranging and delightfully informal first-hand account of Zuni life and culture as related to food. For comprehensiveness and vivid immediacy of presentation it has never been equaled—and, like various other peerless works, it was composed to get its author out of debt.

No doubt with the same intent, he had also become involved, with his friend Adolph Bandelier, in a more covert form of moonlighting. In August 1883, Bandelier had written Cushing inviting him to join an arrangement he had entered into with the Royal Museum of Berlin whereby, for a commission, he was making a collection of Southwest Indian artifacts for them. Subsequent letters indicate that Cushing accepted the offer and made at least one shipment of Pueblo material he had collected. An offer to purchase his finds was also made by the trader Thomas Keam, though no letters have surfaced to indicate whether or not the offer was taken up. The extent of such independent operations was almost certainly quite small. While Cushing several times let his superiors in Washington know that he could easily go into business for himself by selling what he collected, the purpose of such remarks was usually to make them feel better about the debts he had contracted in their name. For the most part, he seems to have been true to the disclaimer he invariably added of engaging in any business but that of the Smithsonian or the Bureau.

The fact was, though, that since before the trip east he had been entertaining thoughts of alternative sources of livelihood. Worn down by the "hard uncertain struggle for a niggardly existence," as he put it in a letter to Lieut. John Bourke in the summer of 1881, he had even thought of joining the army. Inspired by the example of Bourke and Matthews (both of whom pursued their Indian studies under the aegis of the military) and also by the cordiality of various other relationships he had formed at Fort Wingate and at Fort Whipple, Arizona, and believing the army could be counted upon to support the continuance of his ethnological work, he had applied for appointment as a second lieutenant. Despite the backing Bourke won for him from General Sheridan, however, this effort seems to have met with resistance somewhere within the bureaucracy, and the appointment never materialized. Another idea, mentioned in September 1882 and seriously proposed by Bourke at the time of Cushing's recall to Washington, was that Cushing might take up a cattle ranch somewhere near the pueblo, with financial backing from "Boston and New York capitalists," and thus be free to carry on his work independent of the Bureau.

Cushing was plainly both reluctant to leave Zuni and uncertain of his future in the Bureau of Ethnology. Even assuming the continuance of his appointment (which he did not take for granted), there was the sensitive question of his footing in the establishment. As a transplant from the Museum, he was not (at least not yet) one of those close to the throne of the Director, and he seems to have felt himself still something of an outsider. "So far as intercourse with Washington ethnologists is concerned," he wrote somewhat standoffishly to Powell, pressing for a postponement of his recall, "I care for the exchange of ideas with *not one* of them save with yourself and Mr. Holmes. No other could enhance my work at present in the slightest advantageous degree [Cushing's italics]." Bourke, who blamed Bureau interference for Cushing's failure to get an army commission, reinforced these uncertainties. Referring to the Bureau as a "congregation of penny-dips [who] will not be disposed to let an electric light enter among them," he told Cushing: "You know well that I have always distrusted those people and that in our communications long ago we both concluded not to lean upon them too much."

For all his restiveness and insecurity vis-à-vis the Bureau at this point, however, Cushing does not seem to have been seized irresistibly by the notion of casting loose from a government berth he had held since he was nineteen. In a few years, on leave from the Bureau, he would get his Boston capitalist backing for a return to the Southwest as director of the Hemenway Archaeological Expedition. But for the present, punctual to his promise to Powell that he would be out of Zuni by the first of May, the last tearful farewells were said in time for the Cushings to be in Albuquerque on April 26; at 11:30 that night they boarded the train for the return to Washington.

Thus ended one of the most remarkable chapters in the annals of anthropology. Nothing quite like Cushing's sojourn among the Zunis had happened before, nor has anything like it happened since. For Cushing himself, of course, it was not the end; he had much of his major work still to do. But not only did the Zuni experience provide the subject matter for a large part of this work (certainly that for which he is best known), it also shaped and informed his approach generally. More than that, it contributed significantly to the shaping and informing both of Southwest studies and of modern anthropology as a discipline.

Perspectives

To appreciate the significance of Cushing's pioneering experiment in fieldwork, one needs to have in mind at least one or two facts concerning the "state of the art" in anthropology at the time when he embarked on his venture among the Zunis. The most salient of these with respect to the Bureau of Ethnology in particular is illustrated in two of Cushing's first letters from the Southwest. In these we learn that Professor Baird's general injunction to "find out all you can" had been reduced by Major Powell to a definite assignment: making the measurements for a model of the pueblo and, more explicitly to the point, doing "whatever else . . . to get at the social structure and system of land and house tenure of the Pueblo Indians."

Glossed by Cushing's own later allusions to *gentes, phratries,* and the "primitive system of the consanguinity and affinity of the Zuni people or their ancestral races," these instructions reflect the guiding influence of Lewis Henry Morgan on the science of anthropology as it was to be pursued in Powell's Bureau, and indeed as Cushing himself had already been schooled to think of it.[73] To Powell, such data of social organization represented evidence bearing on the place of the Pueblos in the general evolution of man from savagery through barbarism to civilization.

The idea of man's rise to civilization through evolutionary stages had long been current, of course, as had the notion that American Indians and other living "savages" could be explained as remnants of an earlier stage in the process. Morgan's great contribution to this line of thought, growing out of his ground-breaking studies of kinship systems, was to correlate the evolutionary changes he postulated in these kinship systems with changes in other social institutions in what he saw as one great universal process of development "running in different but uniform channels upon all continents, and very similarly in all tribes and nations of mankind down to the same status of advancement."[74] In a period taken up with the theme of evolution and with the questions raised by recent discoveries showing man's great antiquity, it is no wonder that Morgan's grand scheme represented an epoch-making step forward. His demonstration of the underlying uniformity of the human mind as it advanced everywhere, inventing parallel technologies and institutions at parallel points in evolution, seemed to provide what was needed to establish anthropology as a genuine science. Certainly, it provided a central foundation for Cushing's thinking.

One other figure must be also mentioned—Edward B. Tylor, whose formative influence on Cushing's thinking (and on that of anthropologists generally) was almost certainly even greater than that of Morgan. Cushing encountered Tylor's *Researches into the Early History of Mankind* when he was a boy of thirteen or fourteen, and it seems to have been this book that first exposed him to the study of anthropology and to the idea of evolution as applied to human history. Through this book and through Tylor's later masterpiece, *Primitive Culture,* a book Cushing listed among those he had frequent occasion to use in his early years in the National Museum, he became acquainted with terms, problems, and principles that would remain central to his thinking for the rest of his life. If he was indebted to Morgan and Powell for introducing him to the intricacies of social organization, Cushing owed to Tylor his introduction to the concept of culture—in Tylor's classic definition "that complex whole which includes knowledge, belief, art, morals, law, custom and any other capabilities and habits acquired by man as a member of society."[75] Also from Tylor, he learned the notions that cultures grow and decline; that inferences about earlier states of culture may be drawn from traces still present in traditions and myths, in language, or in anomalous customs ("survivals"); and that primitive thought processes do not include the distinction between "subjective" and "objective." The list could go on, but it may stand as sufficient to suggest Tylor's considerable contributions to Cushing's tool kit as a journeyman ethnologist on his first major assignment. They are contributions of which the reader will be aware in more than one of the writings collected here.

Of all that Cushing carried with him to the Southwest, however (apart from his own highly individual gifts and predilections), nothing was more crucial than what was stipulated in the assignment itself—to focus a study of the Pueblo Indians upon one single typical village, and to take as long as necessary to do the job. If Cushing's report can be trusted, credit is due to Major Powell for the very firm instructions he gave on this point at the outset, somewhat against the grain of the general surveying and collecting mode otherwise followed in the expedition. "I would much prefer that one Pueblo be investigated thoroughly than that all the twenty-seven should be seen and collected from superficially," Cushing quotes him as saying, "and if you can't do it in one month, take six, or even more."

The idea of a study concentrated on one single community was probably the product of Powell's own experience in the field a decade earlier, when he had spent a few weeks in the Ute country of northern Colorado learning the Ute language and collecting information and artifacts.[76] Whatever the impetus, it was a portentous choice of research strategies, for it established a condition essential for this original "modern" fieldwork experience. The result would be, in Powell's later words, to make "traveling ethnologists" a thing of the past.[77]

A few further observations remain to be made about the fieldwork itself and what came of it. The first concerns Cushing's famous exposition of the sevenfold division as the key to Zuni mentality and social organization. According to the Zuni way of seeing, as he learned, all reality in the universe is ordered in reference to a division among the spirit worlds of the six directions and the center on which they converge, which is the pueblo of Zuni itself, the "middle ant hill." This sevenfold division, notable in the myths and ritual reenactments of the Zunis' original wanderings in search of their abiding place in the middle of the world, was an idea, according to Cushing, which reproduced itself symbolically not only in the identification of the winds, plants, animals, seasons, colors, and other phenomena of nature but in architectural design, housing location, agricultural practices, totemic, clan, and priesthood organization—in short, in every facet of that "complex whole" comprised by the social and cultural life of the pueblo. It was Cushing's elaboration of this "model" of Zuni society which helped to inspire the theories of Durkheim, Mauss, and Levy-Bruhl regarding primitive thought processes and their relation to social organization, and which prompted Levi-Strauss in turn to grant Cushing "a seat on Morgan's right as one of the great forerunners of social structure studies."[78]

Now as Alfonso Ortiz has pointed out, in an essay which also owes something to Cushing in this connection, the assumptions that make up a society's "world view" are never entirely explicit, much less among the Pueblos, who have

> no tradition of philosophical speculation as to the nature of all things. . . . we cannot just walk up to any Pueblo Indian and ask him to unfold his world view. It must be inferred from what is known about other aspects of Pueblo reality, and this knowledge, in turn, must come from many statements and actions of many people on many diverse occasions.[79]

This, of course, was exactly what Cushing, as the first anthropologist to study a particular community intimately and at length, was the first to discover—without benefit of an existing concept such as "world view" or even any prior reason, such as Ortiz himself had, to suppose that a primitive people like the Zunis would *have,* in Ortiz's words, "underlying premises which unify the various aspects of [their] existence."[80]

Granted that Cushing may have inferred too much at times, or got an unbalanced view by relying too exclusively on the old priests and tribal leaders who were his teachers and chief informants. The point is simply that the new departure in anthropological thinking represented by his inference of the "notion of the 'middle' and its relation to the rest [as] the central fact indeed of Zuni organization" was the result of a kind of relationship that none of his nineteenth-century mentors had entered into with a "primitive" people.[81] Cushing's readiness to conceptualize this pattern in the complexities of Zuni culture, the "systems within systems" of its organization, doubtless owed much to both Morgan and Tylor. But for the perception itself, what he required was the density of contact afforded by his sharing in the life of the community, along with, of course, that gift of his for entering into another point of view—what Robert Lowie a generation later was to call "that sympathetic projection into alien mentality which anthropology is supposed to foster."[82]

The same point applies to that corollary innovation of Cushing's pointed out by Joan Mark—his use of the term "culture" in a way that anticipates its modern meaning, not as *the* single "complex whole" comprised by the totality of man's accumulated acquisitions as a social being at any given stage of evolution (Tylor's meaning) but as the pattern of belief and behavior distinguishing *any* ethnic group.[83] For this change in perspective to occur, or begin to occur, and for the idea to dawn that a preliterate society might have a culture and history of its own, someone had to become sufficiently immersed in the way of life of at least one such society to discover how complex and whole, as well as how different, it was. In keeping with this development, Cushing, who went to Zuni primed with theories about the evolution of culture, became increasingly caught up with the evolution of *Zuni* culture and its ramifications.

What we are discussing here are extensions of

consciousness associated with a pioneer experience in participant observation (predating the invention of that term too, needless to say). One further instance deserves mention: namely, the consciousness Cushing acquired relating to the nature of the anthropological enterprise itself. Aware of the problem posed in "such researches as this" by the tendency of observers "to read into their renderings of things [their] own personalities," as he put it in one of his unpublished notes, he was far ahead of his time in seeing this "personal equation" as a fact of life for the ethnologist. Indeed, though acknowledging that it constituted a "grave contingency," he argued that it was also "supremely essential," for without the involvement of the total person "at all points, practical, sensational, emotional, and intellectual," there could be no real comprehension.[84]

To a degree, no doubt, this sort of reflection simply mirrors (as it attempts to deflect) a criticism to which Cushing himself was already being subjected and to which he has ever since remained particularly vulnerable. "His observations," Alfred Kroeber remarked, "were of the keenest, but almost impossible to disentangle from his imaginings."[85] So they may have been—as whose, in the last analysis, are not? The point here is that his defense, if that is what his note was, articulates a perspective on observations in general and cross-cultural observations in particular that not only was unique in his own intellectual milieu but was long indeed in gaining general recognition among social scientists. It is a distinctly *modern* perspective.[86]

Among his peers, Cushing's ability to enter into the "alien mentality" of Indians and to explicate the logic of their orientation was legendary. Less well known, and in a sense even more remarkable, is that in the course of saturating himself "at all points" in this other mentality he learned something about his own as well. Having gone to the Southwest to do his part in the general collecting of facts about Indians, he became conscious of the opaque and shifting nature of such facts in themselves; that is to say, he became aware of their *symbolic* nature and of the role necessarily played by his own relationships within the community and his own participant imagination in penetrating their surface to the patterns of meaning beneath. In this perception he not only predates but points beyond several later generations of participant observers toward the kind of thinking represented by Clifford Geertz's notion of "interpreting" a culture.

Within this picture of Cushing as anthropology's pioneer modernist there must still be room, of course, for the ways in which he reveals himself as a man of his own time. For example, he seems to have seen no contradiction between established evolutionary doctrine and his own pluralizing of the term "culture," as we see in various late references to "primitive peoples in their status of culture" or to other cultures, like that of Zuni, as "earlier" or "older" than our own. Nor did his expositions of their cultural complexities prevent him from making periodic references to the childlike simplicity of the Indians themselves or to the special insight into their mentality which he thought was vouchsafed to him by virtue of his clear and sympathetic memory of his own mental processes as a child.

Like a host of other American images of Indians, Cushing's conception of them as childlike seems to tell us more about him and his culture than about them and theirs. It also lights up a side of Cushing which seems to bear out George Stocking's description of nineteenth-century anthropologists generally as a "proud and aggressive" lot sustained "by their self-confident belief in the superiority of their own culture and by the evolutionary concepts which gave this belief theoretical legitimacy.[87]

That Cushing shared some of these Victorian tendencies, or susceptibilities, is all too evident in some of the letters and journals collected here. The yen to "master" "his" Indians has already been mentioned. One notices, too, along with his use of such terms as "children," "savages," "simple natives," and the like, how sensitive he was to criticism from his own side of the cultural boundary for choosing to adopt the life and dress of such people. He repeatedly justifies this "voluntary degradation" as consistent with his "self-respect" in that it was done only in the interest of science.

Also evident is a species of cultural and professional "self-confidence" less easily laid to rest with the Victorians—an attitude manifested, for example, in a reference to his "understanding of Indian feelings and consequent management of them" for the purpose of collecting "everything venerated." "Of course, a degree of deceit has been necessary," his friend Baxter remarks in one of his articles. "This kind of deceit cannot be called treachery, however," Baxter continues, "for the results will not bring harm to them; . . . and [again the invocation] what he does is done in the name of science."[88]

Like other individuals, but more dramatically than most, Cushing was a figure of many facets, some of them contrary to one another. The proper Victorian who viewed (or at least represented) his hard life among the savages as a sacrifice for science coexisted with the romantic adventurer who was living out as fully as possible his boyhood dream of becoming "truly an Indian." The young defender of the traditional authority of the Zuni priests against subversion by the missionaries coexisted with the zealous young reformer who ordered a set of handcuffs from Fort Wingate to force one of the tribal holy men to put in his allotted hours of labor on the brick-making project. The reverent novice in the Zuni rituals coexisted with the methodical collector of ethnography who ransacked the sacred caves and spoke of fleeing the pueblo when he had "penetrated to the Arcana of the Zuni traditions." Perhaps Edmund Wilson had something like this in mind when he spoke of Cushing's having internalized the struggle between the white man and the red man within his own "dislocated human spirit."[89]

It is obvious that complexities of this sort, though personal enough, were not unique to Cushing. As both creature and critic (at least occasionally) of his own culture, both stranger and friend (or more than friend) in a society outside his own, Cushing represents an early prototype of a personality pattern that at least one self-conscious practitioner, Hortense Powdermaker, has identified with anthropologists generally.[90] He is also a representative American of the Victorian age, feeling his way between the nineteenth century and the twentieth and at the same time embodying in his own polarities a conflict in the spirit of his generation.

If the dominant public mood in America in the last decades of the nineteenth century was one of buoyant confidence in science, progress, and the manifest destiny of the civilized to rule over their cultural inferiors, there was another mood as well. Beneath the gilding it was a period of violence and ferment, and as the forces of civilization were completing their conquest of the continent and initiating the new age of industrial capitalism, an articulate minority had been growing increasingly conscious of the blight as well as the blessings in the path of their culture's progress.[91]

To get a balanced view of what Cushing meant when he spoke of Indians as a childlike people in an earlier phase of cultural development, it helps to have in mind this sort of minority reaction to modern man's progress in the "conquest" of nature. In his own way, Cushing shared this reaction, manifested then, and since, in a fascination with earlier or exotic peoples against whose presumably still *un*dissociated sensibility, *un*disinherited mind, *un*mediated vision (a hundred terms have flowered) may be measured the cost of civilized life and consciousness.[92]

Neither historian nor philosopher, Cushing was little given to discourse on such subjects. Indeed, he never ceased to identify with the progressive and optimistic ethos of the scientific circle to which he belonged, as well as with the manners and sentiments of the Victorian bourgeoisie generally. What "childlikeness" could mean for him, however, is conveyed in occasional passages, such as that which describes his first visit to a Pueblo village outside Santa Fe. In that context of frontier rapacity and violence, he remarks "how much more human were the merry, industrious people whom I had just left than those who call themselves their superiors and boast [of] the city which they have built and so badly misnamed." In a similar mood he comments in a letter: "My Indians have more sense of honor than most of my own people and associates."

"Of all the people on this continent," Cushing declared in a late address to the Board of Indian Commissioners, "the most profoundly religious . . . are the American Indians, especially wherever still unchanged from their early condition."[93] "We know," he mused elsewhere, "that the primitive child-woman I have told you of is mistaken in believing as she does that, for instance, by touch or breath she can infuse into the insentient household things she makes [the same kind of] life she gives to her beloved little children. Yet, after all, [those] who actually believe [that] have lived the better therefor."[94]

Though he considered it mistaken, moreover, this "earlier" way of thinking in no way betokened to Cushing a deficiency in intelligence—only a difference in focus. "In stoic wit excellent; in repartee scarcely surpassed; in punning unconquerable, these Zunis," he wrote in one letter, "are not such bad companions after all." Cushing's relish for such wit is evident in the examples (often at his own expense) encountered in any of his accounts of life in Zuni. More generally, what is conveyed in the dialogues scattered through these accounts is a sense of the vitality of the traditional Zuni way of thinking. In the company of Zunis, as he presents them, it is he who appears childlike and in need of "cooking"; his Zuni teachers, even when confronted by the technological wonders of the East, are never at a loss for explanations in their own terms. Though they are sometimes amusing in Cushing's report, the effect of their grave and trenchant interpretations is also to throw into relief the flat, unsignifying materiality of the "real" as understood by civilized folk—and thus to expose the relativity of this "reality" to a cultural point of view.[95]

Whatever else is to be said about Cushing's view of the mentality of Indians, then, it is clear that it was not *merely* ethnocentric in the way Stocking suggests as typical of nineteenth-century anthropologists. Though the "science and practical sense" bred into him by his own culture obliged him to regard as superstitious most of the beliefs held by the Zunis, the more he learned of the interrelationships comprising the complex whole of their culture, the more he came to appreciate how much was upheld by this "superstition," including the very aspects which he admired most in their culture and missed in his own: the great body of unwritten myths and tales, the richly elaborated rites and ceremonies, the intricately complicated unity of the social order, the reverent demeanor before the gifts and powers of life.

We cannot know exactly how much a sense of deprivation in his own society had to do with the "craving" Cushing avowed in a letter of 1884 for "knowledge of savage lore and life." But there is no mistaking the expression, in his talk before the Indian Commissioners, of his identification with "the simple people of the blanket" in their "sadly unequal struggle with an advancing and alien civilization."[96] As a scientist in a government bureau whose evolutionary party line affirmed the inevitability and justice of the Indian's demise in that struggle, Cushing did not question the outcome. But he may have been the only one in that company to whom it would have occurred to use the word "alien" in reference to his own society's advancement.

Here, too, of course, one must expect to find some projection. Alienated romantics have greatly enriched the literature of the "white man's Indian" over the years. Such alienation as may have been involved in Cushing's own case, however, was as much the product of his fieldwork as it was the motivation for it, and served as much to generate perception as to color it. In his background, by the time he returned to the East, were the opportunities his venture of living as an Indian had afforded him to experience "civilized" society from the point of view of its victims. Not only was he witness to whatever nineteenth-century America was doing to the Zunis during his residence in the pueblo; by virtue of choosing to share their life he became vulnerable to the same kind of degrading treatment they were subjected to. Through the Zunis' reaction to *his* abasement, moreover, he gained insight into his own sensibilities as an American as well as into theirs as fellow sufferers. Looking back years later, he recalled the humiliation he had suffered at Fort Wingate when he turned up there with a Zuni companion during the first winter of his stay. Seeking shelter after a long trek down out of the mountains, they had been refused a room and offered instead, grudgingly, a corner of an unused hen house. Considering all the assurances he had given the Zunis about his important status as a "Washington man," Cushing expected nothing but scorn from them after this exposure of his low estate in the eyes of his compatriots. The reaction was quite different. "Well, you see, *we* are Zunis," said his fellow traveler; and he found upon return to the pueblo that his standing in the community had been, not weakened, but strengthened.

Through such experiences, Cushing's pioneer adventure in search of an insider's understanding of an alien culture led to increased understanding of another kind as well, even more profoundly anthropological than the appreciation of cultural differences. His evolutionary mentors had theorized about the "psychic unity" beneath the racial and cultural divisions of mankind; for him it was a matter of direct experience. Strange and fascinating as were the beliefs and customs of his Zuni hosts, the ground on which he found himself meeting them was that of their common—and equal—humanity. Nor was it merely as Zunis that he loved and remembered and wrote about them, but as vividly individual *persons*.

THE FINAL YEARS

Zuni provided Cushing with his only experience in ethnological fieldwork. In the sixteen years remaining to him after the close of his life in the pueblo, his career consisted of extensions from this formative experience—in archaeological explorations, in museum work, in lecturing, and in the production of his theoretical and scholarly writings. These were years in which Cushing was recognized as one of the leading scientific men of his time. At the end of 1886, sponsored by the wealthy Mary Hemenway of Boston, he returned to the Pueblo country as director of the Hemenway Southwestern Archaeological Expedition, a large-scale project aimed at tracing the origins of the Zuni people and their culture through the systematic excavation of ruins along the "migration track" of their ancestors prior to the settlement of Zuni itself. This was the first venture of its kind in the Southwest. From it dates the history of modern archaeological investigation in that part of the continent. Over the next several years, the expedition's progress was national news, commencing with the almost immediate discovery, under a mound in the Salt River valley near Tempe, Arizona, of what turned out to be one of the largest pre-Columbian settlements in the area.[97] Then, a decade later, he matched his finds in the Southwest by unearthing, in the Keys off the Florida coast, the remains of several other ancient settlements—the work of another pre-Columbian people, hitherto unknown, who had constructed town sites of elaborate design on mounds built up out of seashells. Both were stunning discoveries, accompanied by massive shipments of a great variety of recovered artifacts, many of impressive beauty.

Stemming from this same period is a list of some two dozen publications on such subjects as primitive copper-working, the evolution and lore of the arrow, the influence of hand usage on culture growth, the development of Pueblo pottery, Zuni creation myths, and his famous theory of the sevenfold division.

Bristling with brilliant intuitions and grandly sweeping hypotheses, some of these papers are still classics in their own right. For both Cushing and his readers, however, they were but "preliminary" works, giving promise of more compendious, definitive, scientific monographs to follow—the expected fruit of his years in Zuni and his archaeological discoveries in the Southwest and Florida. Unfortunately, such large-scale monographs were not to be part of the Cushing legacy. Plagued by debilitating, often prostrating illness and a formidable writer's block and at the same time possessed by a spirit ever restless to be off on new explorations, Cushing struggled over the years with one after another of these projected exhaustive studies, eventually laying each of them aside to work on other projects. He was still working on the Florida materials when, eating dinner one evening in April 1900, he choked on a fishbone and died.

Cushing's failure to produce the monumental works which were expected of him, and which he expected of himself, left about his life a sense of tragic unfulfillment. Worse, from the professional standpoint, was his failure, in the eyes of most later anthropologists (and even some of his own contemporaries), to be altogether convincing as a man of science. Among the burdens of his later years was a scandal created by accusations that in two separate instances he had used his fabled skill in native crafts to fabricate or "doctor up" objects he had presented as purely aboriginal artifacts.[98] About his writings, too, there have lingered suspicions, not so much of deliberate falsehood as of holding too loose a rein on his imagination. "He leaves us wondering," Robert Lowie complains, "how much of his interpretation reflects his own rather than his native hosts' mentality."[99] As anthropology, moving into the twentieth century, came to identify itself with the "exact" sciences and the ideal of a purely objective methodology, Cushing was—at least in America—more or less written off as a wayward genius whose work, as Franz Boas said, would have to be done all over again.[100]

If Cushing had his shortcomings as a scientist, however, they were perhaps the defects of his virtues as a pioneer modern anthropologist. In a piece written after Cushing's death, his friend the Dutch anthropologist H.F.C. ten Kate recalled a visit to Zuni in 1883: "There I saw Cushing in his element. I saw here an Indian among Indians, loved and revered by many, the ideal student of ethnology. I saw then that Cushing really was a 'Zuni familiar.' "[101] As for the problem the scientists were already having with Cushing a century ago, ten Kate had seen that too. "Even his own colleagues in Washington did not leave him in peace," he wrote of Cushing in another report, adding a remark which seems to describe the dilemma still posed by this unique figure in the history of anthropology: "On the one side was the distrust of the work of the young ethnologist; on the other, excitement over the rich treasures of knowledge he was bringing to light."[102]

Part I
Becoming a Zuni

1. *August–December 1879*

On the Way to Zuni

On Monday, August 4, 1879, Col. James Stevenson was given his official orders for the expedition to the Pueblo country of the Southwest; on the following day, the Stevensons and Cushing set out by train from Washington on the first lap of their long journey.[1] *Joined by John K. Hillers in St. Louis, the group proceeded to Las Vegas, New Mexico, where they paused for several weeks to collect the provisions, mules, and wagons needed for the remainder of their travels and to trade with local Indians for artifacts. From Las Vegas, the trip across to Zuni required about three weeks, with stopovers in Santa Fe and Fort Wingate.*

What follows is an account of some of Cushing's adventures en route. Evidently intended for circulation through the newspapers but never completed, it survived in the form of a penciled (and not altogether legible) draft among the papers now housed in the Southwest Museum. Date of composition may be inferred roughly from the date (November 6, 1879) entered on the other side of one of the sheets on which it was written.

An Ethnological Trip to Zuni

One sunny morning in late August, our party, after long delays, left Las Vegas [New Mexico] on the old stage road for Santa Fe. I rode ahead on mule back, not only from necessity but also from preference, as this enabled me to make short trips to either side of our train for the purpose of exploring any ancient remains which might be along the way.

Just as the sun was setting behind one of the most beautiful mesa mountains in the world, we rode down into the valley of the Pecos and stopped at the little Mexican town of San José where it nestles in the shadow of the hills. At about nine o'clock a Mexican dance was given in our honor to the music of the guitar and violin. The men were awkward and roughly clad, but the women were graceful and quite pretty.

The sun was above the mountains [when] we again started. Our road, along great valleys, over hills and meadows, [was] so beautiful that one could scarcely believe that for miles and miles the most diligent search would not reveal a drop of water. It was about three o'clock in the afternoon when we rounded a hill and again beheld the Pecos, green and flowing as before, but here dwindled to a mere rivulet ever and anon disappearing in its hot, sandy bed. To the right, on a high mesa-head, red with the setting sun as the red hills around them, rose the rugged walls of the oldest church in the United States.[2] Beneath the diminishing shadows of these walls themselves, washing away year by year, stand the ruins of the once powerful Pueblo of Pecos.[3] We made camp for dinner, and at my urgent solicitation the rest of the party consented to remain there for the night. I spent the afternoon in sketching and planning [diagraming] the still distinct rooms and courts. The pueblo entirely covered the little mesa on the end of which stands the church. It is arranged around [a] central, irregularly square court with entries at either end. On the terrace below either side are traces of a defensive wall which once encircled the whole pueblo, and at the western end, opposite the court, is a well-preserved stone corral, where the dung of two centuries' accumulation covers deep the primitive rock floor of the mesa. In the western court, excavated into the solid rock, are two round estufas, one at either end (each forty feet in diameter). The great log which supported the roof of one still lies in its place, and the stone wall yet stands the test of a century. Just above is the house of the Alcalde, which, fireplace and all, still remains perfect.[4] The front wall has fallen forward and revealed the white-washed interior. . . . Upon the roof of this house the lady of our party excavated nearly all the parts of a charming olla, and in the debris which covered the floor Col. Stevenson found a broken loom treadle and some beautiful bits of pottery showing . . . painting and . . . glaze. I planned [measured and diagramed] till the close of the day. Then, just as our campfire died out, the moon rose full and clear over the front of the old church and lighted up grandly the two estufas. . . . Candle in hand, [I made my way] to some ancient remains which I had discovered. . . . How strange these smoky walls should still support a ceiling as perfect as on the day when it was made, [and] that from the latter should hang the same strings which supported the dance trappings of the days when all was new, and held the loom on which were woven

Zuni and Western New Mexico (Bureau of American Ethnology *Second Annual Report,* 1880–1881).

the beautiful fabrics. In one room I found a perfect fireplace, the cinders still lying on the hearth which had not been warmed for a century. In another, the rafters had broken under the weight of superimposed timbers and had been rudely notched with sharp stone and spliced with ropes of fibre.

Into one small room I broke and, searching about, found the small entrance to another. Squeezing through with difficulty, I entered a room which, save for the sand which the wind had drifted in, was not changed from the day it was abandoned. On either side of its two doors I found the beautiful tracing of a young woman's hand. The boys and girls of her great grandchildren now sport about the mud walls of Jemez, yet still in this dim chamber where the laughing maiden came in from her marriage dance remains the paint which with her beautiful hand she pressed against the wall above the doorways of her future home.[5]

The moon was low among the mountains, as was my candle in its socket, when, long after midnight, I crawled out from these lonely chambers. All of our party were buried in slumber, as they were in the thick shadows of the ruined church, and as I ran down to the river to wash from my hands the soil of centuries, the howl of the distant coyote, and the low note of some nigher kind, sounded to my ears like the moaning wail that went up from the fugitive tribe as they left the burning house of their fathers to seek shelter in that of their distant cousins in Jemez.

On the following morning, heartily laughed at, I gathered a quantity of pot shard specimens [before leaving] with the rest for Santa Fe. Toward evening we came to a hot, sandy valley high up among the mountains, where we stopped to gather a few topazes, hundreds of which lay scattered in the sand. Here in my search, I came several times upon the remains of stone relics in a valley now so desert that it scarce harbors a living creature. Then, just as the sun was setting, we rode over the edge of the Santa Fe Mountains. Tired as I was, I scarce knew whether I would not rather tarry among these sun-emblazoned peaks and haze-curtained valleys, so beautiful were they, than seek shelter far below in that mud town which they call the capital of New Mexico.

During the few days following, we were engaged in making collections which Indians from the various Pueblos brought in for trade. One evening, after these had all been labeled, fearing that our party would leave without visiting the not distant Pueblo of Tesuque, and impatient to see people like those among whom I must live for a season, I saddled my little mule, strapped a couple of blankets to his back, and rode out, determined to spend a night there.[6] The pueblo was farther off than I had suspected, and the moon was high when, peering ahead, I saw the flashing of campfires among dark trees. Galloping forward and with difficulty crossing the arroyo of the Tesuque, I rode up the bank and saw above, blackly silhouetted against the clear, starry sky, the blocks and ladders which books and pictures had taught me were peculiar to Pueblo dwellings. To the left, nearer me and on the same bank stood also, gracefully outlined against the sky, the silhouettes of three women and a little girl. They had been dipping water from the spring and one had already balanced her olla on her head when the sudden appearance of a horse and rider had transfixed them with surprise. I called out to know the way into town; still as statues stood the three and the little one. I called again, yet no answer, no motion. Then, spurring my mule, I suddenly made an advance toward the frightened creatures, who, finding legs, dropped ollas and dippers and scattered among the tall weeds which covered the bank.

In a moment the village was in an uproar. Dogs barked and babies cried, but I rode up to the wall of the town, determined to reach a point where I could seasonably demonstrate my peaceful intentions. There was a huge campfire in the outer plaza where a woman was burning pottery. Out from among the dark fruit trees and into the circle of light which this shed around came a man whom I immediately recognized as one with whom I had traded in Las Vegas. He reached both hands toward me and asked where I was going. When I replied, "to Tesuque," he bade me dismount, and within ten minutes my mule was munching corn in a little corral while I, following my delighted host up a ladder and into a quaint little room, was seated cross-legged on a roll of skins waiting for an olla of fresh water which his squaw had immediately run to fetch; and when this came, a rude feast of tortillas, cold meat, and melons was placed before me. That night, alongside the two rolls of skins and blankets which contained my host and his family was a third—my own. And when I awoke at midnight and along the four-sided terrace saw gleaming in the moon beams the bare faces and arms of silent sleepers, I thought how similarly had been received the lonely Vaca and how slightly had those centuries changed the hospitality of this little Pueblo.[7]

Just as the sun was changing the eastern gray to another hue, I heard a long drawn chant rise from some part of the town, and a moment after, from the top of an opposite house, wrapped from head to foot in a red blanket and facing the east, the Alcalde rapidly called out the orders for the new day. Almost instantly the rolls of blankets began to move, and within a few moments smoke rose from a hundred olla-capped chimneys and the odor of as many breakfasts scented the morning air.

Purchasing a large and beautiful collection of pottery and storing it in my host's house, I galloped off for Santa Fe to get transportation. Midway, I met our ambulance and turned back. We gathered still more specimens and went home literally with a wagon load of quaint curios.

Once more, a few days after, with my friend Mr. Brown of the Geological Survey, who, [now] with the Land Commission, surprised me by appearing in Santa Fe one evening, I spent a night in Tesuque, in the morning sketching novel features and collecting still more specimens while my friend started for the city.[8]

While crossing a stream on my way home at midday, I was twice shot at by a Mexican because, notwithstanding something he shouted at me, I paid no heed to what he had said; and on the evening of the following day, just as I was about to enter my hotel, a sharp pistol shot echoed across the Plaza, and a man who had been calmly smoking his cigar fell with a groan across the door sill. I reflected how much more human were the merry, industrious people whom I had just left than those who call themselves their superiors and boast [of] the city which they have built and so badly mis-named.

Three or four days after, with one six mule wagon, a four mule escort wagon, and an ambulance, myself again mounted on a mule, we left for Zuni via Fort Wingate. That evening we camped beneath the great lava hills at Peña Blanca in the valley of the Rio Grande.

Ere the sun was higher than the lava hill we had climbed down the day previously, I was off through wide planted fields of waving maize toward the yellowish red adobe blocks which indicated Cochiti.[9] Riding some six miles, I entered the town which stands on a bluff above the river valley. The first man I met happened to be the Lieut. Governor. I had a talk with the latter, visited the estufa, the house of the Governor, sketched some sacred objects, and again mounted and was off to catch our long departed train.[10] Riding down into the valley of the Rio Grande, I thought to cross the stream where the water seemed shallow and the bed hard. About midway my animal sank nearly out of sight in the quick-sand. I leaped from his back, pulled at his head until the bridle broke, sank deeper, and finally abandoned the mule to save myself. The little mule struggled mulefully, as I manfully, to get out, and at last clawed up the bank, like myself wet but well. My dismay was great. My saddle bags had been nearly submerged, and I feared my sketches and books were ruined. [But] examination showed them to be only a little injured, and repairing the broken strap, I again mounted the saddle to gain the now distant party.

Among the mountains to the west of the river I came to many roads and for a little time was lost. Not unfortunate was this, however, for there in a lone valley I came upon the deserted camp of some wandering Indians and found my first traces of ancient remains. By watching for the tracks of our mules, I was able to assure myself of the way, and toward evening regained the [trail of the] train where they had rested for a lunch. The close of evening showed us, in the green little valley of the Jemez, the hamlet of San Isidro.[11]

In descending from the low mountains which bound it on the north, I came upon some rude remains. Dismounting to gather them, I stepped into an ant hill. In a moment, those red-bodied villains were all over me. I paid no attention to them at first, but presently their bites became great red blotches and their pain became so intense that when I galloped into camp I was utterly crazed. Waiving all prudence, I rushed to the river and threw myself into its cooling waters, lying there, so intense was the relief, until I was so chilled I could hardly regain camp.

In the morning, the poison had left me. I sketched a young Indian who visited our camp and decided to ride over to his Pueblo some five miles distant. This is the Zia of Spanish celebration.[12] It was late ere I started, again alone, as Col. Stevenson had gone to visit the hot springs and others of our party did not care to join me. An old Mexican guided me to a point where a bend of the valley showed, perched on a little mesa, the dark, smoke-brimmed Pueblo of Zia. I rode up the steep pathway into one of the plazas, tied my little mule to a corral, and started on a tour through the town. A mild looking old man bade me enter his house. Strangely enough, he proved to be the Lieut. Governor. A rude feast was spread before me on the floor, and when I had finished, my host [conducted me on a tour of] the town, showing me the estufas, of which he informed me there were two.[13] He led me to one, a round underground structure just like those of Pecos, but when I asked to see the second, he guided me to the church, and paying no heed to my remark that this was not an estufa, he strode on to his house.[14] There I sat down, playing with his children, [and] showed him pictures, one from the estufa of Cochiti. On seeing this, he arose and left the house.

After about half an hour, he returned, laid the tip of one finger on my head, another on my sketch book, and pointed then toward the plaza. I took up my book and followed. He crossed the plaza, entered first a walled enclosure, then a long room with hand marks on the rafters. From this he went into still another [room], in the eastern end of which hung a great shield of Montezuma.[15] To the left of the latter was a door. He pounded this nine times and with bent head waited. Presently the door swung open with a loud rumbling sound like thunder, and I entered a large apartment, the walls of which were painted with signs for all the agricultural products, figures of lightning, the day sun and the night, the stars, and the Serpent of the sky. An altar was suspended under the latter in the end of the room, and underneath stood a long row of symbolic masks—in their midst a bowl of clear, yellowing liquid. My conductor kissed his hand and motioned me in.[16] In the middle of the room, naked and old, sat the chief of the estufa. He was spinning cotton for the masks which some silent young men were making. One ground paint in troughs of stone; another decorated those masks; another trimmed them with evergreens, while yet another was drilling shells to make ornaments for their animal-shaped ears. Strange was this sight where all worked as silently as did the workmen of old on the walls of Solomon's temple, where no sound save the clattering of spindle on the paved floor, the creaking of the steady little drill, and the scraping of the stone paint mill disturbed the sacred silence of this ancient sanctuary. I laid my hand on the head of the scowling priest, who forthwith smiled; turned to my guide, and thanked them for a privilege which, as they informed me, had never been accorded to a white man before, and retired. I was begged to stay all night, but, pleading [other obligations], I rode back to camp, promising to come early on the morrow and sketch the figures on the walls of the estufa. It was late [morning], however, ere I was in the saddle; yet, when I again rounded the valley and gazed off toward the mesa, I saw upon its edge, four men wrapped in serapes and watching the point which I rounded. They no sooner espied me than a young man galloped headlong down the steep path and, heeding neither growing corn nor irrigating ditches, dashed to my very side, stopping so suddenly that it scattered sand in my face. He reached both hands toward me, grasped both my own and giving me a violent squeeze, pointed to the men standing on the mesa edge. I understood by this that they were waiting for me and made breakneck haste to the base of the hill and up the steep path. As I dismounted, a man took my mule, and those who had been watching advanced, each gravely extending both hands to me, and escorted me to a large room facing the main court, which appeared to be a council chamber.

Here some melons were sliced and placed before me, and while I ate, the principal men of the Pueblo gradually gathered in and sat down to smoke. I had just finished when I heard approaching steps outside the door. Suddenly every one in the room rose from his seat and waited with bended head. I turned and beheld, slowly advancing, the most aged Indian I had ever seen. He was naked save for the short native mantua or tunic, and his legs were mere bones with a wrinkled and shriveled hide stretched lightly on them. His hair hung down in great tangled white masses over his red, blinded eyes and to his hollow cheeks and toothless mouth. With shaky and uncertain step he advanced, supported by a handsome, well dressed young man, to where I was sitting. Guided by the young man, he placed his arms around me and feebly embraced me. I returned his salute by laying my hand softly on his head. He was then seated beside me. Placing one of my hands in one of his own while with the other he ceaselessly felt for nothing up and down his crooked staff, he began, with head bent almost to his knees, a low tremulous speech. I observed that those who had happened to touch him had each kissed his hand afterward, and that while he spoke, all sat with bowed heads, maintaining perfect silence. I was therefore not surprised when, after he had concluded and dropped my hand, the principal of the four men who had received me moved nearer and began his low-toned translation by saying:

"The Cacique of the Sun, the Son of Montezuma, Son of the Sun, bids you welcome and is glad to number you among his children."[17]

In return I merely thanked him and his people for the privilege they had accorded me and for the distinguished compliment which he thus paid me; and when he arose to go I supported him to the door and breathed on my hands as I had seen the others do. This excited universal comment and approbation. So soon as the old man had retired, I was bid again to the estufa which I had visited the day previously. As the door swung open and I glanced in, I saw that all was changed. In the place of the busy workers of yesterday were only some weary and grotesquely costumed dancers—seven men sitting along the right wall and the same number of women along the left. At the head of either row and near the altar was an extra man costumed to represent a grizzly bear, his conventional mask of that animal held hanging just above and before him. The man who had translated for me proved to be the Governor. The others were the Lieut. Governor, the Alcalde, and a captain. With these dignitaries I stepped into the estufa and advanced to the front of the paintings of the sun and sky (the altar), the Governor and Alcalde on my left, the Lieut. Governor (my host) on my right. There we stood a moment with bowed heads until the aged and naked priest rose from his place near the fire which he never suffers to go out, and going up to the bowl under the altar, dipped up a long scoop full of its contents. Ideas of black drinks and others unmentionable passed through my mind, and I confess I rather dreaded the ceremonial through which I was to pass.[18]

Zuni: Making a Start

According to Cushing's later report to Powell, the group reached Zuni on September 19.[19] *Again riding alone in advance of the rest of the party, Cushing was the first to come in sight of the pueblo. Hence the thrill of personal discovery experienced upon emerging just at sunset at the top of a long, winding mountain pass and finding stretched out, a thousand feet below, a broad, sandy plain on the western horizon of which, just midway between the northern buttes and the opposite grey mesas, he beheld what looked like a little terraced hill, "held in the great outstretched arms of the setting sun."*[20] *This "hill" was, of course, Zuni.*

The Zunis, as Cushing was to learn, were the descendants of those Pueblos who had peopled the legendary "Cities of Cibola." Described by the chroniclers of the Spanish conquest of the Southwest, they were the subject of much speculation in Cushing's own time. When they were discovered by the Spanish in the sixteenth century, the Zunis had occupied at least six pueblos in the vicinity of the present Zuni reservation; by the time of the great Pueblo Revolt of 1680, however, they had abandoned these pueblos and taken refuge on the mesa tops. As they came down from these strongholds over the course of the next decade, they consolidated in a single settlement, now called Zuni, adjacent to the old pueblo of Halona on the Zuni River. At the end of the nineteenth century, the village was occupied by something over fifteen hundred souls (1,602 by Cushing's count the following year).

From the fragmentary draft of a letter dated September 27 from "Casa del Gobernador," it would seem that Cushing made his move from the expedition's camp into the house of Palowahtiwa (Patricio Pino), the Zuni governor, within little more than a week after their arrival (a shorter time than he would remember it to be in the account below). Two weeks later, the Stevensons and Hiller were back at Fort Wingate, en route to the Hopi towns in northern Arizona, and Cushing was alone in Zuni.

The first view presented here of his early experiences in the pueblo is actually a retrospective one, from a talk, "Life in Zuni," which he gave in Buffalo, New York, on December 10, 1890. Along with four or five other selections, it violates the rule of comtemporary witness generally followed in this collection. While in this respect it is a bit out of place with the notes and letters that follow, it is included for its vivid images of some of Cushing's first "adventures in Zuni." Indeed, it amounts to a kind of alternate version of an early segment of the published account of those "Adventures," the differences in detail only demonstrating that verisimilitude is as much an act of creation as of memory.

The reminiscence is also noteworthy for the glimpses it provides of Cushing's method and manner of approach at this crucial beginning stage of his fieldwork in Zuni—particularly of his cultivation of friendships with Zuni women and children as a means of entry into Pueblo society. Whatever stress he later placed on the importance of his demonstrations of intrepidity among the Zuni men, clearly the qualities that appealed to the Zuni women and children—his gentleness, consideration, playfulness, and sheer charm, as well as his ministrations to their wounds and illnesses—were of equal and perhaps greater importance, not only at the beginning but throughout his stay.

The earliest Cushing papers that date from the Zuni period, however, are two notes addressed to influential men: the governor, Palowahtiwa, or Patricio Pino, and his father, former governor Pedro Pino. Here we see that the role Cushing came to play as a spokesman for the Zunis, though urged on him by the Indians, was also from the beginning a strategic proposal of his own, aimed at winning acceptance in the pueblo.

Reminiscence

The first time I ever went into a Zuni house I took my pistol, hunting knife and spurs off at the doorway. I left them there. Then, as I entered, I removed my hat. The room was low, scrupulously neat, with whitewashed walls and low, wattled ceiling supported by huge round rafters. The floor was paved with smooth slabs of sandstone. At one side was the black-throated fireplace of stone and clay—very large, shaped like a box diagonally divided and set sideways against the wall. A jointed vertical row of bottomless pots leading up through the ceiling served as chimney. To one side of this was an enclosed line of graded trough-shaped stone slabs: the mills, coarse and fine, of the household. Opposite, depending from the ceiling was a long blanket-pole, covered with beautiful native fabrics. Exquisitely decorated jars and dishes stood along the walls, some filled with water, some with food. A loom was stretched from floor to ceiling under one end, under the porthole-like windows—glazed with a plate of mica—and little stool-blocks eighteen inches long and six inches high to the number of six or seven [were] placed near the hearth, for mealtime was approaching. A man was sitting under another window knitting. Two women were quietly working about, and a beautiful young girl had just come in with a water jar on her head, and, still balancing it, stood gazing at me through the part in her hair. Two small children scuttled out of the way as soon as I appeared, one down through a trap hole, the other under its mother's skirts, yelling heartily, and their elders busily coaxing and rebuking them for their incivility—as they had noted my actions at the door and were desirous of showing their appreciation thereof. I greeted them with gestures and was bidden first by the women, then by the men, to sit and eat, but I pointed to the children, laid a trinket on the floor, and departed. As evincing both the value of politeness toward savages and their power of observation, I heard every detail of my behavior during that, my first call in Zuni, related in council years afterward, and the character it gave me stood me in good stead at a critical moment.

After that I wandered about day by day making notes and sketches of everything I saw (drawing, I now see, wrong conclusions invariably). It was a busy place. The men, except the very old ones, were away in the fields; the women, except very old ones, were busy in and out of doors unceasingly. Along the sunny sides of the terraces, aged men and women sat chipping with pick of jasper or flint in clean and beautiful lines, a household utensil of lava, or spinning with a humming top-shaped distaff the fibers for the household loom, all the while singing in perfect accord the songs of their industry—songs so born of the arts that one would think that the work had given rise to the music of that people and that the winds which howl over their desolate land at night and in the morning had added their singular harmonies to the strains of labor.

Everywhere I wandered, the little children, shy as prairie dogs, would dodge in and out of the sky holes or scamper away far ahead, calling to one another so that the chance of seeing a man of such strange race and costume as we Americans then were to that people should not be missed. As time went on, my chief duty was the taming of these little wild urchins. I would hold out a bit of sugar or a gleaming strand of beads to them, and speak to them as softly as I could. By and by they began to venture toward me, would take my presents and scamper away, more often rebuked than not by their olive-skinned mothers when espied from some near porthole. But day by day they grew more familiar, until one day a woman came along my way with a very little child in the soft, dark-blue tasseled mantle at her back. The child's face was covered with scars, and its shoulder was bandaged, and it cried, poor thing, incessantly. I quickly, but with a smile, spoke up to the woman, who was about to flee from me. I laid my hand on my heart, touched her forehead lightly, and then my own, and diving into the wallet which I always carried, produced a box of ointment. She hesitated a moment. I stepped up to the child and breathed on my hand. Then the woman came nearer, holding the child closer to me also, and brushing off the shreds with which it was bandaged, I applied the ointment and covered the sore place with clean bits of cloth. In a low and wonderfully soft voice she said the one word, "*elahkwa*," which I knew must mean "thank you"; and thus I learned my first Zuni word.

After that, intercourse with the people became easier with me. Others brought their children to me. I plied them with my ointments, effecting what seemed to them wonderful cures, and both the children and their mothers grew as fond of me as I did of the children, for wonderfully beautiful they were with their smooth, round, bronze-colored cheeks and large bright eyes, fringed with long lashes, and their little dimpled mouths. As they became more and more familiar, I would catch one or another of them up in my arms, and, resolutely bent on making a slow conquest of the tribe, would kiss them, heedless of their abundant dirt, until before the end of a month my progress through this town, whether along the turning streets or over the high housetops, was a sort of triumphal march, leading a procession of shouting, laughing, expectant children. Through the children I became tolerated by the mothers, who, as I passed their door would thrust their hands forth and beckon me in, asking me to be seated; and gradually through the mothers I was made, first very grudgingly, and for many weary months most suspiciously, welcome by the men.

Col. Stevenson, the chief of our party, negotiated with the people in council and secured for the use of the expedition and of our photographer a couple of long, low-roofed, quaint rooms at the southwestern corner of the pueblo. Thither, considering that I had made sufficient progress in the good graces of the people, I one night bore my hammock, blankets and a few possessions and took up my abode. No one noticed my insinuation. At dusk an old man with a wonderfully clear-cut face, strong eyes and fine intelligent expression, whom I knew to be the head chief [governor] came into the room.[21] He looked at me a moment blankly. I did not know that by the right of marriage, as well as rank, he was the master of the house. A dog happened to stray into the room. My visitor snatched up a convenient rung from the ladder near at hand and vigorously assaulted the dog; then caught him up by the nape of the neck and flung him howling out of the sky-hole. Never a word did he utter, but he pointed to the disappearing dog, to the club, then to me, and dusted his hands. I pretended the blankest stupidity, and again he gazed at me, wonder-stricken, and with a disgusted shrug of the shoulders disappeared through a mysterious doorway at the end of the room.

The exit was guarded all night—and many a night after—but otherwise I was undisturbed. When I awoke the next morning, I saw an old, white-headed woman, very small, a child on her back, its face carefully secreted in the folds of her blanket. She was staring at me, an expression of extreme disapprobation and bewilderment on her face. I did not know that she was the grandmother, and therefore by tribal right the sole proprietor of the house. She looked at me long, with a stare so troubled, and a mouth so drawn down at the corners, that one would have supposed I was the chief figure of a horrible nightmare. Finally, she pointed to the East, whence we had come, and then to me, and calling out loudly, as though thereby to make me understand, motioned how bad it was for a stranger, and a tender young thing like me, to live in such a house. That sort of welcoming, and (as my knowledge of the language progressed) the invariable question of every man who chanced to come in of how soon I might be going back to Wassintona, was what I experienced, with no variation, until after the departure of our party for other fields.

No less absurd and ill-advised was my remaining among the Indians supposed to be by the principal of my associates than by the Zunis themselves. They attributed my resolution to youthful folly (nor do I now blame them); but finding that I persisted, they decided to give me the best opportunities for my experiment, and one morning, somewhat sooner than I had anticipated, I woke to find myself alone among the Indians. Of provisions I had almost none; of money, almost none, as it chanced; of resources aside from these, none whatsoever. All day long, wondering what I should do where so unwelcome, I wandered dejectedly about the town or stayed within the doors of the empty council chamber. I was too melancholy to eat, and even had I not been so, would have felt fearful of attacking my small store of provisions. But toward night I kindled with some pieces of brush a small fire on the hearth, and laying some slices of fat bacon in a skillet, endeavored to fry them, and, with the grease and flour and water, to make a kind of gruel. The blaze was so strong that the grease in my frying-pan was soon aflame, and ere I could extinguish it had sent up such a volume of black smoke that presently I heard the scuffling of feet. A pair of legs appeared on the ladder through the sky-hole.

I had placed the frying-pan by the side of the fire and retired, woebegone, to sit in my hammock and think. The pair of legs developed into the same old man who had expelled the dog. I had seen little of him since. He now came and stood before me, his hands behind his back, his head on one side, looking at me critically. I glanced up, but he neither moved his gaze nor his lips. He stood there looking at me until I lowered my head again in an attitude, I suppose, of extreme dejection; for presently, in sepulchral tones, he exclaimed in Spanish, of which he knew a few words,

"Pauvle?" (Poor?)

"Yes," I nodded.

"Muy pauvle?" (Very poor?)

To which I was also forced to assent.

"Ha! Ha!" exclaimed the old man, and resumed his contemplation of me.

Presently he approached me, thrust two fingers under my chin, lifted up my face, and sawed across his stomach with the edge of his hand.

"Hungry?" said he.

"Yes."

"Very hungry?"

"Yes."

"Ha! Ha!"

Then he turned and caught sight of my bacon. He curled his lip contemptuously and pointed to it.

"Pig's grease?" said he.

"Yes."

"No good," he remarked in the first English I had ever heard him utter. That was about all he knew, too. He went over to the fireplace and picked up the skillet, made a motion as though he would throw it into the river outside, then suddenly hesitated, a gleam in his eye. He smelled it.

"Good!" said he, making a gesture of relish and pointing to himself.

Then he wheeled around and, taking my all with him, disappeared up the ladder. I didn't know what to think. I sat down in my hammock again. After a while I heard a scuffle on the roof. Then the old man peered down through the sky-hole, showing the edge of the skillet, as clean and polished as though never used. With another chuckle, he vanished.

After some time, I heard his footsteps slowly approaching. He came down the ladder. Presently he was followed by his short and not over good-looking, though always well-meaning, wife. The old man poked in the fire and held my skillet before it in triumph. It was over-loaded with highly peppered, exceedingly well cooked slices of mutton and venison, deep in smoking grease, while the old woman bore along behind him a great basket-tray loaded with the most singular forms of bread. Little crescent-shaped cakes in corn leaves; little wrapped-up doughnuts of meal in carefully tied packages of corn-husk; and long, beautifully light semi-transparent rolls and sheets of paper-like bread [the often-mentioned *he-we*].[22]

"Here," said the old man, plainly motioning his meaning. "Now sit down with me and eat food fit for *men*!"

"Yes," said his wife, averting her face from me as from a pestilence, for having no children, she remained as yet unconquered. "Sit and eat," she said, and then hurried up the ladder.

I put forth my hand (there were neither spoons, knives nor forks), took a morsel in my fingers and was about to taste it, when the old man grabbed my wrist and pointed to the fire, then to the food, and then, lifting his palm upward:

"They," said he, "must always be remembered." He took a tiny morsel of each kind of food, breathed on it, held it near his heart, and uttered a short prayer; after which he cast the food into the fire and again breathed from his hand.

"There now," he said, or seemed to say, "you are a barbarian, and no wonder your people foresook you. Did they? Are you poor? Very poor?

"Well," he managed to explain, "unless you are a fool, you shall be poor no longer. You shall have brothers and sisters; I and mine; uncles and aunts; fathers and mothers; and where such are, no man need be poor.

"Now, will you be a Zuni? Or will you still be a fool?—in which case"—he pointed toward the northern mountains—"you will have to live beyond with your kind. Zunis live here, not fools."

I meekly acquiesced.

"Ha! then eat with me, little brother," said he; and ever after that, as truly as any man living, he was my elder brother and almost always with me.

FHC: Two Notes

Zuni, September 28, 1879

I would be the friend and plead the cause of the industrious and peace loving Pueblo Indians of Zuni, who have ever been kind to me, especially of their Cacique Grande, Pedro Pino.

Frank M. Cushing
In Chg Ethnology
Smithsonian Institution
Washington

[blob of wax, presumably as seal]

Zuni, October 1st, 1879

I am and shall remain always the friend of the People of Zuni, whose kindness, industry and intelligence speak most highly for the Pueblo civilization and deserve from superior nations commendation as high.

Whenever a good word can be said for them, a

good act done for them, I shall not hesitate to say and act for the People of Zuni.

The friend of Patricio Pino,
Gobernador de Zuni,
[signed] Frank H. Cushing
Ethnologist
Smithsonian Institution
Washington, D.C.

Draft: FHC to Thomas and Sarah Cushing

Zuni
Evening, October 7th, 1879

My dear Mother and Father,

An Indian just brought to the Pueblo some mail, and with it {your} letters, which are such prizes to me now.

Tomorrow morning our party leaves Zuni for Cañon de Chelly and the Moqui {Hopi} towns—all save poor lonely me, who remains, as he said he would, at Zuni. . . . {unfinished}

Diary Note

October 12, 1879

Sunday. Arose rather late and breakfasted with the Governor, who cooked the breakfast and was mightily pleased afterward by the compliment which I paid to the Zunians, saying they cooked as well as the Americans, which of course he most illegitimately took to himself. The forenoon was passed in attending to my two patients, who had been getting worse. The smaller one was very badly off, and I doubt if my medicines do him any good. The other, notwithstanding his night, is better, except on the shoulders.

Draft Fragment: FHC to {Emily Magill?}

{Zuni, October 14, 1879}

{I would give anything} in the world (save my love) could I remain but to do part only of what I wished to. How *can* I come home without it? The sum of money which was turned over to me {to} use I have seen but one sixth of, and the other day the Col. quietly informed me that it and his were all gone and he depended upon Washington for more for Moqui trade. So much for Mr. Leech's friendly interest.[23] I bear him no happy will for it. I may yet eat my Christmas dinner at 1515 {i.e., back in Washington}, but while I shall be happy, it will be with a heavy heart, I fear.

Well, dearie, I must go to work. If I have but short time here, I must work the harder, if that be possible. Good night, dear Love, I dream of you every night, and I hope I may this night, for I feel very unhappy.

Your loving Frank

Morning, Wednesday 15th. It is cold and windy but clear and bright this morning, and I feel . . . {unfinished}

Draft: FHC to Col. Stevenson

Zuni, October 15, 1879

My dear Colonel:

The wagon came last evening and, agreeably to your wishes, I have today packed everything save the large bowl and a small olla, which we had no room for without great risk of breaking. . . .

The Governor was gratified with his present (the axe wanting, by the by), and he wished me to say that when you come two small boards like ours would gratify him much. I find the Indians expect a great deal from you, which under the present condition of affairs you will be unable to give them. Of your arrangements with them, however, I know and say nothing—and in my own dealings with them I am most careful in what I promise—not caring to mortgage the possibility of a future among them for present prosperity and good will. They are remarkably kind to me, furnishing meat and every delicacy which their poor lot affords and asking in return only a drink or so of coffee and enough of sugar to sweeten it. It was therefore with regret that I found so small an allowance of these things in the wagon, although I doubt not you did the best you could by me. . . . I cannot too strongly urge upon you the importance of using all means in your power for enabling me in *any* event to remain here as long as you gave me reason to expect it would be convenient for me to. You remember that our instructions were to remain as long at the Pueblo we should choose as typical as I should deem it necessary, after the collecting was done, for measuring and research relative to the sociological organization of these people.

You remember that Major Powell said to me, "Find out these points by all means, as they are of primary importance, and if you can't do it in one month, *take six,* or even more. I would much prefer that one Pueblo be investigated thoroughly than that all the twenty seven should be seen and collected from superficially." The object, therefore, of the Expedition, as I understand it, is not merely collecting, which in itself is of great importance, but observing as well, which work I believe I have the honor of being trusted with. Now in order to secure points which cannot otherwise be done, I have labored assiduously to acquire a partial knowledge of the language, a work in which I have made fair progress but which requires with other things still more weeks ere their ends can be attained by it.

If I find it necessary to abandon this work at the very early day which it now seems necessary that the party should return to Washington, personally I shall be only too glad, as a solitary sojourn among these people, living as I have to, is not pleasant; but I deem it only my very clear duty to do what is in my power, and in a manner which probably seems to you unwarranted to urge you to do the same toward my remaining at least a month or six weeks longer at Zuni.

I am,
Respectfully Yours,
F. H. Cushing

FHC TO BAIRD

Zuni, Casa del Gobernador
October 15, 1879

My dear Professor Baird:

I had wished to write you many times ere this. I do not, however, give my reasons for failing to do so. They would be as tedious as they are numerous and true. Before I say anything regarding the success of our Expedition, I desire to express what has been in my heart all the while: namely my gratitude to you and Major Powell—mainly to yourself—for the happy opportunities which but for your kindness in appointing me to this trip, I had not enjoyed. I trust almost as I hope that when you see our collections you will not regret having sent me, as I have reason to believe that their number as well as their quality has been colored by my presence.[24] Discovering at the outset that my activity and success in collecting at Tesuque Pueblo, whither I proceeded alone from Santa Fe and remained two nights and as many days, excited the envy not to say jealousy of others in our party (especially of the *lady* member who has constituted such a leading spirit in it), I withdrew, upon our arrival at Zuni, entirely from such work, busying myself with measurements, sketching, and note-taking.[25]

I may mention here that during the afternoon I have among others written you a letter of no fewer than twelve pages. On reading it over, however, I think best not to send it as it is composed chiefly of complaints which without producing any good would only serve to annoy you. I therefore roll it up as of possible use, and must beg of you to pardon the brevity of this, the other having encroached so much upon the limited time which I have ere our wagon leaves.

In deference to the wishes of Col. Stevenson, I do not, [much] as I long to, tell you what we have acquired in the way of collecting, and I cannot have the gratification of speaking as happily of the results in the way of observations, which for completeness and value require more time and a practical knowledge of the language of these people. With the hope, however, of making these as full as circumstances will admit of, I have remained alone here while the rest are absent on a visit to Cañon de Chelly and the Moqui towns.

The trouble in Utah threatens, by preventing issue of more stores to us, to shorten our stay in this country very considerably, and while a longer one would hardly be productive of valuable results in the way of collections, every thing thus far gained in the way of observation will be comparatively valueless without reinforcements. . . .[26]

Feeling that I can never too highly regard the opportunities which through your kindness I regretfully see drawing to a close,

I am in the greatest haste,
Your Obedient Servant,
F. H. Cushing
Ethnologist, Eth. Exped.

[Spencer F. Baird]
Director, Smithsonian Instn.

From Unsent Draft of FHC to Baird, October 15, 1879

. . . .

I regret that Col. Stevenson and I should have started out with such entirely different impressions regarding my position on this Expedition. He has seen fit to regard me as a boy and to treat me since he reached the field entirely as he regarded me, but of this I do not in the least complain. He is an able and most excellent *business* manager, and, I think, as kind an executive officer as ever went into [the] field. Yet, for purposes scientific and reasons egotistic, I suppose, if Heaven, or rather, Professor Baird—of whose identity I am rather more certain—ever blesses me with opportunities for visiting this country again, on coming I shall insist that it be alone or as head, even with but half the means with which our Expedition was vested; and if the Powers that be (our subsistence and transportation, the War Department) are accommodating, I shall promise, as strongly as I insist, more than half-results. The "horizons for future work," which you [instructed] me to look out for in this country, don't require much looking for. I've even noted several *prominent* "pinks" in the middle ground which are vastly rich in scientific material objectives as well as philosophic. This country has been in most respects—in none more than ethnologically—badly misrepresented by my predecessors, largely, I think, on account of insufficient data. To be able to correct these misrepresentations and to produce something in the way of a report at least worth the writing, I shall require some more time here. . . .

Previously to the departure of Col. Stevenson, I had arranged with him to remain here after the rest had returned to Washington, until mid-winter, as there was little that they could do after the close of this month, and much of my work which necessarily remained undone. I was rather surprised, however, when I came to look over the stock of provisions etc. which had been promised to me . . . to find that I had no tent, barely half a camp kit, half a pound of sugar, a little coffee, *no* cloth, four coffee mills, and six dollars for trading. I confidently looked forward to the coming of the wagon for that all-essential tobacco and trading material for making food and industrial collections as well as an increase of provisions, to which effect I wrote to Wingate by means of an Indian who was going that way. When the wagon came, it brought a sack of flour, four or five pounds of sugar, the same amount of coffee, the articles I had named as necessary for my camp kit, and no trading material or money, save six skeins of yarn and five or six yards each of white and red cotton cloth. I do not write this complainingly but as indicating, I think, together with the remark which the Col. made in the presence of one of the men, that he should allow me to remain here but fifteen days longer, as indicating that he intends my stay here shall be as limited as my means. Yet, in the name of candor, it seems strange that in his letter he makes no mention of this intention. He only wishes me a pleasant time, all success, and a great increase of information, while he hopes I shall have my measuring as far completed as possible when he returns.

The notes which I shall be able to make in such a limited time, together with the completion of my measurements, must add little to those I already possess. Nor can a fair picture be drawn of these people before December, when all the inhabitants of the three or four dependent Zuni pueblos are gathered in and the winter ceremonies and festivities begin. It is solely with the wish to make my visit to this Pueblo of a little scientific use that I would even *consent* to remain here. Communicating by means of Spanish as yet imperfectly understood by myself and hardly better by the Indians, living in constant discomfort from cold, the eating of disgusting Indian food, etc. etc., together with the unceasing apprehension of a change in the manner of these people toward me, to say nothing of the wish to be once more at home, you can judge whether it is mere personal desire, or interest in the work, which causes me to appeal to you (as I do) to use your power in lengthening my stay here (if comformable to your wishes and conveniences) to the end of December or the middle of January. If I can trust my memory (I have here nothing else to rely on), the instructions which were given to Mr. Stevenson and me were to the effect not only that I was to have the sum of one hundred and seventy five or two hundred dollars or its equivalent placed at my disposition for filling up gaps [left by others in the collection] and the rations, tobacco, etc., of four men, but also that the *Expedition*—not myself alone—should remain, nothing of a business nature interfering, wherever I should judge it desirable for observations and collecting until such observations and collecting were completed. Moreover, I was specially instructed and directed by Major Powell to make complete measurements for a model of Zuni on a large scale, as well as whatever else I might find to do, to get at the social structure and system of land and house tenure of the Pueblo Indians, and "that if one month were not sufficient for this to use six or even more." I have labored faithfully to accomplish these two objectives, have diligently studied to this purpose the language, which I am gradually acquiring, and without a partial knowledge of which the task laid on me, difficult in any case, is absolutely hopeless. Perhaps all these instructions were shams. If so, their falsity has not been revealed to me; and in the event of not hearing from you I have nothing to do but to follow them out, believing that by investigating these and other even more important questions, which all ethnological works are so at fault about, I shall be not only obeying orders as a private, but also doing what you would most wish me to do.

The expense of living here (as I live) is nominal—chiefly drawn from the bank of health in which I had, when I reached Santa Fe, a large capital invested, though it must be admitted I have considerably reduced it since. Nevertheless, the residue is amply sufficient. The chief actual expense will be in my railroad transportation home, which will amount to more than it would did I accompany the others.

I was advised by Col. Stevenson to get two small sketch books and twice as many memoranda books. I bought twenty four of the latter and ten of the former and at this moment leave it to Providence to tell me where I shall make all of my memoranda, as several of the books are filled, the Col. has relieved me of eight, and four of my sketch books are filled with pencil and water colors. I promised the gentlemen who exclaimed so loudly at my extravagance that for anything not actually required for our work I would willingly pay the bills. I shall have but a dollar and a half to pay.

Begging you to pardon my long delay as well as an irritating letter, as hastily scribbled as it is irritating as an apology,

I remain, dearest Professor,
Your Very Humble Servant,
Cushing
Ethnologist, Eth. Exped.

Note [N.D., circa 10/17/79]

We entered a room where there was a company of several persons eating—men, women, and children. The fire was bright on the hearth, and by its light I could see three great bowls of meat, chili, and corn cooked together. . . .

As I entered, [someone] said, "Sit, eat," and made a place for me in the crowd, placing two blankets for me to sit on. The Governor went to the end of the room and sat down by himself. Presently he asked me why I did not eat, and I asked him why he did not, to which he replied he had already eaten much. So I sat down with the rest and ate from the bowls in common with all, using my fingers and a little wooden spoon with which I was provided.[27] All were greatly pleased—and also happy to see me wearing the head band which the Governor had tied for me in the morning, with the remark that it was good to do at Zuni as the Zunians did, and that [as] I ate like them, why not wear a head band. . . .

Daily Journal: "*Ho-ma-tchi*" Dance

The two entries which follow represent the contents of a 3¾" × 6¾" notebook labeled Daily Journal V, Zuni, October 20th to October 30th, 1879. *It is the earliest such journal known to be extant, and in this book the last third of the pages have been torn out. Five other notebooks similarly filled with daily journal entries are all that seem to have survived from the whole Zuni period. The proportions of the loss are so great that it is best simply to concentrate gratefully on what we do have, and there is a particular fortuity in the survival of this earliest of the notebooks, since almost the whole of it is devoted to meticulous field notes of the kind that Cushing generally has been supposed never to have taken. The subject—an enactment of what he understood, perhaps mistakenly, to be the* "Hō-mā-tchī" *or "Knife Dance"—is also of particular interest for several reasons, not least among them Cushing's own brief but very memorable part in the proceedings.*[28]

When he took his place on the pueblo roof on the morning of October 20, 1879, to record the ritual events of the day, Cushing had been in Zuni just a month; hence, he was severely limited in his knowledge about what was transpiring. Through the medium of his keen and detailed observation there emerge the lineaments of a remarkable ceremonial, but exactly what ceremonial it was remains something of a mystery. It seems evident from the date and from the prominence of corn, melons, peppers, and feasting of one kind and another that it was a harvest rite, and in fact Matilda Stevenson too described a "thanksgiving festival for the crops"—the O'winahai'ye*—which she said was celebrated annually in October ("The Zuni Indians," pp. 205–17, 578). A production of the Bow Priest war society, the rite reported by Stevenson, like that reported by Cushing, combined features relating to the harvest with features common to the war dance, such as burlesque and various gestures signifying destruction of the enemy.*[29] *There, however, the similarities seem to cease. Stevenson described a two-day-and-two-night-long festival in which the war society figured prominently and in which dancing in "the dress of the anthropic gods" occurred only at night and indoors. Cushing described a one-day festival ending at sundown which featured kachina dancing in the plaza and predominant roles for several societies that went unmentioned in Stevenson's account. On the other hand, Cushing himself failed to mention the Bow Priests (of whom he may not yet have heard). In other respects, too, what is most striking in each of these accounts is absent from the other. Were they describing the same ceremonial? Brief references to the* O'winahai'ye *by several later anthropologists suggest that they probably were, but none of these later anthropologists was actually present at a performance of this rite; they only heard about it from informants as something discontinued long since or performed very infrequently.*[30]

In any event, the enactment we witness through Cushing's account is a colorful and highly dramatic one, alternating between humor and ferocity, mock violence and real violence, stately dancing in unison and wild leaping about, a well-ordered feast of cooked food and the frenzied engorging of raw peppers and ripped-out dog parts, being victimized and victimizing in turn. It was filled, in short, with the sorts of oppositions that would interest modern anthropologists of a structuralist bent as well as those who might see them as an advance warning against any one-sided application of the term "Apollonian" to Zuni culture.

As Cushing had recognized by the time he got around to mentioning this "Ho-ma-tchi" *dance to Baird (letter of July 18, 1880), the gorger clowns who play so important—and so un-Apollonian—a part here were members of the* Newekwe *clown fraternity. Specialists in healing disorders of the stomach, they demonstrated their powers by their capacity to eat and drink* any*thing. What is involved in the present instance, however, is a kind of progression from feats of sheer ingestion (raw peppers, urine) to something more complex, more akin to the frenzies of the Dionysian maenads tearing apart their victims. Seen in this light, the "killing of a Navajo" becomes an act of sacrifice, the victim in this case (at least as it turns out) being a kind of scape-dog who, instead of being cast out, is "taken in" by the all-digesting* Newekwe.

Cushing's own part in the day's events occurs late in the afternoon (and almost at the end of the notebook), when, with startling suddenness, he becomes the endangered center of attention. Critical as the moment seems clearly to have been, it is entirely unforeshadowed in his account of the preceding hours, save for one brief and seemingly humorous exchange with some of the dance figures. Does this mean that he had simply been ignorant of the warning signs that would have identified him all along as the intended victim—indeed, as the raison d'etre of the entire performance? Or does this on-the-scene account suggest rather that his part was an incidental, almost accidental one (no less perilous, to be sure, once he was noticed with the hated sketch pad) in a ceremony whose motives were more generalized in origin? Cushing himself (professedly informed later on by the Zunis themselves) of course held to the former explanation, which was far more interesting from his standpoint and in keeping with his treatment of this episode in "My Adventures" as the climactic turning point when his courage in the face of extremity sealed his acceptance in Zuni.[31] *On this point the reader will have to decide for himself. In any case, the notebook tells us a great deal more about this ritual event as performed a century ago than has hitherto been known.*

MONDAY, OCTOBER 20TH, 1879

Arose late on account of last night's late writing and illness. Pedro Pino came in this morning for the first time since the party left, and while the Governor was baking and making bread, I went down to Dr. Ealy's to get coffee and a piece of calico and ask for medicine for Lupolita's mother's eyes.[32] When I returned, the Governor cooked me some meat, impaling it on a rod and roasting it over the coals most deliciously, then serving it with salt and chili. Just finished breakfast when the dance began. The dancers had already issued from the estufa opposite the church (across the alley).[33] Whenever not dancing, they were hopping from one foot to another and going about in a sort of crazy zig zag course. This dance is called the *Hō'mā'tchī* and is distinguished from all others by the presence in the right hands of great stone and wooden knives. I therefore name it the Knife Dance. It contains several characters. The most numerous I first describe. Of these [Bow priests in *Homachi* masks?] the dress, with the slightest exceptions, was precisely like that of the *Tcha-kwi-na,* save that the shoulders, instead of being painted with yellow, were covered by the skin of a gray fox, and the body, instead of being painted black, was nearly of the normal color, heightened a little, perhaps, by Indian red, the arms below the elbows and the legs below the knees being painted yellow.[34] The wrists of the right hands had a bracelet of two strings of oliva shells and a slight binding of dried grass. Those of the left were bound by the same leather and silver bracelets I have before described. Round the left leg below the knee, and not visible in the dance—therefore probably having some superstitious significance—was bound some dried grass like that which encircled the wrist. To the calf of the left leg—and there for noise, not for show—was the invariable tortoise shell and deer hoof rattle, bound on cross-wise. In the left hands were carried the bow and the green wand, and in the right an ancient stone knife somewhat like the N[ew] Z[ealand] *Patu patu.*[35] Those who did not happen to possess these had made some in close imitation of wood. All had been dipped in blood, and over one or both sides had been scattered eagle down. I observed one who, having lost his knife, had extemporized by using a trowel.

The masks of these common dancers were straight pieces of raw hide, bent around to cover the faces, the eyes being little protruding balls, and the mouth bearded by red skin lips, the upper one of which was surmounted by a short moustache and the lower one below by a long beard of human or horse hair, black, gray, roan or even green, according to the character of the dancer. The shorter front hair had been beautifully frizzled and combed in beautiful wavy masses over the upper portion of the mask and down the sides of the head. The painting was in the greatest variety. The first in the line had the mask painted black, the eye band (1) being green and the eye balls green socketed with black tips. The face was specked all over with tiny red and blue spots, and the beard was light gray.

The second was half black, half pink. Eye band green holes, not balls, for eyes and beard black.

The third—carmine spotted with black and white, green eye-band, balls for eyes, green sockets, black tips—and black b[ea]rd.

The fourth—white, black-spotted & black eye-band, balls for eyes, gray beard.

The fifth—Indigo, green band, balls for eyes, green sockets, brand-iron gray duck-head base to feather head-tuft.

Sixth—red, blue band, balls for eyes, sockets white, beard red.

Seventh—green, black band, balls for eyes, green beard.

Eighth—vermillion, black band, balls, white sockets.

Ninth—duck mask.

Tenth—green, black band, balls for eyes.

Eleventh—blue, two rows of white spots, two of red below eye-band which was green, holes for eyes.

Twelfth—white, red and blue spots, black band, balls for eyes.

Thirteenth—green, white and pink spots, black band, holes for eyes, bl[ack] beard.

Fourteenth—red, black and white spots, black band, balls for eyes, gray beard.

Fifteenth—black, green band, balls for eyes, gray beard.

Sixteenth—yellow, black band, balls for eyes, yellow beard.

Seventeenth

Eighteenth—green duck.

Nineteenth—pink, bright green band, balls for eyes, gray beard.

Twentieth—green, red band, balls for eyes, green beard.

Twenty-first—duck, regular spots.

Twenty-second—half crimson (right side), half black, white spots, black eye-band, holes for eyes, black beard.

Twenty-third—white, black spots, black eye-band, balls for eyes, black beard.

Twenty-fourth—crimson, regularly disposed white spots, green eye-band, balls for eyes, black beard.

Twenty-fifth—right side black, pink and white spots, black band; pink other side, white spots, green band; holes for eyes, black beard.

Twenty-sixth—black, white and carmine spots, green eye-band, balls for eyes, gray beard.

Whenever the color of the sockets is not mentioned, they are the same color as the band, except when this is black, in which case they are white. For example of full figure, see sketch-book, fig. 1.[36]

The second class characters consisted of three, all dressed nearly like the others save that one wore the long, fringed kachina belt instead of the embroidered kind which the others wore. They wore round-topped, round masks, straight front, back and sides, covering the entire head and distinguished particularly by great black beaks of wood,

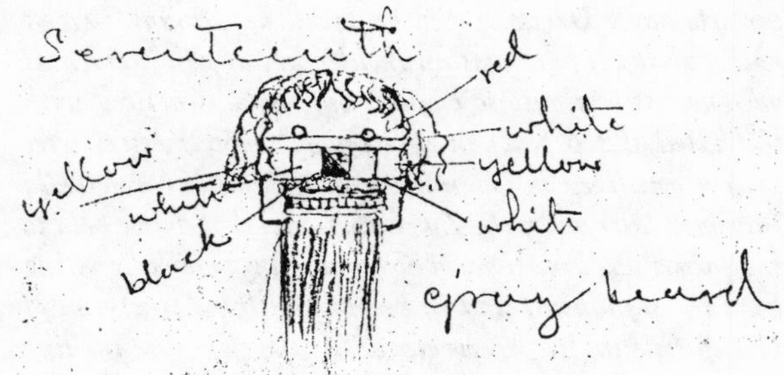

Fig. 1 Seventeenth Homachi (Cushing sketch).

made evidently in imitation of that of the duck. Two were white and spotted, one distinguished from the other only by the greater regularity of the spots. Each was surmounted by the stuffed head and neck of the wild drake, into the nostrils of which were bound two *maya* [crested bluejay] feathers and two small plumes of eagle down. To and over the base of this neck was bound eagle down, in front of which were two or three brown feathers pointing forward and behind which was a wide-spread fan-shaped ornament made of the reddish brown feathers of the *Pe-pe* or falcon with the down, and under the feather work was a tuft of black or brown hair which hung down in all directions over the top of the mask. The eyes were represented by tiny white balls, the tips of which were painted black and underneath which were two short black streaks, in which, invisible, were the holes for seeing. At the sides were holes for the ears, very small and square, and over these and the eyes, meeting on the front of the forehead, were two conventional serpents, one yellow and the other blue. On the back of the mask was the painting in crimson of the Horned Toad (conventional) and on either cheek, that of the coyote's paw.[37] Round the base of the mask, forming a great collar, was bound a gray fox skin.

The third differed from these in having the face green, having a simpler head dress (wanting the duck's head, and in its place having two painted black feathers). Neither were the two serpents painted upon it, but the coyote paw was a trifle larger and more elaborate, having in the base a round white spot. In the place of the serpents were two immense frizzled tufts of hair on either side, which gave the mask a very different appearance. The girdle of this one was the long fringed white kachina belt. The skirt was more scant than those of the rest, revealing the right leg and showing the dancer to be an albino, the legs and arms of whom were magnificently developed and rounded. He carried a knife of stone, the point of which had been broken and ground off.

The one with the regular spotting carried a very broad gray stone knife, chipped and slightly rounded, on one side of which had been painted in black a number of short streaks and tadpoles. In addition, like all the rest, it had the blood and eagle down spotting.

One of the dancers, the fourteenth, carried in addition to the knife, wand and bow one of the common gourd rattles such as are used in the *Tcha-kwi-na* dance. It was his office to give the warning by long and loudly shaking the rattle. Otherwise, he was indistiguishable from the others. Aside from this one was the invariable *Awen Tatchu* [leader] carrying a different, though generally similar, bowl to that of the *Tcha-kwi-na.*[38] The feather baton differed also in that the tip feathers were blue and some of the others must have been those of the parrot. Of course there was the usual profusion of eagle down, and the base was of most beautiful yellow basket work. He wore white cotton pantalettes, and the primitive knitted woolen coat of Zuni, the sleeves open at the shoulders and closed at the wrists. His hair was combed down as before, and, as before, he wore in it at the crown a large white plume of eagle down.

They came out of the estufa in single file, hopping about on its roof as I have described, rather violently from one foot to the other, coming down the ladder in single file and running off toward the court of the church, the first out pausing and running about in a confused mass near the large space at the corner of the church until the others should come up. Then running in or hopping to the center of the court, all the while keeping up the cry of "*Hū ū lī, Hū ū lī, Hū hā, hū hā, hū hā*," which being uttered in a deep tone and out of time, some calling "*Hū lī*," while others were snapping out "*Hū hā*," made a fearful din, and, together with their crazy prancing about and brandishing and wriggling of their great bloody, down-covered stone knives, gave the impression that a lot of mad monsters had been let loose and were seeking whom they might haggle and devour.

Suddenly the rattle rustle is heard through the clatter of the tortoise shells and immediately every one, just where he stands, begins the regular step by lifting the right foot, bringing it solidly down, raising the left an inch or two as though to get a better footing, and again stamping the right—in rapid succession. Soon the confused clatter becomes rhythmical and the worse confused cries of "*Hooli, Hooli, Hū hā, Hū hā*" merge into a song or chant to the rhythmical clatter, as the dancers gradually—never breaking step—assume their definite places in the line. These are shown in diagram on the following page, and were but slightly varied throughout the day. The *Awen Tatchu* (1) was at the head, facing the dancers; next came the common dancers, as I have described them in detail, the eighth being the Duck mask, the captain of the dance, standing midway (3) between him and the second duck mask (regular spotting, 4), and the duck mask with the green face coming two below the latter. The rear of the dance was brought up by a very short and probably hunch-backed person, and indeed all the latter ones were ranged in the order of their height, from the *Awen Tatchu* down, giving the line a regular and most beautiful appearance.

Dancing some fifteen minutes. The captain at the close of one of the measures of the song gave the warning rattle, and the dancers, *pell mell,* as before, began their crazy prancing. The *Awen Tatchu* gravely marched off through the covered way toward the next stopping place, the front of the cacique's house before mentioned. Some time in making their noisy transit, they at last arrived, the *Tatchu* awaiting them and the dance beginning promiscuously as before. The order was as before. The step the same and the figure which I describe here in more detail. The front was being constantly turned, never looking, never more than for a moment being faced one way. Nor was the turning simultaneous. It began at one end and continued to the other, just as a row of bricks fall, the end one being knocked over, one after another. This gave a very pretty effect.

On each turn, the *Tatchu* dipped his fingers into the bowl, took up a pinch of the meal and scattered it on the ground in front of the first dancer, who at such time was facing him, and who then immediately turned, followed by the next, and so on. After a short interval, the song ceased, and all, raising their knives and pointing them toward the horizon, cried out "*Hū lī, Hū lī, Hū lī, Hū hā, Hū hā, Hū hā*," again resuming the song, lowering the knives and only raising and thrusting them forward in time to the dance and at the end of some emphatic measures in the song. The absolute regularity of song, stamp, turn and thrust of the knives was as remarkable as it was beautiful in effect.

Whenever any part of the attire on one of the dancers became disarranged, the *Tatchu,* leaving his place, walked to the one in question, placed his bowl and baton carefully on the ground, resting the latter over the former, repaired the defect, and leisurely resumed his place. When again the dance broke up, they all proceeded around the corner and to the Old Court. Here they assumed a line, the *Awen Tatchu* standing at (1), the green duck at (2), the captain at (3), the regularly spotted duck at (4), and the others at (5). Next to him always danced the dancer with the red buckskin skirt.

Continuing here about the same length of time, they proceeded to the Dancers Court through the covered way, taking considerable time for the transit. The first duck, and the red-masked *Hō-mā-tchī* (see figure) remained behind all the rest and wriggling their knives at each other, one bending one way while the other bent down the opposite. After the others had remained in the Dancers [Court] long enough to resume their dance in the regular semi-circle they were joined by the duck and the red mask, the latter with the other remaining out through nearly half the dance. The green duck, on the contrary, always danced regularly with the others to his place, joining the line as soon as the rest. Although essential, he appeared to have no special part to play. Breaking up from this, they rushed to the estufa opposite the church, remaining there about half an hour, chanting meanwhile and two or three of them always in motion, as I inferred from the rattling of the tortoise shell.

When they again came forth, they were headed by the *Awen Tatchu,* who, as he descended the ladder, sprinkled flour on the ground. Again they made the round of dancing, first in the Church Court, then at an intermediate point in front of a new house, again in front of the cacique's house, [in] the Old Court (1) and [in] the Court of the Dancers. As may be seen by the diagram, they were not all out this time, the green duck and three or four of the main dancers lacking.

After completing the circle this time, they retired to the estufa for nearly two hours, women and young men bringing great quantities of cooked food for them to feast on. At about two o'clock, they appeared as before, and as before, danced the round, all being present this time. When returning through the covered way leading from [the] Old Court, they were met at the end by the *Koyemoshis,* headed by an *Awen Tatchu* with streaks of flour drawn across his eyes and mouth (fig.) and bearing a pitcher containing flour and a baton of feathers but slightly differing from the one carried by the other *Tatchu.*[39] They received the others with their usual shout and passed on in single file to the Dancers Court. Some of them carried melons made into packs with Spanish bayonet fibre; others carried long strings of corn—one red, another black, and others white. The *Awen Tatchu Koyemoshi* (the one with feathers in his ears—see sketch) bore a short-handled axe and a section of a knotty pine stump, both covered with flour so that the latter was hardly recognizable [distinguishable] from bread. They were accompanied by a young man bearing a drum, who took his place near a ladder in the north east corner and began beating, first calling attention by a series of raps.

The *Koyemoshis* faced about and began to dance along by hitches, gradually assuming a circular course. While in progress, they sang sharply and in time to the drum in the usual Zuni strain: "*Hē kōn tē, Kī kâ ko Hē kōn tē Kī kān hō.*"

Each hitch took them a few feet; then they stopped, faced inward, and, dancing, sang the following:

Hē k on ī
hē hâ ō
Hēk on i
hē hâ u,
etc.

and so on until they had completed the circle, when they formed a semicircle, all the while singing and stepping from one foot to another. Then they ceased, and the *Tatchu Koyemoshi* stepped in front of the cacique and, taking a pinch of flour from the pitcher, raised it to his mouth as though to kiss it, stepped to the middle of the circle, and, bending low, breathed on it and muttered over it, then sprinkled it on the ground in the form of a cross (E), carefully and, to the great chagrin of the other trembling *Koyemoshis,* depositing his stick of wood over the intersection. When the latter touched the ground, all the *Koyemoshis* jumped as though it had fallen on their toes. Then he placed his axe alongside the knot and deposited, a little way off, his melon. Another placed a second on the opposite side, and so on, until, on both sides equally, all the corn, melon, calabashes and onions were placed one on another in neat little heaps. A considerable number of spectators, women and children had gathered by this time in their usual place at the south side of the Court. Presently the drum struck up and the semi-circle began to dance and sing as before, while the *Tatchu Koyemoshi* again advanced, took more flour, sprinkled it over the heaps of fruits and the wand and axe. Then [he] took two eagle feathers from the cacique and waved them over the wood to the time of the dance, with which he kept step. Meanwhile, the [other] *Koyemoshi* went up to the crowd of women and touched two on the shoulders. They came forward and stood quietly near the wood. The dance stopped. The *Koyemoshi Tatchu* went up to one, [who] bent her head and moved her lips a few times, then to the other, who did the same, and then he took up the axe and advanced to the younger. She laid aside her blanket, and carefully adjusting the stick, began to attempt splitting it. Whenever she hit a blow which seemed likely to split off a stick, the *Koyemoshis* flew about and trembled as though it were one of themselves. Not succeeding, the axe was presently handed to the older woman, who ultimately struck off a stick. Succeeding no further, she was dismissed and a young man touched on the shoulder approached as they retired.

He succeeded in splitting off a stick and was rewarded with a string of corn as he went, a middle-aged man next being summoned. He did not succeed better, and a finely made fellow sitting on the estufa was called and beckoned. He sprang up, tearing off his frock as he descended the ladder. Running up to the stick, he grabbed it in both hands, terribly frightening the *Koyemoshis* by his bustle, and turning it over and over, carefully laid it down on the ground, striking several tremendous blows with all his might. Again placing the stick, he struck it so hard that he glanced his axe and fell, amid the cheers of the spectators and the frightened shouts of the *Koyemoshis.* He was on his feet in a moment, and pulling off his breeches, so as to be nude save for his breech clout, he again fell to, harder than ever, striking off several sticks. Then he was directed to rest, and the older man tried again. Not succeeding, he was mocked by the *Koyemoshis,* one of whom ran up, turned around, raised his breech clout and exposed himself in the elderly man's face, then skipped to his place as the latter succeeded in splitting off a stick. Then the younger man was again permitted to try, furiously and blindly striking, a small chip flying and hitting one of the *Koyemoshis* in the head, who staggered and fell under its tremendous force, not being able to resume his legs until helped to them.

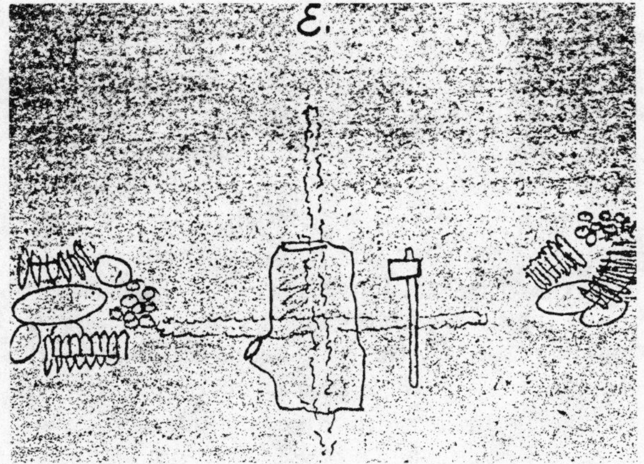

Fig. 2 Peppers and Wood Chunk (Cushing sketch).

At this point the *Tatchu* appeared at the entrance, with his yelling, prancing dancers in tow, and immediately the two men went forward to the cacique of the *Koyemoshis* and, taking their fingers full of flour from his pitcher, bent low their heads before him, moved their lips as [though in] confession and prayer, and then the first (the younger) advanced to the *Koyemoshi Tatchu* (who bent his head) and sprinkled some of the flour above his forehead; then the next, and so on to the last, meanwhile moving his lips rapidly, like a priest at the altar. The older man did the same. Then they gathered up the chips and sticks in a blanket, a gray haired man and a woman doing the same with the melons etc., and the *Koyemoshis,* headed by the cacique and followed by the drummer, began the hitchy march out, as they had come in, some little children running in and picking up every chip and scrap of wood, not only to get them out of the way of the dancers but to preserve them.

The *Koyemoshis* went out as the others were coming in, shouting to them as they had on entering. The line was then taken up, and the old *Homatchi* dance resumed as before. A long interval of feasting then succeeded, during which quantities of cooked food were issued to groups of young men and children standing about the estufas, and some of it was taken to the neighboring houses.

When next the dancers issued from the estufa, they went directly into [the] Dancers Court, accompanied by two of the *Koyemoshis,* blanketed. Gradually they were joined by more and more of the latter, until all were assembled. Then the dancers retired and the *Koyemoshis* remained behind to cut about and play the fool as is their custom. One was standing, and another sneaked up and laid a spider on his foot. The victim seemed to be unaware for a few moments, then fell over, and the others cut and hid behind a ladder. The victim, recovering, got a large stone and began to pound at the mite of a spider as though it were a serpent, missing it each time. The aged *Koyemoshi* must needs be mixed up with the affair, so he advanced cautiously, and the other began to search for the spider, with stone in hand, pretending to have lost it. [Meanwhile,] three or four [others] were [also] looking about for the [the spider,] hands on knees. One snatched it up and put it on the foot of the aged *Koyemoshi,* the latter still hunting in the sand for it. Then the one who had placed it on his foot sneaked up and, taking a small pinch of skin with the insect, pulled them off together, utterly upsetting the aged *Koyemoshi* with astonishment and pain, the latter not recovering for half an hour but going about on one foot and rubbing the bitten one (as he supposed) with the other hand. Then one found a string and was holding it up to his eyes and stroking it. Another stepped up behind and pulled it gently out of his hands, a third taking it out of his, and a fourth out of *his*—all, from first to last, pulling and stroking at the string as though entirely unaware it had been taken from them [and then] finally discovering, with such surprise that they almost lost their balance, that they had been stroking and tying knots in nothing.

One caught sight of me trying to sketch him. He tumbled over, got up, ran against the wall to find his companions, and then communicated the fact to them. It paralysed them, so that I sketched two before they could hide. One got behind a ladder, just showing one eye to me. The aged gent, entirely unaware that I could sketch *him,* held a blanket to hide another. Suddenly turning, he saw me looking at him and lost his balance, recovered, and turned his back, which I sketched. Another discovered me at this and informed the one of age. Then he ran and hid behind a ladder, another behind him, and another, and so on. The most ridiculous sights I ever witnessed, I think.

No more joking until the dancers came, and the whizzer took his place, and the others ranged around to shout. One told a *Homatchi,* about his [illegible] and presently a half dozen of those devils were gathered round my ladder, brandishing their knives at me, as though [to] drive me away—which they did to a pack of brats, greatly to my relief, though I held my ground, as had been the case several times before today. And as before, they retired like Christians' lions. The dance lasted about the usual time, they retired, and the *Koyemoshis* remained, beginning now to play ball with a buckskin pad [bag] by hitting one another anywhere and as hard as they could. When one was hit, he ran to the other side, and so on. Finally they lost their ball and their senses together at the sound of a drum advancing through the covered way and accompanied by a loud rapid song: "*Hǟ' hō' chur ch chur ch Chur ch*!!!" repeated over and over again, with a series of words between. As the sound approached, I observed two men advancing side by side, and sidewise, by shifting their feet along without taking them off the ground, exactly each time the drum was struck by the first and larger man, who carried it resting on his toes.[40]

They were costumed alike, wearing skull-caps of white fabric, with a tuft of split husks on the crown and sides. The face and body were painted white, a black streak being drawn along under the eye and down the cheek, and another over the upper lip and down the corners of the mouth, like a moustache, which it exactly resembled. Around the neck was a loosely twisted black woolen string tied in a sailors knot, the two ends falling down on the breast like the ends of a scarf. A little out of keeping with their profession (as afterward revealed) was the wearing of pantaloons. One had a black pair, the other white cotton. The first (as I shall call him hence[forth]) wore large silver ear-rings but was otherwise indistinguishable from the other, save by his size and expression. They entered with their heads thrown back, singing and grimacing like wild beings, as they were, and when they neared the corner, began to throw interjections into their songs in the way of witty speeches, which never failed to excite laughter [in] the by now great crowd of spectators who thronged the house tops.

When they reached the corner of the court, the larger set down his drum and picking up the lost ball, struck one of the timid and inoffensive *Koyemoshis* in the back, laying him out senseless on the ground. This began war, the *Koyemoshis* hauling the clowns down and pounding them, singly or in body as best they could. Whenever one of these fellows (who were all the while shouting out witticisms with a readiness quite worthy of a Yankee and were always ready with repartee to a most astonishing [degree]) happened to get pounded by a *Koyemoshi* and the other stood innocently by, he fell to pounding him as though he were a *Koyemoshi* [himself], or if he happened near a ladder and could seize a round, then as the teasing *Koyemoshi* disappeared, with evident satisfaction he began pounding the ladder in his place. Though wonderfully ready with their speeches, and as greatly feared as they were pounded by the *Koyemoshis,* they made themselves to be quite as great fools in many respects. Thus things went on until the moving of the distant *Homatchis* warned them to begin to get their places. As these entered, the *Koyemoshis* assumed their places and the clowns joined in with the former as though they would get into the line, from which, however, when it was formed, they were ignominiously crowded out.

When the dancers again retired to their estufa, the sporting was resumed. Presently I heard a great yell and, looking up, saw a strange painted and masked figure dart into the midst of the *Koyemoshis,* hit one a peck on the head with a stuffed deer-skin, and as quickly dart out of the court. Never before was such terror exhibited by the *Koyemoshis* and the clowns. They hid behind ladders and little stones, ran against one another, the one hit swoon[ing] away, and ere they had recovered, another identical figure, save in colors, darted in upon them and pounded *Koyemoshis* and clowns alike, the latter pounding in turn not only the ground where they had passed but any poor *Koyemoshi* that happened to stagger near, or even his own compatriot, if he could get hold of him.[41]

The clowns in question were painted and costumed, having only a black breech clout in the way of clothing, the body being painted all over and the head covered with a large painted rawhide mask (see fig), around the base of which was a bound fox skin (a). The top was surmounted by a tuft of hair (b) from the crest of which arose a cluster of chilis, two or three being red, the others green. The nose was a little loose, twisted, each alternate twirl being painted a different color. The mouths of all, made in like manner, were skewed down at one corner, giving, together with the white radiating marks under the black eye holes, a most diabolical and at the same time pensive and foolish expression to the character.

One had half the body painted blue, half white. The mask was blue with white zig-zag streaks running down the sides. The tuft of hair was reddish yellow. His bunch of chili was fuller than that of the other. He was first to appear and oftenest appeared after. The white portion of his body was ornamented with darker streaks made by drawing the fingers along the surface in wavy lines. This man was remarkably nimble in his motions, as were all, and as with all, the paint on his body showed beautifully the relief and play of muscles. Another was painted a little unevenly white all over the body. He wore a whitish mask streaked with dark on the sides, red nose and mouth. His tuft of hair was a patch of black sheep's wool.

A third had the mask painted pink or a light flesh color. The hair was yellow and black, unevenly intermixed, and the body was slate colored.

The fourth had the mask painted blue [and had] yellow and black hair, and slate colored body, the streaks made by drawing the fingers along the surface being apparent on him as on all the others.

They had continued pestering the *Koyemoshis* and clowns but a little while when the dancers came in, these four characters then settling down and crossing their legs just as if nothing had happened—in perfect peace. Both the clowns and *Koyemoshis* attended to any defect which appeared in the dresses of any of the dancers. When again the dancers retired, the persecutions were recommenced—this time with greater vigor. A painted man would dash in, sneak rapidly up in bent posture before a *Koyemoshi* and suddenly straighten up before his eyes, paralysing the latter. He would then belt him over the head with his pad, run, dodge in and out among them, striking anybody anywhere he could and bringing consternation wherever he came.

Finally, the larger [*Newekwe*] clown grabbed the blue and white one round the waist and began to pull off his chilis, which, hot as they were, he ate voraciously. The brother clown and some of the *Koyemoshis* rushed up to his assistance. Soon the chili was all devoured with great grimaces and coughs, and the *Hē-hē* was tumbled to the ground, rolled over on his back, deprived of his breech clout, and pulled by the penis, the prepuce of which was tied until he would call out shrilly "*Hū ū, hū ū*," which meant that he was ready to submit. [Then] he was released and sent naked to the corner of a court, where a blanket was lying, in which he folded himself. Soon another, and one other were captured and served in the same way, being deprived of their chili, which the big clown voraciously devoured, and slapped and pulled by the penises [until] they were sent to the side of the first.

Suddenly the clown who had eaten so much chili was seized with a severe fit of coughing in consequence, and his companions ran up a ladder, brought down a bowl of stale urine which may always be found standing on the house tops, and handing it to him, he quickly drank off at least a pint as though to quench an intolerable thirst—after which he seemed to recover, never in fact seeming to be pained but merely making grimaces etc., as though he were tortured to death, but instantly after breaking out into some wild witticism which caused the myriad spectators to shout and laugh as we do at a clown in a good circus.

Here the revelry was again interrupted by the advent of the dancers, the two clowns having procured two or three dry tortillas and busying themselves in making witty remarks and munching the dry bread. The dancers retired, [and] the sun was getting low so as to flood one half the court in red light, redder from the red walls, and to shroud the other in twilight shadow. The spectators lined the house tops and terraces, and [the] south side of the court was filled with women and children, who had come and spread their blankets, on which they were resting and watching. The last (fourth) of the painted men was captured and carried triumphantly to the corner. Then the *Koyemoshis* repaired hither and began a shuffling dance. The clowns came up and began to take charge of proceedings, and directed the subjugated He-he's to join. Immediately they arose, ducked their heads and uttered their only note, "*hū ū, hū ū*," and began to dance most ingeniously until ordered to stop, which they immediately obeyed in doing, by ducking the head, responding in the same way and standing about on one leg like so many storks.

Pretty soon one was called forth and told to go and get *hē-wē*. "*Hū ū ū ū*," and immediately he was off. Another was called out and directed to go and get dried venison. "*Hū ū*," and off. Another and the last were directed to go off on a scouting expedition. Away at once.

Then the two clowns stood talking a few moments, grinning, smacking the lips, snapping the tongue, frightening the *Koyemoshis,* winking, calling out, h[umming] little snatches of song which they would interrupt in the middle to make a remark which set the village in a roar, then off with the song again. Presently one rushed frantically forward from where he had been serenely sitting with crossed legs by the side of the other and shouted out something which caused the *Koyemoshis* to scatter headlong in all directions and the women to move nearer to each other. He snatched a ladder round wildly from its place. The other sprang forward and grasped the other, and both began to talk rapidly and wildly—the significance being that they must have blood. Looking wildly about the court, the first had his eyes directed by a *Koyemoshi* to me, sitting calmly, notebook in hand, at the top of the estufa. He brandished his club, stepped up to where I sat and glared a moment, striking the ground with his club. The cheers died out. The women, some of them, uttered subdued cries, and the court became as still as at midnight. I gazed calmly down, laid my hand on my hunting knife, and continued my notes—or appeared [to].

Presently he gave a scream, started for the base of the ladder, and struck it with his stick. I laid my notes by, folded my hands, and burst [out] in a laugh which an American would perhaps have detected as forced. He then waved his club aloft, pointed to the covered way and resumed his harangue, which was loud, fierce and long. I leaned forward and listened attentively—all the while smiling. As he closed his wild speech, the crowd burst out in a shout. He repeated his closing speech with a brandish of the club and, whirling, with a wink at me and a word to his companion, rushed out through the covered way.

The *Koyemoshis,* relieved of such unpleasant restraint, recommenced their fooleries. Suddenly a long howl arose from without. The spectators hushed. The *Koyemoshis* ran and hid behind each other, ladders, and in the corners, and the howls and yelps, mingled with the fierce cries of the clowns, came nearer and nearer, until in rushed the yelling two, dragging by his tail and legs a great, shaggy yellow dog. The latter was yelping and in vain snapping at his nimble and frantic captors. They rushed with him to the center of the court, threw him against the earth, where he cowered and howled and cringed in mortal fear. The smaller [clown] brandished his club and shouted. The larger one made a rapid foaming [sic] speech, pointing at the howling dog with glaring eyes, and then, waving the club high in the air, struck the brute with full force across the muzzle. For an instant, the dog staggered. Then, rearing, he glared wildly at his captors, looked aloft as though to leap over the high houses and cheering spectators, and, turning, lifted his head in the air, gave one long piercing yell ere he turned with glaring eyes to the one who had struck him. How his crazed eyes gleamed in the red sunlight! How his howls and the fierce execrations of the two maddened clowns echoed in the old court! Just as he lifted his forefeet to spring or flee, a blow from the smaller man's club laid him on his side with a broken back. Another blow from the bigger man's club caved his ribs in, and drove out his expiring howl and breath. While yet the blood was gushing from the mouth of the beast and in the throes of death his back was drawn up and his legs were twitching, he was seized by the larger man, who was held, as [if] to restrain his wild fury, by the other, by a strap around the waist, and raising the brute aloft, he seized its nose in his teeth, shaking it from side to side until he had gnawed the cartelagenous substance off, which, resigning the dog to the other man, he swallowed with many grimaces and speeches. The other fastened his teeth in the dog's upper lip, but no sooner had he got a hold than the former rushed forward, seized in the same way the other lip, and, snarling and fighting, the two men pulled in opposite directions until the one detaching a piece, the other rolled with the dog he was wildly biting at, in the dirt and blood. Then the tongue was bitten off and eaten, with grimaces and duckings of the head, like the efforts of a gorged turkey to gorge more, while the smaller [clown] rushed wildly about and called for "a knife" "a knife."

The knife was thrown down. The first clown made a wild speech, hitting with tremendous force the already pummeled dog, and then, snatching the knife from the hands of the other man, he seized the dog by the middle, cut with one slash a huge gash in its belly, and, clutching one of the smaller intestines, began cramming the steaming duct double into his mouth. The other [clown] darted forward, seized the other end, tore the long intestine from the viscera of the animal, and began cramming the other end into his mouth. Tearing, grasping, and stuffing as though famished, the two approached one another, eating as they approached, spitting out excrement in every direction like the seeds of a melon and eating the intestine until it grew short between them. Then, both together, they clutched for the animal, the larger seizing and ripping forth the bleeding liver, which, in morsels almost unheard of, he began to bolt, [covering] face and front, where not smeared before, with blood. Then, with a sigh of contentment and a smile of the greatest satisfaction, he approached the ladder and laid his dainty bit on a round, not moving from it more than a few feet ere he would re-approach it and take a huge morsel, twisting himself, grimacing, and closing his eyes as the huge black morsel passed down red lane. How these fiends yelled and skipped about, cuffing *Koyemoshis,* ready with tongue to deal out a readier wit. They would run up to the drum [and] sing and dance, joined by all the *Koyemoshis.* Then the first clown (the other never drummed) would drop his instrument and re[turn] to his bit of liver. The *He-he*'s returned, one by one, and deposited their load of *he-we* and dried meat, melons, etc., which the clowns would take, ravenously bite a piece or two from, and then scatter recklessly among the spectators, who scrambled like Father Brady's urchins for the bits.

[The clowns] were sitting contentedly eating when the dancers came in for the last time. The whizzer took his place, the *He-he*'s stood about on one foot or [illegible], and the clowns gradually worked their way to the middle of the court, where they kept laughter going until the *Tatchu* with his bowl of flour advanced down along the line of dancing figures and, going to the head *Koyemoshi,* began talking to him in a low hurried tone. He bowed his head, and the cacique went on from one to the other, sprinkling a little flour on his bent head. Then he sprinkled the *He-he*'s, then the line of dancers as they still danced, omitting to do the same with the two clowns, and keeping up the same low, hurried talk all the while. Then he took his place at the head, the rattle shook, the dance broke up, and all save eight or ten of the dancers rushed out of the *Southeast* [Cushing's italics] covered way. After remaining and brandishing their knives a few moments, the others, save one duck and a red mask, followed suit, and presently, after a few more freaks and witticisms, the dog-eaters walked down among the *Koyemoshis,* one uttering an order like the Alcalde's, ending with a laugh and a hiccough, and the spectators then began to disperse. The duck and red mask ran off after their companions, the *Koyemoshis* went for the estufa, and I strolled along down to see at what place they would stop. The dancers were hurrying toward the estufa in lower Zuni where, until the *Awen Tatchu* passed out and down the darkening street, the two last remained, prancing around, calling out "*Hū lī, hū lī, hū lī, Hū hā, hū hā, hū hā,*" and wriggling their knives and bodies at one another. Then they entered the estufa, and as the sound of their rattles died out, I retired to the house of the Governor.

On my way, I met Lupolita's little companion, Sā-wā-tīā-sīt-sā, who looked at me and smiled. I stepped up and patted her head, and she raised her hands to mine, as though to detain them there. When I turned to go, she timidly motioned me to follow, so I did. She led me to the house next [to] Lupolita's and asked me to sit down, running to bring her sister, who wished to see my pictures. I told her they were not good—would be when they were painted. But it was all the same. She must see them, so I showed the book to her. She immediately recognized every one of the half-finished sketches, to my great surprise, as I find but few Indians who can do so before they are painted, though none fail to do so afterward.

Reaching the house considerably after dark, I found the Governor baking bread for our supper. The coffee was singing and the fire was bright, and we were all in excellent humor. Everybody treated me well that night; everybody smiled on meeting me; and I was not long in finding out why, for the Governor soon translated the fierce speech which the dog-eating clown had made to me. Among other things, he had said that I was not a Zuni but, though an American, I was a good man and that all Zuni was glad to have me here. That he addressed me as a "Little Cacique Capitan." But whereas they loved me, they (fiercely) hated the Navajos; that they were all the same as coyotes and dogs, and they were going to kill one. With this, he had wheeled and started for the dog with his companion.

The Governor was pleased when I said, "Thanks to all Zuni for wishing me with them and being glad with my presence. Thanks still more to the brave dog-eater for his good and kindly speech; most glad am I that Zuni cares to make me such speeches." As pleased was he when I told him that the dance I had seen was more beautiful than the most beautiful I had seen before, and he told me that when in the same way a dance was thought good and beautiful, Zuni much glad was to see it and had it two days, and that therefore on the following day the same dance would be repeated.

TUESDAY, OCTOBER 21ST.

After eating breakfast, which consisted of a chili and meat stew and the usual coffee, fried bread (tortillas) and *hē-wē,* I went out, just as the dancers had issued from Church Court and taken their place at the front of the house mentioned second yesterday (remaining pages missing).

First Reports

In spite of the instruction to "write frequently," the first letter Cushing addressed to Secretary Baird had been that of October 15, a letter not only dated more than two months after the expedition's departure from Washington but also quite uninformative about his activities. As Baird's response indicates, this was not, from the Washington standpoint, an auspicious beginning; but it was more than redeemed by the letters to follow. As an initial report of what he had been learning in the first month and a half of his stay in the pueblo, Cushing's second letter to Baird (dated October 29) signaled clearly that he was, in Baird's words, "on the inside track." From a later perspective, this letter is of particular interest as Cushing's earliest articulation of his new "method" of fieldwork, an approach which he was only just taking up but the advantages of which over the investigative methods of his predecessors he was already self-consciously delineating. From this point on, until his transfer to the Bureau, Cushing was a model of regularity in keeping his supervisor informed.

Baird to FHC

October 25, 1879

My dear Mr. Cushing:

I am in receipt of your letter dated at Zuni & am glad at last to hear from you, after so long an interval of silence.

The omission to report to me from time to time of your whereabouts and operations I have considered a very serious offence. I do not think the circumstances you mention constitute a sufficient explanation or excuse. I am not accustomed to being so continuously without official information of what is done by assistants of the Institution.

I am very sorry to hear of the existence of any internal jealousies in an expedition in which all parties should cooperate towards a common end. But unless you are more communicative, I can form no idea of the circumstances. During the rest of your sojourn I shall expect to have at least a weekly word, if no more than a postal card, stating at what point you are.

Yours Truly,
Spencer F. Baird
Secretary

Draft: Cushing to Stevenson

Zuni, October, 29, 1879

My dear Colonel:

The wagon bringing your letter of the 25th came Sunday, and I am gratefully thankful for the supplies—especially the sugar and coffee. The canned materials, which up in Zuni I do not need, I have been enabled to trade for the latter articles with Mr. Ealy.[42] You were kindly thoughtful too in sending the overcoat, which will prove a great blessing when the colder days of November advance.

I have regret in telling you that the little things which you ordered from Wē-wē are not completed; since the warmer weather began, she informs Miss Hamaker that the preparations for the winter festivities—meaning blankets, grinding corn, etc.—will so occupy her that she cannot make them.[43] I am sure Miss Hamaker has been very faithful in reminding Wē-wē of her promise, and I know that I have done all that several visits could do to make her fulfill it. I trust, however, to the persuasive powers of Mrs. Stevenson—which are very great—for bringing this obstinate woman to terms. . . .

As for trading, I have as yet done none. I believe that you have but small confidence in my ability, as pertaining at least to practical things. I entertain this belief the more readily in that such an impression with you would be only rational, if not indeed unavoidable from the manner in which you have heard me talk and seen me act and from the representations regarding money matters which my friend Mr. Leech made to you. Therefore, and in view of the confidence which I have in your ability—founded as it is on long experience—to trade to greater advantage than I could, I am content to carefully note any scientific desiderata to our collection, which list I will submit to you on your arrival to be dealt with as you may see fit. On the other hand, should you expressly wish it and acquaint me with such wish by mail, I am very willing to go on as well as I can until my trading material is exhausted.

Once more, let me ask of you to do all in your power to enable me, in case it seems as desirable as at present, to remain here as late as the middle or end of January. I can no longer doubt that every additional month among these Indians will increase my stock of data sufficiently to warrant any additional expenditure—if not too great—made necessary. My especial anxiety is to witness and record the festivities of early winter and to see the whole people when they are gathered in from their summer stations to this central Pueblo. With a slowly increasing knowledge of their language many things at first blind are cleared up amazingly, and if I could know that I could depend on two or three months more here, I should devote some two or three weeks *exclusively* to its study.

I have witnessed two dances since your departure—one of them the most varied, wildest and handsomest I ever saw. Both I carefully recorded, painting all the characters in detail.[44]

I live exclusively with the Indians, eating in common with them, and to their great gratification, wearing the head band and blanket—the former by their request.[45] The advantages accruing from this course seem to me very great. Their confidence and closer acquaintance are thereby secured, and I am enabled to gain a close knowledge of their cookery, domestic habits, etc.

I am glad to inform you of their good will toward yourself and their continued kindness to me, the latter which is as inexplicable as it is gratifying.

Believe me,
Yours Sincerely and
Respectfully,
F. H. Cushing

FHC to Baird

Zuni, October 29, 1879

My dear Professor Baird:

As a wagon leaves for Wingate in the morning, I take the occasion afforded by the evening of a busy day to write you a few words.

As the winter approaches and the corn is gathered in, the dances become more frequent, and unlike those of other Indians, they are all *observances* which, without variation, year after year, have been repeated by this people for centuries. In these strange festivities the Zunian throws off everything foreign. His dress, where not fantastic, is primitive; his axe and knife are of stone; his gorgeous scarfs and feather ornaments are much as Cabeza de Vaca saw when first he climbed the mesa and saw the city which afterward was Niça's Cibola.[46] No less primitive are the names designating the characters and forms in these ceremonies; hence I find them teeming with suggestions of the Pre-Columbian Pueblo.

In view of these things, on all days and nights when these dances take place, I note the important details, and sketch at least faithfully and in color, all personages or characters figuring in them and all minutiae of costume. And it is in view of these facts that I am using every argument in my power to induce Col. Stevenson to make arrangements for my sojourn here until mid-winter—if such prove not an unfavorable plan to you and to Maj. Powell. My anxiety would not be so great were there not a possibility that I am among the last who will ever witness all this in its purity, as the proposed advent of the Rail Road next fall will, with its foreign influence, introduce all sorts of innovations.[47] Even when a company of officers and ladies from Wingate came here with our party for a day or two, the Indians varied the *Tchā'-kwī-nā* or blanket dance which we found them dancing and which I have since witnessed in full, not only cutting it short but also casting out of it all obscenities—or rather indecent observances—on account of their presence.[48]

As gradually their language dawns upon my intellect, not the significance of these things alone but many other dark things are lighted up by its morning. They are the People who built the ruins of Cañon Bonita in De Chelly.[49] In their language is told the strange history of these heretofore mysterious cities, each one of which has its definite name and story in their lore. The hand marks on the rock faces, and the "Pictographs of a 'Primitive Civilization'" in the light of this language and tradition [thus] reveal their mysteries at once with their *proof*. Each mark of conventional ornament on their earthen vases, I recently learn, has its name, and this name its significance, with the knowledge of which latter comes the perfect revelation of Zuni art.[50] Perhaps not a more conventional people can be found than are in many respects these Pueblos. I lately discover that their apparently endless variety (in ornamentation) of *tinajas* or ollas may be reduced to from seven to ten types, each bearing its definite name, and the ornaments of which you never find occurring in foreign forms.

Before these investigations too, if long enough continued, much of error must be swept away. Already the eagle which "is to bear Montezuma back" becomes a bird kept in common with the wild turkey—for its feathers—the latter sacred, but the bird no more so than is the soil on which is grown the sacred corn.[51]

The literature on these people, with the exception of one or two recent brief articles, is utterly worthless; and if again I turn my face to the field, I shall hardly be faint hearted because an authority tells me he can do more with books than I can with ears and eyes, and a filibuster says that the tribe scientifically is "bed ridden." I do not count myself a man of as much ability as those possessed who have preceded me; but my *method* must succeed. I live among the Indians, I eat their food, and sleep in their houses. Because I will unhesitatingly plunge my hand in common with their dusty ones and dirtier children's into a great kind of hot, miscellaneous food; will sit close to [those] having neither vermin nor disease, will fondle and talk sweet Indian to their bright eyed little babies; will wear the blanket and tie the *pania* around my long hair;[52] will look with unfeigned reverence on their beautiful and ancient ceremonies, never laughing at any absurd observance, they love me, and I learn. On account of this, the women name me *Cushi K'ok shi, Cushi Tihi Nima* (the good Cushing, the sweet Cushing) and the speakers of the dance call me (in Zuni of course) the little Capitan Cacique. On account of this, thank God, my notes will contain much which those of all other explorers have failed to communicate. But do not fancy that all this is lightly purchased. Were I to paint you the picture of my daily life here—of my *meals*—you would, I fear, for some days, enjoy yours as little as on all days, does your poor servant his. I am the "good Cushie" for I take a child, dark with inherited disease, and cleanse and annoint its great sores that they heal. As such, therefore, I am entitled to distinguished courtesy. Hence a woman at a meal picks up from the floor (which is our table) a wooden spoon. It is *not* clean. She therefore wipes it across her moccasin (I do not tell you what that moccasin has repeatedly stepped on today), she draws it along her mantle (which was once white), and bethinking that it is the Good Cushing who is to eat with it, she quickly raises it to her mouth (I will not tell you what that mouth has been used for today—wait till my Report comes out) and in a manner most natural and expeditious, cleans (?) and immediately with the most irresistible smile hands it to me. Do you suppose that I refuse it? No! I plunge it into the huge bowl of steaming food, for I only know that her hands squeezed up the *hē-wē,* not how dirty they were, and trusting to its abundance and heat to cleanse the utensil sufficiently for my blunted perceptions—and, thinking that on this very day while I was doctoring her baby, I was indebted to her for showing me how she loosed it from the cradle board and—etc. I utter between my gulps of hot soup "*E-lu-kwa, E-lu-kwa,*" [thanks], with a smile quite out-rivaling her own in breadth, if not in genuineness. Is this all of my price? Ah! no. I told you that my capital in the bank of health was large (would to God the other kind were equal). *More* than that, I have drawn on it, like the worst of spendthrifts since I began to eat Indian food. Never a prize fighter through weeks of training who was more "Devilishly physicked" than I have been, never! and if Providence spare me to ever reach Washington again, it must be with but half a stomach.

Well it is very late. Two caciques who have been discussing "affairs of state" with the Governor and a medicine man who has been kneading the Governor's sick wife are about to depart and I must close.

Believe me, dear Professor,
Your Faithful
Cushing

Professor S. F. Baird
Dir. Smithsonian Instn.
Washington, D.C.

FHC TO BAIRD

Zuni, November 7, 1879

My dear Professor Baird:

Certainly the circumstances which I mentioned in beginning my first letter to you failed to *explain,* as, I regret to learn by yours of the 25th inst., they [also failed] to excuse my protracted silence; for I made mention of them only by allusion, not by name.

The relation to you of the one cause which more than all the others deterred me from performing that duty which I had looked forward to as one of the pleasantest in store for me—the communication to you of every success with which we might meet—would have been as inconsistent with my silence as it would have rendered the latter useless.

While at Santa Fe, we made large and valuable collections principally at Pueblo Tesuque; and my nights were occupied with labelling and cataloguing, as were my days in assisting to collect these. But it was not this which deterred me from sending you word, as I found time, and have since, to write several letters to friends in Washington and one of many pages to my home in New York.

I had already begun a letter to you shortly before our departure from Santa Fe, in which I had intended not only to detail all our operations but also their scientific results, when I was requested by Col. Stevenson not to mention in any communication which I might address to you anything definite regarding the collections which had been made, etc., as he wished the communication of such official information left to him. At the same time, he requested me to make a copy of my catalogue, which he said he would forward to you through Major Powell, under whom he was directly employed and to whom he wished primarily to make such official reports of our progress. But he said also that before leaving for Wingate he should write to you as well as to the latter gentleman. Looking upon Col. Stevenson as the executive officer of the Expedition, while I had charge only of a branch in it, I was compelled to forego the pleasure, the anticipation of which had grown the greater as the greater had grown our collections, and feeling that a communication containing little more than personal items would seem to you almost as much out of place as it would prove unsatisfactory, I had, thenceforward, as little of heart as I had of time to write you.

After our arrival at Fort Wingate, the thought that in thus deferring to Col. Stevenson's request I might be proving traitor to a benefactor to whom I owed much more kindness than to any other I had ever known, save for perhaps my early friend Mr. Ledyard, without whom I had not known this one, I was again tempted to write you. And at last, believing that you would be pleased to hear of our success in examining and collecting from ruins along our route through New Mexico, many of which, being on horse back, I was able to discover and examine, I again summoned spirit to begin a second long letter to you—which, by accident, I think I still retain. The Colonel, visiting my tent as was then his kindly custom frequently to do, asked me what I was writing, and when I replied "to Professor Baird," he once more repeated his request, and once more, reluctantly, I abandoned all idea of communicating with you ere I should have results exclusively my own of which to inform you, or some matter of a business nature to urge me to do so. For I reflected that which I now know to be true, that unless I wrote you a frank communicative letter you would be perhaps more displeased than if I wrote nothing at all. I now deeply regret the step I took.[53] But it was an error of my judgment, not of my heart, which has remained as loyal to you throughout as it must ever remain, how much and for how many kindnesses I am indebted to you.

Perhaps from my last, and I suppose equally unhappy, letter you can gather something regarding the things I am called upon to endure while among these people, but you cannot gather all. Not my health alone has suffered but my personal security was for some little time at stake. Only a few days since, I was compelled to brave all Zuni for the chance of sketching their sacred dance, the *Ka-kok-shi,* which they did not propose I should sketch or record and which proceeding provoked a council at which my talk and manner in reply to the accusations brought against me fortunately resulted in assuring for me high and I trust permanent favor with the principal men of the Pueblo.[54] When, tensed by like annoyances, tired from constant watching and sketching, or ill from the food I am compelled to eat here, I have had late at night to square up my notes or prepare for the morrow, the thoughts that my labors were being and would continue to be appreciated by you, that I was now enjoying the opportunity at one stroke to gain rare scientific information and earn perhaps the confidence you had reposed in me, have together rendered the few weeks of my life here among the happiest I have ever known. That is ended. . . .

Your letter contains the first reproach I have to remember as coming from you, and it comes at a time when, more than ever before, I am or was performing or trying to do my duty toward you as far as I could see it. Had it not been for this consciousness of duty done, the best of all consciousness, I should have been crushed by that reproach and I do not think Washington had seen me for some years.

Col. Stevenson is here for the last time. The wagon which brought him brought also your letter. I read it to him. While he does not blame himself that you have been kept in ignorance so long regarding our whereabouts and operations, but rather the accidents, or other [causes] which have kept from you his communications to Major Powell, he refrains from blaming me. He says that the same mail which shall bear this letter to you should also take an explaining one from him. I have been at a loss at times to understand what were his own motives in instructing me as he did. But at such times I have thought that he designed for you a pleasant surprise—as indeed it must prove, and a grand one—and [hoped] at such times that you as well as he would thank me for keeping my peace. But at other times this has seemed to me a childish explanation. Whatever these motives be, I know, or rather believe, they were not bad ones. . . .

The work of recording the ceremonial festivities and observances of early winter over, I aim to visit on my way to Santa Fe several of the principal Pueblos, etc., for the purpose of laying out plans for future work, or rather data to that end, as well as to gain by these a more comprehensive view of the Pueblo civilization.

The Indians are growing less and less reserved in their relations to me. Recently they have given me information of the sacred source of rain (a natural well) and two caves, or as they call them, houses, two days journey to the west from here. These have heretofore been kept secret from American as well as Mexican. When I manifested innocent interest in their story, they drew a complete map of the land of Zuni showing not only the whereabouts of these caves but also the road leading thereto. These caves have been used as the "Birth" or starting place for certain characters or officers which figure in their sacred dances, ever since the time when their traditions say the Zunians occupied the remarkable ruins of the cañons of Arizona.[55] As the Apache hostilities render a visit to the caves of Silver City as dangerous, as, according to Col. Stevenson, it would be impracticable on account of expense, I shall make it a point to visit these traditionary caves [instead].[56] Although there is possible danger to be apprehended from wandering Apaches, I think that with care the trip can be made in safety. Those who informed me are now distinctly opposed to such a visit, but I believe I can ultimately win them over or go in secret.

In accordance with your wishes and expectations, I shall be pleased henceforth to make frequent reports to you of my whereabouts and doings, although the merely accidental manner in which I shall be able to send and receive mail here may cause their receipt to be irregular. I remain,

With Respect,
Your Obt. Serv't,
F. H. Cushing

Prof. Spencer F. Baird
Director of the Smithsonian Institution
Washington, D.C.

P.S. I regret that circumstances have called upon me to mention that which I have of Col. Stevenson. But I would not allow you to believe that either disloyalty, ingratitude, or mere laziness was the cause of my silence. That which I write is true, as, in case my word seems insufficient, my notebooks can testify to. But I sincerely hope it will bring upon the Colonel no censure; for, although I have suffered some from what I regarded as thoughtlessness on his part, I must say that he is the most industrious, most thoroughly good natured and I believe best intending man I have ever known in his capacity. I have [attributed] all difficulties which to me have appeared as such [to] one over whom, through this same large good nature, he chooses to exercise as little control as that one [i.e., Mrs. Stevenson, presumably] exercises much over him.

FHC to Baird

Zuni, November 14, 1879

My dear Professor Baird:

In accordance with your wish, though in extreme haste, I write to let you know where I am and how I am getting on.

I am glad to say that the Indians are still very friendly and daily becoming more and more communicative regarding those matters concerning which when I first lived among them, they only replied to my questions, "*Quien sabe?*." This morning they communicated to me the beginning of the story of Montezuma, of which name they denied all knowledge when I first questioned them about it. They say that the name Montezuma is only adopted from the Mexican and give his real and universal name among the Pueblo people as Po-shai-an-k'ia.[57] They promise to tell me the whole story concerning his comings, doings, and departure in five weeks, if I remain good—and to show me plumes and relics which are supposed to belong to him. I shall consider this a great acquisition as the notions which have been circulated regarding the "Montezuma" of the Pueblos have been crude and erroneous in the extreme. This beginning of one of their most sacred stories has [an] importance [all the greater] in that I think it will be followed by much more that is interesting as bearing on their ancient institutions and history.

Col. Stevenson is still here although he expects to leave daily for Wingate on his way home.

I remain
With Sincere Respect
Your Servant,
F. H. Cushing

Baird to Stevenson

Washington, D.C.
November 18, 1879

Dear Mr. Stevenson:

I was very glad to get your letter of the 7th, as furnishing some information as to your operations. We have been completely ignorant even of your whereabouts, much more, of the nature of your success, until a few days ago, when Mr. Pilling sent me your catalogue.

I have just written to Mr. Cushing to say that it was not so much the lack of any information of results as that of the whereabouts and post office address with which I found fault, as I had repeated occasion to communicate letters and memoranda but had not the slightest idea where to send them.

I am very glad to find that you have been so successful, and look for much gratification in the receipt & inspection of the collections. . . .

I think very well of the idea of leaving Cushing in the Pueblo country to complete his investigations. It will be difficult for him to get so completely on the inside track of his people again as he appears to be now.

I have just had a letter from J. R. Metcalfe of Silver City, in which he says he is informed you have exhausted your appropriation & cannot visit him. He had several lots of choice things ready for transfer, & was, I think, willing to exhaust the contents of the cave in our behalf. Will it be possible, perhaps, to have Mr. Cushing go down there & superintend the exhumation & packing of the collections? It would be a pity to have this done carelessly, & especially in the interest of some other party. . . .

Sincerely Yours,
S F Baird

Col. James Stevenson
Fort Wingate, Valencia County
New Mexico

FHC to Baird

Zuni, New Mexico
November 19, 1879

My dear Professor Baird:

As Colonel Stevenson leaves in the morning for Wingate, I take occasion to add this little note to my communication of a few days since.

On the 16th inst., the Grand Dance and Festivities of the season began and with this, day and night, I have ever since been closely occupied; as I shall be until the twenty-second.[58] The dancing and ceremonies are carried on in seven or eight different houses in widely separated parts of the town, and as the nights here at this season are intensely cold, I suffer not a little in trying to keep abreast of it all—with notes and paintings. To add to my difficulties,

I am compelled to do my sketching in secret, as some Isleta, Moqui, and other Indians who come here to take part have persuaded some of the principal men that my work is for no good, and that if the Mexicans—who are not allowed to witness these ceremonies—see my sketches, great calamities such as drought and famine will fall on the nation. Yesterday and today, however, by appearing in the ancient national costume (at my Zuni friends' instigation) I have succeeded in lulling their newborn suspicions to such an extent that this morning they were very free with their information regarding the meaning of certain plumes and prayers.

The sound of the dance drama summons me out to my ceaseless duties, and I am thus in haste.

Ever Your Devoted Servant,
F. H. Cushing

STEVENSON TO PILLING

Fort Wingate, November 21, 1879

My dear Mr. Pilling:

Your two letters, one enclosing draft for $250 salary for October and one enclosing draft for $700 reached me at Zuni. I thank you ever so much for your kind attention. I have just returned from Zuni, having completed the survey of the town for a model, and brought with me nearly a wagon load more of collections not previously obtained. I secured from the Old Church of Zuni two large images 4 ft high, and out of one block of wood, and the center piece of the altar representing a crown with a large heart carved on it below. Got them in the dead hour of night.[59] I have left Cushing at Zuni provided with provisions and transportation for a stay of two months, provided the Major approves of it. If not, he can come on immediately. . . .

With best wishes and kind regards to you all.

I am Very Truly Yours,
Jas. Stevenson

J. C. Pilling, Esq.
Chief Clerk, Eth. Bur.

FHC TO BAIRD

Zuni, November 24, 1879

My dear Professor Baird:

The Governor of the Pueblo, in whose house I live, leaves tomorrow morning for Wingate, and as Col. Stevenson failed to take with him my mail on the morning of his departure, I send you these two letters already written and, together with them, the present hasty note.

As I had anticipated, the story of Po-shai-an-k'ia was followed by much more—which, if written, will be read with interest and will, to minds more gifted than my own, throw great light on the origin and peculiar character of Pueblo culture. I am in so far gaining, too, that I was able openly, on the closing day of the ceremonies before mentioned, to make my act of sketching complete, and the figures this added to my portfolio are, perhaps, the most valuable of all.

I am still engaged with the notes of the Great Annual Fiesta. So soon as these are completed, I shall write you a long letter detailing my journey here, and some of the more interesting features in the life of these people. This letter—in case such meet your approbation—I shall design for publication, in whatever organ of the press you shall deem proper. I have two objects at least in wishing for its publication. The one is that our work here may be known, in order that the chances for its continuance may be increased. The other, that the many questions and letters from friends and others which I have received since my arrival here may be answered at once, as to reply to them separately would consume time which is too valuable for other purposes.

I feel the more inclined to thus popularly publish something since I learn that two at least, if not several, letters have appeared in the East from the pen of Mrs. Stevenson.[60] I am not a little surprised at this, for ever since our departure from Washington until a week since I have been urged by this lady, as well as by the Colonel, not to send anything back for publication—as such would interfere with the latter's plans. I know now with what motive such request was made—and feel bound no longer to respect it. I do not deny that I wish personally to secure popular credit for the peculiar work in which I am engaged—more, I am sure, as the means of an end in which my whole heart is enlisted than for the mere gratification of vanity.

On his return to this Pueblo, the Colonel had so exhausted his means that he could leave for my use here only twenty dollars, and could promise to deposit at Wingate only thirty more, to serve me in my journey to Santa Fe via the various Pueblos. This had been amply sufficient with the amount which I might have realized by the sale of the bacon which constituted part of my rations, but I learned on the day after his departure that the Colonel, without apprising me of the fact, had turned a large portion of this over to the missionary here. This circumstance, together with the fact that also I have since become aware of, that the rent of the large room which the Col. took for the season remains unpaid and of course devolves upon me, will considerably reduce my means and leave me in actual need. As I wish, moreover, to go as far as possible in filling up large gaps in our collection, I should be very glad, if, say, one month's salary might be forwarded to me at Wingate. This, however, I leave entirely with you, as, without it, I *can* get along, because I *must,* and I am only too glad to be able under any circumstances to remain here this extra amount of time.

I neither murmur, nor do I complain of Colonel Stevenson. If he has gone beyond, or up to his depth in chalk, it has been in a good cause, in which my interest and hopes are enlisted and founded, as much as or more than his own. I only think that if he had treated me more as an officer of this Expedition insofar as to have been more communicative regarding his plans, work would have gone on more smoothly and fewer chances for misunderstanding had occurred.

Very Respectfully, Your Devoted Servant,
F.H. Cushing

I hope to get ink with which to write my next letter to you. My good word to all.

FHC to Baird

Zuni, November 27, 1879

My dear Professor Baird:

A Navajo brings my mail from Wingate this morning, and in it I find your kind letter of the 18th inst. . . .

I am also very much pleased with the prospect of being enabled to remain here a couple of months longer. Toward the end of this time, although it will greatly delay my return to Washington, I shall be very glad, in case Col. Stevenson can make financial arrangements for it, to visit the cave near Silver City, as I learn that I can make the distance on horseback within a week and at no very great expense; and the additional cost is merely a question of living and labor. . . .

I have within a few days made a still more important discovery. It is accurate information regarding the location of the Indian mines for turquoises and jades so much remarked on by the early Spanish chroniclers, and so much prized and worn even at the present day by the Zunians. The place is surrounded by evidences of centuries' excavation and is hidden away in the Zuni Mountains some fifty miles from here, its location being indicated by the Indians merely by heaps of stones surrounded by stone pointers. This I shall also take early occasion to visit.

While nothing short of an absolutely perfect knowledge of the Zuni language will enable me to make an exhaustive monograph of the people internally, the entire amount of time which you kindly see fit to permit me to spend here will enable me to make a complete *descriptive* report and a passable one on their institutions, political, religious and other. . . .

I remain, dear Professor,

With Sincere Respect,
Your Obt Servant,
F H Cushing

Trip to the Chalchihuitl Mines

> During the month of December [1879] I explored, with the loss of my mule and consequent great suffering, the Zuni Mountains, in search of the ancient green-stone and turquoise mines of which the Indians had told me, but the location of which they refused to reveal to me. These were found, sketches and plans made of them, and a brief epistolary report concerning them was forwarded to Professor Baird.
>
> —Report to Powell, July 6, 1882 (SWM H-C 37)

Turquoise, in the words of one modern researcher, was in times past "the most important substance mined by any Indians in what is now the continental United States, {and of North American miners of this substance} the Pueblos were by far the most persistent and prolific."[61] In this first—or first recorded—of Cushing's ventures of exploration we see one of the early investigations on which that modern generalization depends. Given his interest both in the technology and in the history of the Zunis, Cushing had been intrigued by remarks made and a tradition described by his Zuni friends implying that they had "somewhere in the Sierra Madres to the eastwards old mines of Tchalchihuitl, or green and blue stones." Opportunity to see the mines for himself (and thus, among other things, test the value of oral traditions as clues to history) was afforded by an encounter with "a sort of wandering prospector and artisan named Williams," who was staying for a few days with the Zuni trader, Douglas Graham.[62] As Cushing wrote later, Williams "had rambled all over the Southwest," thought he had seen the mines in question, and, since he was setting off in that direction a few days hence, offered to take Cushing to them.[63]

The documents relating to this frigid expedition (whose object turned out to be mines not of turquoise but of soft green and blue stones used for ceremonial paint) are of several sorts. They include a diary kept by Cushing over the period covering both his initial trek and a second trip to the mines made within a few day of the first; letters written by him in the course of these journeys; an account of the trip, undated but written presumably not long after, while he was still at Zuni; a reminiscence recorded some nine years later in a newspaper interview; and a letter written to Mrs. Cushing by an important witness twenty-one years after the event. The "Account of Cushing's Search for the Tchalchihuitl Mines, December 1879" was evidently written with publication for a popular audience in mind, but like the account of his initial journey from Las Vegas to Zuni, it survived only in a hand-written copy among the papers turned over to the Southwest Museum after Cushing's death. In some respects the earlier diary and this later account supplement one another, but they also cover much the same ground, though with somewhat different aim, the former being simply a record of events and observations, the latter focusing more on the adventurous aspects of the expedition. Less complete (and probably somewhat less reliable), the later account is printed here as an appendix at the end of the book.

An additional opportunity afforded by Cushing's December treks to the Zuni Mountain mines (one to which he actually devoted more journal space than to the mines themselves) was that of inspecting various ancient Pueblo ruins encountered en route and thus of increasing his knowledge of territorial and technological aspects of Zuni history. The letters Cushing wrote following his return from the mountains demonstrate the further development of this important ground-breaking interest in the historical and regional context in which he was learning to place Zuni itself—in relation to other pueblos, both ancient and contemporary, and in relation to the conditions and resources of the area as a whole. By the time he wrote to Baird on December 24, he would have worked out a plan (never realized in full) for visiting all the principal pueblos in the region.

In Zuni itself, moreover, owing to his improvement in the language and to his adoption of the "entire costume" of his hosts and conformity to the December "feast of the New Sun and other observances," he found in the weeks following his return that he was being accepted "as one of their people." All in all, he reported, December was a month in which he had "made more progress . . . than in any one month heretofore."

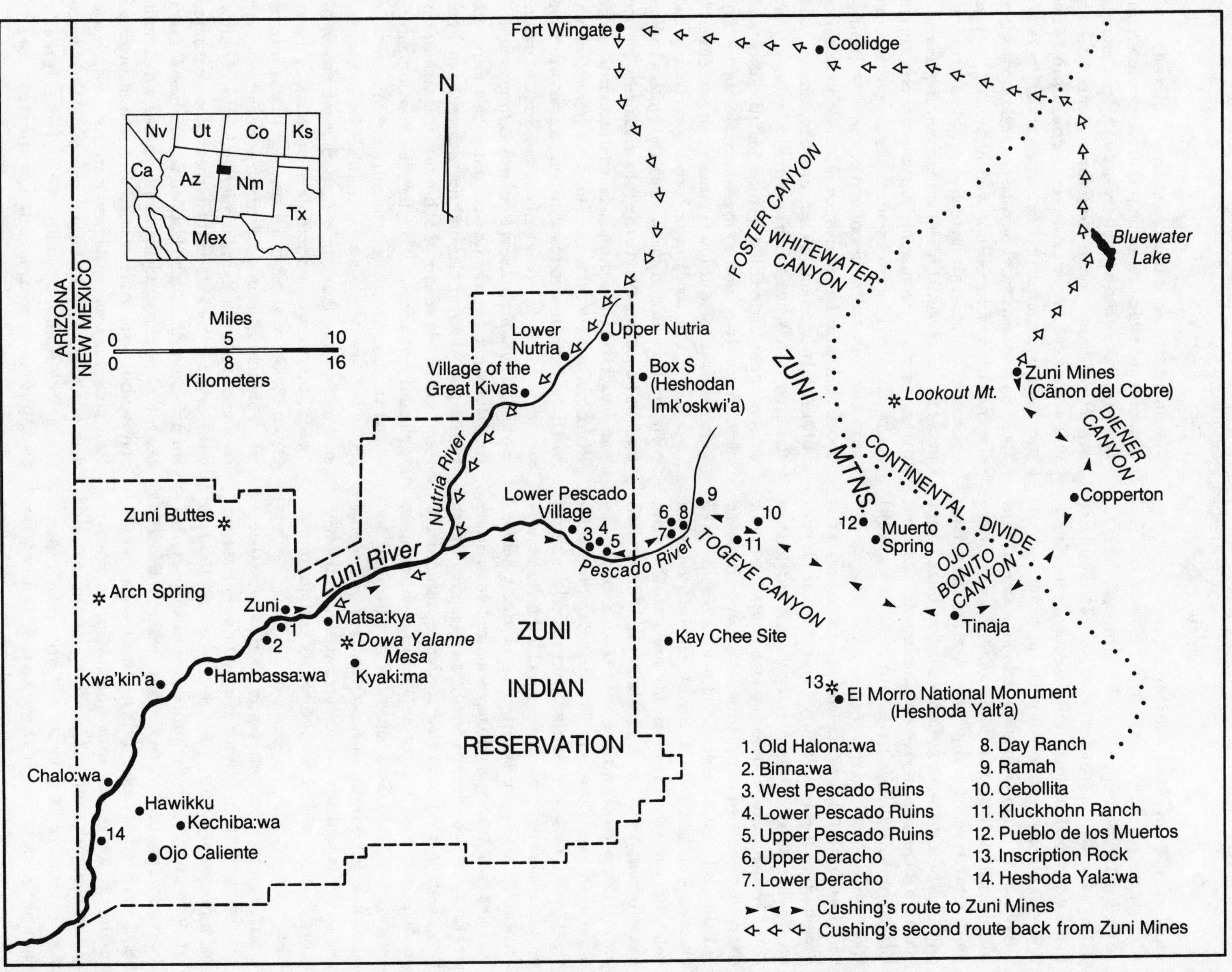
Fort Wingate
Coolidge
N
Nv
Ut
Co
Ks
Ca
Az
Nm
Tx
Mex
FOSTER CANYON
WHITEWATER CANYON
Bluewater Lake
ARIZONA
NEW MEXICO
Miles
0 5 10
0 8 16
Kilometers
Lower Nutria
Upper Nutria
Village of the Great Kivas
Box S (Heshodan Imk'oskwi'a)
ZUNI MTNS.
Zuni Mines (Cãnon del Cobre)
Lookout Mt.
DIENER CANYON
Nutria River
CONTINENTAL DIVIDE
Copperton
Lower Pescado Village
Zuni Buttes
Muerto Spring
Zuni River
Pescado River
TOGEYE CANYON
OJO BONITO CANYON
Arch Spring
Zuni
Matsa:kya
Dowa Yalanne Mesa
Kyaki:ma
ZUNI INDIAN RESERVATION
Tinaja
Kay Chee Site
Kwa'kin'a
Hambassa:wa
El Morro National Monument (Heshoda Yalt'a)
Chalo:wa
Hawikku
Kechiba:wa
Ojo Caliente
1. Old Halona:wa
2. Binna:wa
3. West Pescado Ruins
4. Lower Pescado Ruins
5. Upper Pescado Ruins
6. Upper Deracho
7. Lower Deracho
8. Day Ranch
9. Ramah
10. Cebollita
11. Kluckhohn Ranch
12. Pueblo de los Muertos
13. Inscription Rock
14. Heshoda Yala:wa
Cushing's route to Zuni Mines
Cushing's second route back from Zuni Mines

Zuni Area.

Daily Journal[64]

November 30th

Decided last night to accompany Mr. Williams [and] a wandering mechanic, to the Zuni Mountains, in the Eastern part of which he says he has found traces of ancient mines for *chalchihuitl,* or turquoise. I told the Governor I was going in the morning to take a five day journey. He asked where, [and] I told him about where [and] that I would not get back for several days. I did not inform him what I was going for, as this would have excited his opposition.

This morning I flew about and made ready. The Indians all helped to get my breakfast and prepare me for the journey in a way which was quite gratifying, the Governor sitting meanwhile and ordering the women how to prepare this thing and that. We did not get started until nearly eleven o'clock. I repassed the gorge in the rock boundary of the Valley of Zuni and the various ruins which I described on my way in from Wingate. After we had passed the road leading to Wingate, remains of small Pueblo dwellings became more frequent. At Ojo Pescado I found a very flourishing little farming pueblo—quite as large as Tesuque.[65] At the beautiful spring just above occurred two round pueblos, one on either side—originally constructed of stone and adobe, so poorly, and moreover so ancient, that they are now almost leveled to the ground. Above [east] a few rods is another spring, which flows out from under the rocks which rise perpendicularly from it eighteen or more feet. On the top of the rather round mesa thus formed I found other ruins.[66] All of these I hope to plan [diagram] on my return.

The spring is of interest from that fact that I identify it with the second spring of Zuni described in Whipple's report.[67]

Continuing on up the valley, we came to a number of small ruins, and to the left, where the valley turns and beyond half a mile is joined by a cañon, I discovered a circular ruin of great size, near to which were two stone-paved reservoirs (one in an excellent state of preservation).[68] Above, facing and running along the edge of the cleft, was a beautifully laid stone wall nearly three hundred feet long, of which every stone had been perfectly dressed with some sort of edge tool. The prehistoric character of the work was shown, however, by the presence of corrugated pottery and flint implements.[69] I am now convinced of the positive superiority in workmanship of the ancient Pueblos over the modern, though in architecture the modern is far superior to the ancient, as a rule—not wholly.

Across the valley diagonally was another mud pueblo ruin, very large and much better preserved than the first.[70] From some of the finest portions of the walls stones had been torn and drawn away by ranchmen so as to disfigure one of the most beautiful ruins I hope to see in New Mexico. Four miles farther on, we came to a cliff ruin which in the cold and growing darkness I drew a ground plan of.[71] It is a beautiful little thing, which I shall sketch and more minutely record on my return.

In the wall of the lower division I found a peg embedded in the wall. The portion protruding has been worn almost thin by use, showing what an immense length of time the ruin was used. Smoke had deeply blackened most of the interiors of the rooms, of which three or four were perfect. They had little doors fifteen to twenty-six inches wide and tiny holes near the rock roof for the exit of smoke. On the wall of one I observed marks of fingers which had been dipped in red paint and drawn downward. In the adobe cement of another a dotting in lines intended to represent the horned frog from the appearance of the wall bit left; in two or [three] others the impression of corn cobs and in a room of the lower division a stone fire box like those now used for cooking *Paiu-chi* in Zuni. The rock floors of some of the rooms were smoothed in places by use as grinding stones. At dark we remounted and started for the ranch of Ammon Tenney, a Mormon.[72] We journeyed through the cañon into a beautiful valley in which the rocks assumed the shapes of men, animals, and even cathedrals on the grandest scale. My ride back through this cañon will be a treat and may reveal many more remains, but seen by starlight alone, it was only interesting from the grandeur of its dark forms. Our whistle of "Home Sweet Home" echoed from rock to rock and deep gorge to mesa summit in a strange way, reminding me indeed how far away I was from home.

December 1st

Stayed at Bishop Tenney['s] all night. Passed a bad night, but on a good supper of bread and milk, and came away at sunrise without more than four biscuits and the good breakfast which was kindly supplied us. The Mexican work boy there I suspect to have taken my belt (Zuni), and after I went into the house last night, he went through my saddle bags, spilling some of the oats and leaving them open so that the dogs went through them, eating all my meat and bacon and most of my biscuits, leaving us (three men) with five biscuits and two Indian husk corn-cakes. We discovered all this only two or three hours since. Soon after, we lost our way, and, leaving the road, struck out for the mines which I wish to investigate. Night overtook us, and here we are, in a little cañon where we have found a little grass free from snow which our jaded animals may brace themselves upon. Should a snow storm overtake us tonight or tomorrow, our "cake will probably be all dough." So we bivouac tonight in the Zuni Mts., where the water, when there is any rain in summer, freezes slightly. It is not terribly cold tonight, and our immense pine campfire at once warms us, gives us light, and melts snow for drinking water—which we accomplish by gathering the snow and placing it in a sheepskin before the fire.

December 2nd

Miner's cabin, on the little Cañon del Cobre, Zuni, fifteen miles S.W. of Agua Azul, and about seventy five [miles] east of Zuni.

We passed a fairly comfortable night, getting cold at about three o'clock and rebuilding the fire. After warming [ourselves] and looking after the animals, we again rolled up in our blankets. I slept well enough to dream of all sorts of comfortable things. At sunrise we arose, rekindled the fire, and saddled again, setting out for the mines. Mr. Williams at last saw the [word missing] of the monuments of which he had told me, and then, passing a little cañon and crossing the divide, we entered [the] valley of one [i.e., cañon] which he pronounced to be that of the mines.[73] Soon he shouted, "There's the boy's cabin, but no one's there." We rode up to the door, and it suddenly opened, revealing a young man with a handkerchief tied over his left eye, who proved to be alone—in charge of the snug little cabin of Stevens and Co[mpany]'s claims.[74] This gentleman [Stevens] and his guide, old "Smid" [?] as he is called all over the Territory, were gone prospecting. We jumped off and Williams walked familiarly in. He discovered, some three years since, the claims now owned by this company. After a while, we watered the horses, and one of my two companions picketed mine to a tree down the cañon. Then the young man got a breakfast of fried bread and coffee. We ate heartily, and soon after, the whole party went down the cañon and up on the left bank to examine the ancient remains. Coming to and examining these, Mr. Williams and Buck bade me good-bye and set out. I immediately commenced planning the ancient ruins. These were in a group of four. The first (most northerly) consisted of a series of three or four rooms and were divisions of parallel walls with two semicircular rooms facing west—very irregular and now almost levelled to the ground. The three first groups, including this, were nearly on a line, and the fourth was to their rear, midway between the two last (most southerly) in the front (western) line. The rocks were coarse sandstone or fine conglomerate resting on a copper-bearing conglomerate formation in which the small pieces of blue and green stones occur of which the Indians make paint and, when hard enough, their green stone necklaces. About these old ruins I found a few pieces of pottery, both painted and corrugated, also some chips of various silicious stones and a hammer stone as well as a pretty white crusher of quartz.[75] The walls, partly from age and also from the inferiority of the mud which these Indians must have been forced to use, were nearly level with the ground, though in places standing three feet high and unbroken inside. The first described was the most perfect. Others are reported as existing on the other side of the cañon, but I have not found them to examine them.

From the ruins we went south a few rods and came to one of the primitive pointers or monuments, at once distinguishable from the modern miner's by their greater perfection and size and more worn appearance.[76] Between this and another some thirty yards farther is a bed of washed sand producing the little green nodules, though very soft ones, in great abundance. I sketched both monuments (see Books I [and] II),[77] and we then went nearly west and about half a mile up the hill, where we came to two immense excavations—one seventy-five by forty feet in diameter and joined above by two others half as large. Great pines grew on them, showing them to be at least one hundred years old.

We then crossed the Cañon and near the top of the hill—well up—came upon a series of five fresh holes where the Pueblo and Navajo Indians still dig for the precious material. Further down, we picked a few specimens out from the little hole which has been dug to start the copper mine. This was commenced on an ancient excavation, and the Indians have this winter pecked about it. Just to its right was a little brush hut, made by binding saplings together, laying sticks against them, and heaping pine needles over the apex. It is now nearly rotted down. Near it I picked up a pine digging stick, well worn at both ends and showing with what infinite labor the work of mining has to be done.

From here we struck off to the right, down the slope some three hundred yards, nearly north east. Here I found and planned twelve excavations, the upper right being very ancient. Five of the latter large and in a line along the ledge and three scattered between these and the more modern works below. The little hollows made by brooks and all the ground about had been scratched over, and all stones had been turned in the search for the green stone. One digging in the half decomposed rock and soil was fifteen feet deep from the upper bank. We were fortunate enough to find one of the well preserved though evidently very old digging sticks with which this work must in the main have been done. It was but little larger than the other (two feet long) and of the same material, though better made.

Since Mr. Tyzack has been here (the young man before referred to), at least a dozen Pueblo Indians have been here to dig or scratch about. At one time there were six Zuni Indians, and other parties came, usually by twos, mostly from the former place, Laguna and Acoma. They never stay more than two days and usually only one. Navajos also sometimes visit the place, both to gather stones and to hunt, as the mountains abound in turkey deer, bears, and smaller four-footed game. Also panthers and wild cats and wolves are quite numerous and bold.

The sun was nearly down when I finished sketching and we came down to get dinner. When I went to re-picket my little mule, I found that my companions had taken Mr. Graham's magnificent lariat and substituted one of their broken ropes. They advised me to always beware of the Mexicans, but great thieves as I know the poorer class of the latter to be, I have learned they do not steal from a friend. I am now writing by the firelight, and at the same [light] Mr. Tyzack is sketching a rough plan of the mining claims here, showing the directions of cañons and the approximate locations of the ancient diggings.

Mr. Tyzack is kindly aiding me in every way possible, and I put this address down here [so] that he may receive anything I may be happy enough to publish on this country. He is most worthy of encouragement. His home is Council Bluffs, Iowa, and his name, Herbert Tyzack.

Later.

The moon is just rising over the mountain divide to the right of the canon. A little while since, I went out to see that my mule was quite secure, for on him everything depends. Although we tied him securely and examined each [and] every knot in the old rope, nevertheless I found he had broken it and scampered. I searched the valley over, told Mr. Tyzack when he came from the spring, where he had gone to fetch some water, and was joined by him in the search. Then it occurred to me that he would go directly to our last night's camp. We hastened over to it, a mile away, but he was not to be found by the moonlight. I have again carefully searched the cañon, its forks and sides about here but have seen or heard nothing of the mule.

"Good-bye, Smiler. You are a little fool—that's all I've got to say. You will probably spend your days among a lot of Indians now, and maybe, badly as I've treated you, you'll find their whips a little more stingy."

In the morning I take her track. If it go toward Zuni, all right; I'll go there too. If not, I follow it a short distance—although I cannot go far, as I must get back to record the dance which takes place four or five days hence. Meanwhile, I must sleep, and that well too. Nice dreams I'll have, for they always come whenever anything occurs to make me believe more firmly than ever that everything is for the best—even the substitution of a rotten rope for a lariat. It will keep the other fellow's horse from getting away and teach me to trust still less and less those who call themselves my friends.

FHC to Baird

Cañon del Cobre
Zuni Mts, N.M.
December 3rd, 1879

My dear Professor Baird:

Three days since, in the company of a Prospector named Jonathan Williams, of Albuquerque, and a wanderer named Buck (Miller) I started for these Mountains to explore the supposed jade and turquoise mines of which I had received information. These I have found, together with interesting ruins in connection with them, and the sketches, notes and specimens which I have made and secured, form important additions to our collections and facts concerning the aborigines.

While I was searching for ancient remains yesterday morning, my two companions changed a knotted old rope for the magnificent lariat which I had procured from Mr. Graham of Zuni just before leaving. With this rope I was compelled to picket my mule last night, although before doing so Mr. Tyzack, the young man in charge of the mining cabin here, and I carefully examined and strengthened every knot. After I had finished my notes last evening, I went out to once more look after the mule, and he had broken the rope and stampeded. This morning I shall track him if possible; if not, I shall strike off over the mountains for Zuni, where he has probably gone.

In this altitude among strange mountains, and with scant provisions, the chances are about equal that I get caught by a snow storm and freeze, get lost and starve, or reach my destination in safety. I therefore leave with Mr. Tyzack this letter with the request that he, if I do not return after two weeks for my saddle, bridle, specimens, etc., may conclude that I am lost and forward this letter to you by the first opportunity.

Therefore should this reach you, you may conclude that I have perished, and I would suggest, as the easiest way of informing all my friends and relations, that a paragraph be put in the press to that effect. In case this happen, I regret that the material I have collected this summer, much of which is new, may never be worked up, as my notes in the hands of another would be unintelligible. I am not much troubled about my difficulty. My philosophy is that everything happens for the best, if not for the individual, yet for others and that's all I have to say save to thank you for all kindnesses.

Ever your Devoted Follower,
F. H. Cushing

I am grateful to you for all you have been ever ready to do in my behalf, and asking you to give my remembrance to all I loved, I say good-bye.

Daily Journal

December 3rd [1879]

Bivouac at the foot of the divide.

Mr. Tyzack was out early kindling the fire by which to cook my bread. I also got out and began to prepare for my search and journey. By passing the strap of my pouch through the middle ring, thus forming a loop for either shoulder, I made a tolerable knap-sack. To the top of this I have tied one double and one single blanket, thus making a complete outfit for the mountains. After eating a breakfast of bread and coffee, I strapped on the knap-sack, wrote two letters, one to Emma, the other to Prof. Baird, and giving them into the keeping of Mr. Tyzack, started out with him to track. We made an entire circuit of the valley, finding only traces of Smiler near the spring where she had last seen the other animals. We found no more tracks; and taking the two bread cakes and half a dozen strips of bacon, I started.[78] It must have been as late as eleven o'clock, and thus, although I walked uninterruptedly, save for a hasty lunch, yet I only made this point by dark and must wait until morning to resume my tracking. I am in hope that it will not snow. If not, I shall get over the divide safely. But if it snow, I have as much reason to believe that I shall be days in finding my way out as that I shall get out at all. From the intense exertion of climbing up and down not fewer than ten cañons and one mountain in reaching this valley, and then coming some fifteen miles, I am so lame I can scarcely move.

I have built a little fire with a pine tree, scraped together some of the comparatively dry needles and thus made myself comfortable. The only water to quench my thirst has been made by heaping snow on my little canvas sugar sack and waiting for it to melt—the water being retained by little sticks laid under the edges of the sack. These mountains are infested by the cougar, the cinnamon bear, the wolf, lion, coyote, and many other smaller animals of prey. Their tracks in the snow were yesterday everywhere abundant. The deer, elk, and turkey are also abundant in parts, though I have seen none to help me out today. I shall sleep with my carbine as a pillow, and trusting to the Providence which has brought this hard lot upon me, lie down again to pleasant dreams.

December 4th [1879]

I have passed the night—not comfortably—and have, nearly exhausted, reached Mason's ranch, the last habitation which we left in going out.[79] The warm coffee and *So-pai-pias* [Mexican fry bread] which were placed before me have much revived me, and I shall attempt to reach Tenny's tonight, where I shall make this account more complete.

As it darkens, I find myself still unable to go with sufficient expedition to reach the next ranch (eight miles away).

When I had built my fire last night, laid down in my blanket—not to sleep to any extent, as the wind circled about fiercely in every direction, threatening at any moment to set my blankets on fire. At last finding at which point the wind blew least, here I scraped away the little snow which had fallen. I placed my litter of pine needles there and prepared to get a little sleep. The wind pierced my blankets as [well as] matting, but by building a great fire I managed to keep half warm. I fell asleep, but the crackle of a branch caused by the footstep of some large animal aroused me, and I found to my dismay that the snow was steadily falling. So again building my fire, I half sat, half laid down, napping now and then during the [remainder of the] night. Toward morning, the storm grew fiercer, and the snow fell faster. So strong was the wind on the mountain side where I waited for morning that a great tree snapped and fell, above me, with a noise like the report of a cannon, its echo bounding from mountain to mountain and cañon to cañon. After this, feeling weary and cold, and knowing that my watching would neither stop the wind nor lessen the snow, while it *would* weary and chill me, I resolved to sleep. I rolled up in my blankets and slept—save for frequent starts—as calmly as though at home.

Finally, I awakened, parched with thirst. I peered out of my cold blanket and saw, through the clouds and snow, the gray of dawn. As yet, however, one could not see his way clearly, and where life and death were the two things staked on this, I resolved that haste was not prudent. I ate some snow and slept. In about half an hour I awoke. The lameness brought on by yesterday's travel was nearly gone. During the night the pain in my legs, breast and back had been so intense that I had feared I could not, from lameness, resume my journey—but now I felt not only well but strangely merry, and as I munched my cold piece of bread beside the snow-blinded fire the woods echoed with my snatches of self-cheering song. Drawing on my frozen leggings and stiff, nearly worn out moccasins and rolling up my sleet-covered blankets, I prepared to scout for a little evergreen branch which, not dreaming I would be thus compelled to use as a guide, I had broken as I descended the divide. Not ten rods away I found it, and knew that I had slept near the hidden trail which leads to the summit of the mountain ridge which divides the waters of the Gulf of Mexico from those which flow into that of California. Getting my pack on my back, I slowly labored up the steep.

Though not lame, I did not realize until after starting to climb how weak I was. Finally reaching the top, I could of course find no trace of our trail, which led to the cañon which should take me out of the mountains. The tracks of our animals were buried under five inches of snow. From habit constantly on the alert for ancient remains and strange natural features, I had seen and unconsciously recorded several burnt trees and one or two artificial piles of stone on my way out. When, after wandering round and round, I came upon these, one by one, I gradually found the cañon, as I thought, which we had come up. Taking out my compass, I found that it led east. I therefore struck for another, also in sight from the trees and stones, and determined to go down it at all hazards, as the wind which swept over the peak was chilling me through and through.

As I descended, my delight was great to find that many a strange feature which I had seen on my way up was present—and I knew that I was in our trail. Mile after mile of the rugged pathway I climbed down, never slackening my pace although I was becoming weaker and weaker, and my hands were nearly useless. I had left everything not absolutely necessary at the mining cabin, my soldier [?] coat with the rest. My body was therefore protected by my usual indoor flannel shirt; my hands were bare, my moccasins soaked, and my head protected only by my long hair and the Zuni paña, to which, however, I had become accustomed. As I began a more western course, I passed cañon after cañon and at last concluded that I must have strayed. Soon, however, I observed a Navajo deer shelter which I had noticed and commented upon on my way up. Then I knew that four or five miles would bring me to the first ranch. Soon an opening in the cañon revealed the bleak, sandy plains below, and I soon came to a little dam at a spring just at the beginning of the cañon. There I passed into the plain. All the way down, after leaving the shelter of the mountain pines, I had found the wind intensely piercing and cold, and when I at last stepped into the plain, the snow, borne on a fiercer blast [was] well nigh overpowering. I met an Indian with some burros. He was a Lagunan and had heard of me. He offered to shake hands, but when I attempted to draw my hand from my pocket, I found that the arm was so far paralysed that as I brought it forth it dropped uselessly to my side. Over the hands I had no control. When I entered the door of the ranch, I was just played out, and it was many minutes ere I could get the use of my hands to take off my pack. The Mexican owners treated me kindly. They built a large fire, and ere I knew it had some coffee and fried cakes (native) before me on a chair where I reclined near the fire. These revived me, and as I warmed, I thought I might again set out, but found myself so lame that I could not think of going.

And now my lameness is a little lessened, but it is too late to go further. The sky is once more clear. The cold is intense.

December 5th.

As night closed in, I suffered intensely from colic, brought on by eating snow in the mountains. The Señora gave me a dose of some hot medicine which temporarily revived me, but a slight supper brought on the pain again, and I could do no more than sit by the fireplace and groan. The young women came a little after dark and asked for my serapes, with which to make my bed. Then I was led off to another little cabin, where a comfortable bed had been prepared for me. The cabin was aglow with the pinewood fire in the ample hearth, and around the floor were spread the beds of a groaning old man, a middle aged Spaniard, and my host's brother-in-law, Señor Mason. The warmth and comfort of my bed somewhat relieved me, and I slept deliciously until morning.

When I awoke, I was recovered both from my sickness and lameness. After eating breakfast, I came out of the house and asked what should be the value of my accommodations. The woman replied that the amount was at my pleasure. I paid the woman a dollar and saw at once that she was disappointed, but as I could not get them to name the amount, I had to let it stand. Then, once more strapping my pack to my sore shoulders, I struck out along a trail over the hill.

I had proceeded about five miles to where the trail turns to join the main road when I saw by the side of a stream called the Ojo Muerto an interesting ancient pueblo, nearly square and laid with stones which had been dressed.[80] There were traces of two estufas—one four sided and the other round. The many little rooms were indicated only by hollows in the four walled or sided heaps of stones. The pottery of the place was of superior coloring and decoration, some of it being almost intensely red. Hastily pacing this ruin and picking up three or four representative pieces of pottery, I started along down the stream, attained the main road, and came on about four miles farther to the Mormon Ammon Tenney's place—Savoita [Savoia].[81] Here I found Solomon Barth, the contractor, camped with his many wagons and 137 head of oxen.[82] I was very lame and tired when I entered the house of the Mormons, and after sitting before the fire a few moments was hardly able to move without great pain. Old Mrs. Tenney received me with great kindness and said she had feared the Navajos of the mountains, who sometimes take advantage of solitary travelers, had killed and robbed me. A meal was hastily prepared for me, and I was urged to stay until the morrow. This I had decided not to do. Unable to get a horse from Mr. Barth, I applied to Mr. Tenney Jr. He could give me but an old and slow but good mule, though he had neither saddle nor good bridle. Deciding to halve the price with Mr. Graham here, he saw me [sentence unfinished] But the mule, like many others, not caring for my stick, moved so slowly that I saw he would not get me out of the valley before sunset, although the sun was two hours high, and I decided for this and for the reason that Mr. Tenney had feared the mule might get away, that I might lose my road or that I could not get back within two days, I turned back and stayed here for the night.

During the evening I have talked with the family a great deal, and I found to my surprise that old Mrs. Tenney was not only from New York but that she was also a Strong and was also included in the Strong book of genealogy, [and] that her grandfather was John Strong. As this gentleman was my grandmother's uncle, I suppose I must claim, or rather, accept, relationship which is claimed.

With discussing Mormon subjects and reading Mormon literature, it was late before the old lady went into the outer room to make me a bed of blankets on the floor, meanwhile explaining how she dipped candles, made soap, and cut up pigs. If every woman were as strong and energetic as this old lady, there would be more pioneers (Mormon, presumably) and less work for the men of this world to do.

December 6th.

Passed a comfortable night, although the wind shrieked through the cracks in my loose log room, and the Mantua windows proved little protection against its biting. Yet the abundant blankets with which I was provided, compared with the two with which I slept in the mountains, made this a night of luxury. The old lady came into my room early to cook breakfast, and I crawled out from my comfortable nest. I sat down in front of the fire, and while breakfast was preparing wrote the memorandum of yesterday. Prayers were said. Then we went in to breakfast and grace w[as] asked. Then we ate, and I strapped on my pack and started out. I was footsore and lame, but I determined to reach Zuni before I stopped. Half a mile this side of Tenney's place I examined some ancient ruins composed of two pueblos. One was somewhat square, the other almost round. They lie on either side of the road to Albuquerque.[83] As at all other ancient pueblos, fragmentary pottery was abundant, showing the usual red decoration which characterizes much of the earthen ware of all the Pueblos Viejos of the Zuni Valley and mesas.[84]

Toiling along some ten or twelve miles further, [I] pass[ed] two miles to my left the celebrated Inscription Rock and near[ed] the three round pueblos of Pescado.[85] These, though in an advanced state of ruin, must have been more recently occupied than the others, since they show a nearer approximation to the modern pueblos in the remains of their art. On the sandy road which approaches the first of these I was warned by the jingle of Indian bridles to step from the road. As I did so, three young Zunians who had been hunting two days in the mountains rode up. They stopped and gazed at me a moment, then exclaimed, "*Tim Cushie, Hop-tan-i!*" ["Hey, Cushing, where are you going?"] I told them my story, gained their sympathy, and asked one if he [would mind taking] my serapes on behind. Instantly the principal one dismounted and strapped them there. I then wrote a hasty note to Dr. Ealy and told them to take it to him, and with the [serapes] to give it to him. According to my usual practice, I translated it, telling them that it said I was very lame and tired, that I was beyond Pescado, and that I should some time in the night reach his place.

They looked at one another, then at me, but did not start. Then they spoke a few words in which I heard "Why not this," and "Why not Cushie this," and the constant exclamation "*Ma-i-me*" (I don't know). Then the same one ask[ed] me why I would not get on his horse with him. I told him his horse went fast and that [if] I rode with him, he [the horse] would not go so fast, that he would get tired and be sick, and that he was a good man and I did not want his horse to get so. They all laughed at this, and he said *no* Zuni horses, I must know, were like that. It was only Mexican horses that were so foolish. "Get on, get on. Will you sit in front or behind?" I jumped on behind, and while I knew that, as these Indians never let their horses walk, I would—sitting as I was on its hips—have a hard time of it, I reflected that it would be better than to travel all night, so we came on.

This galloping behind an Indian on the hips of an Indian pony is a hard business. Yet with whatever breath I could get, I breathed thanks both to the Indians, and to Providence for this good fortune. The pain of this ride was a change from the intense pain of the walk, and I was content. At the entrance of Zuni Valley, as I saw that the Indian pony was getting jaded, I said I would go afoot. The Indian replied "*Wānāni*" [wait a moment]. So I waited. In a few moments he set me down, and I rewarded him with some silver, and saying thanks and adding a post scriptum to my note, bade them "*Hlano*" [good-bye].[86] So they galloped away, and with ten or twelve miles still before me I painfully resumed my journey afoot.

The day, though cold, had been clear and sunny, and as I entered the Zuni [valley], covered with its dry grass and deserted fields and cut diagonally in twain by the abrupt arroyo of the Rio Zuni, I do not think I ever saw a more beautiful sunset. Nor have I ever, under the happiest circumstances, enjoyed one equally. The red rays of the sun threw the thousands of little turf mounds which cover all the valley bottoms of this region into twice their natural relief and scattered their shadows like the strands of a fan toward my eyes, which were sheltered in the shade of [the] great lava rocks which bounded the rugged path down which I was climbing. And away on the edge of the horizon, rising from its bed of sands, was the silhouette of Zuni.

The wind was from the north and just strong enough now to drift away a great banner of blue smoke which floated up from the whole southern side to join the sun clouds of the west. Of nothing could I be reminded by the silhouette but a terraced volcano—the smoke rising from its myriad craters.

Then down into the plain and across the river and four miles more of hard sandy walking, and with the advent of darkness I was at the gate of the house of the Maestro.[87] When I reached the door, it was opened and the good doctor rushed forth and shook me warmly by the hand. Mrs. Ealy and Mr. Graham, who was also there, received me warmly; but in mock coolness, as a "tramp," was I received by the young lady. Supper was prepar[ed] for me, and eating of it heartily, I prepared to leave for the pueblo. When I arose to go, I could hardly step, but I managed to get over, bade Mr. Graham, who accompanied me, good night, and went on to my room in the house of the Governor. The little windows were curtained, and the door locked, but the light of a warm fire sparkled through the cracks. When I pounded at the door, a glad voice responded "*Wānāni*."

Presently, after a long attempt, the Governor succeeded in unlocking the door, which he had religiously kept locked during my absence. He could hardly wait for me to enter, but grasped my hand and turned with beaming manner to the interior, which lo! he had entirely made smooth, white and cozy. The forge removed, a new pole for my serapes, everything in the best Zuni style.[88] I knew that tired as I was, I must express surprise, [as well as] thanks, which I did. But the pleased smile faded from his face. He looked at me and said "For why sad?"

"No sad, no more. Tired."
"Yes, sad."
"No."
"*Hōpi mu-la?*" [Where is your mule?]
"*Qua-ku*." [Not here, gone]
"*Yā-o Nāi!*" (Great God!)

The story was told. The Governor told me what he thought of the two American companions and reminded me how he had labored to convince me how far it was, how much I would be absent from Zuni. I meekly admitted [that he had], rested a little while read[ing] some letters from home, and cracked jokes with all who had more warmly and clamorously than even the Maestro's people rushed forward to welcome Kū-shi. But the governor looked grave all the evening, and when I said that I had written letters in the mountains to tell Washington that I was dead if I did not get back in ten days, and that I should therefore again start in two days, he arose and said he was going to have a talk and smoke at his uncle's house. He wanted to sleep in my house. I said yes and rolled up in my blankets for the night.

December 7th.

Was wakened early in the morning by the Governor, who entered to kindle a fire. Then he brought me a bowl of water to wash in and told me to get up. I arose, dressed, and ate of the breakfast he had meanwhile prepared, while he told me that the blue stones which I had found were of great value to Zuni and Acoma and that from these two pueblos men had from times of old gone to get their blue paint and green.[89] He very coolly went through my sack, taking out all the blue stones he could find. I said nothing. I humor them when it's policy [sic]. Then he spread a little cloth and told me to put there all the green stones I had in my pockets. I did so immediately. He looked them over and selected all but two specimens of copper ore which I had. Then I knelt down and took out ten little bits of blue and green and put them in a cartridge. He took the cartridge and poured them back again. I looked at him and asked why he did that. He said I did not want that paint. It was not good that Washington should have it. I told him, as I again picked up the specimens and replaced them in the cartridge, that I wanted them. He said no. I said yes, and I must have them. I laid the cartridge down again and told him, "You see it? It is mine, and you let it alone." For some time he and Roman were very sullen.[90] When they began to recover, I told them why I wished the specimens, and the Governor, who is always reasonable when fully informed, became good again. He said I must stay at home today, as Juan Citimo would come to cut out my pantaloons.[91] He said he had spoken to Juan for horses and that much [sic] would come.

Forgetting that it was Sunday, I went down to the Doctor's to see if I could not raise some money in case it became necessary to buy a horse, by offering him some of my clothes. When I arrived there, however, I was reminded from the stillness that it was sabbath and did not make the proposition, merely got sugar, coffee and flour instead.

When I came back, I found that my tailor had not been here, and the Governor told me he had perhaps lied to him. "Never mind," said he, "*Yo sabe*."

Nor did he come, and the Governor told me that he might have lied also about the horses. He said he had this excuse, however—that he was probably making plumes for the coming dance, which was deemed so necessary that it excused him. He was also making plumes [himself] and told me the varieties, uses and origins, what they were destined for, etc.—which, with his traditions of ancient ruins related during the evening, I must write up in books specially devoted to these subjects.

Listening late to the Governor's talk, I did not retire early. He again spoke of my proposed trip to Silver City, endeavoring in vain to fix to his satisfaction where that place was. He still insists that it is wrong for me to go alone, as much as I persist in telling him that if the letter from Washington comes I shall go. "Well," he says, "I know it all—where your little bows and arrows are and all.[92] And I know where there is another cave like it too, and I know the names of all mountains and streams between those places and this, and if you must go alone like a fool, why, before you [leave], we must go together to a high mountain and I will talk to you a whole day. *Como*." He also told me where *chalchihuitls* were found, drawing a map to show precisely the locations. It is in the Sierra Blanca just above Camp Apache, and when I visit the ancient dance houses I shall also go there, though it is two days further away.[93] It is a great privilege to be thus informed by an Indian about the source of their treasure, at once sacred and the most precious they possess.

December 8th.

The horse with which I was to have gone this morning came as promised last night, but trouble arising about some distant sheep, a young man, without speaking before, took the horse and rode off. As I also find myself a little lame this morning, I concluded not to go but to wait until tomorrow, when I shall have the pleasure of Mr. Graham's company. The Governor said he would go and speak to the Alcalde. . . . When he returned, he remarked after about half an hour's silence that the Alcalde, who had good horses coming in this evening, would give me one and insisted on taking another and going with me. He said they did not wish me to go alone and that moreover he wished to get some blue paint stones. I said, "Very well." I had told the Governor of getting my *Pihlan hli-an* [sinew for hunting-bow string] from Lucero's brother and asked him to tell me what the price of one was, but he said he did not know. He said I must ask Lucero. Although he knew what one was worth as well as anybody, I could not by any means get him even to hint. Toward evening I said, "Well I must go and pay Lucero three or four dollars." He laughed at me and said I was a great fool—then held up two fingers. He went out with the remark that perhaps he must talk. Soon Lucero's brother came and sat down. I drew out two dollars and asked him if it were good. He replied, "Yes," and thus ended the bargain. When evening came, I began to get supper and cook a great deal of bread. He asked me why I did so, and I said, "For tomorrow's journey."

"Perhaps you will not go; the Alcalde's horses did not come, and he says he can't go."

"Yes, I will go. When [Zuni?] wants to get horses for a man, she can. And I will start on foot and get a horse at Masons."

"Why not take a burro?"

"*Burros no bueno para Americano. A pie mas mejor bueno.*" [Burros are no good for an American. Much better to walk.]

I had seen a young acquaintance riding a pretty yellow pony during the day and suggested getting him. The Governor did not reply, [but] within an hour the young man in question came in. I proposed supper and meanwhile spoke to the Governor about it, before him—both understanding Spanish. They had a talk. The Governor went out to "oblision," at the same time remarking that I must do my own talking, as he would not.[94]

I proposed to hire the young man's horse. He said all right, but he would go too. I saw that they were evidently bent on someone's going with me, but fearing they would expect reward and being unable to give more than the hire of a horse, I stoutly opposed it. I went to see the Alcalde. . . . [When I] went back to the room, Governor was there, also young man. Told him [Governor] latter had said I could get a horse from him; but that he was going too. I asked why, and suggested that they thought I would lose their horse and not pay them for it. He said *no.* Then that they thought I lied to them? Again he said *no.* That I was a bad man and would run away with the horses?

See my trunk, my papers, my all, here. Do you think I would run away from them?"

"You are a little bit of a fool. Were you not a good man, we should not care, but it is because you are that we wish a man to go with you. He will keep the fire at night. He will go and get the horses, he will make the camp for my friend Cushie, who not knows how Zuni."

Then I told him fairly why I objected; how poor I was, that I did not feel able to reward a man for going with me. I could pay for a horse but not for a man. If a man wished to go with me, I would be glad.

"See that boy" (the young man)? You say you will pay a dollar for each day, one for one day, six for six. Pay that to this boy and *you* shall have a horse for nothing. But I want some Zuni man to go with you."

"Well, well," said I, "I don't like that, but thanks for *your* kindness. I'd rather take a horse alone and give you all than pay him all and give you nothing."

"It is good," said he, and he got up to leave with his woman and the boy for singing a night "*oblisia*" and I went to sleep.

December 9th.

Arose early in the morning and prepared to leave. At breakfast time the young man came. Soon after, Mr. Graham, who said his horse had run away but that a young man had gone after it. He said he would go around and get Jesus's in case the other did not come. Went, secured the latter, came back to tell me, accompanied by latter, who sat down to smoke. It was getting late to start, but we could not hurry the Indians. Jesus wished to smoke, and smoke he would. The Governor said "my boy," his nephew K'iesh-pa-hu (Mex. Luciano Martina), was at his house preparing, that it was useless to hurry as we couldn't go without our horses. I knew their ways and sat as unconcernedly as though I had no intention of making a journey; but Mr. Graham was considerably excited, taking their apparent indifference for impertinence. Soon K'iesh-pa-hu rode up to my door, on a rather poor animal, accompanied by a poorer looking gray pony—one eye banged out. Forthwith, all was astir. In spite of my declaration that I should go bareback so as not to tire the animal, they went off and got another saddle. I growled vehemently about my horse, but the Governor only smiled and said I was a fool and that was for why I talked bad—that I didn't know that an old and tough animal, even if he *didn't* look nice, knew more about the mountains. "Besides," said he, "if you don't stop talking God-dammy, I may not let you take the horse."

I bade them good-bye surlily and set out for the store, where Mr. Graham was ready and joined me. I wore, as usual, the *Ohl pane* [head-band], a Zuni belt and a serape confined, Zuni fashion, at the waist—not so much from desire, as they thought, as from necessity. However, this excited approval, and all, as I rode through the village, were loud in the "*Hlū-ū*"s and "Look at Cushie!" We rode out of the valley, to meet a piercing wind, the breeder of a storm. Mr. Graham suffered greatly—but immured by my recent experiences, I did not feel it much. On an elevation near the Wingate road, where the wind was fiercest, my bag of provisions tore apart. Not until my Indian and I tried to gather them up did we realize how cold it was. It was a terrible task. He took a serape from his roll (of three) when it was done, and in a twinkling all was inside, *a la* saddle-bags, and it was securely strapped behind my saddle.

At Ojo Pescado we stopped to shoot a duck and again got chilled. Then we rode hard past the ruins before described, under the little cliff houses, and around the great cathedral rock to Tenney's ranch, reaching this place just at night. I spent the evening in talking and *churning*. Passed a dreadful night—for, hospitable as it is, I think their house (without the serapes) colder than any other in New Mexico.

December 10th.

On this morning I started out in company with the Indian alone. Mr. Graham had decided to go no further on account of the cold, but to stay at Tenney's and hunt one day, then return to Zuni. We rode against a raw wind by road and trail to Masons. Near there, my boy got off and picked ten or twelve Spanish bayonet leaves. At Masons I fed the animals some oats, warmed and again started, following as nearly as I could the trail by which I had come out. This, after leaving the spring, was entirely blinded by the severe winds and recent snows. Save for an occasional broken sage brush, a rift in the snow, or a point where the wind had swept the sand bare, it was undiscoverable. I learned more in trailing it during this one day than I had learned by the years of reading in a study. When we left the ranch, a dog followed us. I used English invectives until I was hoarse, but he was a Mexican, it seemed, so I used Mexican in trying to persuade him back—to no purpose. Evidently a Zunian. I employed my small stock of Zuni. He only pricked his ears and continued on. I soon passed the Navajo deer shelter, and then various objects with which my painful trip down the mountains had made me familiar, and thus knew that I was right. At last, in the face of a freezing wind, we crossed the great divide and descended into the Valle de los Argones.[95] The wind swept up it fearfully. The sun was setting, and clouds were gathering. We found good grass and looked for a place in which to camp. Found one, but it was not suitable, and we rode on several miles. At last, where the two streams of the valley meet there shoots off a cañon or two, broad where they join the valley but narrow and protected above and their bottoms splendid pasture. My Indian said, "Ah—cold! And here yonder, good pasture, good camp."

"Good," I said, and he galloped on to the entrance. There, two trees had fallen. He dismounted, and I suggested nothing. I wished to see how he would make a camp. He caught up a little stick, scraped the snow away from a spot close to one of the logs, and in a twinkling had our saddles etc. placed there, and the horses hobbled and started out to feed. A kick of the foot four feet in front of the cleared space indicated where the fire was to be made. While I prepared the place, he brought wood and pine needles, and with two trials we raised a hot blaze. Then more wood was piled on, more snow scraped away, tufts of grass pulled and laid before the fire to dry, and plenty of wood gathered for the night. Then the Indian sat down on one side of the fire and I on the other. The wind blew smoke in our eyes and sparks against our serapes, but we managed to shift about until we found a spot where it blew least. The cold was intense—so much so that our ride had almost benumbed us. But for our serapes, which, Zuni fashion, are far superior to heavy coats on horse back, we could not have endured it. Now to add to our misfortune, snow began to fall, but we piled on wood and calmly prepared for the night.

K'iesh-pa-hu seated himself and took out some goat skin which he had brought and began to soften it by melting snow on it. He then drew forth his knife and Spanish bayonet leaves and began to make a pair of over-shoes. While I gathered the scant grass together near the fire, placed a saddle for my pillow, and rolling my two blankets around me, prepared to sleep.

The dog had gone as soon as the horses were turned loose, and digging a hole in the snow had laid down to watch them. Accustomed to traveling, evidently, and a good animal. I tried to entice the poor thing to the fire, but he would not come until toward morning, when he laid down close behind me.

Before sleeping, we ate our supper, which consisted of bread, sugar and canned salmon, which, partly for want and partly for the can, to cook coffee in, I had brought along. Then I slept. At about midnight K'iesh-pa-hu woke me and asked me if I wanted water. I said yes. He went around to the other side of the fire. There he had dug a hollow in the ground into which he had heaped snow, which had melted and, constantly replenished, had filled the hollow with water. He threw a handful of snow into the middle of the pool—which was muddy of course—and applying his mouth, took a draught through this cold mouth-piece. I added to it and did the same. The snow acted as a strainer and sponge at once, and the muddy water reached the mouth clear, cool, and to the lips of thirsty travelers, delicious.

Again I slept. I was awakened three times during the night by snow. But when at last dawn came, the sky was clear. K'iesh-pa-hu was sound asleep, and as all night when I had awakened I had found him attending the fire and looking after the horses, I did not disturb him but silently replenished the fire and, hauling the strange dog into my blankets, tried to get warm and sleep. At about sunrise I again woke, got up, replenished the fire, woke K'iesh-pa-hu, and eating a hasty meal prepared to go. In getting our salmon—which, though it had stood a short distance from the fire all night, was frozen solid—I had to use my hunting knife, and this unfortunately put a hole through the [bottom] of my future coffee can. K'iesh-pa-hu mended it with a rag, but that didn't stand fire very well. So, melting some snow and drinking it, we saddled and packed and again started off—the sun clear, the air keen, and the snow crumpling under the horses' hooves.

December 11th.

Thus [we] rode on, having no trouble in detecting the trail, as I had learned by hard experience to detect the faintest trace of human passage. We rode over the little rise where the two arroyos of the valley have their sources, one flowing Southeast, the other Northwest. Followed the valley to where it turns at right angles and, instead of undertaking the laborious crossing of the mountains, followed down this Valle de los Argones. Until we had reached this turn, the cold was severe, though the sun shone in summer splendor. Down the valley a mile, we came to a deserted sheep ranch, after which we followed a trail four or five miles until we came to a little cañon mouth, opposite to which was another sheep ranch. The walls of the cañon on the right were high, bold and beautiful with their bands of red and gray strata, and off to the right were the central peaks of the Zuni Mountains. Turning in to the ranch, we rode up the hill or mountain, following a trail some four miles. Finding that I was one or two cañons below that in which the cabin stood, I turned off to the left, and soon struck, to my great joy, the little basin-like valley in which my mule had been picketed. Riding down this a little way, I saw the top of the cabin, and as a further relief of my apprehensions, heat and smoke rising from the chimney.

I rode up to the door and shouted. The renowned old "Smid"—"Don Pedro"—was inside, laid up with lameness. Tyzack came to the door, the rag off his eye but the usual [bread] dough in his hands. He greeted me boisterously, dough and all, and K'iesh-pa-hu and I were soon sitting down with Tyzack and Don Pedro to a mountain feast of venison and good bread, for Mr. Tyzack certainly knows how to make griddle bread. I took care to get my two letters which I had deposited with Mr. Tyzack—visibly before K'iesh-pa-hu. I learned [that because of] shortness of provisions and fear of snow they were about to leave for the nearest settlement. Had this been the case, a mining pick would have been left for me to draw the lock and enter the hut, though this was deemed unnecessary, as it was thought I had perished. The letters therefore would have been mailed on the day following, and it would have been reported through all the East that I was dead.

After eating, we went to the mining sites to get specimens. On the edge of an abrupt cañon opposite the del Cobre, in a vertical dyke I got some good specimens of galena and silver. Copper is abundant all over the hill. I took specimens from the opening visited at first, as also some of the conglomerate in which they occur.[96] Got also specimens of the granite and talc of the higher beds, and a few bits of the blue stone. While I was getting all these, K'iesh-pa-hu was busy picking up the blue stone, an occupation which he quit with reluctance as the coming darkness compelled us to go down. We took up a supply of water, brought wood for the night, made a roaring fire, our beds, and prepared a big supper of venison, bread, and coffee. I promised "Old Smid" that, should he remain lame in the morning, he could ride one of my animals and I would walk. He decided to avail himself of the offer, to go down, get another animal and come back.

The night set in clear, cold and starry. No thought of a storm crossed our minds. After writing up notes and studying a map for a while, I rolled up to sleep. During the night I could frequently hear K'iesh-pa-hu passing out to look after the horses, to see that they were about, safe from wild animals, and where they could get food. Once toward morning I went to the door. All were sleeping. I opened it and looked out. It was dark and cloudy,

December 12th.

and the snow was falling so thickly that it covered everything deeply with white. I turned in, bitterly. Everything was against me. If this continued twenty-four hours, it would make the mountains impassable. Soon light appeared, and the others awoke to our misfortune. We at once decided to quit the hut [and head together down the eastern slope]. We cooked a last good meal at the cabin, ate two *he-po-lo-k'ia* and packed for the journey.[97] I was forced to leave a blanket there, as also an interesting basket olla which some searchers for blue stone had left before me. Even then, Don Pedro wished to take so much down that one horse had to be led with his pack. I walked all the way.

At the foot of the cañon I procured a specimen of the red rock which immediately underlies the paint-bearing conglomerate. Then as we turned to the Valle and followed it south west, the stream became larger, containing trout and beaver traces in abundance. Passing down about two and a half miles, the Valle suddenly narrows to form a cañon, then turning abruptly down the eastern slope, winding from side to side and presenting spectacles at once grand and beautiful. The snow was quite deep and the trail sometimes narrow and hard to travel. Two miles down this cañon the cottonwoods grow abundantly from one inch to fifteen in diameter. Large and small, the beaver makes such havoc with them, I observed not a few a foot in diameter which they [had] laid low. One [of] ten inches they had cut in a single night.

The walls became abrupt, grand, wild, and beautiful. At one point in the downward course they were of limestone [and] were rugged and grotesque. Very fossiliferous, producing the Rhynchonellids and Productus in abundance. I collected several of the latter in the hope [of] determin[ing] by them the geological formation.[98]

Just below where the limestone formation begins a natural rock shelter midway up attracted my attention. I climbed to it and found there traces of habitation, rude and only temporary, but evidently Pueblo. I regard it as the work of primitive Acomites who, in their passage up the mountain for blue stones, would have to camp frequently and in protected places, from fear of Navajos. The walls were chinked with grass and sticks and had been partially roofed with rafters ready cut by beaver. One of these showing the work both of man and the latter animal I broke the end from and brought along as a specimen.

After this I came upon no ancient remains claiming attention until we reached the lower country, when about three miles from Agua Azul we crossed a jasper producing hill which had been extensively worked. I found a fine point as a sample. Just at dark we reached the ranch of Señor Provencay, a Canadian Frenchman.[99] All the lower country was without snow, but the San Mateo, which stood out against the clear sky all our way down, making, with the mesa landscape between, a picture beyond my descriptive powers, was covered like marble with a mantle of snow. Near the very summit, where a great banner of clouds floated away, even now dropping snow on the other side, Old Smid pointed out where a sacred cave is situated in which have been deposited *chalchihuitls* and beads with wooden carvings and gave me one of the beads and some other bits picked up there.

I was heartily glad to gain shelter and warmth, as the rugged walk had told on me. Soon supper of stewed meat and coffee was spread, and we sat down to eat a prodigious meal. While at it, one of the mail riders who makes a stop here gave me some idea of what I had got to go through to reach Silver City. He said a thousand dollars in cash could not induce him to make it in the face of the Apache hostilities, obscure trails and snows of winter. After seeing to everything, I rolled up in the corner, told K'iesh-pa-hu to sleep by my side if he wished, and slept well till near morning, when I went out to feed the horses, taking K'iesh-pa-hu. Then came in, slept a little while, and proposed to start. Ate breakfast and saddled, paid for accommodation, two and a half dollars, and started toward Wingate via Crane's ranch.

December 13th.

The road was plain and soon joined the one I had ridden over on my way out [i.e., en route from Fort Wingate to Zuni in September], but the cold was intense and the wind severe, according to all my luck on this ill-fated expedition. Some fifteen miles from Crane's I turned in to a Mexican ranch to water my horses. They charged me a quarter for the privilege. At about three o'clock I made Crane's, having accomplished a ride of some thirty miles between the hours of nine and four. I was kindly met by Mr. Crane, whom I had seen nearly three months before.[100] He led me in to a fire, had a room nicely prepared for me, and I found myself within half an hour sitting in as comfortable quarters as I have seen since leaving home. When the time came for supper, I was summoned by dinner bell. I found the table spread with beef, potatoes, nice white bread, coffee, and—more than all to me—sauce. Of the latter I ate beyond all reason, but I couldn't help it. A fellow who's gone without fruit of any kind for more than a month wants it pretty badly at the end of that time.

I talked long after supper with Mrs. Crane. She said that much had been remarked against Dr. Ealy, his family and their work. I then told her what had been said at Wingate to the Indians concerning an effort to get him turned out and another in his place. She said she would write to the Mission Board at once, as well as to others who might be influenced, and begged me to tell Dr. Ealy all about it at once.

I had a talk with the buckboard driver concerning the trails leading through the Apache country. He said snow, the Apaches, and bad trails made a trip difficult and hazardous even when undertaken by a party. Like everybody else, he advised me not to undertake it. But he and Mr. Crane advised me, in case I did attempt it, to get a rather small pony for the purpose and one not less than five years old. [end of Notebook VIII]

Herbert Tyzack to Emily Cushing[101]

Vernal, Utah, March 30, 1911

A short time ago I picked up a copy of the Salt Lake Herald which contained an article in reference to the work being done by the government in the matter of irrigation and reclamation among the Indians of New Mexico and Arizona, and while glancing it over I happened to catch the name of "Lieutenant Cushing." To get at the point I will state that this brought to my memory the fact that years ago when I was a boy about eighteen years of age I became acquainted with Mr Cushing under conditions that stamped themselves on my memory. It was when Mr Cushing was living at the Zuni Indian village, when he was living among them in such a way as to be almost one of them, with a view of learning all the old traditions and beliefs, all their old superstitions and fancies and I remember too that he was very enthusiastic in his work. At this particular time I with others was interested in some mining claims in the Zuni Range that we dreamed would make us wealthy some day, and in this particular locality there were many evidences of human life in the long ago.

It seems that Mr Cushing had learned of many things of interest to him in that particular locality and it happened that one day in November I think it was, a fellow whose name I have forgotten, called at the Zuni Village and Mr Cushing learned from him more things that interested him about that section and he persuaded this fellow to guide him to our camp, believing that he could find his way back to the Zuni Village after he had completed his investigations. He stayed in the camp for two or three days, and I will also state that I was alone there when he came and was alone after he left, but to continue my story I remember that the night before he was to start back he picketed the government mule that he had ridden over, near the cabin for the night and when he went out to see that the animal was safe before going to bed he discovered that he had broken the lariat and was gone. Mr Cushing hunted for hours that night but without avail. The mule was gone, and to make matters worse it started to snow and the next morning the country was covered and of course no tracks could be found. After hunting all that day Mr. Cushing made up his mind to start out for the Zuni Village 75 miles away on foot, with only moccasins on and a red hankerchief tied about his head as was the custom of the Indians. That night before he started he told me the history of his life and his aspirations.

He told me of a young lady in Washington who was more to him than the whole world and he wrote two letters to leave with me with instructions to get them to a post office if I did not hear from him in a month after he left; one of these was to the president I think it was of the Smithsonian Institute and the other to the young lady whom I supposed was his betrothed. I will never forget the next morning when he started away. The snow had fallen to a depth of about three inches as I remember but the clouds had cleared away partly but it was threatening to storm again and I thought as he started away across the hills in that wild country that I would never hear from him again. With moccasins on his feet and a red hankerchief tied about his head, some meat and biscuits in his knapsack and his gun over his shoulder he disappeared from view. About three weeks afterward he came back to the camp after his outfit that he had left at the cabin, and this time he brought an Indian with him, and then he told me the story of his experience in the hills, and which you of course have heard from him. Now the reason I am writing to you Mrs Cushing is this: At the time that he came back he told me that it was his intention to write a book covering the traditions of the Zunis and that when he did this he would forward me one, and in it he would mention his trip to our camp. I left New Mexico shortly afterward and he lost track of me. I learn now that he died some time ago and I am writing you for one of his books in which he covers the Zuni Indians and his experiences. If you will kindly advise me what the cost will be and whether you can send me a copy I will remit to you all expense of same. Hoping that I will hear from you I remain;

Yours Truly
Herbert Tyzack, Secretary
Uintah Abstract Company, Inc.

FHC to Baird

Fort Wingate, N.M.
December 14, 1879

My dear Professor Baird:

The prompt receipt of your kind letter of the 6th inst. is very gratifying, as it assures me at once that my lonely work receives your much needed approval, and that you are willing to allow me time for satisfactorily completing this work, and that the money which I asked for will reach me, at a time when I was arranging to sell my clothes for the purpose of raising means.

I have recently passed through a series of most trying and unlucky events and adventures. In my last (of the 27th inst.) I believe I mentioned my desire to visit an ancient mining region in the heart of the Zuni Mountains. On the first of the month, accompanied by my informant, a prospector of Albuquerque named Williams and a stranger named Buck (alias Miller), who were to pass within a few miles of the region, I set out. . . . [*There follows an account of the stolen lariat and the runaway mule.*]

The mule had broken loose and gone, leaving me, my specimens, and equipage seventy five miles from Zuni, in the highest, snow covered, most untraveled portion of the Zuni Mountains, and thirty five miles from the last inhabited place. . . . Knowing that to be at all safe I must make at least thirty miles before the following mid-day, I made up my pack and wrote you the enclosed hasty note.[102] This note, from my haste and condition of mind, was neither well considered nor detailed; yet, as it was sealed I send it you, not caring to re-read it from fear that I should condemn its sending, and thus fail to present the facts it bears witness to.

I need detail neither my adventures nor sufferings in that walk to Zuni. Overtaken at night by snow storms, by day following deep covered trails, I reached, after two days' wanderings, the first ranch—weak with hands and arms rendered useless by cold and the tension of my pack but with spirits cheerful. Two days more brought me to Zuni, where I was received with kindness and every demonstration of joy by my Indian hosts—a fact which I mention as in contrast with what I shall be compelled to record presently. I told them of my intention to again start within three days. After no little trouble, they procured me horses, and, never heeding my wishes to the contrary, detailed a man to go with me. The trader, Mr. Graham, also started, but, unable to endure the severe cold, left us on the second day. . . . On the third day we reached the cabin in which my things and letter were deposited. Most unfortunately, during the night and on the following morning, snow fell to such an extent that it was impractical to re-cross the divide. I was thus forced to come down the eastern slope and return toward Zuni via Fort Wingate—a distance of more than a hundred miles. On my arrival here (a few hours since) I was met by indifference and insult such as I can never cease either to remember or to resent. Nor would I have had extended to me even the constrained courtesy which I am now compelled to suffer, had not my conversation convinced the commanding officer that I am still a civilized being and not the beast and savage—nor the "merely tolerated boy" that idle gossip and intentional malice have represented me as, to the conservative society of Fort Wingate. This experience is one more of the many which I owe to a presence in our party of which I have before made mention—a presence which, from the beginning, has been incapable of recognizing in my self-inflicted degradation to the daily life of savages any motives other than such as, from their rather low character, I trust I shall in future be, as I have in past been, quite incapable of.[103] Could I have foreknown the experiences of today, I would have turned back over the threatening divide; for I had rather have faced the storms of the highest peaks of the Sierras of Zuni than the contempt that I have this day faced. The one chills only the body and freezes the skin, but the other chills all faith in humanity and freezes the heart. Yet this is but one more of the little things which the course I have adopted calls upon me to endure. Need I feel surprised if, on the strength of the same gossip and conjectural representations, which I naturally expect must precede me in Washington as they have in Wingate, my friends there come to class me—in desires and motives—with drunken sailors or enlisted soldiers. I should think one thing might appear quite plain—that desires of the nature above hinted at could lend but little enthusiasm to a solitary mountain trip of two hundred miles through the hostile Apache country or to the exploration in mid-winter of mountain mines and uninhabited caves, or at least that the man who bent his whole heart toward doing those things was sometimes capable of a purer enthusiasm. Pardon me, I know that much which I have said is out of place in a letter to you; but I feel stung through and through with mortification and must say something to one whom I believe *knows* why I have adopted the means I have. . . .

The mail is not yet established between Wingate and Zuni. Letters reach me only when I send for them or by the hands of passers by, Indians and others. Hence, perhaps your present way of addressing letters to me is as good as any.

I remain, dear Professor,

Your Obedient Servant,
F. H. Cushing

Reminiscence: Reception at Fort Wingate

. . . When I went on the first trip I made away from Zuni, . . . I was lost and snowed up in the mountains and had a terrible time reaching a frontier post, foot-sore and nearly starved, only a single Indian in my company. I was totally ignored; worse than that, I was humiliated in every way in which I could be humiliated. When there were plenty of clean and comfortable rooms, it was represented to me, nevertheless, that there were no rooms in which I could be invited to stay and that I would have to occupy an old shed that was formerly a hen-house.[104] I expected that my day was done in Zuni, for the little man who was with me (and who afterward became my brother by adoption) had to share the same fate. But he surprised me by turning to me and saying (I understood him but dimly at the time, for I had not acquired the language), "Well, you see, *we* are Zunis." I did not fully understand him, or I would have taken heart. . . . I had supposed that it would ruin my prospects with the Zunis, that they would think me a man of no consideration, and they did, in one respect: they said I was very poor. But they also said, "That is your baptism in Zuni."

—*San Francisco Examiner,* July 1, 1888

Draft: FHC to Baird

Zuni, December 24, 1879[105]

My dear Professor Baird—

When I was at Wingate a few days since, during the evening on which I wrote you from that Post, I called on the commanding officer, Capt. Bennett, as well for the purpose of talking over with him the Southern Country, as for attending to some business relative to the Expedition.[106] He told me that to go to Silver City alone would be hazardous in the extreme, as the Apaches who range over the mountains lying between that place and this are very hostile. He extended to me, however, an invitation to join Lt. Emmett and his small party of scouts, which is to leave the Post for Ft. Bayard within only a few days. As the safer Rio Grande route would require nearly twenty days of continuous travel, whereas by passing straight through the mountain country but from eight to ten days would be needed, I have decided without further authorization from you than that which I already possess, to avail myself of this liberal invitation, in case, that is, I can raise sufficient means seasonably. . . .

I shall return from Silver City by the Rio Grande route not only as being the safer of the two but also because it will enable me to visit, without in any case going more than nine miles out of the way, the Pueblos of Isleta, Sandia, Acoma, Laguna, and the chain of ruins this side of the Cañon del Zuni, lying between the latter place and this.[107]

So soon after my arrival here as the condition of my animal will permit, I shall visit the new cave, possibly also making a trip from the latter point to a cave two days southwest in Arizona—intimately associated with Zuni tradition, and from which the Indians for centuries have drawn a portion of their supplies of turquoises and jets—then return, to close up as hastily as possible my Zuni investigations. Finally, on my way to Wingate I wish to make an excursion two days out of the way to the Moqui Province. Thence to Wingate, Albuquerque, Santa Ana, San Felipe, Santo Domingo, Silla [Zia], Jemez, Cochiti and Santa Fe. If the plan meet your approval, I further wish, rather than ride at once to the R.R. terminus, to take a direct course North West along which, at intervals of half day and day rides, lie the Pueblos of Tesuque, Nambe, Pojoaque, San Ildefonso, Santa Clara, San Juan, Picuris, and Taos, two days from which is the Railroad juncture at Trinidad. The time consumed in going to Silver City will be, if through the mountains, ten days, there being cañons and ranges to pass, of which, from the want of detail in my maps, I was unaware before consulting those who had been over the country. Of course, the length of my stay there will be regulated largely by the amount of work I find to be done, and the means I shall be able to command whereby to accomplish it. My return, if via the Rio Grande, will require between two and three weeks—the distance [being] nearly three times as great as by trail. The reconnaissance of the Pueblos mentioned will not materially lengthen the time of this journey as all save Acoma, which lies eight or ten miles to one side, are directly along the way. From here (Zuni) two days will take me to the new cave, in the exploration of which I shall occupy only the same length of time. Two more days to the turquoise cavern at which one day, I think, will be sufficient; from which in four days I will again reach Zuni. The side trip to Oraibi in the Province of Tusayan—one of the three only Pueblos at all closely related with Zuni tradition—will consume a week, and one more via Wingate will take me to Albuquerque.[108] From this point I can make a fair reconnaissance of all the Pueblos (Indian) of the Rio Grande del Norte within from twenty five to thirty days, encountering the Railroad more than one hundred miles north of the latter station (Santa Fe) to the saving of that much transportation.

I shall thus have seen all existing Pueblos, have greatly extended my knowledge of the most peculiar phase of human culture which they represent, and more than all, shall have *thoroughly* prepared myself to point out the most promising horizons for future collecting and research, together with the most advantageous means for accomplishing these works.

Thus, leaving the Silver City exploration out of the question, you will see that such a tour could be made in from five to seven weeks. Nearly three would be consumed in a mere ride to the R.R. Terminus. That by the *extra* expenditure of (at the outside) one month of time and no means, or very little above such as would otherwise be necessary for the payment of travelling expenses from Wingate to Trinidad, I might accomplish no inconsiderable end. To be sure, there is another expense which I have not taken into account. It is purely of a personal nature: the risks, discomforts, and hardships incident to such an undertaking. The cold is the chief difficulty—it being, here, in the lower regions, by day, about equal to that of Washington; but at night, and on the elevated mesas or in the mountains, it is much more severe. Traveling on horseback (as would be unavoidable), scant living and frequent bivouacs would be necessary; yet not as a hardship but as a privilege and, in a certain sense, as a pleasure, shall I—in case the scheme of it meet not with your disapproval—embrace this opportunity.

My investigations would have been greatly facilitated, and my traveling expenses greatly lowered, had I been on the departure of Col. Stevenson, furnished with the proper papers for identifying me with the Expedition of which I once believed myself to be a member. I made a request to this effect, but was very reasonably refused by the Colonel on the ground that he wished all letters, orders, etc., for his own use until he should reach Santa Fe, from which place, immediately on arriving there, he promised to send me at least some of them. When I was at the Fort, Captain Bennett informed me that he had learned by letter from Mrs. Stevenson of the arrival and departure from Santa Fe of the Colonel and his party. Three mails had failed to bring me any intelligence to this effect when I left, and once since I have sent over [to inquire] with a kindred result. Unless he further explains himself, which he is not apt to do, maintaining both under the persecution of hot words and the persuasive administration of flattery the most tranquil silence, I shall be compelled to believe that he designed to extend to me no more aid than was officially necessary—this either because, as "that *boy*," I was considered undeserving of such recognition, or else because, through motives of a more personal nature, he wished to hinder my progress and thus render my chances for advancement more unfavorable, to his own possible advantage. I can understand why he should have left me with scant resources and scanter means. He had exhausted his resources in a noble work in which my sympathy, if not my personal interests, were as much enlisted as were his own; and this condition of things I accepted without a murmur, glad under *any* circumstances to be enabled to extend my stay here. But I cannot understand why, unless the above conjectures be true, he should not have supplied me with that which would be neither an expense to the Government nor, in Washington, of the slightest value to him; yet, to me, alone in this country, of the highest importance. Even including myself, my petty vanities, and worthless ambitions in the question, I think my request was only reasonable, inasmuch as it related to a work which, though admitted to be thus personal, was also identified with the interests of the Institution under the auspices of which we had the honor to come out, and from which we had the rare advantage of so many favorable letters and papers.

I am glad to be able to add that since my return from the mountains I have made more progress in my work of observation, than in any *one month* heretofore. With the partial acquisition of the Zuni language, and the entire adoption of their costume and habits of life, I have not only opened an easy way to their more obscure relations but also have overcome that superstitious prejudice with which all observers of savage life have most to contend.

Can you get some one about the Institution to gather up some very white shells (thick) or pieces of shells [and] also to break out the purple portions of a few Quahogs for me? Useless there in Washington, I find recently that they could be of more use than even money here, to a certain extent. If you can procure me some green or blue argillite or any thing approaching in appearance or texture either jade or turquoise, any cheap imitation of the latter, or malachite which I might break up into pieces of about this

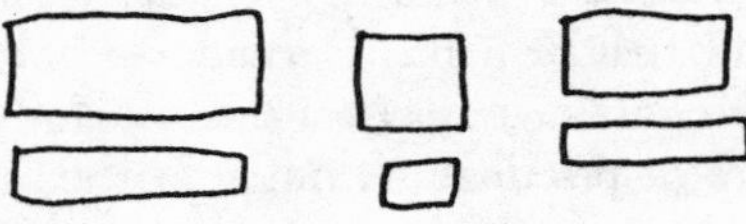

size, I would be able to use them in procurring one of the old heirloom necklaces of which these people have numbers, but which they value at from one to six horses.[109] These things—comparatively worthless there, would aid me immensely here, and I would also have the advantage of studying their methods of manufacture when they came to work up my material. They might be sent in small packages by mail. Anything like fragments of pink or reddish shell, or pieces of red coral would be worth their weight in gold to me; and if it be not too much to ask, I would be deeply obliged if you could have some or all of the above thus sent. I have much more to communicate but must delay to a future letter, as I cannot afford to miss the chance for mailing which just now awaits me.

Very Respectfully and Sincerely Yours,
F H Cushing

P.S. I have not yet received the money but suppose this mail will bring it. Should you send the shells etc., please send at once.

Baird to Cushing

December 30, 1879

Dear Mr. Cushing:

I received your two letters of Dec. 3 and 14, & regretted very much to hear of your difficulties & embarrassments. I can understand your feelings in regard to the reception at Fort Wingate, & your disgust at finding the misconstruction of your sacrifices in the course adopted in your relations with the Indians, & which I am entirely satisfied were dictated by the best & wisest motives. I do not see how in any other way you could have obtained the confidence of the Indians & secured access to their sacred religious ceremonial rites. It was exactly what Major Powell did before you, with equally satisfactory results. Of course in such cases a man's conscience is an important element of strength. So long as you keep your own self respect, the disdain of others is of less moment.

I was very much worried to find on inquiry that the instructions given a week or two [ago] to send you some money were overlooked, the difficulty, according to Mr. Rhees, being the lack of vouchers signed by you on which the money could be drawn either from the Interior Department or the Smithsonian.[110] I, however, advanced your salary for November & and gave it to Mr. Rhees, who forwarded it Saturday in a registered letter to Ft. Wingate. I telegraphed you to that effect & I hope you will get the information very soon. It has been suggested that I send a check to Mr. Johnson of Santa Fe, whose nephew is post trader at Wingate & who can easily give you credit to the former for the amount.

I will take the first opportunity I can get of talking over with Major Powell the subject of your troubles. At present he is busy day and night with the Land Commission.

You say nothing as to the practical results of your trip to the turquoise & jade mine. Did you actually find either of these minerals *in situ*? . . .

Very truly yours,
S. F. Baird

2. *January–May 1880*

Widening Vistas

> During the winter [of 1879–1880], by diligent study, I largely acquired a conversational knowledge of the language of the Zunis and made numerous sketches and notes on their sacred dances and on the meetings of some of their secret societies, which I succeeded in surreptitiously observing. In consequence of exposure while observing one of the latter meetings, as well as the scant protection afforded by my native costume, I suffered, during the spring of 1880, from a severe attack of pneumonia, from the effects of which I did not recover for many months. . . .
>
> —Report to Powell, July 6, 1882 (SWM HC 37)

*Cushing's illness (which accounts for the long gap between his February 23rd and April 8th letters to Baird) seems by no means to have rendered him idle. As he tells the story in "My Adventures," even the stretch of confinement in his hammock was filled with practice and instruction in the Zuni language (MAZ 34–35 {*Zuni 105–07*}), and the remarkable series of letters on his findings (linguistic and other), beginning with the long report enclosed with his letter of May 5, attest to the uninterrupted acuteness of his observations. Addressed jointly to Baird and Powell and lost somewhere in the shuffle between them, this long report "relative to {his} season's work" fortunately survived among Cushing's own papers in the form of a draft, evidently begun on February 18 and worked on over the next six weeks or so. It is an impressive document, showing in the fifteen "salient points" set forth an anthropological vision which at once synthesizes major ideas of Morgan's and Tylor's and opens wide new vistas for research. Based at this point on a five- to seven-month exposure, it is the first of Cushing's brilliant "preliminary" examinations of the field before him. Among the more remarkable discoveries he relates is that of the* "inote," *or ancient talks, containing, in "unvarying language {handed down} from generation to generation," formulae governing a range of learned behavior from the measuring of material for clothes and the painting of designs on pottery to the burying of ceremonial sacrifices. In the* inote, *as he recognized, he had found a key not only to the "arts of this Civilization" but to the "religious, social, and political organizations and institutions" of what he was already at this early date calling "Pueblo Culture." As we see in Cushing's report, the questions that had come to preoccupy his attention were those of the origin and history of this Pueblo culture—a development in keeping with but also to be distinguished from the preoccupation of his mentors with questions of the origin and history of human culture generally.*

In the inote *and the conventions regulated by them, Cushing found a special instance of what Tylor had termed "survivals." He was also investigating other avenues of historical research opened jointly by his earlier reading and by his growing acquaintance with the Zuni language and lore—exploring the ruins named in the Zuni legends of ancestral migrations, studying the artifacts he found, applying to this study what he learned about the various social divisions of the tribe and the traces by which they could be recognized, and sorting out the clues buried in the language itself. By summertime, he would also have associated what he had learned about some of these ruins, including their Zuni names, with the "Cities of Cibola" he was reading about in extracts from the old Spanish chronicles of the discovery and conquest of New Mexico, thus pushing the boundary between what we call history and what we call prehistory three centuries back into the Zuni past. This first half of 1880, in short, was to be a period of intensive study and intellectual ferment. Perhaps the most far-reaching perception of all to emerge from it was a methodological one—that of the essential linkage between the various lines of inquiry he was pursuing. Here, indeed, he was envisaging the lineaments of a new anthropology. Recognition of the interdependence of linguistics, ethnology, ethnography, ethnohistory, documentary history, archaeology, sociology, economics, and geography would shape his thinking from then on.*

In this same period, as we see in the documents, he was beginning to take on a role in "pleading the cause" of the Zunis in questions of land rights and other current issues of concern to the pueblo, an involvement (probably as much insisted upon by the Indians as volunteered by Cushing) which would carry him in time to a position of leadership in the community. It would also compete with his research, win him enemies both outside and inside the pueblo, and ultimately contribute to his removal from the scene.

FHC to Baird

Zuni, January 11, 1880

My dear Professor Baird:

I have your kind letter of the 30th inst., as also the registered money and an equally kind note from Mr. Rhees. Much as I needed the money, it was not more acceptable to me than were these words of sympathy and reassurance.

The ancient excavations which I examined were neither jade nor turquoise mines but sources from which the Indians of Zuni and Acoma have for centuries drawn their supply of sacred paint. The rare occurrence in them, however, of turquoise and of a hard green nodular stone greatly resembling the true *chalchihuitl*—and accepted as such by the aboriginal miners—has greatly stimulated the work, abundant traces of which I have found and noted. The sole material result of this trip was the acquisition of some ancient wooden picks, samples of the paint and accompanying minerals, and one or two of the stones referred to. I was compelled from want of transportation to leave other specimens behind. The scientific results, however, embodying sketches, plans, and notes, far exceed, I think, the cost, although so great, of the exploration.

Since my return, I have definitely ascertained the principal source of supply of both these varieties of precious stone; but as it lies across the Rio Grande far north toward Santa Fe, I have entertained, with a great wish to do so, very little hope of visiting the place.

The Zuni myth which accounts for the origin of these stones, as also for that of a peculiar black bead equally prized, and of salt, is somewhat as follows:[1]

> Centuries ago, there was a great cacique who lived in the Sierra cities of Sierra Azul, north of San Mateo. Wherever he urinated, his drops of urine became beautiful blue and green stones. When the Zunians and Acomites came to know of this, they flocked to and camped in such numbers near his place that the stench of their excrement and urine became so great that the god was offended and fled westward. On the top of the Zuni Mountains (where my excavations were made), he stopped to rest and urinate; but, so great was his haste and anger that the urine never all became pure *chalchihuitl*.
>
> This side of the latter point, he met the woman whose urine, like his own, was transformed—not into blue stones but into salt. He took her, according to Indian custom, and settled only a mile or two eastward of the present Pueblo of Zuni.[2] Again in anger he fled from the house he had built, around which the foolish people once more flocked and stayed—this time northward to the desert where no one lived. Here his wife begged him to settle, and her urine formed the Lake of Salt ("Salinas") which to this day is the source of supply to all Indians of the country.[3] In the course of time becoming angry with him, she drove him from his home and he sought refuge in a cave in the White Mountains of Arizona, from which he disappeared, no one can say whitherward. Since then, a strong wind has blown out of the north of the cavern with such force that all torches are extinguished ere one can reach the point in it where his urine was transformed. Notwithstanding this, people entered without lights and found the precious stones by feeling. On this account, a part of them were turned black, and large flies were caused to live about the place in summer [and] in winter the snows [were caused] to fall. Yet in all generations since, men have persisted in going there; for many bows and other things are found in the cave, and many necklaces of the discolored beads are still worn by the people of Zuni. At this place, the cacique's urine was changed at once into perfectly finished and drilled stones, and in that condition—black and blue—they are still gathered.[4]

Of course the cave in question is one like that of Silver City, both being identical in use with the sacred dance cave of Zuni where paraphernalia are placed and costly sacrifices of *chalchihuitl* are made even at the present day.[5] The original use of the former place having passed out of memory, the old myth has been ingeniously enlarged to include it as the last halting place of the God of Green Stones.

I have given you this rather extended account because it will serve to show you partly wherein I consider the examination of the paint mines of importance and partly to show my interest in visiting the cave I called Turquoise Cavern (the last stopping place referred to in the tradition). . . .[6]

I leave this morning for Fort Wingate, for the

purpose of getting the mail and attending to some things which were left over for my use with the Post Trader. As the ride is a long one, the start has to be made early, and this, I pray, will serve as my excuse for haste and brevity.

Very Respectfully, Your Faithful Servant,
F H Cushing

Give my kind regards to all.

FHC to Baird

Zuni, February 23, 1880

My dear Professor Baird:

The long letter which I promised in my last I cannot send, as, having been handled by the Indians, it is hardly in condition for sending. Moreover, since the receipt of my last Washington mail I have concluded, from what you say regarding my relations to Major Powell, that it is best to address to yourself and him jointly, as it concerns not my progress with the Indians alone but particularly plans for future work amongst them.

You will pardon, I hope, my failure to make weekly communications during the past month. Some five weeks since, a great snow storm rendered the Zuni Mountains impassable, in which condition they have since remained until within the last six days. Although the snow is now gone, they are yet very difficult to cross, on account of mud, and [it is] by mere chance [that] I am am able to send [via] the Ranch of Navajo Springs, this hasty scrawl, that you may know I am still alive to my duty to you . . .[7]

May I, without offense, ask you once more to have shell matter and green stones sent? Especially imitation turquoise (which are very cheap at manufacturing jewelers). The request was well considered. It mean[s] almost *everything* regarding collecting among these Indians, and also much regarding my favor with them.

My health, from night exposure, entire Indian food (my supplies having long ago given out), and the fearful condition of weather, has suffered badly for the past few weeks, and all in all I am having pretty up-hillish work. But my progress appears to me as good, as it certainly is constant, and I trust that in the end you will be glad I have stayed here.

Some recent discoveries, through initiation into a winter ceremony, entirely account for the deposits in the Silver City cave—even for such details as the cane cigarettes and the little bows and green stone beads.[8] This makes me more than ever anxious to explore that deposit, as it could be important ethnographically as well as archaeologically. I think best, however, not to attempt going there before I get word from Col. Stevenson regarding funds, unless otherwise advised by yourself.

Let me thank you for having so liberally advanced for me my November salary, and at the same time beg that you will not feel required to do for me anything so personally inconvenient in future.

Asking for your charitable consideration, and hoping to please and repay you in the end, I am,

Hastily yet Faithfully,
Your Obedient Servant,
F H Cushing

FHC to William Jones Rhees

Zuni, New Mexico
February 23, 1880

Dear Mr. Rhees:

I enclose herewith the vouchers which you kindly sent. Do please be liberal with me. You do not know what I have suffered during this winter, nor how much that suffering would have been lessened by a more liberal allowance of means. Were I to communicate actually what was left to me on the departure of our party, you would wonder whether I told the truth or not. Will you also kindly try and see to the shells etc., of which I speak in my last letters to Professor Baird. . . .

I cannot say what is in my heart. Your sympathy has struck chords in it which have very rarely vibrated this winter, and I shall not forget your words of encouragement. . . .

I am now using some of the backs of leaves in my sketch books and for this reason, unless I could receive more, . . . would fear to send them home; but in case you could get an order for, and send me four or even six more of the small (medium) size, I would take pleasure in following your good suggestion. My life is insecure here, and in case I lost it, nothing I have done would be of account save my sketches, and even *they* would amount to but little.

I would write more, but it is by mere and unexpected chance that I send this, which bids

God bless you for your kindness to
Your humble friend,
F. H. Cushing

Wm. J. Rhees, Esq.
Chief Clerk
Smithsonian Institution

DRAFT: FHC TO UNKNOWN ADDRESSEE

Zuni, April 7, 1880

Gentlemen:

Inasmuch as I closed a bargain, some days since, with Sr. Pablo Candelario, whereby I was bound orally with such Indians as I might choose, to furnish him with one horse and three blankets or equivalent value, whereby and for which he was equally bound to turn over all his rights to the *ojo* [spring] of Pi-tchai-a-kwi acquired through labor or occupancy—which bargain made in good faith in the presence of witnesses renders all papers in his possession or bearing his name or signature as guarantees null and void.[9] I have to request that you shall at once deliver such papers into the hands of the Indians for my examination.

Moreover, in case you consider said bargain not valid, I, as an officer of the Int[erior] Dept., Washington, D.C., and as a vindicator of the legal rights of the Zuni Nation, have, and hereby exercise, the right to examine all papers, letters, etc., whereby you claim the right to exclusive possession of said *ojo*.[10]

Hoping that you will at once comply with my request, and assuring you at the same time that if you fail to do so I shall speedily be compelled to pay you a visit of examination,

I have the Honor to be, Señores,
Yours etc.
F. H. Cushing
Ethnologist, U.S. Bur. Eth.

DRAFT: FHC

Zuni, N.M.
April [1880?]

To Whom it May Concern:

According to an article providing for the settlement of unsurveyed lands of N.M. approved by the legislature of said Territory, any Pueblo or other Indian not drawing annuities from the Government and proposing to carry on improvements for agricultural purposes on such tracts [and] who also manifests his willingness to pay taxes as a citizen of the United States, is entitled to such lands equally and on the same conditions with Americans or Mex[ican]s.[11]

On these grounds, two Zuni Indians, Antonio and Juan Thomas, propose to settle and build at Kia-ma-kia, four miles east of El Ojo del Jaraliso.[12]

Any person therefore molesting them will be [subject] to the correction of the law.

Very Respectfully,
F. H. Cushing
and
Rev. [space for signature by Taylor F. Ealy]
U.S. Teacher and local Ag't of Zuni

FHC TO BAIRD

Zuni, April 8, 1880

My dear Professor Baird:

I have been, during the past six weeks, very much prostrated by an attack of lung complaint—brought on by exposure, I presume.[13]

This explains, I hope, why I have not finished the long communication repeatedly heretofore mentioned, and why my letters have been so unworthy of you.

The money came as a blessing. It will last me some time, but as Col. Stevenson long ago said another fund and transportation facilities would be furnished me, I await his advice before proceeding to Silver City and the Casa Grande.[14]

I can assure you most unhesitatingly that I am losing nothing in information gained by remaining here in waiting. I believe today that there is no ethnographic field in America, if in the world, so rich in uncollected material and fact as the Pueblo, of which I have come to regard Zuni as the highest representative. . . .

I hope you will pardon the wording as well as the brevity of this letter. I am actually unable to do better this morning, as the Indian who dispatches this is waiting restlessly, as he has fifty miles to ride with it before sunset.

Very Respectfully,
Your Obedient Servant,
F. H. Cushing

Deposition[15]

F. H. Cushing: Testimony as to Boundaries

On the 19th day of April, 1880, before me, Walter G. Marmon, Notary Public in and for the County of Valencia, Territory of New Mexico, personally appeared Frank H. Cushing, of lawful age and who, having been by me first duly sworn, deposeth and saith in answer to the following interrogatories:

Question: State your name, age and place of residence?

Answer: My name is Frank H. Cushing, my age is twenty-three years, and I reside at Zuni in Valencia County, Territory of New Mexico.

Ques. Are you acquainted with the Zuni Pueblo grant, and if so, how long have you known it?

Ans. I am, by reputation and through reference to it in contemporaneous documents now in possession of the "Caciques of the House of Zuni."

Ques. Do you know the location of the Old Pueblo of Zuni; and if so, where is it situated?

Ans. I do. It is situated on a high table land in a southeastern direction from the present [illegible word] of Zuni and distant about three miles therefrom.

Ques. How do you know of its location?

Ans. From personal knowledge, and general reputation.

Ques. Have you any interest in said grant?

Ans. I have not.

(signed) F. H. Cushing

[seal]

Subscribed in my presence and sworn to before me this 19th day of April, 1880.

Walter G. Marmon
Notary Public

FHC to Baird

Wingate, May 5, 1880

My dear Professor Baird:

More than a month since, I began the long letter which—still unfinished—accompanies this. No fewer than three times have I confidently promised its hasty coming, but many causes have conspired to delay its completion.

Chief among these has been my suffering health. I have been for more than two months midway between the bed and my feet—of a pulmonary difficulty from which, although the chances are I may be long in fully recovering, I am certainly rapidly mending. At times, I have been unable for two or three days to write anything more than my daily memoranda—with difficulty even these—not from suffering but from general debility. At other times—when better—the Indians have claimed and even compelled my exclusive attention. These reasons, with no fewer than six expeditions with and at the urgent demands of the Indians into parts of the country from one to three days distance, have been the causes of this delay—a delay the more lamentable in that it has compelled me to violate one of your requests of many months ago.

I know, however, that in the end, if my results prove good, you will forgive this and other delinquencies. If the contrary come to be the case, the most scrupulous attention to such incident duties would have availed me nought in your eyes.

Regarding the accompanying communication, I beg that you will, both from its imperfectness and incompleteness, defer any final judgment on it until after reading its conclusion.

I have always made my paramount duty here in Zuni that of collecting not material but data, yet always, when opportunity presented, have gotten together what I could toward filling up some of the gaps in our collection. The costumes primitive and modern which I had once despaired of securing I have at last, through increased influence, obtained. I think they will prove very acceptable to you, and instructive to a scientific public.

Regarding this subject of collecting from the Pueblos, I have much to say in the letter to follow the accompanying, which my enlarged knowledge of Indian life suggests as profitable, and which I hope may prove so in your eyes.

The means left me on the departure of our Party were of little avail for collecting. They were:

$6.00
8 yds of Mantua (1.00)
" " red calico
6 boxes of cups
1 bunch of lead bars
1 string sleigh bells (20)
½ box of refuse dentalium shells
½ plug of tobacco

This was and is all I have had.
Of provisions I had:

2 sacks of flour (1 partly used)
2 sides of bacon
45 lbs of sugar
30 " " coffee
2 cakes of chocolate
4 cans of canned milk
2 boxes (1 lb each) dried apples
3 cans of sardines
1 can of salmon
1 can of beef
4 lbs of rice
24 cans of baking powder

I stretched this out until mid January with the aid of Indian food, since which, with the sole exception of sugar and coffee, I have lived exclusively on the latter, tasting nothing in the way of vegetable or grain, save the Indian preparations of corn, native beans, or dried green squashes and chile. This, with mutton, horse flesh, occasionally game and goat, has made up my diet, except when I have had the good fortune to be invited to a meal at the missionary's.

You will therefore not expect, I hope, too much from me. Little would get *much* of the kind of material which Mrs. and Col. Stevenson collected; but that which they left behind was left either from ignorance, want of influence [with] the Indians, or, *more often,* from its high price. Now I can get in Zuni anything for the price that a Zuni himself would have to pay; but just those things most needed for our collection are the very things which can be had only for a high price (comparatively) in things which they value—like plumes of the turkey, shells, and blue or green stones or imitations of the latter.

Yet do not despair. I have some *five* costumes [and] can get a complete Food, Medicine, and to a lesser extent Industrial collection—the two former on the eve of my departure, as they would spoil if collected long before.

I have received the shells of which you speak, and, when worked up, they will accomplish more than you would imagine. Many thanks for them. Remember the *blue* (turquoise shade) and green stone material. Soft [or] hard turquoise—imitation or the genuine—*anything* blue or green will work up to great advantage. I find that even a soft blue serpentine which, very anciently worked up by the Indians, so resembles turquoise as to have until recently deceived me, is highly prized.

You remark that you will "try to send me a surplus of beads, turquoises, corals, etc . . ." I hope you will not fail to do so, as, even though they be too dear to be furnished *me,* my selection from them would be of value, I think, to any future collecting party among the Pueblos.

I still await advice from Col. Stevenson regarding the Silver City and Casa Grande matter. To the former I *must* go now. Since I have learned so much concerning the meaning of such deposits as it contains, it would be a sin to leave the country without doing so. When, however, it matters but little, as my time is *just as full as ever* at Zuni.

Will you investigate the matter of papers, forage, transportation recommendation letters, etc. etc.

And am I entitled to still draw rations from the Government? I have drawn absolutely nothing since the departure of Col. Stevenson. I could reduce my living expenses to nothing if I had the ration privilege, and oh! I would be *so* glad to have some flour to eat once more; yet I will continue willingly to live on corn, if no such arrangement exists.

You will pardon this [letter] its illegibility and incoherency when I tell you that this is midnight after nearly a hundred miles ride of two days over a mountainous country.

Ever Respectfully,
Your Obedient Servant,
F. H. Cushing

My kind regards to Mrs. and Miss Baird, as to all at the Institution.

DRAFT: FHC TO BAIRD AND POWELL[16]

Zuni, February 18[–April 13], 1880

Honored Sirs:

I have long been thinking of points relative to my work, progress, and plans, and making memoranda of them with the intention, so soon as time would permit, of embodying them in a communication to you. This communication, with other matter, I now have the honor to submit.

At the outset, let me sincerely ask your pardon for intruding upon you a letter of such wordiness. I have a thousand things of interest and value to claim my eye and time, leaving but little of either to devote to this and other communications. I am, moreover, far from well. Even at my best, it is a task of great magnitude to write a small letter, requiring an increase in the length of time, at an inverse ratio to the decrease in the length of the epistle.

The examination of the two caves so often referred to in previous letters, I have from lack of means for travelling, not yet undertaken.[17] As, however, I have recently acquired an Indian pony, this obstacle will stand in the way no longer, and I shall, so soon as the Indians have performed two or three more dances which it is imperative I should witness and sketch, go to explore them. They promise—in the one case with certainty—much more than did the survey of the ancient mining region in the Zuni Mountains.

It is hardly to be regretted that during January I could not command a riding animal, as, had I been in possession of one, or of the means of securing one, I should have gone off to visit these caves soon after the New Sun Festivities, and thus have missed numerous ensuing ceremonies, as well as most important progress in my Zuni life.

The contrast between the present results of my labors and those which even greater exertion secured before the departure of our party is pronounced. Instead of getting unfriendly and overbearing, as Col. Stevenson believed they would [be] in his absence, the Indians became more communicative and unconstrained than ever, sparing no pains to please me, and permitting me to go pretty nearly wherever I pleased. After I adopted their entire costume, and conformed to their New Sun feast and other observances, they insisted on counting me as one of their people.

At about the same time, nearly the whole tribe became interested in trying to secure my marriage to a young woman who, according to their peculiar custom, had chosen me. The only drawback I have had since my adoption was caused by [my] refusal of this girl, leading to a difference so marked in their friendship for me, that, serious as the move had been, I almost regretted when I thought of the ground lost, that I had not made it. Since then, I have received no fewer than five kindred messages, but their refusal has created no more disturbance than would have resulted had I been a genuine *Shī-wī* [Zuni]. My friends at last concluded that I had not refused because I did not wish to be a Zuni, in heart as in life, but simply because I had not been pleased with the messages; and they still look forward to ultimately satisfying and marrying me into the Tribe.

Near the close of January, one of the greatest dances of the season occurred, partaking of a social as well as of a sacred character.[18] This, the principals told me, they would expect me to join. Embarrassing as it was to me, so soon after my experiences at the Post, I consented—even with apparent alacrity—thinking thereby to win back their lost confidence, as well as to get a more perfect knowledge of this peculiar observance. I was mistaken in neither supposition; my dancing secured for me, not only both these ends, but also, a much coveted costume, and admission into the sacred houses during religious ceremonies, a privilege which, being sought in vain, I have ever since enjoyed with, of course, the most important advantages.

With the closer intimacy thus formed and with a knowledge of their arts, first initiated by the manufacture of a primitive style of costume for me, I have made some unexpected discoveries, which entirely change my *wishes* at least regarding my future work amongst them.

When one of the old men was preparing to make the costume referred to, I observed that he only looked at me for a moment and then, with his fingers began measuring in different directions on the material to be cut out. He moved his lips as he measured, like a child attempting to read. The occasional whispered utterance of a word or two led me to suspect that he was working by rule, and on questioning him, I found that it was true—that he was guided entirely by a formula, so to speak, framed in short sentences, and so nearly approaching a metrical arrangement, that it could be easily acquired and remembered. After that, I ascertained by more closely watching the women engaged in painting ollas and bowls, that the decorative arts were likewise guided by rules even more rigid.

I had often wondered, as have all others who have watched this process of painting pottery, how a woman would sit down and without any pattern before her, commence painting on the rim of a *tinaja,* and not only produce an elaborate ornamentation, *identical* with that made by her great grandmother or by another woman in a widely separated part of the Pueblo, but also have the pattern join without a hitch on the other side of the vessel. I had also wondered why I should find that, numerous as the styles of *tinaja* decoration appeared to be, there really were but seven or, at most, eight distinct types, all others being slight variations of these, resulting from imperfect knowledge of rules, or individual genius, or else recent innovations.

Of course, on learning that rules of the most definite, concise, and curious nature existed for the guidance of all indigenous arts and manufactures, which rules, like our "a b c's," are almost universally acquired at an early period in life, I ceased to thus wonder.

My initiation into the Estufas during the religious ceremonies accompanying dances, and my partial participation in the latter, were no less prolific of results relative to their mythologic institutions; for I definitely learned thereby what indeed I had often before surmised, namely that their religious observances and ceremonies were no less, or even more, rigidly and anciently regulated.[19]

I cannot help believing that the discoveries thus hinted at form the most important revelations yet made toward an understanding of the conventional aspect of Pueblo Culture. To repeat: that the arts of this Civilization, industrial as aesthetic, are regulated by rules or *formulae* handed down in unvarying language from generation to generation. That the religious, social, and political organizations and institutions are no less rigidly ruled by instructions contained in myriad prayers, "ancient talks," and songs, dating back at least as far as the prehistoric period. I speak of the latter as myriad advisedly, for I know of them by the hundreds, yet am only beginning in the knowledge.

Most curious and instructive among the industrial formulae are the traditional directions for building a stone house, such as may be now seen in ruins by hundreds all over the territory, but such as at present are never or very rarely built by the *Shī wīs.*

Equally, if not more, interesting are the ancient regulations regarding the burial, at the close of the New Sun (New Year) fast, of the God *A-hai-iu-ta*—the father god or creator of the Zuni Nation, and four other branches of the Pueblo race. The hold these ancient institutions have is strikingly shown in their effects on this ceremonial. Loaded with shells and precious stones, the god is carried to his house in the Sierracitas, some ten miles to the South, and on the mesa of Ta-ai iallonne [Dowa Yalanne], where, with prayers and sacrifices of flour and plume-sticks, he is planted.[20] His bearer and high priest is one of the *Pi-hlan Shi-wa-ni Mo-so-ne,* or Captain Caciques (Mex. Matalone Cacique).[21] Now, although the Apaches have long since retired to the South, and the Navajos, hereditary enemies of the Zuni people, are, through the force of American arms, at peace with them; nevertheless the *Pi-hlan Shi-wa-ni,* in addition to his sacred paraphernalia, is costumed in armor from head to foot. A buckskin helmet or skull cap protects his head, his body and thighs are covered by a thick elk skin cuirass, impervious to arrows, his legs by wrappings of the same material, and, although for many years this people have been in possession of fire-arms, not the sign of such appears about [his] person; nothing but the great stone battle-knife dangles from his belt, and the primitive cougar skin quiver and awkward bow, hung at his sides. Equally if not better armed are his two attendants, one of whom walks four feet in advance of him, bow and arrows ready for instant use, the other following at an equal

Fig. 4 Ahayu:da Shrine (Bureau of American Ethnology, *Twenty-Third Annual Report*).

distance, bearing the sacred plumes and flour-dish and also plying the whizzer which serves as a warning accompaniment to all such processions of the gods. The necessity for protection and escort being out of date, yet its apparent employment and, in case even of hostility, the superiority of fire-arms over the rude weapons of a period of stone, yet the sole employment of the latter, serve to show the tenacity with which these people hold to the *i-no-te* or ancient usages and the prehistoric character of the "ancient talks" (*in-no-te pe-ie-we*) which I above refer to under the name of instructions.

If my belief be well founded, that these *i-no-te* are unvaried from a remote period of prehistory (and in numerous instances besides the above the proof seems sufficient), then we have, amongst a people possessing no written literature, nevertheless records or gleanings of their remote history more reliable than simple tradition, because they bear into the daylight of the present century material attestation. For instance, were we uncertain that the Zunis were once surrounded by enemies, rendering it unsafe to sally forth even a mile from their stronghold, we should have proof positive of such a condition, as also of the ancient manner of equipment for war, [in] the observances accompanying the burial, in these peaceful times, of the god *A-hai-iu-ta.* And again—[we have evidence] that these were the people who built the numerous ruins throughout their territory, in that an ancient traditional formula for building explains how they may be and were able to make their stone wall straight and strong, as is the case in many of these remains. I do not mean to say to those who deal with American Archaeology that this is the only evidence I have regarding these stalwart problems. I have unearthed the most valuable traditional evidence bearing on this point, which, without the evidence afforded by such formulae, might be regarded as possibly uncertain but which, with it, lacks not for substantiation.

So closely connected are the traditions of ancient ruins with many of the religious usages, etc., of the present day that the Zunis have looked upon all questioning relative to the former as invading the sacred province of the latter; and have hence maintained such consistent silence regarding them that travellers have time and again asserted, "They have no knowledge" of these (to me avowed) places of their ancestors.

Perhaps a more pertinent instance of the importance of studying closely these ancient formulae, instructions, and forms, as throwing light upon archaeological speculations, as well as on the present condition of culture, exists in the ceremonies which followed soon after the New Year fast.

Four men, equipped as for the burial of *A-hai-iu-ta,* bore little painted bows, arrows, smoking canes filled with native tobacco (unused at the present day save in old ceremonies), plume sticks, precious shells, and green stones, which with lengthy prayers and exact forms were deposited as sacrifices to the *Na-na-kwe* (spirits of dead ancestors) and the *Kâ'-kâ* (spirit of the sacred dance) in a distant cave.[22] [These deposits being] identical with [those] in the Silver City cave, does not all this serve to explain them? And would not a full understanding of it show relations of yet a wider and more interesting archaeologic import? Still more curious, if not so important, would be a record in the exact words, if not in the identical language, of the prayers which more than a thousand years ago (judging from Metcalfe's guess of the age of his cave) took place at the Silver City deposit. On account of the permanent traditional character of all these prayers and instructions accompanying ceremonies, even this apparently impossible thing could be effected, merely by recording the prayers *now* in use with the Zunis on occasions of similar deposits. Six weeks before I witnessed this instructive ceremony, I had heard traditions regarding the origin and meaning of such deposits and, incredible as it may appear, of the exact Silver City locality as well. I told my adopted brother's father and others of my intention to make a solitary horseback journey to the latter place, and in trying to dissuade me from the *hal-ai-shon* (crazy) attempt, they told me the name in Mexican (Burro Mts.) of the mountains at the foot of which the cave is situated, the Zuni name, and the number of mountain ranges and cañons etc. I would have to cross in reaching it. They said "Why go there, where no man can ever travel in winter without death, when, if you must see a 'death house,' we can guide you to three or four other places, far nearer, just like it, and connected, moreover, with our own people?" They did not claim that their own people made the deposits in the Silver City cave. They only said they "might have," and remarked that they would like to know. "If I would bring them plume sticks from that dark place, they could tell at once, on seeing them." But they knew perfectly well what the deposits were and why made, and added that if I believed them not, to wait a little and I should see the whole thing here in Zuni, a promise which was fulfilled in the performance of the above described dances.

It is my conviction that it is the *duty* of some one to record, word for word, in the original language, and with faithful translation, these prayers, ancient instructions, and formulae. And that this duty is more clearly my own—to which I ought to be willing to sacrifice every other motive and wish—is my equal conviction from the several facts: that I have already acquired a conversational knowledge of, I suppose, half the language in which they occur; that I have run the gauntlet (not without suffering permanent injury) of accustoming myself to Indian fare, mode of life, etc., as I think no other man will, and have thus won the confidence and esteem of the Indians, as no other man can, without equal sacrifices.

To effect the above work, the first requisite would be the acquisition of language, not merely a vocabulary language of it alone, but a knowledge as well of its grammar—more particularly of its etymology. Judging from the progress in this direction which I have already made, the result of no little industry, about a year would be required for this purpose. (Of course, near the close of this period it would be necessary to devote but little attention to this preparatory branch of the work, and much more could be turned toward the recording and other matters.) After the kind of knowledge of which I speak had been gained, I think with hard work and constant attention to the note book, the prayers, formulae, songs, etc. etc., might be recorded in the way mentioned—at least the important among them—in about six months.

Holding this to be the primarily important work, there yet remain hosts of other things to be accomplished and acquired: as, for instance, a mere material series of results in the way of all the sacred paraphernalia, all dance masks, some of the most important symbolic tablets and altars, ancient war equipments, and, in fact, everything venerated from its connection with the *I-no-te,* which could not be obtained without great length of time and the most unlimited understanding of Indian feelings and consequent management of them; yet which I have already paved the way toward sufficiently far to feel confident in asserting that I could acquire them.

In this material series, take for example the one item of sacred dance costume. As you may gather from the color sketches which I shall presently send home, they alone would be well worth the expenditure of the amount of time I have named, as well as all the expenses incident to such a stay. The masks belonging to this series, possessing all the fanciful variety of Northwest coast collections, have the greater value in that they are produced after ancient oral models, with such unvarying faithfulness, that although I have witnessed the reappearance and manufacture of several of them, I could detect no deviation either in shape, line or plume, from the ideal, or previous examples. As with the pottery, they are made with no pattern before the artist. Yet an elaborate *He-ma-shi-kwe* head dress and mask made in one estufa was indistinguishable from one made in a separate estufa, by another individual.[23] Thus, their models grounded in antiquity, these costumes assume the importance of being richly suggestive of ancient dress, customs, etc., and are actually, moreover, what is claimed for them by the Indians: material representations of the personae of their ancient mythology.

The collections which our party took home, although the most extensive and truly the finest ever gotten together at once, were (but one department excepted—ceramic) neither complete nor representative. They contained mostly only such specimens as could be obtained for small sums and without the aid of great influence [and] consequently were lacking in all *sacred* material and in the rarer and more valued articles of art, costume, and even use. The stay which I plead and the means which I shall mention below as necessary to it and its work would enable me while carrying on other investigations to make our Zuni collection, with what we already possess, the most exhaustively representative of any ethnographic gathering from a single people in the world.

Naturally connected with collecting would be the study and acquisition of a complete set of Zuni plume sticks. I have seen placed upon one stick plumes from eleven different species of birds, the feathers from each kind being, moreover, varied in size and shade. Each of these plumes has its appropriate traditional use, significance and place in the prayer and songs, serving as powerful memoranda and bearing possibly a closer analogy (in that color is employed) to the ancient Peruvian *quipu* than to the wampum belts of the Iroquois.[24]

A fertile source of speculation have been pillars or posts of stone, arches of stones, etc., in various parts of the old world and new; some claiming them as religious, others as astronomic monuments. Such mnemonic structures are, in both senses, still in use amongst the Zuni—even my partial understanding of which would, being properly presented, throw a flood of light on these archaeological mysteries of two continents. The House of the Sun, though infinitely cruder, bears a remarkable resemblance to the older Peruvian structures of similar designation described by Squier and others.[25]

In this, in the possession of a material incipient literature comparable to the *quipu* in the story of *Po-shai-an-k'ia,* his sudden coming and mysterious disappearance, and in many other matters relating to mythology and tradition which I cannot here mention, the Zuni bears a strange resemblance to the Peruvian and other ante-Columbian cultures.[26] To the better understanding of these analogies, if not relations, would I additionally wish to continue my studies here.

The use of Signs as a distinct mode of expression

has ceased to be among the Zunis; yet a most elaborate gesticulation accompanies excited or emphatic oral demonstrations—very many of the signs thus used being too artificial to have had origin in simple natural conceptions; and from this not only but also from their close affinity to those of other tribes, we must infer that they have been remotely acquired or at least that they are survivals of an ancient intertribal gesture speech.

As such, they are for many reasons more interesting than these speeches as they exist in their fulness today among such nations as the Arapahoes, Cheyennes and Sioux. A full knowledge of the language, however, would be necessary to a perfect understanding of the relation of this gesticulation to speech.[27]

Another department of the enquiry which from want of proper instruments, diagrams, etc., I have been compelled to almost entirely neglect is Anthropological research, such as measurements, surgical and medical data, etc. Such researches, properly carried out, would be interesting supplements to the investigations of Humboldt and others on the Physical effects of high altitude—[and also] as showing the results of division of labor between the sexes, which here reaches the fullest development, perhaps, among the nations of this continent.[28]

That most valuable source of Ethnographic information, the study of Sociology as exemplified by indigenous systems of consanguinity, I have been but to a limited extent successful in, since it—*here* at least—imperatively requires a full knowledge of the language. The vocabulary of consanguinity is in some respects most unnecessarily elaborate, in others most meager. But while today I can find no name for cousin except "brother," yet I find in the forms of address every day used when smokes are interchanged (I use them myself) remnants of a system once more definite, designating degrees of relationship with great minuteness.[29] To search out, with the aid of etymology and a familiarity with traditionary lore, this primitive system of the consanguinity and affinity of the Zuni people or their ancestral races is a task which, otherwise hopeless, would, with patience, be mastered by the means I have mentioned; which means, however, lie open only to one who has acquired the language.

While my investigations in this direction are by no means satisfactory, they have availed me something by introducing me into a very wide and ancient, yet fresh, field of enquiry. I have learned that like most other crude nations, the *Shī-wi* is divided into gens, or as they style them, families, each, as with the Iroquois, bearing the name of some animal or plant or grain.[30] The number of these families in the Zuni nation, once much greater, is now sixteen. It has diminished to the present number merely through the dying out of representatives—a process still rapidly going on with some of them, one of which is at present represented only by five persons or "one house." As with the Iroquois and for the same assigned reason, the descent is on the side of the mother. That is, a son or daughter takes the name of the gens or family to which the mother belongs and is supposed to be the property of that gens; and while there is no obstacle to the union of a person to a member of his or her father's gens, union with one of the same gens as the mother is strictly prohibited.

The exclusive possession by certain of these gens or families of particular dances and other religious ceremonies of particular estufas or worship houses as the fountainheads of these observances, led me to believe that, in tradition at least, separate points of origin or of primitive occupancy were assigned to these divisions. I have, following up this idea, found it to be true that while originally all are supposed to have issued from the same birth place, they subsequently separated, occupying pueblos (now in ruins) widely apart before finally, for the sake of mutual protection, again coming together as one people like the present. While I have been able to find the original houses of the two great divisions of the gens and to trace by tradition and ruin tracks their migrations toward the present pueblo, I am still ignorant of all save five of the minor divisions.[31]

For the final settlement of this great question, as of the myriad others of almost equal interest which it involves, extensive observations throughout the ruin tracks included in the traditions, as well as perfect, even etymological familiarity with the language of those traditions would be essential.

Of course, as complements to these field observations (which could be carried on during the sowing and harvesting seasons when nothing worthy of attention is going on here), extensive archaeologic collections and a magnificent series of ruin photographs and plans could be made. As illustrating more definitely the extent of this field of observation, I applied a list of the successive stopping places of the *Tchu-a-kwe,* or Corn People (*Ko-ha-kwa-kwe, Kwin-a-kwa-kwe, Hlupi-si-kwa-kwe, Shi-lo-a-kwa-kwe,* and *Ca-tcha-tchu-kwe*—White, Black, Yellow, Red and Pinto Corn People) in their migrations southeastward from the Colorado Chiquito, north and then west again to their final place, occupied at the time of Coronado: Ojo Pescado (*He-sho-ta tsi-na*).

Tradition points to the place of origin of the Zuni and three others of the Pueblo nations (Taos, Oraibi, K'us-ni-ni or Cos-nina?) as from under the ground in the "mountains west of the West."[32] It is not until this tradition brings these nations to the regions of the Colorado Chiquito that it begins to emerge from fable and mythology into almost definite history.

South from the latter river, near the *Y'ahl-a K'o-herie* (White Mountains), was the first stopping place of any length, very primitive ruins still marking the site, which indeed may be said of all the points I mention below, more than half of which I have personally examined.

In order, they were as follows:

1. Ke-e-a-ti-wa
2. Ki-tu-tu-ma
3. Op-kwi-na Kia-na
4. Pa-na-tu-ma
5. Kia-ma kia-kwi
6. Kia-tsu-ta-ma (and Ha-wi-ku)
7. Kia-nai-tu-ma
8. Pi-kia-kwi
9. Kwa-ton-na-kia-nu
10. Su-kia-nu
11. He-sho-ta Yah'l-ta
12. Ha-pa-na-a-kwa
13. He-sho-t'i Ti-wa-kia-na
14. He-sho-ta Im-kos-kwa
15. Mo-kwi te-lu-hla
16. He-sho-ta Tsi-na (Ojo Pescado)[33]

By this list, which includes only the sites occupied by the Corn People and their tribes (the above specified divisions), it will be seen that in the southern half alone of the traditionary territory of the Zunis, no fewer than sixteen ancient pueblos occur, all abounding in ancient remains. Of these pueblos, the *He-sho-ta-we* ("round towns"),[34] which were among the last built, are magnificent specimens of aboriginal art—the stones of which they were made having been dressed and laid straight, the walls often standing, even yet, twelve feet high. A *scientific* series of photographs of these ruins in their proper succession, even with the most meager descriptions, would be in itself of immense archaeological value.

The Pueblo sites of the *Hle-to-na-we,* another great division composed of the Crane, Bear and Badger gens, who, dividing from the Corn People, went north, are far more numerous.[35] Their first great settlement was at Cañon Bonito, whence they migrated as far northeast as Shipap-po-lima (already inhabited by the Taos nation)[36] and, making numerous stops on the way, returned southward as far as Las Nutrias, which place, like Ojo Pescado, still occupied in summer, was their home up to the time of the Spanish invasion.[37] One who examines the ruins marking the traditional pauses of this great division of the *Shi-wi* people cannot fail to infer at once that while more energetic and restless, they were by no means so advanced in the peaceful arts and all pertaining thereto as their southern relatives.[38] While the ancient remains at Cañon Bonito evince that at the outset they were equally advanced, the series further north shows that they gradually, through long wandering, became like the nomadic savages by whom they were ever surrounded and harrassed.

One point lending additional interest to, and throwing more light on, this question is that the larger divisions of the gens, such as those spoken of above, probably had distinct dialects; not only this, but that the original *Zuni* differed—like our old English—from the modern. The former is inferable from the fact that the name of a cave spring [called] *K'e'e-a-ti-wa* at the outset of the Tchu-a-kwe migration had changed to *K'wa-ton-na-k'iana* (Go in water) at the 9th stopping place. The latter [is inferable] from the fact that there are preserved remnants of this variation of the ancient language from the modern in the various prayers, songs, and forms of address used during sacred ceremonies. For example, members of the Winter *Kấ-kâs,* or "Good Dances," when they come out of one estufa in their passage to another converse in a language differing quite as much from the present as Captain John Smith's narratives differ from the writings of Irving or Kennan. This *I-no-te* style of speech is affected, on account of the vague belief that these night dancers are either representative of the *Na-na-kwe* (spirits of the ancestry) or else possessed by them.

This differentiated condition of the language, exclusive possession of special religious ceremonies, medicines, incantation songs, etc., of special estufas, and, I believe, of types of ornamentation, as exemplified in *tinaja* decoration by one great division of the gens and another, seems to prove that the *Shi-wi* nation is but the confederated remnants of several nations, all belonging to one stock—indeed (as I have reason enough to believe) the true Pueblo stock itself—but still formerly inhabiting different points, and possibly maintaining distinct or at least independent governments.

In this great and gradual migration eastward, tradition hints that the *Tchu-a-kwe* left portions of their number at many of the pueblos they established; as, for instance, at *Ha-wi-ku*—inhabited at the time of the Franciscans, as shown by the ruins of a church I have discovered there. Also *Kia-ma-kia, Pi-tchai-a-kwi,* and some of the *He-sho-to-we.*[39] That some were abandoned altogether while others continued to be at least partially occupied is proved, indeed, by the much more advanced state of ruin in which we find them, even when they occur late in the series—as the sixth and fifth to the last named above, which from their much dilapidated condition would appear almost as ancient as the first. *Kia-ma-kia,* the fifth in this series, is wonderfully preserved considering its traditional antiquity; for there is one wall in it—the northern—four and five feet high, straight, and more than six hundred feet in length. The outer stones are all dressed square by the pecking process and laid in a kind of mud and ash mortar.

I may add parenthetically here that the *Tchu-a-kwe,* under the more modern name *Ta-a-kwe* (one meaning grains of corn, the other corn in the abstract) form nearly one fourth of the Zuni nation of today. Their religion, dances, and ceremonies, where separably distinguishable, are superior to all of the others save only those of the *Pi'tchi-kwe* (Mexican Parrot family). Most of their ruins are of dressed stone, where workable stone was procurable, and they claim to have possessed not only knowledge of agriculture but also of herding an animal the name of which implies that it was regarded in the light of a relative of the deer or antelope.

In a conversation with me only three nights since (April 10th), one of the principal representatives of the *Ta-a-kwe,* Lotchi, nephew of the chief priest of all their dances, told me without a leading question of mine, when trying to convince me of the superiority of his gens and of its claim to certain southern ojos, that the reason why his people's ancestors' ruins are so much finer than those credited to the *Hle-to-na-we* division is because they have been built of dressed stone.[40] The country being warmer, his ancestors had more time to spend in picking the stones out, to make their villages strong against enemies; more time also to devote to their ancient fabrications, which were therefore also superior. The name of the gens itself, he further explained, proved their pre-eminency because, having a warmer, richer soil and being attentive to their sacrifices, hence in favor with the gods who gave them rain, [and] being more skillful in agriculture and all kindred arts, they raised such quantities of corn as to merit the name *Tchu-a-kwe* (Nation of Corn-growers).

It is curious to note that the theory of this savage cacique, founded on tradition, agrees with the most advanced opinions of anthropologists, who would account for the early appearance of civilization in tropical and subtropical countries on the ground of favorable physical environment.

Not only in arts but in government, this people seem to have advanced beyond the others, as shown by a fragment of their primitive laws which I caught from the instructions of the *Kian-a-kwe Kâ-kâ* [*Ky'ana:kwe kachina*], the principal traditional dance of the *Tchu-a-kwe.*[41] Of this dance, Lotchi is the leader in the song, while his uncle and the *Tchu-kwe Mo-so-na* (Cacique of the House) [i.e., leader of Chuppawa kiva] are the chief priests, all three offices being strictly hereditary. At the close of each measure in the song and step, the two priests approach each other and the one gives to the other directions as to how his people shall raise corn and save it, how give the "Good share" to those who govern, protect and care for them, and how and why give attention to their ancient religious usages and duties.[42] My very limited understanding, at the time, of the words used was torturing, since I knew that so much of interest and archaeologic value which was being rehearsed within my hearing was not for me.

This great dance, in which from fifty to seventy five act, occurs only once in four years, and I had the inestimable advantage of seeing and sketching it.[43]

Lotchi tells me that so soon as I understand their language so that it will be "not hard," he will rehearse to me all these instructions, prayers and songs word for word.

I believe the comparison tenable, if not lucid, that the *Shi-wi* nation of today is like a stream which, once rushing along [and] carr[ying] every thing before it, has now scarce the power to push the straws which oppose its progress. But just as the grand banks, and rockrifted ravines of this stream show how great it once was, so the grand mythologic ideas and ceremonial forms of this people, the widely separated and even grander ruins claimed and indisputably covered by their traditions, quite as surely evidence a former greatness and a somewhat more energetic culture.[44]

That many of their institutions and forms *must* have originated under the influence of a higher state of culture and association seems evident from the fact that those who practice some of the most beautiful of them have partially lost knowledge of their original meaning and credited religious value, observing them on the ground of primitive usages and in conformity to ancient instructions. A more complete understanding of these spiritually extinct observances and the instructions and usages which give origin to their practice today must necessarily reveal much as to the former condition of civilization.

It is not alone in the strict harmony of the native architecture, to the terrace-like configuration of the mesa-covered desert in which it exists, not alone in the absolute conformity of the decorative arts to this architecture—showing that they are of contemporaneous or subsequent growth to the latter, that evidence is found of the *indigenous* character of Pueblo culture; but the religion, no less in all its prayers, songs and forms than in its "myths of observation," distinctly bears the stamp of the country in which it occurs.[45]

True, the religion retains enough of an original personality to indicate that it was possibly conceived in the womb of some of the more advanced ante-Columbian cultures; but to one who gets the slightest insight into it, it must appear evident that its subsequent growth and development have been entirely indigenous, or else that, already grown, it has, like the architecture and arts, so entirely conformed to the environment as to appear thus indigenous.[46] In either case, its study, as evincing the effects of environment and natural phenomena on native belief is of vital interest; and, I may add that the latter study could no where be more satisfactorily carried on than amongst the Pueblos, where the physical environments are so unmistakable and the natural phenomena so pronounced.

From the drift of the paragraph preceding the last, you might infer that I would join that more theological than scientific class of theorists, those who regard all savages as the degenerate descendants of a higher civilisation, the fallen representatives of a higher moral condition. Not for a moment. The causes which have acted to make the Zuni nation of today less strong in all pertaining to its physical state, less vigorous in its social, political and religious institutions than it was three hundred years ago, are three, and natural as they are recognisable.

First, the defiling influence upon native belief and politics of the attempted engraftment of a foreign religion and government; an attempt which, though it signally failed, could not but maim the native institutions which it tampered with.

Second, the thinning out and cramping effects of an ever pressing savage enmity—which second cause led, by uniting the several tribes or divisions of gens into one nation occupying a single pueblo, to the

Third and greatest of all: depopulation and degeneration (mental and physical) resulting from excessive intermarriage.

For example, as I have before stated, union with one bearing the name of the gens to which the father belongs is not strictly prohibited. Moreover, the dissolution of the marriage contract is attended neither with censure nor inconvenience amongst the Zunis. Hence it may happen that a young woman's father—a *Kia-kial-i-kwe* [Eagle clansman]—has married successively members of the *Sus-ki-kwe* [Coyote], *A'in-e-shi-kwe* [Bear], *K'o-lok-ta-kwe* [Heron or Crane], and *Pi-tchi-kwe* gens—the last union resulting in her birth.[47] Her mother being a *Pi-tchi-kwe,* she is, according to the rule of inheritance, the same—[and] is hence at liberty to marry members of either or all of the three other gens into which her father has married. Thus it may happen that she marries one of her own half-brothers, as he would bear the name of, and be looked upon as, the property of another gens, and hence there would be no legal objection to his union with her. Any issue of such a marriage, according to well known laws of heredity, would have redoubled in him the mental or physical weaknesses of the single family to which his parents belonged. I do not mean to assert that such an exaggerated instance of intermarriage is common. Indeed, since I have begun to talk the langauge I have heard animated discussions against such a very case. But as the population thinned down by war, as various gens came closer together, living in one pueblo and on more intimate footing, as this population became sexually unbalanced, as is at present the case (the men exceeding in number the women by seven to every hundred), the chances for such or kindred marriages would be increased. Hence it is not hard to understand that the old stock, which is dying out here in Zuni, is immensely superior to the younger, which is presently to form the bulk of an inferior nation—notwithstanding the fact that the younger has had vast advantages over the older. Also that certain families are notable for their brilliancy above others.

I don't think this latter process of degeneration extends back more than six or seven generations—and thus it happens that the present [generation] retains a mythology and ceremonial religion which must be an inheritance from a far greater people because it is superior by a great deal to anything which the present would be capable of conceiving.

What was the original native perfection and state, as shown by the present when viewed in this light, is one more of the many interesting questions which my researches have suggested, yet for which more study is required to pave the way toward a solution of.

I forgot to mention in its proper place another matter which is, so far as I know, a peculiarity of the Pueblos, though appearing to a lesser extent amongst other nations ancient and modern: the sacred character of games, all of which, save those played by children, being held as having originated with and for the gods.[48] These games are regulated by the caciques and render betting a religious duty as well as a pleasure—certain of them appearing only at certain seasons or under peculiar circumstances, others being ordered by the caciques and *Pi-hlan shi-wan-na-we* [Bow Priests]. Some of them are accompanied by elaborate ceremonies, songs, ancient instructions, and prayers to the sun. To get at the philosophy of these games would, it seems to me, lead to important results toward a knowledge of Pueblo life.

I have also failed to state heretofore that with a full knowledge of the language it would be a matter of small difficulty to record specimens of the native oratory (which is peculiar), noteworthy biographies, and, in addition to the mythologic stories, to get a vast amount of folk-lore with which the latter is more or less intimately mixed. I might reiterate until you were weary—if indeed you are not so already—what I have before stated regarding the native etymology, without impressing you with the importance which I attach to its study, as related to all the questions I have heretofore touched upon. Sometimes, for example, with the etymology of a word the whole savage philosophy regarding some natural phenomenon—incomprehensible before—is revealed to me.

Now, I believe, I have presented the salient points which appear to me open for research to a future student in Zuni.[49] All the many minor and almost equally important ones which crowd upon me I fail to make mention of, from the fact that I have already written too much, so much, indeed, that I may have made this communication confusing; hence, for the sake of clearness, I venture a few more words in recapitulation.

First, then, among the objects of extended residence with the Zunis would be the acquisition of the language, as essential to all the following:

Second, the recording, in the original language and with faithful translation, of the industrial and art formulae;

Third, [the recording] of the "Ancient Talks" (*i-no-ti pe-ie-we*) or religious instructions for ceremonies, dances, etc. and of the prayers and songs;

Fourth, the collecting of a vast amount of material (costumes, altars, masks, wands, etc. etc.) illustrative of this study;

Fifth, study of the plume sticks with collecting of a series;

Sixth, [study] of the astronomic monuments, structures, etc., with photographs, plans, etc., illustrative;

Seventh, [study] of the Zuni culture as compared to and illustrative of the other indigenous civilizations of America;

Eighth, [study] of the survivals of gesture language in use among the Zunis as an accompaniment to an oral speech;

Ninth, [study] of the Zuni system of consanguinity and affinity

a. present
b. primitive
c. geographic origin of the groups ("divisions") of the gens, including the special histories of these groups, etc.

Tenth, [study] of the *I-no-te* as related to ancient ruins, including the exploration, planography and photography of and collections from the scene;

Eleventh, [study] of the primitive condition of the *Shi-wi,* its culture, etc., as compared to the present;

Twelfth, [study] of the import and origin of certain mythologic usages now in vogue but only [partially] understood;

Thirteenth, [study] of the effects of natural phenomena and physical environment on native belief;

Fourteenth, [study of the] philosophy of games;

Fifteenth, the recording of specimens of native oratory, folklore, mythologic stories, poetry, etc. etc. (Continued in letter to follow)[50]

Baird to FHC

May 15, 1880

Dear Mr. Cushing:

I have just finished the perusal of your fifty-page letter, with the greatest interest, & do not wonder at the enthusiasm you feel in regard to future work. I am quite willing to have you remain until you accomplish all your objects, or until your presence here is absolutely necessary in the re-arrangement of the collections. . . .

I will advise with Major Powell in regard to various matters in which he has a common interest, & let you know the result. Of course, now that you have got the inside track of the matter, your chief object will be the recording of that part of the history of the people which is less evident to aliens; although the gathering of illustrations of their habits & customs should be prosecuted as far as opportunity permits.

I am glad to know that the shells sent you have been received. I will endeavor to send some imitation turquoises, coral beads, & the like, of which I now have samples. Do the Indians prefer transparent or opaque stones? Advise me on this head. . . .

Very Truly Yours,
Spencer F. Baird

Draft: FHC to George Kennan[51]

May 12, 1880

My dearest Friend:

I cannot tell you how glad I was the other night, after a ride of forty miles in the cedar crested and sand covered mountain mesa to the south of here, after a starlight descent of the most difficult and hazardous rock trail I've ever seen; after running the gauntlet of fifty wolfish curs to my little mud house in Zuni; after slinging a few hard-worded sentences at my harder headed and most provokingly reticent brother, El Gobernador; and after eating a meal of native tortillas, *wyavi* [corn meal], and stewed [meat], to roll my own husk cigarette and squat down to a letter of twenty pages from my dear old boy George. . . .

Were I to attempt a full relation of my curious experiences since we last spoke together, I should at once—leaving the question of encroachment upon my scientific duties entirely aside—intrude upon my own powers of endurance as well as on those of the most charitable of friends. Yet I cannot deem it fair that I should pass them over entirely. As being more full in this respect than anything I now have time to prepare, I am going to take the liberty of introducing a copy of a lot of notes on the first part of my ethnological trip which I long ago prepared during leisure moments, for the newspaper press with the intention of sending them to Professor Baird for official revision but which I neither had time to finish nor the courage to send.[52] [draft ends here]

FRAGMENTARY DRAFT: FHC TO UNKNOWN ADDRESSEE, UNDATED: ON ZUNI LANGUAGE[53]

Thenceforward, I began to live entirely on Zuni food, dress as a Zuni, sleep on a bed of skins and blankets, and in fact, in all outward things, to conform my life exactly to those of the natives.

I conversed at first in broken Spanish, which after the end of two months proving insufficient for my needs, I began earnestly to study the native speech. Whatever other accessories to my success I may have neglected, I have never neglected this. Too ill at times to write my field notes, I have nevertheless set down my little daily acquisitions in this direction and thus, word by word, I increased my store until I could carry on a broken, strange mixture of Zuni and Mexican conversation, gradually dropping the latter until toward the end of three months, I rarely returned to it, save in abstract terms, hard to get unless by accident or rarely occurring occasion, and which, after all, as I now know, the Zunis understood as little of, save by intuition, as I did of their own corresponding expressions. Whatever accessory to my success I may have neglected, this, as the very *first* of *all,* I have labored at incessantly, and my reward is that today at the close of eight months' study I speak a strangely complicated tongue not perfectly but fluently and easily; a tongue so difficult to the Anglo-Saxon, on account of its remarkable grammar and combination of aspirations, gutterals and *Klicks,* that of all the traders, missionaries and [others] who have been in contact with the tribe—some for years—not one ever gained a knowledge of its commonest nouns or simplest idioms.

The Zuni is, so far as it goes, though of course lacking in metaphysic and intellectual terms, one of the most complete, full, and expressive languages I ever knew of. Abounding in nice synonyms, grammatic refinements, etc., far above other aboriginal speeches, it is at the same time so *primitive,* or perfectly preserved from [word missing] with other speech, that many of its words are absolute imitations of the actions or objects they represent.

I'm going to give you one or two examples illustrating this point, both because I know they will interest you and because I wish to find out what you think of them. I will first give the Zuni numerals and their derivations. But I charge you, my boy, to guard this first item very carefully, for if it be correct, I esteem it one of the finest, most satisfactory, I have acquired in all my research. And although I am not so selfish as to care much for the credit of it, yet it is a duty I owe to my Institution to have this and all other original facts preserved to its credit. So, should you give it any publicity, make sure that my Institution, if not my own name, be clearly identified with it.

I give you concisely my system of writing Zuni words that you may better understand what follows:

ā as a in father	ĭ as i in it
ä " " " hat	ō " o " no go
â " aw " bawl	ö " o " not
ē " a " mate	ū " oo " fool
ë " e " met	ŭ like you
ī " e " be (ee in meet)	ü as u in but

' placed after consonant representing click made by pressing tip of tongue against roof of mouth suddenly opening latter on exploding breath,
'h [indicating] emphatic aspiration,
' before a letter denoting omission or abbreviation,
¯ placed over syllable [indicating] silence,

> diminishing to inaudibility,
¯ above and between syllables [indicating] sudden stop.

It is a curious fact that the Zuni numeration is not decimal but arranged by fives; while the Apache language, inferior grammatically and almost in every other way, has, like our own, a decimal system. This is a significant fact—very—which, however, I will not here dwell upon. Below I give the Zuni numerals:

One	*Tō-pïn-ta (Tā-pïn-tē)*
Two	*Kwī' lī*
Three	*Hā'-ē'*
Four	*A'wī-te*
Five	*Op-tī*
Six	*Topu-likīa*
Seven	*Kwe-lī-likīa*
Eight	*Ha-ē-likia*
Nine	*Tīn-ā-likia*
Ten	*As-tem-hlan*
Eleven	*As-tem-hlan to-pi-iühl-te*

The Zunis, although they have the words for the expression of numbers which I have just given, *always* use the fingers in counting. Beginning by grasping with the right hand the little finger of the left hand back outward, laying it down on the palm, and then the second middle finger, forefinger and lastly the thumb. The same process is then repeated on the right hand by the left. Evidently in the following remarkable series of compounds the objects representing numbers referred to are the fingers, as evidence by the derivation of the word for ten given below.

A dissection of these words one by one reveals very interesting facts regarding the origin of systems of numeration, facts the possibility of the existence of which has been hinted at by Tylor but which he had not the material to establish.[54]

Tā-pīn-tē or *tō-pīn-tā*—from *tā-pī,* to take, catch or grab, i'-nāī-ē, an in-dwelling quality or condition of a thing (as for instance the price, size, form, color of an article is its ī'-nāī-ē) and *tē'-ā* = *tai'* (imperative), let it be thus.

Tā-pī ī-nāī-ē tē-ā-tū [becomes]
Tā-pīn-tē [which becomes]
Tō-pīn-ātā.

Hence a very liberal translation of this compound, and yet a correct one, would be: *The* (finger) to be grabbed or that is grabbed, grab-finger = *one.*

Kwīl-lī—from *Kwī-ho-ū'* (imperative), throw down or throw away, *ī-wī-lī* (or *īllī,* its contraction), together with or with, and *ī'naī-ē.*
Kwī-ho-u, i-wil-li i-naī-e [becomes]
Kwi-īll-ī [which becomes]
Kwī-lī.
[Translation:] The (finger) to be thrown down or laid down with (the other) = lay-down-with finger = *two.*

Ha-ī or *Ha-īn*—from *ha-pō-na,* more than two together, and *i-nāī-e.*
Ha-pō-na ī-nāī-ē [becomes]
Hā' īn [which becomes]
Hā'ī.
[Translation:] The (fingers) together = *three.*

This must be illustrated:

I sat, *hâ-i-mo-k'ia.*
We sat, *hon-atch-i-mo-kiā.*
We altogether sat, *hon-hapona-imokiā.*

Thus you see there are two plurals in Zuni—one relating to two objects, the other to any number above that.

A-wī-tī [or] *Ā'-wī-tīn*—from *Ā'* (a prefix indicating *all*), *i-tī-wā,* middle or midst, and *in-āī-ē.*
A' ītī wā in āī ē [becomes]
A-wī-tī n [which becomes]
A-wī-tī.
[Translation:] All the *middle fingers* together = *four.*

O-ptin—from *op-tsi,* to cut or cut off, and *ināī ē.*
Op-tsi and *inaī ē* [becomes]
Opt in [which becomes]
Op-tī.
[Translation:] The finger cut off (thumb), cut-off finger = *five.*

Topa-lī-kīa—from *Topa,* the other, *īlī* or *ī-wī-lī,* with, and *K'iā'* (termination corresponding to our *ed,* always indicating past tense).
To-pā, īlī-kiā [becomes]
To-pali-kiā.
[Translation:] The (finger) put with the other (five) = *six.*

Kwī-līl-li-kia—from *kwil-lī,* two, *iwīlī* or *ī'lī,* and *kiā.*
Kwīllī-īlīkiā [becomes]

Kwī-lī-likīā.
[Translation:] Two (fingers) put with the other (five) = *seven.*

Hā-ē-līkīā—from *Haī,* three, and *ī-lī-kia.*
Haī'-ī-lī-kīa [becomes]
Ha-i-lī-kīa.
[Translation: Three fingers put with the other five = *eight*].

Tē-nā-likīā—from *tē'-nān,* to be or being exhausted or run out, empty, and *i'likia,* put with.
Tē-nan īli-kīā [becomes]
Te na likiā.
[Translation: All four fingers put with the other five = *nine*].

Äs-tem-hlän [or] *Äs-tem-hlā*—from *As-sī,* finger, and *tem-hlā,* all, and *īnaīē.*
As-sī-tem-hla-īnaīē [becomes]
As tem-hlan [which becomes]
As'-tem-hlā.
[Translation:] All of the fingers [= ten].

As-tem-hlan-to-pa-i-äthl-to—from *As-tem-hlān* (ten), *tō-pā* (one) and *ī-ä-thl-tō-āī-ē* (laid upon). . . .
[Translation:] All fingers and one laid on = *eleven.* And so on.
Kwilli-ken-as-tem-hlän (all of the fingers two times) [= twenty].
As-si-as-tem-hlan (all of the fingers ten times) = one hundred.

I ought to have mentioned that the Zunis, while they have the bones and *parts* of the hand and arm named, have *no* name for the hand as a whole or for the fingers other than adding the diminutive *tsana* to the name used for the whole limb or arm, hand and fingers as a whole.

If the derivations of these names of these members as I have given them be correct, don't it give *date* to the Zuni language, old boy? It takes it back, almost just as it *is,* to the time when the Zunis or their ancestors could not express numbers without the use of the fingers; and knowing of nothing with which to express by sound so abstract an idea as number, neither having any distinct name for the fingers, they named other numbers in the order in which they used them, up to *five,* then borrowed a finger from the other hand, the name of which they cemented on to the names of the first five, and so on up to ten. Then beginning over again, they got a finger from the left hand and "laid it upon" all the other fingers, making eleven and so on up to twenty, which was two times all the fingers, and up to one hundred, which became "All the fingers ten times," one thousand being expressed by "Ten times ten times all the fingers."

REMINISCENCE: THE ZUNI LANGUAGE

. . .How long was it before you became familiar with the language?"

"I began to talk the language moderately well in about nine months. I could not have possibly learned it in that time had it not been a matter of sheer necessity and desperate determination. I worked at it constantly; they never let me rest day or night, but were always drilling me, and were far more impatient to have me learn their language than I was to learn it. They would never permit me to use, uncorrected, any inaccuracy. . . ."

"Their vocabulary is large?"

"It is very ample, and like the German, is capable of being indefinitely extended in any direction at once."

"By the adding of syllables?"

"Yes, by the perfectly regulated combination and accentation of different roots. If they have occasion to change the mood or tense of such a sentence-word as one of these coinages, they simply add the requisite prefixes or suffixes or interjections of a single word, and that makes a single word of many. The promptness with which they will manufacture a word is surprising, and the promptness with which the applicability of that word will be recognized by another man who knew nothing of the coining of it is a little more so. This was illustrated one day when I showed the pole which accompanies a theodolite to an old man. I asked the old man if he didn't think the Zuni language very inferior to the American (I was joking, of course; I often took that means of drawing them out). 'No, why?' 'Well,' said I, 'a language that hasn't a name for every object must be inferior.' He picked up on the very spur of the moment an article of the Zunis' paraphernalia and held it between his fingers and shook it. It was a kind of combined bell, amulet and rattle. He said: 'What is the name of this in American?' 'Well,' I said, 'Americans don't have those things. There is no name for it.' 'Ah ha,' said he; 'now ask me the name of something.' So I turned around. I was sitting in a room where there was an engineer's apparatus. I turned round with equal promptness and grabbed one of the poles and set it up. 'There,' said I, 'what is the name of this?' 'What is it for?' 'It is for measuring the relative heights of the land.' 'Oh, yes,' he said, and gave me the following name for it: '*U'lahnananitetchunakyathlam.*' The meaning of it in English is, 'the heights of the world progressively measuring stick.' That would be the etymology, as best one can get at it. It is cleverer than that, and, of course, it is a sentence in a word; and if our language could be used in the same way, I could have told him the name of the Zuni article. But a Zuni could put the case-ending to that whole long thing and make a single word of it, and then, such a word being more and more closely amalgamated by use, it would become a short and extremely expressive word. I put it in my note-book, and the next day I took that measuring stick to the extreme corner of the pueblo and began to flourish it around to arouse the curiosity of somebody, and, sure enough, a middle-aged man came along presently and said: 'What in the world is this?' I repeated the Zuni name given above. 'Indeed,' he said, 'can they actually tell how far up and down journeying the world is?' It is on this account that no foreign expressions (with few exceptions, such as the names of domesticated animals) have ever entered into the Zuni language. It is absolutely pure."

—*San Francisco Examiner,* July 1, 1888

3. *June–December 1880*

Rediscovering Cibola, Conquering Zuni

> During [this time] I continued my investigations into the mythology, traditions, and ecclesiastical as well as governmental institutions of the Indians and explored many of the traditional ruins within a radius of fifty miles of Zuni. Before the close of the year, I had so far acquired knowledge of the Zuni language as to take an important position in the councils and was made Chief Councilor of the nation. This increased knowledge also enabled me to learn traditions bearing on historic matters.
>
> Among these was one concerning the ruin of Kia-ki-me, at the base of Ta-ai-iallonne (Thunder Mountain), a mesa stronghold three miles east of Zuni, which related to the death of "the Black Mexican with thick lips," in whom I failed not to recognize the Barbary Negro Estevanico. [*Cushing had learned of this guide of Marcos de Niza's and of his death at the hands of the Indians in the excerpts he had been reading from the old Spanish chronicles. This story from the Zuni side, added to the phonetic similarities he recognized between town names given in the Spanish accounts and Zuni names he had heard for local ruins, would clinch his identification of Zuni as the locus of the Spaniard's Cibola.*] Inquiries . . . led to the specific determination of the sites of nearly all the Seven Cities of Cibola . . . [and] to the belief, ultimately confirmed by old Spanish records, that there was no one city of Cibola, but all together were known by that name . . .
>
> —Report to Powell, July 6, 1882 (SWM HC 37)

Cushing's progress during this period in learning about the Zunis and their history was accompanied by equally dramatic developments in his relations with them. As his later report indicates, he was by now so far along on his "inside track" that he was not only accepted in the community but beginning to make his weight felt as a person of consequence. The records surviving from the summer and fall of 1880 afford some particularly vivid, and from a later standpoint occasionally rather shocking, glimpses of the young ethnologist in his double role as researcher and man of affairs—commencing with the remark in a letter of July 18 that he was "pretty much master of his situations," having "pounded" the war captain and governor. Perhaps the heavy-handed and confrontational behavior sometimes evidenced is to be explained, as George Stocking explains the sexual fantasies and hostile references to "niggers" recorded by Malinowski during his sojourn in the Trobriand Islands, as the reflection of "the psychological demands imposed by the new ethnographic style"—the strain of "sustained immersion in the strata of native daily life" and of being "alone with his instincts in the heart of darkness."[1]

Certainly in Cushing's case, as in that of Stocking's Malinowski, empathy for the "natives" manifested itself not only in identification with them but in ambivalent and sometimes aggressive behavior. Unlike Malinowski's diary, however, Cushing's—at least those that survive—are singularly free of expressed animus against the "natives," however he may sometimes have lorded it over them. True, Cushing simply kept a less introspective record, and the fact that he didn't write down sexual fantasies or feelings "decidedly tending to 'Exterminate the brutes,'" as Malinowski did (echoing Joseph Conrad's Kurtz), doesn't necessarily mean that he didn't have them. Another, less profound explanation of Cushing's aggressive behavior among the Zunis is suggested, however, by the complaints of Bandelier and other "civilized" associates of Cushing's about the latter's overbearing manners as director of the Hemenway Southwestern Archaeological Expedition—simply that it was in his nature to be ardent and headstrong and that power could go to his head. After months of abiding the benign "tyranny" of the Indians, he was by mid-1880 enjoying a turn of the wheel.

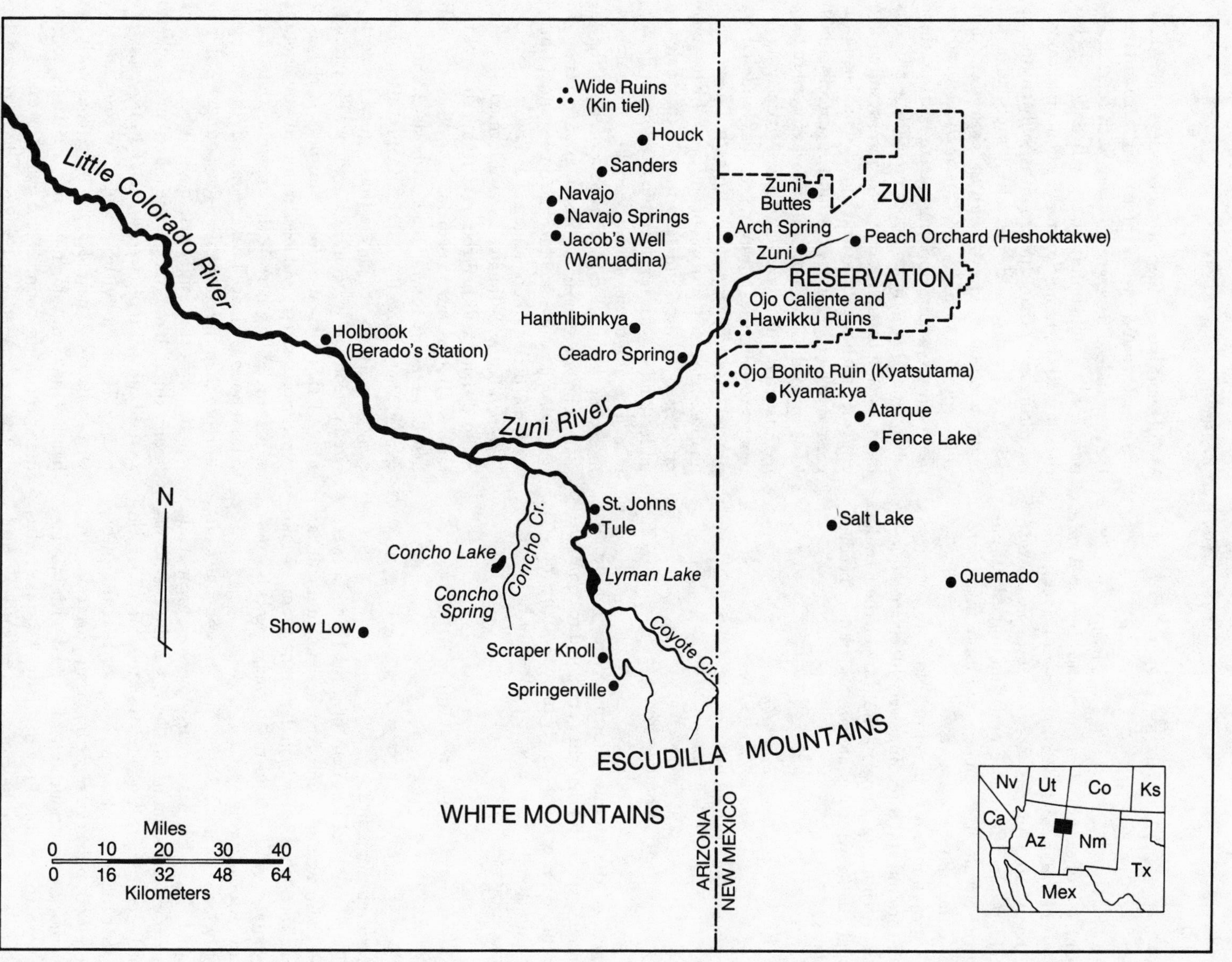

Zuni and Its Southern Environs.

Note

15th June 1880

Cutting of sacrificial prayer wands by the *A-shi-wa-ni* and *Kâ'-kâ A-shi-wa-ni* or *a-mo-si* is followed in the evening by the *Ko-ye-mo-shi a-wa-nu-thla,* special priests of election, nude and unmasked, going the circuit of the houses to prophesy and pretypify the coming of waters.[2]

They join hands to hips from oldest to youngest, going around and threading every block and *pi-la-ni* [plaza], shuffling along to the time of their traditional chant, which is archaic and pronounced as follows:

Tu me tchim tchim
Ai a tchi a wa we na
Tchi a na we na
Tchi a na we na
Weh weh
Tu me tchim tchim

which is the chorus informing the inhabitants (women especially) that they are called to come out, for the rain is coming (surely to be brought? now?). As this is archaic, it can at present only be paraphrased by me.[3]

FHC to Baird

Zuni, June 20, 1880

Dear Professor Baird:

The final establishment of a mail line between Fort Wingate and Camp Apache, via Zuni and San Juan [St. Johns] of which I just now am to take advantage, will enable me to make weekly communications to you. . . .

My interest in the Silver City cave continues unabated. Indeed it has recently received great stimulus from the account of Lieut. Gardner, who recently returned this way from a scout after Victorio in that region. So long as I do not hear from Col. Stevenson, however, regarding transportation, etc., I cannot carry out our long cherished wish in reference to this place. Providentially, I suppose, has this delay occurred heretofore, as recently Victorio has wiped out pretty nearly all the inhabitants of the Mesilla and Eastern Rio Grande valleys, save those of Silver City and two or three other large villages. He may indeed have gotten away with Metcalfe—but that, though unfortunate, will only have left the coast all the more clear for our final operations.[4]

During more than three months, only ending six days since, a dry, cold, excessively sand-laden and severe wind has swept through the valleys of Zuni. On warmer days this has become at times an actual monsoon. Constant, blinding and suffocating, these sand winds have, in conjunction with a previous indisposition brought on by exposure, resulted in a difficulty with my lungs and thorax which had progressed so far that for days I would be scarcely able to leave my bed in the morning and was forced to have recourse to it during the day. Except in delaying my reports to yourself, [however,] this has hindered my progress scarcely any, for, although I have been unable to do much writing of any kind, I have so far progressed in the Zuni language as to speak and understand it with considerable freedom and readiness. The times when I have been illest have always, moreover, been filled by conversation with the Indians who, never absent from my room, keep up an unceasing flow of talk which of course cannot but be very instructive to one engaged as I am. . . .

When last at Wingate, I was informed by Lieut. Stafford that I still had the right to my share of the rations allowed our expedition but that it would first be necessary for me to get authority from yourself or Major Powell to sign receipts in my own name, or else to get papers thus signed by authorized persons ere he would issue to me. He strongly advised that I should do the former, as the most expeditious, safest, and least technical way. Flour is at present selling here at the enormous rate of ten cents a pound. Hence I have refrained from using in all more than thirty or thirty-five pounds—which I purchased during my worst days to help me as a luxury through my illness. Sugar and coffee sell also at the high price of twenty five and fifty cents per pound. These, notwithstanding their cost, together with tobacco, I have had to keep constantly on hand—the former for home use, the latter to give me a seat in the councils and sacred estufas.

The gentleman with whom I have traded has agreed that, should my allowance in rations be granted, he would allow me to return in kind the material I had purchased, without reduction. Could I draw rations for the entire time of my stay on the first of January, I would be enabled by judicious management to cover nearly all of my proper expenses for the winter and spring as Lieut. Stafford is very willing to issue from any class of Commissary stores. . . .

[*The following two paragraphs, taken from two earlier drafts for this letter, were omitted from the final version:*]

Taking their cue from the Apaches, who . . . only a short time past spread terror and devastation throughout the region sixty miles southwest of here, . . . the Navajos have become bold and arrogant, some of them threatening to take the war path. Only two weeks since, they killed one, and severely wounded another American (the latter an acquaintance of mine) and more recently two or three men were killed within ten miles of Fort Wingate. I do not, however, share in the general fear that they will break out—a fear which has driven dozens of families to the Post, and others to desert their homes; and which has caused the almost entire temporary suspension of trade, travel and freighting on the road through this valley. Nor have I ever ceased to vindicate in council the rights of my adopted people against these wandering coyotes—driving them mercilessly from Zuni territory and compelling them to return or repay stolen property. Thus more than ordinary Americans, I am in danger when traveling solitarily about the country. No less am I, in the opinion of men of these parts, in at least some risk from the Mexicans who, on account of the restraint which my presence imposes upon them, and on account of my revealing several of their relations with the Indians, hate me much with the spirit of past times. Moreover, I have, through testifying to the traitorous character of some of the Mormon relations with the Indians, won the displeasure of a large proportion of these people, who, I am informed, would on the first occasion of finding me alone either cause me to be killed by Navajos or do it themselves.

While I fear in none of these cases, I value just now the fruits of the opportunities I have enjoyed, too much to run any unnecessary risks, and I am informed by gentlemen in both official and civil life, that I must arm myself securely—for effect if nothing more.

. . . .

The chief of the Rio Puerco Navajos, a friend of myself and the Zunis, told me that in one moon he would return to Zuni and exchange his necklace (the finest Pueblo production of the kind in the world) for clam shells—yellowing red or pink shells—and a small quantity of green and blue stones, from this

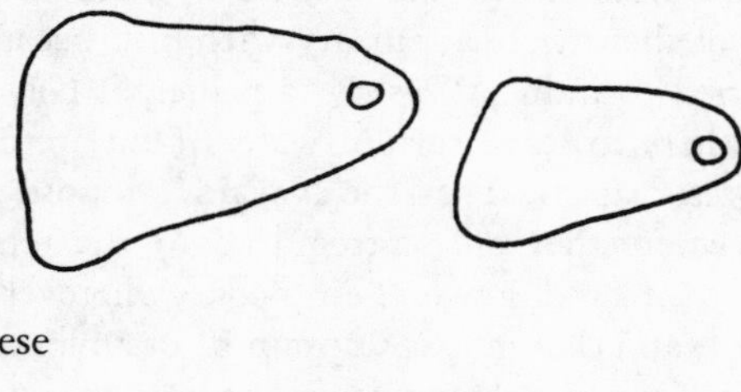

to these

sizes and shapes. Absolute imitations of turquoises or any whitish blue stone—not necessarily hard—with an almost imperceptible green tinge rank highest in the scale of Pueblo possessions. Next are jades, after which [come] coral [and] red, pink, white, or purple shells. Any of this material which you can procure and send to me I can and will make good use of.

Begging that you will kindly consider the above requests,

I remain, Respectfully and Truly,

Your Servant,
F. H. Cushing

DRAFT: FHC TO UNKNOWN ADDRESSEE

Zuni, N.M.
June 27, [1880]

In a private talk in our presence and in the house of Dr. Ealy, Palowahtiwa, Governor of Zuni, in company [of] Nai-iu-tchi, Chief War Cacique, [and] Lai-iu-ah-tsai-lu (Pedro Pino, ex-Governor), said that on Friday night Ti-ni-tsu-se, a Navajo Indian living at Coyote Springs, came to Zuni and remained at the house of Wa-mun, a Zuni Mormon, until Saturday morning, June 26th.[5] That the object of his visit was to assure the Zunis of the friendly feeling entertained for them by the Navajos, and that he (the Navajo) was delegated by the mass of his people to say these things to the Zunis. He then further stated that a great Capitan had just come from Washington to the Navajos and had a council with them at Defiance. That the Captain had displaced their Agent and put Captain Bennett in charge.[6] That his people were not as fond of Captain Bennett as was generally believed; that many of them were at enmity with him because he had tried to induce Washi—a principal Navajo—and others to leave certain waters [and] return to their reservation. That the Navajos propose to remain where they are scattered about the territory or to roam and graze their flocks wherever they pleased, and that in case Captain B. or anybody else attempts to force them within the lines of the reservation, they should resist it and fight until [they] wipe out all Americans. That they had dispatched messengers to the Moquis as well as to all the Rio Grande Pueblos assuring them that the Navajos would do them no injury, and that they desired to sustain friendly relations with them all. That messengers had been dispatched to the different bands of Eastern Apaches with assurances of friendship and a desire in case of trouble that they should unite with them (the Navajos) in fighting the Americans.

FHC to Baird

Zuni, July 2, 1880

Dear Professor Baird:

In consequence of two excursions to Ta-ai iallonne, the sacred mountain of Zuni, as also of the visit of Special Indian Commissioner Col. E. W. Townsend, Lts. Gardner and Gatewood and Dr. Martin, U.S.A., I did not succeed in posting my last letter by the mail I had designed it for.

Since the departure of these gentlemen, I have been very ill, but tonight finds me better than for many weeks.

Two dances have recently taken place, together with important ceremonies relative to the Sun, thus introducing once more my old, ever interesting but very wearing task of watching, recording, and sketching.[7]

It is my good fortune to have here one of the R. R. Route Exploration volumes containing occasional extracts in quotation from the journals of early Spanish adventurers.[8] Also I have recently, through the courtesy of Padre Brun, enjoyed the privilege of searching over some of the Mss. records of the now deserted Zuni church—which was one of the earliest established by the Franciscans in New Spain.[9]

Through studies of these ancient records I have been drawn into a department of research in reference to the Zunis, interesting from its connections with History and important from the light its results throw on early conditions and still existing traditions.

This line of investigation is founded mostly on the comparison of old Spanish names of people, kingdoms, and towns with corresponding terms in the Zuni language of today—a task which, heretofore impossible, is now comparatively easy to me. By this means I have already *definitely* located the celebrated City or Kingdom of "Civola," discovered three hundred and forty years ago by Padre Marcos Niça, the ruins of which stand within rifle range of the present pueblo of Zuni.[10] This ancient town, having been the first of the pueblos subdued by the efforts of Coronado, and the center of all subsequent early operations, it occurred to me that many of the native names to be found throughout the first Spanish accounts must have been derived from the language of the Civolatese—or Zuñis—and this I find to have been the case, more than two thirds that I know of or have in hand being directly traceable to this source. For example, the principal "Citie of Cibola"—according to Casteñada—Muzaque (pronounced *Mū-tsa-kī*) finds a correspondence in the Zuni name of a ruined pueblo at the foot of Ta-ai iallonne, called Ma-tsa-ki [modern spelling Mats'a:kya].[11] Also the largest city of the "Kingdome of Civola" according to Niça and Coronado, Ahacus (Spanish pron. aspirated *Hā-hā-kūs*) cannot but be presented by the splendid ruins ten miles west from here—called by the Indians Ha-wi-kuh [*Hawikku*]. There is certainly no more discrepancy between these words than before the known name in the church records of a Pueblo (now ruined) which one hundred and fifty years ago stood just across the stream from here, the Spanish being Alona, while in Zuni it is Ha-lo-na-wa.

Among other things, it has been remarked by nearly all modern writers that the accounts of Padre Niça are utterly unreliable. These remarks are founded mostly upon his statement that there existed not far from the Province of Civola, "at the Southwest, a Kingdome called Marata where there were wont to be many great cities which were alle builded of houses of stone, with diverse loftes." Also upon Coronado's refutation, who, coming to Civola a year afterward, failed to learn of any such "Kingdome" and in his Report to the Viceroy of Mexico, said of the "Father Provincial—and to be briefe, I can assure your honor he sayed the truthe in no thing he reported, but all was quite contrarie. . . . The Kingdome of Marata is not to be founde, neither have the Indians any knowledge thereof." When, in translating to the Indians a few days since, some of the passages I have on hand, I pronounced the word Marata, they at once corrected me by say *Ma-kia-kwu-ta-hna* (the syllables marked with diminuation points and slur, being very rapidly and slightly pronounced so as to sound at a short distance like *Ma-kia-tah*). This word simply means "The land or place of the South"—the term always used to denote that direction or quarter. There, today, is the remarkable series of stone ruins mentioned in my April communication. Having knowledge of the real meaning of Marata not only throws credit on the heretofore questioned authenticity of Padre Niça's *Relaciones* but also gives additional proof to the Zuni tradition that the *Ma-kia-kwu-ta-hna* series of ruins were still inhabited, though sparingly, at the time of the Spanish Discoveries.[12]

I make mention of these examples, not presuming to call your attention to the importance of the comparison of records, names, etc., of three hundred years ago with the traditions and corresponding terms of today, but only to try and prove to you that I am on the right trail and that the value *I* attach to this species of investigation is the outgrowth of conviction, not of enthusiasm alone.

On the strength of this, I make bold to ask your kind cooperation toward securing, for immediate use, at least the following works:

1—Hakluyt, *Voyages* Vols I to III
2—Ternaux–Compans, *Voyages,* Sirie I, tome VI
3—Davis, *Conquest of New Mexico*
4—Sitgreaves, *Report*
5—Smithsonian *Report*—containing Coronado's March to the Seven Cities of Cibola
6—*Popular Science Monthly*—number containing Dr. Loew's article on Zuni
7—Bancroft, *Native Races of {the} Pac{ific} States*—Vols. of Linguistics and Mythology
8—Spanish Dictionary
9—French Dictionary[13] . . . .

I am now in the heart of the country treated of in all those works; I speak the language which the writers of them listened to, and took the names of Kingdoms and Cities from. In my rides throughout these deserts, I constantly stumble upon the half buried ruins of the identical towns to which these names related—and daily, I pass under the shadows of the first church which the zealous hands of those old authors fashioned and established in the outlying realms of their Nuevo España.[14] If I may have access to these few works while I am yet among the people and scenes to which they relate, I shall be able to accomplish much, I think, of real importance. If I may have this privilege granted to me, I will pass whole nights with the old men of the tribe, translating passages to them, eliciting traditions from them, comparing Spanish names with theirs, or listing their suggestions (as in the one instance of Marata) as to what old words might have been designed for.

If, on the contrary, I am forced to defer these investigations to the time when (God knows when) I again reach Washington, it seems almost as though they had best be deferred altogether, so different would the two results in the end prove to be. . . .

Because of the unsettled condition of the eastern Navajos, who [besides] the Mormons, are my special enemies, I have been constantly advised by the officers of Wingate and Camp Apache to fully equip myself, for effect, if for nothing more. Hence I accepted the kind offer of Major Jewett to get me at officer's rates, a government outfit. Though his kind office will considerably reduce the cost, it will still amount, probably, to thirty or forty dollars. I hope, therefore, that I may not be disappointed in my expectation of an early remittance.

Very Respectfully and Most Faithfully Yours,
F H Cushing

FHC to Baird

Zuni, July 18, 1880

My dear Professor Baird:

. . . .

[Were it not] for the ethnologic interest which it still has for me, my exile here, [owing to] the superstitious character of the natives, the desert character of the country, and the absence of all vegetable substance from my diet, as well as the stale character of the flesh and utter flatulency of most Zuni cereal preparations, [would be] absolutely unbearable. Yet I am gratified more than I can say with the decision which both yourself and Major Powell have reached regarding my case. [*Cushing had just received their approval of his continuing on in Zuni.*]

Such a prodigious task is the collection of psychologic material of savages, and so incomparably valuable is this species of information, that one can scarcely gain too intimate a knowledge of the language which is to a great extent its embodiment or, thus exposed, devote too much time to its investigation. Every hour conscientiously put into the work of research now avails me that which, knowing it is to realize its indispensability. And from the present outlook of things, it does not appear that this kind of essential information is lessening in the least degree, but on the contrary, as I near and grow into the subject, I see infinitely more to be gained. Hence it is that I am pleased with your decision. . . .

The matter of superstition which I above alluded to is, while very interesting and all that, not so pleasant. The Zunis have, within the past ten days, killed one of their own men from its dictates. His trial, on the absurd ground of sorcery, I attended personally and as in every other public debate of the tribe, had more or less to say—of course, so far as possible, for the defense. His death took place in the night [and] was horribly violent—although partaking more of the character of a sacrifice than of an execution. *I* have been more than once—on the ground that I had become a Zuni—Americans being considered free from sorcerers—subject to the same accusation.[15] But I hold my friends from doing me violence by a bond of *brotherhood* which you have but to be conversant with the Indian character to appreciate the strength of; and my enemies I have equal power over from their absolute dread of me.

I have never flinched from their worst demonstrations—[and] have hence established a reputation, very valuable among Indians, of absolute fearlessness.

Once on occasion of the *Ho-ma-tchi,* or Zuni War Dance, which was gotten up to intimidate me from collecting sacred articles and to infuriate the tribe against my sketching dances, sacred ceremonies, etc., I was calmly painting and taking notes when the cry arose among the officer of the Dance, of "Kill him! Kill him!"—whereupon two of the naked painted devils called *Nē-wē-kwe* rushed to the foot of the ladder near which I was sitting, brandishing their stone knives and wooden war clubs, and taking up anew the cry of "Kill him! Kill him!" I stuck my pencil behind my ear, calmly smiled (though I confess I didn't feel like it, but there were a thousand eyes upon me), drew a big hunting knife out of my wallet, laying it down before me, and still smiling, took up my sketch book, drew out my pencil, and continued as though nothing had happened. Immediately the *Nē-wē-kwe* set up a cry that they had made a mistake in their man, that he was no Navajo, neither like one, but perhaps a creature of great value, and they killed, in the most revolting manner describable, a big yellow dog instead.

Since then—it is many months ago—I have been pretty much master of my situations; pounded the War Captain the other day in a crowd of fifty opposers; settled in the same way the Governor, who attempted to interfere, and since then I've had no trouble with the Zunis.

I never espouse any cause in which there is not justice—never have any trouble which is not connected with my work—which, with the other, I always carry through, no matter what the risk. The result is that by my friends I am treated with unbounded respect and by my enemies with that which amounts to the same thing, though the outgrowth of fear.

I don't mind the risk of this thing; however, I cannot help recognizing the fact that there is some in it. I have no fear. Only the superstitions of these fellows, and the things they ask me to do in conformity to them, are at times exasperating in the extreme.

My living is simply horrible, unmentionable. I thought I couldn't bear too lightly on that subject last Autumn; but the Spring living of the Zunis I'd better not mention at all. Until now (July 18th) no green has appeared in all this valley.

The rains have at last come, and, with the dying away of the sand storms, my health has been on the gain constantly, although I continue to lose flesh rapidly. I hope, nevertheless, that Major Powell will not pass lightly over the consideration of my ration assignment.

Although on my arrival here I understood neither Spanish nor Zuni, could converse with nobody save my books and by signs for many days and weeks, I do not remember during all my Zuni experience having had a single attack of genuine nostalgia. And, however full my life be of hardships (from the civilized point of view) and my work of discouragements (from the scientific), yet, both have their bright sides, and the only actual depression I ever suffer from is when I see my health failing, and I sometimes recognize my inability to fill the time properly with work. For instance, when I make a long sought discovery, the pleasure is fairly so intense that I forget how I live and all. Besides, the Indians, though exteriorly so reticent and apparently gloomy a people, are, when known and when viewed from the standpoint of one of themselves, about the merriest race I have ever known.

When the evening comes and we all sit round the meal of the day, no Christmas dinners I have known have been filled or seasoned with so much badinage, reparté, and hearty laughter as these. In stoic wit excellent, in reparté scarcely surpassed, in punning unconquerable, the Zunis are not such bad companions after all. Yet if they hate one, all these points or traits only go to make them the more unendurable.

I can sum up in one sentence what my life here has been—physically, so far as the appetites are concerned, paralysis; socially, exile; ethically [and] theoretically, a feast, a peace of mind unapproached in all my previous experience.

And as to results—probably impaired health during life; a strengthening and development of moral character in *every respect,* and aside from a more practical and cosmopolitan view of humanity and its institutions, I hope and pray (though sometimes dubiously) that it will make *a worker* of me.

On the whole, then, while it is a pretty hard thing, I am *far* from sorry you have decided to keep me down here till I've done something. I have made this long digression from proper official correspondence with you, neither complainingly nor, I trust, from egotistic motives, but that you may the more freely grant me pardon if I seem sometimes disposed to ask too much consideration, which *realizing* my situation, you would not find it hard to do.

I remain, dear Professor Baird,

Very Respectfully,
Your Humble Servant,
F H Cushing

I am very grateful for the kind compliment and really practical benefit you bestowed upon me in addressing my last mail as "Agent of the Smithsonian Institution" and for your kindly mentioning to Mr. Rhees my necessities in the way of stationary and money, which, though not arrived, I expect by the coming mail. FHC

Daily Journal

July 21, 1880

Warm cloudy day with a very little rain toward evening. Was called this morning to a house in Onawe to administer sacred rites to a little girl who was scared at me on the day I struck the war captain.[16] They consisted of taking a lock of my hair, throwing it on coals held in a little bowl, then crouching the little girl over it and spreading a blanket so closely over her that scarcely any of the smoke could escape. This exhausted, I breathed into her mouth and nostrils three or four times, said a sacred word or two, and the ceremony closed. Preparations and rehearsal at night in my house for *Hla-he-we.*[17]

July 22, 1880

Warm, somewhat cloudy day. At about noon the dance of the women (*Hla-he-we*) commenced in the house below my father's. It began to the song of *Shoh-k'o*—the women who sat in one end of the room rising, preparing, being led a short distance by the *mo-so-ne* [leaders] of the dance, then gradually dancing to their place, keeping both feet close together, with arms extended, hands grasping ears of corn, elbows crooked. There were at first six or seven young women engaged in this dance. It gave way, prayers were said by the caciques and other *mo-so-ne* present; then the *Hla-he-we* dance was initiated, which consists simply of two girls with a sacred blanket folded, bound with [a] woman's belt, and laid across the head from front to back. The step is the same as the former, though the arms are more widely extended. Regularly the *Hla-he-we* consists of two to four virgins, with one immaculate young man, dressed as for the *Hle-we-kwe,* in the center.[18] All hold and consecrate ears of corn.

The dance closed at about eight o'clock in the evening, and not long after[ward] the *Hla-he-we mo-so-ne* and singers came to my house, where they sang until twilight, the two women *mo-so-ne* dancing some of the time.

In this dance there are four men *mo-so-ne* and four women, who are forbidden from sexual intercourse for eight days.

Friday, July 23rd, 1880.

Slightly cloudy, somewhat hot. Dancing suspended until night, when in two different houses the dance—*Shoh-k'o* in one, *H{la-he-we}* in the other. Latter in my house. Lasted until early morning (rising of morning stars), when I was called up to partake of the sacred drink of *Ale-kwe-uwe* and water, sanctified by the two women who acted as the *mo-so-ne.*[19] Dance was conducted just as on fast and K [illegible] nights.

Rained toward evening and at night. Only slightly here, though to a greater extent above. Got beginning of story of flood.[20]

FHC to William Jones Rhees

Zuni, July 24, 1880

Dear Mr. Rhees:

. . . .

My work of observation still progresses quite satisfactorily, adding to the wealth of material I had already at my last writing acquired, as well as constantly nourishing a healthy growth of my mental and perceptive facilities.

I confess that the longings for my Eastern home, the intense desire to grasp once more the hands, one and all, of my dear friends, the isolated and at times intensely suffering life which I lead here, would all be too much for the stoutness of my heart, were I not borne up constantly by the love, ever increasing, of the studies which I have chosen for life and which here, where all else is misery—death even—find their fullest development and widest green fields.

Hoping you are passing the time pleasantly where, in a land bright with God's civilization, it seems to an exile like me, it would be mere bliss to live,

Ever I remain,

Your Humble Friend,
F. H. Cushing

Daily Journal

July 25th, 1880.

Warm, cloudy and somewhat rainy day. *Hla-he-we otiwa* [dance] and *Shoh-k'o otiwa* for the day *tchu-ni-kia* [stopped].

Toward evening, I was apprised that there was trouble with Dubois at Ojo Benado and that my letter to latter gentleman had not yet been delivered.[21] I was angry and fear the matter of Antonio's impertinence may cost the Zunis some trouble.

At night had at my house as usual the *Hla-he-we* rehearsal.

Draft: FHC to Daniel Dubois

Zuni, July 25, 1880

Sir:

Some three weeks since, the Indians unfortunately, in carrying out some of their religious observances, set fire to one of your cedar fences.[22]

Immediately after, the principal men of the tribe called together a meeting and commissioned me to write you expressing the sincere regrets of the Governor and Alcalde and their willingness to repair whatever of your corral had been burned. They however stated that they could make no further atonement, as the fact that you had fired two pistol shots at their party, as well as retained and thrashed one of its members (thereby breaking up their most sacred exercises) did away with any payment on the ground of trespass.

Unfortunately, the letter which I wrote and at once dispatched was impertinently detained by Antonio, the principal property holder of Ojo Caliente.[23] I did not learn this until yesterday, and not only make haste to write you this communication but also to order the immediate delivery of the former.

Inasmuch as these Indians hold no grudge against you, save that aroused by your driving upon them, [and] that they meant no personal harm toward you in firing your corral, but on the contrary that this firing was merely an incident to a sacred ceremony which has been observed by them every four years for centuries. I hope you will have at once the kindness and good sense to consider their offer to make good your fences sufficient reparation. [final salutation omitted from this copy]

Daily Journal

July 28th, '80.

Wednesday. *Hle-we-kwe* commenced final preparations this morning by *Hla-wap tis-li-kun* [cutting prayer sticks], after which we were all feasted. I am supposed, for having made the wand, to be also one of them; was therefore instructed not to speak loudly or angrily for three remaining days and nights.[24] Toward noon, the ceremony of bending the cane to the wands took place in the estufas. Under the great temporary house other ceremonies followed, ending in evening [with] songs by firelight, singers being arranged in rows to left (*Hle-we-kwe*) and right (Shoh-k'o-kwe).

When this closed, there was a great bus[tle], the seats being arranged, and here they pass the night sitting, neither sleeping nor being other[wise] engaged than in religious exercises.

July 30th, '80.

Slightly cloudy, very hot. End of *Hla-he-we* and *Shoh-k'o otiwa,* as shown in notes.

Council about detainment of my letter and about Zuni trespass on Dubois's ranch.

Talk in afternoon about wars of the *Kâ'kâ.*

Talk at night about ancient times traditions and more of the wars of the *Kâ'kâ.*

Hla wap tshish likia [Cut, or prepared, prayer sticks].

July 31st, '80.

Very hot, cloudy and toward evening slight scattered rains. Noteworthy: the one on my Brother's fields *alone,* who was engaged as priest and chief singer of the *Hla-he-we.*

Very little of ceremonial nature. Council in great square today concerning church, two saints, Dubois, war of Mexico, Mexicans, etc.

At night, visit at my house resulting in vast acquisitions mythologically.

FHC to Baird

Zuni, August 2, 1880

My dear Professor Baird:

The last two mails have been, through your kindness and the prompt execution of your requests by Mr. Rhees, very rich ones for me, the first, in ample supplies of stationary, of which I have already had great advantage, and the second in sufficient money, I trust, to meet my expenses for some time to come, as well as to enable me to make my long contemplated expedition, during the latter part of this month, to central Arizona for the purpose of examining the remains marking the courses of the ancient Zuni migrations, as well as to examine and collect from three caves of which I have learned from the Indians. And in view of all that this will, with good fortune, enable me to do, let me acknowledge with sincere thanks your kindness in causing it to be sent.

Although I can make no use of more than an *eighth* of such of the trinkets, trimmings, etc., as remained unbroken in the five boxes which Mr. Rhees sent me, nevertheless I cannot but offer in gratitude and equal terms, my acknowledgements for the liberality which dictated the sending of them. Strictly a conventional people, as the Zunis are, even to the extreme of Chinese conservatism, one can introduce no articles among them—especially those for personal adornment—which have not received the sanction of years of their recognition and usage. They do not share with other nations inferior to us the love for showy articles which have not a *universally recognized* value. For their own use, therefore, like the Patagonians and other horse owning people of South America, you cannot get them to purchase and wear articles of gold, nor can you *give away* to them yarn or other stuffs of bright yellow, blue, purple, or like shades of colors.

It thus happens that I could dispose of the really valuable lot of millinery goods etc. which were sent me only by giving them away or trading them, to great disadvantage, to children for toys etc.

If Col. Stevenson visits the Rio Grande Pueblos during the season, where the same prejudices, while they once existed, have been largely overcome by long contact with the whites, he might be able to use them to great advantage in his general collecting. And if either you or he will let me know some point in his proposed route to which I could address them, I would take pleasure in carefully repacking and inscribing them to such destination.

Could you, however, succeed in procurring for me *Blue or green stones, hard or soft, imitation turquoise, beads, as well as the unpierced material; coral beads (large); all kinds of ocean shells, broken or whole, bivalvular or univalvular, red, pink, purple and white, and the oliva, pecten, pyrular {ficus} and plain bivalve varieties* being preferable, I could do *ten times* more with them than with the amount they would cost, because all these articles were once the *staple currency* of the Pueblo race, with fixed values which, even up to the present late day, have remained unchanged in at least four out of the twenty seven Pueblos—Moqui, Zuni, Acoma, and Picuris—also probably Silla [Zia].

Aniline dyes (crimson etc.), extremely red and black dye-stuffs, mineral or vegetable [and] cotton in the *raw, rough state* would enable me to make exchanges for rare and highly valued ancient sacred articles of costume, obtainable in no other way.[25]

I doubt not that some of my friends who have gone with you on Fish Commission service, as well as the children of various of your employees on the sea coast, would take pleasure in collecting such shells as I have mentioned, and thus, *without cost* to the Bureau, I could have at my command that which would do *more* than *money.* I experience no difficulty or expense in getting such things as come by mail delivered at my very door.

And the imitation turquoise and green and blue stones, while they might cost something, would be used, as I said before, at ten times their first cost in my field.

I am so thoroughly conversant with the tastes of this tribe, and with the prices of articles of native fabrication, that there are traders who would pay me large sums for the results of my knowledge for use among the Pueblos and Navajos, yet I can name nothing which would be more useful than that above mentioned.

Hoping that I have not burdened you too much with this and the last request concerning old books (about which I feel even more anxiety),

I remain, dear Professor,

Your Obedient Servant,
F H Cushing

P.S. I returned yesterday from an expedition to some most remarkable ruins, and the sacred caves so often spoken of.[26] So satisfactory were the results of my observations that I have determined to make the long and difficult trip to central Arizona above referred to.

Daily Journal

Wednesday, September 1st.

Cold, cloudless until toward evening. Somewhat windy. Zunis, family by family, leaving to gather wheat. All over valley may be seen at night campfires built to protect fields of corn and melon from coyotes.

Capitan and Jesus went out *tsupiak'ien* [yucca gathering] today.[27] Came in with blankets full of *Tsupia*—fruit of soap plant—mostly green. The ripe far superior to bananas.

Called at Dr. Ealy's about mid-day. Met Mr. Dennison, who came over to have a tooth pulled. Squaw wished th[e] same favor of me. . . .

Mr. Burges' wagons came in tonight.[28] My kerosene oil ($4.50) arrived as a grand addition to my resources for work.

Thursday, September 2nd.

Clear, cold, warm during mid-day. Flies almost intolerable, rendering painting beyond the question. Called two or three hours at Dr. Ealy's, as little girl is seriously ill—in his absence. Pulled D's tooth this morning. He and I got up nice dinner today—a great boon. Have felt rather indisposed during latter half of day. Proposed killing Navajo today—who has murdered Mexican and American recently. Indians talk great deal about it. Learned of serious divisi[on] between *Tchukwe mosone* [Chuppawa kiva leader] [and] *Pe-kwi-ne* today.[29]

Friday, September 3rd.

Clear, very cold in morning, but warm at midday.

Last night preparation for *Sa-te-tchi.*[30]

Saturday, September 4th.

I did not get up so soon as usual this morning, for I was very faint from coughing and pain in the lungs.

Clear, cold in morning, but very warm during latter part of day, and not cold tonight.

Called at Dr. Ealy's two or three times today. Ruthie better.[31] Burges went to Ojo Navajo today. Between flies and my sickness I am not able to do much. Brother finished my buckskin coat today except fringing. Beautiful fit.

Sunday, September 5th.

Somewhat cloudy and warm.

Moqui traders with women's dresses and fine dressed skins came in today. This evening I proved by them the correctness of Major Powell's observations.[32] The celebrated Rain Sign is correctly as follows:

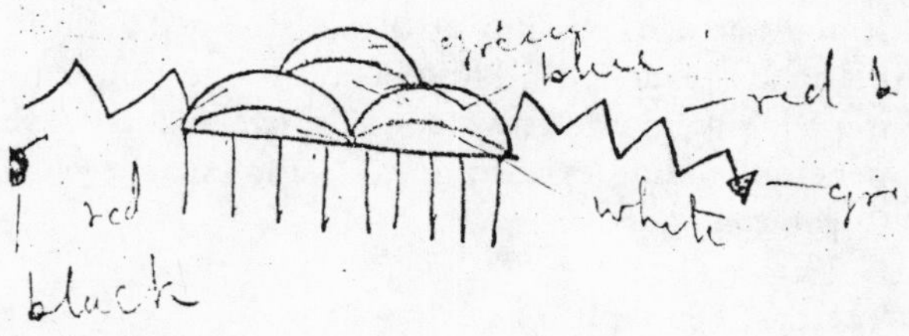

Fig. 7 Hopi Rain Symbol (Cushing sketch).

Oraibi and Taos are the last two resorts for the *Shi-wa-ni* when all other resources fail. Met today Mr. Martin and wife, who are stopping with Burges family.

Mailed to Baird, Gatewood, Reed.

Monday, September 6th.

Cloudy and quite warm.

Was wakened by Moquis this morning. Very much pleased with me and wish me to visit their country. Ate with me, then ceremoniously took leave. Came afterward (5) when my house was alone and amused themselves in looking everything over. Stole nothing. "Were afraid," was the sententious remark of my brother, who thinks no people but *Shi-wis* can be honest.

Sa-te-tchi-otiwa today. Two young men in red leggings, red blanket thrown over shoulders, buttons along parting of hair. Shield in one hand; spear, gun or bow and arrows in other. Dance made up of double walking step back and forth for about two rods, to accompaniment of song and drum. Singers three. Two young men followed each by girl decked with necklaces, earrings and Kachina dresses. Long edged *eha* [black kachina dress] and eagle plumes.

Tuesday, September 7th.

Quite warm and cloudy today. Fru and Ruthie better. Self worse with pain and itching sensation in lungs.

About noon, *Sa-te-tchi*. Very poorly represented. Only six singers and twelve or fourteen dancers. One Flag and party. Looked upon by most of the older people reproachfully, who said that as soon as the melons were ripe they would have it again, saint and all, as it was last year.

Last night, story of origin of lice told me, and ancient instructions given to young about smoking, sitting, eating, waiting, etc., which not being obeyed were punished by the falling of lice (*nu-we*) from the *Me-la-nai-e* constellation.[33]

Wednesday, September 8th.

Warm, cloudy and toward evening slight rains. Received mail this morning. Letter from Emma, George [Kennan?] (*two*), Prof. Baird (one), father (one)—*all* fraught with good. Got milk for and

Fig. 8 Kia-nis-ti-pi (Cushing sketch).

called two or three times at Dr. Ealy's. Also for Burges.

Began to discover remarkable facts regarding terminations of various parts of speech in Zuni.

Thursday, September 9th.

Moderate temperature, cloudy, and hard short shower in afternoon. Got milk again for Dr's people, which took down, then returned to writing.

Graham came last evening, Dr. this.

Friday, September 10th.

Cool, cloudy and rainy. Nearly all Zunis gone to gather wheat. Dr. Ealy came home last night.

Will go to see ruins at Navajo, get my mare, etc. Also visit, if possible, ruins of Rio Puerco. Have made some important discoveries today regarding "evolution and survival of fittest" in Zuni language, specially illustrated by numerals, descriptive and imitative words, as also interjections.[34]

Saturday, September 11th.

Cool, cloudy, somewhat rainy in direction of Zuni. Came today with Fru to Navajo Springs. Shall ride about tomorrow to examine ruins. Passed celebrated *Wa-nu-a-ti-na,* nearly 75 feet deep, and filled at bottom with drift-sand.[35] Very sacred to Indians. Ojo Nara, ranch of first order [?]: two corrals, four or five springs of soft water from which mud oozes at edges, giving Zuni name of *Ho-kwai-na-kwin* (mud exuding place, Mud Springs). Ruins all about.[36]

Sunday, September 12th.

Cool, cloudy, very rainy at evening toward Zuni.

Find ruins on all the hills about, some half-mile distant provided with tanks. Ojo Navajo in midst of [illegible word] valley plain sloping toward Rio Puerco. Sage brush and grass sole vegetation of importance. Cottonwoods and cedars very distant. Once fertile, probably at time inhabited. Picked up fine specimens of pottery. Met Mr. Davis, formerly of Washington. Splendid scholar, though much reduced. Great treat to talk with him.

Monday, September 13th.

Cloudy, cool and rainy.

Visited, with Messrs. Dennison, Davis, and Meekin, ruins a few furlongs from ranch to south west (see sk[etch] book).[37] Fragments of pottery abundant, amongst them spec[imen]s *showing Zuni designs.* From here went to low isolated large mesa, on Eastern ledge of which were some pictographs—notably *Ta-kia* [Frog], *Kia-nis-ti-pe* [Water-skate] and Man of *To-na* [Turkey] tribe.[38] Returned and started for Zuni. Examined on way *Wa-nu-a-ti-na,* seven miles east of Navajo about acre in extent, cañon tending into it from east; nearly hundred feet deep, bottom made up of tracked mud. Rapidly filling. Same described in Pac. R. R. Reports. Found fragments of ancient pottery on banks. On two or three hills far from water, abundant pot shards. Signs of other sinks about, however. Three near *Wa-nu-a-ti-na.* One yet filling. Probably served as water supply.

Over first divide on plain—very large, long straight arroyo, possibly artificial. Reached Zuni in night, desperately ill. Found Navajo chief and Capitan in my room. Governor, *Tatchu,* and Alcalde gone on trading expedition to Camp Apache with Coyoteros.[39]

Tuesday, September 14th.

Cloudy, cold, slightly rainy. Mr. Burges and family, Fru, and ladies of Dr. Ealy's household went to

Albuquerque. Invited me, but can't leave. Ill all day. Hlah'mon visited me. Preparing for expedition to caves.

Wednesday, September 15th.

Cloudy, cold and rainy. Mail came, and brought letter from Prof. Baird, anticipating my stay until spring. Also letter from Father.

K'esh-pa-he returned day before yesterday.[40] Brought my beads of turquoise from Lt. Domingo.

Ill all day. Had moccasins prepared for expedition to caves.

Saw first sweet corn brought in all ready cooked, strung up in bunches for winter.[41]

Thursday, September 16th.

Cold, cloudy, and during afternoon very hard rain. Moccasins not done, so go to visit He-shok-ta-kwe to north of Zuni Valley, in midst of peach orchards.[42] Two sets of ruins very perfectly preserved. Kia-u went with me, and K'esh-pa-he, also Da-poto and Maki.[43] Going up, passed Zuni ranches, attended as usual by old women. Took right trail, winding by difficult passage up the face of the mesa. Not far south from this trail on left side stands a phallic altar. It is a rock pillar with large head, somewhat like section given here, and about 20 feet in height. It has, six or eight feet above the base, a cavity corresponding to sexual part of a woman. Near base between it and trail is a large heap of pebbles which have been cast at fissure and, missing, have fallen down.[44]

A young man passing must always cast his rock at the fissure, and if it enter, breathe in from his hand, uttering the prayer—"*hom te ko ha ti a lu.*"

In the face of the great mesa mountain above the He-sho-ta-kwe N[orth] is a black hole, which Nia-k'i told me was A-tosh-li's—the Demon of the Children.[45] Visited a strange spring around the corner of this sheltered, in a natural cave-like recess many feet high and wide. This *Osh te-k'ia-na,* or House of Water.[46] The walls are covered with pictograph, ancient, and pintegraph [sic], modern. *Ya-to-kia-tatchu* (sun dance) *Kia-kwe-nai, Ya-a-na, Shu-lu-wit-se, Cha-la-k'o* (6), *Sai-a-ta-sha,* and *Kia-na-kwe* dance costumes are quite fancifully reproduced.[47] I sketch them later.

Fig. 9 Phallic Altar (Cushing sketch).

On my way home, saw at crest of each difficult ascent in foot path (2) the heaps of stones which are accumulated by the passers who sacrifice to gain strength. A stone is caught up, waved around head three times, then cast upon pile; spit, then pray "*Home-hla-vi-a-tu*" (strengthen me), and breathe in from hand.[48] Took K'i-a-u on behind horse and rode in at about sunset.

Friday, September 17th.

Morning cold and cloudy. Prepared to go to Navajo Springs. K'i-a-u remonstrated—everybody remonstrated—but friends all mournfully helped prepare. K'i-a-u prepared my food with tears in her eyes and murmurings about the *Kwa-an-pi-kwai-a-ni* (waywardness) of her *hani* (little brother). Jesus and K'esh-pa-he offered, if I would wait, to come with me. But I design a visit to sacred lake; hence don't want them.[49] Am in no small danger from Navajos, but am well armed. Reached Navajo at about eleven o'clock in evening. At one, Mr. P.O. Fazende and Le Noir, joint proprietor of Star Line Trans and Mail Co. from Albuquerque to Prescott, and Division Agent, respectively. Polite, refined and admirably educated men of Washington.

Saturday, September 18th.

Had delightful conversation with gentlemen who arrived last night. Fazende is a Frenchman of wealth, station and wide travel. He took intelligent interest in my work and suggested I should search records of Santa Fe and Spain for abundant material in ancient Pueblo history.[50] Gave me following references of gentlemen presumably able to help. Personal acquaintances of himself. Says *must* go to Spain. [in another hand: P. O. Fazende; Archbishop Lamy of Santa Fe; Rev. Father Trouchard, Vicar General, Santa Fe; Cardinal McCloskey, New York]

Rested animals and self and repaired [illegible word] and pouches. Visited little ruin in valley and collected pottery. Appear to have been outlying [illegible word] *ham-pous.*[51] Like the Zunis, taking advantage of waterholes.

FHC to Baird

Ruins in Rio Puerco
Apache County, Arizona
September 18, 1880

My dear Professor Baird:

I write this in reply to your very gratifying communication of the 2nd instant, in the hope of being able to send it via buckboard tomorrow or next day. I am now investigating ruins the extent, beauty and interest of which I have never yet seen equalled. Not only are they important on account of their state of preservation and the relics abounding in them, but also as the traditional homes of the *Hle-e-to-kwe,* or northern division of the great Pueblo race from which the *Shi-wis* claim to be descended. The remains of the Sun monument and the six communal *ki-wi-si,* or estufas of the *modern* Zunis are strong evidences of the reliableness of these Zuni traditions, although the ruins are in the heart of the Navajo country, and I have had to ride nearly a hundred miles to reach them.[52]

I leave for Zuni tomorrow or the day after. I had hoped to visit on these trips the sacred lakes and adjacent caves, but my horses are worn out and I must wait until some future time when they are fresh and when I can safely elude the watchfulness of my Indian friends.

With reference to the jay to which you referred, any number of nests and eggs could be obtained by the aid of my Zunis during the months of March and April.[53] In rambling over the ruins of the *Ta-a-kwe* [Corn People] south of here, I have myself secured the young of several species or varieties of the woodpecker, which is peculiarly abundant in this region. Two species of the eagle (which I do not know) are annually captured by the Zunis, for domestication, together with two or three species—one very large—of the hawk and falcon. I have also collected the names of five species of owl, as recognized by the Zunis, and doubt not more are to be found among them. In fact, the *ava fauna* of this immediate vicinity—on account of its comparatively frequent rains—is very rich in numbers and kind[s]; and were Titskematse to come out while I am here to interest the Indians in assisting him, I could warrant a very rich harvest both in skins and the nests of rare Southwestern species.[54] If supplied with facilities (such as alcohol etc.), he could, moreover, add vastly to the more important collections of the Institution, of reptiles and the fishes found in isolated springs among the mountains of the ancient Zuni region.

I value very highly the prospect of having him as an assistant either in the field or at Washington, as he is—like the Zunis—a constant and very important study to me.

I will write more regarding these points on my return, until which time,

Believe me as ever, Very Respectfully,
Your Humble Servant,
F H Cushing

Daily Journal

Sunday, September 19th.

Had to wait for horse today, but employed time in repairing still, and visiting other little ruins. [Many] ruin[s] are Zuni. Don't blame Zunis for believing theirs the favored land of the gods, as it rains there almost always if in country. It is a year since I came to Zuni, today.

Monday, September 20th.

Would have gone to sacred lake today but for rain which was pretty constant and severe.

Had to remain, and have planned for tomorrow an expedition to ruins twenty miles north.

Made five small collections of pot shards today.

Tuesday, September 21st.

Beautiful warm clear day. Started with Mr. Davis for ruin. Arrived at about two o'clock.

The ruins are approached by trail almost due

north from Navajo Springs, 20 miles. They are situated upon and nearly equally divided by an arroyo [through] which once flowed water, the form being a somewhat irregularly rounded parallelogram. At East and West corners the walls inside and out nearly perfect—12 and 17 feet respectively, showing in center of mid and upper story square doorways two feet by three (a). All walls more or less well preserved. Also walls very high and two rooms nearly perfect at mid-point between S.E. corner and arroyo (b). At arroyo, washed away. Again perfect on hill rising north from arroyo. Near N.E. corner, remains of covered way like those of Zuni (c). Beyond which, rounding corner, are 12 rooms more or less perfect and all of Northern wall well preserved. Descending West side Southward, walls much fallen. Crossing arroyo, defensive wall ran to join house wall of N.W. side, perfect only at commencement. The N. end, filled with debris of houses, and Eastern side evidencing seven or eight terraces. Two *Pahl toie* [*pahlto*: stick used in stick race; something indicating a boundary]. In either corner circular depression indicating *ki-wi-si* (2). At arroyo through E. wall, evidence of protected covered way (d), and to left of this wash reveals floors of six or eight rooms paved with thin slabs; in one, bake stone *inside* on hearth. Rafters in many places, all cut with stone axe. Brought away portions of these and *Katta* [stalks of wheat?].

Near arroyo on North and West sides, pillar of Sun still standing firmly planted in rock. Four other *ki-wi-sis* (estufas) in this end on either side and two or more *Tchu-kwe pahl-toie* [*tchu-kwe*: corn kernels; hence, boundary markers made of corn kernels?]. I name this Pueblo *He-sho-ta pahl-toi-e* (Deserted City of Refuge) in place of Zuni name yet to ascertain.[55] It has been remodeled since primitive building, the great northern entrance having been walled up with new stones (e) and all exterior windows or openings having been closed. The walls are exquisitely finished by pecking both outside and inside.

An estimate gives the total number of rooms as more than a thousand. Ground rooms were almost always used as storerooms; two rooms is the average Pueblo allowance for a family—giving a total of more than three hundred families. The average family in Zuni is *three,* giving approximately one thousand as the population. Public labor was communistic, as in Zuni, as shown by difference in quality of stone and workmanship on different divisions of exterior walls.

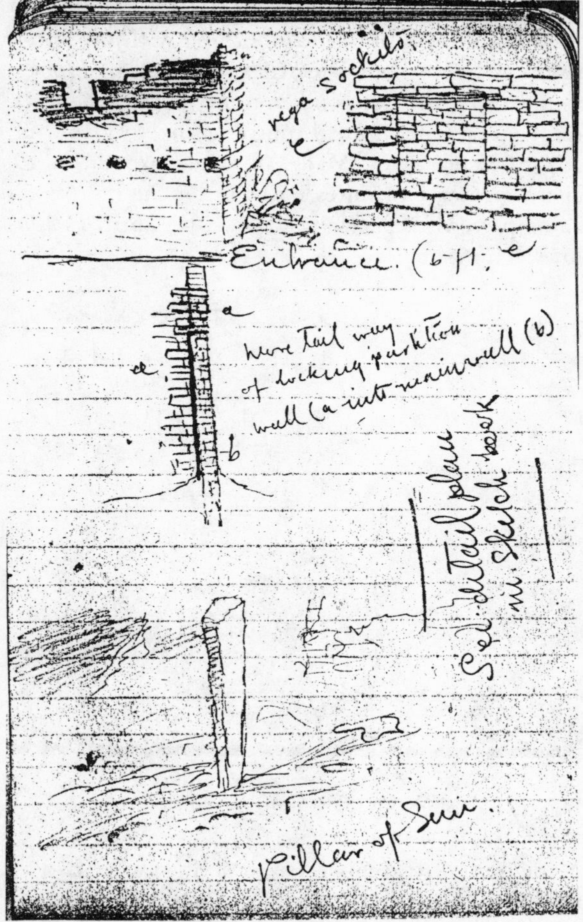

Fig. 10 Pueblo Ruin (Cushing sketch).

At Taylor Springs found another, though small, *He-sho-ta,* and two miles north of Bennett's ranch a large mound-like *He-sho-ta* with exterior, deep, *very* well preserved reservoir.[56]

Found mail awaiting me when reached ranch at 1 a.m.—from Emma, George, Father, brother, and Prof. Baird. Latter apprises me of Rusby's motions, Father's asks detailed letters of my life (possibly designs publishing).

Wednesday, September 23rd [*sic*].[57]

Was occupied until near morning with my letter reading; hence slept late. Clear and warm. Horses found to be in poor condition for journey; hence I resolved to remain until morning and to give over trip to sacred caves. Made, however, expedition to ancient ruins two miles north of ranch. Pottery of Zuni patterns, especially abundant. Form as follows:

Fig. 11 Pueblo Ruin (Cushing sketch).

Made pretty little collection by sunset, when had to stop.

Thursday, September 24th [*sic*].

Slightly cloudy, but fine day.

Started home at 11 a.m. with both my ponies, one packed, other rode. Reached second divide at sunset. Made camp to wait for moon up. Then came home at about three a.m. Found Brother (Governor) waiting. Greeted me cordially but in a shamed [*sic*] way.[58] Built me fire, got water, cooked me supper, and then we talked until nearly morning, relating mutual experiences. Read him some of my letters. Laughed at my chagrin at being ordered to remain longer in Zuni.

Friday, September 25th [*sic*].

Cloudy and toward evening sprinkled; at night fierce thunder storm.

In morning quite ill, but at evening feeling my best. Indians all greeting me like a prodigal son with "*Ke-esh-tosh-e-kia*." [How are you?] Very very lonely, although Indians more friendly than ever. Dined with Mr. Graham. Had long talk in evening with Dr. Ealy.

FHC to Baird

Zuni, September 25, 1880

My dear Professor Baird:

I have been unable to send my last letter, written while I was in Arizona last [week], but I shall take occasion to send both it and this by the next mail from here.

Rest assured that I shall do all in my power to interest Mr. Rusby in our behalf, as I wish as far as possible to have the Smithsonian *monopolize* the whole Pueblo business—archaeology and all.

I shall, moreover, throw him, should he come in my way, as much off of track as possible, because the collections which might be made from a cave in the domain of the Ancient Pueblos would be rendered almost utterly valueless scientifically by the disturbance of its superficial deposits.

Furthermore, in the light of being *traditionally* important, these caves, if meddled with by any not thoroughly conversant with methods of cave exploration, would be practically undeserving of a second examination. It has been just with a view of examining other cave deposits (of which I have vague information) in the region of Silver City that I have looked forward with so much interest and expectation to a visit to the latter places.[59]

Very Respectfully,

Your Humble Servant,
F. H. Cushing

Daily Journal

Saturday, September 26th [*sic*].

Last night it was very cold, so that I had a fire built, and now begins the new struggle against cold. Quite severe save at mid-day, but clear and sunny—one of the blessings of even cold weather here. Nothing of special importance. Swash [squash?] strings and festoons of chili appearing again. Wheat being brought in on burro back from farming pueblos.

Wagon of Americans (O'Donald and Murphy) came in today. Latter two gentlemen entertained during evening. Gave me insight into what is most striking in my Zuni life.

Sunday, September 27th [*sic*].

Very severely cold last night, so that Juan, with whom I talked for improvement in Spanish, said he found ice.

Today at evening, Governor, at my request, wrote a letter to Mr. Kennan which I translated literally and in full. These are grand aids to my Zuni.

Monday, September 28th [*sic*].

Most bitterly cold last night, so as to destroy squash, melons, etc., but as in matter of our rains, Zunis (religiously) say not a word against the misfortunes, counting it the will of *Ona-weti* [the one who started our roads, the Creator] and the *Na-na-kwe* [spirits of the ancestors]. ("It has gone to them, and in return, if we revile not, they will make us, who suffer most, the most abundant harvests and bring us prosperity in coming years.")

Had call from Captain Stoner (of San Juan) and Mr. Monroe, who a year since asked me to intercede for him with Mr. Stevenson. He remarked I was a little poor, much tanned, and must suffer dreadfully. He remembered the enthusiastic youth who came out through Santa Fe more than a year before.

Today Lai-iu-ai-tsai-lun-kia wrote a letter to my family. *Very* characteristic. He came this morning, humbly held out his arms (at the door, for me to embrace him). I forgave, and did; couldn't help it. He took me home to eat, brought me *the melon,* etc. etc.[60]

Boys today went to Ta-ai-iallone [Dowa Yalanne] and dug me *Tse-kwa-we* (*assi*) [see below] to dye deer skins for my coat and other new garments which the Governor will make for me to meet Enos in.

Tuesday, September 29th [*sic*].

Cold again last night, but a little warmer today. Cold again tonight, cloudless. Zunis want rain.

Worked translating letters. Hardest imaginable work. Never speak the terribly mixed up Zuni save as a Zuni, not as expressing so many American ideas in Zuni talk; hence it comes harder than I can say to furnish—not an exact equivalent but a literal equivalent.

The skins dyed today. About equal quantities of *T'si-kwa-we* (alder) [or birch-bark] and *assi-tse-kwa-we* (a red root). Salted bark boiled, forming red decoction; former chewed, then ground to pulp and applied with corn cob and abundant decoction on both sides (skin being laid down on blanket).

Wednesday, September 30th [*sic*].

Clear and comfortable. Mail came this morning. Letter from Father asking again for my permission for the publication of my Santa Fe letter. As it does not concern my researches, think will give it. Also record of Gilfredus Cusin of 1327, the remotest ancestor of whom we have any record.

Letter from Mr. Rhees stating that Davis' *Conquest of Mexico,* Bancroft's III vol., Sitgreave's *Report,* Smithsonian *Report* '69, French and Spanish Dictionaries [were sent]. Did not arrive; are probably in Wingate.

Na-wa-lush-ni-kieu today, one more left.[61]

Thursday, October 1st [*sic*].

Cloudy mild day. Brother, father, Tsa-wai are at work on my costume in preparation for my going to Wingate and getting my brother and works which Mr. Rhees's letter informed me had been sent.[62] Today *Shi-wa-na-kwe Hla to kia.*[63] Evening things almost done. I have written to Emma and Prof. Baird, also two oration letters, one by Governor to Kennan, my friend, and the other by "father" (cacique of the *Pitchikwe*) [*Bikchi:kwe*] to my parents, comforting them on my absence.

Friday, October 2nd [*sic*].

Cloudy and somewhat rainy. . . .

I am in Toia-kwe on my way to Wingate.[64] Brother, Father and Sha-tsi-tiwa are with me on way to Wingate. Fine ride over, full of jokes which are now sounding in my ears, distracting my attention. Tested the Zuni sight today. At great distances able to see very quickly any living thing but not as able to discern as closely as myself.

The Indians last night played a practical joke on me. When I asked where to sleep, one said, "How sky about?" I looked out of ladder hole and said "right all." "Then sleep on the roof, if you will." I said not a word, took my two blankets, my saddle for pillow, and passed the night painfully and in cold. At about eleven o'clock, laughing and chatting, they closed up house, built big fire and went to bed, laughing at remonstrating of women and saying "it will do him good." I said not a word next morning until one began to groan of having to sleep on one blanket and "make much cold." Then I said "You're pretty fellows. Sleep in the house and grumble when I slept outdoors with same amount of bed and never have said a word." Silenced them entirely. They respect my endurance highly.

Saturday, October 2nd [back on calendar time].

Bright day, few clouds and little rain in direction of Zuni. We all started for Wingate early, which place reached at about midday. Found every[one] glad(?) to see me, and an entirely new set of officers, with the exception of the Surgeon, who remains the same, Dr. Turney.

Was introduced to Mr. Sullivan, who has been sent out as agent for Moquis.[65] Pleasant elderly gentleman, and wished me to give him some information about Indian character and the religion of the Pueblos. I promised to give him a native prayer translated, for a society of which his wife is a secretary—in case he should promise in return to state it came from an officer of the Bureau of Ethnology, Smithsonian, etc. He would, willingly. First met among officers, Lieutenant Hovy, who invited me very courteously out to shooting practice, where he introduced me to others—Lieuts. Bishop, Buck, Ferney, and Capts. McArthur and [blank space]. These gentlemen treated me with the greatest politeness. In evening I called on General Bradley.[66] He is the kindest and most intelligent old officer I have known in these parts. Invited me to call at his house in morning.

Quartermaster sergeant called my attention to a letter from General Sherman entitling me to commissaries. It was received on the 19th of May. How much I have suffered for want of knowledge of this. I learned that Col. Stafford had designedly kept me from a knowledge of this.

Sunday, October 3rd.

Clear in morning, afternoon slight rain at Nutria. Took Indians up to see dress parade and hear music, then to General Bradley's. He treated them kindly, chatted with them, showed them Napoleon's picture and the signature of George Washington, also a Sioux [illegible word], and gave them tobacco (speeches in other part). Drawing some commissaries, I went about my business and prepared to go. Lt. L. brought me from Capt. McArthur [a] present of fifty rounds of amm[unition] of which I was greatly in need.

Monday, October 4th.

Cold but clear. Left Nutria for Zuni today, stopping to gather up a herd of horses of the Navajos, who pay no attention to rights and laws; hence I shot into their herd, and also with Governor gathered it together to take to Zuni, sixty-five in all, but a Navajo (Ashonnetsana) came in humbly and explained their presence; hence I pardoned and gave him back the horses with a good lot of sound instructions which he promised to follow. Reached home at about five o'clock, at the crossing of the river meeting the Burges wagon, minus the latter and Mrs. Ealy and her children, who remain ill in Albuquerque and Laguna. Mr. Davis of Washington accompanied.

Tuesday, October 5th.

Clear, wonderful day—nothing of special interest going on. Visited all the corners[?] today. Mrs. B[urgess] ill, and Miss H[ammaker] very downhearted. Dr. [Ealy] busy on his house. Indians related very especially how the captain at Wingate treated them.

Evening Mr. Lacombe's son and a peon came for former's mail.[67] Remained all night with me. Read some of the *Relacions* of Niça, Coronado, and Casteñada in "March to Seven Cities of Cibola" and Davis' *Conquest of New Mexico* to Indians who gave me traditions evidently bearing very closely on the subject. (See Colls. of Myths and Traditions.)[68]

Wednesday, October 6th.

Clear day and pleasant, toward noon very warm.

This morning I shot by order of the Governor and some Indians two hogs which were in corn. Had some high old councils and about one third of the Pueblo ready to eat me up for it. I told them to shut up and asked them, "What can you say for yourselves?["] *Muy seguro,* I am Boss here just now.[69] I told them they should listen to the calls of their Governor and then they would not get into difficulty, and if they didn't shut up I'd shoot half a dozen more. [One] bullet pierced through heart and other through middle of body still singing on its way.

At noon received letters from Father and Enos, former asking privilege of publishing and latter informing me of coming last week of my brother.[70] Also following books, for which I thank God:

Velazquez, Spanish Dictionary
Spiers and Surennes, French Dictionary
Native Races of Pac{ific} St{ate}s

FRAMENTARY DRAFT(S): FHC TO [GENERAL BRADLEY?]

nd

[The following, penciled on sheets of tablet paper, may be parts of a draft for a single letter, though there is no certainty of this. Indeed, the second could be simply a note Cushing wrote on paper at hand in the absence of one of his diary notebooks. The surmise that the intended recipient, if there was one, might have been General Bradley is based on the indication in the journal entry following that Cushing did write *a* letter to Bradley on the subject concerned in the note.]

Dear Sir:

I am able to give you perhaps fewer names of Indians who have bought or else sold whiskey than I promised, but I hope those which I furnish will be sufficient; and before long I can procure more.

The following may be implicitly relied upon:

Patricio Piño (Palowahtiwa)
Capitan Lochi (Lotchi)
[space for several more names]

The second mentioned, besides procurring spiritous liquors for himself, also saw a small party of Navajos purchase from Jesus Mason for one burro, some serapes and other Indian sundries, two small kegs of whiskey of which they drank freely and then placed behind the saddle on one of their burros, and soon after appearing at Nutria and shooting at random among the people there, though to the injury of no one. The latter circumstance I remember well, as it caused a council in which I participated. It occurred during the latter part of April or the early part of May.

. . .

On my way into Nutria on the night of my departure from Fort Wingate, I saw a band of Navajo horses on the grass lands bordering the fields of unthreshed wheat, for which reason the Zunis had to guard this highly prized harvest during the night.

On the following morning, as I started for Zuni, I observed just below the wheat fields a band of sixty horses and five colts, belonging to some Navajos whom I have constantly warned by message to keep away, by advice not only of Captain Bennett but also of the Pueblo Agent, Dr. Thomas.[71] The reply to my messages has been that they did not believe what a Zuni said, and if I or any other American officer sent a letter to them, they would tear it up and stamp it into the ground—that if Captain Bennett wished to see them, let him come there, and the same to Dr. Thomas, and what would they have to say for themselves if they came? I have constantly warned them, moreover, in council and out, that should they persist I would shoot their sheep, horses or oxen. I therefore, in the hope of luring the herd away, cut off by a pistol shot some of the tail of one of the horses in this band, as the Navajos had sent word I was a liar and had told the Zunis I was afraid to do anything with them or their stock.

Then I commanded the Governor to drive the herd into Zuni and [announced] that I thereby authorized the Zunis, after due warning, to shut up horses or sheep stock and demand payment for damage or trespass before releasing. The owner of the horses [came] up very humbly and apologized, promising, moreover, to take all his stock away and not trespass any more and to hold himself in readiness to go to Cañon Bonito whenever our officers or their agent should order the same.

Yesterday the chief of the Rio Puerco Navajos, who is a friend of mine, paid me a visit and confirmed my action as aiding his own express but unobeyed orders. I have today, however, had a very hot council with a young Navajo who came to see the Governor and other Zunis to prejudice them against me and to call [for the dismissal of] the Governor from office for carrying out the instructions of *Americans* and myself.

Reminiscence: Duties of a "Chief Councilor"

". . . The Zunis still maintain the matriarchal institutions which, perhaps, have developed more highly among them than with any existing people I know of on this continent. For example, unless I happen to be a priest and a member of an esoteric society, I cannot will my property in land, house and orchard to my own children, for they belong to my wife's brother, not to me. In such an organization my sister's children are my children or heirs, not my own, and what I have in real estate goes to my sister's children if she be dead. If she be alive, it goes to her for her children. A great many tremendous contests in councils and lawsuits are founded on the difficulties of adjusting those things, which have of late years arisen. Our people have come in and inoculated the Zunis with the ideas of our institutions. It makes a terrible lot of work for them. I have had to spend many a night without sleep in such councils."

"How are such councils composed?"

"The head chief is supreme judge, the second head chief is adjutant, so to speak—that is, the chief councilor. That was the position that was earliest given to me. Then come the assistant chiefs of the second political chief and the head chief, the chief councilor having no assistants. These assistants, six in all, range themselves on one side and another by choice of their understanding. They plead for and against the case, and I, as chief councilor, sit on the left side of the head chief, saying not a word excepting to keep order. You may call me in that part of my function a sergeant-at-arms. They have got to wrangling too much. I have a club and rap the floor, crying 'Be more moderate, my children. Moderate yourselves. Be more aged with dignity,' and the like.

These trials take place always at night. The evidence is first taken. Then the chief councilor turns to the head chief and recapitulates absolutely everything that has passed, though the trial may have been going on several hours. He must touch the case off rapidly and very briefly, and yet not miss a single significant part of it on either side. He must be so impartial in his representation to the head chief (who is supposed not to have heard a word) that all of those men hearing him can only say, 'Most true and correct,' and when he has finished, the head chief gives his decision, not on what he has heard from the witnesses but from the recapitulation made by the chief councilor. He turns to the chief councilor and gives his decision absolutely to him. 'You have told me so and so. It is therefore so and so.' Sometimes, if the question is about a blanket or something of that kind, and the evidence is exactly balanced, the man's sense of impartiality leads him to walk up to the blanket and cut it in two, thus to divide it as the evidence stands—equally—though it renders the blanket utterly worthless."[72]

—*San Francisco Examiner,* July 1, 1888

Daily Journal

Thursday, October 7th.

Slightly cloudy though not cold. All the forenoon engaged in council which ended in a council of war with a young Navajo, the son of Ke-ihl-to, an influential Navajo. The Navajos design to have a council with the Zunis about getting rid of me in a few days or weeks (for council, see copy of letter to General Bradley).

Ki-se-wa told me ever so much about ancient religious traditions today (see Coll. of Myths and Traditions).[73]

Mrs. Burges much worse. Took her down to Dr. E's to spend night with Miss Hammaker.

Friday, October 8th.

Cloudy and toward evening rainy. Night cold.

Was routed out this morning by a messenger from Capt. Kraemer of Camp Apache, who visits Zuni in search of two deserters who the Indians say passed here two days since in [the] night. He came to see me, as he had heard of me from time to time from Lt. Gatewood, and to invite me to visit him at Camp Apache. Also Mr. Warner [?] visited me and remained overnight.

Alcalde's boy died last night. Mrs. Burges some better. Been to see her three times.

Saturday, October 9th.

Cold and very windy in morning, very rainy at night.

Captain Kraemer departed this morning and Mr. Warner soon after. Toward evening Mr. Dubois and family came on a visit to Mrs. Burges.

Ki-a-u told me that the reason why Lache's [Lotchi's?] child was so badly burned and dangerously ill was because her father had failed to be [in]formed [?] of the coming of the *Sha'lak'o* on the day of the *Hai-to-sha* so as to make the sacred plumes as a *Shiwani*.

Monday, October 11.

Very rainy night and followed by rainy, cold, dark, muddy day. At about noon people were gathered together for a council at which I was employed. Substance: the establishment of obedience to officers and the initiation of the support of the school by work and furnishing of wood, forage, etc. Also scolding about witches, most ably replied to by Ki-wi-si [Kiasi], the *Pihlan shi-wa-ni Mosona.* He stood erect, his blanket around him, and said (see Speech).[74]

Speech on the whole well received, save regarding my punishment of those who stole from the Laguna stores by sentence of two days' work. The man principally guilty took it in good part and promised to work out his sentence, but the Governor wished to pay for his brother. Got angry and went with me down to Dr. Ealy's to tell the Agent that he would not submit, but on reaching latter place drew in.[75]

Mrs. Dubois and sister accompanied me down and back. Very muddy and somewhat rainy.

Tuesday, October 12th.

Experiment of working the Indians began by ordering five off for grass, three for wood, and ten for straw. Latter all went—one with wagon and oxen.

Governor and Alcalde very blue and much engaged in their new work. Not very confident of success and always looking to me for backing.[76]

Wednesday, October 13th.

Clear warmish day. Experiment of getting people out to work on adobes. Men mixed mud and women made adobes.

Three hundred and thirty made. Not very successful. I shall take the matter actively in hand tomorrow.

Mail brought in at two o'clock—a letter from Father and two from Enos, who has reached Albuquerque. Wishes me to come out to Ojo Gallo, but will get my letter and come on to Wingate, I guess Friday.

Thursday, October 14th.

Clear good day. Took matter of aiding officers this morning into hand. Well pronounced success. Had nearly fifty men and many women at work. Did well, though had to watch them and stop some from running back home. *All do as I say.*

Wish to go to Wingate tomorrow, but Dr. Thomas has been ill for two past days and wishes before leaving to have a council at which he would like to employ me. May send Lai-iu-ma.

Friday, October 15th.

Clear cold day. Went out man-hunting early, got the Indians at work on adobes at about noon. Made some six hundred and fifty.

Sunday, October 17th.

Clear cold day. Council nearly all day in my room. At about two o'clock, Governor called out, "Your brother has come." I looked up, saw Enos through the window and rushed through the back door to meet him, tripped [on] a riata which a horse was tied with, came near getting my breath knocked out, and ran around to receive the poor boy.

Thursday, October 21st.

Clear, warm day. Many adobes made. Tchushi refused and is to be punished as soon as the handcuffs come.[77] Plume making and *u-pu-i-ki-en* still going on in preparation for the *Pū-ān-ī-ki-en* ceremonies.[78] Was told the ceremonies accompanying the *pū-ān-ī-ki-en* of the *Sho-a-kwe* [Arrow-point people]. Sitting naked in fireless room eight days, body painted with ashes, hand bound tight with willow sprig. Ended by the rubbing of the sharp edge of an arrow point against the forehead until blood appears, then the laying of the latter down and exclaiming of the prayer: "*Si a tatchu; lihl hom sho oti, hom ton an ko hatiatu.*"[79]

Crowd at my house last night to talk—among other things of the approaching *Sha'lak'o* ceremonies. 36 days left.

Monday, October 25th

Slightly cloudy though warm day. Had some Indians draw adobes today. Had to take the *Pihlan Shiwani mosona* an[d] son by force and violence, but succeeded.[80]

Was forbidden in evening to go into the sacred ceremonies of *Pu-an-i-ki-en*. Told Indians they would *have* to let me go in. If they attempted to hinder me by force, by force I should enter. At eleven o'clock, therefore, I went, taking my lamp. Was very well received, as the old priests had concluded to make the best of me.

So I presented candles, tobacco, etc. to the council.

Has lasted four days. *Papa* [elder brother] high priest to come on eighth. Tonight *Pu-an-i-ki-en*. Begun by entrance of officers and deposit, through *Awen Tatchu,* of *mi-ile* and prayer.[81] Then singing. Then two young men dance over pinch of ashes, dip imaginary influence from it with eagle wing feathers, and shout: ——— [sentence unfinished]

Road [of sacred meal] made from door to altar. Four, all small save one young woman, crouched between so many of fi——— [remaining pages missing]

Daily Journal

November 12th [1880]

mu-luk-ta-kia oti-wa [*Muluktakya* dance].

Clear but very cold. Dancing commenced about ten. *Koyemoshis* came out and performed the ceremony of shooting the effigies of deer, elk and antelope, made of dough. Afterward distributed to spectators. Dance round first—followed by shooting.[82]

Ceremony of *iak-to-hani* [whipping] the children who had been *pu-an-i-kia*. Came into court, the *Sai-a-hle-an* (four) (see sketch), then line of *Koyemoshis,* along a line of sand.

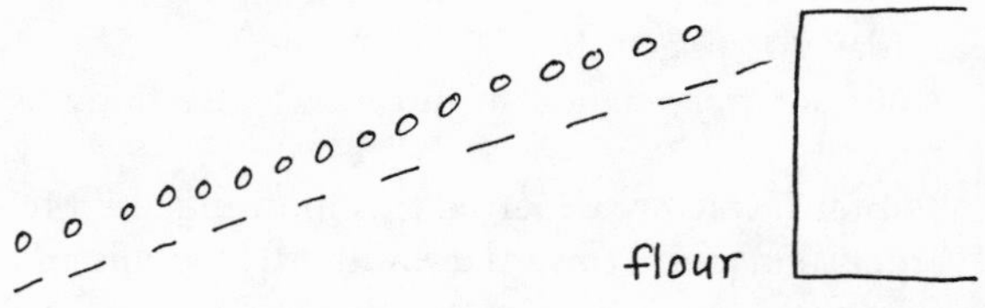

flour

Then Lotchi with his boy on his back, covered with skins etc., passed along line and each *Ko-ye-mo-shi* hit him four times. Then passed into the estufa, where were assembled the caciques, the *Na-hla-shi,* the four *Sai-a-hle-an-a-kwe.*[83]

November 14th, Sunday [1880]

Cold and clear. Nothing ceremonial going on, but at night preparations for *Tcha-kwe-na* [Chakwena Kachina Dance].

November 15th, Monday [1880]

Cold but beautiful. *Tcha-kwe-na. Wo-tatchu* of *Pihlan shi-wa-ni mo-sone* for *Hla-ta-kan* [grandfather of the Bow Priests, head man of the hunt].

Burges and Branford came, in night.

FHC to Powell

Zuni, November 21, 1880

Dear Sir:

Two weeks since, I received from Dr. B.M. Thomas, Agent of the Pueblo Indians, a letter stating that he had written you to obtain permission for my taking the census of the Tribe of Zuni and asking whether, in case such permission were granted, I would be willing to undertake the task or would consider the asking of it too great a liberty. I immediately replied that while this would involve a vast amount of labor and the possibility of failure, I would gladly attempt it if agreeable to my superiors, not only on account of our mutually friendly relations but also as a work indispensable to my line of research.

During the summer, I [secured], with the aid of the officers of the Pueblo, the census in grains of corn; but the feeling of resentment which for superstitious reasons this proceeding created prevented me from securing either full or current results, and greatly prejudiced the priests and secret orders of the Pueblo against me as well.

Although the overcoming of this prejudice required only the exercise of a little tact, yet I have heretofore deemed it advisable not to allude to it a second time. When, however, I received by last mail, not only from Dr. Thomas but from the Department of Interior as well, authority as an officer and Enumerator to carry out this work, I at once called a council of the priests, caciques and principals of the Pueblo, gaining through my personal influence their good will and through my new-born authority their most substantial cooperation.

The task is an immense one, which absorbs nearly my whole time for the present; but it has so many features of importance to our work, especially in the sociologic line, that I have grown very enthusiastic in it and would defer it for nothing save direct orders to the contrary either from yourself or Professor Baird.

I am requested to turn finished results in by the first of December, a thing which I scarcely hope to accomplish; yet in my attempt to do so I beg your generous patience until I can complete the more extended communication which, promised in my last, is only now well commenced.[84]

Could you spare for my present urgent use a work which I have once or twice unsuccessfully sent for: Morgan's more recent and popular edition of *Systems?*

Very Respectfully,
Your Obedient Servant,
Frank H. Cushing

Major J. W. Powell
Charge of Bureau of Ethnology
etc. etc.

DAILY JOURNAL

November 25th.

Cha-la-ko a-we-kia [Shalak'o came]. Cold, hence at evening the *Ka-ka* did not all come out, but in evening (24th) danced through the consecrated houses. At our house today was the ceremony of the Baptism of children of the *Ta-a-kwe* [Corn clan], and the acknowledgement of a young man as the *Tikia mosona.*[85] *Ta-a-kwe* and *Tona-she-kwe* [Badger clan] taking part.

November 26th.

Rather cold. *Kâ'-kâ a-we-kia* [Kachinas came]. Only *He-ma-shi-kwe* [performers of Jemez Dance]; rest remained. *Koyemoshi itinikia* [Mud-heads settled down].

At night *Kâ'-kâ tem-la* [all of the kachinas] and some of the Eastern Pueblo dancers, among them the *Ha-kiu-kwe* [people of Acoma]. *Koyemoshi* danced about the tops of the houses, calling the *Ka-ka* out. Then came down from Estufa the boy who was beaten at bottom of ladder, when four *Koyemoshis* hit him same number of times. Then on back of Lotchi, behind *Mu-luk-ta-kia,* hit the same way. Then entered and had the final ceremony of hitting by the *Sai-a-hle-an.* This is very severe on the children.

Then suddenly *He-he-a* came on the scene.[86]

Fig. 13 He-He-a (Cushing sketch).

Then a dance occurred, after which the *Sai-a-hle-an-a-kwe* came out, hitting whomsoever they came across. The hitting was by no means gentle. This over, dance again, women bringing food to the *A-shi-wa-ni* in the Dance Court estufa.

November 27th [1880]

Today *Kâ'-kâ a-we-ki-a.* Very fine day. *Mu-luk-ta-kia, He-ma-shi-kwe, Kia-kwe-na, Wo-tem-hla, Ka-k'ok-shi.*[87] At night dance of *Ko-ye-mo-shis* and the lifting of the gourd with the eagle quills.[88]

Fig. 14 Quills and Gourd (Cushing sketch).

A-hla-shi.[89] In event of failure, goes back to respective owners. *Awen tatchu* contributed the buckskin.

In this case not guessed, as hoped, to be a cedar leaf.[90]

Clear cold but very pleasant day. At night *Kâ'-kâs. Wotem-hla Tcha-kwe-na, Tem-tem-shi, Ka-k'ok-shi, Mu-luk-ta-kia, Tchi-tchil-tchi, Apa-tchu awen,* etc.[91]

Fig. 15 Male Dancer (Cushing sketch).

November 28th [1880]

Beautiful day. Dance of the *Ko-ye-mo-shis.* The guess. Four pairs, each guess four times for the heap contributed to by each of the *Ko-ye-mo-shis* and

FHC to Baird

Zuni, November 28, 1880

My dear Professor Baird:

I am in receipt of your letter and enclosure re-

Fig. 16 Female Dancer (Cushing sketch).

Fig. 17 Captain of Navajo Dance (Cushing sketch).

garding the Census of Zuni, and I write to express once more my ability and entire willingness to undertake the enumeration. . . . I have, with some schedules furnished me by Dr. Thomas, already begun and have progressed so far with it as to regard it indispensable to the results of my researches with this tribe. . . .

I am a good deal gratified to learn in a note dated Nov. 14th that you are corresponding with Captain Pratt about sending Tits-ke-matse to Zuni.[92] I remain very willing and extremely desirous of having him.

I have formed many plans relative to the exploration of a large ruin-covered territory down in Arizona, including not only Pueblo and cliff remains but also a number of caves, which, without Tits-kematse, would hardly be feasible. Then, in addition, he would be able to secure specimens for specific determination of the large class of birds sacred to the Zunis, a matter which would aid to clear some parts of a very obscure and complicated mythology.

Adducing my work on the census and the necessity of attention to the great *Kâ'-kâ* (a ceremonial of eight days, now going on) as excuse for the brevity of this letter, I remain, dear Professor,

Your Very Humble Servant,
F H Cushing

PILLING TO FHC

November 30, 1880

My dear Sir:

Yours of the 21st to Major Powell, who is in California, is just rec'd. I take pleasure in sending you by mail today a copy of Morgan's *Ancient Society* asked for by you. It belongs to Maj. Powell and I may be taking a liberty in sending it, but the difficulties experienced by you are sufficient, I think, to justify it.

I wrote Prof. Baird a day or two ago requesting him to ask you to make us a picture of a Zuni room—and such articles *of their own manufacture* lying around as your fancy may suggest—the picture to be 7 × 9 and to accompany a work by Morgan on House and House-life of the N. A. Indians.[93] I did this because I did not feel at liberty to ask it direct from the office.

I am sure Major Powell will be glad to hear on his return of the lively way in which you have taken hold of the Census matter. I am

Truly Yours,
James C. Pilling
Chief Clerk

FHC TO BAIRD

Zuni, Dec. 19, 1880

My dear Professor Baird:

I have to thank you, very truly, for the grand additions you have recently made to my means for conducting researches and making collections among the Zuni. Already, they have proved of advantage in both connections, without the material diminution of any kind. They especially advance my influence, as they give me the reputation and standing of a holder of sacred property. Although some of the shells will not prove as useful as others, which are almost invaluable, yet *all* will be useful, and together with the dyes, they will be such important acquisitions to me that I cannot but express over and over my gratitude for them.

The two great ceremonials of the New Sun, now over for the second time during my residence in Zuni,[94] I shall have more leisure not only for communicating with you and writing little articles for publication as you may see fit but also for working up the archaeology of this region, which has such an interesting connection with the Zuni history and traditions.

I therefore, after so many long delays, find my opportunity for visiting the several caves of which I have so repeatedly spoken to you and which, from additional information I received only last week, bid fair to surpass in every respect the Metcalf deposits.

I shall of course take pleasure in completing at the earliest moment the sketch asked for in Mr. Pillings' letter to you, although from my lack of artistic skill I fear it must prove far from attractive. It shall, however, be ethnologically correct and representative.

I am minded by this of the fact that a communication of many pages, including the cream of my researches into the etymology of the Zuni language as well as involving many days' labor, which I addressed to yourself and Major Powell (as also valuable mail matter both before and subsequently), has been lost between this place and Fort Wingate. As there is no post office between the latter place and this, the mail is necessarily sent both ways open; hence, as I design to make many communications of the kind above referred to, which should they be lost might fall into other than proper hands, may I be so bold as to ask if you will see whether or not a mail bag with a special lock and two keys—one to be entrusted to me, the other to the Post Master at Fort Wingate—might be procurred from the Department for use during the remainder of my stay here?

Have you learned anything more regarding Tits-ke-matse, whether or not he will be sent to join me? I shall welcome his coming as a great aid to my operations, and I do not think, situated as I am and accustomed to Indian ways, any one could be named who would be of such practical service as himself.

Pardon the paper which I use; my stationary has been exhausted more than a week since.

On my return I will immediately communicate the results of my reconnaisance, and until then

Believe me, though in haste,

Very Respectfully,
Your Obedient Servant,
F. H. Cushing

DRAFT: FHC TO L. W. LEDYARD[95]

[Zuni, December 1880]

My dear Friend, Mr. Ledyard:

It has been many months since I left Washington to enter into researches among the Pueblo Indians of Zuni and to investigate the archaeology both of traditional and prehistoric connections in this paradise of ethnography, the great Southwest. I am sure—my silence and all not excepted from consideration—that it is needless to explain to you that I have never seen a single realization of the hopes we used so happily to discuss together, never found a beautiful remnant of some primitive people, never looked upon a single one of the thousands of grand monuments which these sandy deserts have revealed, but I have thought of the kind—more than kind—*dear* friend who stooped to rescue me from obscurity; who made himself the companion of my friendless rambles, [despite] the disdain, mildly spoken but apparent, of those in whose society he moved who scorned a country boy; whose kindness and understanding; whose generosity and warmth of friendship fired me with an enthusiasm which has never in long intervening years died away; and who by all this and more laid upon my soul a debt of gratitude which though unspoken has proved one of the strong motives of my life. . . .

For many months my suffering and loneliness were dreadful. I neither understood the Spanish language universally spoken by the whites here, nor the native Indian. My means were scant, my position—as a pryer into secret and forbidden rites—precarious. The Indians were all my masters, and with the kindest intentions—those of making me a member of their tribe—they prove[d] tyrannical. I was forced to adopt their mode of dress and manner of living, to live with them, and to share their food in common. By policy and patience I won, in long months, their confidence, respect and esteem, gained authority over them, and with the acquisition of their language, became their chief councilor, so that at present the table is turned and I am *their master.*

Perhaps no young man of my age ever had such grand opportunities, such chances for distinguishing himself as are now in my grasp. Success beyond my most sanguine dreams must crown my labors if continued and completed. Nothing but industry and health remain to insure this; yet of the latter I am sadly doubtful, and of the former I am in fear, for my health, by the absolute change in my mode of life and from my terrible and repeated exposures, has suffered—I dare not hope to the contrary—permanently.

But I have many rewards. I have gained knowledge which has [eluded] my predecessors, and by the acquisition of the native standing among the natives, and of their language, I have [opened] the road to ever richer harvests.

I wish that without intruding upon your time I might give you more facts regarding the strange people of whom I am today considered one, of my yet stranger life and adventures among them, but I hope at some future time, either in conversation or by letter to allude more fully to these things.

I have found the most valuable evidence of the existence of phallic worship among at least one class of American aborigines, and I await only to get better sketches before communicating further with you on this, a subject which has for years claimed your enthusiastic attention.

I am on the eve of departure for the exploration of some very interesting caves in Arizona, in which I hope to discover the rarest treasures of ancient art and glean facts rich in the archaeologic revelations which they shall make. On my return, I hope to be able not only to write you further but also to make some curious additions to your little exhibit. [end of draft]

4. *January–June 1881*

Explorations, New Friends

During [the last week of December and the first two weeks of] January, I made a trip with burros . . . along the line of ruins marking the sites of the pueblos referred to in the Zuni ritualistic recitals—as far west as the valley of the Colorado Chiquito [Little Colorado River].[1] I not only discovered a grand series of monuments but also verified the correctness of the recitals by a study of the mythologic pictographs with which many of them (and the surrounding rocks) were covered. South some fifteen miles from the town of San Juan, or Bardito [now called St. Johns], I found in the same valley a remarkable line of conical hills containing craters which, from the mineralogical character of their deposits, I regarded as extinct geysers, and the caverns of which had been used by the ancestors of the Zunis as sacrificial depositories. In these I had the good fortune to discover numerous well-preserved [sacred objects]. . . . Returning to Zuni, I proceeded at once to Fort Wingate with portions of my collections, which I there catalogued and prepared for shipment.

—Report to Powell, July 6, 1882 (Southwest Museum HC 37)

Most notable among the important discoveries made by Cushing on this trip were the sacred lake of Kolhu/wala:wa, believed by the Zunis to be the dwelling place of their ancestors and kachina gods, and the adjacent cave shrines to which pilgrimage is made every four years at the summer solstice to make votive offerings. As was the case in his explorations earlier in the fall and in the previous December, Cushing was both guided by and attempting to confirm stories told and hints dropped by his friends in the pueblo—for instance, what he had learned at the summer solstice about "the lake where live 'our others' and whither go our dead" (MAZ 49, Zuni 142). Also, as on his earlier trips, he was pursuing his explorations in secret and against the expressed wishes and taboos of the Zunis, violating in this instance the most sacred of all their holy places. "For centuries under Spanish and Mexican rule," as E. Richard Hart points out, "the Zunis had peacefully used their shrines at Kolhu/wala:wa, unmolested and freely. But within four years of the time when the first U. S. representative [i.e., Cushing] learned of the shrines, they had been looted twice by government employees and a third time by someone out to make a profit by selling Zuni religious relics."[2] Cushing, the discoverer, was the first of these looters.

He, however (according to a later recollection), had the distinction of being caught at his illicit collecting activities and brought to account—thus being provided with an additional field experience as well as an unexpected bonanza of information about his finds. Compelled to lay out his "dear-bought relics" in a council chamber and "undergo a trial as for sorcery by the tribunal of the entire secret priesthood of the tribe," he was saved by the reverence he evinced for the sacred objects (and by the evident tolerance of the gods themselves, who had let him escape alive from the shrines). He "learned, without the necessity of asking a single question, what each object had signified 'in the days of creation.'" Cushing's later account of this expedition, "Extract from Catalogue of Prehistoric Zuni and Cave Remains," may be found among the Appendices of this volume.

"During the succeeding spring," according to the Second Annual Report of the Bureau of Ethnology, *Cushing "again set out for the cave country, with one soldier and a citizen, re-exploring not only the caverns before visited but also other important grottoes on the Rio Concho, and the caves still used as sacrificial depositories by the Zunis, near La Laguna del Colorado Chiquito, north of San Juan. The collections, the greater portions of which were cached, aggregated over two thousand specimens" (p. xxvii).[3]*

Meanwhile, another sort of development was also occurring, one whose importance for Cushing would be reflected

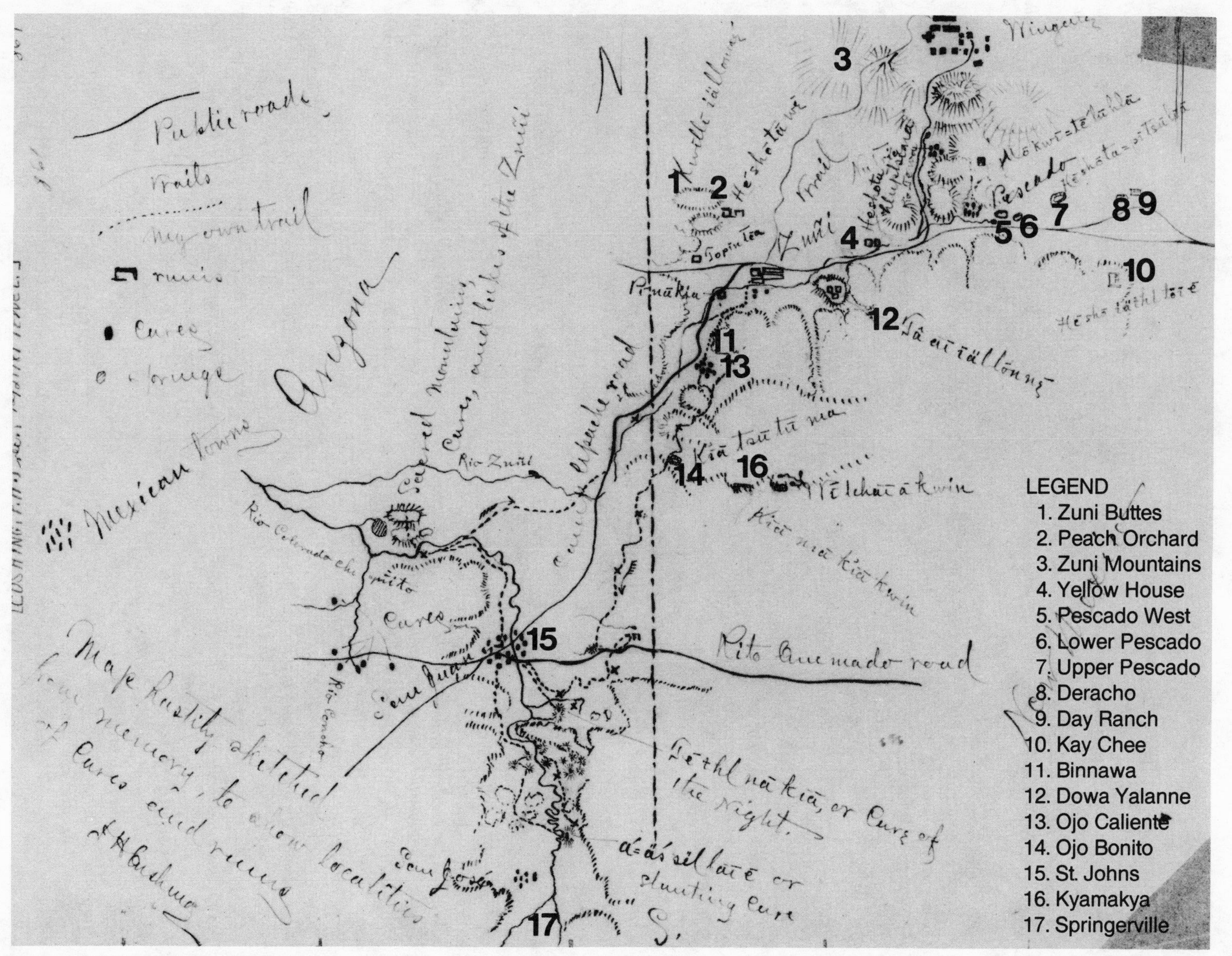
LEGEND
1. Zuni Buttes
2. Peach Orchard
3. Zuni Mountains
4. Yellow House
5. Pescado West
6. Lower Pescado
7. Upper Pescado
8. Deracho
9. Day Ranch
10. Kay Chee
11. Binnawa
12. Dowa Yalanne
13. Ojo Caliente
14. Ojo Bonito
15. St. Johns
16. Kyamakya
17. Springerville
Public road
Trails
My own trail
ruins
Caves
Springs
Arizona
Mexican towns
Rio Zuñi
Rio Concho
Pescado
Zuñi
Pinakia
Rito Quemado road

Cushing's Map.

in his correspondence. He was beginning to gather a circle of friends with ethnological interests like his own. The first two of these were army officers he met at Fort Wingate: Washington Matthews (the post surgeon) and Lieut. John Gregory Bourke, both of whom would also be prominent figures in early Southwest anthropology. Matthews, who was interested in studying the Navajos, had gotten the appointment to Wingate in late 1880 with that aim in mind.[4] *He and Cushing met early in 1881 and quickly became friends. Bourke, whose interest in Indians and their customs had developed in the course of more than a decade's service in campaigns against them as aide de campe to General George Crook, met both Matthews and Cushing while visiting Wingate in the spring of 1881—a visit which in fact coincided with that of the Boston journalist Sylvester Baxter and the young artist, Willard Metcalf, who was traveling with him.*

Recorded by both Baxter and Bourke, this propitious encounter caught each of the three eager ethnologists at a point of particularly high anticipation. Matthews was just getting started in the Navajo studies which would occupy him through most of the next quarter century and would lead to his classic accounts and translations of the great Mountain Chant and Night Chant ceremonies. Bourke, at the beginning of his career in anthropology, was on a tour of the Southwest which would take him to Zuni, to the Hopi villages (where he would be "the first white man to carefully note" the celebrated Snake Dance), and to other Pueblo as well as Apache and Navajo communities.[5] *Cushing himself, just in from his second trip to the cave country in eastern Arizona and packing off his finds to Washington, was on the point of departing again, this time on the journey to Havasupai. Between their anticipations and the projects they were already engaged in (especially Cushing's experiment as live-in anthropologist among the Zunis), there was much to discuss and much to interest the journalistic visitors from the East.*

This cordial meeting was of special significance for Cushing, since it secured, along with Matthews, an important new ally in the field (Bourke), a first-rate interpreter and supporter in the national press (Baxter, whose stories in the Boston Herald *and* Harper's Magazine *made him, and Zuni, famous),*[6] *and a gifted illustrator (Metcalf, who did drawings for "My Adventures in Zuni" as well as for the Baxter pieces). Among all five men, what resulted was a personal and professional fellowship which lasted the rest of their lives. With respect in particular to the anthropologists in the group (to whose number the names of Adolph Bandelier, Alexander Stephen, and others would later be added), what is perhaps most notable in the exchanges that followed—given the usual tendency to view Cushing in the light of his singularity—are the evidences they show of mutual assistance and, indeed, mutual stimulation. For all the competitiveness abroad, there was, among these men at least, a genuine sense of community.*

Samples of the correspondence between Cushing and these friends will be found scattered through the remaining pages of this book. Both Bourke's and Baxter's accounts of the Fort Wingate meeting are included in the following section—the latter abridged to a few fragments chosen to convey the more salient points and at least a suggestion of the romantically picturesque light in which the scene, the hero, and the exotic subjects of his investigation are cast. In a sense, it could be said that Baxter set the tone for Cushing's own ventures into popular writing, and thus may be partially responsible for the image, at once attractive and suspect, perpetuated in such works as "My Adventures in Zuni."

FHC to Baird and Powell[7]

Zuni, January 13, 1881.

My dear Professor Baird, and Major Powell:

I just return from the exploration trip referred to in a former letter, after an absence of twenty days, and a journey, with burros, of more than two hundred miles. . . .

The Indians, who, from superstitious reasons and the wish to have me constantly with them, opposed my going, failed to bring in my ponies; hence I was compelled to set out only with burros and a small camping outfit. A friend, Mr. Chas. A. Kirchner, temporarily stopping in the Pueblo on his way East, kindly volunteered to join me, and at about noon on the 19th of December, we started via the Ojo Caliente road and *Kia-tsu-tu-ma* trail, for the land of the caves in Arizona.[8]

Accompanying other plans, you will find a map on which my wanderings, stopping-places, etc., are indicated, giving you a fair idea of the Geography of the country through which I passed and showing the relative positions of caves, monuments, ancient Pueblos, etc., which I visited.[9]

I will not trouble you with an itinerary, although it might serve to make the nature of my work more clear to you. I will remark simply that, opposed by the difficulties of having a companion unused to the hardships of the rough-and-ready life and fare of the Indians, to which I have become thoroughly inured; of being compelled to walk nearly every mile of the way; by snow storms and sleet, accompanied by cold winds and the severest weather at night, I reached, after six days wanderings, the first of the ancient caves of which the Zunis had informed me, and the related Pueblo ruins of the *Tâ'-a-kwē* [Corn People], of which *Punatuma* forms the chief.[10]

The location of this most remarkable pit or cave, is, as you see by reference to the outline map accompanying, some six miles South East of Bardito or San Juan [St. Johns], in the basin of the Colorado Chiquito.[11] Here is encountered a series of peculiar round hills or mountains, composed, if I mistake not, of calcareous tufa, inter-stratified with thin bands of gypsum and indicating, at no distant Geologic period, the occurrence in this region of hot volcanic springs or possibly even geysers. These peaks are often several hundred feet in height, solitary or double, round, concentrically stratified, and especially characterized by the occurrence at their apexes of a crater-like opening which, when unfilled with debris or talus, varies from fifty to three hundred feet in vertical depth, by an average diameter of from thirty to one hundred feet, the North and South axis usually exceeding the East and West by about one-third, although sometimes varying slightly to conform with the direction of the river valley. The edges of these craters are invariably lower by from three to eight feet on the Eastern than on the Western side.

By uniting my pack-rope with a riata and tying both to the roots of a cedar tree, I managed, with the assistance, yet against the strenuous upbraidings of my companion, to descend to the floor of the pit or crater. My perilous descent and many days of hardship and search were more than rewarded, at once, by the discovery of well preserved plumesticks (many *in situ*) and other sacrificial paraphernalia of the *Ī-kwī-nā-k'īā* ceremonial which is annually performed during the month of December, by a religious community of the Zunis known as the *Teth*-na-kia-a-she-wa'-ni (Priests of the Night).[12]

I must take the liberty of remarking that it accidentally happened [that] on the precise day during which this very interesting ceremonial was being observed at Zuni, I entered the crater, and at just the time when the two Priests go forth to make deposits in an *Osh-te* (rock shelter), near the Pueblo of Zuni, I was laboring up a rope, bearing the spoils from the repeated similar sacrifices of centuries ago.

The importance of this discovery—to me—I cannot over-estimate. It proves absolutely and completely not only the general correctness of the Zuni migratory traditions, but also an opinion which I have long held as probable, of their close or direct connection, in the far past, with the builders of the Ancient Pueblos throughout Arizona and New Mexico.[13]

Unfortunately for science, the two principal sacrificial accumulations had been burned, either by Mexican herders or by Navajos; yet enough relics remained to furnish from three to four hundred plumesticks, etc., several of which had still attached to them remains of plumes, and miniature bows, arrows, and war-clubs of the younger brother God of War, Ahai-iu-ta. Although I secured from the surface, including the plume-sticks, more than two large coffee-sacks full of relics for the most part still so perfect that their specific sacred characters were afterward at once recognizable by the Zunis, yet enough remains which careful digging might reveal, to fill a small wagon. This includes stone-age carvings, painted wooden weapons, and sacred paraphernalia, paint-pots, etc., etc.

Among my finest finds at this cave, though by no means the most important scientifically, were the figure of the War-God above mentioned, A'hai-iu-ta, and his plume-sticks,[14] the former of which I send home by the hands of Mr. Kirchner, who bears letters of introduction to you. This is the form used not at the annual New Sun or New Year ceremonials, of which I have so often spoken, but that which was set up at the time following some signal victory gained by the people of the cave over some inimical band.

These remains, almost without exception in themselves of great value as Museum specimens, have that value vastly heightened by their direct connection not only with the traditions but also with the customs and ceremonies of the Zuni of the present time.

Between twenty and thirty miles South and West from the cave just described, I found two others of the same physical character. The smaller was situated only three or four rods East from, and eight or ten feet above the level of, the Colorado Chiquito. It was of about the same size and shape as the one first examined, although not so deep, and contained, besides the coals and ashes of a sacrificial fire, an ancient War Club, bearing a notched record exactly corresponding to that of the Zuni Calendar sticks. All other remains had been covered by the introduction of sand and other debris, and by accumulations from vegetable growth. Digging in this place would, of course, be amply rewarded by the finding of rare remains.

By far the largest and most curious of these crater-like caverns was the other of the two last named—situated from the first about a mile South and East and some hundred feet above on the adjoining table-lands.[15] It occurred in the very peak of a conical mountain, and had a longitudinal diameter at the top of seventy-five or eighty feet and a depth (the size gradually increasing downward) of between two and three hundred feet, or possibly more, since a stone dropped from the upper edge required six slow counts, or about three and one-half seconds to reach the bottom. In the dim light, near the Northern portion of the floor, I could distinguish the invariable ashes and cinders of the sacrificial fire, and to one side, the end of a *shoh' k'on* or sacred flute, such as is used in one of the mid-summer night ceremonies of the Zunis called *Hle-we-kwe o-ti-wa,* or tablet dance.[16]

I discovered this place very early in the morning, and my first and almost uncontrollable impulse was to enter it by means of my pack-rope and riata. This, however, was practically almost impossible from the shortness of my ropes and the vertical or receding character of the walls. I was further detained from doing so by my companion. It is needless to add that a thorough exploration of this crater would be very desirable; but in order to effect this, one would have to be supplied with cable, ladder, and grappling-hooks. Of course, [owing to] its isolated location and difficulty of access, it has never been entered, nor is it apt to be, save by the most enthusiastic; yet this circumstance makes the working up of it the more urgent. [Judging] from the immense labor which must have attended the aboriginal visits to this place, it must have served as an annual depository for some sacred dance of great superstitious import. In view of all these facts, my anxiety to make a reconnoissance of it is almost unendurable. . . .

Leaving this cave, I visited six other similar caves, without, however, finding any considerable openings or traces of ancient remains.

On the same day, however, about three miles South, I had the good fortune to discover, in the West face of a mountain, on the Eastern bank of the Colorado Chiquito, the second cave, of which the Zuni had spoken as one belonging to their *Ta-a-kwe,* or *Cera* [Corn] tribes. It proved to be simply a subterranean crack on a large scale extending through the middle of the mountain, descending at least fifty feet, at an angle of forty-five degrees.[17] From the entrance to the terminal crevice of this cavern it is one hundred and fifty-one feet. Its course, though zig-zag, is generally North North West, and some of the passages in it are almost impenetrable. Before any of these are reached, however, a point is found at which the cave enlarges to a width of seven or eight feet, and in which the deposit of bows, arrows, war-clubs, plume-sticks, cordage, matting, masks, etc., must once have exceeded five feet in depth. The work of destruction, as in the first, has, however, not removed but rendered worthless every trace of ancient art. Of this *whole cave* I have only to say that I never saw a foot of ground so rich in archaeological remains. Older than the first, its floors and debris are filled and strewn every inch of the way, with both broken and perfect examples of stone-age implements, weapons and sacred appliances to the dance.

Beyond the burnt region I discovered, very high up, a narrow passage, which, with great difficulty and the loss of much of my long hair by fire from the candle, I managed to get through. A sudden descent of six or eight feet and a turn to the East revealed a chamber not quite so large as the first mentioned but filled—packed—to the depth of ten or twelve inches with long cane arrows (some with stone points), bows, images, image slats, plume-sticks, etc., etc.

The place had never before been penetrated save by rats and animals of prey; hence many of the remains were undisturbed. My feast was consequently so engrossing that, unknowing of the flying time, it was long after the appearance of Orion ere I came forth.[18]

The two gods A'hai-iuta and the accompanying sacrifices, numbering in all more than three hundred pieces, I managed to get safely out from this dark recess by wrapping them in blankets, and pushing them forward as I crawled—not, however, until I had spent a day in laying the whole crevice off in square yards, and carefully mapping it.[19]

Amongst the "dress" (*Khŭān klē-ā-pa*) of the two gods were several image-slats and sticks, made from a pithy vegetable substance which the Zunis say was derived from the mountains of the Apache country. These were covered with painted figures of the dragon-fly, sacred lizard and frog, the *Wi' ili* [lightning worm?] and *Kia-nis-ti-pi* [water-skate] (two sacred beings of Zuni tradition), the tortoise, lightning, the morning star (emblem of A-hai-iuta), etc.[20] All or nearly all of these are emblems still painted on sacred bowls, altars, and pendant slats, and still used in the various religious orders of the warriors of Zuni.

I send by the hands of Mr. Kirchner four examples—although I was compelled to retain the most important of these curious slats, on account of their length and the delicacy of their figures.

The failure of provisions—twice replenished on the way—compelled me to relinquish the preliminary overhauling of this cavern before it was properly accomplished, although at the necessity of suffering a good deal from snow and short rations, I managed to remain long enough to insure it against the disturbance of any who might visit it ere I could return to complete operations.

By sacrificing my riding burro, I was able to bring home—with great risk of breakage, however—some two hundred plume-sticks, nearly as many broken arrows and bows, idol slats, image-sticks, and in fact, examples of all the above mentioned things, including some perfect war-clubs and matting. Among those things most interesting were some rain-pots and an ancient plume-cob, such as are now used among the Zunis *in all* ceremonies, and which they (the Indians) are giving me considerable annoyance about.

Aside from these few remains, I secured perhaps more than a thousand specimens which I cachêd for some future visit when, re-inforced by proper transportation facilities, I could bring them safely and bodily away.

Returning to San Juan, I learned of the existence to the West of three other caves rich in ancient remains, and of two to the North, which latter I was already acquainted with through their modern connection with the Zunis, and *their* freely communicated information regarding them. They are caverns which, although more than sixty miles from the Pueblo of Zuni, are annually visited by this people for the invocation of rain and "light."[21]

At the risk if not of life, yet of my standing among the Indians, I determined to visit and partially explore the two latter.

Having meanwhile dispatched a letter to the Governor of the Pueblo for horses, this became comparatively easy; sending my young men back with the burros, I took only my companion, and after a few hours ride, reached the first cave. It is that of the *Ka-k'ok-shi* or Good Dance and possesses the advantage of being ethnographic as well as archaeologic—the ceremonies pertaining to it having been performed during my stay at the Pueblo and a visit of fifty warriors and priests having been made to it during the past summer. All of the sacrifices made on that occasion, in almost perfect preservation (numbering more than a hundred) I secured, together with remains pertaining to the stone-age, although of the same specific character. Wishing to mislead the volunteer Mexican guide who accompanied me, I did not enter the rear passage, where, by the flickering of my candle I could discern large numbers of still more primitive remains.

The companion cave to this I did not for the same reason visit, since through the freely communicated information of the Indians I had months ago come to regard it as extremely rich in modern as well as ancient remains and neither wished to give it away nor risk early detection by the Indians.

I went near enough to it, however, to satisfy myself that, as in all other instances of the kind the Zunis had not deceived me in their accounts. From familiarity with the subject, I was, moreover, convinced of the truthfulness of the representations of my Mexican informants regarding the remaining three caves, of the situation of which they even furnished maps, and I therefore left them until such time as I could make their investigation thorough and conclusive.

Finally, through the traditions and accounts of the Indians, corroborated by the statements of travellers and guides, I am informed of the existence of yet other archaeologic caves. One is in the White Mountains fifteen miles South East of Fort Apache, the name of which is, in Zuni, *Re'-la-hlim-na-kwa* (Home of the Snows).[22] From this I already possess a beautiful stone necklace several yards in length. The others are situated respectively South West of Camp Apache thirty miles, and in the Coconinos mountains, the foothills of the Sierras San Francisco, nearly three hundred and fifty miles West of San Juan.

During a brief visit, since my return, of Lieut. Gatewood of Camp Apache, who also bears letters from me, and who has kindly aided me in many ways, I learned of yet other caves in the neighborhood of his Post, which, although unexplored, are yet known to contain remains of the same general character as those above described.

I have in view, then, no fewer than a dozen caves, four of which I have personally examined, and all of which are by far richer in archaeologic remains than any ever yet discovered in the East. The thorough examination and working up of these would simply bring about a repetition of the Bransford, Swan, and Schumacher eras in the history of the growth of the Museum;[23] and they, moreover, possess the added interest to me of being directly related and necessary to the Archaeologic History of the Zunis.

From time to time during the past year, as leisure would be afforded, I have made horse-back trips—in pursuance of the object mentioned in a former letter—some of them exceeding three hundred miles.[24] I have thus examined many of the ruins spoken of in Zuni tradition, and with one or two exceptions, I have made caches of greater or less extent at all of them—especially of such relics as either from their fragile or bulky character [were] impossible to transport on horseback.

I have, moreover, during many months past, been told of a people called in Zuni, *Kuh'-ni-kwe* [Havasupai], numbering fewer than a thousand grown persons, dressing in the costumes of the Zunis, possessing also their religious, and to some extent their political customs and institutions, who have held themselves ever aloof from Americans and Mexicans through early prejudice toward the latter, and who, by virtue of their isolated deep cañon home, are unknown to either of the two latter nations. All prospectors, save one, who have entered their little world have never returned. The latter published an account of his visit to the cañon in the *Arizona Miner,* some two years since and owed, I believe, his escape to the avoidance of the Kuh'-ni-kwe.

Scarcely able to credit this strange history, I caused all Zunis who claimed to have ever visited Kuh-ni, to assemble in the council house. They were five in number and stated that not only did the new tribe resemble them in costume, etc., but that they understood Pueblo agriculture, and that there were in their languages at least verbal similarities. Finally, since my return from the cave expedition, I have received directly from the Kuh-ni-kwe, through the Moqui, who are their nearest Eastern neighbors and many of whom understand the Kuh'ni tongue, assurances that, as the "Washington Zuni," they are anxious to see me and wish me, with some of the Zuni officers, to visit them.

Their country is in one of the almost inaccessible box cañons of the Colorado River, near the Northern slope of the Sierras San Francisco, eight days by horse from Zuni via Oriabi, the four last days of which lie through a waterless desert which can be passed only in winter or early spring.

It is an earnest desire on my part not only to take advantage of this invitation but also, as hinted in a former letter, and enlarged upon in the communication to you which was lost, I wish, aside from making exhaustive researches in, and collections from, the caves above described, to visit, survey and collect from all the ancient Pueblos throughout the territory covered by the earlier Zuni traditions.

It is this end, in view of the facts embraced in the preceding pages, which emboldens me to submit the following suggestions, or queries:

Could not the four-mule team and buck-board offered me last winter by Col. Stevenson for the Silver City Expedition be turned over for use in these various missions until such time as it shall be again required for the field operations of the Bureau? The caves are all, in common with the ancient Pueblos, accessible to wheeled vehicles; and such points as are inaccessible to such conveyance could be reached by employing the mules as packers. . . .

A most desirable addition to an outfit of the kind I mention would be a field photographic apparatus, which I could manage myself, and some surveying instruments, such as a standing compass, gradiometer, chain, and engineers' paper in large quantity.[25]

I have long been anxious to secure the former, for the purpose of photographing ruins, pictographs (significant to the Zunis and of the highest importance in connection with tradition), Phallic and other monuments, the House of the Sun at Ma-tsa-kia and the temples of the two War-gods, A-hai-iu-ta, which I alone have been guided to by the Indians. . . .[26]

I shall ever consider my work at Zuni as having been only half done, if it be not, in the end, re-inforced by such accurate and convincing records and testimonials as photographs and instrumental surveys.

My camping-outfit, already tolerably complete, would need the addition of an A-tent for protection against the rain and sleet-storms of spring, and this or anything else of the same nature could be, without difficulty, obtained from the Quartermaster Department, since not only the commanding officer, General Bradley, but also all of his officers including the Quartermaster and the Surgeon, Dr. [Washington] Matthews—the latter a thorough Ethnologist—treat me with great kindness and even distinction, and extend every aid to me in their power. Nearly the same will apply to the officers of Fort Apache, Arizona, at the other extreme of my route. . . .

I need not inform you of my strength to endure (through my Indian education) any amount of hardship and suffering or of my ability to care for such an outfit properly. My familiarity with this country, with its people and their languages, and with the charge of all kinds of animals, even wild Indian ponies, has somewhat increased my experience since the loss of my mule.

Whatever sums might be available for labor etc., I would expend as judiciously as possible; in their absence I would do (necessarily at the waste of much time) the best in my power.

Hoping that my plans will commend themselves, and not seem officious,

I have the Honor to be,

Your Obedient Servant,
Frank H. Cushing

Draft: FHC to L. N. Hopkins[27]

nd

My dear Sir:

Will you please send by the bearer, if procurable, half a pound of Vanity Fair smoking tobacco . . . and the [same] amount of Perique.

In case you have neither of these, kindly send a plug of the army tobacco and, say, a pound of the best cigarette smoking tobacco in your store—such, in fact, as *you* would be willing to use in the absence of cigars.

This trade stuff is killing me, and yet I am forced to smoke when I am present at the estufa observances of the Indians.

Hoping all goes well, I remain,

Truly Yours,
F H Cushing

Matthews to FHC

Fort Wingate, N. M.
February 14, 1881

F. H. Cushing, Zuni, New Mexico
My dear Friend,

Your brother came today bringing your letter of the 12th *inst.* and a red rug for which I am very thankful to you. I will send back by him some vaseline and perhaps some other things.

You certainly had a series of horrible adventures on your way home and you have my hearty sympathy.[28] But now that you are safely housed and that it is all over, do you think the Indians could have seriously contemplated making away with you? It seems to me that they would not dare to do it. If men of no consequence are travelling unmolested through the country, why should they attack one whose loss would lead to an immediate and rigid investigation? And your horse and accoutrements were hardly sufficient temptations. I must admit, however, that their actions were very suspicious and might reasonably have alarmed anyone. . . .

Now to the question of your health: That medicine I gave you for your heartburn was not "Cream of Tartar"—"may Heaven forfend"—or if it is Cream of Tartar, it is certainly not what I ordered for you. Cream of T. would only make the acidity worse. The medicine you have for heartburn is—or should be—Bicarbonate of Soda. Now whenever you have a heartburn, take soda, and take enough of it to stop the heartburn, come what may. Never allow your stomach to remain acid for five minutes if you can possibly help it. . . .

I have got your sacred pot and will take the best care of it. Is it one of the sacred pots you found in the cave, or is it the promised facsimile thereof?

Perhaps you should give up your smoking altogether.

If you think of it when next you write, you might mention what books you received from Powell. If there is anything new among them which I have not got, I want to apply for it.

Mrs. Matthews sends her regards,

Yours truly,
W. Matthews

FHC to William J. Rhees

Zuni, February 16, 1881

Dear Mr. Rhees:

Encolosed please find receipt for one hundred and thirty dollars, on account of salary, which came as greatly to my surprise as to my relief by last mail.

For this, as for your many kind responses to my requests I am ever grateful.

I suppose ere this you have heard of or read my report on some preliminary explorations of caves in Arizona. What do you think of my scientific "bonanza?"

I learn from Doctor Matthews, surgeon of Fort Wingate, who is an esteemed friend and valuable collaborator, of the very recent discovery in the mountains above Jemez Hot Springs of an ancient cave rich in archaeologic remains, a few of which the discoverer collected and presented to the Historical Society of Santa Fe. The exploration, on account of haste and fear, was very imperfect, not even extending to the limits easily passable in the cavern. It might be well for me to ride over and secure the results, as I now learn these troglodytic deposits possess such *inestimable* importance to ethnography that I wish to *monopolize* them for our Institution and Museum. . . .

Remember that the little scraps of information which you incidentally give me in your official letters are all I ever get regarding the operations of the Institution, and when you reflect that I still take a *little* interest in the latter, you will know that I am more than a little thankful for them and hope you will never leave them out, however small.

With best regards and respects to your ladies, and all friends,

I remain

Ever Truly Yours,
F. H. Cushing

FHC Note

nd

Last night the story of Creation and the Ancient History of the Zuni people was told me by a council of the *Pi'hlan Shi-wa-nis,* including the Caciques and other principals of the Pueblo. This council followed the signing of their names and the council with Dr. Ealy and the great religious race.[29]

When all were seated, they led in by his cane a very old white-headed blind man named H-ku-an-a-si and seated him in the center of the room. He smoked the cigarette I had rolled for him, and with bent head began the recital of the ancient story of the coming of men. He is blind, very old, and the historian of the most ancient of *I-no-te.* Thus he proves to be a second Ossian or another Homer, for he tells the ancient story of his race as a rude savage song, an unrecorded history, an unwritten Bible.

He cleared his throat and began:

Before men knew their Father Sun, their mother Moon, their brothers the Stars, before they knew the world of light,

There were four worlds (*A'wi-ten Te-hu-li-wa*), one below the other, in the mountains west of the west, the last one low down in the earth, and dark as the black in the chimney and the dye in dyed deer skin.

And in this fourth world, where it was dark as a cloudy night, where men never saw their Father Sun, their Mother Moon, their brother Stars, men multiplied and filled it full and had no room to move about, or if they passed to and fro they stepped upon one another. One spit; another said, "*Cu tchi!* Why do you spit on me?" "Why I could not see you." And if he spat in another direction, another would say "*U sa!* You have spit on me!" "*Ha na ha!* I did not see you." If one made water, another would say, "*A le!* Who is wetting me?" "Alas, I did not see you," And if he turned another way, he wet another who cried, "*Sho ma!* Who is wetting me?" "Alas, I did not see you."

The place became fuller and fuller, men were always running against one another, always spitting on one another, always wetting on one another, and stepping in one another's manure, and the place was stink full, and thus they became discontented.

"Where are the *Pi'hlan Shi-wa-ni mo-so-ni-we?*" said one, and "Where are the *Pi'hlan Shi-wa-ni-we?*" said another, and another and another. "Why, you know," answered one; and "You know," answered another, and another and another, until all were asking, "Where are the *Pi'hlan Shi-wa-ni mosone?*" and all were answering, "You know."

"Let us find them," said one; and "That's it," said another; and "Let us search for them," said one; and "That's it," said another; until all were saying "Let us find them," and all were answering "That's it."

And when the *Pi'hlan Shi-wa-ni mo-so-na* heard this—"What is it, my children?" they both said, and they said. "Our world is small and dark, and we are filling it, and we run against one another, we spit on one another, and it is full of stink." "Why, that is indeed true," said both, "and what is it you would have us do, my children?" they both said.

"Where is our Sun father, our Moon mother, our Star brothers? Go and search for another world, for here we are not glad."

"Why you shall say," said both, "and we will search for our brother caciques, and we will ask them where is our Sun father, and where is our Moon mother and where are our brother Stars, and our children are not glad in their world, for it is dark and small" and etc. etc.

So they went and found their brother caciques and said, "Our children are not content, for their world is dark and small and full of stink," etc. etc.[30]

FHC TO BAIRD

Zuni, March 12, 1881

My dear Professor Baird:

The receipt of your letter dated February 24th must have been delayed by the late snow storms and irregularity of the buckboard, as it has only recently come to hand.

I am surprised and disheartened at the fate which all of my more important communications to yourself and Major Powell are attended by. The one which you refer to as missing consisted of about sixty-eight closely written pages, accompanied by plans and sections, giving an account of my recent operations in four rich ancient caves, and of my discovery of seven others equally deserving of exhaustive overhauling. Two sheets of it were devoted to the description of a *new* Pueblo tribe, of which I had at first learned among my Zunis, and afterward from travellers and prospectors through these territories. In only one instance has this tribe ever been visited by white men—two years since—by a couple of gold hunters—one of whom lost his life in consequence. It referred to an invitation which I had received only a short time before through the Moquis, directly from this people (the *Kuh'-ni-kwe*) [Havasupai] to visit them with an embassy of my tribe, of the partial arrangement of the latter, and urged the desirable nature of such a visit for the purpose of investigating linguistic affinities said to exist between the Kuh'-ni and the Zuni, by the latter, as well as other ethnographic features, and finally asked your advice on the subject together with the transportation facilities to be used not only for this purpose but also for exploring some twenty-nine ruined pueblos and the caves.

I cannot enter into such a thorough account either of this matter or of the caves in the present letter, as I have not slept for thirty-six hours, and the mail carrier is at this moment awaiting my motions. I will, however, during the present week, try to rewrite as well as possible the letter, which to no purpose I finished at the expense of considerable time and labor.

The money referred to came to hand a month since, and I hope the receipts I signed therefor have long ere this been received. I shall, however, require more money very soon.

With regard to collections, I have on hand, not only that which I consider a very valuable although incomplete series of modern Zuni specimens but the five or six hundred ancient articles which I brought home, at the expense of walking, on our burros. While I am aware of the War Department transportation facilities to which you call my attention, it is impossible for me to send in any of my collections for the simple reason that I can get them neither to [Fort] Wingate nor to any other military post. I am supplied with no transportation, nor with authority for commanding such as Mr. Stevenson had at his disposal, while the means with which I am supplied are far from sufficient to secure the freighters of this country. True, I might secure the boxes and lumber (entirely lacking here of course) for packing such collections, from the Post, had I the proper papers, but it still would be necessary to have transportation from the latter place to this, as well as from here to there.

Moreover, as my letter informed you, I have cached at one of the caves more than a thousand specimens, at another, five hundred, and at a third a trifle more than the latter. It is not only expensive but very dangerous to transport such things on horse-back, and it would be quite impossible thus to carry the collecting and investigations at these places much further.

The Indians have only within the past ten days consented to my collecting any of the paraphernalia of their sacred dances, or of the ancient trophies of their tribe. They now promise to *help* me get such things together, and I expect as the result, one of the finest ethnographic collections, although time will be required for its completion, and additional strategems and watchfulness.

Of the collections "made by Col. Stevenson" few specimens were such as possessed great intrinsic value among the Indians. Such alone were left for me to collect, with but a fraction of the means and facilities. Of the money which I have received during the past eighteen months all or nearly all has been expended incidentally—my whole strictly private account probably covered by *less* than twenty five dollars. The fine lot of imitation turquoises and corals sent me by Mr. Stevenson consisted simply of *three* of the former, of the size here given ● [and] ◓, and of a quantity of wax beads, which though of interest at first, very nearly ruined my reputation when they came to melt upon their wearer's necks—not withstanding the fact that I warned the Indians of their character.

Of the really magnificent series of shells which you sent me, I find I can make disposition to a very much greater advantage in the worked condition, and hence sent East at the expense (private) of nearly a hundred dollars for a lathe, turner, knives, etc., of my designing, with which to work upon this rich material—which will show at once whether I am in earnest, and that I want, laboring under the disadvantages I do, to come out as honorably as possible.

This machine, I am informed by letter, was shipped from the railroad several days since, and I am expecting it with every sunset.

I find that the clam shell such as you sent works up magnificently and would like a great deal more, as it is entirely inexpensive. And *all that I could get* of the oliva such as I enclose would be of very great value.

I am terribly weary, terribly cast down. It does not seem at times as though I could endure longer this terrible work, or wait longer for the call which shall summon me to Washington. Yet with the acquisition of the Zuni language, I have laid open a field which without presumption I can say is the richest ever within the reach or sight of an American investigator, but it widens with each step and to leave it *now,* after my struggle to acquire it, would seem not short of sacrilege to me.

I fear that by all and after all, I have not won the commendation of those for whose opinion I care most.

Very Resp'y Your Ob't Svt,
F. H. Cushing

P.S. I am at work by day constantly on the Herculian census designed by Major Powell, and put into my hands by Agent Thomas. By night I am as busy with my more proper pursuits. I am making more rapid progress in the study of the *inner life* of these wonderful savages during the past few days than ever before. Familiar as I am with their language, and one of them by adoption, I have not until within a week secured anything like a complete vocabulary of their consanguinity terms, or any conception of their *true* belief in immortality and its conditions—notwithstanding that this has been one of the facts I have constantly searched for during a year and a half.

Why is it that Major Powell designs everything on such a grand scale that the very object he aims so well to cover is defeated at the outset? An example is his census. In this he leaves for most enumerators—except they have limitless time and thorough familiarity with the native language—only two alternatives: either to turn in incorrect results—worse than none—or deceitful ones—worse than either.

Were it not that my honor was involved, I should have given it up long ago, for this extra work has been the source of many personal as well as official sacrifices.[31]

Very Respectfully,
Your Humble Servant,
F. H. Cushing

BAIRD TO FHC

March 26, 1881

Dear Mr. Cushing:

Your letter of the 12th of March reached me just as I was on the eve of starting for Philadelphia, & I take the first opportunity after my return to answer it, & to say that the letter referred to as missing came to hand four days later. . . . I trust you have not gone to the trouble of reproducing the communication. . . .

I was not aware that you wanted to be recalled to Washington, but supposed your longer stay was simply due to your desire to accomplish your work of research. You must use your own judgment & exercise your discretion in this matter. I shall be glad to have you back whenever you come, & leave the time of your stay entirely optional with you. Of course there is plenty of work here that you can do, especially now, [as we are engaged in] preparation of the new Museum building.

Yours Very Truly,
Spencer F. Baird

FHC TO POWELL

Zuni, March 26, 1881

. . . .

Accompanying your census, as I did, with one of a gentile, phratral, religious, and architectural bearing (for ethnological purposes), it became an almost impossible undertaking and, completed, as I am happy to say it nearly is, I regard it as at once one of the most difficult and important works I have accomplished in Zuni.[32] I was opposed by the superstitions of the Indians almost violently, and it was only by virtue of my position among them as a chief and my understanding of their language that I was enabled to carry it through after more than two months of hard work. I also made a census, separately for Dr. Thomas, of the population, and I hope this gentleman will forward the one or both to you soon after its receipt at his office.

I am recently informed by telegraph from Professor Baird that a four mule team and accoutrements have been ordered for me at Wingate by General Hatch. Am I wrong in believing that my thanks are due as well to you as to him?

I have the honor to remain,

Ever Faithfully Yours,
F. H. Cushing

POWELL TO FHC

April 15, 1881

My dear Cushing:

The Kuh-ni-kwe whom you mention in your report to Prof. Baird and myself are known to travelers and scientific men as the Coçoninos.

In 1870 I saw a small party of them myself. As you suppose, very little is known of them. When I met them, they claimed that they had been Pueblo Indians at one time and lived near the Zunis so that the statements you have received concerning them are abundantly confirmed.

I hope that you will be able to get a vocabulary from them even though it may not be greater than two or three hundred words. Can you not take a census of them?

I am

Yours cordially
J W Powell
Director

FHC to Baird

Zuni, April 15, 1881

Dear Professor Baird:

. . . .

I trust that the money which you say you will try to send with the stationary etc. will reach me early, as I am in pressing need of it. I intend to visit Wingate tomorrow or the next day for the purpose of getting my transportation facilities and shall, as soon after as possible, lay in a large supply of commissaries preparatory to an extended tour among the caves and ruins of Arizona. Do you wish that I should make, during my tour among the Arizona ruins etc., a visit to the *Kuh'ni*? I learn more and more of interest concerning them as time goes on, which increases my desire greatly to see and casually study them.

I have yet to ask, as very desirable if not essential to my work of exploration, especially for cliff ruins, a pair of small but powerful field glasses. In case there are none available about the Institution or Bureau, I would esteem it as a great favor if you would kindly—personally—attend to the purchasing of a pair and either deduct from or charge to my account with the Museum. The price, in case you do not deem the expenditure a proper one for the Institution or Museum appropriation, need not—within reason—be considered, as I wish to secure the best possible instruments for service, with especial reference to *clearness of definition*. A good price for appliances of this kind I do not hesitate in the least to pay, as their usefulness does not terminate with one excursion or season. It was due to a pair of excellent opera glasses belonging to Mr. Kirchner that I made some of my best discoveries last winter, and it was then that I was made aware of their usefulness in such work. . . .

And now, dear Professor, I come to thanking you once more for you last kind letter.

As I have said to you before, I am always wishing to come home, but cannot but think that after spending all the time I have making the sacrifices I have, enduring the criticisms I have, in order to gain a knowledge of the language and inner life of the Indians, it would be a sin—not more nor less—to desert my field at its present stage. The more since that stage has reached a point at which I can see how much there is to be acquired—and how to acquire [it].

I am perfectly well aware of the opinions which some people hold of me—so much so that I am constrained to remark that my Indians have more sense of honor in some things than most of my own people and associates. But I never lose sight of one very pleasant and encouraging fact—that my chief—yourself—is ever my friend and supporter—my defender if necessary—and do you suppose I am not going to deserve his confidence?

Anything you wish me to do, mention it and I will do it if it be in my power. Your wish is my law. I remain, ever faithfully,

Your Ob't Servant,
F H Cushing

John Bourke's Diary[33]

April 27th, 1881. . . . During our brief stay at Fort Wingate, I had the great pleasure of making the acquaintance of Mr. Cushing, of the Smithsonian Institute, who has been living among the Zuni Indians since last summer. They have regularly adopted him into the tribe, made him a chief and invested him with their costume. Noticing a string of sea-shells around his neck, I inquired whence they came. "From the Pacific Ocean; the Zunis make pilgrimages there every four years." Cushing is a man of intelligence, persistance and enthusiasm: just the character to carry through to a successful conclusion the mission he has undertaken. . . .

Yarrow to Baird[34]

May 9, 1881

Dear Professor Baird:

I send by messenger the scalp of Pi-ho-na for Mr.

Cushing, about which I wrote to you some time since. Will you be good enough to have it forwarded to him.

Very Truly Yours,
H. C. Yarrow
Surgeon General's Office
U. S. Department of War

FHC TO BAIRD

Camp Waterless, Mesa Prieta, Arizona
May 12, 1881

Dear Professor Baird:

. . . .

I am most happy to know that Titskematse *is* ordered to join me in New Mexico, as his assistance will enable me to make the collection of birds, etc., which you wish, and which I am also very desirous of securing, as illustrative of the sacred fauna of Zuni.

I am feeling greatly encouraged by the kind recognition and many favors which I am lately the recipient of at the hands of yourself and Major Powell. Moreover, those among the officers at Fort Wingate who have an interest in, or any understanding of, my kind of work, notably Dr. Matthews and General Bradley, look upon my proceedings so flatteringly, and I am received so kindly by them and their associates, that I am quite devoid at present of that melancholy spirit which has heretofore haunted me so much, especially of late.

Of all you communicate—Major Powell's appointment excepted—nothing proves more pleasant than that concerning Harry Biddle.[36] Both of your letters speak of his wish to assist in exploring the cliff reimains and of your disposition to help him, and hence I feel certain of being, ere long, associated with him—and am more glad than I can here say on that account. I have always since the cave days at Carlisle taken a great interest in him. Can you not arrange to have him with me or in my party? I think a season or two in this country, and some experiences kindred to those which I have had, would do more toward making a man of Harry than almost any thing else; I speak advisedly of this sort of thing, as it has helped *me* in this respect marvellously.

Harry is an *honest* boy, and it requires more honesty than has qualified those who have hitherto entered this field to do—as I would like to see it done—the work of archaeologic research and ethnologic collecting. So far as I have been a witness, this has been a lacking element, but we all feel quite certain it will not be thus with Harry. . . .

I am glad to say that I am popular with all the officers and their ladies at Fort Wingate, save only one remaining from those who were stationed there during the winter of 79–80. I am distinctly aware of the source of even their ill feeling, and I count the days of the present happy state of affairs, for I feel that they are numbered or limited to the time of certain arrivals which will exert a different influence with regard to me. It is an unwise policy in a scientific expedition to be accompanied by supernumeraries—especially when these develop malicious influences toward any of the proper officers of such expedition, or tend to turn the tide of interest in collecting into any other than the Public channels.[37] Pardon this little confidential interpolation—I write out not the half which I know or feel, because I know it is not always best.

The popularity has resulted very favorably in many instances for my work—in none more than in aiding to furnish me a handsome camping and working outfit. I had also an excellent soldier turned over to me, and a young man named Wm. H. Baily accompanies me as assistant without pay, for the purpose of continuing in my company during at least this trip. He is very efficient, hard working, steady, and a frontiersman, and I should like to be able to employ him through the season. I will possibly be allowed another soldier by General Bradley (who was absent when I left the post), but even in that event my force will be very limited, as I have almost constantly to excavate to produce good results, and could not have too much of a force with me. As I have no motive other than that of advancing the work with which I am entrusted, I have taken the liberty of mentioning Baily's case, and of asking if arrangements cannot be made for remunerating him as an inducement to the continuance of his services. I have had many applications like his but none which suited me; and he was so disappointed when I told him I was unauthorized to employ citizens that he volunteered to accompany me through this trip not as a "beat" but as a genuine workman, as he has proved to our advantage.

I met during my brief stay at Wingate a young officer, Lieutenant [W. W.] Wotherspoon of Washington, who told me he had heard you speak of me and who is much interested in archaeological matters, and wishes to assist me if possible. He is post adjutant and Quartermaster at Fort Whipple, Arizona, and of course a powerful friend if he choose to be. He suggested that I write you, using his name, and ask you to have orders for assistance and transportation facilities furnished me at Fort Whipple (District Headquarters of Arizona) or that you write personally to General [O.B.] Wilcox (post commander), to whose staff he belongs. He says such facilities are more abundant at Whipple than at Wingate, and that there will be no difficulty in securing them. He further promised to personally accompany me with an escort to the cliff ruins of Beaver Creek (some of the most ancient of the Zuni)[38] and to the borders of the Ha-va-su-pais, or Kuh'ni country, of the existence of which tribe he is aware, in confirmation of all I have said concerning them. As Whipple lies much nearer my line of operations westward than any other post, he planned that I should go there with my present or even a more limited outfit, and resupply in exchange there, in case you took active measures in the matter.

I have by this mail the box of olivas which you kindly sent; though not of the special variety which I desired, I think they will prove quite as useful, and return many thanks for them. Of course your judgment was much better than mine with regard to the photographic apparatus. I now see that it would have interfered with my more legitimate work—which even now I have none too many minutes for.

I hope, however, that ere my researches are concluded, I may enjoy the advantages of a specialist in that line to do work under my specific direction for the illustration of at least the archaeologic portion of my work, which, from the amount of time already given to it and in prospect, will be more important, perhaps, than I ever dreamed it might become when I initiated it.

I am delighted to know that you have interested yourself in procurring for my use a pair of pocket field glasses. I am already sorely in need of them and hope their arrival and that of Titskematse will not be delayed, as, with regard to the latter, the season for Maximilian [jay] eggs is passing.

I remain, Dear Professor Baird,

Very Respectfully and Faithfully,
F. H. Cushing

[P.S.] Of the two shells enclosed, the smaller is taken from the wristlet of a *Pihlan Shi-wani* (Bearer of the Bow or warrior), the larger from the sacred necklace. Both represent the most valuable of white shells among the Pueblos and Navajos. A large quantity of them would enable me to accomplish a great deal, I think, as they are also ground into the native shell money. A few oyster shells might be well to experiment with, and if it is not too much that you should send such, I think I may be able to repay you richly in time.

John Bourke's Diary[39]

May 28, 1881. Saturday.

. . . Reached Wingate at 2 p.m., read my mail and called upon General Bradley and family. Had the great pleasure of meeting Mr. Frank Cushing at the house of Dr. Matthews; had a long and delightful conversation with him concerning our S. W. Indians and their customs. Showed him my list of the Zuni clans which he pronounced correct except that two, now extinct or nearly so, were not properly given; these were the "Rattlesnake," of which only one man is now living, . . . and the Agua or Water clan, which Cushing claims is now extinct.[40]

Saturday, May 29th, 1881 [*sic*].

Had another conversation with Mr. Cushing, after breakfast. I found him to be the most intelligent ethnologist I had ever encountered. Dr. Matthews is also well up in his knowledge of Indian manners, customs and languages. . . . In the evening, called upon Mr. Hopkins, the post trader, and his charming wife; thence to General Bradley's, where I met, besides his family, Mr. Cushing with Patricio, the "gobernador" of Zuni, Dr. and Mrs. Matthews, and Lieut. Chance. Mr. Cushing read us some poetry in the Zuni language, an invocation to the spirit of the antelope, showing rhyme, rhythm and melody. Patricio said that it was a song they sang to the spirit of the antelope before starting out on a hunt and, as we seemed to be so pleased with the words, he would sing the song itself, if we so wished. Need I say that we jumped at the chance and begged Patricio to gratify us. He sang in a sweet voice, a little bit tremulous from nervousness, the invocation or chant beginning: "May-a-wee, May-a-wee!" (Spirit of the antelope, Spirit of the antelope!)

Just before he began his song, Mr. Baxter, the correspondent of the *Boston Herald,* and Mr. Metcalf, an artist of the staff of *Harper's Weekly,* entered the little circle and took down notes of all that occurred. They impressed me as very bright young gentlemen. . . .

Cushing says that the Zunis have societies for everything—dances, festivals, etc. He told me that he was having made for me one of the sacred blankets of the Zunis and we have arranged to go together to the Moqui villages, to witness the "rattlesnake dance" which comes off in August; thence, to the Grand Cañon of the Colorado and perhaps to the country of the Ava-Supais. Mr. Cushing thinks that the See-vitch, of the Grand Cañon, have a common origin with the Zunis or Ah-see-vitch [A-shi-wi].[41] The Zunis themselves admit as much. They called the people of Taos their "older brothers" and say that four hundred years ago the buffalo roamed around Taos. . . .

NEWSPAPER STORY

SOLVED AT LAST: Mysteries of Ancient Aztec History Unveiled by an Explorer from the Smithsonian Institution. Wonderful Achievements of Frank H. Cushing
(from our Special Correspondent)
Fort Wingate, June 10 [1881]. . . . It was here at Fort Wingate, while getting ready for a trip to the famous Indian pueblo of Zuni—the largest pueblo in America—that I had the rare good fortune to meet Mr. Frank H. Cushing, a young gentleman whose name will soon rank with those of famous scientists.

As a result of Mr. Cushing's labors, Aztec history will have to be rewritten. Much of what has hitherto been received as such falls to the ground, a mass of rubbish. There are no other people as distrustful of strangers as are the Indians, so reticent about everything concerning themselves. Therefore, when questioned by strangers about their religion, their past and their traditions, they have answered, to be sure, but these answers, accepted as sober truth, have been uniformly a pack of very ready and ingenious lies. Mr. Cushing, therefore, adopted the only sensible method of getting at the bottom facts: that of becoming one with the Zunis, learning their language and living with them. . . .

He has discovered a mine of mythological lore, beliefs and superstitions, gods and spirits, that throw the full light of day on the mysteries of the Aztec religion. . . .[42]

The most marvellous thing which he has discovered in connection with their religion is the grand fact that their faith is the same thing as modern Spiritualism. The Zunis have their circles, their mediums, their communications from the spirit world, their materializations—precisely like those of the spiritualists of civilized life.[43] Their seances are often so absorbing that they are kept up all night. Their belief in the phenomena explains many strange things about their religion which Mr. Cushing was unable to account for until he hit upon it—they had kept it carefully guarded months after he was on most intimate terms with them—by telling them about certain spiritistic phenomena he had witnessed, thus gaining their sympathy as apparently a fellow believer.

Their language has proved a most interesting study. It is thoroughly grammatical, and has a finely arranged system of declensions and tenses. The Zunis are most careful to teach their children to speak correctly, and drill them thoroughly. They have words for "grammatical" and "ungrammatical" ("good talking" and "bad talking" literally translated). Strange to say, they have an ancient or classic language, just as English has its Anglo-Saxon. This dead language has been handed down in their religious rites and is, for the most part, known only by the priests. Many of their sacred songs are worded in it, and these songs are of unknown antiquity. This is a striking illustration of the conservative influence of religion in preserving the institutions of the past. . . .

[There follows a disquisition on the extensive unwritten literature of the Zunis—the songs, prayers, fables and proverbs handed down from ancient times and embodying the Zunis' "marvelous knowledge of their past."]

Mr. Cushing has also deciphered the secret of the inscriptions or pictographs that cover the cliffs in this part of the country. One of the most important results of this acquisition is the proof they give of the correctness with which the Zunis had related to him the history of the ruins they mark and of the extent of the country once covered by the race.

An achievement of which Mr. Cushing has reason to be specially proud is the success of his effort to locate exactly the cities of Cibola, a question which has been the cause of many an archaeological dispute. This he has settled beyond a shadow of a doubt, the result of his explorations corresponding exactly to the descriptions of Coronado. . . . His proofs, which are indisputable, require too much elaboration for a newspaper article, and to attempt to give them in an abridged form would be an injustice. Therefore the simple statement must answer here, placing the credit for the discovery where it belongs. His report will consider the subject in all its bearings and will throw quite a new light on the narratives of Niça and Coronado. I have seen the ruins of the original Cibola and the mountain from which Niça looked off upon it—the mountain where, with the aid of the Indians, he raised a heap of stones and erected thereon a small wooden cross, taking possession of the country in the name of the viceroy, the cross standing as a symbol of taking possession. Mr. Cushing found this stone heap still standing, and the father of Pedro Pino, formerly the Governor of Zuni—Pedro Pino is now an aged man of something like 80 years, and his son is now Governor—saw the remains of the cross on the spot. One of the finest proofs of the location of the Cibola pueblos is the tradition which the Zunis have of the killing of "the black Mexican with thick lips." They told this to Mr. Cushing of their own accord, and with no leading questions on his part, under circumstances most convincing that this was the negro Estevan who accompanied Coronado. Mr. Cushing knows the exact pueblo where the deed was done. . . .[44]

Mr. Cushing is confident that the mystery of the magnificent ruins of Yucatan—a mystery that has generally been supposed to be impenetrable—will some day be solved. It will be done, he says, by someone who will follow a course like that he has pursued. He must go among the Mayas, the fierce people who inhabit the mountain wilds of Yucatan and who are the lineal descendants of the builders of those grand ruins, and let himself be found among them some day, helpless and alone. Then, learning their language and becoming one with them, the explorer will find himself rewarded by a clear, full knowledge of their history—a knowledge that will also enable him to read the mazes of inscriptions on the stones of the ancient palaces as readily as he would read a book. Perhaps it may be the mission of Mr. Cushing to do this work. . . .

—S[ylvester] B[axter]
Boston Herald, June 16, 1881.

Sylvester Baxter: from Account of a Visit to Zuni in Early June 1881

The Governor of Zuni, whom we had already met at the fort [Wingate] a few days before, was at Pescado attending to his farm. He was at work in a field near the road as we approached, and came to meet us. A joyful gleam illuminated his dusky face as he recognized "his young brother," and as he walked along beside our slowly moving team he humorously responded to Cushy's [Cushing's] playful queries. A member of the most powerful family of Zuni, Patricio Pino is a man of middle age, with a thoughtful, reflective face, and a profile that is almost classicaly Greek. . . .

After supper we lay back upon the sheepskins in the Governor's rooms in the Pescado pueblo, quietly enjoying the novel scene about us. Sticks of piñon wood had been placed on end in the corner of the fireplace, and their bright crackling flame sent a ruddy light through the large room, touching up the nearer side of all objects in sharp relief against the intensity of the shadows. Gay-colored clothing and blankets, hung on poles suspended from the ceiling, caught the dancing light; curious pottery was ranged along the floor by the walls; and here and there in the walls were little niches, just as we had seen them in the walls of ruined cliff dwellings. In these little niches were conveniently arranged little articles of domestic use, which had a delightfully bric-a-brac suggestiveness. The scene was just the same now as it had been within those walls hundreds of years before. We were away back in the centuries, and living the life of the remote past. . . .

Mr. Cushing's room at the house of the Governor's [in Zuni] was a picturesque mingling of culture and barbarism. A writing-table, a case of bookshelves with the books necessary to his studies, and the volumes of valuable notes that recorded his investigations, a stool, a student lamp, and a hammock, completed the inventory of the civilized furnishings. But there was the wonderful addition of a telephone which Mr. Cushing and his brother, who was visiting him, constructed out of a couple of old tin cans and several hundred yards of twine, to prove to the Zunis the truth of what he had told them about the triumphs of American invention. The telephone was connected with the house of one of the caciques on the opposite side of the pueblo, about a quarter of a mile away. . . .

—from "The Father of the Pueblos,"
Harper's New Monthly Magazine 65
(June 1882), 77–80.

FHC to Baird

[Fort Wingate] June 10, 1881

My dear Professor Baird:

I return[ed] via Zuni to Fort Wingate to find awaiting me the field glasses—a most excellent pair—and your very kind letter of the 25th of May. Thanks for the former, and for the latter I need not say how grateful I am. . . .

The letters which you promise to write Generals Hatch and Wilcox will be of almost vital importance to the successful prosecution of my archaeologic work, since such facilities as were allowed me recently—while they enabled me to secure an important collection and transport it to the post for shipment—were nevertheless inadequate, necessitating as they do one or more visits to the cave region before its stores can be exhausted.

I am regretting today in almost despondent terms the repeated delays of Titskematse, as, in awaiting his arrival, I have missed possibly the finest opportunity of my life—priority in the description of the *Kuh'ni*. I learned last evening, through a letter from Lieutenant Wotherspoon to Mr. and Mrs. Mathews, that a cavalry expedition with Dr. Coues as Surgeon and Naturalist and Lieut. Palfrey as Engineer Officer had been fitted out at headquarters of Arizona (Whipple Barracks) and left on the 4th of June to penetrate, explore and survey the country of the *Supai* or *Kuh'nis*.[45]

I have never before experienced a disappointment like this, and I know not how to dispel the cloud which it casts over all my work and endeavors; but I suppose, like all other things, it will regulate itself.

I also learn through the same kind letter that Lieut. Wotherspoon is now (temporarily) chief quartermaster of the Department of Arizona. With the increased power which this gives him he can extend to me greater facilities than could have been expected from a less kind and true friend to my cause.

Hoping to yet do something with the Kuh'ni, I have telegraphed Lieutenant Wotherspoon, today, as follows:

> Am very anxious to reach Supais Country before departure of Expedition from it. If I reach Supais within fourteen days, will I be in time?
>
> Have seen your letter.
>
> Cushing

Fort Wingate June 10th "81"

Should the reply, which I shall receive some time tomorrow, warrant it, I shall set out at once by horse from Zuni, accompanied by the Head Chief and an adopted Moqui named Na-na-he as guides and interpreters. I shall take only a pack animal and one or two saddle horses, going by trail from Zuni to Oraibi, and thence through the great Moqui Desert—if possible at this season—to Kuh'ni—a journey in all of nine or ten days. My ever kind and true friend Dr. Matthews, in whose hands I placed my last receipts from you, knowing that my limited means would not carry me through the possible emergencies of such a trip, has generously offered me an advance of one or two hundred dollars. In case I start soon, I shall accept one hundred of this sum, and I hope your next installment to me will be in his name, to that amount, instead of my own. By this unlooked for means, I shall be enabled not only to provide for the possible accident of finding no facilities awaiting me at Fort Whipple on my return from Kuh-ni but also for making, I hope, a small yet representative collection—which I hope to get the Expedition to transport to the latter post.

From the tone of the letter in question, I have no doubt that, had I been at the Post when preparations were being made for the Expedition, I should have been considered its proper Ethnologist or at least should have received facilities for prosecuting my work, of a very desirable kind.

I have finished cataloguing, labeling and packing the small collection I was able to bring in, and both trust and hope it will please you. Yet another trip to the caves will result in a much more extensive gathering. I will send the catalogue on as soon as it is properly copied, in order that you may know what has been turned over for shipment.

Some of the results of my recent expedition have been the discovery of additional crater caves—which it is impossible to enter without long rope ladders, yet which contain ancient remains as abundantly as the more accessible caverns—and of wonderfully fortified *Malpais* or lava pueblos so cleverly constructed among the high craggy edges of cañons and mesas as to have escaped observation heretofore.[46]

With the old conveyance broken down and my mules jaded, I came in very slowly and was forced to leave all heavier remains cached for the future. Reaching Fort Wingate, I was told by the Indians that their annual *Wo'-tem-thla* would be performed within three or four days—and, accompanied by Lieut. Emmet and some friends from Boston, I returned to witness it.[47] I am therefore late in replying to your kind favors.

On my arrival at Kuh'ni, not later than fifteen days hence, I shall at once join the Expedition mentioned above, and, in case I can complete enough work on the people, shall return with it to Whipple; there, should there be orders authorizing it, I shall get facilities for exploring and collecting from the cliff and Pueblo remains of the Verde and Beaver Creek cañadas [valleys] and cañons, which promise, according to descriptions furnished me by Lts. Wotherspoon, Palfrey and Bourke, an abundant harvest. In this work I may be detained several weeks, returning in time to execute whatever mission Major Powell may have for me, and to receive Harry [Biddle]. During the approaching two months few ceremonials occur, none save one which I have on a former occasion witnessed, of sufficient importance to make any material difference in my Zuni work.

In consequence of the severe sand storms and droughts which initiated the season of last year, the crops of the Zunis failed almost entirely to reach maturity. Their condition, therefore, made worse by the constant ravages of grasshoppers during the past five or six years, is, relative to food, very pitiable. I represented [this] matter to the Pueblo Indian Agent, Dr. Thomas, in one of my letters of more than two months since, without, however, eliciting the poor honor of a reply from him. The Indians having named me one of their chiefs and regarding me as a "child of Washington," look forward to my being able to relieve them. If I prove unable to be the means of so doing, I fear I shall lose all standing among them, and hence, not only but also on purely philanthropic grounds, I pray you to intercede with the Commissioner of Indian Affairs or to direct me how to proceed with this question, which has become a serious one. Only about two thirds of the tribe (numbering sixteen hundred and two) are in an actual condition of want, and all they ask for is flour, corn, beans, and some coffee and sugar which may be distributed among the richer families to avoid dissensions and jealousies which are so common to all Indians. I hope I am not taking too great a liberty in bringing this matter before you and that you will write me early your views about it. I have heretofore deferred speaking of it, through courtesy to the Agent, but since he takes no (small even) measures, I come to you for advice. . . .[48]

Ever your Faithful and Dutiful Servant,
F H Cushing

FHC to Powell

[Fort Wingate] June 11, 1881

Dear Major Powell:

Having just returned from an archaeologic trip

into Arizona, I take occasion to reply to your two kind letters which have lain so long in waiting. . . .

I believe you are aware that I am now almost *thoroughly* familiar with the Zuni tongue, have been for more than a year an adopted member of the tribe and of one of the gentes (the latter not, however, to be confirmed until marriage) and one of the head chiefs of the Nation. With my peculiarly good opportunities, I am making happy progress with the study of the inner life of the Pueblos—the sacred institution of the dance, to some extent of the secret orders (of which there are twelve), the folklore, the myths of observation, mythical and rhythmical oral bible, etc. etc.

I have discovered the existence of fifteen gentes and of three *kinds* of phratries—the *U-loch-nan* or Geographic Phratry, the *Tikian* or Sacred Phratry (secret medicine orders), and the *Ki-wi-tstin* or Estufal Phratry—the latter resembling more nearly the true phratries of other tribes. Each of these kinds of phratry is divided into from three to twelve minor phratries—if such all may be termed.

The amount of knowledge which I have to gain of these curious institutions will throw much light upon them not only as they now exist but as to their origin and growth. . . .

Learning . . . that a cavalry expedition, with Dr. Coues as Naturalist, left [Fort Whipple] five or six days since for the country of the Kuh'nis, . . . I am making rapid preparations to set out, with some of my Indians as interpreters, across the Moqui Desert in order to secure priority of description and pure results for the Bureau and myself.

Hoping that this will sufficiently explain the haste and raggedness of the present letter and that I shall be able to return in time to execute any missions you may have for me on your arrival at [Fort Wingate], I remain, very respectfully and faithfully,

Your Obedient Servant,
F. H. Cushing

Daily Journal

Saturday, June 11th, 81.

The day was pleasant, and I not only made all preparations for leaving Wingate but Dr. Matthews made up a party to accompany me to Zuni, consisting of himself, Mrs. Matthews, Lieutenant Fornance and Mrs. Fornance. An escort wagon was ordered by General Bradley to accompany our ambulance and carry my things. The Lt. went with orders to inquire into the Navajo matter, and the Doctor to vaccinate the children.[49]

Laid in a stock of commissaries ($56.54). Wrote on census until I fell asleep, and also scribbled a letter or two. No mail.

Sunday, June 12th, 81.

This morning rose early and prepared to go in to Zuni. Concluded to ride silver mare (my brother's horse), and he rode Jesus' black. Ambulance left at about 9 a.m., and I followed soon after, my brother remaining behind. We reached Nutria at about noon, and camped a couple of hours, We-wa entertaining us very nicely. The wagon not coming up, I left note of directions with Indians. Secured as pay for trampled corn $5.00 and an ox hide of a tired animal which I directed the Indians to kill and eat. Reached Pescado early, I going by trail.

Wagon did not come. Received handsomely by Governor, but passed uncomfortable night on account of scarcity of blankets. Ladies slept in house of Pedro Pino, and I took my friends to Governor's house, where a nice straw tick had been stuffed for them by Gov. A talk ensued, after which Lt. fell asleep. Dr. and I quizzed Gov. on Navajo Gentes and clans, with very satisfactory results to former. I did translating.

Monday, June 13th, 81.

Early this morning the Alcalde, Hla-ko-a, and an assistant came by trail with my two buck mules loaded with the bedding which Enos had sent from Nutria with note saying that the wagon was broken slightly and late in getting in; hence had not come on.

I sent note back directing driver to be sure and come through, and we then prepared to leave for Zuni. Ambulance went on, and an hour or two after, I followed. Found my friends comfortably waiting for me in my room, although the inquisitiveness of the Indians had so disgusted them that they wished me to get another house, which I did, although with many forebodings—that of Na-wi-ku.[50]

A little dinner was soon prepared, to which Ten-atsali was invited by note. In evening, went about with the party, showing parts of town. Council was appointed and heralded at dusk, and at about 8 o'clock I summoned the Dr. and Lieutenant. The attendance was good. First the Navajo question was attended to, the Lt. making notes. Then the matter of vaccinating, and finally the Kuh-ni question, in which my friends aided. Tsai-iu-tsai-ti-wa, one of the five young men who had been there, agreed to act as guide, and Na-na-he, the adopted Moqui, as interpretor, if his wife would be willing. Council broke. Spent a long time in conversation with a young man named Barret, who called on me today. As the Indians told me, he had been awaiting my coming several days, being dressed as perfectly like a Navajo as I was like a Zuni. Trade and mines are his objects, and learning of my success he has imitated me. He [showed me] on map several ruin and crater [locations].

Tuesday, June 14th, 81.

About as warm but less wind and sand today than yesterday. Spent most of time writing and showing the pueblo to my friends—also helping them to get curiosities.

Spent pleasant day, although wearisome one. Did not succeed in getting to Ta-ai iallone with Doctor, on account of rest of party. Probability of Navajos breaking out. Old men must always be the first. If there be but one shuck, give it . . .[51] [Several empty pages follow.]

5. *June–December 1881*

Expedition to Havasupai

Late in June, having meanwhile carried on under increased facilities the investigations into the inner life of the Zunis, I received . . . authorization for the proposed expedition. . . . I procurred at once the services as guide of a Zuni Indian named Tsai-iu-tsaih-ti-wa, who had before visited the country of the Coçoninos [Havasupai], and accompanied by Tits-ke-ma-tse, a Cheyenne Indian who had been sent by Professor Baird as my assistant, I proceeded at once across the country to Moqui. At the pueblo of Tewa I also secured as interpreter and additional guide a native trader named Pu-la-ka-kai. The season was uncommonly dry, and the only practicable trail led through the Deserto Pintado and the adjacent still more formidable waste over the eastern borders of the Grand Colorado Plateau, in all a waterless journey of more than one hundred miles . . . [to] the great cañon of Cataract Creek. After a [further] journey of more than twenty miles down the solitary trail leading through this cañon, we reached the village of the Coçoninos, . . . more than three thousand feet below the level of the surrounding plains. Here I found about thirty huts occupied by two hundred and thirty-five Indians—men, women, and children. . . . During the four days I was enabled to pass among the Coçoninos, who call themselves *Ha-va-su-pai*—"People of the Willows"—I collected a vocabulary of more than four hundred words, recorded the creation myths of the tribe, and succeeded in securing a complete series of notes regarding their manners, customs, industries, and to some extent their religion and mythology."

—Report to Powell, July 6, 1882 (SWM HC 37)[1]

Daily Journal

The remainder of Cushing's June–July diary is taken up with the Havasupai journey—also the subject of his "The Nation of the Willows," originally published in the September and October 1882 issues of the Atlantic Monthly.

Camp Shoia, Sunday, June 19th, 81.

Very warm morning. Awoke early, and had gratification of seeing Jesus with his horse. During night Ma-he-kwe's mules got away. Let them go, of course. So had to get horse three years old with white face (stallion) for Tits-ke-ma-tse. Tsai-iu-tsai-ti-wa came early. Sent him to get ready. Second horse for Mr. Miller. Wrote Lt. Bishop about adobe pay, General Bradley about boards etc., Solomon Barth about oxen, Dr. Matthews about departure, L. M. Hopkins about Governor's bridles, and Dan'l Dubois about sending my mare. Indians gathered in to see us off. Large crowd at noon when we were ready. Pedro Pino bade us good-bye, and while holding hand of Tsai-iu-tsai-ti-wa said prayer for light, good fortune for us, etc. etc. Bade all good-bye and set out. Was caught by some friends as we passed out of the valley, some saying "Happily may you go. Then the time will come, we think, when through the good fates we shall one another see"—a prayerlike and set form of giving the farewell greeting.

Mules behave tolerably well, boys excellently so. Both understand their business, Tits-ke-ma-tse as well as the other.

Road led north west past Kirilli iallon [Twin Buttes] through an ascent covered with cedar and latterly piñon woods. Scenery subdued and beautiful. Two valleys passed, then woods again, finally quick descent from highest point to plain below, beyond which was the green of the Shoi'a Spring, from which I name our camp Camp Shoi'a.[2] Mule in mud tonight, but rescued.

Monday, June 20th, 81.

Night warm. Tsai-iu-tsai-ti-wa herded the animals nearly all night, but came in at the rising of the moon. No fear about Tits-ke-ma-tse; he is an adept at camping and stands thirst, hunger and riding stoically.

Boys awoke me at sunrise this morning, and disposing of a can of apples etc., which means coffee, we were off in a Southwesterly direction for about two miles, where we struck the main trail which leads nearly west. Soon after joining it, was shown by Tsai where two young Zunis were once waylaid by Moquis. The spot is marked under a cedar tree where they had been resting. The *Suia thlina mosona* [Priest of the West] is one of them. Continuing West for some six miles, we again turned Southwest, down a broken trail to the Spring of A-hok-k'ia-na [Houck's Tank]. Here we were furnished a meal of meat, and I purchased more, and a blanket, with beads and five bits, giving Tits-ke-ma-tse the blanket for the beads (mine) he had so reluctantly parted with. We then left the Valley of A-hok-k'ia-na and mounting a great undulating plain, covered with cedar trees and good grass, we continued until about three o'clock, [when] we reached Tam-ellon iallon, or the Mountain of the Standing Stake—so named from a post placed there to indicate the middle point between Zuni and Moqui. From this point the Ku-ti iallon [Mountain of Tree Trunks?] was in view, the worst part we have to make. Passing over about three miles of very broken white sandy trail, we came to the brow of the latter, from which a wide arc-shaped plain or valley stretched off magnificently to the West, running nearly North and South and from which the terraces of tomorrow's mesa were shown to be two.

On the farthest Western border gleamed the traveler's life, water, in two bright silvery patches, intensely brilliant in the setting sun. Glasses showed a Navajo hogan below them, and grass for the animals. Far beyond, S.W., start the San Francisco Mountains, hedged in, apparently, by terrace after terrace and mesas of black rock so distant and hazy as to look like spectral images. One of the two or three best scenes my eyes have ever drunken in.

Hastened to camp, watered, shaved, washed, helped Tits to make necklace, and retired.

Tuesday, June 21st, 81.

Night cold but delightful for sleeping. At moon rise, mules in Navajo corn, and sent Tits to drive them out. Latter getting unfrozen, and free in the vicious [sic] use of signs. Navajos came to see us and traded saddle blankets for a few beads. Breakfast over, I saddled up and came on ahead, passing a Navajo corn field on first plateau and waiting atop of a breakneck trail on last for the boys.

Busy with writing, noon came with Tsai hunting for me. The road I had taken had no water on it, and hence he detained me. Tits had been left behind with the mules. Hence our road bears only a trifle N. of West, through broad plains surrounded by black mesas on the South. The most desert place I was ever in. Desert shrubs, sage and grass luxuriant but gray with dryness. Here and there an antelope too far away to shoot, an occasional prairie dog village, hot sand and hazy atmosphere, with smoke fairly issuing from the earth, and a cloudless sun and sky. Soon as we found Tits, he went off alone to get a shot at some antelope. When he joined us further on, his horse was tired, and five or six miles further on we had to relieve him. I gave him my horse and sent both on ahead to water, one being unable [missing words] and the other unable to go on foot. I gave them instructions to water the animals and bring back water for me. Continuing over about seven miles in the blazing afternoon sun, I came to a black mesa, round which the trail leads to water. As I turned it, I saw Tsai coming at full run with a canteen of water. My mouth was parched and lips bleeding freely from thirst. After a drink, we resumed our journey.

The water is in a sort of rock shelter at the foot of a huge black conglomerate cliff. Good and icy cold. Navajos live round other side, houses scattered over

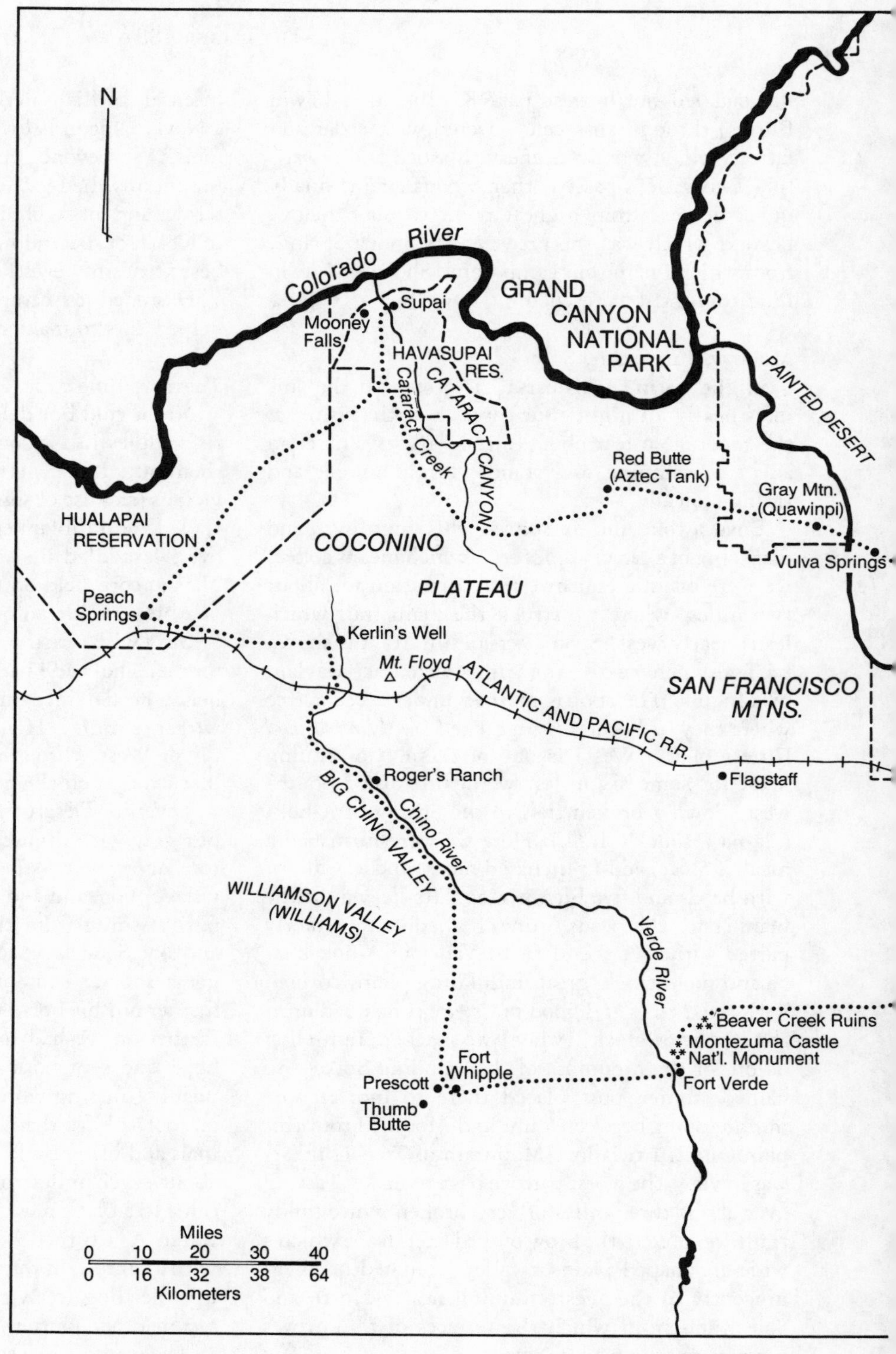

Journey to Havasupai

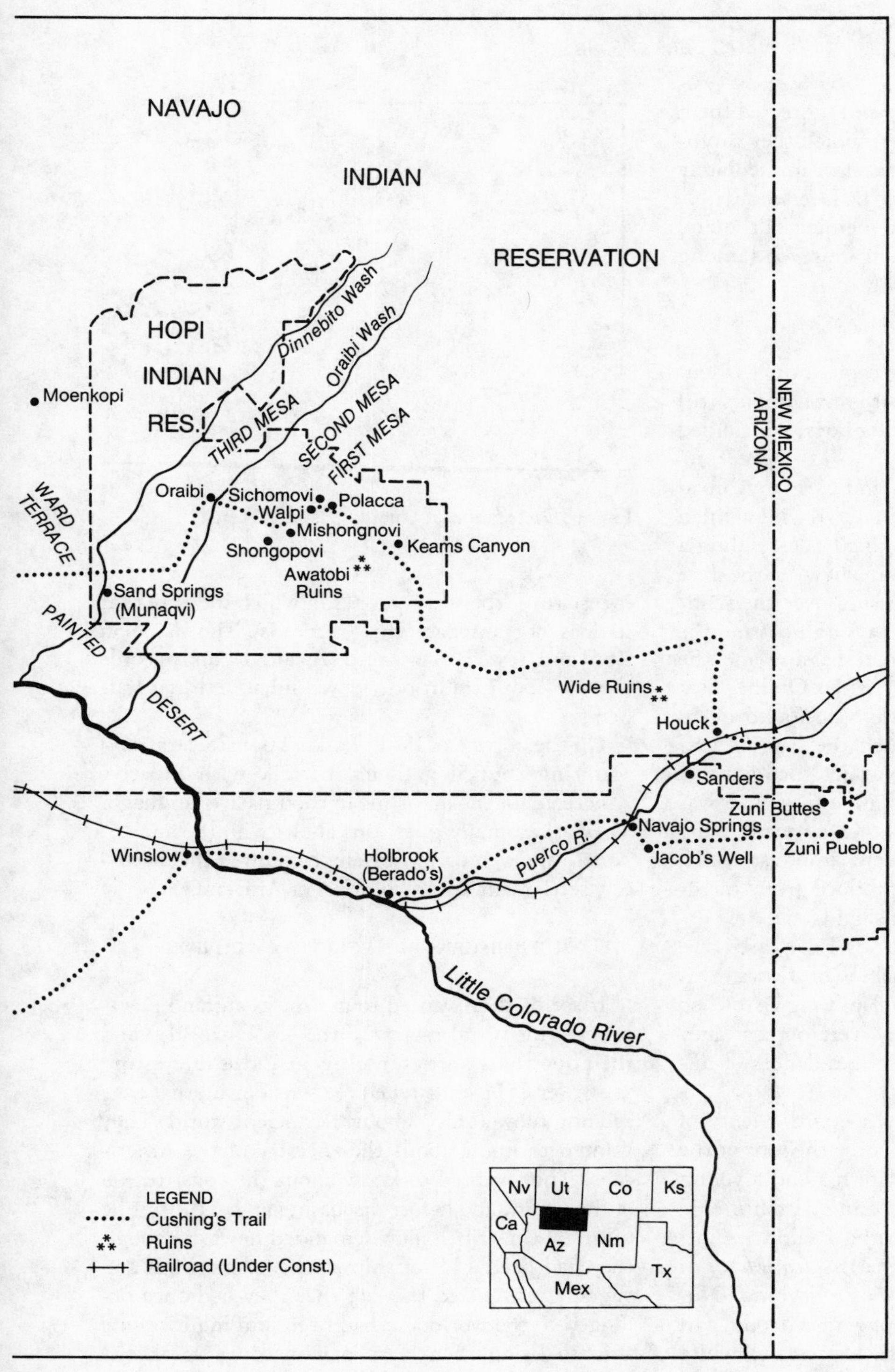
NAVAJO
INDIAN
RESERVATION
HOPI
INDIAN
RES.
Dinnebito Wash
Oraibi Wash
THIRD MESA
SECOND MESA
FIRST MESA
Moenkopi
WARD TERRACE
Oraibi
Sichomovi
Walpi
Polacca
Mishongnovi
Shongopovi
Keams Canyon
Awatobi Ruins
Sand Springs (Munaqvi)
PAINTED DESERT
NEW MEXICO
ARIZONA
Wide Ruins
Houck
Sanders
Zuni Buttes
Navajo Springs
Jacob's Well
Zuni Pueblo
Winslow
Holbrook (Berado's)
Puerco R.
Little Colorado River
LEGEND
Cushing's Trail
Ruins
Railroad (Under Const.)
Nv
Ut
Co
Ks
Ca
Az
Nm
Tx
Mex

plain below. Two came to see us and I directed them to bring me a sheep in morning, which they promised to do. Ate supper at sunset and immediately retired. Tits-ke-ma-tse proves to be Deer *anote* [i.e., member of the deer clan] and a member of the 2nd order of warriors, of which there are seven [among the Cheyenne].

Wednesday, June 22nd, 81.

Arose at sunrise. Navajos came but without sheep. Traded the tired horse with seven dollars [to] boot and came on ahead to wait for boys, who joined me before nine o'clock.

We passed over two plains and as many broad valleys, bounded on the South by Kwinna thlan imnia and other black mesas. Finally descending a sandy plain or hill, we came in view of the first patches of Moqui planting. Passing over the sand, sand, sand bottom, we came to a rough pass on the top of which a Moqui met me, passing me the information that Kuh-nis had visited Oraibi. Lost my knife, but returning a little way, found it. In passing over the ridge on which the pass occurs, found two or three hogans of Navajos. Below was a small spring, at which a pretty Moqui woman was getting water. In the valley yet lower were many picture writings, most prominent amongst which was the following, which I produce from memory—which I take to signify a shield.

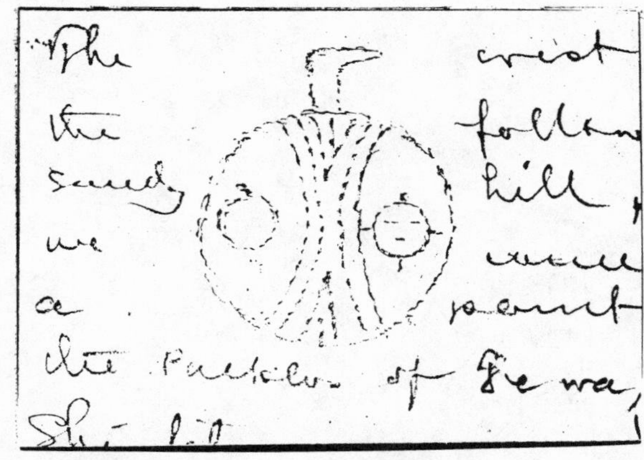

Fig. 18 Pictograph of Shield (Cushing sketch).

The crest of the following sandy hill passed, we came to a point where the pueblos of Te-wa, Shi-tcho-movi [Sichomovi], and Wal-pi were visible, so like the high narrow mesa they were on that they were scarcely recognizable as the residences of human beings.[3]

One more very long sandy slope with plenty of grass, a broad valley, and I was near the foot of the fearful mesa. Near the great cistern stood a young Tewa man. I passed the Zuni greeting with him. He stared at me. "Where is the road?" I said in Zuni, and in same he said, "Ha!" (What!) "*Hop is huitl on na-we? Ma ath-la*" [Where is the road going? Nowhere]; and I thought the young man would fall over with surprise. Rode up such passes as white men would not in the East attempt and at last was heartily welcomed by a former Zuni, Pu-la-ka-kai.[4] On the ridge this side of the spring stands an immense ruin, the straw adobes in which indicate that it does not antedate the Spaniards. The name in Zuni and Tewa is A-wa-te-u [Awatovi], and according to Moqui tradition, it was inhabited by Oraibians.[5]

On the portico of Pu-la-ka-kai's house a large and admiring council gathered to talk with a native American for the first time in their native language. They asked many questions about who the ancient Americans were, and I briefly recounted the discovery, settlement and revolution of America.

Reminiscence: Reception at Tewa

It seems they wanted to use me as a grand newspaper—historical review of the whole world—and their questions were as intelligent and as interesting as any series I ever listened to, considering that they did not know a thing about the ancient world. They wanted to know about the ancestry of the Americans. They wanted to know about the constitution of the world, and before discussing any of the public affairs of the tribe, they demanded news as though they had been a lot of shipwrecked Americans and vaguely recognized the fact that they had once belonged to the world and had been longing for some ship to bring them a man who could speak the language of the world in their language. It surprised me almost unspeakably, but I finally learned that the thing that had caused their curiosity directly was the many relations they had received from visiting Zunis, or trading Zunis, who had come there and told them of the many things I had told the Zunis of the world. In Zuni I used to have classes in history or philosophy. Of course you can imagine what a tremendous harvest that was for my notes. Even the inquiries that these men made! Running through it all was that wonderful conception they have of the world, never in the slightest degree fazed by any statement or explanation that I could make.

San Francisco Examiner, 8 July 1888.

FHC to Baird

Moqui, June 24, 1881

My dear Professor Baird:

On my way to Kuh-ni, I reached the Pueblos of Te-wa, Si-chom-o-vi, and Wal-pi night before last, and visiting the Agency today to receive authority for the employment of a Zuni-speaking Indian as interpreter, which the Agent, Dr. Sullivan, kindly grants, I learn that a mail leaves tomorrow and take this occasion to redeem my promise of a week since.

Just before my departure from Zuni, Tits-ke-ma-tse arrived under the escort of two soldiers, and I take him with me as an assistant to the Kuh-ni country. I am very much gratified and thankful for his timely arrival. I shall take vocabularies and a census of the Kuh-nis and such other notes as possible, which second work I hope will come to account in defraying the expenses of my trip. As I have a desert of three days to cross, which at this season is dry, I am making preparations accordingly, which will probably detain me some. I am universally welcomed in Moqui, and have already been religiously adopted by the Cacique of the Walpis. Should I ever have occasion to work among any Pueblo aside from the Zunis, my ground is broken, as several Moquis speak the Zuni, and my position among the latter people secures me the same privileges among other Pueblos.

I will write you as soon as possible, giving a report of my proceedings from this point on.

And remain, Very Respectfully,

Your Faithful Servant,
F. H. Cushing

Daily Journal

Thursday, June 24th [sic], 81.[6]

Rested all day. Evening visit to Wal-pi and reception into tribe, with prayer and ceremonies by *Kia-kwe-mo-so-na* [town chief].

Everywhere this morning the Moquis watched me. When I awoke, they were on the house top to talk, and admire me. When I looked around, I saw my little Zuni friend Chilota, who had returned to his tribe. He had been sitting in waiting for me since sunrise. He came and kneeled by my bedside to shake my hand and then patiently sat down to wait for me. I arose [and] dressed, and he with his uncle (who had called upon me in Zuni) motioned me to Wal-pi. I went with them, to disgust of Tewans.

The village [is] situated on extreme end of mesa, connected only by narrow passage with stone steps cut. Moccasin path worn six inches deep in rock. At edge of village his sister was waiting for us. She shyly but confidingly dropped her hand in mine and accompanied me to their house, which was on the third terrace. His people received me with great joy. Food was placed before me—jack rabbit stew and rolls of crisp *he-we.* Ate and had a smoke, my little girl with her giant virgin coils of hair on either side of her head sitting close by my side all the while.

Returned, laid down and took a sleep. Awoke to find a council assembled, awaiting my awaking. More about old America. An intelligent curiosity of value in estimation of character. Evening, another visit to pueblo. Two—an old man and a youngish woman—waiting for me. Understood Zuni and came for a talk. Woman home-sick for Zuni. Night, my reception. Embrace, prayer, breathing, etc.etc. Council about Navajo. Begged me to get Agent and have a talk. Promised to do so. Talk till midnight. Little girl all the while nestling in my lap or at my side.

Friday, June 25th [sic], 81.

Visit to Agent. Reception, letters written, council arranged. His aspect toward the Moquis.

In morning, accompanied by Pu-la-ka-kai and Tits-ke-ma-tse, started on horseback for Agency. Ran all the way nearly, passing everywhere little sand-patches of corn. Agency reached at about noon. Found Dr. Sullivan, who received me cordially. Also his son, physician of tribe. Kind men, and good ones too.[7] Would not allow me to return. I sent Indians back, with message that council would come off in morning, Agent Sullivan promising to go out to Tewa and Walpi with me. Agency of substantial houses. Fine store of Mr. Keam's, kept in latter's absence by "Prof." Stevenson of prospector fame.[8] Latter gentleman advised me to return.

Dr. Sullivan wrote order and pass for Pu-la-ka-kai to go with me as interpretor, at $1.00 per day. Passed pleasant evening purchasing two files (.75), beads ($1.00), and a dozen boxes of matches ($1.00). Wrote at night to Prof. Baird, Major Powell, Dr. Matthews, Enos, Mother, and Father. Retired late after discussing Moquis with Agt. Sullivan. His views good, and plans broad and philanthropic.

Omit[ted] to mention call on and introduction to Mr. and Mrs. Robertson, missionaries to Moquis. Same old story.[9]

Saturday, June 26th [sic], 81.

Return from Agency. Council with three Pueblos. Talk afterward. My little girl again. Arrival of Dr. Sullivan.

Rose early—with vegetables as luxury—lettuce especially—for breakfast. Wrote Dr. Thomas concerning census, blankets, etc. Visited store, bade all good-bye, and prepared to go on with Agent S., who had hitched fine team to buggy and was ready. Had some difficulty in leading bronco behind wagon but succeeded after breaking riata several times. Reached Pueblo mesa at about noon, received by four or five men who immediately cared for our animals.

Sunday, June 27th [sic], 81.

Arrangements for leaving. Visit with Dr. S. and with Keh-ti and wife. Evening with my little girl.

Fine morning with some clouds. First work, wrote Father and Emma, then notes, then had long visit with Dr. S. and prepared to go to Walpi.

Monday, June 28th [sic], 81.

Preparations for Kuh-ni. Departure. Arrival at Oraibi. Reception as Mormon. Otherwise as American.[10] *Kia-kwe mosona*'s house. The *Apa-tchu awen otiwa* [leader of Apache, i.e. Navajo, Dance]. Behavior of girls. Wander over pueblo. Departure at sunset for spring.

Tuesday, June 29th [sic], 81.

Visit of two Oraibi chiefs to our camp. Talk on Mormons. Wrote paper to call attention of Mormons to their duty concerning trespass.

In the morning two Oraibi chiefs—the *Kia-kwe-mosona* and another—visited us and had a talk on the Mormon question. Mormons told them same story as Zuni. Would become children of sun by baptism. Could keep their own wives, and when they learned English, to look Mormon girls over, and when they saw one they liked, the chiefs would give her to them. To live together and divide equally the crops. Oraibians believed; hence the Mormons took their wheat and cotton fields away from them. Whenever the Mormon stock got into the Oraibi wheat and did damage, they refused to pay. If pay were demanded, they took a whip and drove their Oraibi friends away. They said that Washington was of no account, but stated that they had been sent by their [own] Washington to rule the Oraibi[an]s and guard them against the lying Americans. Not to trust us, not to tell us what the Mormons said, as, if they did, we were bad and would send soldiers after them.

They must not go to their Agent for any question but come to them, as the Agent would lie to them and could do nothing.[11]

Let spring guide our course Westward. Passed over sand hills and down a long, gently sloping plain to the valley of Mo-e-na-ka-ve, where, in a sandy arroyo we found water—the last that is assured.[12] Oraibi herder gives us a sheep and visits us. Evening Pu-la-ka-ka gives long account of his wanderings to California. The ocean, people, steamboats, porpoises, *and* dolphins, sea shells, printing, book stores, street cars, wheat and fruits, etc. etc. A good observer, and description wonderfully realistic.

Wednesday, June 30th [sic], 81.

Awoke early and prepared to leave Mo-e-na-ka-ve. From latter place we continued almost due west over a very sandy rolling plain for perhaps seven miles, then turned South in an old beaten trail, reaching within three or four miles the painted desert, a wild, sublime series of terraces cut into a thousand fanciful forms by wind and rain, and descending almost constantly to the valley of the Colorado Chiquito at the foot of the San Francisco Mountains. Descending from the sand plain over the first terrace, we came, in a dry arroyo, to a spring or tank of yellowish-green water, almost oval and about four feet long, from all of which it derives its name of *A-shon-kia-na*—Vulva Spring.

The water, although full of insects, was good, although astringent. Making three additional descents, the last over a beautiful cliff of red and brilliant pink sandstone, we reached a sand-dune region which was perhaps nearly eight miles long. Very laborious, though beautiful. Rattlesnakes and lizards of several varieties in abundance.

From which point, continuing So[uther]ly, we followed the sandy bed of a rainstream (dry) in gradual descent to the arroyo of the Colorado Chiquito, marked by a long line of *Polas,* or Cottonwoods. Night when we made camp. Found pool of water, although feed very poor.

Thursday and Friday, July 1st and 2nd [sic], 81.

Journey from Colorado Chiquito to Ka-win-pe cañon. No water.[13] Journey by night and into next day to *Leo-koi-ni-mash-re'e,* or the tank of stinking water. From latter to Aun-she-kiana [Bear Water, from *anshe*: bear, *kiana*: lake]. One more drink. Beautiful forest and grass country. Rain and impressions of my companions. Kind of sacrifice and cave found, Kuh-ni relics. Our camp.

Morning was a little cloudy but warm. I rode on ahead, the trail leading Westward and a little North. Came to a grassy spot and stopped to write notes and let horse feed. Found numerous little lava nodules, brilliantly black. Passed on to red shale hills, entered *Mal pais* region.[14] Road terrible, grass good. Two ravines passed, came to third with water-hole *dry.* Passing three or four more ravines, came to one deeper than rest, long valley leading N.W. thru which trail ran. Mounted the great mesa and again waited for Indians. At about four o'clock all came, went on. Some two miles from brow of mesa came to ravine. Entered with immense difficulty. All water pockets *dry.* Drank a meager allowance each from our goat skin, with *He-pa-lokia* meal, and prepared for journey of fifty miles more.[15] Got out of mesa with great difficulty. Passed through *beautiful* grassy country, wooded, game abundant. At nine o'clock found stinking water pocket which contained two or three gallons of black water. Deer tracks abundant. Drank black stinking water mixed with meal. Rested. Again took road. Country of pine forest. Beautiful glades. Reached Aun-she Kiana at about four o'clock.

Saturday, July 3rd [sic], 81.

Took a good sleep, and we arose to breakfast at about 8 o'clock. I went out to hunt, as deer are abundant everywhere, but the lack of water explains their temporary absence. We shot several pigeons and made dinner of them. Spent afternoon in talking [of] our travels. Pu-la-ka-kai tells of printing, distribution of mail, fountains, his dancing, his presents, the friends he made, animals of the ocean steamers, Americans who spoke a different language, a museum, graftings, Chinese store, silk, ribbands, lacquer-ware, houses of prostitution—Talk with captain of steamer, landing of passengers. His minuteness of observation unsurpassed, and faithfulness of description. Affect on his companions.

We thought of leaving by night, as we have to pass another desert. Two days hence we shall reach our destination. Clouds and rain led us to pass another night here. It is late and we are still talking. The boys have been telling the following of their courtships. [Unfortunately, the remainder of the page was left blank.]

Sunday, July 4th [sic], 81.

Today we left Bear Water (Aztec Tank) [Red Butte on modern maps] for the Cañon of the Kuh'nis. Passing over a country for a few miles quite grown with piñon pine but gradually less so as we went on. Rain again to considerable extent. Course generally North West. Grass good. Saw an antelope and deer or two of remarkable size—which accounts for the superior size of Kuh'ni skins. Came to head of cañon at about 3 o'clock. The descent, into the grandest of cañons, crooked and steep, no where less than 45°C, sometimes steeper. Three turns [took] one through a very steep, narrow passage which led into the open, though very rapidly sloping valley. Over a thousand feet before the base is reached, at which point vegetation changes—palmettos much larger, absence of soap-weed (replaced by Century plant and variety of cactus). Not much water. Rain water abundant below, in rock pockets. Rather late into bed.

Monday, July 5th [sic], 81.

Left today at about half past 10 o'clock. Descent rapid. No water save in pockets. Again, slightly rainy. Course: turn after turn, at 5th of which some pictograph shields with Zuni emblem (see sketchbook).[16] At 9th turn some cliff houses. Last grass. Further on, more cliff houses and pictographs—some wonderfully fresh.

At about three o'clock a sharp turn (now between 2 and 3 thousand ft. below mesa level) brought us to the cottonwood and willow groves above Kuh'ni farms. Water suddenly appears in great volume, clear as diamond over a white sand bottom bordered with willow fringe. Caves etc. everywhere.

Here saw our first Kuh'ni. South American type distinctly, with dress and hair like Pueblos. Short cotton trousers, calico shirt, head band of twisted and dyed fiber. Fine physique, like European races. Well developed legs. Entered town attended by considerable sensation. Went to house of Pu-la-ka-kai's friend, a handsome young Indian. Were well fed—on mescal *He-kusna* [mush] and *green corn*—well on toward ripening. Corn everywhere luxuriant. Irrigation etc. excellent. Council—in which reference to relationship to Zunis. Same story of Creation. Met American—Mr. Sample, miner.[17] Gold and silver below. Retired after long talk.

Tuesday, July 6th [sic], 81.

Arose rather late. Had delightful bath in stream. Rested badly last night; hence rather indisposed. Paid Navajo visit this morning. Purest type of fine Indian in character. Received us quietly, our greetings thankfully, yet reservedly, etc. Visited house of Su-pu-hovi and several others. Took vocabulary. Bathed at noon. Returned to council and trade. Everywhere well received and always invited to eat. Supper of *chuhawe* [young corn] and venison. Excellent council with traders. Visit from Navajo and talk with him. Left about about 9 o'clock and prepared to sleep, first writing and regulating notes. Have decided to leave five days hence, Mr. Sample kindly offering to guide me to Prescott, the boys to be sent home with Moqui. Compelled to make haste on account of animals and provisions.

Wednesday, July 6th, 1881.

Spent day in writing and eating. Did a great deal of trading, which, after the start, went very fast. Blue beads, blankets, brass bracelets, beads and buttons in demand most. Silver buttons more valuable than anything else. Was visited by Mr. Sample. Heat excessive. Crowd worse. Found Sample a good man. Brought horses down to river. Race between Tits-ke and Su-pai boys—about equal, T. a little ahead. Called on Navajo but succeeded in making him understand but little. Have written a letter of recommendation and another regarding a horse which fell over a cliff and which he feared the prospectors would accuse his people of having stolen.

Thursday, July 7th, 1881.

Very warm day. Wrote notes during cool of morning, and with Mr. Sample as guide visited falls below. The river descends in three cascades from village to the lower line of Reservation about $1\frac{1}{2}$ miles below, where the fall is about 150 feet. Cave or grotto below of carbonate of lime once inhabited by Su-pai who was killed by Apaches and place never again occupied nor gardens cultivated. Trail of great difficulty down rocks by means of notches like those of Ta-ai iallone.

One mile further down, another fall, over which the prospector Mooney was precipitated a year and three months since. Descent over two hundred feet. One stream of spray. Scenery grandest possible, and beautiful with verdure. Shape of cliff: horse shoe, with water falling over toward right of middle. Color of rocks red. Visited Sample's mines. Very rich. Carboniferous mostly and rich in galena. Returned to find that horse had gotten into river and drowned. Indians in trouble about trade with Pu-la-ka-kai; [I] would not consent to his trading back—manifestation of ill will which I give no attention to.[18] More trading.

Friday, July 8th, 1881.

Warm day. Propose to leave tomorrow on account of animals and lack of provisions. Shall be able to make no collections this time. Shall be very busy with notes today—which must be very imperfect from difficulty of interpreting. Inner life not to be investigated without study of language. Mr. Sample will accompany me to Prescott. Plans are to leave tomorrow. Navajo particularity in exacting faithful interpretation.

Expect hindrance from dissatisfied Kuh-ni respecting horse, but prepared to stand grounds for reputation of my people. Question broached this evening. I would not listen to more, I told them, and that twenty-four hours' council would not change my mind.

Talk through old blind interpreter on language and mythology. Some names of heavenly bodies collected.

Saturday, July 9th, 1881.

Warm day but breezy. Left cañon. Packing up early this morning, distributed some presents to my hosts and to the old blind interpreter and prepared to leave. Went to Sa-la-sa-ho-vu's house, where found Mr. Sample making ready. Hasty breakfast over, gave Pu-la-ka-kai paper, talked a little while, and bade him and Tsai-iu-tsai-ti-wa farewell. A large crowd assembled to see us off. All merry and good-natured. Navajo came to Sa-la-sa-ho-vu's and told us there was no water at head of cañon. We therefore headed through S.W. cañon to A-ga-sha.[19] Trail for ten miles terrific. Over hedges and precipices of terrible heights and insecurity. Course S.W. Last stretch along edge of cañon with but ½ or 2 feet, below which from 600 feet to a thousand. Only determination would pass it. Wonderful engineering skill exhibited in its construction.

Sunday, July 10th, 1881.

From Yo-hua-ka-ho-na to A-ga-sha. After a [stop for] water at above place, climbed above described trail, and stopped in vale at top. Below, found Maidu tanks containing water, pure, sweet and soft.[20] Very welcome, and good supper. Divided as to journey, but decided to wait till morrow. Made beds together and passed comfortable night. Early this morning started. Windy and cool, though cloudless. Course generally S.S.W. Saw two bunches of antelope, of two and five respectively. No grass for twenty miles, at end of which stopped to lunch and rest animals. Very hard on latter. Reach piñon and pine forests—scattering—further on. Most beautiful glades, similar to those passed from Col[orado] Chiquito to Kuh-ni Cañon. At about 8 o'clock reached old log cabin at A-ga-sha, a spring dug 10 or 12 feet deep in bed of dry grassy arroyo. Only panful apiece for animals. Desperate. Found on way by old beggar of Supai named Tishiyez.

Monday, July 11th, 1881

Camp at Agasha, Walapais. Beautiful though cold night passed. Camp, as soon as made, visited by one Walapai and one adopted Paiute. Rattle and medicine incantation heard during half night at Walapai wigwams over knoll. Similar to Supai. Visited this morning and wakened by O-kou-ia, old Walapai chief whose place is here. Most good humored and kind old Indian, as incapable of absolute wickedness as anyone. Visited by whole camp and begged to come and see sick woman. We all went. One double and two single wigwams of cedar bark, supported by sticks and branches. Leaned against cedar trees as center poles. Noticed antelope decoys, guns, bows and arrows, baskets, panniers, trays, roasting bowls, etc. etc. Tame dogs and hawk, young pigeons and several children. Women better made than Supai; all dirty, never washing, prolific. Men same, though smaller. Sketched young man in decoy.

Tuesday, July 12th, 81.

Camp at A-ga-sha, more of Walapais.

Found in rafters of log cabin biographical sketches of revolutionary heroes and Prescott's *History of Conquest of Peru,* 3rd book. Read with interest.

Made another call at Walapai camp. Sketched O-kou-ia, squaw, wigwam and sweat house. Hunter came in, bought two quarters of antelope from him for $1.25. Women roasting grass seed with live coals in trays protected by thin coat of pitch and some mineral substance. Very dextrous motion circularly around grass seed to side of center. Roasting complete. Ground and added to meat soup. *Very* rich and wholesome, though dirty.

Another medicine incantation over squaw. Latter will not live, suffering from inflamation of stomach; had been incised twice over pit {?} and sucked, cauterized.

Sent animals to spring in cañon three miles N.W. Plenty of water.

Wednesday, July 13th, 81.

From A-ga-sha to Peach Springs—S.W.[21] Again sent animals to spring and decided on account of Indians to go around by Hackberry, near Western boundary of territory, more than a hundred miles further, on account of lack of water.

Changed course, and after securing services of Walapai boy (2.00) started for some tanks called *A-ke-hual-le*. Traveled into evening, saw antelope. Found trail leading S.E., which, after some fifteen miles joined other {trail} to the A-ke-hual-le tanks. East, within mile or two of latter, left it, in dark, and started out northeast. Within two miles, Indian shouted and said "Heap shoot." T. shot twice and was answered once. Struck out. Mountain of obsidian found by two Indians. Soon found camp in little vale. Camp of Ke-thutch, sub-chief of Hualapai. Three wigwams, three men, four squaws—two very pretty—and five children. Found little water below. Ate hard supper and dug more water from lower tank. Signs of rain. Made bed of juniper and passed delightful evening.

Thursday, July 14th, 1881.

Passed day in camp at A-ke-hual-le. Very oppressive and cloudy. Traded little blanket for woman's dress. Bought some meat and paid Indian $3.50. Plenty of antelope. Visited Ke-thutch's camp. He made a speech about how he was surrounded by people but that he always remained at home minding his own business and hunting. He said his people did not raise corn but depended upon grass, reeds, etc., for cereals. His squaw asked me if I would eat a cake of grass-seed if she would prepare it, and I said yes. She toasted some as before described, and then grinding it into an oily paste, patted it out into an oblong cake and presented me with a dark, oily mass extremely palatable and rich.

Decoys made same as Zuni masks, save stuffed with cedar bark in drying.

Wrote and read some. Slept more. At night rained to some extent and raised our hopes.

Friday, July 15th, 1881.

Still cloudy, very warm and a sprinkle of rain. Prepared to go to Kerlin's Wells this morning.

Walapais came around camp and I traded a pair of black moccasins for Ke-thutch's heavy three-soled ones, as he said wherever he went, whoever saw him, they would look at his feet—shading his eyes at the same time and intently regarding the imaginary feet.

Sprinkled and clouded. Watered animals limitedly and packed up, the Indians at the same time leaving for a distant hunting tank. Took S.W. course over obsidian and *malpais*. Ground everywhere soft. Grass moderate. Country rolling, almost mountainous. Passed broad valley S.W. by W. climbed a big *malpais* mountain and left S.W. again. Just after dark struck a crooked cañon, and two miles down came upon a dry tank. Dug in ground and found a few pans full of water for thirsty animals. Camped in mouth. Passed good though undecided night. Rain to South.

Saturday, July 16th, 1881. Kerlin's Wells.

Morning sultry, though cloudy, with rain to S.E. Sample and I went on to examine Kerlin's wells. Found what we supposed to be abundant water. S. immediately went back to get T. and animals, while I remained behind to dig. Found supply to be limited. Doves and crows in myriads flock about tank.

"Kerlin's Wells" is inscribed on the face of the black rock cañon just above the tank. This is situated a few rods south of the celebrated road to California constructed through the desert by Lt. Beal. Kerlin was an officer under Beal, and the well may have been discovered by him—hence name.[22] I took little nap and boys returned. They had given all water to animals and we had none even for ourselves. Desperate case. I ordered them to get dinner and pack. That we must travel that day and all night for Roger's Ranch became certain. While eating, sprinkled and gave no hope.

Followed trail nearly due South. Some sixteen miles on, saw that Southern rains had wet ground very much. Hoped Wickiup tanks would contain enough for horses and selves.[23] One narrow strip about latter, not twenty rods wide, was dry and dusty. Of course no water. General disgust and desperation. Resolved to camp in Wickiup until rising of moon. Slight rain to South. At midnight were wakened by T. and packed again. Started S. [and] myself leading on foot.

The pictographs on rocks about Wickiup tanks are of Pueblo, if not *Shi-wi* origin.

Sunday, July 17th, Rogers Ranch.[24]

After continuing about four miles down cañon, crossing and re-crossing arroyo, came to Little Chino Valley, crossing which, struck a road. Continued to low bluffs, where I awaited the boys. We had breakfast just before daylight. Had been heavy rain. Horses ate damp grass ravenously from thirst. Discovered loss of silver bridle. Continued down road into broad valley which appeared greenish gray and fresh in morning light. Here a railroad road joins that of Chino Valley where it becomes Big Chino Valley.[25] Some seven miles [further] we saw our haven not of rest [but] of water. *Water.* Rogers Ranch. Tits. suddenly left trail. Soon we heard report of rifle. Looked back and saw he had wounded and was chasing an antelope. Latter passed valley. We (S.) fired but did not hit it. T. came up, drank, took rifle and struck out on trail. Went on to Rogers Ranch. Animals drank excessively. Found camp of eleven R.R. men, who supplied us with baking powder, sugar and tea. Ranch consists of a little plaster and scantling house, with saloon in process of construction, to right, near one side of valley. In front, large corral with long trough into which water is lifted by horse power. Supply unfailing from well of sixteen feet. A valuable suggestion to ranchmen, as this place is capable of supporting 2000 cattle.

Tits returned with antelope on his back and pride in his heart. We feasted greatly, noon and evening.

Heavy rain evening.

Monday, July 18th, 1881. Rogers Ranch.

Very hot day, although cloudy. Slept in incipient saloon, passing miserable night. Rose late. Had good breakfast. Just learned today of attempted assassination of President Garfield. Shocking. I wish I could see Joe, as he is now the President's private secretary.[26] Sent Titske after bridle. Very unwilling to go. Indications of rain. Hope to get off tomorrow. Sergeant from Camp Walapai came with orders to Rogers about noon.[27] A post to be established somewhere in this section. Verde being abandoned. Learned today of ancient ruins and fortified mounds in upper part of William's Valley—from Mr. Sample, who has frequently examined them.

Very terrific rain at about 3 o'clock. Tits. returned at sundown. Brought bridle, but no reins. In evening did a little banjo picking. Broken up by arrival of three R.R. contractors, one of whom had met me at Wingate. Retired early.

Tuesday, July 19th, 1881.

Left Rogers Ranch at about 11 this morning, after passing uncomfortable night and having difficulty in getting horses this morning. Day cloudy with indications of rain. Bought a workman's (Irish) valise. Offered him $2.50, which he refused, saying it was too much—paid under his protest $2.00. Rare honesty for Arizona.

Country rolling and in patches dry. Rain covered only about three miles, to appear some ten miles further down, where T. went to shoot an antelope. His maneuvers very Indian. Hit his horn. A mile further, passed Sullivan's cattle ranch, a typical one, well improved, and passed into farming settlement of Williams [Williamsons] Val[ley]. Cottages, very Eastern life. Two *painted* white. Rain drove us into an uninhabited shanty. Very hard thunderstorm. Very soon, sheet of water came gushing down from Granite Mountain. Rain only of a few miles extent and observed one today which remained around two little mountains and extend[ed] only half a mile into the valley in any direction.

Reached Breon's Station in rain near evening and put up there. Found comfortable quarters and fine board with *potatoes*—which are raised in the valley abundantly. Breon has frequently ploughed up green stone ornaments on his farm.[28] He has flowers, vines and pets—birds and dogs. A little cottage above (west from here) shows his thrift and taste. Four beautiful willows (which he planted) shade it—all in all a very civilized little place and man.

Take a warm bath and retire. Shall reach Prescott tomorrow. Look forward to, yet dread it on account of my costume, but then "Duty" and all is well.

Coues and party passed here last night for Walapai, where I shall call on them if possible.

Fort Whipple

{Arriving at Fort Whipple, outside Prescott, Arizona, Cushing reported:} I was most kindly received and greatly aided in the investigations of ancient ruins, etc. in the neighborhood of Prescott and Fort Verde. . . . Between Camp Hua-la-pai {Walapai} in western Arizona and the cliff ruins of the Rio Verde I discovered a remarkable series of mesa strongholds exhibiting a crude form of the Pueblo architecture and undoubtedly furnishing a clue to the origin of its terraced features" (Report to Powell, July 6, 1882, Southwestern Museum HC 37).

Wednesday, July 20th, 1881.

Rose late. S[ample] decided to go to see a partner or to visit Phoenixville. Bill with Breon 6.50. Treated admirably by that gentleman. Came on early. Animals within 8 miles of Prescott jaded. Therefore did not get in until late (4 o'clock). Was received very kindly by Lieut. Wotherspoon, whose example was followed by everyone else. I am honored and made at home and ease, notwithstanding my costume. Met at Lt. Wotherspoon's Lts. Von Schroeder, Wilson and Smith, {and} Maj. Egbert. Had excellent bath and at dinner at Mrs. Egbert's met lat[ter] lady and Major Egbert. Passed pleasant evening in company with Dr. Smith, Capt. {space} and Lts. {space}. Was called on by Lt. {Carl F.} Palfrey, a keen observer and very cultivated man. Was invited to Captain's house and Dr.'s quarters. My apprehensions are over. Learned of papers relating to my transportation. Wrote Doctor Matthews and Enos, also Emma, and commenced to Prof. Baird.

Matthews to FHC

Fort Wingate, N. M.
July 21, 1881

My dear Friend:

I thought that on your arrival at Prescott you might like to find a note telling how the world here wags, so I write:

I got your letter from Moqui, and had many misgivings as to your future safety on account of your mishaps before reaching Moqui. Soon after I got your letter, I met Mr. Sullivan, the Moqui agent, and he said he saw you going off in good shape and in high spirits. Now to the brief news of the place.

Your brother Enos is still here and seems to be doing splendidly. Everybody is gaining confidence in him and he is kept very busy. Your census papers were fixed up by your brother and were sent off some time ago. Your specimens have not yet been shipped. I sent Lieut. Wotherspoon your $50 and you will find it there when you arrive. Many flattering articles have appeared about you recently in the papers—either copies of what Bourke and Baxter have written or extracts from the same. The Santa Fe *New Mexican* had a complete copy of Baxter's *Boston Herald* letter. I sent a copy of the *New Mexican* to Prof. Baird with the article marked, and have a few more copies on hand if you want to use them. Extracts have appeared in the local papers at your home, in the *Army and Navy Journal,* etc. A party of Austrian noblemen came here with the intention of visiting Zuni, but when they found out you were not there they did not go over. And Thomas Moran, the great artist, was coming to Zuni, but hearing from Fornance at Albuquerque that you were not there he did not come further than Albuquerque.[29] He may come here yet but will not go to Z. Mr. Ealy's successor went over about the time you left, so I think E. was contemplating leaving Zuni about the time that you came down on him in your might, and probably had made all his arrangements long before.[30]. His successor is one of those cadaverous sky-pilots who wear a stereotyped smile on their faces. . . .[31]

Your Sincere Friend,
W. Matthews

Daily Journal

Friday, July 22nd, 1881.

My birthday, I believe. Went down to office with Lt. W. and from there to Sutter's store—who treated me very well and ushered me into the officer's room. Was called on there by young Wilcox, who begged me to come up to stable and see his fine Arabian, which he kindly offers to sell me in event of failure of my own. Insisted on my going to his house. His room most elegant I have seen in West. Very lusty and dressy young man. Was invited to dinner. Met Misses and Gen'l Wilcox. Plain mannered and very good people who have the best courtesy possible and make one feel at ease immediately. Compelled to remain until quite late. Called at Lt. Palfrey's but not at home. Returned in time for dinner. Passed pleasant evening chatting with Lt. Schroeder and called with him at Lt. Palfrey's. Latter not at home but called on us. Appointed to meet him on morrow 11 a.m.

Saturday, July 23rd, 1881.

Passed pleasant night. At Lt. W's house met some other gentlemen. Everyone was very kind. Made engagement to visit inscriptions at Thumb Butte with General Wilcox yesterday, who arrived before my departure. Splendid old gentleman. Calling at Lt. W's office, met and had most interesting conversation with Captain Eugan. Very cultivated and pleasant gentleman, more observing than most officers. Invited me, as all have done, to call on him. Called at Lt. Palfrey's house, was very well entertained, the Lt. being a prime scholar. Has splendid collection of books and maps. Latter most perfect on America extant. Saw in a *New Mexican* immense notice of myself, which, however, oversteps the mark and modesty.

Very threatening rain clouds. Called at Gen. W's but found him, Miss W., and the Lt. decided on going mounted and had pleasant ride with them to place, which is perhaps half a mile this side of Thumb Butte. Distinctly Zuni. On high rock which caps a natural heap like pyramid. Face literally covered. Among symbols—*Mo-yu-tchun* [star], *Sai-an-ne* [horn, antler], *Na-a-li* [deer], *E-la-we Mi-kai-a-thla* [standing young corn], *Hle e-to-we* [large turtle], *We-lo-lo* [lightning], etc. etc.[32] Returned through town with Lt. and purchased gloves. Returned to tea with General and daughters. Excellent wines and fare. Passed most pleasant evening. . . .

Latter very kind—more so than any commander I've met. Will see me through in everything—men, transportation, etc. etc. To make expedition Monday to Verde with Lt. Wilcox. Cliff ruins, graves, etc. etc. Gen'l anxious to have my photograph, my company, and to get me to give a little lecture before a select audience. His daughters most kind, wish to get up a reception for me, which I dread.

Rumors of Navajo war. So ho! on account of Eastman.[33]

MATTHEWS TO FHC

Ft. Wingate, August 8th, 1881

My dear Cushing,

I received your letter some days ago. "Colonel"!! Stephenson [sic] came down on us a week ago with half a dozen tenderfeet, including Professor Gore, Harry Biddle, the son of a Virginia Senator, a young Mr. McElhone, brother of a potent newspaper man, Mr. Mindeleff, an artist, and several other "judicious" appointments.[34] Stephenson staid with us, and we blew your trumpet all the time he was here, & he kept rather "mum." A portion of the party are gone to Zuni to get materials to make an immense model of the Pueblo, the biggest model they have yet made, to be about 15 feet square.[35] Enos quit his work and went over with them. Gore and two others stay here to make a number of those valuable "base-lines" which are scattered all over the west. Stephenson has gone to Santa Fe for some inscrutable purpose and expects to bring Powell back with him in a few days. Mrs. Stephenson came to Crane's Ranch & stopped there, so we have not seen her fair face nor listened to her gentle voice. Perhaps she wanted an invitation to Wingate but she didn't get one.

Did you see Dr. Coues' wonderful etymological article in the *Nation* on the name *Yava-Supai*? His derivation is from *Agua Azul,* "Blue Water," which I think is "stuff."[36] He just wanted to rush into print. I wish you would get into print on the subject as soon as possible. If you will send me a full description of your trip, written in a popular shape, I will send it to Baxter, or you can send it to him yourself and ask him to rewrite it, over his own name. But you should get your work before the world just as soon as possible.

Lieut. Bourke came here three days ago and went right off to Moqui to see the rattlesnake dance. Peter Moran, an artist, and brother to Thomas Moran of Holy Cross Mountain fame, goes along with Bourke.[37] B. regretted much that you had gone to Kuhni; he had hoped to go with you. I think

Bourke is really a good friend of yours. Please keep all this scandal to yourself, except that you may reveal my sentiments to Lt. Wotherspoon.

Mrs. Matthews sends you her kindest regards,

Very Truly Yours,
W. Matthews

Please burn when read.

Dubois to FHC

Deer Springs, A.T. Aug. 9th 1881

Mr. Frank Cushing, Zuni, N.M.
Dear Sir:

The bearer who says that he is a brother of Jack's has had one of my horses for the last sixteen days. We hunted for the horse for fourteen days, but could not find for the reason that the Indians kept it hid and moved it from place to place, wanting pay for telling where it was. Besides they have ridden the horse damn poor and made his back sore and left him in a hell of condition generally. Now I wish you would do me the favor to tell the Zunis that I will not pay them a damned cent for picking up my horses when they see them running on the range. My horses are not lost nor would there be any trouble if they would let them alone. There are horses and cattle belonging to the Indians at my place the year round and they never have any trouble in finding and getting them. Now besides causing me to ride from thirty to forty mile a day for two weeks they hunt deer with my animal hunt horses and lend from one to the other to keep it out of my sight and then want to be well paid for giving it up after stealing a bell off of it that cost me $4.

Now Mr. Cushing please to tell Mr. Ingin that the next one of them that I catch riding a horse of mine is going to get hurt as sure as hell. Besides this some of them killed a cow of mine a short time ago. I will give $25 cash to find out what Indian done it.

Yours Truly,
Dan Dubois

Draft: FHC to John G. Bourke

Fort Whipple
August 13, 1881

My dear Lieutenant Bourke:

The condition of the railroads, of which you have doubtless been informed, resulted in the detention of my mails which were forwarded from Fort Wingate and reached me only last night on my return from Camp Hualapai.

By the same mail I am informed that the Snake Dance comes off within five days from present date—exactly a month sooner than I had been informed it would by the Moquis when I visited them in June; and I telegraph you today that you may not miss the ceremonial in case you have waited for notice from me, as we had unfortunately arranged. From the Moquis I gathered that there were to be performed *two* snake dances during the season—the one by the Walpi and the other and later by the Oraibi Indians, the latter which I naturally looked forward to visiting with you, as it occurs in the largest of the Moqui pueblos and takes place at the full of the moon in the month of ripened melons and corn. As a warm friend of mine among the Tewa Indians who speaks both Moqui and Zuni fluently promised to come for me (at Zuni) two weeks in advance, I decided to await his arrival and then communicate with you definitely by telegraph. Should you miss the great ceremonial through this mistake of my judgment, I shall never cease to deplore it. Hence I take every ready means of mending my error.

By the same mail which brought to hand the kind letter I now acknowledge, I received also a very happy note from you containing some highly complimentary, valuable, and—notwithstanding their rather strong estimations of me—equally pleasing newspaper notices of my Zuni work, for all of which I am indebted so deeply to yourself that I cannot attempt to adequately express my earnest and affectionate gratitude to you for them.[38]

Yet more evidence of your kindness—inexplicable kindness—came as the result of your favorable conversations with Generals Sheridan and Crook in the form of an encouraging, noble, generous communication from the former—whom I met at Fort Wingate last winter and whose goodness bears out my then unconscious estimation of his character. I do myself the honor to acknowledge his letter by this mail.

Whether I am pleased to hear of your intentions to visit the Navajo and do work among them, the

Grand Cañon, and the Moquis in my company I do not pretend to say. You know I am—so much so that I leave the attractive fields for archaeology which I find in Arizona *immediately,* that I may possibly reach Zuni in time to yet join you—when it may happen that we will again work down this way, visiting the Ha-va-su-pai and Huala-pai—very important tribes for *you*—and sharing together that which is too good for me alone, the pleasure of finding each day new facts regarding the abundant archaeologic remains of this marvelous ancient country.

You may perhaps have noticed an article in *The New Mexican* which copies from the *Boston Herald* a rather enthusiastic account of myself in which it makes mention of my "*undoubted*" discovery of the Seven Cities of Cibola. I *have* gotten, since my conversation with you at Dr. Matthews' which awakened me, some pretty strong, although by no means infallable, facts regarding the subject. On my return from Wingate I was joined by Lt. Emmett, Mr. Baxter and Metcalf of Boston—which latter gentlemen plied me incessantly with questions, thus giving additional cause for my making a rather interesting investigation of the matter—all resulting as you may have seen it. And yet more, after my arrival in Moqui: I learned considerable concerning the Province of Tusayan which I had not known before, all of which together with much that is new regarding the three sets of clans among the Navajo—gentile, sacred (or phratral) and territorial, which your earnest enquiries and a desire to help you inspired me to search up—I hope to be able to talk with you about when I see you again.

I now come to a totally different matter, which you are peculiarly and perhaps alone able to give me advice and direction in.

I have decided definitely only last night to seek an appointment as Second Lieutenant in the U.S. Army. Not alone because I have always wished to enter the Public service, as evinced by an early inclination toward one of the academies, discouraged, however, by my friends and relatives, and by my subsequent medical studies, which were made with a view to the same end but cut short by my detail on the Indian work two years since; but because the army offers unparalleled advantages for social, institutional and scientific cultivation, the possibility of following up one's mistress not in a hard uncertain struggle for niggardly existence but as a love to be cultivated for the love that is in her, not for the money and fame she may afford, which are to such as I secondary, unattractive, repulsive. Such a course would be, I am aware, unsuited to me were I alone ambitious for a name in ethnological science. But the well spring of my interest is far apart from this, which I can explain only as an instinct—a deathless enthusiasm, an ever present, silently urging voice, which I follow because I cannot resist. Had I, on the other hand, been actuated in my choice of calling by a desire for money, I should have chosen that which my talent fitted me for—sculpture—or that which my father destined me for—medicine.

I cannot give you in a preliminary letter all the reasons I have for wishing to enter the army. Perhaps, after all, it is inexplicable—as I had the wish when all motives in life were more obvious. But I *want to,* and I ask you to give me all directions and advice rendered possible and easy to you, perhaps more than to any one else, with no more cold water than truthfulness requires.

So far as my qualifications are concerned, my physical education has been peculiarly fit, my understanding of Indian character, from the *inside,* of the sign language of the plains, of the base language of the Pueblos and of the Mexican patois might be other advantageous qualifications.

The privations I have undergone and the habit of accepting very hard details in the pursuance of my line of researches would enable me to follow unmurmuringly such distasteful orders as might come to my fate, or make me submissive to the necessity of occasional isolation—neither as great as I have already endured in lonely posts.

In brief, I wish to enter the army that I may cultivate arms as a profession and science as a recreation and love.

What do you think of it all? Expecting to meet you soon in New Mexico with the best hopes for and abundant trust in the success of your Indian investigations, I am gratefully,

Your Humble True Friend,
F H Cushing

Initiation to the Bow Priesthood[39]

A prerequisite for admission to the Bow Priesthood (or, from the Zuni standpoint, a circumstance requiring *membership in that order) was possession of an enemy scalp. Cushing had tried, and failed, to fill this requirement with two scalps sent him for the purpose from the East. On the return trip from Prescott to Zuni, however, his need was met. "The timely outbreak of the Apaches enabled me . . . to secure an additional scalp. On the strength of these and of my standing with the tribe, I was admitted to full membership in this society soon after my arrival at the pueblo" (Report to Powell, SWM H-C 37). This was indeed a crucial turning point for Cushing, "the most important step {he had} ever taken in {his} work," as he wrote to Baird; for initiation to the Bow opened the doors to all the other religious societies in the pueblo and put him on a whole new footing in the community and in his quest for knowledge of pueblo life. Moreover, the experience of the sixteen-day-long ceremonial was itself without doubt a profoundly significant one for him, a true rite of passage from which he emerged with altered consciousness and with much deepened capacities for understanding, from the inside, what it was to be a Zuni.*

What prompted the Zuni leaders to accept Cushing at this point into the highly prestigious order of the Bow? It is evident from one letter that the decision was made with some reluctance, the possession of an enemy scalp being in Cushing's case a necessary but not quite sufficient condition. According to one of his letters, what tipped the scales was his warning that, if denied, he would soon leave the pueblo and return to Washington. This they seem not *to have wanted, having by this time discovered the uses to which he could be put as a mediator with the outside world. Indeed the Zuni headmen were not long in recognizing the possibility of his usefulness in the Bow (war) society, which was, in effect, the defensive arm of the secular government in dealing with threats from without as well as within the community. Once the decision was made to admit him and his membership was sealed by the sacrament of initiation, they moved almost at once to make the best of the situation by putting him into the position of military leadership which he translated as "1st War Chief."*

Draft: FHC to General Bradley

Navajo Springs
September 12, [1881]

Sir:

On [the] way from Prescott to Zuni, I saw yesterday morning, two miles this side of Berado's, a dozen shots exchanged between sixteen mounted men and several ranchers.[40] The ranchmen ran and mounted party galloped to hills toward S[outh] in two squads single file. As nearly as I could determine with field glasses, they were Apaches who are reported four miles from Berado's. Ranches of region deserted and people [are] at latter place.

If you judge right, let Gen'l Wilcox know, as I promised him all such items. Will reach Zuni day after tomorrow.

Respectfully,
F. H. Cushing

FHC to Baird

Zuni, September 24, 1881

Dear Professor Baird:

As I informed you in my letter from Fort Whipple, August 25th, I left that Post on the fourth day following, reaching Zuni on the 16th inst., after a severe journey—four days of it through country raided by Apaches. This matter, far from being disastrous, enabled me to secure a scalp, which, with the ones furnished by my father and Dr. Yarrow, enabled me to get a hearing in the secret council, be named a candidate for entrance into the Order of the *Apithlan Shiwani,* or Priests of the Bow, and subsequently confined and fasted four days and nights in preparation for initiation, which, with this slight interval, is to be on the fourth day hence. Having been in close confinement, I have heretofore had no opportunity for writing you, and even now my communication must be brief.

I have been for more than a year, anxious to join this fraternity of the Zunis—the almost universal Masonic order of advanced Indian tribes, the repository of all the sacred recitations and prayers so often mentioned in my letters, and the only means I had of progressing further with the study of the secret religious institutions which, without membership, are barred even from the Zunis.[41] I am now compelled to write these things as one of my duties and, as rapidly as possible, acquire or memorize them. I see nothing but hard work for more than a year in order to accomplish this, a year which will cost me the sorest exercise of will in case it be deemed advisable to spend it. The most important step I have ever taken in my work, which but a few days old, yields results I have labored seven months for—and I therefore did not hesitate at the expense of it, which is and will be very considerable, as I, in the character of a novitiate, have to give a grand feast to the tribe and to my order.

This, with the expenses of the Kuh-ni and Verde and Hualapai expeditions, during which I lost by thirst three animals and nearly an Indian, leaves me today more than two hundred dollars ($237.00) in debt, and I beg that you have sent at once the sum of three hundred dollars.[42] Knowing the importance of the step I have taken, together with the fact that my expenditures are always judicious and economical [and] my life consequently frugal and hard, I do not hesitate to make these demands or requests—the more as they are measures of *necessity.* I know that my results are going to please you [and] are of importance, and whenever a liberal yet judicious use of means is likely to affect favorably my progress, I shall not hesitate. . . .

My notes of the Havasupai were very considerable and complete. As they were taken systematically, I have already succeeded in writing about two thirds of my report on the trip and reconnaisance. So soon as the ceremonials of the present cease to claim my attention, I shall complete and forward it to you for immediate publication if you like.

Promising to write very fully at an early day, I have the honor to remain

Very Respectfully,
Your Obedient Servant,
F H Cushing

DRAFT: FHC TO MATTHEWS

Zuni, Sept. 30th, 1881

Dear Friend—

I have been so busy with the ceremonials of my initiation ever since I returned that I could not hunt up the beads which you asked me to get. I have had no rest until this morning, and I am now scarcely able to write. I have just returned from a meeting of the *A-pi-thlan shiwani* (it is after midnight) and shall be compelled to continue these for the sake of schooling in sacred songs and dances for four nights, when the final ceremonial of my initiation will be completed. This lasts . . . [torn out] days and takes place in the Grand dance of the *Oi-na-he* which I made mention of to you.[43]

I despair of ever being able to record fully all I have passed through and seen during the recent few days. The initiation is a terrible tax on endurance, but was grand beyond power to describe. I often thought during it that I would give much to have you present, for I know you would have been intensely interested in the marvelous regularity of all forms observed. It was weird and impressive—more so than anything I've ever seen. I have taken an elephant on my hands, but it is a white one. I wear upon my right wrist no longer the silver bracelets but four rows of medicine shells—never to be removed until I take my second degree. In the adjoining room hang my medicine pouch, war club, bow and arrows. I look upon them all with pride, for there are many Zunis who have passed the meridian of life who have longed and striven for this honor in vain.

Each day I record some prayer or acquire more and more of the marvelous dead language songs of this order. One of these which requires three hours for its repetition has not one modern Zuni word in it—and thus I find it is that the medicine and spirit of these institutions are kept secret. Wonderful, isn't it?

Will you kindly send over by Mr. Chappell the memorandum book in my reticule? I wish to collect data regarding the Solomon Barth matter.[44]

My kind regards to Mrs. Matthews, to whom present with my compliments the bear skin.

Very sincerely yours,
FHC

FHC TO BAIRD

Zuni, October 12, 1881

My dear Professor Baird:

I am glad to write you of great successes recently

in the line of our researches. As hinted in my last letter, I have just been passed through the ceremonials of initiation into the secret order of the *A-pi-thlan Shi-wa-ni,* or Priests of the Bow. In order that I might be made eligible to this position, I had first to be made "son of the Parrots," or adopted into the Parrot gens; "child of the Eagles," to establish the paternal gentile relations; and "child of the Sun," a matter of religious significance. I have the position of "Junior Priest of the Bow," with the privilege of taking the twelve other degrees of the society, or entering any of the ten medicine orders of the tribe.[45] This order is the Masonry of the North American Indians, if for the sake of happy, yet not misleading comparison, it may be referred to as such. It exists among many, if not all, of the advanced Indian tribes, as with all Pueblos, the Navajos, the Mandans, Arickarees, and Hidatsas of the North, [and] the remnants of the civilized Indians of Mexico in the South. There are prayers and songs in this order, embodied in ancient and obsolete language, which would require many pages of foolscap for their transmission, and which I was compelled to vow sacredly I would never weary of until I had acquired or written them. The priests above me have required me already to write carefully ten of them, and these alone are worth all sacrifices I have been compelled to go through in entering the order: the four days—first the day of motionless attitude and silence, the three nights of dancing in the estufa, the last of which was continued until physical exhaustion compelled some of the members to retire, giving me the same privilege. The feast I had to give in common with my four brothers, was expensive, but not so much as I had anticipated and has been a hundred-fold repaid. As a consequence of my initiation I have had a world of facts opened up to me, which I had despaired of ever reaching. I had from my former standpoint exhausted the subject with the exception of a few details, and was preparing to come home permanently during early January of 1882, in case your decision would prove favorable; but from the present I see nothing but the most constant work, with the best of facilities for at least four years to make my work *exhaustive.* I can never give this amount of time to the work, even with your heartiest concurrence, however important it may seem, as I have interests in life apart from Zuni. But I would be willing to devote, say, a year or two more to it, or at least parts of such a period. Indeed, my disappointment would be almost irreparable, were I unable to study for a period almost as great, from the *inside,* the life of the Zunis, as I have from the outside. After having secured the two necessities, the absolute confidence and language of the Indian, I feel it my duty to use these necessities or advantages to the fullest extent of their value, toward the end which I acquired them for.

I have decided to ask your permission for my return in January with four or five Indians to Washington, and with this view, I have begun negotiations for securing free passage for myself and party via Omaha and Chicago. Some excellent connections which I have made during the past two years, will, I think, render this easy. Some of my enthusiastic friends in the two cities mentioned will aid me strongly; and the ladies of Boston have extended cordial invitations to me, to bring my party on if not to Boston, as far East as New York and Washington, promising their aid, etc.; also I wish to make this move principally to advance my future work in Zuni, as the Indians have each day, for more than a year, spoken of this, begging that I should bring it to pass. They wish to see my great cacique's house, see what we will do with their things, and if in the end they prove satisfied, they promise to furnish me a series of their sacred costumes for the dances, etc., than which nothing can be more interesting, beautiful, or valuable for an ethnographic museum. Inasmuch as after the New Sun festivities and ceremonials, nothing save the night *Kâ'-Kâs*—which I have faithfully seen for two seasons—occurs during the months of January, February, March, and April,[46] I could remain in Washington during those months, retaining my brother, the head chief, working with him on the dictionary and grammar and a part of the ethnography and getting together material for the final work in Zuni.

Through the promised aid of Col. Stevenson and my friends, the completion of this scheme would not involve great expense, would be the last remaining policy-stroke with the Indians, and, according to the colonel, would aid immensely in popularizing—not more mine than his own part of the ethnographic work.

I remain, Very Respectfully,

Your Obedient Servant,
F. H. Cushing

FHC TO RHEES

Zuni, October 15th, 1881

Dear Mr. Rhees:

I am cheered by the arrival last night of your kind note and enclosure, for which I write to thank both yourself and Professor Baird for your prompt responses to me in my need. I had begun to feel very gloomy.

You are kind to take cognizance of my success. It has been *really* such—success greater than I have ever before achieved. I am now constituted Son of the Parrots, Child of the Eagles and Sun, and Junior Priest of the Bow, with full secular and sacred rights of clanship and title of "Commander of the Zuni People"—*A-shi-wi-awen aunthla*."[47]

I enclose receipt, and requesting that you remember me to all kind inquiring friends,

Believe me

Very Faithfully Yours,
F. H. Cushing

Wm. J. Rhees, Esq.,
Smithsonian

I am this morning engaging time on a brief account of my initiation into the Priesthood of the Bow, as the ceremonials were so remarkable, I think they will interest you all; and I therefore prepare an account of them, not for publication but for private reading of Prof. Baird and his friends.[48] I hope also within the next two weeks to finish my Report of Kuh-ni, or the Inhabitants of Cataract Cañon, Arizona, whom you will remember I have just completed a reconnaisance amongst.

FHC

DRAFT: FHC TO BAXTER

[Opening missing] nd

I regret that your box of specimens reached Boston in such poor condition. But remember that you have a friend among the Indians whose address is Zuni, New Mexico, and who would deem it a meagre opportunity for showing his gratitude toward you, were you to signify a desire to have him secure more of the kind.

Your article in the *Boston Herald,* which I have seen copies of, save for its rather enthusiastic exaggerations of my own abilities, leaves no room for doubt that its author can manage the *Harper* piece, detail and all, quite satisfactorily.[49] Yet send along the proof, and it will give me pleasure to [read] and return it speedily to the giver. The sequel will show you why I have not been more prompt in executing the Governor's Profile.

You see I am back from Kuh-ni. It was a terrible but ah! a grand and beautiful trip, of which I shall have more to say to you in a future communication—now in course of preparation—through Dr. Matthews, who thinks that the account of a people living isolated from all the world in a lone cañon three thousand feet deep will interest some of your readers, and that to quietly give it you is my duty. I rode into Zuni only less than a month ago, after an adventurous trip of over eleven hundred miles.

Do you remember mention made of the Masonry of the Zunis, of the prayers, unwritten bible and ancient songs, obsolete language, etc., reposed in the order of *A-pithlan Shi-wa-ni,* or "Priesthood of the Bow"? And of my desire—through securing a scalp—to get into this wonderful organization? The scalps procured for me by my father and officers of the Army were insufficient in themselves for this purpose; but the timely outbreak of the Apaches enabled me to acquire another and far more genuine article with right and title to possession; for I passed through country constantly raided by these boys for four days, and nights, saw very effectively a fight between them and some ranchieros. Moreover, grand old rain poured down over New Mexico—the valley of Zuni in particular—and washed away the foundation of the scalp house, destroying all save one of the trophies of centuries of Zuni valor. My Zuni brethren were therefore ready for the story I had to tell them, made me bury my insignia, guarded me all day, took me under the cover of night to the chamber of warriors, convened a council, smoked me, listened to my tale of blood,[50] refused absolutely my entrance into the order, consented to listen to a strong speech from me in which I mentioned former allusions tending to my initiation, my service to the god (*Kia-pin-a-hoi*),[51] my love for my people (*A-shi-wi*), the sadness to think that as a *Pithlan Shiwani* my heart would be always Zuni, [but] as a baffled warrior I should return forever, ere two moons passed, to Washington—Here it was broken. Fifteen minutes after the [ensuing] discussion as to which clans should adopt me—the Parrots for my gens, the Eagles for my fathers, [it was] decided—the vows of eternal fidelity to the Zunis and obedience of rules [were] administered. Then I was hustled off, without warning, guarded by four warriors and two priests until morning, taken out to the burial place of the scalps, where a sham fight with prayer, song and ceremony ensued. A pole was then prepared, and the scalps being tied to it, I was directed to shoulder it, and at the head of my little party I was marched to the vicinity of the western gardens, where, the pole planted, I was perched, bareheaded, on a sand-hill filled with ants, compelled to sit motionless in the hot sun watching my scalps until evening, when the prayers and initiation into the clans took place—the pandemoniac march round the pueblo, the killing of twenty-five or thirty dogs, and ere I knew it, I was hustled off to be baptised as the son of the Eagles and child of the Parrots, locked up in the chamber of the warriors, tabooed from exit, fire, salt, meat, tobacco, the touching of outsiders, the looking at women, and what not for four days. How fearful, these four slow days, with their motionless sittings, their nights of only five hours sleep, their emetics, sacrifices, etc. etc. But I must stop here. I cannot describe the multitudes of prayers, songs, ceremonials, which the following twelve days brought forth. I can only say that fresh in my memory as they are, they seem to me the grandest, most interesting, weird and terrible experiences and days my life has ever seen, and open up the sublimest depths of meaning to my researches in Zuni. And it is not an American who writes to you now. It is a *Zuni* by right of his "clanship with the Parrots," his "sonship of the Eagles," his "birth from the Sun" and the *Kia-pin-a-hoi,* his membership in the "Order of the Bow," and his sacred position as "Junior Priest of the Bow," and secular status as Commander of the *A-shi-wi*. Surely the gods have favored me. Eighteen days have changed the possibilities of my life and labors, and opened up a new significance to the study of Indian ethnology. It may be that when I see you I can tell you more about this, or at some leisure time write more. But I can only add now that I have told you only the beginning and most uninteresting part of my new experience, that these have revealed to me the fact that all my previous work amounts to nothing as compared to that which is at hand, for the Indians have already compelled me to learn by heart five long ancient prayers and commit to paper for memorization as many more, with songs and rules of the order—all which, you remember, I was using every means to record and had about despaired of during your visit.

Give my humble and grateful thanks for Mrs. Goddard's kind intentions.[52] I have no doubt that with the Head Chief, the High Priest in my order, Pedro Piño, and the Lieutenant Governor, I shall be able to reach the East some time in January, my plan being to leave Washington by steamer for Boston and New York ere the final return to Zuni; but my plans may be frustrated.[53] I shall, however, make my best efforts to secure to-and-from passes to the East and have fair hopes of success. At any rate, my work in Zuni is not done.

Write me, my good friend, and command me as

Yours Ever,
F. H. Cushing

Baird to Powell

October 27, 1881

Dear Major:

I enclose herewith a letter from Cushing [FHC to Baird, October 12, 1881] which is very interesting. Please note his project of bringing some Zuni Indians east & working out here some of the problems connected with their history. Can you do anything to aid it? So far as I am concerned, I have given him liberty to do as he pleases in the matter.

I hope to see you before long, either at your house or the Museum.

Yours Truly,
S. F. Baird

A Busy Season in Zuni

The last months of 1881, from the time of his return to Zuni on September 16, seem to have been extraordinarily active ones for Cushing. Following the Bow Priesthood initiation, which must have taken up most of the second half of September, he had greatly expanded ceremonial responsibilities to attend to, in addition to his duties as assistant to the governor and as "first war chief." At the same time, heavy claims were being made on his services as an employee of the Smithsonian. The Stevensons had returned to the Southwest on their third collecting trip, and in October they arrived in Zuni. As Powell explained in his Director's Report for 1881–1882, "the large quantities of valuable material, both ancient and modern, possessed by the Pueblo tribes made it important that the work of collecting should be prosecuted energetically, in order to secure as much as possible before the objects should be carried away by visitors and speculators. . . ."[54] *In the course of two months spent at Zuni on this trip, Stevenson "secured" some 21,000 pounds of "specimens" (seven wagon loads)—over 3,700 items, many of a sacred nature—for the National Museum.*[55]

As in earlier Stevenson enterprises, Cushing was much depended upon for assistance in this operation. In his Introductions to the "Illustrated Catalogues" of these huge collections which appeared under his name in the Bureau of Ethnology Annual Reports *for 1880–1881 and 1881–1882, Stevenson acknowledged his indebtedness to Cushing for help both in the collecting itself and in the preparation of the catalogues—as well he might. According to a Stevenson letter of November 10, he, Cushing, and a third Bureau staff member, Victor Mindeleff, had "been at work night and day for a week numbering and labeling the specimens."*[56] *More significantly, one notes that the 267 page manuscript of the Zuni portion of the 1881–1882 catalogue, on file in the National Anthropological Archives, is in Cushing's handwriting, and it must also have been Cushing who was responsible for the text.*

During the last half of November, Cushing was visited by his new friend John G. Bourke, who came to witness the Shalak'o *festival and pursue his own study of the Zunis (already begun on two briefer visits in May and September).*[57] *Further claiming Cushing's attention during this eventful period, apart from his visitor, his tasks for Stevenson (which continued through the month), a heavy schedule of ceremonials continuing on through December, and negotiations for the upcoming trip to Washington—was the trouble developing with the new Presbyterian mission schoolmaster, S.A. Bentley, who had evidently formed an offensive alliance with Mrs. Stevenson. Since Bourke's diary provides an engaging lateral view of Cushing in the midst of such adventures in Zuni, some fairly lengthy excerpts have been included in the pages to follow. Cushing's own journal shows him learning his new responsibilities in Zuni ceremonial life as a member of the Bow Priesthood.*

John Bourke's Diary

November 16th, 1881. Wednesday. Breakfasted with Dr. and Mrs. Matthews [at Fort Wingate]. Drove forty-two miles to Zuni Pueblo where I put up with Mr. Frank Cushing. . . . Took supper with Mr. Stevenson, Cushing and Mindeleff—a good plain supper. Then went to call upon Mrs. Stevenson, with whom I found my friend Pedro Pino, Patricio (the Governor), and the Cacique of the Sun. Stevenson displayed before my delighted gaze a wonderful accumulation of idols, obsidian and flint arrow and lance heads, awls, and knives. The idols were rudely shaped to represent bears, lions, birds, antelope, and deer with eyes of chalchihuitl and other stones. Arrows were fastened with sinew to the backs of these animal gods. Pedro said that they were smeared with blood of deer and antelope and worn in the belt that the possessor might catch plenty of game. He seemed greatly oppressed by the idea that these priceless treasures of the religion and antiquity of his people were to be carried away to Washington. . . .[58]

While I was writing these notes, Cushing collected about him a score of copper-visaged listeners and began the recital of a fairy tale. Looks of wonderment, nods of approval, and peals of laughter greeted the work of Grimm's, whose red children became as much absorbed in the efforts of his genius as their white comrades on both sides of the great Ocean. . . .

When we went to bed, to our amazement, we found it was 3 o'clock in the morning. Cushing told me that the Zunis had a tradition that the horrible custom of Human Sacrifice was kept up among them *in secret* until about twenty years before the coming of the Americans.[59] Cushing also said that one of their Sacred Orders is obliged to dance, once in every generation, and that it is obliged to resort to human sacrifice.

The Zunis claim that now they only go through the form, but Cushing, while not absolutely certain inclines to the suspicion that they may still adhere to this unnatural rite.

November 17th, 1881. Thursday.

. . . .

The Nehue-cue {*Newekwe*} sent word to Cushing that they were going to do us the unusual honor of coming to our house this P. M. to give us one of their dances, something which Cushing said was unprecedented. The women of the house put the long "living room" to rights, sweeping the floor and sprinkling it with water to lay the dust.

Soon after dark, they entered: twelve in number, two being young boys. The center men were naked, with the exception of black breech-clouts of archaic style. Hair *au naturel*; bunch of wild turkey feathers in front and one cornhusk over each ear. White Bands across face at eyes and mouth. Black cloth neck-cloth or collar. Broad white bands, 1 inch wide around body and arms at navel, and breast; legs at mid-thigh & knees. Tortoise rattles at Right Knee. Blue woolen knit leggings, moccasins. In R. hand, the wands of their order.

Others, with one or two exceptions, dressed in old American suits. All had cotton night-caps, cornhusks at top of head & at ears. Generally had white goggles painted over eyes and a white line at mouth. Tortoise rattles or strings of brass sleigh bells at the R. knee.

One wore a long India-rubber gossamer overall & had a pair of goggles painted in white: his general get-up was a capital take-off upon a Mexican priest. The other was a very good counterfeit of a young woman.

To the accompaniment of a drum and the rattles & bells spoken of, they shuffled into the long room, crammed with spectators, Indian and Caucasian, the former of both sexes and all sizes and ages. Their song was apparently a ludicrous reference to everything and everybody in the room, Cushing and Mindeleff receiving special attention to the uncontrolled merriment of the savage auditory.

I had taken my station at one side of the room, seated upon the banquette, having in front of me a small bench upon which shone a small coal-oil lamp. I suppose I had a striking resemblance to the church picture of some old Roman Catholic Saint in a Mexican Church (if I had, my ugliness ought to kill me): to such a resemblance at least I attribute the performance which followed. The Indians suddenly wheeled into a line, threw themselves on their knees before my table, and with extravagant beating of breasts began a ridiculous and faithful, even if censurable, mockery of a Roman Catholic (Mexican) Congregation at Vespers. One bawled out a parody of the Pater Noster—while another rambled along in the manner of an old man reciting the Rosary—while the fellow with the India-rubber coat jumped up & began a passionate exhortation which for faithfulness of pantomimic representation was, like the mockery of the others, simply inimitable. This kept everybody laughing with sore sides for a few moments until at a signal from the leader, the performers marched out of the room, in single file as they had entered.

An interlude of ten minutes. Floor sprinkled by men spitting water from their mouths with great force. *Nehue-cue* re-entered; this time 2 were naked. Their singing sounded like a chorus of chimney-sweeps. Their dance was a stiff-legged jump: heels kept 12 inches apart. (The naked men were dressed like the God of their order, pictured in their club-room). . . .

After dancing a few minutes, Cushing announced in their language that a "feast" was ready for them: at which they loudly roared their gratification, and advanced to shake hands with the "Americanos" addressing us in a funny gibberish of broken Spanish, English, and Zuni. The feast [was] of tea, hard bread, sugar & such things as my supplies afforded.

The Indians set to work with a will and consumed great ollas full of tea and others of hardtack and sugar. A squaw carried in a small olla of urine of which the dirty brutes drank heartily(!) I couldn't believe the evidence of my senses and asked Cushing if that were really human urine. "Why, certainly," replied he "and here comes more of it." This time it was a large tin pail full not less than two gallons. I was standing by the squaw as she offered this strange refreshment. She made a motion with her hand to tell me that it was urine and one of the old men repeated the word "mear" in Spanish. My sense of smell demonstrated the truth of that statement: it was urine and was miserably stinking rotten urine to boot.[60] The Indians swallowed great draughts, smacked their lips & amid the roaring merriment of the spectators remarked that it was very, very good. I counted 87 Indians in that one apartment & six white men, not including Mr. Stevenson and Mr. Bentley, the Presbyterian school teacher, who had just left.

Another of the clowns ate a piece of corn-husk pronouncing it good, saying he thought it was bread: and still another started to swallow a piece of dirty rag.

This disgusting work enlivened by an occasional smutty joke, which gained the dignity of chastity by contrast with vile actions, is said to be ascribable to the purpose of the order of *Nehue-cue,* to make each of its members proof against the troubles & privations of famine and inure and prepare them for those of war. . . .

The smell of our room, arising from the presence of such a jam of dirty Indians, indulging in such filthy practices, became, as might be expected, almost intolerable. The dance did not last very long, and none of our party manifested the slightest desire to detain the clowns when they announced their intention of departing. . . .

After the dance was ended, a small detachment of the head-men remained in the room, saying they wanted to speak with me. They were:

1. Pah-loati, or Patricio, Parrot clan, Governor.
2. Nayuchi, Eagle clan, Cacique of War and Grandfather of the Order of the Bow.
3. Lah-wah-tzi-luh-ti-wah. Parrot clan, Cacique of the Temple.
4. Isé Pallé, Cacique of the Maiz clan.
5. Pedro Pino, Aguila [Eagle] clan, Warrior of the Order of Fire.
6. Lyah-tzi-lunqui, Parrot clan, Cacique of Temple.
7. Tiwah-wi-chiwa, Parrot clan, Lt. Governor.
8. Way-hu-si-wa, Sun clan, Son of No. 6.[61]

Pedro Pino acted as spokesman. He addressed me in Spanish.

I want to advise (avisar) with you. They have told us this afternoon, the Schoolmaster (maestro) and Mrs. Stevenson (la mujer del Coronel Stephis—"La cacique mujer"—the latter term used in contempt) that Cushy (Cushing) is not a chief at all: that he commands nobody—that he is only a muchacho (boy) and has not been sent here by order of the Great Father. We have come to talk with you: is it true?

Lieut. Bourke: My friend, Cushing is one of the President's favorite sons and has come here by his, the Great Father's orders. The Great Father is much pleased with all that he has heard from Cushing about his children, the Zunis. If the schoolmaster says that Cushing has not come here by the President's orders, the school-master lies and you can tell him I said so. If Mrs. Stevenson said so—it makes no difference. She don't know. Among us, women don't know much about what the G.F. is doing. Here is one of the Great Father's Books—it has Cushing's name in it. I'll read what it says (translating an extract from Smithsonian Report of 1880.) I am an officer—a soldier—you all know me, I have never told you a lie. You must believe what I tell you now. I know Cushing and I tell you that he does come straight from the Great Father. Anybody who tells you anything different tells you a lie.

I am going to put our talk down on paper so that the Great Father may know what we have said to each other and who are the enemies of his young son Cushing.

The chiefs bade me good-night, each shaking hands then lifting his closed hand to his mouth.

On my way to bed, I passed through the room in which the dance had been held. This was the common dormitory of the family, every member of which, big and little, lay sprawling upon rude mattresses of sheep-skin and covered partially by Navajo or Zuni blankets. . . .

Nayuchi and Lah-wah-tzi-lu-ti-wah told me that Cushing was a "Zuni capitan." They pointed to the bracelet of olivette shells on his wrist and said "See—capitana—Zuni." Before I got into bed, Cushing made me a delightful present of a stone fetich—a panther with arrow on back—a beautiful little idol. Also three tortoises in pottery.

November 18th, 1881. Friday.

. . . .

Went to Pedro Pino's house; on my way, stopped in to look at Mr. Stephenson's collection once more. . . . On my return home, I found Cushing in a high fever and the squaws preparing an emetic for him. "Patricio's" [Palowahtiwa's] silver moulds were lying at the door: made of baked clay bound with iron. The Zunis also understand how to make cupels—one, of inferior workmanship but showing its object very well, is in the collection made by Mr. Stevenson. . . .

Pedro Pino lunched with me. I told Pedro when I first reached the Pueblo that I should be glad to have him with me at every meal. He accepted the invitation in good faith, and come weal, come woe, I know that he'll stick to me like Banquo's ghost, so long as I remain.

His collection of letters is one of the utmost value and great interest, surviving back as far as the Treaty of Peace made with the U.S. in 1848, which was signed by Pedro as Governor of the Pueblo. . . .

When we got back to the house, darkness had set in. Cushing was sitting up in bed and with him were Stevenson, Mindeleff and half-dozen Indians. . . .

The subject of Religion being broached, I recalled what I had read in Pedro's papers this afternoon. First the Treaty of 1848 entered into by the U.S. through its representative Lt. Col. Basky, 1st Ills. Vols., 1848 with Pedro Pino and other representatives of the Zunis, which treaty expressly stipulates that they (the Zunis) shall be protected in persons, property and religion.[62]

Secondly, a paper, purporting to be an agreement between one Sheldon Jackson of the Presbyterian Church and the principal men of Zuni relative to the establishment of a school at Zuni. By an artful arrangement of terms, the Zunis are made to promise to build a school & set apart garden-land for the Presbyterian Missionary while he, on his side, merely agrees to supply window sashes and doors. There is no quid pro quo expressed or implied & the paper hasn't the least legal value. The agreement (!) never would have been signed by the Zunis had not Jackson been fortified by a letter couched in most emphatic and mandatory terms from Agent Thomas to the Zuni headmen. This action is a perversion of authority and a stultification of a holy office. Under the provisions of this agreement, ignorant, bold and impudent missionaries have compelled the Zunis to furnish them with fire-wood etc. threatening to burn up their sheep-corrals in case of noncompliance.

The Agent of the Pueblo holds his place without a shadow of law.[63] Thomas, in most respects, impresses me as a very good man, but the above hurried memoranda suggests a bitter line of comment & censure upon the questionable manner in which missionary enterprises are conducted on our frontier. . . .

At this moment word flew around the Pueblo that the *Coyamashés* or mud-heads were "out."

To don our outer clothing took but a moment and but another to join the tail end of the garrulous procession, pushing its way under low, forbidding arches to the recesses of the middle or enclosed plaza. Darkness was before me, behind me on all sides of me. Cushing held me by one elbow, Mindeleff by the other. . . .

Back at our house, found the usual concourse of old men, nine being on their haunches, smoking corn-fodder cigarettes. They had come to see how Cushing was getting along and were happily in a conversational mood. . . .

Before separating for the night, the Indians told a great number of proverbs, and nothing but the fact that Cushing was so very sick kept them from giving us a regular benefit in the way of folk-lore, maxims, myths, and traditions. . . . I was surprised to see what night-owls the Zunis were. They will remain up until very late chatting and telling stories of which they never seem to grow weary. . . .

November 19th, Saturday. . . .

After breakfast, Cushing, Pedro Pino and myself went to the upper story of one of the highest houses on the Eastern side of the Pueblo; here in the West wall was an old blue china plate fixed there, so the head of the house said, in the time of the Spaniards, to conceal a painting of the Sun, which faced a small rectangular aperture in the eastern wall. When the sun shown through the aperture farthest to the North, Spring had come and the season of planting had arrived; the more Southerly aperture allowed the rays of the Sun to fall upon the center of the plate (in ancient days upon the face of the Sun picture) about the period of the Autumnal Equinox—and when the light struck a certain point in the Wall, it was the time of the Winter Solstice.

"But," said the man, Pedro coinciding with him,

> we are getting very careless about these things now. When the last Cacique of the Sun was living, he used to come here constantly and watch the Sun and used to go out to the Stone pillar erected by our ancestors and there make sacrifices and watch the Sun. This cacique either don't know or he don't care. He will go out on the top of any hill and watch the Sun and don't do things as they used to be done. . . .

Cushing said that generally their winter solstice had been determined at December 19th, but this year, by the mistake above spoken of, it had been brought on some weeks earlier. . . .

Cushing, Mindeleff, Pedro Pino and myself took tea together. In the course of the conversation, Cushing emphatically asserted his belief that human sacrifices were still kept up, altho' in the deepest secrecy and at rare intervals. More than that, he said that a year ago, a certain order, the Tulushtulu, gave a sacred dance, sacrificing, in the daylight, in the presence of the Pueblo, a young puppy; but that night a young boy and the next morning a young orphan girl were offered up.[64] Cushing enjoined me not to mention this matter outside of my notebooks, fearing to excite too much bitter comment. . . .

November 20th, Sunday. . . .

Ké-ā-si, second in command in the Order of the Bow, called upon me this evening, bearing upon his wrist, the string of olivette shells from the seashore, indicative of his high position, which may better be styled the "Second War Cacique." At Cushing's suggestion, I withdrew to put on my uniform. This old man told me that one of his duties was to preserve mnemonically the Sacred Genesis of his people, handed down by word of mouth, from successor to successor from the earliest times. The record, he said, was called in his language "The words of the doings of the Ancients in the days of the New, or the Record of the doings of Gods and Men in the Beginning." (The word Ancients, as he explained, includes both Gods and Men.)

From what I have learned through the kindness of Cushing, I am convinced that the *Ah-shi-wi* have, in addition to the Mythology which every nation, savage or civilized, has evolved for itself, a theology and a theogony as consistent and well defined as those of the Ancient Greeks and Romans. Not to have some narrow-minded man say that my views were prepared for me by Cushing himself, I have made such independent personal investigations, through Pedro Pino, as my limited knowledge of Spanish would permit and have, in no case, servilely followed Cushing's ideas, but have combatted them if they did not strike me as purely logical and consistent. . . .

The old man said to Cushing: "My friend, I am glad that you are telling your friend what I have just told you. Do not tell it to the common people, because ignorant persons do not understand such things; but do you think that I have brains enough to make up such a story? No. Nor have you brains enough to compose it. It is the story of our Ancients, handed down from the Old Days, and, as you know, given to me by (mentioning the name of his predecessor who had lately died in office) who sat up with me by day and night pouring it into my ears."

The Zuni priests preserve bottles of sea-water from the Gulf of California or the Pacific Ocean.

The Zunis are great believers in witchcraft: a witch was put to death to-day in this year of grace 1881, Keasi and his Order superintending the execution of the culprit who met his death with fortitude.[65]

Cushing and I walked around to the house of Nanaje [Nanahe] to ask him to come and explain what he knew of the "Snake Dance of the Moquis," he being by birth a Moqui of the Snake Order. . . .[66]

I invited Nanaje and his friend, Old Nayuchi, the story-teller to come in and have a cup of tea with me; they accepted. Nayuchi said to Cushing that Nanaje represented a "medicine order",—that its secrets were Sacred, but if I laid before him "a little bundle," (i.e., an honorarium) as a token of friendship, according to the rules of his order, he could give me, a foreigner, some information about it. "You, being a foreigner and ignorant of our language, can do us no harm and cannot divulge our secrets to the mean and vicious in our tribe or among other Pueblo tribes who would scatter them to the four winds and destroy our Order. A Secret Order is for the benefit of the whole world, that it may call the whole world its children and that the whole world may call it Father; and not for the exclusive benefits of the few who belong to it. But, its privileges are the property of its members and should be preserved with jealous vigilance; since, if they became known to the whole world, they would cease to be secrets and the Order would be destroyed and its benefit to the world would pass away."[67]

My conversation with these two uneducated Indians upon this topic filled me with astonishment. . . .

Cushing arranged with Nanaje to return with his friend to-morrow evening and promised by that time his "present of ceremony" (i.e., the "little bundle") should be ready and we waiting for them in my room apart from all idle or unnecessary spectators. . . . [For the full account of these interviews, with Nanahe, see Bourke, *Snake Dance of the Moquis,* pp. 180–95.]

November 24th, Thursday. . . .

For some days past, the heads of the Zuni people have been much concerned about Cushing, whose initiation into many secrets and Sacred Traditions has been attended with this grave inconvenience that he cannot, by laws of their tribe, ever again abandon the Pueblo. They have communicated their views to Cushing and intimated to him that, as he is now a Zuni—a full member of their tribe—it is his duty to marry without further delay and become the father of children who shall grow up among their people.

To his objections that he had not yet been able to make a choice and that where there were so many lovely and accomplished damsels, it would be no more than justice to them and to himself to weigh well the claims of each, before making a definite and irrevocable selection, they replied that they had weighed well all his arguments and appreciated the difficulties under which he labored; and to assist him in his perplexities, they had carefully considered the merits of many worthy young maidens and had finally determined that ——— "who regarded him highly and was anxious to become his wife, was in every way worthy of the honor, either on the score of family position, personal beauty or accomplishments; she would take good care of his home, be a good breadmaker and blanket-weaver and, in every respect, make his life happy."

Pedro Pino came to me yesterday and, in a very mysterious and consequential way, said that Cushing had now become a full Zuni; that he had taken a scalp, danced the Scalp Dance, been made a "matador" ("killer" or Warrior) and that he could never leave Zuni. "But then he can never take my old friend, Pedro Pino, to Washington, to see the Great Father, to take him by the hand, to see the wonderful sights of the "Estados Unidos" and receive beautiful presents from the "Americanos."

This greatly disconcerted the old man and modified his views of the situation to a more considerable degree than he would be willing to admit.

Cushing's position among these people is becoming fraught with increasing responsibilities and, perhaps, some little danger. While each day he is taught more and more of the Esoteric life of these Zunis, the meshes are weaving tighter and tighter about him, and, in the end, his departure from the Pueblo will be a desertion and a flight.

The young lady spoken of came up to our door the night before last and waited patiently until Cushing appeared: she addressed him frankly and modestly but in a perfectly self-possessed manner, asking him whether or not he would "cut her a buckskin." (This means "to cut out a pair of moccasins," which, he said, her father would sew for her; this, as hereinbefore mentioned, is equivalent to an offer of marriage.)[68]

Cushing excused himself, saying he had not yet learned the art of making moccasins neatly and rather than present a young lady with a botched pair, he would not give her any. This answer did not satisfy the young girl, who said that her father would cut out and make the moccasins and leggings if Cushing would simply present the buckskin.

Hoping to escape the dilemma, Cushing determined yesterday to use diplomacy. He took a fine buckskin, walked to the house of the girl's parents, asked if the girl was in and, seeing her, laid at her feet the present he had brought. Her daughter sat by her side until this refreshment, called the "food of welcome," appeared when she took it, set it out on the floor before Cushing, and squatting down by his side, began to partake of it with him. While they were eating, blankets and rabbit-skin "cobijas" had been spread for them in an inner room.[69] Cushing said to the girl: "Come sit by me, I want you to know that I have given you that buckskin because I think a great deal of you, but I don't wish to marry you. That is not the custom of the Americanos; among them, when a young man thinks a great deal of a girl, he makes her little presents, tells her how much he thinks of her and speaks to her parents about her. He don't marry for some time afterwards: sometimes not for a few weeks, sometimes not for a few months, and, occasionally, not for a few years. He goes to see her & she gets acquainted with him. They learn each other's ideas; each knows what the other likes and what the other dislikes, the other's good qualities and bad; and, with this knowledge to commence upon, they are more likely to live happily together.

The girl said nothing but her mother observed with some petulance: "That may be a good way for the Americans, but it is not the custom of the Zunis. Among us, when young people like each other and a young man gives a girl a buckskin or a pair of moccasins, he is received with the "food of welcome," their bed is spread for them, he takes up his abode in the house of her parents and from then on, he has no further cares. She takes care of him; keeps his house in good order; bakes bread for him and weaves his blankets."

Cushing was obdurate and refused to change in that point from the custom of his people.

This action has deferred, but it has not cancelled the reckoning which must come. Cushing understands this and says that within the next six months, he hopes to penetrate to the Arcana of the Zuni traditions and, if worse comes to worse, shall then be ready for flight.

Upon this point, I wish to make the note that, from close scrutiny of his life among these people, I feel prepared to assert that Cushing's morality is beyond reproach: I fully believe his statement that from the first moment of his coming among them, he has been forcibly impressed with the necessity of avoiding all entanglements which would impede his investigations.

At the present time, his marriage with the daughter of influential people, would, beyond a doubt, largely enhance his influence; but he is not prepared to blight his future prospects by any such connection; and he hopes his manoeuvre of last evening may accomplish almost the same results.

Time alone can tell; if he deport himself with circumspection, he may for a brief period—six months at the uttermost limit—throw dust in the eyes of the leading spirits: but they will not long remain deceived and when they discover his duplicity, for such it must be, his influence will be destroyed, unless he consent to the ceremony so long delayed.[70]

This is Thanksgiving Day! Cushing and I have done the best we could under the circumstances. Gordon has had the foresight to bring back with him a small quantity of beef-steak and fresh bread. Brown has done his level best, and, with my assistance, has compounded a very appetizing rice pudding from goat's milk and two fresh eggs sent over by Mrs. Stevenson yesterday. We broiled a tempting steak, set out a loaf of bread, a can of cranberries, half a dozen boiled sweet potatoes and a pot of hot coffee; and each admitted to the other that this was a Thanksgiving indeed.

We dined alone; but, later in the evening, Colonel Stevenson, Mr. Graham and Mr. Hathorn dropped in and chatted with us for an hour or so, while Pedro Pino, Jesus, and one of two others of the Zunis lined the walls.

November 26th, Saturday.

Cushing, before breakfast, had a great wrangle with a party of Zunis, who were hoping to change his resolution about deferring his marriage. Cushing has won over Patricio and the head men to his side of the question, but the friends of the would-be bride are determined, if possible, that the wedding shall take place and the marriage be consumated without delay and Cushing is equally determined to fight them off by all sorts of excuses until he can no longer evade the issue, when he will sever his connection with the Pueblo and return to Washington. . . .

[Toward the end of the day, a procession of masked gods led by *Shu-lu-wit-si,* the Little God of Fire, arrived, crossing the river on a little foot bridge constructed for their passage and making a grand progress around the pueblo.]

The last rays of a golden sun were now flowing back from the sandstone battlements of Toyalani; the bleating herds trotting slowly to their folds; children in swarms chasing each other across the streets; and lordly Navajoes, wrapped in blankets whose gorgeous hues rivalled those of the Sun god, squatted upon fences or housetops. It was a scene of savage beauty and savage characteristics. Tits-ko-matski, Cushing's Cheyenne Indian, educated at Hampton, Virginia, yielding to the fascination of the occasion, threw aside the habiliments of Civilization and appeared in the savage adornments of red paint and Navajo blankets. We could see the giant servitors of the Fire God, (The Coyamashés) dancing about him, and running like swift, clumsy ostriches in the sand, where, I was told by Pedro Pino, that they were depositing the great plumes of sacrifice.

The priest, from whose mask protruded the long horn, is known by the name of "Long Horn" and is the warrior of the ancient Sacred Dances, which in turn represent dramatically the Ancient Hero-gods of the Zunis or Ah-shí-wi. He wore, at his neck, a red abalone shell, inlaid with a so-called turquoise or malachite, a very ancient relic, no doubt many hundreds of years old.

Cushing, with his usual gentleness, rendered me very valuable assistance in making rough but valuable sketches of the Little God of Fire and the principal members of his retinue, which I shall endeavor to reproduce on the following pages. . . .

November 27th, Sunday.

[The following episode was the sequel to an incident which occurred at the end of the *Shalako* festivities. When the procession of kachinas passed back across the river in the early morning, they had been followed, counter to Zuni propriety, by a number of Navajos and by Mrs. Stevenson and Mr. Bentley, the missionary school teacher. Eventually, Patricio, the governor, had ridden over and told them to move back.][71]

I was at breakfast with Cushing, Col. Stevenson and Mr. Mindeleff being in the room with us, when Patricio entered: he said (to Cushing) "I told that maestro that he mustn't stand up so close to those sacred dancers—that he must come down further this way—that he had no business there. I don't see what he wants there. He always says that he don't believe in those things and that they are no good—then why does he want to see them? Nobody goes over there of our own people except the dancers and a few who want to pray and make sacrifices.

I should say to be absolutely exact that Patricio was in our room before the other two—or rather he entered and departed a number of times—I remember this because I asked him to breakfast with me and he declined, having already eaten.

Mr. Bentley, the school-teacher, stopped and in a very excited manner said:

Mr. Cushing, I wish you to say to Patricio that he came up to me a few moments ago when I was over at that dance with Mrs. Stevenson. I couldn't understand what he said but I did understand his manner and you can tell him that if he does that way to me again while I am in this Pueblo, I will whip him and if Mrs. Stevenson hadn't been with me, I'd have whipped him anyhow.

Cushing: Patricio says that as you didn't understand his language, you, of course don't know what he told you: that he simply didn't want you to stand up so close to the Sacred Dancers. That he asked you to move a little lower down. That you had often said that you didn't believe in these things and for that reason, he couldn't understand why you wanted to go there. That those were cermonies by which his people have lived for generations and that they were grumbling because you went even where the Caciques didn't go.

Mr. Bentley: (Hotly) The Caciques *were* there.

Cushing: (firmly) I beg your pardon, Mr. Bentley, they were not. There was only one of them—José Pellé, who went across the river.

Mr. Bentley: Well, I saw José Pellé.

Cushing: Patricio wishes me to say to you that he didn't do anything more to you than he would to anybody else under the same circumstances. You and Mrs. Stevenson were the only strangers, except the Navajoes, who crossed the river. You mustn't think that there is anything personal in this, Mr. Bentley. Last year, I myself went over and pushed in among the dancers and there was a terrible hubbub kicked up. I had to strike a man's horse twice over the head with a whip to keep its rider from running me down—

Mr. Bentley: (Interrupting Cushing, in a very excited way) I don't care a straw about what they did to you, Mr. Cushing, I am speaking about what they did to me, and I want you to tell Patricio from me that if he ever again addresses me except in the most respectful manner or orders me away from anyplace, I'll knock the stuffings out of him. That's the kind of man I am. I want him to know that I am master here and propose to go where I please and see what I please and if any man attempts to interfere, I'll knock his head off. That's the kind of man I am and the sooner he knows that the better.

Patricio listened patiently to this outburst and then said to Cushing: Say to him, Do as you please. Not a muscle quivered, not a note of his voice faltered as he said these words and his entire demeanor was in noble contrast to the unfortunate want of dignity and self-possession displayed by Mr. Bentley.

Mr. Bentley (continuing): Tell him that he raised his hand when he was talking to us. I don't know whether he meant to hit us or not, but tell him that if he had laid his hand on Mrs. Stevenson that he'd have come off that horse mighty quick and he wouldn't have gone back again either. Tell him that if he ever speaks to me in a manner that isn't perfectly respectful, or attempts to interfere with me in any way, I'll knock the stuffing out of him and he may as well know that I am master here and I'm going where I please without regards to anybody.

Cushing: He says that he wasn't going to strike any of you: he simply raised his hand to wave you back and point to a place a little further off from the dancers where you could stay without interfering with them or being molested yourselves. As to the striking, he says again, "Do as you please."

No one else said a word, but it was easy to see that the sympathies of all present, even of Mr. Stevenson, were with the Indians.

Mr. Bentley departed in a towering rage and I've no doubt that when he has cooled off a little, he will regret as deeply as we did the exhibition he made of himself. The whole trouble lies in a nutshell. Mr. Bentley's one of those aggressive natures which cannot digest the meaning of the motto "festina lente."[72] He wishes within a few week's time to subvert the teachings and traditions of generations and in his over-zeal has been betrayed into many indiscretions. Added to this he has an over-estimate of his own importance and is afflicted with the habit of bluster that would suit admirably in a bar-room, but is not adopted to the position of a teacher among savages.

Patricio's conduct throughout the whole interview was very commendable. He never alluded to Mrs. Stevenson—but quietly directed all his remarks to Bentley himself and in doing so, never raised his voice above a whisper. When Mr. Bentley turned to leave the room, he said quietly to Cushing:

He can do as he pleases, I belong to the "Order of Warriors."

Mr. Stevenson said: I didn't go over there myself as I didn't think any one had a reason to. Mr. Bentley has taken a very indefensible position if he imagines that as a school-teacher here he has any right to go where he pleases. These Indians have their religion and their sacred rights and if they don't want people to see them, their scruples should be respected. They have a right to the exercise of their religion—. . . .

Pedro Pino came in during the evening and with him two Indians of Isleta,—one of the Maiz Amarillo and the other of the Huacamayo clan. They said that the "Muchacho" was "Maiz Blanco." The object of the Isletas was to induce Cushing to give them a paper by which they could sell a burro they had brought with them to the Pueblo. Cushing complied with their request.

November 28th, Monday. . . .

We had a spicy little episode this evening which is well worthy of a brief place in this Record. Ramon Luna, the old Mormon Indian, of whom mention has already been made, has of late become very obnoxious to the Governor and head men of the Pueblo from the aggressive and defiant manner in which he has avowed his sympathy and connection with the Mormons and his contempt for the Washington Great Father—

What do I care for the Great Father in Washington? He's an old liar. I am not afraid of him or his soldiers. The Mormons are my friends. They will help me. This

Great Father's soldiers do nothing but chew bacon and drink coffee. With one gun I could go to the Mountains and if they came after me, I would kill 50 of them. I do not pay attention to anybody but Mormons. They are my friends. I don't care for the Governor, nor for the Caciques. I am a Mormon.[73]

Thinking that today would be propitious, because besides Gordon who came back this morning, there were now in the Pueblo, One Sergeant and three enlisted men of the 13th Infantry, sent out by Genl. Bradley to guard Mr. Stevenson's wagons back to Wingate, I sent for the Sgt. and his detail, had each man appear in Military uniform, 40 rounds of cartridges in belt and rifle in hand, and then marched them all, a total of Six including Gordon and Brown to the house of Ramon Luna where a dance was in full swing. We drew up in a line in front of the house awaiting the conclusion of the dance, which we did not wish to disturb. As the dancers came clack, clack, clacking down the ladder, Ramon himself sprang out on the roof, rifle in hand, and in a very defiant way cried out that we couldn't take him; that if we wanted him, there he was. I did not wish to provoke an outbreak of any kind, kept my men in place and told Cushing to say to Ramon that we hadn't come to hurt him, didn't wish to be unkind, but he had to go with us to the house of the Governor, there to talk with the headmen.

Ramon descended and I advanced and shook hands, at same time taking his gun and handing it to one of the soldiers. With Cushing holding one elbow and I the other and the Sergeant and squad closed up behind him, we marched Ramon to the house of Patricio (our house) and there held a conference, in which I told Ramon that the Great Father in Washington was a kindhearted man and loved all his children, not wishing any evil to any. That he was very fond of the Zunis and regretted very much to learn that any of them should show disrespect to his authority; that this was all his country and all must obey him, white, black, red or yellow—that if the Mormons gave him much more trouble, he would send his troops to clean them out. That if Ramon wanted to join the Mormons nobody would hinder him, but he would soon be sorry; that if he didn't behave himself, he would suffer. He would be put in the Guard-House, made to work, have no food and be ironed. He could take his choice—this was no talk of Babies—men were speaking now, men who meant what they said and shot when the time came. If Ramon gave any more trouble, he would regret it all the days of his life. I wanted to be friendly to him and to all the Zunis, but he must behave himself and obey the orders of his Governor and the Caciques who were the Great Father's children.[74]

The speech, crude as it was, produced a great effect, not only on Ramon, but on all the others. Ramon said that he would obey, that he wanted to take me by the hand and be friendly to him. Which was done and I then let him go to his home, and dismissed the squad. . . .

November 30th. Wednesday.

November leaves us with the gentlest of breezes, the most cloudless of skies and the brightest of suns. Cushing and myself had an early breakfast and then started for Toyalani [Dowa Yallane], the mesa upon which stands the ruins of the Pueblo inhabited by the Zunis at the time the Spaniards entered the country. This perpendicular escarpment of naked sandstone lies between 2 and 3 miles to the East of the present Zuni, above whose plain it towers grimly to the dizzy height of 1000 ft. (by actual measurement).

A drive of fifteen minutes brought us to the foot of the precipice where we left our ambulance under Gordon's care and began, with much panting, the tedious and dangerous climb up the face of the rocky wall.

The old moccasin tracks of the Zunis of long ago were still plainly discernible in the solid rock, and treading carefully, and, for my part, with fear and trembling, we slowly advanced by foot to the summit. (Cushing wore soft moccasins; my boots were too thick to be trusted; for which reason, I took them off and carried them in my hands.) In one place—for 50 yards, the trail followed the sheer face of the bluff, winding along a little shelf, from 1 to 4 inches wide, where a false step would have sent a man crashing down over a hundred feet. Cushing here led the way to examine every inch of the path, as he called it grandiloquently, and then returned to guide me onward and upwards. He said there was plain sailing from this on, and there was. That is it was perfectly plain to me that I had about one chance in ten of ever getting out of this business alive. The trail (!) now climbed straight up the rounded projection of an immense monolith, little foot-prints being nicked in the rock every 15 or 18 inches. I turned once and once only, to look down into the valley—beautiful and impressive as a finely engraved map of a country, with which we have nothing more to do. "There's your ambulance," said Cushing, pointing to a black mark, with four mice tied to it: "Yes, and I wish to Goodness, I was back in it," was my feeling reply.

Acoma is the merest child's play to it—not even the faintest spice of danger, comparatively speaking to recommend it, after one has "done" Toyalani—"One hundred feet more and we'll be all right," said my cheerful guide. As I wouldn't go back again over our trail for ten thousand dollars, there was no way out of this extra climb, which was not, after all, so very bad. The path was precipitous, shallow and dangerous in the extreme, but a few branches of half starved scrub oak peeped out from the clefts to lend a helping hand or foot-hold. I breathed freely when I stood upon the crest and repeated to myself Dante's lines,

And as a man with pitiful short breath
Forespent with toiling, scaped from sea to shore,
Turns to the perilous wide waste and stands at gaze,
E'en so my spirit that yet feared,
Trembling with terror, paused to view the straits
That none had passed and lived.[75]

FHC: DAILY JOURNAL

[Here begin Cushing's entries in the fifth of the surviving Zuni diaries, covering December 1–8, 1881.]

Thursday, December 1st, 1881.

Was wakened very early this morning by Laiva Tsu, who came to make bread. Learned that *A-shi-wa-ni* counciled nearly all night. Arose at sunrise. Very cold. Heard a great deal about recent *i-an-a-pe-na* council [council of the chief *A:shiwani*].[76] Consulted Lieut. Bourke about it. . . . Younger *Pithlan Shi-wa-ni mosona* [i.e., Kiasi] came in to bid Lt. adieux, together with Pedro. Lt. scolded P. for talking too much. I wrote letter to Dr. Thomas regarding our affair below, requesting him to come and investigate.[77] I am *not* in the wrong. Went as far as store with Lt. B, bade him good-by.

Called on Graham. Went over to get vouchers for him. Returning, got Pablito *antatchu* [my father] to go with me to Mr. Bentley's, where I asked him politely for some things which had been left by Col. S.'s party for me, and for mule and horse.[78] Was politely treated in return.

Returning, went to see *Kia-kwe mosona* [town chief] about lamp, [which was] not there. Had talk with latter about recent difficulties. Find him more my friend than had imagined. Went to give Nai-iu-tchi his tobacco. Found him at home. Had pleasant talk with him. Found by Younger Kiasi. They are good friends of mine and say in common with all the other chiefs that I have been carrying out only such directions as I received in their hearing from Major Thomas. Returned home. On way accosted by Wi-wi-an-tsita, who wished to know why I had not been to see her people. "Perhaps you are estranged from us," she remarked. Took a much needed nap. Arose and ate something. Arranged room for white-washing. Had talk with Cha-ko-na. Lent *ha-sho-a* [kilt] and *mum-pa-lo* [sash] to dancers. Preparation for last *Kâ'kâ* going on. Grinding of meal and killing of sheep for *Koye-mo-shi*. Tomorrow ceremonial of their presentation and journey to be performed.[79] *Pa-u-ti-wa* and *He-we* to come. Latter with his *tsu-tich-kivi-e* and former to bring water (*Kiap-thle-ia*) and to go east to plant plumes to look *Westward*.[80] Went over to see Mr. Graham regarding bill. Wrote him letter sanctioning and recommending it to be forwarded. Found Mr. Fru present. Had long conversation with both. Find them, as well as Indians, all well disposed toward me. Engaged Jesus to care for my horse and mule. Went out to dance. *Wo-tem-thla* danced at uncle's house. Went to house of Muma [Roman Luna] whom I had friendly conversation with, telling him that on account of his having gotten wood I considered him a good man and friend and that whenever he had trouble would be glad to have him come and tell me about it, and do what I could to help him out. At his house dance of *Mu-luk-ta-kia, ya-to-kia an o-ti-wa* [dancers with branches, dancing to the sun]. Left for uncle's house where I had jolly time waiting for the *A-pa-tchu* dance.[81] Told Indians where I came from, why here, what my position was in East, etc. etc. They are all marvelously friendly. *A-pa-tchu awen-o-ti-wa* was performed once, and on exclamation of "*Te-a*!" [More!] again, and the third time.

Came home to write.

Friday, December 2nd.

Rose early with bad headache. Cloudy, with prospects of rain. Went over to Mr. Graham's. Met there Mr. Hubble, Mr. Aldrich and Señor [space] from St. Johns on way to Albuquerque.[82] Indians after him not to go near dance. Bought of Mr. G. 35 yards of calico, two tin plates. Came home and began to fix old room, covering ceiling with white and blue cloth. Worked hard at this most of day. Wrote letter for Mr. Graham, recommending his bill. Was visited by Mr. H. and G. Some Indians also. Jesus came in with leg of mutton and promise to care for horse and mule. Helped me. Governor very ill. Cheek, nose and neck badly swollen. Visited by his mother, father and younger brother today. Lotchi and Sui coming in helped me to remove boxes for Kia-u, to plaster floor. Went over to Mr. G.'s. Bought 1 pound of nails. Indians all remarkably pleasant today.

The great ceremonial of *Kâ'-kâ' a-wi-a* over today.[83] Dances of nearly all today. The *Pa-u-ti-wa* arrives with water, *Ne-we-kwe* attending. Two *Pithlan shiwani mosone atch* [chief Bow priests] went carrying *tethl na-we* [plume prayer-sticks] in hands, whirling the *to-he-pa-ti-na-kwin* (whizzer) to change water brought by *Pa-u-ti-wa.* Returned just after dusk. Distribution of flour took place, and the *Cha-we* of the *Ko-ye-ma-shi* wandered about the pueblo for tythes, carrying sacred plumes in left hand and blanket for foods on back. Chanted very curious song. Mr. G. took bag of flour to them, causing much merriment and good feeling. Went down to store, had little talk and returned to resume regulation of room. Explained notes to Indians, which excited much curiosity.[84]

Saturday, December 3rd.

A-pi-thlan shi-wa-ni ha-po-kia te-thlap-a [Bow priests gather together in a group, go into retreat].

Fine day. Engaged pretty constantly on room and assorting books, papers, etc.

Governor very ill with sholine, a kind of neuralgic inflamation about face on left side. Received three *very* pleasant letters from Emma, Father and Mr. Baxter. Father awaits my visit, and Emma is overjoyed with the prospect. Baxter gives me news about my intended tour, which overjoys both the Indians and myself. Jesus brought sheep in today and took my animals out.

While reading, a herald called at at the window,

She? [Hey].
Ye! [Yes.]
Tash n tche. [Are you in?]
E! [Yes.]
Ta ha po kia tu. [You have to go the meeting.]
Ya! [Fine.]
Lah yam kia kwan pathl-to kwi. [reference to one's own (*yam*) collection of (*kia*) sticks used in stick races (*pathlto*)?]
Ya! [All right.]

I accordingly made haste to eat and then started for the chamber of warriors. No one there. Deposited my lamp and went to house of Nai-iu-tchi. Old man was not at home. Returned to chamber; still no one there. Came to house of Wi-we, visited a little while and went back. Pi-tchi had come. Gave him some tobacco and again went out, this time to house of Tsu-i. Had jolly visit, returning to find a *mo-so-na* and three or four other members present. Was questioned regarding some things Mr. Bentley had been telling the Indians. Gave them a verbatim report of our conversation the other night. Effect was very favorable to myself. The *mo-so-na* then commenced a prayer, which was interesting but very long and which I cannot reproduce verbatim.

Thus many have the days gone by; we Fathers have, the Gods (beings to whom water is needed) their days are at hand, and our Fathers for them, one day theirs shall we labor; hence, this day, with words of prayer do I teach ye, my children—Even so!—when the days were new, that it might be well it was said that one day should the Priests of the Bow gather together their children to labor for the gods, to grind meal for their fathers (the caciques).

I have fathers, the gods, who have possession of the spaces—*A-hai-iuta* the yellow, the blue, the red, the white, the variegated, and the black, by whose will we are beings, and theirs do I now draw in the wind for ye, my children (E'n so, thanks!) that we may walk the right road. And I have children of the descending ladder, whose blessing I breathe (verily!) that they may be happy.[85]

I have gods also, the Priests of the North, Priests of the West, Priests of the South, Priests of the East, Priests of the Firmament and Priests of the lower world, and this day this night do I breathe in for ye my children their wind—(E'n so, thanks!)

And in the world of waters have I gods: *An-pis-kai-a,* floating hair and [space]; their medicine hence I breathe in this day, this night, for ye, my children, their wind. And I have also a father, the Sun, he who sees everything as one, who rushes up from the East, stands midway, and goes on ever in his course, and I breathe in this night for thee my children his wind and await with anxiety the days he may provide for me (E'en so, thanks!). To the spirits of our ancestors and the gods do I send out words of prayer, that for one day my children may labor for the gods and make for their fathers meal, for thus in the days of the new was it given out, and all of ye, my children, may you happily pass the night until the morning, and in the times to come, forever, may ye be happy to the evening of each day, and may the light of the gods be made to meet ye.[86]

May the light of the gods be made to meet us. Our fathers the gods, may they send us rain and hail and snow, and light, and may our father, who makes the road of life for all and who sees everything as one, grant unto us good fortune, age and light to meet us.

I have as well as possible repeated the substance of the prayer, though not the words entirely. It is at once a prayer to the gods and spirits and an exhortation to the members of the Priesthood of the Bow.

Niesto then began to speak of the days that were while the younger high priest upbraided his children for failing to abide strictly and heartily by the ancient instructions of the order.[87] Niesto said that these were the days when small boys had their say while the old men had to sit back as if in modesty and see it all. "A young man or even a boy who talks wisely is entitled to a voice in council, yes even to chieftancy, but a young man who talks after the usual fashion of young men of our day was a shame to those who listened to him." He said to me:

The laws of our institution are very ancient. Our gods A-hai-iuta were in ancient times the grandest of beings, though only small boys, and masters of all. They did not come out of the four great caves with ourselves, but at the time we reached Han-thli-pin-kia they appeared in the mist of the wars of the *Kâ'kâs,* in a cloud of vapor, and were dressed in the costume of war—buckskin armor and helmet, a quiver of lion skin, bow, arrows, war club.[88] Their appearance struck mankind, and caciques asked them, "Whence come ye? It may be that through your will the people may be saved. Do you think you can right things at the Pueblo beyond—Ojo Caliente?" "We do not know; we can only try," said the young men, for like every true member of the Priesthood of the Bow, they never told what they would or could do but waited to do. Then they commanded the great cacique: "Call forth your people." And when they were gathered together: "Then call forth those of the Coyote gens and order, their song masters, and place them in a circle round the sacred kettle drum and tell them to sing as we dictate—and when the song of four words is finished, they shall strike the kettle drum, and ye shall behold our grandfathers." So they were placed, the song dictated, the drum was struck—lo! the mists rose from below, the ravine of Hanthli-pin-kia widened and the great monsters appeared—[space] and *U'he-po-lo-lon.* Great monsters whom we know not in these days, save their *names.* But the A-hai-iu-tas said, "These are our grandfathers, and in them and us shall ye believe." And the people were wonder stricken. "There is a monster woman of the *Kia-kwe-na Kâ'-kâ* [Chakwena Kachina Woman] whom no one can overcome, and through whose will the world is filled with anger and bloodshed, and no one can conquer her. She is invulnerable; although you may drive arrows into her body, breast even, she dies not; neither does she fall, but walks back and forth ever between her people and ours, shaking her rattle. Go ye of grandeur and power—however boys and yet our fathers—and subdue her. Can ye do it?" said the great cacique to both. "We know not," they replied, and preparing themselves, they went forth at the head of the *A shi wi.*

True as the sun's rays were their arrows, yet the woman was as untouched but went back and forth crying her note and shaking her rattle, and at the end of four days' fighting neither side had advantage. "See, let it be thus much for the present," said the both, and they went away by themselves. "Oh what shall we do?" said they to one another—for, etc. [sic]—and the younger brother said, "Let us go to the house of our father the Sun." "Go thou," [said] the older to the younger, and when the sun had risen and was resting in the mid-heaven, the younger went up, and as he drew near, the Sun said, "You have at last come." "Yes," said A-hai-iu-ta the younger. "Ah, I knew it would be so and have prepared for you." Then the boy told his story. . . . "A ha!" said the Sun. "My son, I knew of this and have made you an arrow of lightning, here! You may shoot the woman through and through; it is of no use. Saw you not the rattle she carries? In it is enclosed her heart, so little. Go now, my son, and with the arrow I give you shoot not at her head or breast but at her rattle, and ye shall conquer." "It is well," said the son, and bidding his father farewell, he descended to where his brother awaited him. "Ah, thou comest." "Yes!" "Well, what of it?" "Why, it is quite true that it is useless to fight her; her heart is in her rattle which she always carries. Go now and strike at her rattle and you shall conquer." "No, *you* go." "No, for you are the older and should go first." So the older went forth and drew near to the old woman and struck at her rattle, but missed it by a small breadth. Then the younger brother raised his arrow of the Sun, drew it and let go. A ha! it struck and shattered the rattle, and woman with a cry fell to the earth dead and disappeared into the hollows of the ground.

Then the two gave the command, and the mists rose from the ground, and the two led the people Eastward.[89]

FHC to Baird

Zuni, December 4, 1881

My dear Professor Baird:

. . . .

During Col. Stevenson's presence here, I extended every hospitality and aid in my power, also giving him my personal assistance in the collecting and turning over to him much, both ancient and modern, which I had collected. My efforts and influence with the Indians were not, I think, without avail, for not only was the quality of specimens collected an improvement on those of two years since but the number lacked only a few dozen of being doubled. I also prepared for the Colonel a catalogue in both English and Zuni, adding to it such notes on the uses of objects and on the significance of the decorations of pottery as limited time would permit. This catalogue might have been made far more complete, valuable, and elegant had I not been compelled to keep pace with the packers. But I arranged with Col. Stevenson to have it returned to me for completion, prefacing, and appendicing after it had been examined by yourself and Major Powell as a report of his progress. I have little faith, however, in this arrangement, and in case for any reason it not be carried out, I will try during my visit East to get it into shape. . . .

I surmise that, accounting the Alaska collections, which I find mentioned in your Report for '79 and '80, together with the gathering of last year in New Mexico, I shall have much that is new to see and arrange when I return to the Museum.

Having, during the past two years, turned my attention almost exclusively to the acquisition of facts, I have lost to a great extent the avidity for gathering *material,* which characterized the earlier years of my acquaintance with you; but I still have the most enthusiastic interest in the progress and aggrandizement of the National Collections, without any trace of the old enthusiasm for accruing a private cabinet.

My progress is most happy in the study of the Zuni inner life. Being now a *Pithlan shi-wa-ni* or Priest of the Bow, I am secured the privileges of this strictly exotic society, as well as entrance into any meetings of, though not for the present membership in, all the other secret, medicine, or sacred orders of the Tribe. I bent all my energies toward this supreme order of the Zunis for more than a year, and my success in gaining admission to it is the greatest of all the achievements of my life perhaps; for it breaks down this last shadow of objection to my gaining knowledge of the sacred rites, not only of this but of the Moqui tribes and others as well.

Were it not for my membership in this order, the day of my ruin would now be at hand, through the interference of the Missionary here. And it now becomes my duty—an unpleasant one—to inform you of some recent relations with him and to ask you to determine his standing etc.

I have the honor to submit the following:

During the autumn of last year ('80), you will perhaps recall to mind the fact that I wrote you I was visiting Dr. Thomas, the Pueblo Indian Agent who was then here, and that my position here as chief councilor gave me great advantage in this. On account of this position and the influence I had over the Indians, Dr. Thomas requested me to take charge of some matters for him, such as through my chieftancy to aid the native chiefs and to insist upon both his own and my authority in vindicating and carrying through their mandates.

At the time there was a refractory convert of the Mormons named Wa-mu'n, or in Mexican, Roman Luna, who ever since his conversion had defied the authority of all the chiefs and council of Zuni and who refused on the grounds of his Mormon claims to listen to the commands of either "Washington" or any of his emissaries. He went off to his farm at Pescado and refused to either submit or come to the Agent. Dr. Thomas, being compelled to leave without seeing him, gave directions to me before the council to bring him, with the aid of the chiefs, to terms and make him pay the penalty of his disobedience by twenty days of hard work or by furnishing wood to the Mission. He promised, in case the man proved refractory, to either furnish me irons or request the commanding officer of Fort Wingate to do so. Roman, being informed of this, sent a message of defiance to me, saying that if I came after him he should kill me or die himself. At the head of five of the chiefs, I started the day following for Pescado. Arriving, I entered the house in which Roman was living, without opposition, offered the cigarette of peace, which he accepted, told him I had come after him, accepted no refusal, and took him back to the council. All of the chiefs were present and gave with myself the order that he should get a four ox team wagon load of wood for the Mission. The debate was hot, but he acceded. I gave the man his own time. Several months passed by. Roman began to talk again, and went off to visit the Mormons, one of whom, named Samuel Tenney, told him they would back him up, and he again became defiant, saying that he had refused the council and that any Zuni who listened to its voice would be a fool. At this time, contrary to the orders of the head chief, my "brother," he permitted a Navajo to plant and pasture his sheep on the Reservation, and became so impertinent as to personally oppose my entrance into one of the summer ceremonials. I had the war caciques and chief shut him up, entered, and soon after sent into the Post for hand-cuffs, which were in due time given me. I then called a council to which we had to bring Roman by force. He at first refused our commands, but afterward promised to abide by them. During my absence in the Coçonino Country, he became desperate and unruly again, seizing another man's peach orchards on the claim that they belonged to him by right of gentile descent.[90] On my return, I was informed of this and begged by my brother chiefs to assemble another council. I told them to wait my movements; meanwhile, Roman again reported that he should kill either the Governor or myself if we again entered his house to call him to council. I immediately ordered a council to be heralded, and Roman not coming in, I started alone for his house. He had loaded a gun and placed it in the corner of his room. I entered and commanded him to come to the council. At first he refused, making a start for his gun; but I laid my hand roughly on his arm, commanding [him] to come or he should be bound and brought by force. He followed me. He again came to terms and I gave him ten days in which to execute his promise. The ten days passed, and meanwhile Lieut. Bourke came to pay me a visit before his return Eastward. He had a small detachment of soldiers with him. Roman, without reference to this, prepared his arms and said he intended to kill me. Learning this, I informed Lieutenant Bourke of the state of affairs, showing him a letter from General Sherman which you kindly had him write for me at the time of my Wingate troubles. I asked him if I could call on him for his moral support, and he replied that I certainly could, as a measure of protection. Accordingly, on the evening of the 28th we filed out and drew up before the house of Roman, backed by the request of the council, which assembled for the purpose. A dance inside was the occasion for some delay, when suddenly Roman, armed with an immense rifle, sprang up through the roof and cocking it, leveled it at my breast, calling out that I should die that night and that then he should—that he was ready.

I commanded him in a loud voice to come down or I would fetch him down. A second command (when he saw that I did not flinch) brought him to the ground, when the Lieutenant and his men disarmed him and marched him off to the house of the Governor, where we made him acknowledge before the council his obligation to the Great Father, the Agent, and the chiefs of Zuni, foreswear his allegiance to the Mormons, and promise on the day following to get the load of wood. This he did, expressing his regret to the council and saying he had been led to suppose by the Mormons that he could do as he pleased. On the morning following, he took a load of wood to the Mission, where he was questioned, received promise of pay for his wood, contrary to Dr. Thomas's directions, was told that he had done right in refusing the council and Cushing, and assured that Cushing would be sent off the Reservation and the captain of soldiers would be severely punished.

The name of this missionary is S. Bentley. The most proper and elegant term for him I can find is a Spanish one—"*uno ladrone y fanfarron*" [a thief and a braggart]. I would like to give its English equivalent, but under such circumstances quotations from foreign languages are considered more gentlemanly, while quite as expressive. I have met several of these whining "martyrs (!) to the cause of Jesus" in my sojourn in this country, and they have invariably proved to be most unscrupulous rascals and unchristianly breeders of trouble; opposing the progress of science and, by their overbearing dispositions, jealousies and canting zeal, defeating their own ends as well as those of the government in permitting their presence—the education of Indian youth.

I believe the one at hand is here as "U.S. Indian Teacher," although he claims to be Agent and supreme master of the Zunis, with the privilege of turning me or any of my party—without reference to their moral standing or scientific objects—out of the Pueblo and off the Reservation. I beg you will ascertain, so far as practicable, his standing and the extent of his authority; for I began my investigation believing that I was under the orders of Spencer F. Baird and Major J.W. Powell, of Washington, D.C., which gentlemen, by virtue of a bill passed by Congress and the U.S. Senate, had secured special privileges for their assistants and officers, either in trading for material with which to enrich the National Museum or in the pursuit of ethnographic researches on behalf of the Bureau of Ethnology and Smithsonian Institution. I should infinitely prefer to die by the bite of a rattlesnake than to be compelled to give up my investigations at their present stage on account of the rantings of this "Don Fanfarron."

When I returned from the country of the Coçoninos, I found Mr. Bentley here as new Teacher. His plans were good, and I promised to further them to my best ability—so far as possible without jeopardising my own work. I have not once forgotten this promise and have, on several occasions, aided the man in his studies of the Zuni language, turning over to him one of my vocabularies and writing out several grammatical rules for his use. He begged my advice, and I had it to offer on one occasion only. He was constantly talking about how, if an "Indian—chief or any one else—" offered opposition to him, disrespect, or in any way offended him, he should "knock the stuffin' out of him," or "break his head," or give him a "side winder," or take a "fence-pole to him"; or if the Indians didn't furnish wood for him, he should "tear down the corrals"; and any man who opposed him would be "laid out, that was all!"—I quote *verbatim* the elegant and constant expressions of a laborer in the "Fold of Christ," who believes that "Except ye become as little children, ye shall not enter the Kingdom of Heaven." I did remark after hearing a few such speeches that the "science" [of boxing] was unknown in Zuni, and that during a residence here of two years, I had never seen one Indian strike another, and that as I once tried the game to my own disadvantage, I did not think its employment would speed the work of conversion or advance the cause of education or popularize the gentleman who introduced it.[91] But I was informed that I "knew nothing of Indian character." If I "had passed twenty seven years among Indians," I "would know more about them." Since then, whenever the good word of advice has risen to my lips I have swallowed it.

Some days before these occurrences (regarding Roman), one of the secret medicine orders being in session, the high priest came and asked me if I would not like to have his society give me a dance in my own house and an exhibit of some of their medical powers in honor of Col. Stevenson and Lieutenant Bourke. I replied gratefully, "yes"; for it was the highest possible honor. The dance was performed, in the presence of Col. S, Mr. Mindeleff, Mr. Bentley, and myself, but the missionary got up with a frown and left before the ceremonial was half completed. Having never been thus honored by the Indians, he felt jealous of the distinction they gave me.[92] Since then he has constantly been casting mud and slime in my pathway by telling the Indians I was not what I had been representing myself, that I had come here to write about all their secret affairs, and when I sent my papers East I was paid for them and that was the way I was enabled to live; that Washington did not give commissions to *boys* but only to *men* like *himself*; that they must not come to me any more for counsel but to him; that I was a liar and would get them into trouble; and that if they asked me to interpret for them I would surely deceive them, etc. etc. etc.

When, unaware of all this, I paid a visit to the man and asked him if he had received his wood, he replied by requesting the immediate presence of Lt. Bourke and myself. Lieut. Bourke sent his compliments to the gentleman and declined his invitation, stating that he had a room in the house of the Governor, where he would receive and listen to the missionary; to which the latter retorted by saying that he had "merely thought to save himself the trouble of reporting Messrs. Bourke and Cushing to the Departments." Col. Stevenson urged me to have a conference with the irate, bull-dozing representative of the Home Missions, promising to be present, and I accepted the invitation. On the evening of the 29th I went down in company with Col. Stevenson. My missionary friend talked of the weather and health etc. etc. until I respectfully drew his attention to the fact that he had requested my presence for a cross examination. He replied that he had sent for Mr. Graham, the trader. I informed him I had done the same, and that the gentleman would be at hand shortly. His arrival was the occasion of a second reminder from myself, which nettled the missionary, a little, and he began:

"Mr. Graham, Mr. Cushing is a dangerous man. At my face he is a perfect gentleman; behind my back he tries to undermine my authority with the Indians." "Address your remarks to me, Mr. Bentley. I will hear you through, sir, and then reply," said I. But the gentleman, like a hound that has stolen a bone, did not like to speak directly to me but continued his remarks to Messrs Graham and Stevenson. To be brief, the substance of them was as follows:

That I was a liar; that I had made grave charges concerning the former missionary (which I would substantiate, I replied);[93] that I had caused the governor to remove him and Mrs. Stevenson from the sacred dance a few days previously—as he had been informed by Pedro Pino and other Indians (to which I replied that it was a question between the veracity of Pedro Pino and the other Indians and Mr. Cushing, and that Mr. Cushing would state that either Pedro Pino and the other Indians, or else their reporter, were liars;[94] but the reverend gentleman remarked that he preferred the testimony of the Indians and that I was not only unreliable but that I was in the habit of interpreting falsely between Indians and Americans; that I claimed to be a chief to the Americans but that he denied my position as such among the Indians. I asked him to inform me how it was that the Indians obeyed my commands; but he didn't inform me; and why it was that no other Americans questioned the veracity of my translations—even those who were intimately associated with me—Lt. Bourke, Mr. Mindeleff, Mr. Graham, and others—to which he replied no one understood Zuni but myself and therefore no one's testimony amounted to anything—he knew how to put two and two together and had not been a lawyer seventeen years for nothing. He said that his authority was supreme here and that I had no business to make any orders in Zuni. I informed him that by the authority of the Agent, Dr. Bentley and Mr. F.H. Cushing were both at liberty to dictate to a limited extent in Zuni; that Dr. Thomas has specially requested my aid and sanctioned my authority as a chief, had requested me to bring Roman Luna to terms, see that the Indians supplied wood for the Mission, take care of affairs between the Zunis and the Navajos, etc. etc.; that in all other matters the U.S. Teacher was his (Thomas') sub-agent; that on the strength of this I compelled the Navajo Sa-va-ta-he to turn over six sheep to the former missionary for trespass and had, after four councils, by authority of all the chiefs and my own as one of them, compelled Roman Luna to get wood for *him* and that *he* objected to the best service I had ever done him; that I moreover had a right to command in Zuni as a chief of native choice, a right sanctioned by the Treaty of Guadaloupe and a treaty now in Zuni securing to the Zunis the right of personal property, government, and religious protection from the United States;[95] that if the Indians saw fit to choose a foreigner as one of their chiefs, they had a right to do so, and that said chief had the right of executing the duties of his office; that, finally, I should therefore continue to execute such duties and to live much as I had heretofore, relying upon my moral conduct, which no one could attack, and a law of Congress which Col. Stevenson was aware of, and my position in the Smithsonian (which the reverend gentleman denied), all of which accounted for my presence in the Pueblo.

Mr. Bentley then remarked that I had ordered Roman Luna to get wood for him in order to undermine his character and authority; had never received such directions as I claimed from Dr. Thomas, and had done a rash act in which Lieut. Bourke had assisted me without authority (he was unaware of the letter I held),[96] and that if I issued another order in Zuni he should report me to Thomas and the Department and remove me; that if the Department did not back him up in that, he should *ruin* me, turn the Indians against me so that they would drive me out. He should simply and entirely "crush" me and "inform the scientific world how unreliable were my investigations."

I asked him if he saw the bracelet of oliva shells on my wrist and understood the rank it gave me; if he saw more than a few of the Indians with such bracelets and [understood] that my membership in the exotic order (he denied exotic orders among the Zunis) would make the time of my final separation from the Indians a necessary time of difficulty for me, requiring in all probability the assistance of cavalry escort. I told him I thought the Indians believed in me, and even if they did not, each member of our order was sworn to eternal fraternity and fidelity, and that *once* a Priest of the Bow, *always* so.

"Ah, that is a humbug." "Did you not witness some of my initiatory ceremonials?" "Ah well, Mister Cushing, they's a good deal of humbug in all that, and the proof of the pudding is eating it." "Quite true, and although we shall work apart henceforth, I doubt not we shall both chew at one string and find the proof therein." "I shall ruin you, Mr. Cushing," said the "Christian gentleman," "and depend on it." "Very well, sir; do as you please, Mr. Bentley, and I wish you a very pleasant night."

I have since reported to Mr. Thomas in the official form the subjection of Roman Luna and in a subsequent communication have requested Dr. Thomas to pay an early visit of investigation to the Pueblo.

I always await any advice or directions from yourself, and to you and Major Powell alone I look for orders or the authority of my presence in Zuni. My behavior during the past two years in this Pueblo has been invariably honorable and *unrelentingly* moral, for I have recognized the gravity of my obligation to the honor of the Institution and of my supporters in the work of research among the Zunis. The *truth* of my discoveries in the inner life etc. of the Pueblos is wonderful enough, and I therefore never have occasion of recourse to exaggeration in my representations of them.

I have been very lengthy in my relation of the above matters in order that you might be thoroughly informed about them, as is your unquestionable and official due. If the language I have used be disrespectful either regarding Mr. Bentley or as addressed to yourself, please bear in mind that it was written in heat and haste and that any ordinary man laboring under such influences forgets now and then that he is a gentleman.

Col. Stevenson left five days since for Moqui with Mr. Mindeleff and Titskematse, whom, at his request, I turned over to his service.

On account of his presence and of my work on the catalogue (more than two hundred pages), I have been unable to complete my notes on the Ha-va-supai. As a member of the order mentioned, I shall be closely engaged in ceremonials for eighteen days, after which time I shall be free to work on it again.

As you are perhaps aware, I have been engaged since the writing of my long letter of February 1880 in working up the symbolism of the ceramic decorations and pictographs of the Zunis. Another person has entered that field and has drawn largely from my own material.[97] Much time is liable to elapse ere I can publish anything regarding my Zuni work, and not only this but much else is liable to creep out through other channels. I therefore make record to you of the fact that not only in this regard but with reference to the news that may be from time to time published about Zuni: *all* is either a direct or indirect emanation from my researches here. We cannot fail to recognize this fact if we glance over the former meager and entirely erronious literature regarding the Zuni Pueblo Indians up to the date of January 1880. The appearance of several newspaper accounts and notices which have come to my knowledge, some concerning myself, give me no concern, although they have been made quite without my authority. Newspaper men are often unrecognizable and *always* unscrupulous.

Ere long, I shall be in need of some money. If such as may be sent can be turned into silver and forwarded to Fort Wingate by *Express* (as there is a R.R. Express office at that point now), it will be a great blessing to me. My expenses for subsistence alone during the presence of Col. Stevenson and his party were more than ninety dollars, as I had to be free with my commissaries toward one who is, I have reason to believe, now entirely well disposed toward me.

I am receiving very complimentary letters from many parts of the country on my investigations, and everybody is looking forward to my tour East with the Indians. No one so much, however, as myself and the Indians. It seems so glorious and happy a prospect that I can scarcely trust to its fulfilment, yet kind offers from various R.R. officials are beginning to come in, and I have every reason to expect everything I might wish in the way of transportation. The people of Boston extend every inducement for a visit to their city, via the ocean, after the Washington visit is completed, promising to give my Indians a private reception, a public entertainment, etc. Prof. Norton of the American Archaeological Society writes me about it, and Prof. Horsford says that I shall accept his hospitality at Cambridge.[98]

When the Indians see how kind the Americans of the "World of Sunrise" are to them and me, I think they will be glad they have given me such confidence and position, and it will make the completion of my work May Day sport compared with the difficulties which beset its beginnings. I have the honor to remain

Your Faithful Servant,
F.H. Cushing

Daily Journal

Sunday, December 4th, 1881.

A-pithlan Shi-wa-ni again *hapokia te thlapa* [Bow Priests again go into retreat].

Monday, December 5th.

A-pithlan Shi-wani tap se-wa-lu-kia [Bow Priests have been dispatched to contact people]. Was visited by Mr. Graham and Fru at dinner. Mail came.

The proceedings of the medicine men over, Brother . . . [three blank pages]

The first game of *Ti-kwa-we* [stick-racing] of the season, so far as I know, was performed today. Children are again beginning quoits and *La-sho-li-we* [game of the hidden ball], and there is talk of a horse race after the grinding of meal for the *A-shi-wa-ni* takes place.[99]

Note

[December 5, 1881]

The Possible Relationship of the Priesthood of the Bow to the A-shi-wa-ni or Caciques of the Pueblo

My impression is that in former times the Priesthood of the Bow was a powerful secret organization of war. The *Tethl-na-we* which I discovered in the caves of the Concho and Colorado Chiquito give positive evidence of its existence then as now, and the comparative absence of the *Hla-we* of the medicine and sacred orders speaks of the former supremacy of this: that so powerful was it that even the *A-shi-wa-ni* themselves—far more supreme in the old times than the present—were compelled to court its favor and ask its assistance.[100] This accounts for the relationships of the "Grand Masters of the Bow" to the "Masters of the House" in the fables of "The Home of the Uncle," "Pa-u-ti-wa and His Two Sons," "The Maiden of Ma tsa ki and Her Lovers," and "The Crazy Young Man," as well as others.[101] It also accounts for the ceremonial relationship of the Priests of the Bow at present (a relationship which I am to fill tomorrow, Dec. 6th '81) to the grinders of the meal of the Caciques and the gatherers of their wood! And finally it accounts for the presence of the Caciques as honorary guests at some of our sittings and at our initiatory ceremonies.[102]

Daily Journal

Tuesday, December 6th.

A-pithlan Shi-wa-ni, ta-ye-ma Kia [Bow priests go up to watch the dance] at about four o'clock in the evening.

Mail left for Wingate. Wrote long letter, commenced day or two ago, to Prof. Baird. Sent it.

A very fine day. Have been engaged a part of the day with the letter to Prof. Baird. Completed it at about noon and took it over to Mr. Graham's for mailing. Read it to him, as it related to the conversation of the other evening. Mr. G. pronounced it good and just, because correct. At about two o'clock, as I was finishing dinner, Wa-tsai came in after me to join the *A-pithlan Shi-wa-ni* in guarding wood for the caciques. Soon after, we were joined by A-hu-te-nu, Ka-pithlan-tchu-ni-koa, Ain-che, and one or two others of the order who came to ask where I would go. It was left with the high priest, and I was sent with Wa-tsai, Ka-pithlan, and Pitchi to the *Kia-kwe mo-so-na*'s house. We had the duty of carrying little buck loads of wood to our cacique and of seeing that every family furnished a sufficient quantity.[103] *Te-hui-ta-thla-na-tel-e-tchi-a* [the Big Plaza] was the division for the *Kia-kwe mo-so-na* [town chief], *Te-hui-ta-tsana* and *Kia-kwe pathl-to* [the Small Plaza and the House (?)] for the Eastern *Shi-wa-ni* [Priest of the East], *Pish-lan-kwin-tah-na* [the northern part of the pueblo] for the Middle *Shi-wa-ni, So-pi-ah-na-kwin* [the frontage of this latter area] for *Ta-a Shi-wan-okia* [Corn Priestess], *He-kia pakwin* [the Heiwa kiva environs] for Lai-iu-ai-tsai-lunk'ia [another member of the council of high priests and Cushing's adoptive father], and *A-kwi-te-a-la* [four floors down] for *Pe-kwi-na.* Of course the adjunct portions of the pueblo were set aside with the grander divisions.[104]

We were engaged in this duty until sunset, the very old members of the order being stationed on the top of Zuni—*Kia-pa-tchu-kwin* [four stories high]—with the two high priests to give orders while the younger members, divided into parties of three, were engaged as mentioned until sunset, when we entered the *Kia-kwe mo-so-na*'s house, each one of our party grasping his hand and breathing in from it the breath he blew upon it, with the words "*Tom te ko ha ne an i h tchi an apta*" (May the light of the gods meet you). We were then feasted and returned to our homes. Within an hour, all reassembled at my house, and we started out to gather the unmarried girls together to shell the corn for tomorrow's grinding. We gathered together six, the first one accompanying to the house of the second and so on. At one house I fell through the ladder hole and sat down with solidity on the stone floor, a circumstance which did not disturb me in the least but excited considerable comment then and after.

Gathering all, we proceeded to the cacique's house and immediately began to shell corn, it being the custom of the members of the order—while masters of the whole ceremony—to style themselves the slaves of the caciques and shell corn, pass it about, hand water and food, be very gallant to the young ladies in their charge, etc. etc., as examples to their people. We were not constantly engaged in this but went all about the pueblo to attend to matters for tomorrow, summon the singers and direct them to remain overnight in the house of the song master, etc. After the corn shelling, the girls gathered their blankets and some skins together, spread them down in long rows and laid down to rest, side by side. At about this time there [were] loud calls for a story (fable) from me, but I declined, claiming it would keep the girls awake. At nearly all points the song masters of the various sacred orders were together for practice with their singers. Although strictly against the rules, after I saw all was quiet and the three Priests of the Bow were distributed for rest at the sides and feet of the girls—as "guards," although, moreover, a place was left for me, I quietly went home, from fear of adding to an already severe cold, and directing my "sisters" to wake me long before sunrise, retired—not, however, before making these outline memoranda.

Wednesday, December 7th.

Before sunrise, I was awakened by Wa-tsai, who came hastily to find me and get me ready for the day's proceedings.[105] Save our wristlets, we donned none of our paraphernalia, but I observed that none of those of our order who officiated today was without this mark of his rank—even those who did not habitually wear the bracelet.[106]

Preparing a hasty breakfast, I ate and immediately went with Wa-tsai to the cacique's house. The *U-hu-hu-kwe* singers were present, and a number of young women, both married and single, were present—some old women also to parch the half-ground corn and shell.[107] We were engaged variously in helping the women to water, passing the cracked corn to the old women and, as it was parched, back again, etc. Very soon, the *Kia-kwe-mosona* or Cacique Major took his seat on the fireplace side of the room in *Ko-ha-kwa* [white shell bead] necklace, earrings of turquoise, *passi thlian* [big-sleeved] shirt, etc., tobacco, fire sticks and shucks being supplied him.

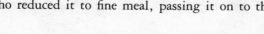

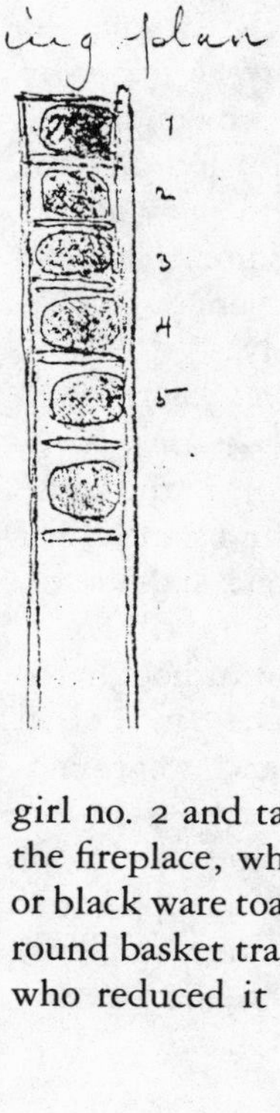

While thus engaged, I observed that in grinding the corn it was put through the process which I attempt to illustrate by the following plan: The *blue* corn [was] first shelled, then sifted and winnowed in a coarse round basket tray and then carried by ourselves to the girl at metate no. 1, where it was cracked, passed over to girl at no. 2, who reduced it to coarse meal a little finer than hominy, [whereupon] it was returned to us by the girl no. 2 and taken back to the two old women at the fireplace, who toasted it in an *al-i-kwi-kiu-te-le,* or black ware toasting pot, lifting it out with a little round basket tray to be returned by us to girl no. 3, who reduced it to fine meal, passing it on to the next, who reduced it to coarse flour and passed it over to the next, who ground it to fine flour, [which was then] heaped up in an immense closely woven basket tray (*ho-in*) as finished, its consistency being that of fine flour. The amount ground in a short space of time was marvelously much. The yellow and white corn was ground likewise, save that it was parched before cracking (in the kernel). The singers went through a few verses of their sacred songs, which of course I cannot translate, and then we went about to gather together those who were to make the round of the dances. Nai-iu-tchi presently came in. As an example, he grasped the hand of the Cacique Major—himself a cacique of war—and, breathing in as we did, took his seat of state beside him. The manner in which these caciques are enthroned and treated leaves little doubt of the former greatness of this office and the supremacy of our order, as [mentioned] in "Stray Thoughts."[108] They were seated on the side near the fireplace about midway of the room, very handsomely dressed and propped up with elegant blankets. Just before we were to start, Nai-iu-tchi arose and indicated me to follow him. He took me to his own house and went to a little wallet hanging on the wall, from which he drew forth a small bag containing a flint arrow point of pink color and some yellow powder. He breathed over this with a brief prayer, and then approaching me, requested me to rise and fold my arms. Using the flint as a spatula, he introduced a small quantity into my mouth, requesting me to wait for it to form paste and then swallow it. At the same time, he took some into his own mouth, masticating it and blowing it first over my head and heart, then over every part of my person, saying, "My son, by virtue of this medicine may the people whom you visit and greet today be all happy at the seeing of you and must the young women look upon you with love"—which latter statement was devoutly repeated with emphasis by his old wife. Nai-iu-tchi said that as I progressed in my order and its etc. [sic], a bag of this sacred flour was being prepared to be always carried about me; that he loved me and therefore sometimes told me things beforehand; and that his ambition was for me to know everything relating to *his* and *my* religion, and prove to be the best and greatest of men in his nation.

Returning, he took his seat as before, and I was hastily summoned to feed "my girls" before starting out. Guavas and peaches were placed alternately in a row through the center of the room, and the girls were called to either side of the luncheon ere they started on their ceremonial visit to the houses of the caciques. All this occurred just after the breakfast of meat, guavas and peaches (stewed) which had been spread by Pitchi and the others and at which we were not present, as we had been engaged in gathering together a company of flute players belonging to the *Pe-sho-tsi-lu-kwe* [Bedbug Medicine Society]. While the members of our order are ceremoniously styled slaves of the Fathers (caciques), yet they are masters and chiefs of the situation, ordering even the high priests of the other orders to get their singers, players, etc. together and calling whomsoever they please of the women to grind meal, yet waiting on them with servile gallantry.

The luncheon finished, we cleared away the dishes etc. and arranged our girls in a line lengthwise of the room, giving the leader and each following a pair of corn ears (blue) apiece. Ke-no-te was chosen from among the singers and dressed by us with dance kilt, embroidered belt and placed midway in the line, also provided with two ears. The flute players, standing around a bowl of medicine water, covered with a sacred kilt, began the song and drum struck, the vacant places at the metates [meal-grinding stones] were quickly filled with young grinders, and the dance performed by the women and Ke-no-te in the usual shuffling manner (heels close together, body inched forward, lifted up and down from the knees upward, ears of corn held, one aloft, the other out at side, and reversed as the dancers turned half around from side to side) was begun. The grinders, the old women at the toasting pots with their long bundles of stirring sticks, the dancers and the drummers and other musicians all kept perfect time. As some of the woman grinding showed fatigue, others took their places. The dance continued, ourselves watching to see that the dresses, leggins, necklaces, etc., were in order on our girls, and arranging them when not so, until the arrival of two of our order with a party of other girls from the Cacique of the Badgers was the signal for the cessation—the dancers shuffling back to the corn tray and one of our number taking the corn from them, first breathing a blessing over the ears toward their nostrils with the usual exclamation and the other distributing the mantles and shawls to the girls and divesting Ke-no-te, the male dancer (*ya-po-to* [symbolizer of corn]), of his paraphernalia.

The girls then formed in a line, headed by Wa-tsai, and followed by myself, as guards and leaders, and we started. Wa-tsai advanced, grasped the hand of the Cacique Major, who gracefully extended it, breathing the blessing of "light" upon him over it, then the hand of Nai-iu-tchi, who did the same, and passed on, the leading girl and the others doing the same in succession, followed by myself. We then took our charges in single file eastward round the pueblo to the house of the Younger Brother Cacique Major. . . . As we entered, the usual greeting was pronounced and the ceremony of hand taking repeated in order described, the wife of the cacique being included. Our girls immediately turned their mantles and shawls over to us and repaired to the metates, grinding through a few verses and then rising to dance as before, a young man being chosen to dance as *Ya-po-to* had done. At the close of the dance—which was signalized by the arrival of the party before mentioned—the ears of corn were blessed by the wife of the cacique—a little while before the close, and at the taking of them. I was much called on by the women here to pass corn and meal to and fro (white) and give the girls water, which the women did to show off the American Priest of the Bow, I presume. I made a cigarette for the cacique, who interchanged smokes with me ceremoniously and elegantly.

The departure was as before, and we went through the *Le hua thlana, etina tsana, So-pi-ah-na-kwin on nan* [the Big Plaza and northern frontage], to the house of the *Shi-wan o-kia.*[109] Here we found some of her relatives, placed in state with her (four) and Niesto, the former high priest of our order, who still nominally occupies his original position although too infirm for the active duties of it. The hands of all were taken and the grinding and dance went on as before; the *woina* cacique this time blessing the ears.[110] While the grinding was going on, I went home and prepared a drink of maple syrup, water, sugar, and peppermint for the singers and flute players, who, as they had been singing since sunrise, were getting hoarse. They drank it devoutly, as medicine water.

Our next place was around to *He-kia pakwin* [Heiwa kiva environs] to the house of Lai-iu-ai-tsailunk'ia (my father). His wife, one or two *Ka-mo-so-we* [*komosone*: leaders of the kachina dances] and Ki-a-si (second high priest of our order) were the *A-shi-wani* of this place. Here was by far the grandest and handsomest company of the day. At the dancing a young man from outside was seized by ourselves and dragged in [to serve as *ya-po-to*], offering the usual cant objections yet of course highly flattered by the matter.

At the *Pe-kwi-na*'s, or Priest of the Sun's, whither we next went, I distributed the last of my medicine. Although as before, the flavor caused grimaces enough, the cooling effect convinced the musicians of its sacred and medical properties, and they gave me, in an ancient sea shell, a sip of their medicine with the interchange of the usual greetings.

At the next point—Cacique of the Badger's—I found [the] *woina* of the house and the two other former high priests, Hu-se-tsana and Pithlan-lo-hai-a, in state. Although I captured a *ya-po-to,* the dance was here left out, and we soon started for the house of the Cacique Major again. Entering, we found the closing prayer already going on, and I saw Mrs. Bentley sitting by the side of the caciques, whom I greeted as pleasantly and politely as possible, although the terms on which her husband and I stand are unpleasant, and she had a look of wonder in her eyes to see me thus associated with the ceremonial—which wonder grew as I sat down in front of the caciques to respond to their prayers with the others (members) of our party. A long prayer was then said by the Cacique Major, which I despair of repeating—the ceremonial of grasping both hands of Nai-iu-tchi and breathing to and from them four times during the closing portion of the prayer being performed.

This prayer changed only to suit the speaker, and, said with more clearness and perfection, was repeated in the same manner by Nai-iu-tchi, being constantly responded to by ourselves. It first concerned our claims as an order and was addressed to the war gods, A-hai-iu-ta, Tsi-kia-haia, Ku-pis-taia; then to the Priests of the North, West, South, East, Heaven and Earth; then to the Gods of the East, who form our roads and grant the winds of water, seed, or reproduction, fortune, long life, and the "finishing of the road"; then to the Gods of the West, or the *Kâ'kâ A-shi-wa-ni* (priests of the dance and caciques), whose attributes were the same; then to the dead of the sacred orders, who still live as our fathers and relatives and whose interposition was besought; then to the High Gods of the Heavens, the Sun Father, the Moon Mother, the two great stars (Morning and Evening), the Milky Way, the Sword Belt of Orion, the Tribe of Seven (Big Dipper) and the *Ku-pa* (Little Dipper [error for Pleiades]) and the *Tsu-ha-pu-hoya tchu-we* (Black lead-graphite [corn kernels]) or twinkling stars, whose attributes were mentioned and intercession besought; then to the Priests of the North, West, South and East, Heavens and Lower regions again; and then to the Priests of the Chase (fetiches); and finally to the Gods of water, all animals, from the worm and "*even* the disgusting *bug* and even the smallest insect" to the great suppliers of food and life—all were spoken of—and the prayer, with the usual benedictions, was closed. It was followed by another, by Nai-iu-tchi, who took my place on account of my inexperience and who addressed it to the singers and all "the children" (of the caciques and gods of water) present and closed it with the usual benediction. The medicine water was distributed to all, to us last, and in the twilight we then hastened to bring out the food—guavas and meat stew well seasoned with salt and toasted chili-flour, the trays of the former alternating with the latter, with stewed peaches on [the] other side in various little dishes. We then called our children to sit down and eat, spreading skins and blankets for them and remaining, two at either end, to await them and pronounce the welcome as they rose one by one and said thanks. On finishing the meal, the guests immediately departed, we having nothing more to do than to distribute salt and show them their blankets as they bade us good-night and we returned the greeting.

Last of all, we ate—for which, of course, it being obligatory, I suffered most of the night with a renewal of my dyspepsia. The caciques joined us, and, the meal over, we bade them the same ceremonious adieux and departed to return the borrowed musical instruments, kettle drums, drum hoop, etc., to the *U-hu-hu-kwe.* I went to the house of the chief priest of the *Chi-kia-li-kwe* (Rattlesnake order) to return his drum hoop—which I did with a warrior's blessing, receiving a priest's in return, as this old man is very fond of me.

This, with the remarks of admiration which I heard (sparingly, as they are forbidden) of my conduct during the ceremonials, with the notice given me by Juan Perca (that most law abiding of Zunis) of the finding of a stray ox of Solomon Barth's in his herd, for which I gave him a certificate of date and circumstances, closed this eventful, weary[ing] and instructive day.

Thursday, December 8th.

Having from fatigue retired early last night, I awoke at sunrise this morning. Soon after, Sister [Kiau] came in and built my fire. I was presently joined by Thla-k'oa, who brought a paper torn from a memorandum book, on which was written a statement as to his having directed a party of ten Americans to the Rito Quemado Road and to which all their names were signed—two women among them.[111] Thla k'oa, who ranks with me as chief in Zuni, when asked who the principal chief was, replied it was me, although he stretched it here a little, and that I had been an American from Washington named Cushie but I was now a *Zuni* named Tenatsali; [at] which he said the Americans laughed. When he had showed them the road, they gave him tobacco, half a dollar, and a dog, whose name they told him (he said) was "*Com-ia*" (come here). I laughed and told him that meant *Kiathl im-a-ne,* and that I would come over and show him how much English his dog understood.

In telling me that five days hence our order must sit up with the two gods A-hai-iu-ta, he made a remark which is worthy of record (See "Stray Thoughts"). Said he, "We make '*imitations merely*' of the two, to show our knowledge of them and our remembrance"—which explains in an Indian's own words their theory of their idolatry.[112]

Presently I was called on by Nanahe and the visiting chief of Shi-mo-covi [Cimopove] (Moqui), who, about to depart, came to present his farewell respects. I made his cigarette and thanked him for his call, which I told him I had awaited that we might become friends—to which he of course replied, "*Krs-an-tcha*" and thanks. He told me I was a great chief and that ever since I had paid Moqui a visit I had been recognized by all his nation as such, and by my speeches then in council they had since tried to live; that he wished to number me among his friends; and that when I visited his village, if it so pleased me, I would ascend to his house and partake of his hospitality; poor as it was, I should be satisfied. To which I replied thanks, that the speech tasted good and did me honor, that I hoped soon to see him back again or to see him at his own home and repeat his own kind words. He was visibly pleased with this speech, and I added, "May you on your journey go happily to the house of your people, your self; and being there, may you, with your children and people, live to see each sunset happily as day succeeds day." To which he replied he could do no better than repeat my last words to myself. He arose, clasped me, uttered a short prayer (I did the same), and then the ceremonial of sealing friendship—breathing on one another's hands—took place; [then] he said, in Zuni, good-bye and departed, Thla k'oa following.

The Lt. Gov., Ti-wahni-shi-wa, came in and, after my breakfast, helped me shake the skins on the floor and clean up generally. Then went in to talk awhile with the sick Governor. Poor Brother! He is very ill, but he never forgets me. Yesterday he filled my lamps with great difficulty, and today when I went to see him he was busy on my shield with file and sandpaper. God grant the old boy's recovery and the journey I pray for him East. He is impatient to get well in order that he may get to work on our costumes for this trip. He is getting better.

Most of the day I have spent in writing, interrupted by no one. Toward evening I went out to walk. Mr. Graham is being fixed up by the women of his house. He is in a pitiable state. Went around to Thla-k'oa's house and showed off his dog to the great astonishment of the inmates. It is a pretty half shepherd black fellow with white nose and feet. Returned at sunset and prepared meal. Was told by Tsai-lu-ai-ti-wa that I would probably have to go on the Navajo expedition tomorrow. In such matters I am chief indeed of the Zunis. They do nothing without my advice or action and always give me unending difficulty if I do not accede to their demands. I may experience hardship and danger, but strict attention to the duties assigned me is the only surety I have to retaining my position among the Zunis, since I now have more to fight than ever—in the opposition of the missionary.

The horses not coming in, the Navajo trip is deferred until after the Fire Fast, as I learn by a conversation with Juan Kelia.[113]

Ti-kia again *hapakia* [sacred societies gathered again].

December 9th. [no entry; no more entered in this notebook]

DRAFT: FHC [TO BOURKE?]

Zuni, Dec. 12th, 1881

My good Friend—

If I have erred in keeping silence this long, it has been on account of strict attention to your own advice, for I have—save during moments of observation which have been many and full since your departure—hardly left my little room. My mails have been larger, my notebooks fuller, and my stomach better than for many months heretofore; and I attribute it mostly to you, as I wish you to attribute my silence to it.

Thus far, the war between Christendom and Heathendom, that is between the missionary and Cushing, has been of no disadvantage to the latter. The enemy, while expending much vile ammunition, and taking many illegal advantages, usually, from inexperience in aiming, flattens his balls against the bulwarks of pagan conservatism or else, in trying to sneak in upon weak places, gets discovered, routed, and has to flee his ground in open daylight. It is likewise not difficult to discover a rattlesnake, for he shakes his rattle, or to avoid him if you know where he be.

Some days since, when that Christian gentleman to whom I above refer was informing the Indians that Cushie had no position in Washington, a wiley buck asked him some pertinent questions, such as "Why did the Washing[ton] food store at Wingate let Cushie have what he wanted, and the teacher who claimed to be a big Washington chief, nothing?" "Why did Cushie go to Arizona with three mules marked with a hook and a rattlesnake 'U.S.' on their shoulders and two soldiers? Why was Cushie known to so many big chiefs with marks laid over their shoulders? Why was Cushie going to Washington with Zuni chiefs, when the other teacher of marks had tried it and failed?

The interrogated, striking a new line of argument, told the Indians if they started to Washington with Cushie, they would not be let into the cars, and if let in, they would go hungry, for all the hospitality their guide could command for them, and if they managed to get to Washington, the great father and his friends would not receive or speak to them, on account of their patron, and finally, they would be left to get home as best they could by Cushie. The aforesaid buck declared for one that he would "wait and see about it all." Others taking up the line of argument, came to my house the next midnight and pulled me out, and took me before a big council, in the house of the Fire Order, where my staunch old friend Nai-iu-tchi was presiding. The sleepless and ever hopeful youth of eighty summers, whom you possibly remember (Pedro Pino) was present also. His and the former's were the only two faces which lighted up in that dark circle with the semblance of a smile, and theirs were only hopeful ones. "Owls and gnomes named *Shi-wis,* why do you pull a fellow out of his bed long after the sword belt of Orion has passed the zenith and told men they need not fear the influence of the Louse Stars but can sleep in peace?" I began, and Nai-iu-tchi gravely replied that I had spoken well, and that he had been laboring with his "children" since eating time, and Pedro Pino had talked about Kenile [Kendrick] and the Navajos, Santiago Arigle [Abreu?] and Monroi [Munroe] in vain.[114] Therefore I had been sent for.

I was in splendid humor and it helped me out, for I heard enough to etc. [sic]. It was just dawn when we broke up our council, but each man in the great chamber shook my hand as we went, breathing audibly upon it and smiling with satisfaction. Four nights since, the caciques all came to my house, closed every crack, and questioned me as to the propriety of making me Head Chief here. They taught me six prayers, which I wouldn't take as many hundred dollars for, and although I am the youngest member of the Priesthood of the Bow, they have given me a chief's mark on my wristlet and made me one of the two priests to go up to Ta-ai-iallone with the war god A-hai-iu-ta, for which I am suffering the penalty of ten days' deprivation of meat and cleanliness and the weakness of two nights' sleeplessness and yesterday's walk to and climb up the aforesaid mesa.[115]

So let these things speak for themselves as to the security of my position with the Indians. . . .

I remain,

Ever Your Faithful Friend, etc.

FHC to Baxter

[ca. December 14, 1881]

[Extracts from letters written during the first several months of membership in the Bow Society]

"I have been going through some of the pleasant (?) little duties incident to a membership of the *A-pith-lan shi-wa-ni,* and writing night and day to keep my notes up. Four successive nights, two of them entirely sleepless, last week, and two already this week; for all the secret orders save mine are in session, and I have, through my membership—a privilege granted by none save it—admission to all the others. I wish I had four constitutions, and two persons; I could then keep up with my opportunities. As I have but one, however, supplied with only half a constitution, I had to content myself with going around and saying my prayers before the altars, and taking a few hungry glances—even which has required until nearly midnight. . . ."

Again he writes: "I have been busy day and night with religious exercises of my order, in which I am already getting very high rank. I had to learn a prayer of more than *two thousand words,* with various shorter exercises."

At latest accounts Mr. Cushing was getting material for a collection of fairy lore which promised to be as rich, imaginative and full of strange conceptions as the wonderful collection of the Brothers Grimm. . . .[116]

Pilling to FHC

December 14, 1881

Frank H. Cushing, Esq.
Zuni, New Mexico
My dear Sir:

Your letter to Prof. Baird relative to your "return with 4 or 5 Indians" to Washington has been referred to this office for reply, and I am instructed by the Director to ask for an estimate of the cost of bringing two Indians—a man and a woman. He is willing and anxious to have this programme carried out if the funds at the command of the Bureau will permit. Please reply by telegram at our expense.

I am with respect

Yours,
James C. Pilling
Chief Clerk
[Bureau of Ethnology]

FHC: Daily Journal

December 22nd, 1881

Was awakened very early this morning by sound of voices inside, calling out for fire to be cooled by *Pa-u-ti-wa* and his *wo-we* [attendant]. At this early hour, it seems that *Shih-kuh-pi* (?) and *Kwe-le-le* go out Eastward to make the new fire.[117] This is done with fire-stick and drill, as in olden time. They then come in with the fire carried in a torch of cedar bark. Young men and old carry from the old fire, which has been so carefully watched for so many days, a few coals which are cooled by *Pa-u-ti-wa,* who gives, in exchange, the new fire.

FHC to Pilling

Zuni, December 24, 1881

Dear Mr. Pilling:

Your letter concerning the Bentley matter is rec'ved, and I write to thank you, as well as Professors Baird and Powell.[118]

I wrote my letter of Dec. 4th to Professor Baird not so much as a request for assistance but as a precautionary measure. Imagining that my principals might from other sources learn something of

Fig. 20 Pautiwa (Cushing sketch).

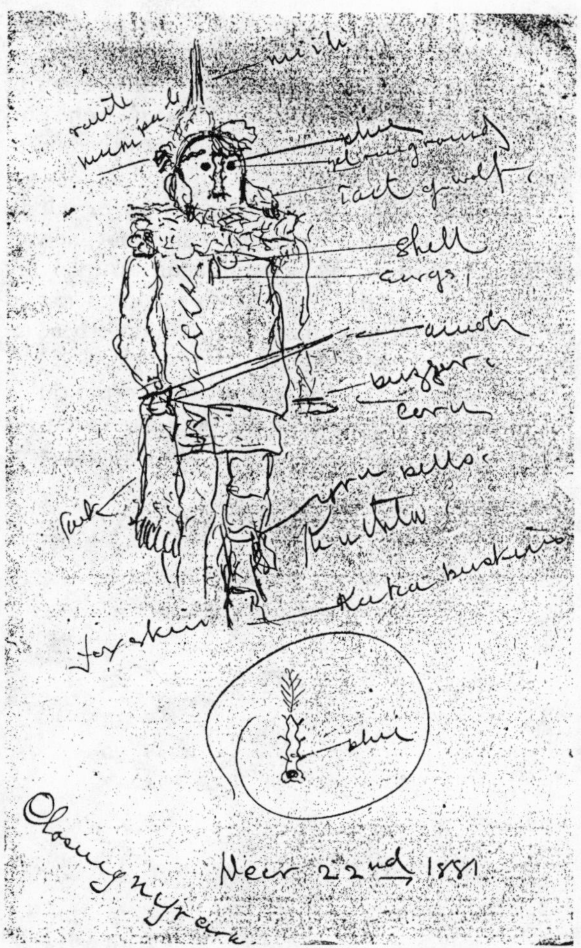

Fig. 21 Dance Figure (Cushing sketch).

the matter, I regarded it as my duty to inform them directly and fully; hence I was both precipitous and verbose in my communication.

I scarcely imagine any interference on the part of either Major Powell or Professor Baird will be necessary, as I propose in future to avoid all trouble with our Missionary Agent by having nothing whatsoever to do with him. I shall continue, nevertheless, to execute my duties as a Chief among the Zunis and as a "Priest of the Bow," with the recently added rank of "Warrior of the Cacique," or Priest of the House;[119] and in case Mr. Bentley, as Acting Agent sees fit to interfere, I shall call his attention to the Treaty which I now have in my possession, between the United States and the people of Zuni, which recognizes the "Rights and Authority of the Chiefs and Headmen of Zuni." In case that gentleman still persists, I shall either follow his own doctrine and disfigure his cadaverous countenance or else use my influence with the Indians, openly, yet legitimately, against him. He will then perhaps realize that which he has denied: my power and authority with the Zunis. The absence of wood from his mission may have led him to a recognition of that fact already. I now live so far *apart* from him that I cannot, however, make any positive statement regarding this point.

Having thus far been left largely to myself in working out my Zuni problems, I shall not, now or in future, obtrude my petty difficulties upon my principals; I shall merely dutifully report them and rely upon myself to regulate them, unless otherwise directed.

I am happy to say that, despite the storm I called your attention to, my progress with the Indians is admirable, my influence not in the least abated. With the absence of Americans, my old opportunities return to such a degree, indeed, that I rarely leave my writing board. Here I sit as I am sitting now, day and night, save only when I am engaged in participating in or observing some ceremonial.

My thanks are due Major Powell and Professor Baird for their kind offer in this matter and to yourself for making me acquainted with their will.

Please present my earnest sympathy to the Director with my wishes and hopes for his speedy recovery and a Happy New Year, with which, Dear Sir,

I am Very Respectfully Yours,

F. H. Cushing

6. *January–August 1882*

Transfer to the Bureau

January of 1882 brought an important change in Cushing's institutional ties—a change reflected in the correspondence to follow. Almost the whole of the known surviving correspondence dating from the first two years of Cushing's stay in the Southwest consists of letters exchanged with Spencer Baird, head of the Smithsonian. This patron, who had supplied Cushing with books when he was still a boy in upstate New York, had been responsible for his first publication (at age sixteen), and had given him his first job at the Smithsonian, had continued to take an interest that was not merely supervisory but paternal and nurturing. Though somewhat august in manner, he was clearly proud and fond of his protégé, indulging his foibles, providing much-needed praise and encouragement, and attending personally to some of Cushing's more urgent needs—shopping for the right field glasses, sending away for the right shells for trading, lending his own money, and so on. Cushing in turn, while sometimes fulsomely mindful of the respect owing to an elder and superior, shared with him not only the results of his experience but much of the experience itself.

In 1882, however, through what appears from the series of letters following to have been an adroit maneuver on Powell's part to get this brilliant (if bureaucratically "difficult") young ethnologist more directly under his control, Cushing was shifted from the rolls of the National Museum to those of the Bureau of Ethnology. While Baird insisted that the move was purely artificial, the Bureau being as much under his direction as the Museum, the fact was that Powell, far more independent of Baird than was the Museum head, at this point superseded him as Cushing's main "principal."[1]

As head of the agency whose expedition had taken Cushing to New Mexico in the first place, and more particularly as the man whose program was to "organize anthropological research in America," Powell had of course been interested from the beginning in Cushing's activities in Zuni and indeed had already taken a hand in guiding his ethnological investigations. From this point on, as the correspondence shows, his guidance was more authoritative, and after a certain initial awkwardness the two gradually settled into the same kind of filial-parental relationship that had obtained between Cushing and Baird and that seems to have been characteristic of the relations between Cushing and his supervisors or sponsors generally. "I loved him," Powell told a memorial meeting in Washington after Cushing's death, "as a father loves his son."[2]

Powell, however, through the stiffly impersonal medium of his chief clerk, James C. Pilling, ran a considerably tighter ship than Baird in terms both of his schedule for publishable reports expected from his agents in the field and of his control of the purse. In both these respects, Cushing's shift into the Bureau would mean a marked intensification of pressure upon a young man who had been used to following his own drummer. Writing, or rather, writer's block, would become a problem ("constipation" as Baird would put it in recommending the employment of a stenographer to help him "effect a proper discharge"), and many were the prim reminders of deadlines approaching and past that Cushing would receive from Pilling "by order of the Director."

Likewise in the matter of money. On this, as on several earlier expeditions on which Cushing had been sent by Baird, he had been accustomed to living under circumstances of extreme penury—mitigated by certain judicious purchases on credit, elaborately justified and ultimately redeemed by Baird. As things turned out now, however, it was precisely the accumulation of his debts in New Mexico and Baird's inability to pay them that enabled the resourceful Powell to effect Cushing's transfer. From this time forward, he would be subject to much more stringent (though still not altogether undodgeable) rules. Most immediately, even before the actual transfer, Powell became the man Cushing had to persuade to support the project nearest to his heart at this juncture—the trip east.

FHC to Baird

Zuni, January 3, 1882

My dear Professor Baird:

I wrote some time since, a letter to Mr. Graham, the trader here, acknowledging the correctness of his account of more than two years' standing with me, which he informs me he forwarded, according to instructions from Col. Stevenson, to Major Powell.

As no reply has been received to his communication, I write to ask if you will look into the matter. It is not an unimportant one, as it concerns very vitally my reputation. Had I imagined there would be any trouble in the settlement of this and other bills which Colonel Stevenson authorised me to make more than two years and a half since, I should not have made them. This and the bill of Mr. Hopkins, which I also enclose for reference to the Bureau, have been made almost exclusively in the prosecution of my researches in Zuni, all matters of a private nature, save a very few items, having been settled for immediately and charged to myself.

I also wrote some time since for some money which I said I would need very soon, but none has thus far come, and I have been compelled to borrow in order to get along.

The expense of my work at Zuni may, at times, seem large to Major Powell and yourself, but the *results also* are large—larger than I can say or you can realise, as I hope you may know ere long.

And in the end, if these results seem to you not what I have represented them to be, I shall be glad to reclaim them, and bear, from my own salary as I am enabled to do, the expenses I incur while securing them, doubting not that with the material I have already on hand, to say nought of that which I am daily amassing, I shall be able to reimburse myself.

I am quite sure, however, that such will not prove to be the case, and meanwhile I beg the hearty support of the Institution and Bureau.

My work in Zuni, while voluntary, is *not* a pleasure, nor is it for myself. It is for the Smithsonian Institution and Bureau of Ethnology; and I have never responded to the many tempting and liberal offers I have had for even the roughest press notes, nor have I, wittingly, given the smallest scrap of information to representatives of the Press. The various notices of my work which you may have seen have been unavoidable and have been ingenuously gathered from my friends or from my unconscious conversations, or else enthusiastic acquaintances, in their kind zeal to aid and please me, have published them personally from their own observations. I have never, either morally or in the matter of etiquette, ever forgotten my honor in my relationships with yourself or Major Powell.

I have the honor to remain, very respectfully and faithfully,

Your Obedient Servant,
F. H. Cushing

POWELL TO BAIRD

January 14, 1882

Sir:

I have the honor to acknowledge receipt of your letter of January 12 enclosing a bill of L.N. Hopkins, Jr., forwarded by Mr. Cushing, and papers accompanying the same. I have also received two other bills contracted by Mr. Cushing—one from Mr. Douglas D. Graham of Zuni, New Mexico, and the other from Mr. S.W. Smillie of this city. The one transmitted with your letter is herewith returned together with the documents above mentioned with the request that you examine the same.

Mr. Cushing has doubtless needed many of the articles included in these bills, and the expenditure in part at least would be quite proper; but there are some articles purchased which he should pay for himself. At any rate, the accounting offices of the Treasury would not pass an account for their purchase.

The chief difficulty, however, in the payment of these bills arises from the fact that Mr. Cushing has made no request for authority to make such purchases, and no authority, direct or indirect, has been given him by myself to incur such expenses. Hence, in the allotment of funds for the present fiscal year to the several parts of the work no provision was made for their payment.

I have from time to time assisted Mr. Cushing in various ways, but have not considered him to be under my instructions and have in no way given him orders or controlled his work.

The three bills are in amount as follows:

Bill contracted with Mr. Graham	$344.29
" " " " Smillie	40.00
" " " " Hopkins	168.71
Making a total of	$553.00

The aggregate is so great that it will be impossible to pay them from the funds under my control without cutting off some branch of the work now in progress. Please give me instructions in the matter.

I am, with respect,

Your obedient servant,
J.W. Powell,
Director

FHC to Pilling

Zuni, December 25, 1881
[mailed January 15, 1882]

My dear Sir:

Your letter of December 14th, bidding me reply by telegram, is at hand; I am so remote from any telegraphic station, however, that I deem it well to write instead, the more so as I have much to say in answer.

I beg you will once more inform the Director—to whom I wrote about a month since—of my reasons and plans for undertaking an Eastern tour with the Indians, which are as follows:

I have sacrificed so much to the Zuni work, have spent so much time in it and have progressed so far that I wish now to see it through. To accomplish this wish I must do one of two things: either marry a Zuni girl or make a tour East with some of the principal men of the Pueblo. I infinitely prefer the latter.

The advantages which might accrue from such a tour would be inestimable. In the first place, all statements I have made to the Indains regarding my former life, my reasons for being amongst them, etc., would be substantiated and their confidence in and respect for me increased. They would, moreover, understand our objects in collecting their things, how "sacredly we care for them in the Great Estufa at Washington," and would then make no objection to our gathering not only sketches but also actual objects belonging to their esoteric orders, sacred institutions and ceremonials. Their objections thus far have been—and are—so great that any work I have done in this direction has been accomplished only by strategem, which falls very far short of complete success.

I am, moreover, desirous of *showing* my principals at once the importance of my work and the progress I have made in it, its genuineness and extent, in order that they will—it matters not what representations they receive—neither accuse me of incompetence or of false views and over-estimations; that they will consequently feel neither hesitation nor regret in extending to me the aid, power and means of their great names and institutions and in granting the few calls I may make on their generosity.

Yet again: there is, in various Eastern cities, a large body of gentlemen—and ladies—of great culture, wealth and position who are anxious to have me bring my Zunis forward and to do all they can to advance, not my interests alone, but also those of the Institution which I strive faithfully to serve.

Finally, and least of all these personal considerations, yet not without its weight, is a natural desire to have attention called to my work, its extent and elements of popular as well as of scientific interest and to its purity of purpose and singleness of aim. For my moral character and earnestness have been often questioned and slandered, and the most undreampt of and frivolous things have been imputed and assigned as my motives.

Nor can I allow all these selfish interests to make me dumb to the voice of humanity.

I owe a lasting debt of gratitude to the people of Zuni. I wish, therefore, to establish pleasant feelings between them and Americans, to solicit for them aid in times of trouble and to show them the wisdom of consenting to education—*not* innovation—and the policy of a course of absolute peace and good fellowship toward our government and people, which policy never, until of late, have they varied from during all their history.

Born in ancient times to the hardships of savage invasion and warfare, they have struggled up to their little incipient civilization, receiving aid from no human agency and asking nothing save the good will of their deliverers, ourselves.

But they are opening their eyes to no advantage from this score. They have been imposed upon by nearly every Mexican, Mormon, and American who comes in contact with them. Within the present year, the second one of their number has been shot down by drunken Mexicans; yet they appeal in vain to their old Treaty with Captain Pfeiffer or to the authorities of this country.[3]

They have been forging for me, during the past two years of doubt as to my genuineness, the keys which enable me to open their vast and ancient treasure-house of ethnologic information, have treated me with strange goodness and distinction; and in my gratitude I cannot but consider a wish to do all I can toward the amelioration of their condition and toward convincing them that I *am* what I have always claimed to be, their *friend*.

I would find it difficult to induce two Indians alone to come on to Washington—first for reasons of their own and secondly because they are detained by the chief and caciques, who are determined to accompany me themselves.

When we first arrived at the pueblo, Colonel and Mrs. Stevenson encouraged the head men to believe that some of them would, through our agency, be enabled sooner or later to go to the Eastern country, a matter they have ever since held me responsible for.

The men of influence in railroad matters, with whom I began to correspond immediately on receipt of Professor Baird's letter giving me permission to do so, would neither give me passes nor like to give me special rates for fewer than five or six Indians, as they wish the party to be representative and impressive enough to attract patronage and stimulate travel over their lines. So that, on the whole, a party of the size which I contemplate bringing on would not cost much more than one of two or three.

As my friends in Washington and other cities which I may visit will for the most part care for us, and as the Indians will take along luncheons of native material, the principal expenses will be *en route* and quite limited.

After all, I have to say, as I have often before remarked, that the largest interest of my life is in the Zuni work. The *completeness* of this depends wholly upon my taking Eastward the party I made up during Col. Stevenson's presence here, and I am prepared, moreover, to say, that if the Bureau find it not convenient to pay the expenses of this enterprise, rather than fail in it now, I will bear them myself; for I believe the savings of more than two years and a half, even from my limited salary, will enable me to do so. Unless I succeed in my Zuni monograph, money will be of little avail to me, as, in case of failure, I mean, as I said in the beginning, to place myself beyond its need.[4]

I therefore beg earnestly that my Directors will do all in their power to assist me. In case the funds of the Bureau be not accessible for this purpose, could they not be loaned to me? I am sure my principals would, by hearty cooperation and good words, be able greatly to aid me. I am quite as sure they would not regret their generosity in the end, or even before the end came.

In conclusion, and in answer to your request for estimations of the probable expenses of bringing on to Washington a man and a woman, permit me to say that I should be able without doubt—even in the absence of more liberal rates than have already been furnished me by railroad officials—to bring my whole party to Washington in good shape for not more than five hundred dollars. The bringing on of two without such special rates would probably cost nearly as much.

If my Director is able officially to allow me such a considerable sum, I shall be very happy; and I should be very grateful if you would cause it to be sent me with the utmost dispatch; and in case this be not possible or expedient, could not the Bureau or my Directors lend this amount to me, to be deducted from my legitimate [payment for] research on behalf of the Bureau during the last two years and a half; or, again, to be paid immediately on my arrival from private sources not accessible in this [part of the] country.

If this may be done, pray the Director that the amount be sent immediately, as the time draws near for my departure.

I have the honor to remain, very respectfully,

Your Obedient Servant,
F.H. Cushing

James C. Pilling
Chief Clerk of the Bureau of Ethnology
Smithsonian Institution
Washington, D. C.

BAXTER TO FHC

Boston Herald
Boston, January 23, 1882

My dear Cushing:

Yours of the 17th just received. The prospect for you brightens. Rev. Edward Everett Hale, whom of course you know by reputation as an author and an eminent Unitarian, feels a great interest in your work and is interesting others in you.[5] He wishes you to make an address in the Old South while here, with your Zunis, and you will receive $100. I have promised this for you, and you will also be invited to address the American Antiquarian Society at Worcester. I think there will be no difficulty about securing the Custom-House steamer for that little excursion you speak of. Mr. Aldrich also wants you to write him two articles for the *Atlantic Monthly* for $100, but I tell him that, I fear, would not be allowed by your principals. I shall do all in my power to secure the transportation from Chicago east that you need.

Yours faithfully,
Sylvester Baxter

P.S. Will write again soon.

Powell to Baird

January 23, 1882

Sir:

On the 14th of January I had the honor to address you a letter relative to several bills involving expenditures contracted by Mr. Cushing. Since that time the arrangements with the Census Office have been completed so as to free a certain amount of funds that can be used during the remainder of the fiscal year.

Under these circumstances I have the honor to suggest that the work of Mr. Cushing now immediately under the direction of the Secretary of the Smithsonian Institution be placed in charge of the Director of the Bureau of Ethnology and that his salary and expenses be paid from the appropriation for the support of this office. If this meets with your approval, be pleased to direct that the bills for debts contracted by Mr. Cushing be returned to this Bureau for settlement.

Some portion of Mr. Cushing's expenditures are of such a character that the items therefore would doubtless be rejected by the Treasury officials and these must be erased from the bills before a final voucher is taken and payment made.

I also request that you inform me what salary Mr. Cushing is receiving.

I beg leave to make a further suggestion that in case this proposition meets with your approval Mr. Cushing be informed by yourself of the action and directed to report to myself.

I am, with respect,
Your obedient servant,
J. W. Powell,
Director

Baird to FHC

January 24, 1882

Dear Mr. Cushing:

I enclose an official letter in regard to the transfer of your name from the Museum roll to that of the Ethnological Bureau. This is not considered in any way to prejudice your connection with the National Museum. Whenever this present arrangement expires, I shall endeavor to place you in your original position in the National Museum. At present Major Powell has funds available for your salary & expenses & the arrangement just effected will relieve somewhat a very serious pressure upon our capabilities. Of course you will continue to communicate with me as freely as ever, although official letters asking special instructions should be sent to Major Powell. The Ethnological Bureau is as much a dependency of the Smithsonian Institution as the National Museum is, only Major Powell is in charge of the one & Mr. Goode of the other.

We had yesterday the delegation of N.M. Indians, among which is your friend. He seems to be a very amiable & accomplished gentleman. I took great pains to refer to you as being our representative in N.M. & spoke of the interest we took in you and all your doings.[6]

Yours very Truly,
Spencer F. Baird

Pilling to Cushing

February 8, 1882

Dear Sir:

Your letter of January 15 concerning your trip to Washington was duly received, as was also yours of same date to Prof. Baird, who has forwarded it to this office. The delay in answering these letters has been caused by our inability until now to procure the necessary passes for yourself and party.

[As of the] date of January 1st Prof. Baird has formally transferred you and your work to the Bureau of Ethnology, and I am instructed by the Director to say that from that date your salary will be at the rate of $100 per month.

In addition to the above this office will pay the expenses of your own subsistence when in the field and transportation by rail when such mode of travel is necessary for the successful prosecution of your work, but expenses other than these above mentioned must be borne by yourself. In cases of extreme necessity due consideration will be given to any estimate which you may propose, but no expense must be incurred until the approval of the Director is obtained therefor.

Referring to your trip to Washington, I am informed by Mr. Stevenson that you are in possession of passes for yourself and party from Kansas City to Chicago and return. I send you (enclosed) a pass for yourself and five [sic] from Albuquerque to the Missouri River and return. Upon your arrival in Chicago, you will please call upon General Sheridan, who has kindly promised to aid you to the extent of his ability in procurring free transportation to Washington and return.

You will confine your party to yourself and six—five of whom should be Zunians to be selected by yourself, giving due consideration to the fact that they should be well versed in the beliefs and customs of their people and one of whom at least should be thoroughly instructed in the government of the tribe. The sixth should be a Moki, and Mr. Stevenson recommends Mahje Vemah, the Rain Maker.[7] The presence of one Moki is especially desirable because of the large collections from those villages now in our possession in respect to which more detailed information is desired.

Instructions have been given the Chief Disbursing Clerk to send you your pay for January and February, out of which the traveling expenses of yourself and party shall be paid—the sum to be refunded to you upon presentation of vouchers in duplicate. These will also be sent you by the Chief Disbursing Clerk with full instructions as to how they should be filled [out].

Wishing you a pleasant and safe journey, I am with respect,

Yours,
James C. Pilling
Chief Clerk

FHC TO BAIRD

Zuni, February 10, 1882

My dear Professor Baird:

Your communication informing me of the transfer of my name to the roles of the Bureau of Ethnology is received; and in reply I have only to say that although it gives me regret to leave the presence of a name which I have always mentioned with pride as that of "*my Principal*," still I am always willing to submit to any arrangements which may tend to the good of [the] Service which I try humbly to represent. I shall in the future years of my life—it matters not to what station I may drift—look back to my service under Professor Spencer F. Baird as an honor; it has been a service not so much of duty as of love, and one the like of which I scarce expect to experience again.

I write in great haste, as the cessation of the mails affords only chance means for sending [letters]. I hope to visit Fort Wingate next week, on which occasion I will communicate with you at more length.

I have the honor to be

Very Respectfully and Faithfully Yours,
F.H. Cushing

In the East

Arrangements having finally been completed, Cushing and his party set out for Washington in late February. Besides Cushing's "elder brother," Governor Palowahtiwa, those selected for the trip were the ex-governor Pedro Pino, Naiiutchi and Kiasi (senior and junior chiefs of the Bow Priesthood), Laiiuahtsailunkia (Cushing's adoptive father), and the Hopi Nanahe. After an eventful train journey and an overnight stopover in Chicago, the group reached Washington on March 3. Their reception seems to have been everything Cushing had promised. Greeted by President Arthur at the White House, they were also given a tour of the National Museum, introduced to the chief luminaries of the Smithsonian and Bureau, shown the sights of the city, and generally feted. Later in the month they proceeded to Boston, where they were given celebrity treatment by the mayor, the governor, and a series of other hosts in the area, including the director of Harvard's Peabody Museum, Frederick Ward Putnam. As a climax to this week-long visit in the cultural capital of the East, the Zuni party and a large crowd of onlookers were taken by steamer to Deer Island, outside Boston Harbor, for the ceremonial collecting of water from the Ocean of Sunrise and a rite initiating Cushing's admission into the Kachina Society. Then, back in Washington, a new round of events followed, including a special meeting of the Anthropological Society of Washington, called so that Cushing could deliver a paper, "Life in Zuni."

Early in May, the principal mission of the trip having been accomplished, four of the Indians returned to Zuni. Palowahtiwa and Naiiutchi remained through the summer, assisting Cushing and others working on Pueblo materials in the Museum and the Bureau and generally sharing in his daily life.[8] *They must have been on hand to witness his marriage, in July, to Emily Tennison Magill, and together with the new couple they spent several weeks at the end of the summer with Cushing's parents in western New York, en route home to the Southwest.*

For Cushing, the season spent in the East could hardly have been more successful. First of all, his efforts as tour manager and host on behalf of the Indians won his release from the pressure for a Zuni marriage as prerequisite for continued acceptance in the pueblo and admission into the Kachina Society—won him, indeed, the approval he needed to bring a non-Zuni wife back from the East. Second, the exposure occasioned by the tour and the scope thus afforded to his considerable gifts as a speaker brought him both fame and a boost for his work. The visit to Boston, in particular, brought him into contact with a circle of leading citizens—Putnam, Francis Parkman, Rev. Edward Everett Hale, Harvard professor Eban Horsford, the philanthropist Mary Hemenway, and others, including their friend in common, Sylvester Baxter—whose interest, helpful efforts, and/or money would in the months and years to come provide Cushing with an important base of support independent of the Bureau of Ethnology and supplementary to the circle of friends he had been making among fellow fieldworkers in the Southwest. Third, it was a productive time in terms of writing. In addition to an important early effort to sketch out his theories about Zuni social structure ("Zuni Social, Mythic and Religious Systems"), he completed his first article for the Bureau's Annual Report*—the classic "Zuni Fetiches"—and the serialized popular accounts of his journey to Havasupai ("The Nation of the Willows" for the* Atlantic Monthly*) and of his Zuni experiences ("My Adventures in Zuni" for* Century Illustrated*). Last but far from least, he married a woman who was apparently not only willing but insistent upon joining him in his life among the Zuni Indians.*

For the Zunis themselves, both the travelers and those who stayed at home, the trip east marked an epoch. This was the first such delegation in the pueblo's history to cross the entire domain of the Americans to its capital city and furthest shore, and what came of their journey was not only a great stock of precious sacramental water from the Ocean of Sunrise. By virtue of the "white Indian" in their number as well as an evident gift for public relations on the part of the native Indian members of the group, the remote and hitherto obscure village they represented was suddenly raised to fame and popularity—and, for better and for worse, opened to a greater influx of travelers and influences from the outside world. The influences would be felt most directly, of course, by the Zunis who had made the journey. When Palowahtiwa was asked whether he was glad to be home again, his reply, according to Cushing's diary, was "Just half." His right side was glad to be home again, but his left side, including the heart, was "still in the East."[9]

FROM BAXTER: "AN ABORIGINAL PILGRIMAGE"

At last the day for departure came, February 22, 1882. Before the Governor's house out-door services were held for the entire population, and the pilgrims were prayed over by an assembled priesthood within. With each there were the parting formalities of an embrace, heart to heart, hand to hand, and breath to breath. Just before the start, Nai-iu-tchi ascended to the house-top and blessed the multitude in a loud voice. The first night they encamped at the piñon-covered foot-hills beyond the summer pueblo of Las Nutrias. They arrived at Fort Wingate the next afternoon. In the evening Mr. Cushing exchanged the picturesque Zuni costume, which had been his garb for nearly three years, for the dress of civilization. The question of his wearing "American clothes" on the trip had been a serious one with the Zunis, and it was a subject of many deliberations. Assent was given only on the representation that it would displease his brothers the Americans should he not do it, their feeling for conventionality in dress being as strong as that of the Zunis. This motive was one that appealed to them forcibly and was readily understood. . . .

At the water-tower in Chicago they were awe-struck in the presence of the mighty engine, and became vexed with Mr. Cushing because he prevented them from touching it, as they wished to, in every part, even where the action was most swift and powerful, with the thought thus to absorb its influence. "What if it should hurt us? It would nevertheless be all right, and just about as it should be!" said they, with their strange fatalism. They prayed before the engine, but not to it, as might have been supposed by some; their prayers were addressed to the god through whom the construction of such a mighty work was made possible . . .[10]

KLEIN TO FHC

Palmer House
Chicago, Illinois
March 2, 1882

Mr. Cushing:

Mr. J.R. Rogers and the management of the Grand Opera House desire to extend to yourself and company an invitation to attend the presentation of the comedy of "My Sweetheart" tonight with Miss Minnie Palmer and R.E. Graham in the leading roles. A box will be placed at your disposal. Please advise me by 5 p.m. if you will kindly accept.

Yours very truly,
J.H. Klein

TELEGRAM: FHC TO BAIRD AND POWELL

Cumberland, Maryland
March 3, 1882

Prof. S.F. Baird and Major J.W. Powell
Will reach Washington on B & O R R at nine twenty five O.K.

F.H. Cushing

FROM BAXTER: "AN ABORIGINAL PILGRIMAGE"

It was night when they arrived in Washington, and when told that they were there at last, they repeatedly stretched their hands out into the evening air, drawing them to their lips and inhaling, thus absorbing the sacred influence of the place. Arrived at the hotel, Mr. Cushing broached the subject of cutting his hair, which was eighteen inches long, and which was making him unpleasantly conspicuous. His *caciques* desired it, he said, and it would gratify his brothers the Americans and show them that the Zunis were considerate of their wishes. The Zunis could not see how it was that the Americans objected to long hair, which was the crowning glory of a man. They were slow in consenting, and could only be made to at last by the promise from Mr. Cushing that he would have it made up so that he could wear it beneath his head-band when back at Zuni, "for," said they, "no one could become a member of the *Kâ'-kâ* without long hair."[11]

MATTHEWS TO FHC

Fort Wingate, March 24, 1882

My dear Cushing:

I am in receipt of yours of the 11th. Many newspapers have been received here giving accounts of you and your party. I have preserved the notices. The only unkind one I saw was in the *New York*

Times, and that was so silly that I wonder a paper of its pretensions would publish it. I am thankful to you for speaking about my affairs in Washington and mentioning my work in your addresses. I saw an account of your lecture in a Washington paper, and an account of your planting plume sticks in the *N.Y. Tribune*. . . .[12]

Now about your marrying I have only this to say. I take such a positively selfish interest in your success as an ethnographer ("selfish" because the progress of our branch of investigation is so near to my heart) that I can only see this side of the question. Will your marriage lessen your influence with the Zunis? Will it estrange them? Will it seal their tongues? When the old Governor can no longer have you with him day and night, when they can no longer enter your apartment when and how they wish, when the last vestige of their fond hope of marrying you to one of their women has vanished forever, will they feel toward you as they once did? Your wife will have to be a woman of rare tact and rare liberality of mind if she does not rather hinder your work than aid it.

Mrs. Matthews, while she admits that you need someone to care for your stomach, your work, your time and your money—in short, that you need a wife badly—does not think that you can have pictured the situation to the lady in all its magnitude. She wishes to know if Miss Magill is aware that she will have no companion of her own sex in Zuni, that she can have little or no privacy, that she can not keep a servant there, that even the masculine "Captain Major" could not stand sights and odors of the rainy season, that while you can mount your horse any day and ride over to Wingate, the roads are often in such a condition that she cannot travel.

Now as to your wife staying with us occasionally or often, . . . I will assure you that we will do everything in reason that we can to make your "little girl" comfortable. At all events we will have no guests here by the time you come back from the east. So if on your return you bring your wife with you, be sure you can bring her right to our house at once, and we will take care of her until you are ready to take her to Zuni with you. . . .

Yours very sincerely,
W. Matthews

From Baxter: "An Aboriginal Pilgrimage"

The ocean ceremony was to be performed at Boston on account of the desire of the Zunis to get the water as far to the eastward as possible and because of the interest felt in Mr. Cushing's work by his scientific friends there and in Cambridge. . . .

After a week of sight-seeing, the day set for the rites at the seaside arrived. It had been a week of chilly March weather, with rain and gray skies, fog, sleet, and a few hours of sunshine, so that the Zunis gave Boston the name of "the City of Perpetual Mists." It was, however, a fortunate city in their eyes to be blessed with so much moisture. In the afternoon, a special steamer took on board a company invited by the mayor and started for Deer Island. The Indians were given seats in the large pilot-house. As the boat sped out into the harbor, the Indians fell at once to praying and did not look up until the boat had nearly reached Deer Island.

Here a tent had been provided, and in this the Indians and Mr. Cushing costumed themselves for the ceremonial in accordance with their sacred ranks in the various orders of the tribe. Nai-iu-tchi, the senior priest of the Bow and traditional priest of the Temple, was distinguished by a small bunch of feathers tied to his hair, over the crown of the head, composed like those of the plume-sticks sacrificed at the summer solstice, with added plumes to the gods of the ocean, or priest-god makers of the "roads of life." He—with the other three members of the Order of the Bow, Ki-a-si, Pa-lo-wah-ti-wa, and Mr. Cushing—was distinguished by bands and spots of a kind of plumbago filled with shining particles upon the face—the war paint of the Zunis, and probably representing the twinkling stars, which are the gods of war. Lai-iu-ah-tsai-lun-k'ia wore a plume like Nai-iu-tchi's, with an added white plume as medicine priest of the Order of the Little Fire. His only paint was a faint streak of yellow, the color of the *Kâ'-kâ.* Ki-a-si wore upon his war-bonnet his plume of membership in the Order of the Bow, and an eagle feather as a member of the Order of Coyotes or Hunters. All the members of the Bow wore across their shoulders their buckskin badges of rank, and the two priests of the order carried war-clubs, bows, quivers, and emblematic shields. Pa-lo-wah-ti-wa wore a red eagle plume, the mark of his rank as chief warrior of the Little Fire Order. Na-na-he wore also a red plume and white eagle plume, indicating his rank in the Little Fire and Rattlesnake Orders, and for the same reason was painted with red about the eyes, with yellow of the *Kâ'-â* beneath.[13]

After the arrangement of their paraphernalia, they were faced to the east, and Nai-iu-tchi blew over them the sacred medicine-powder of the flowers (yellow pollen), designed not only to insure good feeling from the gods, but also to make the hearts of all strangers present happy toward themselves.

Each member took in his left hand the plume-sticks of his order, while the plumes of special sacrifice to the deities of the ocean, as well as the sacred cane cigarettes prepared and consecrated in Zuni by the Priest of the Sun, were placed in a sacred basket brought for the purpose. Nai-iu-tchi, who headed the party, carried the ancient net-covered and fringed gourd which had held the water for centuries and was the vessel to be first filled; Lai-iu-ah-tsai-lun-k'ia followed with the basket and two vases of spar; Ki-a-si and Mr. Cushing came next, each with one of the sacred "whizzers" without which no solemn cermonial would be complete in the presence of the gods. Last came Pa-lo-wah-ti-wa and Na-na-he. Proceeding at once to the beach, Nai-iu-tchi silently directed the rest to a stony point off to the left, which he deemed preferable to the sandy shore for two reasons: because it entered farther east into the ocean and because stony points and wild places are considered more frequented by the animal gods and more acceptable places for the sacrifice of plumes. Sacred meal was there scattered about to form the consecrated bed of the ceremonials, and all squatted in regular order, facing the east and the open sea. Each member grasped in both hands his plumes and began moving them up and down as though to keep time with the song which followed, which was low, plaintive, and filled with expressions of praise and entreaty to the gods of the ocean. At four intervals during the singing of each stanza sacred meal was scattered out over the waves. This song-prayer, or chant, was, like most music of the Zunis, in perfect unison.

With every incoming wave the tide rose higher and higher, soon covering their feet, and at last the rocks upon which they were sitting. Being ignorant of the tidal laws, they recognized in the tide the coming of the beloved gods of the ocean to greet them in token of pleasure at their work. As Mr. Cushing shrank back, they said: "Little brother, be prepared and firm; why should you fear our beloved mother?—for that it should be thus we came over the road unto the land of sunrise. What though the waves swallow us up? They would embrace us, not in anger but in gratitude for our trust, and who would hesitate to have his light of life cut off by the beloved?"

At the close of their song, and urged by Mr. Cushing, the Indians reluctantly moved back to the sandy beach. Here a double row was formed not far from the water, the sacred cigarettes were lit by the two high priests, and after puffs to the six points of the universe—North, West, South, East, and the upper and lower regions—they were handed round. After the saying of a prayer by each, according to rank in the religious orders, the plumed prayer-sticks were invested with the influence of prayer by breathing smoke from the cigarette deeply into the lungs and then blowing it out among the feathers. These were then taken up and cast upon the waters.

The vessels were then grasped by Nai-iu-tchi and Lai-iu-ah-tsai-lun-k'ia, who, with bared legs and feet, waded into the sea and poured upon its surface the "meal of all foods," brought for the purpose from Zuni. Then, first sprinkling water to the six regions and upon the assembled multitude, they dipped the sacred vessels full, and, while they were standing knee-deep engaged in prayer, Ki-a-si and Mr. Cushing advanced, dipping the points of their whizzers into the water, and followed them in prayer. The two priests started up out of the water, and the latter began, the one to the left and the other to the right, to whirl their whizzers, and followed the four others toward the tent. Inside, they formed in a row and sang a song celebrating the acquisition of the waters—a strange chant, which, from its regularity and form, Mr. Cushing considered traditional, yet which he had never before heard of. At the close of each stanza was the refrain:

> Over the road to the middle of the world [Zuni]
> thou willst go!

On each repetition of this their hands were stretched far out toward the west, and sacred meal was scattered still farther in that direction. A prayer in which consideration was asked for the children of the Zunis, of the Americans, and of all men, of the beasts and birds of the world, and of even the creeping and most vile beings of earth, and the most insignificant, concluded the ceremonial. The Indians then seized the seven demijohns given them by the city, which, with their patent wood covering, looked like models of grain elevators, and took them down to the beach, where they filled them without further ceremony.[14]

Before their return to the city a rite unexpected to Mr. Cushing followed, being the first step toward his initiation into the *Kâ'-kâ.* It consisted of baptism with water taken from the sea, and embraces, with prayers. It was the ceremonial of adoption before the gods and in the presence of the spirits, preliminary to introduction into any of the orders of the Zunis.[15]

FHC to F. W. Putnam

Quincy House, Brattle Square
[Cambridge] March 26, 1882

My dear Professor Putnam:

Your son Eben kindly brought my hat over this morning, and I take occasion to send this note by his willing hand.

God bless you, sir, for the happiness you gave me last night, with the added bright honors of the occasion. God bless you! is all I can say until the future opens a way of returning in some way your kindness.[16]

Could you not, in the near future, have some illustrations prepared of your "Peruvian Mysteries" and the sticks etc. ornamented with colored threads and tassles of raw cotton? I would like the honor of writing *with you* a paper on Zuni and Peruvian sacred paraphernalia, which might be of considerable interest to persons interested in Southern archaeology.[17]

Accept my fraternal regards, and believe me

Ever Gratefully Yours,
Frank H. Cushing

My kindest regards to your family.

Baird to Putnam

Washington, April 8, 1882

Dear Prof. Putnam:

Thanks for your kind and considerate note in regard to Mr. Cushing. It gives us great pleasure to have the endorsement of such eminent critics as yourself for our action in keeping Mr. Cushing in the Zuni Country for so long a time and of our intention of maintaining him in that service as long as may be necessary. I expect that his work will greatly aid in unraveling the mysteries connected with the interior life and manners of our Indians.

Yours very truly,
Spencer F. Baird

Prof. F.W. Putnam
Harvard College
Cambridge, Mass.

Francis Parkman to Powell

Boston, April 12, 1882

. . . .

I was very glad to make the acquaintance of Mr. Cushing, of whom I have received a very pleasant impression. I don't know what the newspapers have said to his disadvantage; and it does not matter much, as they are utterly unfit to judge his work. I think that the Smithsonian is fortunate to have found a man so enthusiastic and devoted. . . .

Baird to Powell

April 25, 1882

Dear Major:

It has occurred to me that you will be more likely to get out of Mr. Cushing what he has learned in regard to the Zunis by making some arrangements for the use of a phonographer [stenographer] for a few weeks in taking down what he has yet to say on the subject. He is primed with important facts and many desired generalizations and conclusions; but, like many persons, he is a little constipated and requires loosening, so as to effect a proper discharge. I saw him last night and he was anxious that I should speak to you on this much-by-him-desired subject. His best plan, I think, is to evolve paragraphs in regard to what he knows on any point without regard to order and then, when they are written up, they can be systematized. Should he have to go away or should anything happen to prevent *his* doing this, the notes will still be on hand for elaboration.[18]

Yours truly,
Spencer F. Baird

EDWARD EVERETT HALE TO FHC

Paris, May 5, 1882

My dear Mr. Cushing:

Your two letters from Washington have been forwarded to me here. . . .

I am very sorry that you are so much pained by the scandals put in print about your mission, whether they come from fools or from knaves.[19] Of course such things are annoying, but be sure your real friends rate them at their true worthlessness. For myself, it is enough to say that I was prejudiced in your favor by the opinion which General Crook and Lt. Bourke expressed to me regarding you. But after I had the pleasure of meeting you, you are yourself your own best recommendation. Nor could any man of sense or feeling see you as much as I did without forming a very high respect and regard for you. I am only eager to show that regard by any offices of friendship which I can render you. It seems a little formal to say this. But you will be very apt to be lonely and homesick in the next twelve months, and I wish therefore to reassure you as far as I can by the most explicit statement that you are sure of my friendship and, as far as I can vouch for it, of that of many other friends in Boston. . . .

I have been looking today for what is already rare here—Casteñada's journal, for you. I shall undoubtedly pick up a copy, but it may take time. I wish you could have seen the interest in your discoveries expressed by Mr. Jackson, the Librarian of the Societé Geographique. I was at work in their Library, seeking information about Drake, and about this very volume of Casteñada. He came to me to ask why the Pueblo Indians had that name, knowing Spanish enough to know how the word Pueblo would be used in Spain. Of course he uncorked an effervescing bottle when he talked to me about Pueblos. I found he knew Powell's work, and . . . when I came to tell him of your enterprise, he was delighted. I shall leave your address with him, with the request that if anything of interest to you turns up, he shall send it to you immediately.

I am now on my way to Spain, and I shall spend a week or two in their archives. . . . I wish I had taken from you some definite instructions as to what you would like, but indeed we were too busy in Boston to discuss details much.

Name me personally to my friend the chief and ask them not to forget me. Write to me when you can—and especially when we can serve you.

Always Yours Affectionately,
Edw. E. Hale

P.S. I have bought the Casteñada, & it will go to you as soon as bound. Your best address to me will be Roxbury (to be forwarded).

BOURKE TO FHC

Omaha, Neb., June 7, 1882

My dear Cushing:

I have written a strong letter to Gen'l Sheridan, asking, as a personal favor to myself, that he give you the strongest endorsement in your application for an appointment, and I am certain from what he said to me last February that he will gladly sustain your aspirations.[20]

I am hoping to go over to Chicago next week and will renew my request and not leave until I see the paper drawn up and signed and mailed to your address. When next you come West, I wish you would write a few lines to Gen'l Sheridan saying that you would like to meet me; he will telegraph me wherever I may be.

Did not my prediction come true that in less than a year you would be the best known ethnologist in America? I'll add to that the further assertion that if you come into the Army, you will inside of 3 years from date be the most highly reputed ethnologist in the *world.* You are now among snags; look out lest you run upon some of them. Jealousy has ruined many of the most promising young men in science, literature, and art. Your growing fame will destroy or dim that of many an old plug who has grown fat and prosy in some soft position. . . .

Hoping, my dear Cushing, that I may soon address you by a military title,

I remain, sincerely, your friend
John G. Bourke

Draft: FCH to Bourke

Washington, D.C., July 7, 1882

My dear Captain Bourke:

You are one of the most thoughtful of friends, and I thank you for every proof you give me of the truth of that statement. I am pleased with your admirable notes on General Sheridan's collection, and glad to have them in my possession. Did I tell you that many of the pot shards found with glaze on them may be accounted for by the practise which all the Pueblo Indians had, and some still have, of protecting their new vessels from contact with the fuel by surrounding them with fragments of other vessels? Or did I mention the method employed by experienced squaws of testing not so much the fineness as the consistency of their clay with the tongue and under-lip?

Brief as your notes are, they are incontrovertably the most complete and perfect ever yet published on the Southwestern ceramic art.[21]

Have I yet written you that the little girl whose picture you saw in Zuni will—as a proposition and choice of her own, from which she absolutely and heroically refuses to be dissuaded—accompany me to Zuni? We shall very quietly be married some time next week, and start via my house in New York, as soon thereafter as possible. If I have not told you before, I am very sorry. If I have, no harm has been done in repeating it. I wish you could be here, but of course that would be impossible.

I am Ever Your Faithful and Grateful Friend

When I signed my name to the lower edge of the photograph I just sent you, I was prostrated with illness, from which I have now recovered.

FHC to Pilling

Washington, D.C., July 22, 1882

My dear Mr. Pilling:

Referring to your request for a statement of such linguistic material as I happen to have in manuscript, I beg leave to submit the accompanying list of titles.

I have the honor to be,

Very respectfully,
Your obedient servant,
F.H. Cushing
Ass't Ethnologist

- I Dictionary of the *A-shi-wi* or Zuni language, containing a vocabulary of between 2,000 and 3,000 words. With notes. 76 pages Ms.
- II Vocabulary of archaic words, chiefly gleaned from the ritualistic and folk-lore and ancient songs of the Zunis, with notes. 24 pages Ms.
- III Grammatic forms illustrating the parts of speech, cases, moods, tenses, syntax and orthoëpy of the Zuni. With copious notes and text. 40 pages Ms.
- IV The exclamative and imitative elements in the origin of human languages, as illustrated by studies of the etymology of the Zunis.
- V Collection of prayers, rituals and directions for ceremonials from the priesthood and sacred societies of the Zuni. With notes, 50 pages.
- VI Prayers, rituals and songs of the *A-pi-thlan shi-wa-ni* or Zuni Priesthood of the Bow. 31 pages.
- VII Collection of Zuni songs and poetry.
- VIII Collection of native Zuni speeches with interlinear and free translations—illustrative of Zuni Grammar and Oratory.
- IX Collection of Zuni Proverbs, Idioms and Archaic Figures from the Folk-lore.[22]

Matthews to FHC

Fort Wingate, July 29, 1882

My dear Friend:

. . . .

I did not answer your earlier as I was in some doubt about your movements; but your last letter to Enos leads me to believe that a letter sent to Barre will reach you before you start for the west. Mr. [Lieut. James] Fornance and I paid a visit to the Pueblo of Acoma recently. We were gone not quite three days. Went by cars to McCarty's.[23] Got guide and horses and rode over to Acoma. Staid there less than 24 hours and returned as we went. The Archbishop and Father Brun were there at the same time confirming the little whitewashed pagans. Bandelier had left the village only a few days before.[24] Found A[coma] a very interesting place—in everything but its people more interesting than Zuni. The people don't compare to the Zunis—too much Americanized to the casual observer—but I strongly suspect that one who would go and live among them and get beneath the surface could find many vestiges of the old days still. They are supposed to be good Catholics, but I noticed the little bowls built into the walls and filled with the sacred flour; and late at night I heard the tom-tom beating in a distant part of the village. You should not fail to visit Acoma when you return.

Pilling recently sent me a list of Navajo gentes compiled by Mr. Packard at Fort Defiance from the dictation of "Tci" (alias Henry Dodge) and asked me to revise the same. Which one of the book-carpenters is this information wanted for, do you know?[25]

Mrs. Matthews joins me in kindest regards to your bride and to yourself (I was going to put your name first when I bethought me).

Your sincere friend,
W. Matthews

BAXTER TO FHC

Boston, August 16, 1882

My dear Te-na-tsa-li:

Are you, like the flag, still there? That is, in Washington? If not, of course this letter will be forwarded to you at Zuni. You must write to me from there as soon as possible and let me know all about your welcome back, the council at which the old boys tell about their visit East, our good friends Dr. and Mrs. Matthews, and all the rest. . . .

Do not, by any means, first submit the folkore stories to the *Century,* for you promised to do them for the *Atlantic,* and they are expecting them. . . . Be sure to give the story of Te-na-tsa-li and make the tales as concise and compact as possible.

Do not forget the printing-office scheme, for it will be a great help to you in your work. I think the Zunis would learn very quickly to read and write their language. You remember the wonderful story of Sequoia, or George Guess, the inventor of the Cherokee alphabet, and how quickly that nation acquired it? It is one of the most remarkable chapters in Indian history, I think. You may depend on your Boston friends to help carry out the scheme, as Mrs. Hemenway promised. . . .

May the light of love attend you and your wife in your new home and make it beautiful and happy and a light to guide your adopted people to an ennobling civilization is the earnest and constant wish of

Your faithful friend,
Sylvester Baxter

METCALF TO FHC

Goodwin House
York Harbor, Maine, August 16, 1882

My dear Tenatsali and wife:

I hope you will not think me ungenerous in failing to answer your long letter and also to acknowledge the receipt of the photographs from you.

I have tonight just received the views of Moqui, whither they have been forwarded from home. They exceed even my brightest anticipations. My dear Tenatsali, I cannot begin to thank you for them & your efforts. Oh! but they are fine—not that I can use them in my work, for I fear 'tis now too late. But had I had them in Washington, I might have made use of some of them. What a picturesque place it must be. I wish I had some work to do on Moqui [so] that I might use some of those photographs.[26] 'Twould be simply immense.

I have today just finished the drawing of the ancient mines—which has, I think, made one of my best ones. I wish I could show it to you. Tell the *Century* people, and they will perhaps send you a photo of it. I sent off last week a pen & ink drawing of an interior showing the women grinding—and containing some seven or eight figures. Also the drawing "Making *He-we.*" I have next to do the "Bivouac," which will not take long—and then comes the tough one, the scalp house, which I can't seem to compose in my mind; but as it has to be done, I shall do it. That finishes the second article. . . .

Give my love to papa and tatchu, and tell them

my thoughts are with them always—and wish I could grasp their hands—and if I could see them, how happy I should be. . . .

Your true friend,
O'nok thli k'ia[27]

POWELL TO FHC

August 19, 1882

Sir:

Upon receipt of this you will proceed at once with the two Zuni Indians to the pueblo of Zuni, New Mexico, via the Seneca Indian Agency of New York.

You will keep a memorandum of your necessary traveling expenses en route, the amount of which will be refunded by the Chief Disbursing Clerk.

Transportation Requests from Washington, D.C., to Kansas City, Mo., are enclosed.

A copy of the "Regulations" of the Geological Survey is transmitted herewith, by the provisions of which you will be guided. Your attention is especially called to Section 12, Chapter II, where full particulars respecting this matter will be found.

You will be allowed cabins for two persons. A list of the articles comprising a ration will be found in Section 35, Chapter II, of the Regulations of the Geological Survey. These will be furnished you upon application to Mr. Joseph Brown, Disbursing Agent, in amounts not to exceed a supply of three months.

At the close of the field season you will be furnished with a team and wagon belonging to the Geological Survey by the Geographer in Charge of the Wingate Division.

No expenditure not authorized above must be incurred until estimates are made to and approved by this office.

You will make to this office a monthly report of operations.[28]

Respectfully,
J.W. Powell
Director

Fig. 22 Cushing in Studio Costume, Washington, 1879 (Courtesy of Emlyn Magill Hodge).

Fig. 23 Col. James Stevenson (National Anthropological Archives).

Fig. 24 Matilda Stevenson (National Anthropological Archives).

Fig. 25 Cartoon: Matilda and James Stevenson Responding to Hopi Protest at Invasion of Secret Ceremonial (*The Illustrated Police News* 6 March 1886, National Anthropological Archives).

Fig. 26 Zuni Pueblo and Dowa Yalanne (National Anthropological Archives).

Fig. 27 Palowahtiwa (National Anthropological Archives).

Fig. 28 Pedro Pino (National Anthropological Archives).

Fig. 29 Zuni Chiefs in Boston (Museum of New Mexico).

Fig. 30 Laiiuahtsailunkia, Naiiuchi, and Nanahe with Anglo Child in Boston (National Anthropological Archives).

OF THE ORDER OF THE BOW
FINISH OF THE CERE

Fig. 33 Washington Matthews (Wheelwright Museum of the American Indian).

Fig. 34 John Gregory Bourke 1975 (Museum of New Mexico).

Fig. 31 Zuni Water Rites at Deer Island, Massachusetts (*Leslie's Illustrated Newspaper* 8 April 1882).

Fig. 32 Senator Logan Party at Zuni (Museum of New Mexico).

Fig. 35 (*left*) Adolph F. Bandelier (Museum of New Mexico).

Fig. 36 Willard Metcalf 1885 (Courtesy Elizabeth de Veer).

Fig. 37 Alexander M. Stephen (Stephen, Hopi Journal, Columbia Univ. Press).

Fig. 38 Emily Cushing (Thomas Eakins Painting, Philadelphia Art Museum).

Fig. 39 Cushing House in Zuni (Museum of New Mexico).

Part II
Ethnologist and War Chief

Returning to the Southwest with Emily, Palowahtiwa, and Naiiutchi, Cushing arrived at Fort Wingate on September 18, having visited a Seneca Indian community in western New York en route. After spending several days at Wingate, the party proceeded to Zuni, arriving on the 23rd. Here Cushing resumed making "notes and sketches of Zuni ceremonials and dances as they occurred, vocabularies, and inquiries into the ceramic art decorations, {and} also arranging and adding to papers begun in Washington on the Sociologic System of the Zunis" (Cushing's Report for October 1882, National Anthropological Archives).

Cushing was now on a quite changed footing in the pueblo. His standing as a tribal chief was enhanced by his newly won credibility as an important "Washington man"—fruit of the successful tour east. He had also exchanged the somewhat equivocal position of an adopted junior bachelor for that of a respectably married head of household, and with his new American wife and family entourage was comfortably established in an enlarged and well-furnished apartment whose civilized amenities (including a hired cook) would be extolled by many a visitor. Both accepted as an important member of the Zuni community and able to rely on the company of his own domestic circle and various local white friends, such as the trader and the new schoolmaster, he seemed to have everything he needed for a long and productive stay. Indeed, as an arrangement that satisfied the requirements for continued fieldwork among the Zunis and at the same time provided both improved living conditions and a cover against suspicions from his own side of the cultural boundary that he had "gone native," the establishment of this little enclave could hardly have been more strategic.

Judging by the extant records, however, the second segment of Cushing's sojourn in the Southwest was to be fraught with even more complications, conflicts, and distractions than the first—beginning with those which consumed most of the month immediately following his arrival back in Zuni: a case of horse theft, a murder, a threatened white encroachment on a local spring, and a visit by Major Powell.[1] Under orders from the latter, the next three months were largely taken up with a collecting expedition to Oraibi for the Bureau. And no sooner was that completed than a new set of problems came to the fore—a lost army mule to be accounted for, an imbroglio over some Navajo horses alleged to have been killed by Cushing, the Nutria affair, attacks on his honor and his credibility as a scientist, a recurrence of prostrating illness (the latter brought on by exposure suffered during the midwinter Oraibi trip but almost certainly aggravated by the pressures encountered after his return). Clearly Cushing's newly gained prominence was not an unmixed blessing. If he had been vulnerable before to the charge of reverting to savagery, his much-publicized eastern tour and his popular magazine accounts of "adventures" in Zuni and Havasupai now exposed him as well to the charge of sensationalizing. Then, too, there were the demands made upon his time by increasing numbers of curious passers-

through who had heard of "the man who became an Indian" and were anxious to meet him. As time went on, the pattern continued: more visitors, more problems with horse thieves, continued troubles over Nutria, more controversy, more travels, more illness.

Such is the picture of Cushing's life conveyed by the surviving documents of the year and a half remaining before his recall from the field. Amid this welter one finds intermittent reports of his ethnological and archaeological pursuits, but they are distinctly fewer and farther between. This falling off in itself created additional strain, reflected in more than one letter from Washington reminding Cushing of his authorial responsibilities. How to account for such a seeming change?

One cause, surely, is to be found in the somewhat altered character of the documents themselves—particularly the letters to Washington following Cushing's move from the Museum to the Bureau. At that point, at least, Cushing was not on the same terms with Powell as he had been with Baird; and while the change in supervisors brought about a marked reduction in his correspondence with the latter, this was not balanced by an equivalent increase in letters to Powell, whose primary interest, in fact, seems rather to have been in the official accounts and articles needed for the Bureau's Annual Reports. Hence the record ceases to be dominated by those frequent, informative letters from the field which, with the diaries, provide a strong thread of continuity throughout the first period of Cushing's stay in the Southwest. Unfortunately, too, only one diary survives from this second period—and that a fairly brief one dating from the first few weeks. Leaving aside publications and sundry field notes unsuitable for inclusion here, what have been preserved, with various important exceptions, are the annual and monthly reports Cushing wrote, ex post facto, for the Bureau, letters he wrote on Zuni business and his own, and a considerably increased number of letters and other documents written to or about him.

Fortunately, the existing documents do include not only those collected here but that other product of Cushing's closing period in the pueblo, Zuni Breadstuff, which ought to make up for quite a few missing descriptive letters. In any event, the reader should be alerted to the greater multiplicity both of voices and of threads to be followed in the pages ahead. In this section, the disadvantages of a purely chronological scheme of presentation will become obvious. It is held to, nevertheless, since the alternative possibilities seem merely to exchange one sort of confusion for another and since chronology, as a simple given, does have the distinct advantage in a collection like this of interposing no screen of theory between the reader and the documents themselves.

Given the considerable role of happenstance (the survival of one piece of evidence rather than another), questions of interpretation and judgment abound, though it may be that a trend is discernible—perhaps that of an "experiment" running its course. If he had been allowed to remain, would Cushing's work as observer have been altogether smothered finally under the ever-growing demands on him as a participant? Would the conflicting claims of these two essential elements of fieldwork have been more manageable in the case of this pioneer live-in anthropologist if his own personality and behavior had been different? Why, in the end, was he withdrawn from the field? Was it because of the Nutria-Logan controversy (as he and his friends believed) or because of his ill-health and/or failure to produce the desired monograph on Zuni sociology (the first of several such failures)?[22] And was the deterioration of his health itself but symptomatic of the increasing stress of this requirement for professional validation and the strain of contradictions he was unable to resolve in his situation as a straddler between two cultures and as both an agent and a prisoner of the institutional science and government bureaucracy of his day? But if so, then how can one account for the pure sunshine of Zuni Breadstuff, product of Cushing at his best and in great part written during this same period?

In the face of such questions, the wise reader might take a lead from the notion of "negative capability" propounded by the poet Keats. "I mean," he says, the capacity "of being in uncertainties, Mysteries, doubts, without any irritable reaching after fact and reason." If what follows be found wanting in linear continuity and clear answers, perhaps at any rate in pursuing such questions as these the patient reader will be led to patterns of his own discovery among the figures in this documentary carpet.

7. *September 1882–January 1883*

Return to Zuni

FHC to Powell

South Barre, Orleans Co., N.Y.
Sept 12th 1882

Sir:

I have the honor to report that after a rest of three days I made a visit to the Senecas of the Tona-wanda Reservation in this county, with not only interesting and important results relative to my relationship to the Indians but also scientific gleanings far more valuable than I had hoped to acquire. Concerning the latter I will report on arrival at Zuni.

Having sufficiently rested my sick Indians (meantime visiting my old home), I leave directly for Zuni, via Chicago, tomorrow morning.

Very Respectfully,
Your Obedient Servant,
F.H. Cushing

FHC: Daily Journal

Monday, September 18th, 1882.

Early this morning we arose, prepared for the remainder of our journey, and I went down to depot to look after Abram and the old boys.[3] They had all passed a good night and the two latter were busy smoking and chatting with some Isleta Indians. Emma lost purse of money (?) while at breakfast. Went about Albuquerque, found the town much improved and grown. Found letter from Lt. Fornance requesting me to telegraph Enos. Did so. At train were met by Lts. Fornance, Gilman and Chance. Left Albuquerque station about 10 a.m. Train ran but slowly. Girls much pleased with country. Old boys chatted about familiar scenes; but did not seem particularly contented. Nai-iu-tchi declared himself homesick. Lunched at El Rito and soon after passed Laguna.[4] Met Mr. Marmion Sr. at station. A quiet but pleasant looking man.[5] Walked about at Coolidge (Crane's), the supper place. Cabooses and engines in mourning for accident of few days before. Day cool and delightful. Air just the fit of my lungs. In conversation with conductor learned that A[tlantic] and P[acific] had successfully dug several wells, only one more than twenty feet deep. Gave me courage about my ranch scheme.[6] Toward evening found we were nearing Wingate. Were met at depot by Enos and Stanley, who helped us into Gen'l Bradley's ambulance and away we jolted for Post.[7] Were most cordially received by Dr. and Mrs. Matthews. Learned that Mrs. S. was there. Had accompanied an expedition of Gen'l Logan's to Zuni, the whole thing boding me no good. Lies triumph temporarily![8]

Bade good-bye to our sweet little hostess, who left for a neighbor's house in order to get off early on train for Albuquerque fair. Dr. and Emma good friends, thank God, before bed-time.

Old boys entertained by Prof. Thompson.[9] Abram in hospital. Afraid of ghosts, and I had to go over and settle him. Dr. told me several things worth knowing about my enemies. I found why my commission was not pushed. Enos and George entertained by Mrs. and Lt. Lockheart.[10]

Tuesday, September 19th, 1882.

Arose early and went down to camp. Found all well and a most pleasant place of it. Stanley's rare energy distinctly visible in the order of everything. Met many of my old friends—all the same. Old boys complained of having slept cold, especially after I told them they would have to stay until I could go the second day after. Called on Gen'l Bradley. Found him well and pleasant. All at Post good friends. I am so glad, as I had expected it would have been otherwise. Met Maj. [blank], who seems to be the artist of the expedition. Like clever little Prof. Thompson.

K'esh-pa-he and two other young Zunis came in. Sent one back to tell the Z[uni]s when to expect us. K. stayed to return with us, while three [sic] went on to Alb[uquerque]. Mr. Graham and Dan'l Dubois arrived. Both received me cordially, latter hilariously. At sunset sent three young men off by rail. Have spent the day mostly in working up accounts, writing some letters and talking with Dr. Matthews, one of the noblest of men, he.

This air is splendid. I am happy to be back in this country again. It seems more like home than any other I have seen. This evening many of the Post called on Emma. All impressed her most pleasantly. Learned about a ruin not far from Nutria. Very fine. Indians told me the spring of it was hidden, with ashes, sand, mud and sticks. Will look into it. Passed most pleasant evening.

Sept. 20th, 1882.

Early this morning went down to camp. Found things all pleasant, old men excepted. They complained of having been kicked out by cook. Told them to be patient; they were to go in the morning. Wrote to Baxter, enclosing Dr. M.'s manuscript on Pagan Martyrs.[11] Also communication no. one apprising Powell of my arrival [and] no. two Report on Visit to Seneca Reservation. Wrote to friends and relatives. Had long talks with Dr. M. After lunch took him down to see Indians. He asked them whether they were glad to be back or not. Gov. said, "Just half." His right eye, right shoulder, arm, hand and breast, *liver* and leg, foot and toes were glad to be back again, but the side the heart was in, and the heart itself, were still in the East.

Nai-iu-tchi said, "To my Eastern home I yearn. If you take even an untamed bear and put him in a pen, give him a good bed and fine food, like a horse he would come to know his place and love it. Let him out and he would return to it. Would not then a Zuni think of his comfortable house and friends even among strangers who were ever kind and smiling at him" [pages torn out]

FHC to Powell

Fort Wingate
September 20, 1882

Sir:

I have the honor to report that on the 4th of September I visited, in accordance with your instructions, the Seneca Indians at their reservation in Tona-wan-da (Rapid River) with my two Zuni companions.

Aside from the assistance which this visit afforded to my Zuni work by impressing my Indians with the standing I have even among a remote nation of their own race, it was productive of interesting scientific results.

The Tona-wan-da tribe of Seneca number about five hundred men, women, and children. They have been for three generations in such close contact with our civilization that they have adopted our modes of life and industry nearly altogether and are apparently representative of their race only by name and heredity. Such, however, is not the case.

Although many of them are thoroughly educated in English and are thrifty American farmers, they all still retain, in their primitive perfection, their original language, folklore, and, to some extent, mythology.

On our arrival, late in the afternoon, we were almost immediately received with impressive speeches by the sachem of the council, and within three hours an assemblage of more than three hundred Indians, or nearly two thirds of the native population, were gathered at the Council Hall or "Long House."

Before entering this council, we were entertained at the house of the Grand Sachem, Mr. Abram. A body of elders was there collected to extend to us the first welcome. This welcome consisted of mutual greetings and congratulations and enquiries concerning religion, government, and social matters. First, we were questioned relative to our gentes and formally adopted as brothers into one or another gens of the Seneca tribe. During this enquiry I learned that the Senecas have not only the gentes discovered by Morgan (*League of the Iroquois*) but also other gentes, or at least other gentile names. Nai-iu-tchi, for instance, of the Eagle gens of Zuni, was adopted as the brother of several members of a Hawk or Eagle gens in the Tonawanda tribe. I also found the name for the bear gens among these people. Neither the latter nor the former gentes or names of gentes are, so far as I know, mentioned in works extant on the Iroquois.[12]

Secondly, enquiries were made relative to the chieftaincies, by means of which I was able to ascertain that the office of sachem with the Seneca is equivalent to that of *mosona cacique* or priest among the Zunis.

So also the discussions of religious matters revealed to us the fact that although nominally Christians, the Senecas are yet more or less devoted to their indigenous mythic and superstitious ideas. . . .

[Their] masks were much like those of the Zuni orders, especially in function. They are held in great veneration, the use of them restricted, as in Zuni, to special priests, and are jealously guarded from the whites. So much the latter, indeed, that heretofore no mention had been made either in local or scientific works, so far as I can learn.

Hoping that I shall be able at some future time to follow these investigations to further and more satisfactory results, I have the honor to be, very respectfully,

Your Obedient Servant,
F.H. Cushing

FHC to Sylvester Baxter

[September? 1882]

[Description of his visit to the Seneca Indian community of Tonawanda in western New York]

I went there as a Zuni, with Pa-lo-wah-ti-wa and Nai-iu-tchi; like them I was arrayed in the native costume, ornaments and significant decorations of the Zuni. . . . I was studiously addressed as the Zuni: the expression being "you three western brothers," notwithstanding the fact that some of the Indians remembered me as a boy who had purchased baskets and bows from them in the neighboring towns. After congratulatory speeches [and] inquiries relative to our Gentile standing, . . . a guarded inquiry [was made] about our songs, *sacred* dance institutions, and mystic medicine practices. Imagine my surprise on learning that the sacred war-dance, the sacred incantation-dances for rain, etc., and above all the medicine ceremonials of an *esoteric* institution *still* existed among these copper-colored Yankees. A discussion of dance (*kâ'-kâ*) paraphernalia called out the enthusiasm of the elders and sachems. A sub-chief was dispatched. He immediately returned with a *medicine* mask used in secret ceremonials for the exorcism of disease, identical in function with those used in the *kâ'-kâ thla-na* ceremonials of the Zunis, although made of wood and differing, of course, in appearance. These things are jealously guarded from the most intimate American friends of the tribe, are trusted and venerated with almost Zuni faith, and are used with ancient song and ritual almost as elaborate as are those of the Zunis. During the night we were entertained by exhibitions of the ancient dances. A white witness of their popular war-dances given at fairs was present through his relationship to me (my father), and pronounced not only the dances he had never seen before, but also even the war-dances performed, as totally new to him, and as different in every respect from the popular exhibitions in question. You see how true it is that even a people now clad in American garments welcome my adoption of the Indian regalia and life, lay their secrets at my feet in reply to my Indian speeches, and unveil the mystic symbols of three silent generations. And that is what I believe would be the case could even the most unrepresentative speaker of any Indian tongue be properly approached. . . .

Metcalf to FHC

Cambridgeport, Mass.
September 21, 1882

My dear Frank:

If it gave you pleasure to hear that I intended coming to Zuni, it cannot be as great as the pleasure I feel in thinking of my trip. And I received with great pleasure the letter from your good little wife, for which I thank her. . . . I wrote, immediately after writing to you, to Miss Maggie, telling her of my plans and asking her to please inform me of her movements so that we might arrange things fully. The answer will be along soon, I trust.[13] Now, my dear Tenatsali, let me to business first. Have you a camera? If not, I shall get one, and a good one, for you—and the necessary "fixins." We will fix up a dark room, and by—(well, I won't say it), we will—I should say *you* will—be able to get some things that will astonish people, both artistically and scientifically.

And your aniline dyes—I have not forgotten.

Now tell me what, besides artistic and photographic materials, I should bring, and if there will be any trouble in getting transportation from Wingate to Zuni? Also tell me what in the way of clothing I shall require—for I do not know what the winters are. You know I'm thinking considerably about doing more or less tramping about with you, and possibly, as you once stated, some prospecting. . . .

Your true friend,
Willard L. Metcalf

Let me hear from you as soon as you conveniently can, & tell the old boys that I send them my best greetings, and to Nai-iu-tchi that his son O'nok-thli-k'ia hopes soon to grasp the warm hand of his father & his people.

FHC Note on Return to Zuni

When we made pilgrimage in 1882 to the Ocean of Sunrise, our return and reception of the sacred water was celebrated by an absolutely complete performance of the corn and water drama, occupying two full days and nights.[14] Usually the drama is played through in one day and night, but on this occasion it was regarded imperative that a day and night should be given to each division. As I had been made a Priest of the Bow some months previously and had been baptized for initiation into other orders, including the *Kâ'-kâ,* I was forced to take part with the *A-shi-wa-ni* and remain awake throughout the entire time. Hence my opportunities for observation were, in many ways, unique; but much was lost of the songs and rituals and minor details owing to the fact that my note-taking had to be done by stealth—which price I had frequently to pay for the advantages of being a priest and actor in these and other performances.

—Notes on Zuni Drama

Daily Journal

Sunday, October 1st, 1882.

Arose early and built fire. Cloudy and cool. Slept again till half past nine. Was called out to send food to Nai-iu-tchi. Latter better. American brought to me by Lo-tchi. Two horses lost by Zuni herder. Attended to it. Took food around to Nai-iu-tchi. Went with K'esh-pa-he, after writing Enos and fixing up Hazen questions, to Mission, where Mr. Graham soon joined us. He had no mail; concluded to wait on Hazen matter. Sent K'esh-pa-he to Wingate about noon. Returned to pueblo. Found *Chupakwe* [kiva group] smoothing rafters for *akwe-le-alla-kwin* house.[15] Joked with them. Took off wig. Cause[d] great excitement and much laughter.

Took cane of office and ordered several men and women to sweep about their houses. Some did so. Called sub war chief. Ordered him to summon his brothers in office, at night. Called in new Alcalde, who takes place of Thla-k'oa, who has gone bearing a letter of mine to Esendia Mountain for Chase. Told the chiefs they must send out to hunt Sha-sia,[16] must order the pueblo swept, must order youngsters to school with Mr. Graham tomorrow. They assented to everything. At dinner (4 o'clock) had milk from the house of the Cacique of the Sun. Went out toward evening to summon the war chiefs, first laving [washing] down dust and stuff several had swept. Found Mat-sai at P. P.'s [Pedro Piño's] house. Scolded old man for not coming round since his return three days since. Said his feet were lame, his eyes poor. His wife cried because we had not been to see her. She said she was sad about it. I told them we knew not they were in. They had not let us know. I reminded Pedro how he had wished for thirty years to go to Washington, that against the wishes of his people and mine I had taken him there. He had no thought of this. Left them crying. Reaching home, found two sub war chiefs, 2nd head chief, and two *tenientes* [assistants to governor] present. Gave directions about school; then about having pueblo swept; then about man who had died, who, though poor, was precious because a Zuni being. Directed that orders should be given for bringing in horses. A band of young men should be gathered to go with us to search for man and for the people who had stolen from Graham and possibly murdered the man Sha-sia. Told of our laws and regulations of our government;[17] how the Zunis must henceforth regard their chiefs as precious and obey their commands; when they went away, should give them horses and food for the journey without pay; that the rich must help support the government; the poor aid when their personal strength might be called on, etc. etc.

Monday, October 2nd.

Arose rather early, built fire and found two war chiefs awaiting me. Sent for 2nd peace chief and his two sub chiefs. We designed to call out the people, make them sweep the pueblo and go out after their horses. Emma had a cold this morning but was otherwise better than yesterday.

The orders were barely given when Hai-a-hai-a,

Lesh-ta-u-i, and Yak came in with news of the finding of Sha-si-a's body Southwest from here and not far East from the Rito Quemado Road. The study of tracks led to results chronicled in my letter to the Sheriff of Socarro (copy of which see).[18] They [the trackers] were wonderfully ingenious.

The body was brought in at about five o'clock. With the desire and consent of the chiefs I made a post mortem examination. One bullet entered the body from the right side, between the last rib and the one next it, obliquely from below. This caused the fall, after which three balls pierced the coronal region. The body was in a state of putridity almost unrecognizable. It was brought on horseback and had been almost bruised out of recognition, although Sha-si-a's features and figure could still be traced. He was loosely wrapped in a blanket. According to the old war custom of the tribe, the body was kept outside of the limits of the town, and around it the immediate relatives and members of the father's clan were gathered in rows squatting on the windward side. They rocked their bodies to and fro, patted their hands, cried aloud, sobbed, howled, and exclaimed, "*Ha-na-ha! Hom ta-tchu, hom tatchu!*" [my father, my father]. Especially the widow. She sat on a blanket near the corpse, bowing her head to it, striking its chest, and swaying in agony, casting her eyes to the sky as she repeated the above exclamations. A large bowl with *Amole* was provided.[19] When the time came for me to make the examination, the widow was forcibly dragged away from the (*an-chi-moa*) corpse, and I made my examination hastily, in the presence of Mr. Graham. No animals of prey had touched it, except possibly at the feet, which I did not examine. As soon as I had finished, each member of the clan in question dipped up in the palm of his or her hand some of the foam with a short prayer which I could not catch; [the foam] was dashed upon the body, which was partially uncovered, and then the water was all poured on, the great bowl which had contained it being broken immediately by the presiding women. Quantities of calico, some new blankets, food, prayer meal, and a little money (the latter added by myself) were included in the bundle, and the ceremonial was complete, save that he was buried, as is ordinarily the case.

The custom of bringing to the pueblo the dead slain by an enemy is universal, in order that this last rite may be performed, but they are never taken into their former home, from fear that disease may plague the living in consequence. The brothers and near relatives of the dead beseeched me that the murderers, if found, die not but be brought to the pueblo for retribution.

I have just completed a letter to the authorities, which I sent by the hand of my head war chief to Wingate to be dispatched. K'esh-pa-he arrived with the mail. A letter from Enos, Mr. Brown, Father, Onokthlikia, Mr. Henshaw, two books from Dr. Hale, and proof from the *Century* with an enclosed note was all.[20]

Emma heard from Sister Maggie, Nell, and "Sister." She (Emma) is better tonight and has consented to my going out tomorrow in search of evidence regarding the murder. [Several blank lines follow.]

I asked my little wife what was the difference between a digit and a nigit (idiot) just now, and she replied, "Only a finger's length"—which is a digit's length of course and makes all the difference in the world.[21]

Draft: FHC to Baxter

Zuni, October 3rd, 1882

My dear boy Baxter:

Some days have passed since, with my little wife, my brother and sister in law, and the two old boys, I reached my house in Zuni.

I wrote you how we were received at Fort Wingate, and how also we were met there by some of our tribe. The latter did not know of our coming, having set out for Albuquerque to see a fair and to await, at one of the neighboring Pueblos, our arrival. Among them was my faithful little friend and "brother," Kesh-pa-he. He, with some of his companions, turned back. One galloped to Zuni to bear the tidings. A courier returned to tell us that a dance was being prepared for our welcome.

So, after two days, we all started over the mountains, one of General Bradley's ambulances, our coach, and one of Professor Thompson's wagons bearing part of our luggage. We camped at Las

Nutrias overnight, and the following day, at about three o'clock, reached Zuni. The missionary had gone, and Mr. Graham was occupying the Mission. We first drove up there. As soon as the ladies were provided for, I galloped up into the town. Few of the Indians knew me at first, for my hair was cut. I wore a close fitting suit of gray, and a small derby hat. On second glance, however, as few failed to recognize me. I rode up to my doorway, rushed in, and was plunged in the embraces of my family almost instantly. Before we had finished exchanging greetings and my old sister had shown me with pride two freshly whitewashed rooms made ready for my use, about fifty or sixty Indians were gathered outside riotously awaiting my exit.

October 7th

Some days since, a dire calamity befell our tribe. Some horse thieves, overtaken or visited in the Southern section of the Reservation by an Indian named *Sha-si-a,* shot him down, first taking him to a lonely spot. Expert trailers as the Zunis are, they sent out scouting parties as soon as the Indian was missed and were not long in finding him, when it became necessary, the next day, for me to follow them up on an excursion not after the dead but the living, as the leader of a war-party. We were gone two days, securing perfect evidence as to the identity of the parties but failing to overtake them. This was the first action I had ever taken in my proper sphere as war chief of Zuni.

Another and worse interruption has occurred. It is now October 20th. The other night, as I was beginning again to write you, a long succession of war-cries roused the retiring tribe. They came from over the Southwestern hills. In five minutes a runner thundered at my door. A crowd was already gathering, as, grabbing a gun, I let him in and listened to his story. The party of murderers had been discovered. They were camped some twenty five miles [away]. I bound a serape about me, distributed my small stock of arms among the Indians, took quantities of ammunition, and called for a horse and a band of followers. The word was yelled out from the house tops and corners. A howling, jabbering crowd blocked the doorways and filled the clear space of my outer room. At first word, only five declared themselves ready to go. I used forcible language, and soon sixty men, mostly mounted and armed, galloped off over the western hills in my wake. The night was bitterly cold, but within two hours we were nearing the reported camping place. Here some of our horses gave out, and I ordered their riders to build a fire, capture more horses at dawn, and ride up to us. Some of the Indians were sullen and scared. They started to join the campers. I lashed one of them with my quirt, and they fell into line.[22] So we journeyed on to the ranch of Dan Dubois, which I had appointed as rendezvous. Some Mexicans had camped there, and hence the robbers had not put in an appearance. We dismounted, built a roaring fire, warmed ourselves, and ate a hasty bite of *he-we*. Just as the tail of the Great Comet had appeared in the East, I called my men to the saddle, and, accompanied by Dubois, Mr. Graham, and a couple of the Mexicans, we struck trail. How we followed that trail through the gray light, Dubois and I leading a gang of sixty men! But alas! after almost twenty hours in the saddle, after our horses were used up, we came upon a little ash-bed with all around prints of hasty cautious steps, and we knew we had missed our "game." That night I returned to my poor little wife, having ridden in darkness and daylight over a hundred miles, to find her nearly delirious, for I had. . . . [remainder missing]

FHC to Eastman

Smithsonian Institution
Zuni, New Mexico
Oct. 11, 1882

Mr. Galen Eastman
U.S. Indian Agent
Navajo Indian Agency
Fort Defiance, A.T.
Sir:

Your official communication of July 20th was long in reaching me, as it was unfortunately detained at Fort Wingate during my absence in Washington.[23] It came by courier yesterday evening.

It is quite true that I fired, not twice, but three times into two different bands of horses belonging to the Navajo Indians. It is possible that, as I intended, I killed one or two of them, although of this I cannot be certain.

On four occasions (according to the inter-tribal custom of the Zunis and Navajos) I as one of the head chiefs of the latter requested the Navajos to keep away from our territory at and near Nutria. We moreover warned them that if they did not grant our request we should either take up their stock and claim damage to our pasture lands or fields, or else shoot any of their horses which we found in the Nutria Valley. We also at once reported to the then Navajo Agent our proceedings and intentions and he informed us that he would first order the Navajos away and that in case they refused to give heed to his directions, we might proceed as we had proposed. Some weeks thereafter I found a large herd still frequenting the Nutria bottoms. I called a young Navajo named in Zuni "As-ho-tra-na" to account and asked him if he knew the Agent's wish and our intentions. He said he did and asked me what we were going to do about it. I quietly replied I would show him, and fired into his band. He replied then and there that he would leave with his herd and flocks, exchanged smokes, shook hands and departed.

Early last winter I again saw a band running even nearer to our favorite lands near the Nutria. In the near presence of six Navajos and one Zuni, I repeated my former action and in a council relative to the matter I asked the Navajos if I had not done right. Their chiefs replied that I had and that according to their father's directions they had asked their people to leave, that their people had refused then, and that they might suffer the consequences.

We have also at a recent council informed Kai-a-u-li and his friends Ta-ga-to-he and others that if they did not stop stealing and selling our horses we would make our losses good from their herds. Kai-a-u-li has during the past spring and summer, according to the testimony of Messrs. Dallas and Harper, late of Coolidge, sold to the Americans along the railroad no fewer than fifteen of our best horses. From the two gentlemen named we have no longer than since yesterday secured two of these and at an early day I shall take measures to bring the said Kai-a-u-li with your consent, under the notice of the civil authorities or under the tribal authorities of Zuni.

We have repeatedly made application both personally and through our Agent, Major Thomas, to the Agent of the Navajos for relief. As repeatedly the Agent of the Navajos has, I have reason to suppose, reprimanded his people without however producing any happy result with them.

Rest assured, sir, that of all men I am alike friendly to the Zuni and the Navajo, that with neither will I attempt to transcend the American laws or the laws of my tribe, which in our early treaty with the United States were given the rank of National Laws. That I have acted according to my authority as one of the Native mandators of the latter laws and that when all of our grievances are set right by the Navajos, we shall be then very ready to say amen, and to act all things aright on our side.

Very Respectfully,
Your Obedient Servant,
F. H. Cushing
1st War Chief of Zuni, U.S. Ass't Ethnologist

Eastman to FHC

Navajo Indian Agency
October 21, 1882

Mr. F.H. Cushing, "1st war chief of Zuni"
U.S. Ass't Ethnologist, Zuni, N.M.
Sir: I am in receipt of your communication of 11th instant and am astonished at its contents, and that you have done what you now confess, viz, taken the law into your own hands and with your warring remnant of "Zuni" have pursued a lawless course toward the neighboring Navajos, who, if they presumed to act upon such methods, could speedily make your "Zuni" sorry they had established such a reckless precedent, but while I have acted as their Agent, I have ever counseled and required of them in *all* cases brought to my attention a departure from their former practice of reprisal, believing that it was in the direction of the civilization policy of our Department (Interior) to endeavor to bring the Indian *up* to our standard, rather or instead of going *down* to his—which you now as "1st war chief of the Zuni" appear to have retrograded to, but sir, the fact is, humanity—outside of Zuni—cannot afford it under our form of Government.

In every instance when any matter of difference between the Zuni and Navajos has been brought to my notice I have given the matter the fullest attention, and have never before received any communication from you and believe, except in this case, of your wilfully shooting the Navajos' horses, all has been as satisfactorily adjusted as surrounding circumstances would permit to be done. Only recently I returned horses to the Zuni, said to have strayed on to the Navajo Reservation, and the Navajos consented to my action, instead of doing as you did, shoot them, for unwittingly eating of the Navajo grass and drinking from their springs. Although until the executive order of March 16, 1877 took effect, setting apart the Zuni Reservation, the Navajos occupied from remote time the "Nutria Springs" as they inform me, and in 1879–80 under request from Agent Thomas I did succeed with great effort after three trials, in moving about thirty (30) Navajos and their families from that old "Homestead" of theirs at "Nutria Springs" and some of them did relocate "Homesteads" on the northeasterly side of the "*Crest*" of the mountain a short distance above the Nutria Springs, which "*Crest*" is the boundary of the Zuni Reservation, and these Navajos are the sufferers from your wilful shooting and code of reprisal.

They also claim that the horses shot into by you were northeast of the said "*Crest*" of the mountain when you did your shooting, if so, were off the Zuni reservation, but in my opinion that matters not, spring water coming to the surface and accessible is counted by many on this frontier (especially when it is the whites who are thirsting for the springs of the Indians) as free for the necessities of man and beast as the air we breathe, both being given to all his creatures by the Great Father.

Rest assured Sir, I shall always be ready to aid in maintaining by all reasonable and legal ways the rights of not only your Zuni and others, but of the Navajos too, and with that end in view, I must still press the settlement by you of their claim of $100.00 for the property value of their horses shot by you, and as to the right or wrong of your act, the courts can decide what is the proper rule to be established on this frontier. Trusting that it will result for the best good of all concerned, I am

Very respectfully,
Galen Eastman
U.S. Indian Agent

EASTMAN TO COMMISSIONER OF INDIAN AFFAIRS

Navajo Indian Agency
October 23, 1882

Hon. Commr. of Indian Affairs
Washington, D.C.
Sir:

I enclose copies "A," "B," and "C" of my letters to Mr. Cushing of July 20 and of his reply and my rejoinder dated 20th inst. for your information, with the request for instructions if any further action is required of me in this matter. I did on the 11th inst. call Agent B.M. Thomas' attention to this matter, he being here in person with Capt. Pratt en route to Zuni Pueblo, but I am not advised if he did while at Zuni 13th inst. confer with Mr. Cushing in this matter.

I will respectfully recommend however that the Dept. of Justice take charge of this case and collect the claim of $100, not only, but also establish the proper precedent in this case as the rights of all concerned, or if the matter should properly be brought before the Territorial Courts that you do grant me the necessary authority and funds to properly prosecute the same.

Very respectfully,
Your obedient Servant,
Galen Eastman
U.S. Indian Agent

JOSEPH STANLEY-BROWN TO FHC

Wingate, N.M., Oct. 30, 1882

Personal Confidential
My dear Frank:

Your note in regard to the Oraibi trip duly rcvd., and I hasten to avail myself of K'eshpahe's return to answer it. Major Powell left for the Grand Cañon yesterday, but before he went we talked the Oraibi matter over fully, and he has instructed me to secure your cooperation and that of Mindeleff's party and "clean out" Oraibi—ethnologically speaking. Now my dear fellow, we don't want any "flair" about this. You and I will quietly go over to Keam's Cañon and from there to Oraibi and see what we can do in the way of making a tidy little collection. But remember, the less we have to say about it, the fewer annoying questions we will have to answer and the less criticism we will provoke from "certain" sources.[24] You will only need a good "mount" [and] your blankets. I will see to all the rest. Col. Stevenson goes to Acoma this week. I shall not start for Moqui before today week—so if you are here by that time, all will be well. I shall avail myself of Keam's going out with a buckboard at that time to carry a few needful things. They are trying to get up a party to Zuni for Thursday. If they are successful, I shall come over with them.

Now my dear fellow, a word about another matter in which you may deem me officious. I want you when you go to Oraibi to wear pantaloons and a coat. Your moccasins you can retain, your National shirt, beads, etc. This may seem foolish to you, but my reasons therefor are excellent, as I will explain to you once you arrive. We will be gone about three weeks. Is this not a good time for Mrs. Cushing to visit the post?

With love to all the fam[ily], I remain,

Yours as ever,
J. Stanley-Brown

In Absentia: Preliminary Approach to Oraibi

On November 5, Cushing set out for the Hopi country, "occupying nine days in the journey," according to his Monthly Report for November 1882 (NAA). Brown was waiting for him at Keam's Canyon, and after consultation it was decided that Cushing should "proceed to Oraibi alone and hold a council with the chiefs" to arrange for the intended collection. He got no farther than Walpi, however. Detained there by a snowstorm, he encountered a visiting chief from Oraibi who agreed to make the arrangements for him. Cushing thereupon returned to Keam's Canyon and thence, pending the arrival of the goods needed for trading, made his way on back, "across country," to Zuni in order to "observe more minutely than on former occasions the annual Sun Ceremonial" (Annual report on field work for year ending June 30, 1883, NAA). For the most part, the items to follow were written to or about Cushing during the weeks of his absence on this trip. An exception is the description of some ruins he discovered on his way back to Zuni. Though written somewhat later (in his 1883 Annual Report), it is included here to supplement the one brief letter written by Cushing that is preserved from this period.

Sylvester Baxter: From an Account of a Visit to Zuni in November 1882

Having a friend with me who was desirous of seeing the place, I decided to visit Zuni, although Mr. Cushing was not to be there. [Baxter had just encountered Cushing at Fort Wingate, about to leave for Oraibi.] He said that we should be cordially received and well provided for, since he was now comfortably established in his own household, where his wife would be found, together with her sister, his brother's wife, and Mr. W.L. Metcalf, the artist. Together with Mr. Graham, the local trader, and Mr. Willson, the teacher appointed by the government, with his family, there was now at Zuni a considerable little American community. . . .[25]

It was dusk when we came in sight of Zuni from the elevation of the Black Mesa, and dark when we arrived. As we drove up to the town, the windows gleamed with the cheery, ruddy light of hearth-fires within, and out of many of the stumpy chimney-pots leaped lurid tongues of smoky flame. . . .

We found supper awaiting us at Mr. Cushing's house. . . . It was the same house, that of the Governor, where we had visited Mr. Cushing before, but how changed it was. For twelve dollars and a few handfuls of broken clam-shells Mr. Cushing had bought four large rooms, which had taken about three months' labor to build—pretty cheap real estate that! . . .

The rooms were filled with civilized furniture, and where before we had slept on the floor exposed to sundry crawling things, and had eaten from primitive dishes set on a blanket spread on the same, there were now beds, tables and chairs, with an abundance of nice crockery and cooking utensils. A negro cook brought from Washington, and trained in an old Virginia family, presided at the fireplace, whence he conjured up the nicest dishes, and a cooking-stove was on the way for his benefit. The refining touch of a woman's hand was everywhere manifest. The room which was occupied by Mr. Cushing on our former visit had been transformed by his wife with charming artistic taste into a luxuriant little boudoir, in the decoration of which the local resources had been availed of in a way that gave it a peculiar interest. The floor was covered with the finest of soft sheepskins; the walls were hung with Navajo and Zuni blankets, whose rich and varied hues gave an effect much like Oriental tapestry. A broad divan was also spread with similar blankets, and on easels stood excellent oil-paintings, while rare and curious pieces of pottery were on the mantel-piece and arranged in nooks and corners, with decorations of rich scarfs and draperies tastefully disposed. Pictures, books, and magazines, Japanese screens and a handsome lamp completed the cozy, homelike effect. . . .[26]

Agent Thomas to U.S. Indian Service Commissioner

Pueblo Indian Agency
Santa Fe, N. M., Nov. 22, 1882

Hon. H. Price
Commissioner
Washington, D. C.
Sir:

I have the honor to acknowledge receipt of your letter of the 1st inst.—marked "C" 19070, 1882—

enclosing correspondence of Galen Eastman, Agent of the Navajo Indians, and F.H. Cushing, 1st War Chief of Zuni and U.S. Ass't Ethnologist, on the subject of a claim of the Navajos for $100.00 on account of three horses alleged to have been killed by Mr. Cushing.[27]

I have made copies of the correspondence, and return the originals, herewith, according to instructions. As Mr. Cushing is more than two hundred miles from my office, I cannot have a talk with him now without making a special trip for the purpose, which hardly seems to be necessary, as I shall, in all probability, find it necessary to go to Zuni on other business before the end of the year, and in my judgement nothing will be lost by allowing time for the minds of each party to gradually adjust themselves to the facts in the case. Possibly it may be recognized on the one side that it is an unfortunate necessity which requires a representative of the Government, in any capacity, to actively play Indian War Chief in any of the tribes; and on the other side that Indians who finally suffer loss in consequence of outrageous and exasperating disregard of the necessary rights of others which they have persistently practiced for years, should not receive any consolation.

It is a strange thing that the Navajoes should appear as the aggrieved party on account of anything which could result from their continued invasion of the Zuni Reservation.

I wrote Agent Eastman on the 13th inst. asking him to hold the matter in abeyance till I can give it my attention. I believe the case can be settled, and will undertake it carefully.

Very respectfully, Your obdt. Servant,
Ben M. Thomas
U.S. Indian Agent

Bourke to FHC

Fort Whipple
Nov 25th, 1882

Bourke to FHC
My dear Cushing:

Just before leaving the San Carlos Agency, a very pleasant letter came from you which I will now try to answer.[28] During the time I was among the Apaches, I spared no labor to learn about them all that I could, especially concerning their clans, of which I have the full list. My intention now is to round up the notes already taken just as soon as Gen. Sheridan will allow and then retire from the field. There is more petty jealousy aroused against a man than can be counterbalanced by the small amount of distinction gained; the most sincere and the most appreciative encouragement I've received has been from Dr. and Mrs. Matthews and yourself. I've now obtained my Captaincy, with a fair salary attached and as it don't make much difference whether an officer works or not, I've concluded that I'll soon take a rest.

Now, I've two things of which I wish to speak. The first is that when I am called upon to submit a report, I want to make a special one upon Zuni, writing in a popular vein, quoting largely from my diary and giving in a quiet way, without appearing to do so, a very good insight into your mode of life, the hardships and privations you have suffered in the cause of science, the arcana you have penetrated, and the great work done.[29] I don't mean to say that I can describe the one hundredth part of what you have done, but I can "boom" you in a way which may startle some people. I am going to take the ground that when I visited Zuni, I obtained from Pedro and others who spoke Spanish much information of importance, which I will outline and then take my chance to say that you have done so and so—and under the guise of palliating my own failure, give you a small hoist, on the principle that every little help may be of some account. I'll look after the distribution of the copies myself. You needn't turn your nose up at this—you have done excellently well, but you haven't a friend too many and should neglect no opportunity to gain power. I had a sort of notion of sending to Baxter a monograph upon the Apaches, telling what I knew of them—the fights with them in past years, their habits, some of their songs, a vocabulary of 500 words, their mode of making fire by wood friction, their violins of mescal stalks, their cards of horsehide, and all the usual stuff which you know might be acceptable to eastern readers. I have refrained from writing to Baxter, because he might not like to refuse any contribution to his paper and at the same time could object to becoming the winged Pegasus upon whose sore back I should climb the Parnassus of Ethnology.

The 2nd thing is something which may displease you, because the Stevensons for aught I know are now friends of yours. . . . [There follows an account of several paragraphs concerning Stevenson's pressing Bourke to accept shipment of some volumes of Smithsonian photographs and a model of one of the pueblos in exchange for some writing Bourke was to do. Stevenson had then billed him for these items, and finally, after Bourke had paid the bills, had failed to send the model or to acknowledge payment.] Stevenson is not well thought of by many people and some go so far as to whisper that he and your particular friend, Tom Keam . . . [rest missing][30]

FHC TO BAIRD

Zuni, December 1, 1882

My dear Professor Baird:

I was absent on a trip under orders from Major Powell to Oraibi when your most kind letters came, or at about the time of their arrival, and hence have not acknowledged their receipt more promptly. No one has been more constantly and consistently kind to me than have you; and to say that I appreciate you is to express but a small portion of the gratitude I feel.

Within a week I go again to Oraibi in company with Mr. Brown. I succeeded during my first trip in winning the Oraibians over and confidently expect to make at their Pueblo—the finest collecting point left—a rich and extensive gathering. Above all things, I expect to make the gatherings clean, representative and free of trash and unnecessary duplication. . . .

I met with not a few adventures on my return from Oraibi. They led, however, to important discoveries of ruins heretofore unknown, and in wonderful state of preservation. At some future time I hope to make, at request of the Institution, extensive collections from them. Among my other discoveries was a prehistoric pair of ladder poles—notched instead of bored for the reception of rounds. These I will attempt to secure and forward.

With kind regards—in which Mrs. Cushing joins me, to your family, and for your welfare, I remain, Very Respectfully,

Your Obedient Servant,
F.H. Cushing

FHC: REPORT ON A NEW DISCOVERY IN THE RUINS AT KIN-I-K'EL [KIN TIEL]

En route [back to Zuni], I discovered two ruins, apparently before unvisited, both, according to Zuni tradition, belonging to the *Hlé-e-tâ-kwe,* or the northwestern migration of the Bear, Crane, Frog, Deer, Yellow-wood, and other gentes of the ancestral Pueblo. One of these was the outlying structure of K'in-'i-K'el, called by the Navajo Zïnni jï'nnë, and by the Zuni He-sho-ta pathl-taie.[31] In this remarkable ruin I discovered peculiarities worthy of note. It is a two-story building, almost intact, most of the floor of the second story, the roof, lintels, etc., being in a good state of preservation, built of selected red sandstone slabs around the base and over the summit of a huge outcropping boulder. It is situated in the mouth of one of the arms of Kin-i-k'el, or "Dead Run" Cañon twenty-five miles Northwest of the station of Navajo Springs on the A. & P. R. R. In the ground room of this structure, leaning against a trap opening in the floor of the second story, I found the poles of a primitive ladder notched with stone implements at regular intervals on the corresponding sides. To the lower portion of these poles was bound with yucca fibre (?) a much decayed round, still intact but incapable of disturbance (see fig. 1).[32] In the rooms of the second story, I observed two features indicating the relationship of the building with the ruin of Kin-i-k'el, and thus in a measure confirming the Zuni tradition. These were the oblique (vertically as well as horizontally) loop-holes and the wall hearth referred to in the appended report (Part II of Annual Report on the Oraibi Expedition). By reference to a rough field map (sections etc. reproduced from memory), it will be seen that this arrangement of portholes gave

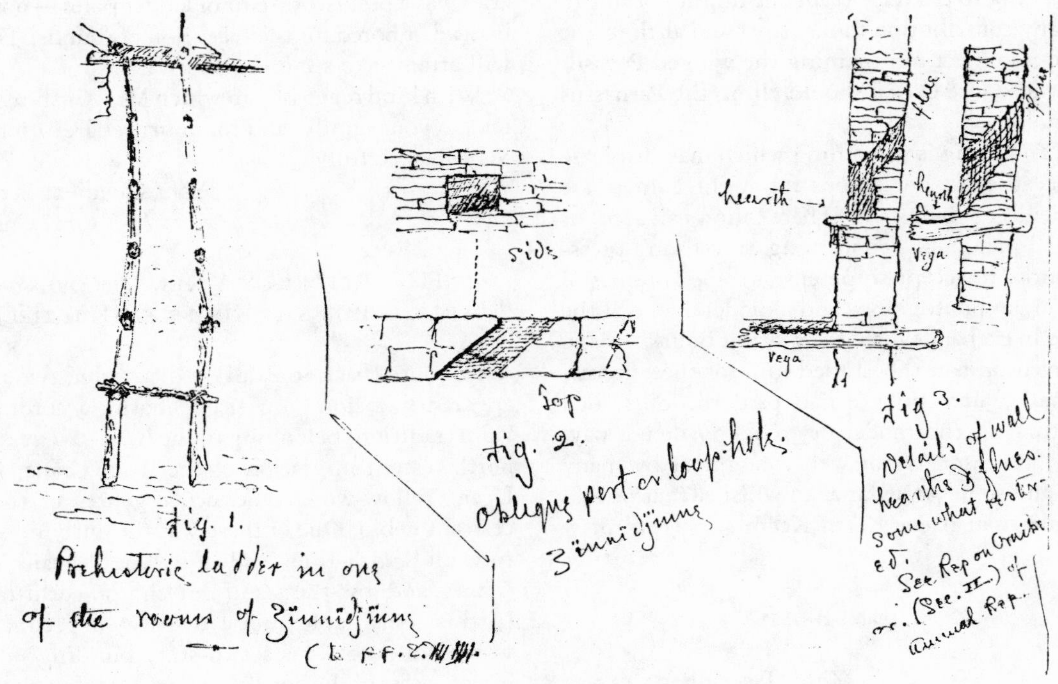

Fig. 40 Kin-tiel Ruin (Cushing sketch).

command of all exposed portions of the valley and arm in which the building was situated. With regard to the use of this splendidly preserved specimen of ancient architecture, the present detached rancherias of the Zunis give the best indication. Plan and sections II represent the corn rancheria of Um-thla-na, an Indian who perished in it during the Navajo raids of a quarter of a century ago.[33] It will be seen that the boulder foundation, the oblique loop holes [portholes] and the flu-less hearth (save that in this latter instance the smoke hole was through the roof instead of the wall) are common to both buildings, and the isolated positions of either, together with their almost equal distances from the main pueblo, are further indicative. Plan III with figures taken from Kin-i-k'el during the Autumn of 1880 for comparison with similar features in the structural works of the Zunis will give yet more details seemingly further confirmatory of the Zuni tradition.

The same arrangement of lintels, the covered way, the flooring of sandstone slabs, and the six estufas (namely of the North, the West, the South, the East, the Upper region, and the Under world) are common to both pueblos, while the protected salle porte is a feature possessed only by Kin-i-k'el. Another ruin of unimportant size yet of great interest was examined [also] during this trip. It was situated three miles East and South of "Houck's Tank," or Ojo "del Coyote" (A. & P. R. R.) on the trail leading thence to Zuni. A hasty examination revealed numerous broken specimens of pottery and, near the summit, a large stone slab through which a circular hole had been cut, and much worn. This stone was broken through the center, probably by the agency of intense heat. It was situated at (a) in the section, whence it had apparently fallen from the roof or walls of the building, which was once continued upward. By aid of tradition and folk lore, I learned that these stones had been used as door ways in a manner shown by the following

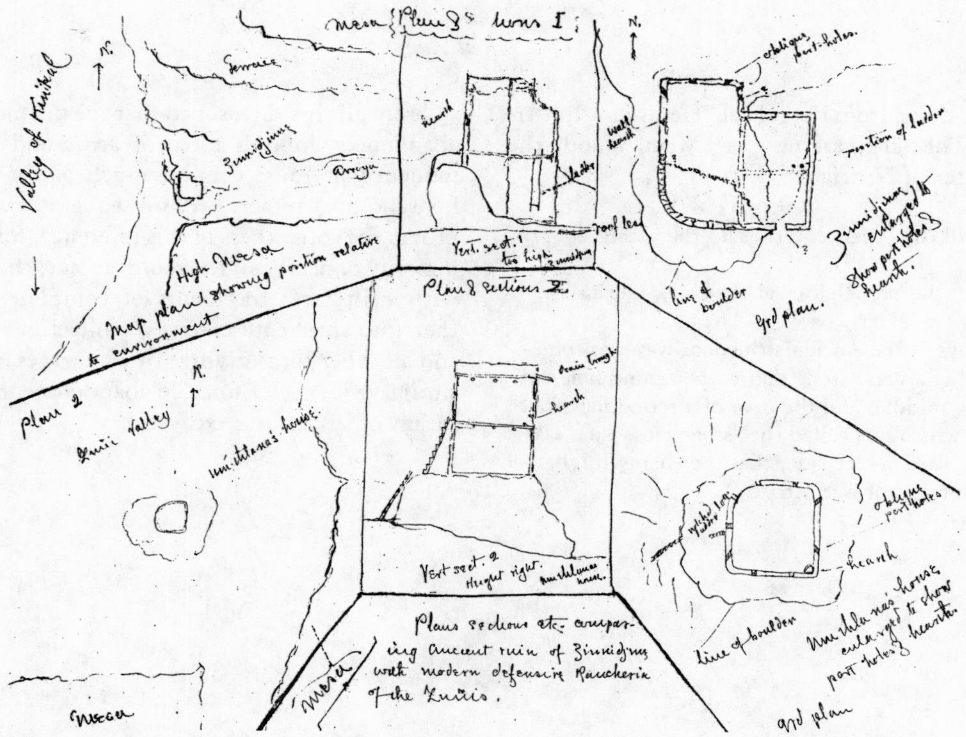

Fig. 41 Kin-tiel Ruin (Cushing sketch).

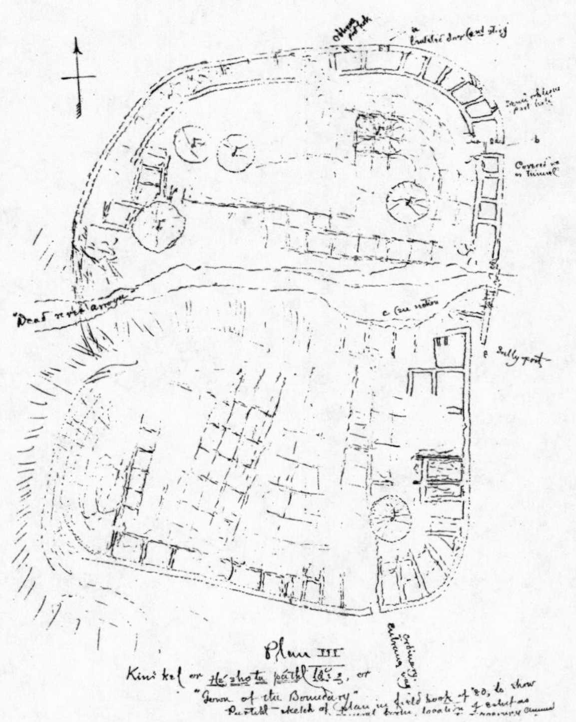

Fig. 42 Kin-tiel Ruin (Cushing sketch).

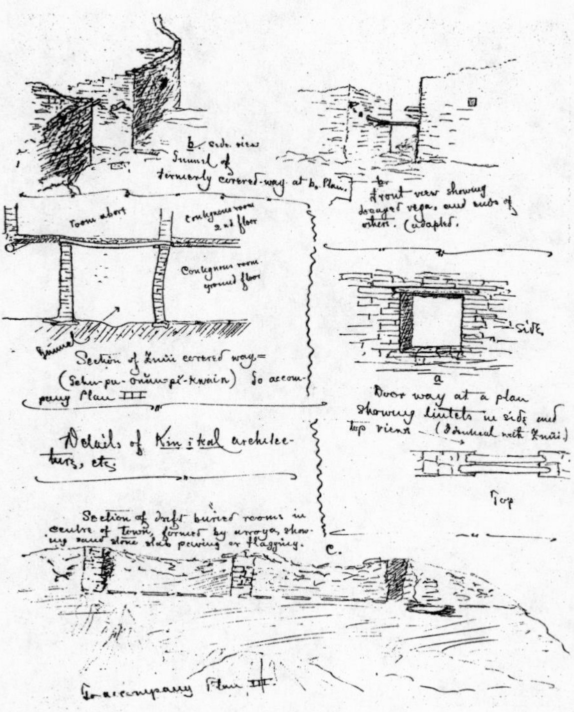

Fig. 43 Kin-Tiel Ruin (Cushing sketch).

quotation, taken from the tale of "He-as-si-a-luh-ti-wa Toi-a Thlu-el-la-kis-na," or "Metal Hand, the Deer Hunter of Nutria":

"How will the others enter?" said the young man to his wife.

"Through the 'stone-close' at the side," she answered.

In the days of the Ancients the door-way was sometimes made of a great stone slab with a round hole cut through the middle, and the door of a round flat stone to close it, which was called the "stone close" and was propped in place on the side, that the enemy might not enter in times of war. Etc.[34]

From all this, I reasoned that the pueblo had been abandoned through force of arms and that consequently it must contain much of the primitive householdry intact. A subsequent examination proves the correctness of this inference, for I find the masonry of nearly all the rooms intact, though filled with drift, and fragments of complete vessels. I therefore anticipate extensive collections from this and all other ruins giving, by like traces of fire etc., similar evidence of forcible abandonment—this by means of systematic excavation.[35]

Adventure in Oraibi

On the 5th of December I left Zuni, via the Rio Puerco Valley, for Holbrook, Arizona Territory, on the Atlantic and Pacific Railroad, accompanied by Mr. Willard L. Metcalf, an artist, and Na-na-he, the adopted Moqui, as interpreter. Four days were consumed in the journey, during which I discovered on the old mail road a ruin evidently abandoned by force and hence offering great inducements for excavation. On arriving at the camp of the U.S. Geological Survey, below Holbrook, I had the honor of meeting [Major Powell,] en route from a visit to the Grand Cañon. I was at once directed to take an invoice and charge of trading material on hand. Also to make arrangements . . . for the purpose of additional goods. . . . On the following morning I received written orders . . . detailing me to service as Assistant on the Oraibi Expedition, and also a copy of orders to Mr. Victor Mindeleff, [who was placed] in charge. . . .[36]

—Monthly Report for December 1882
(National Anthropological Archives)

As a center of Pueblo resistance to foreign cultural encroachments from the time of the Pueblo Revolt of 1680, Oraibi would not in the best of times have been likely to welcome with tranquility a mission aimed at "cleaning out" the village, "ethnologically speaking" (Cushing's orders as conveyed in the letter from Brown). But Cushing was coming at a more than ordinarily difficult time. The Hopis had generally been divided all along between those who had accepted Christian missions and those who had not—and more recently between those who had accepted Mormonism and those who had not—and they were now divided between those who accepted the new government school established in 1877 at Keams Canyon and those who did not. Most Oraibians did not (just as they had also refused the government request for a census in 1871). Now, however, they were themselves dividing into the factions that would eventually split their community into separate villages. The Mormon influence was an important element in this division. In his Zuni diary, Bourke quoted the Hopi Nanahe as saying, "We are a divided people. The young men like myself are fond of the Americans and see that they are a great people whose ways we ought to learn; but all the old men, all those who do the talking and have control of affairs, are friendly to the Mormons, and some of them are Mormons already. This is especially the case in Oraibi" (Sutherland, p. 906). Fear and distrust of Americans ran so high in Oraibi, according to Baxter, that "a recent expedition . . . had found the place entirely deserted, the inhabitants having fled at its approach and concealing or taking with them all their valuables" ("Zuni Revisited," p. 124). Actually, the man who was town chief at the time was inclined to accept the American influence, but he was bitterly opposed by the faction of whom Nanahe spoke. It was into this highly volatile situation, just as it was developing, that Cushing had been sent, on what could hardly have failed to be a highly inflammatory mission. According to Baxter, it was in fact because *Oraibi was a particularly "difficult place to make a collection in" that Cushing had been assigned to the task, being, "by reason of his standing as a Zuni, peculiarly fitted to do the work, which would have been hardly possible under ordinary circumstances" ("Zuni Revisited," p. 124). It may be that he came into Oraibi somewhat overconfident about his standing there. If so, he was to be brought up short.*

For an extended account of Cushing's December 1882 adventures in Oraibi—and, per the usual Cushing pattern, a more colorful *account than that written on the spot in the letter to follow—see his "Report on Oraibi," published posthumously as "Oraibi in 1883," in "Contributions to Hopi History," ed. Jesse Walter Fewkes and Elsie Clews Parsons. Both versions show Cushing in his role as representative of "Father Washington," trying to carry out the aggressive collecting program undertaken by the Bu-*

reau of Ethnology.[37] *Both versions also picture him as behaving with impressive coolness in highly threatening circumstances. But the Cushing who appears in the later version, making provocative speeches and showing a pistol, is conspicuously absent from the earlier one.*

A third perspective is afforded in a journal kept by the eastern visitor who accompanied Cushing on this venture, Willard Metcalf. Described by Metcalf in a note written thirty-five years later as "a youthful record of a winter's exploration trip to Oraibi," this journal provides some telling glimpses of Cushing from the viewpoint of a man not only younger than himself but at least equally touchy and impetuous, particularly in situations (such as that confronting both of them, in different ways, in Oraibi) in which honor was seen to be at stake. Most of Metcalf's account of the two-month expedition is actually taken up with the trials and adventures of the trip itself, a grueling cross-country journey of several hundred miles, much of the time spent struggling through snowstorms in sub-zero temperatures for which neither man was properly dressed and from which, on at least one stretch, both came dangerously near to perishing. The excerpt to follow, however, except for a few pages on the rendezvous with Major Powell's party in Holbrook and a brief subsequent stopover on First Mesa, is limited to the entries covering the critical days in Oraibi.

Metcalf Journal

Holbrook, December 10, 1882

. . . Riding into the town in advance of Na-na-he, I inquired at one of the principal stores for the camp of the Geological Survey and was informed in broken English mixed with Spanish that it was some two miles further down the river on the other side.

Putting spurs to my horses and bidding N— to follow, I made off down the road and after about a mile and a half, I saw in the distance under the trees the white tents and smoke curling lazily upward in the waning light of the afternoon sun.

I was soon in their midst, where I found Cushing (who had ridden ahead) and a number of men to whom I was introduced and invited to supper. . . .

Major Powell, director of the Bureau of Ethnology and Geology, who had that afternoon just returned with his outfit from the Grand Cañon of the Colorado, gave me a seat at supper by his side, and a glorious one it was too, soup, meat, blackberry jam, plum duff, chow chow, &c.

Opposite me sat Mr. Mindeleff, whom I had met in Washington last summer; Mr. Atkins; Col. Shutt of Washington; and a number of mule drivers or skinners as they call them; Jack Hillers, also of Washington, whom I remembered well; Watts and Manuel, two cooks; "Bonny" Hamlin, a stockman but a good quiet fellow; and Charlie, a good natured big fellow called the "Tall Tennessean"—and to-night around the fire [I heard] such stories, expressions and ideas as I never listened to before. Some things I could hardly understand what was meant. . . .

December 13

. . . Today we "pulled out" of camp at about ten o'clock. Two six-mule teams and one four. Mr. Atkins, Mr. Mindeleff, Frank and myself and Na-na-he on horseback, bound for Moqui—there being no road but simply the track made by a buck-board which had gone through some weeks before. . . .

Walpi, December 18

. . . During all this time Cushing had been talking to the Moqui Navajo, our host as I considered him, in broken Navajo and Spanish, finding out what he could of the whereabouts of the team &c. . . .

During supper an incident occurred that was most disgusting, which I must note especially as it was such an ordinary occurrence apparently. We were all in the midst of our feast—for such it was—and thinking how good it tasted, when the little child which was opposite me and which had been crawling about suddenly stopped and, without warning, performed its calls of nature. In a twinkling of an eye there were two of the dogs cleaning, for dear life, the child and the ground, eagerly and furiously whilst others were snarling and crowding near. My feelings at that moment and Van H's, who also witnessed it, I cannot begin to describe. Van H. very foolishly called Frank's attention to it, whilst I mastered the situation as best I could and finished, apparently unconcerned, saying not a word. C[ushing] rebuked Van H. for his making so much of it and said it would be better for him not to say anything more about it, for the less said the better. . . .

December 19

. . . We went over to Te-wa, the most eastern of the three towns upon this mesa. There we were hospitably received by Pulakaki, or Tom as we heard Mr. C. speak of him. He is an old friend of F's, having accompanied him to Hava-su-pai in '81. He had a very good-natured face and did everything to make us comfortable. He is a believer in Americans, has very advanced and common-sense ideas in certain matters, wore American clothes and was quite wealthy. He was, I found, a great linguist, speaking no less than six or seven Indian languages, most of them perfectly, and also Spanish and English. We had supper there and he made us down some fine beds and gave me plenty of blankets when he found out what a time I had had the night before. He had lived in Zuni some years before and spoke the language very fluently, and it seemed good to hear C. and him talking together.

Oraibi, December 21

. . . At last I was near the objective point, and after here, would turn my face Eastward again. At times I am tempted to start off for the old Bay State, but when I remember my object out here, I am forced to remain.

Now came a severe climb for the teams in the ascent to the town, but by means of brake and whip it was finally mastered. Our road was simply a sheep trail and I believe that ours were the first teams that ever visited Oraibi. On the top of the uneven mesa the wind blew and was very cooling to whatever enthusiasm one might have had after witnessing the town off on the western edge. We wound about through peach orchards and gardens and at last entered into the plaza and drew up before a house which afterward proved to be that of the Governor of the town.

We hastily commenced unpacking our wagons, preparatory to taking the town by storm, as it were, and removed our goods to the little room which was up one terrace about 6 feet high. . . .

Our host was a fine looking man with a most pleasing face. He was dressed in Oraibi costume which consisted of blanket, breech clout and moccasins & winter at that. He bade us most royally to be welcome as did also his wife, a bright looking little woman who seemed always to be very industrious.

But to return—During our unpacking the teams, the natives stood looking from the tops of the houses with their blankets from eyes down, thus making it very difficult to tell whether it met with their approval or not, for I had heard previous to my coming that they entertained no very great friendship for the Americans. It was not long before we had emptied the teams of our merchandise, sugar, flour, cloth, blankets, beads, &c., immediately after which all the party started back, excepting C., Watts, Tom (our Indian), and myself. . . .

Soon after supper, Frank and one or two Indians commenced on a council at one end of the room, whilst Watts and I at the other end discoursed on the pleasures of smoking and I also initiated him into the mysteries of corn shuck cigarettes. Frank soon went out to attend a council and see what could be done in the prospects of a collection. Watts and I stayed at home and continued our conversation, I getting little by little a sort of an autobiography of him which was mighty interesting. Frank came back and reported that things were going badly and that the Indians were very much opposed to us. But we thought nothing of that and turned in for the night.

It must have been about 3 o'clock when I was awakened by a shake and saw or heard F. say, "Come, get up! *Quick! Quick!* We have got to get out of here before morning." I, half awake, did not move very rapidly, for I imagined he was excited as he sometimes was, when he repeated his summons again and went for water.

Dressing myself and to myself using some very strong language for having to obey them at that hour, I came out into the large room to find W. out of humor and somewhat mechanically obeying F., who was in a terrible state of excitement. He told his story, which was very long and very exciting; how the Oraibis had heaped insult after insult upon his head and had made him write a very insulting letter to the President of the U.S. and only after that had allowed him to leave there safely, and we must all leave there before daybreak or they would "pierce us." Frank hurried us as fast as he could, and I don't know as I ever was so slow—and to see Watts trying to pack a few dishes and the utter despair pictured on his face in trying to make up his mind what to take and how to take it.

"Now which had you rather do, stay here and suffer the consequences or start out tonight?" says Frank.

"Stay here and d—n the Oros," says Watts. "What do you say, Onokthlekin?"

"The same, you bet," says I, and then followed a long talk as to the practicability of going out into the snow and cold without a blanket or bit of food—for we could not carry them—urged by us and assented to by Frank. "Tell them we will immediately send for the teams and, as soon as they come, will leave as a man should and that we will stand them off for all we're worth if they try anything violent," said we, and Frank started back as he had not finished.

I wanted to go with him and add one more to his side in case of violence, but he said in a tone that hurt my feelings very much that I had better stay where I was—that I was better off there. I was piqued at this suggestion of my cowardice and told him that when he received an honest and conscientious offer to help him in case of need it was not a thing to be sneered at and that 'twould not be my style to do it again soon—at which he melted somewhat, but I did not get over it all night long, although I could not but help going some fifteen minutes later to the entrance of the estufa and there taking my stand with my hand on my revolver, ready to drop in on them and give them the benefit of six barrels if the case needed it.

After waiting there some hour and a half, all seemed to be decent and I was so cold and sleepy that I crawled back to my bed and went to sleep. I am convinced by what Tom told me that Tenatsali (Cushing) did not tell them that we were going to stay. Perhaps he feared violence.

But I awoke this morning, *Dec. 22,* thoroughly expecting to see the town in arms and preparing to drive us out, but after a breakfast during which I was pretty glum, for I had not gotten over what had been said to me the night before, I started out, with my six-shooter in plain sight, determined not only to see what the signs were but also to see the town. I was alone and the first one who stepped out of the house, and I somewhat expected to meet with opposition, but my "dander" was up and I determined to show them—Frank—that I was not afraid in spite of his advice to wait awhile.

I went all over the town and into the houses of some, where I saw nothing but scowls and sour looks from the women and the men were no where to be seen, which I did not quite understand. At one house a dog jumped at me, whereupon I kicked him off the roof and afterwards finished by shooting though not killing. Not knowing but what this might be a signal for the outbreak, after a little reflection I hastened back to the house, but nothing came of it. And so I watched and waited, fully expecting hostilities which came not, but I noticed later in the day that, from under the blankets of a number of the men who had assembled at their estufas, the ends of bows and arrows. So I waited, but with no avail, and I spent the rest of the day in sketching.

The Governor seemed to be in a most embarrassing position, for he said they had told him that they were going to kill him for befriending us. As he told us this and looked at his wife, who sat near him, the tears ran down his cheeks. "My people are all bad," said he, "and they act like fools. I have tried to teach them and show them, as best I can, to be better, and this is what I get for it. I do not know as I shall ever see you again, but you have all been good to me, and I am sorry my people will not benefit by this opportunity," said the old man.

Thus we staid it out until our teams arrived, which was the morning of *Christmas Day*—one which I shall not forget soon. About noon they arrived and we began to make preparations for leaving.

Soon from the housetops we heard the herald announcing to the people that "We must cut off the light of these Americans and not allow them to go from here, for they have defied us," etc. Whereupon we all took an account of stock, i.e., of guns, revolvers, cartridges, etc., and found we could give them some work for a first-class undertaker and straightforwardly proceeded with our work. Soon I noticed the men who had been standing on the housetops begin to get up and move away, and then the women disappeared into the houses. What would have been the results I know not, for we were now done, and so bidding our hosts good-bye, we started out of town—each pretty well armed.

Whether we got away too soon for them or whether they were bluffing us, I can never tell, but I know I got away all right, and glad I was too. F. and I had to walk, as before. After getting some distance from town I put my rifle into the team [wagon] and started off ahead, as I walked faster than the teams were going. Frank started off at a trot, which he kept up for some miles, I following along in a sheep trail which was mostly covered with snow. I walked on and on, deeply wrapped in meditations—in fact noticing nothing except what was right before me and occasionally looking to see if I could see F. At times I would gain on him, and then he would start into a run again, and then I would resume my thoughts and occasionally nibble at some dried peaches of which I had a pocket full I had got of our Indian hosts.

Yes, today was Christmas—and in such a place. . . . If ever I was homesick, here was the time. The contrast, as I thought of it, between home and here. All this and much more ran through my mind as I went on, completely alone. Along about two hours before sundown, I came to an arroyo a little this side of the low mesa which I had been gaining on little by little, and, just before I reached the arroyo, I saw, curling up in the bright sunlight, a thin column of smoke which rapidly grew denser as I approached, and I found C. sitting beside a little fire of sage brush in a sunny spot, evidently as deep in meditation as I had been. Poor fellow, I suppose he was homesick too! I joined him, and, gathering some more brush, sat down to wait the teams' arrival.

We had a lengthy conversation concerning his duties in collecting and his position and Vick's [Mindeleff's] in the party. The teams came and passed us without anyone noticing us, though we were in plain sight for some time. After they had passed, we got up and walked on. . . . During our walk, we had a most pleasant conversation, such as one is rarely met with—for 'twas on his part most beautiful to listen to his sentiments and to hear him express the deep love he had for his wife. The conversation ran on to the excitement at Oraibi, and I rebuked him for his risking himself so hardily when he thought of what could be the result should anything have happened to him. "Were you a young man," said I, " 'twould be different." "Yes! but I can't help it. For you know how little I think of the danger until it's over and above all how I despise anything cowardly."

"Yes, Frank, so do I, and I can't help feeling hurt at your telling me to 'go to sleep,' as you did when you knew I wanted to join you, and more than all, the promise I gave your wife to look out for you to my best ability. And I think you did me a great injustice, for you implied that I was a baby and a coward, and you know, Frank, that such things are not pleasant to hear from one who holds such a place in one's heart as you do in mine."

"God bless you, my boy, what a fool I am that I could not see the kindness, if nothing more, in your proposal. To tell you the truth, I did do you an injustice and more than that. I thought that if anything should happen to you, my boy, what would your Mother and Father say. Their only son!"

"They would be glad, while grieved, to know that I had died as a man should—doing my duty. I am not afraid of death, and they know that, and while I hope to be spared to them, I should have felt worse than they, had anything come of it seriously and I had not been where I should."

"Forgive me, Willard, I was wrong—and right too. You are a plucky boy and I don't think I half appreciated what you wished to do for me. It is not one in fifty—no! a hundred—that would have done as much as you did. God bless you, my boy," said he, as I told him of my watching at the estufa for him, even after his rebuke. That was indeed a very happy talk and did much to bring my spirits back to their proper standpoint.

By this time and about dark, we had arrived at our camping place. . . . 'Twas clear moonlight—clear and snappy. The fire had burned low and was smouldering to ashes. I, from under my tree, lay gazing at the stars and thinking. Quiet; all but the occasional bark of a coyote, a snort, or a rattle of hobble chains from the mules. This was the accompaniment to my thoughts as I lay there thinking that this was indeed the end of Christmas day for me and wondering where next Christmas would find me, etc. etc. Thus musing, I fell into a deep sleep.[38]

FHC to Mindeleff

Oraibi, December 23, 1882

Dear Victor:

I write to you in great haste. I have had a council in which I repeated what was said to the chief last night. I used my utmost with the few who first came and received favorable replies. They, however, told me that while they wished to do as was represented to them, they were powerless in the face of the masses, and that they could help us only by the penalty of probable death. The chief started for the council, designing to advise his people. He was met by a delegation who informed him that if he came he should be killed. Then a large body came into the estufa. They asked me to write a letter to the chief who sent us. Their dictations were full of the utmost impudence and defiance. I kept my temper with them. I made no threats. I just simply said that we were here under orders, and that we must carry out those orders.

Their reply was that we could carry them out only over their dead bodies; that, furthermore, they would give us between this and daylight to leave. That we *must* get out of their pueblo before the sun rose or it would not be well for us.

I told them I didn't propose to go. They said then I would *have* to. I asked them how I should take my bedding and food with me. They said, "If you can take it, very well; if not, you will have to get along the best way you can." I told them I should remain and send for my wagons. They replied I should not, and informing them once more of the same intention, I left them.

At first, I told the boys we must go, as my Indians were very badly scared and begged me to do so, but decided on finding them both willing to stay, that we should do so.

What the Oraibis propose to do about it, I know not. Probably they will, when they see our determination to stay, do nothing. One matter, however, is certain: we can make no collection here, save by force, for the body of the people send word in the letter they dictated to the chiefs and caciques of the Americans, that they wish for war *this month* and no later; that they wish to spare us as the bearers of such message; that they are prepared to die, as through the power of their gods and priests they shall live again, and that too, through the total destruction of the Americans. They beg for war, and say: "When the Caciques of the Americans sit on our decapitated heads, then they can dress our bodies in their clothes, feed our bodies with their victuals; then, too, they can have our things to take with them to the houses of their fathers."

At present it is utterly useless, and even perilous, to continue our attempt; it will be essential to return with the wagons and take our things away. Even were the few friends we have willing to trade, they would not dare, as they tell me, to do so. It is possible that a collection can ultimately be made here; not at present, save through force, and then only in a pueblo empty of inhabitants. The force need only to be small, but force it would *have* to be.

Return, therefore, at once with the transportation, and we will, if you think best, collect at other pueblos, excavate the finds (three) I discovered the other day, and wait for advice from headquarters before proceeding further.

I have passed through no small personal risk this night and left only at the last moment. I am therefore speaking earnestly and faithfully.

They like me, they say. My mission they do *not* like. They will have nothing to do with it, or with the Americans. No, not even though they come with all their power—which they will know of—and with their highest caciques.[39]

Very Respectfully,
Your Obt. Serv't,
F.H. Cushing

Victor Mindeleff, Esq.
Chg., Oraibi Expedition

Out of Oraibi, Into Other Troubles

On the 24th of December we left Oraibi and proceeded to an arroyo under Mui-shon-na-vi [Mushongnovi] and Shi-pau-lovi, where I remained until my final departure, making collections (more than twelve hundred specimens), noting Moqui folk-lore and tradition, and [studying] the considerable collections of antique pottery gathered.[40] On the 19th of January I left camp for Zuni via Keams Cañon. At the latter place we were detained four days by the snow storms and the wretched condition of our animals. . . . Further delayed on our journey by similar causes, we did not reach Zuni until the last day of January.

—Monthly Report for December 1882 and January 1883
and Annual report on field work for year ending June 30, 1883
(National Anthropological Archives).

Meanwhile, other troublesome plots and subplots were unfolding. This holiday season seems to have been marked by a shortage of goodwill toward Cushing, for while he was off about his Father Washington's business in Oraibi, his superiors at the Smithsonian and the Bureau of Ethnology received complaints about him from no less than four separate sources (five, counting a hostile newspaper piece). Two of the letters—reverberations, respectively, from his tangles with the mission school teacher at Zuni and the U.S. Indian agent for the Navajos—may simply have been filed away. The other two resulted in communications from Baird, which awaited Cushing on his exit from Oraibi. The subject of one of the latter two was a hapless army mule which had been loaned to Cushing in September 1881 through the agency of his friend Lieut. Wotherspoon at Fort Whipple, Arizona. Doubly lost, first in the flesh and then in report, amid the combined vagaries of frontier mail service, army bureaucracy, and perhaps someone's inattentiveness to mail actually delivered, this mule had continued to haunt the army ledgers. Whatever Cushing's degree of culpability may or may not have been, by the time he returned to Zuni from his latest trip he had not only a lost mule to deal with but a disenchanted friend and an irritated supervisor as well.

More serious than any of these other matters, however, was the trouble developing over the Nutria spring and surrounding farmlands. While touring the area the previous summer, Senator John A. Logan of Illinois had learned of the inadvertent omission of this vital part of the Zuni reservation from the official description of its boundaries as established in 1877. With his son-in-law, Major William F. Tucker, part-owner of a cattle ranch adjacent to Nutria, the senator had investigated the lands in question. In early November, Tucker and two partners entered claims, each filing for 160 acres under the Homestead Act and 640 acres under the Desert Land Act, to expand and provide water for their ranch.[41] On a return visit to the Southwest, also in early November, Cushing's friend Sylvester Baxter got wind of these developments and sounded the alarm in a story filed from Santa Fe on December 1 (see Appendix). It was this article that prompted the last-mentioned of the December letters bearing ill tidings of Cushing—a note from Col. Stevenson to Baird informing him that Logan was outraged by this attack in the press and held Cushing responsible for it.

It is worth noting that Stevenson's note has nothing at all to say about the substance of the article other than that it criticized Logan. Nor does Baird seem to have bothered to find out what the criticism was about before addressing an urgent request to Cushing for an "authoritative denial" that he had had anything to do with the article. As for Cushing himself, in providing the required protestation of innocence, it is barely possible that he was telling the truth; he was, *as he said, away in Oraibi when the piece was published. But in view of his return to Zuni for the several weeks preceding the dispatch of Baxter's article, and given the kind of information the article contained, it is hard to believe that Cushing was really as uninvolved as he claimed in his response to Baird. It seems, rather, that as a self-consciously unorthodox employee of a government agency dependent on the Congress for its funds he would have divined how lightly a question of justice to the*

Indians would weigh in the minds of his superiors against a threat to their appropriations—and *how discreet he would have to be in a matter of this kind.*

In any case, the Nutria affair and the attendant struggle with Logan were just surfacing in December. Subsequent developments, including Cushing's own contributions and the vendetta mounted against him by Logan and his allies, are reflected in later correspondence and news stories included in this volume, though it was not until long after Cushing's return to the East that the boundary question itself was finally resolved.[42]

News Item

Washington, December 12. A correspondent of a Boston newspaper, writing from Santa Fe, New Mexico, asserts that Sen. Logan of Illinois has taken steps to secure possession of the Nutria Spring, near the land of the Zuni Indians and to establish a cattle ranch around it. This correspondent says that the spring has always been regarded as situated on the Zuni Reservation but that recent surveys have shown that by some inadvertency the reservation lines do not include it. It is further said that the Zunis have had possession of the spring for centuries and that the land around it contains their best wheat fields and that to take it away would reduce their agriculture by half and threaten them with famine. Sen. Logan said tonight that he had not taken the land in question. If it was public land, however, he saw no reason why it should not be pre-empted. He had looked at the land and said that he would take it if he could get it.

New York Times, 13 December 1882

Wotherspoon to Baird

Madison Barracks
Sackets Harbor, New York
December 14, 1882

Sir:

I have the honor to state that on the 1st of July, 1882, a letter was addressed through you to Mr. F. H. Cushing, an employee of your institution, by H.I. Raymond, U.S.A., requesting Mr. Cushing to give all information in his power as to the disposition of a mule which was furnished him by order of Gen'l Wilcox, then commanding the Department of Arizona, to enable him to return to Zuni.

No reply to this letter nor to many others written direct to Mr. Cushing has been received; in fact, he seems to have entirely passed the matter over. I have been informed indirectly that the mule died or was killed during the journey, and, having been responsible for the animal to the War Department, its value is now made a personal charge against me, which I will have to pay unless Mr. Cushing will furnish the necessary evidence as to its death to clear me of the responsibility.

I therefore ask that Mr. Cushing be directed to at once furnish an affidavit setting forth the date at which he received the animal and the place where he received it and giving as fully as possible a statement as to its final disposition, whether it died or was turned over by him to some officer.

At the time this animal was loaned to Mr. Cushing, he was on a trip to Prescott en route from the Havasupai villages under instructions from your office and claiming that his animals were unfit for the service required. The Department Commander courteously furnished him with the assistance he asked. His failure to make any acknowledgement either of the courtesy or the letters sent him upon the subject prompts me to write direct to you in the matter.

Very respectfully,
W. Wotherspoon
1st Lieut., 18th Infantry

Sheldon Jackson to Baird

December 22, 1882

Dear Sir:

Permit me to call your attention to the case of Mr. F.H. Cushing, your collector at Zuni Pueblo. Upon going among those people, instead of cooperating with the teachers of the school at that place, sustained jointly by the government and Presbyterian Church, he has persistently and unnecessarily thrown his influence against the school and, as we have reason to believe, pandered to the lowest passions of the people.

Our Mission Society has quietly borne all this for months, hoping that he would complete his investigations and leave the country, but, as he seems to have settled down there for another term, we ask you to be so kind as to examine into his course and consider the desirability of recalling him and sending another in his place, as we believe that the best interests of your institution will be served by a man who has some respect for himself and will command the respect and cooperation of the teachers at that place.

Very truly yours,
Sheldon Jackson
Superintendent of Indian Schools
Board of Home Missions, Presbyterian Church

Stevenson to Baird

December 22, 1882

Kind Sir:

I beg to call your attention to a conversation I had a few days since with Senator Logan, in which he referred to an article which had been shown him, from the Boston *Herald* of a recent date, post marked Zuni, New Mexico, severely criticizing him as a United States Senator.[43] The Senator stated that he believed this was written or instigated by F.H. Cushing of the Bureau of Ethnology. Senator Logan seemed to be so incensed that I have deemed it proper to call your attention to the matter. I assured Senator Logan that the fact had never come to your attention, and that you did not allow anything of the kind to occur.

Respectfully,
James Stevenson

Baird to FHC

December 23, 1882

Dear Mr. Cushing:

I understand that Gen. Logan is very much incensed at the publication, by the Boston *Herald,* of an article reflecting very severely upon himself, in connection with his recent visit to New Mexico, and charges you as being the writer or the instigator of it.

I shall be glad to have from you an authoritative denial of this, so that I may show it to the General, should the matter come to the case that I think it is likely to attain, namely, his opposition to the appropriations for the Bureau of Ethnology.

No time is to be lost in sending me such a communication as I may use in refutal of the General's impression.

You, of course, are sufficiently aware of Gen. Logan's character—that he is indomitable and relentless; and while he is a most valuable friend, he is a very dangerous enemy.

Yours truly,
Spencer F. Baird

C.H. Howard to Powell

December 26, 1882

. . . There is one other matter relating more particularly to your Ethnological Bureau. Dr. Sullivan at one of the Moqui villages claimed to be in the employ of said Bureau. From all I heard as to his previous character and present conduct, and from what I saw of him myself, I could but conclude his presence there was a positive injury to that people. He may have falsified as to any connection with the Smithsonian Institution, but I have thought it best to tell you exactly my impressions of the man, as I have also given them to the Secretary.

I was exceedingly reluctant to credit some reports injurious to Cushing (with the Zunis), but they came from so many sources I felt obliged to take notice of them also. His shooting of horses of Navajos was brought officially to my attention. From the statements of the Zunis themselves, it was at best but a reckless and lawless act and was in the line of the old barbarism rather than of the civilization which Mr. Cushing ought to exemplify. Worse still is his reputation for licentiousness, which I found to be wide-spread in that country. You will readily see that I could not inspect these pueblos as I was ordered and ignore the presence of such influences or even widely circulated reports of this kind. But you will understand that I have taken particular pains not to cast any blame upon you or any reproach upon your Bureau as such. . . .

C.H. Howard
Office of U.S. Indian Inspector
United States Indian Service
Department of the Interior

Oraibi Dec. 21
In the winter of 1882, when Mr. Metcalf and Mr. Cushing left the friendly pueblo of Zuñi and travelled to a neighboring community at Oraibi they found a different language spoken and a decidedly unfriendly reception for strangers. While this sketch was being made on the housetops, the council was debating in the court below whether it were not best to exterminate the foreign strangers and have no more bother about them. The children were watching their elders intently while the artist busied himself in making an exceedingly careful drawing

Fig. 44 Oraibi December 21, 1882 (Willard Metcalf sketch, *Survey* 1 October 1924, courtesy Elizabeth de Veer).

FHC to Baird

Camp near Mui-shon-na-vi
Moqui, Arizona, January 3rd, 1883

Dear Professor Baird:

Your letter of the 23rd of December was delayed in reaching me, as I have been several weeks absent from Zuni, helping to make collections for Major Powell at the Moqui Pueblos.

Far from having been either the author or instigator of an article in the Boston *Herald* reflecting on General Logan or his visit to this country, I not only have had, previously to the receipt of your letter, no knowledge either of the contemplated or actual appearance of such an article, but sincerely regret that anything of the kind should have been published.

I have no consciousness to justify in me the entertainment of any personal enmity to General Logan, nor can I conceive how he can think I have. Rather, I had hoped that he still preserved the same kind spirit toward me which he seemed to evince on the only occasion of my meeting with him—at a reception in his house of my Zuni party early last spring. You will doubtless recall that it was in this spirit that I mentioned General Logan's name last summer, when I asked your advice relative to seeking a commission in the United States Army—a spirit which had been encouraged in me by one of the General's near friends.

There has been and is much virulent criticism of my connection and methods of research with the Zuni Indians. You are aware, however, as the instigator of such research, that these methods have been the result of my deliberate and best judgment; as well as, I hope, through personal knowledge of my character, that my connection with the Zunis has been honorable and in the constant presence of a sense of self-respect. Feeling this, and knowing from the first that my statements relative to the Zunis would be—as they have been—distorted, criticised and contumned [sic], especially in the West, I have trusted to quiet adherence to my original plans, to the ultimate published results of my researches, and to time to set aright all such matters.

Upon this feeling and upon the dignity of a position which I hope some time to attain, I have hitherto based my conduct and public expressions, deeming it beneath such feeling and dignity to enter, either openly or covertly, into any newspaper statements or controversies.

I have the honor to be, with thanks for your timely letter,

Very Respectfully,
Your Obedient Servant,
F.H. Cushing

Will you kindly have a copy of the article referred to forwarded to me? I have not seen it. FHC

NEWSPAPER COLUMN

January 18, 1883. The admirable article contributed to the last Sunday's CAPITAL by Col. H.C. Rizer, editor of the Eureka *Herald,* on the "hosh-kon" festival of the Navajoes is deservedly attracting general attention and has found its way into several of the leading papers.[44] It is to be said of Col. Rizer's letters on the Indian tribes of Arizona and New Mexico that they have not only shown him to be a writer of more than ordinary grace and skill, but have also dispelled many of the prevalent illusions about those strange and mysterious "first inhabitants" and given us a really intelligent, straightforward and unsensational estimate of their character and condition.

It is particularly noticeable that Col. Rizer's account of the Zunis and other pueblo tribes is very much at variance with the dime-novel newspaper letters and magazine articles furnished on this topic during the last year by certain ambitious young scribes evidently more anxious to "work a racket," as the boys say, than to contribute accurate and useful information. Col. Rizer met and studied the pueblos under all circumstances and with superior facilities for ascertaining the truth about them, and he failed to find any of that romantic courage and hair-raising disposition to make sacrifices out of casual white folks which the young men alluded to have so picturesquely set forth. On the contrary, he found them to be remarkably docile, not to say cowardly, and disposed to view white men with awe and excessive respect rather than to resent their presence or manifest any desire to molest or make them afraid. He was assured also by those who have lived near and among the Zunis, for instance, that they are in no sense bloodthirsty or combative and that a single resolute Navajoe with a piñon club can put a whole village of them to flight.[45]

In respect to the secret, dark and midnight ceremonies of these people, about which there has been so much energetic and thrilling writing, Col. Rizer is constrained to certify that he neither met with nor heard of any difficulty in getting permission to witness any of them. However it may have been in the remote and indefinite past, there is now no particular concealment, so far as he was able to ascertain, about any of the tribal rites or superstitious observances. Anybody is privileged to see them who desires to; indeed it is not uncommon for things of that kind to be improvised without regard to dates, solely for the entertainment of visitors. The "hosh-kon" festival, which Col Rizer described in the CAPITAL, is among the most solemn and significant of a tribe that is in reality warlike, and yet he was welcomed into the "sacred enclosure," and made entirely at home. In the face of such considerations on the part of a people like the Navajoes, it is absurd to talk of danger in witnessing a performance by a subdued and pastoral people like the Zunis, and we must therefore doubt the fidelity of stories to the effect that one must take his life in his hand when he goes to see a Zuni festival, as recently related in such a graphic way, with pictures to match.

To be more explicit, Col. Rizer's observations tend to refute and trivialize all the most striking and remarkable statements in Mr. Frank H. Cushing's much-advertized contributions to the *Atlantic* and *Century* on his alleged adventures among the Zunis. Unless other candid and trustworthy persons who have not only visited the Zuni country for a single time, as in the case of Col. Rizer, but who have lived in and about there for the last twenty years, are to be disbelieved, then Mr. Cushing is a glaring fictionist and deserves exposure. He has been pushing his Zuni investigations ostensibly in the interest of science, under the patronage of the Smithsonian Institution, and he should be truthful if nothing else. He seems, however, to prefer the role of a sensationalist, and to invite attention to himself instead of the facts by embellishing his "scientific" remarks with cheap yarns of personal exploits that occurred only in his dreams or his imagination. It is susceptible of proof, we are assured, by eye-witnesses, that the leading incident of his *Atlantic* account of a saddle-trip to the country of the Havasupai is a pure invention, and that his startling recital in the December *Century* of the peril he braved and the narrow escape he made in witnessing the Zuni "dance of the great knife" lacks the merest foundation of truth. Such impositions are without excuse, and particularly censurable in such an instance as this, where there is a pretense of serving the cause of science and of enlightening the general public on matters of importance. The Smithsonian owes it to itself, we think, to dispense with the services of this elaborate young inflater of the facts; and if prominent periodicals consider it worth while to encourage his talent for what Dickens' old lady called "meandering," they should at least preface his further contributions with a note of warning that as between him and St. Paul, for example, it would be safest to take the apostle's word.

Baird to FHC

January 29, 1883

Dear Mr. Cushing:

I wrote to you a month or more ago in regard to a letter which you received from Lieut. W. Wotherspoon, then at Madison Barracks, Sackett's Harbor, New York, presenting a very urgent request on his part for the data necessary to close out an account charged against him for a mule furnished you by him. Please let me know whether you have communicated direct with Lieut. Wotherspoon. If you have not, I must request you to do so at once, as delays of this kind create an unfavorable impression respecting the Institution and its operations, and may tend very seriously to embarrass us when asking future favors either for yourself or for other parties.

Yours truly,
Spencer F. Baird
Secretary

Pilling to FHC

January 30, 1883

Dear Sir:

I beg to call your attention to that clause of your letter of instructions in which you are directed to submit to this office monthly reports of your operations, and I request that said instructions be complied with.

No reports have been received from you since your return to Zuni—about the first of September last.

By order of the Director.

Very truly yours,
James C. Pilling
Chief Clerk

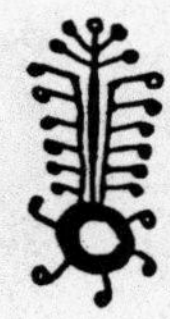

8. *February–April 1883*

ETHNOLOGY UNDER STRESS

To complete the welcome provided by his awaiting mail from Baird, Pilling, and the Topeka Capital, *soon after his return to Zuni Cushing "was severely kicked in the thigh by one of {his} mules." More seriously, the exposure suffered during the snowy trek back from Oraibi, combined with "the irregularity of camp-life and food," brought on a recurrence of "the pulmonary and dyspeptic troubles" from which he had suffered earlier and never fully recovered. He was "thus rendered unable to work, save at rare and short intervals, throughout the remainder of winter and the months of spring" (Monthly Report for February 1883, National Anthropological Archives).*

On the positive side, it was during this season that Cushing made acquaintance with Adolph Bandelier, who was in the area on one of his tours surveying Pueblo ruins and settlements and spent two weeks with the Cushings in Zuni. As attested by the file of correspondence preserved in the Southwest Museum's Hodge-Cushing Collection, the warm friendship dating from this visit was to be lifelong, surviving even what was to Bandelier the considerable trial of serving under Cushing's administration on the ill-fated Hemenway Expedition.[1] Bandelier's own work of reconstructing the history of the Southwest before and under Spanish rule of course rivals Cushing's as a pioneer effort. As Bernard L. Fontana has remarked, "there was no endeavor in the Southwest that could properly be called ethnology until the erudite little Swiss from Highland, Illinois, arrived upon the scene."[2]

What must have excited these two researchers meeting in the field was the discovery of how complementary were their respective endeavors. In their different ways, both were pursuing lines of inquiry initiated by Lewis Henry Morgan—Bandelier having begun his research career as a protégé of Morgan, Cushing having been influenced not only by his own reading of Morgan but by the promptings of Bureau director Powell, whose mission of "organizing American anthropology" was in considerable measure shaped by Morgan's theories of social evolution. In his Annual report for 1883, Cushing refers enthusiastically to Bandelier's investigation into the social structure of the Rio Grande Pueblos and the archaeology and history of Mexico and reports that

> *through this gentleman he {Cushing} learned that his own discoveries relative to the esoteric priest, medicine, chase and war organizations of the Zunis had important bearing on the ethnography both of the ancient Pueblos and the village communities of Mexico. So far as his health permitted, he followed up these discoveries with additional research, with the intention of including the results in {his} treatise on the "sociologic system of the Zunis" (National Anthropological Archives).*

Subsequent Cushing letters evidence the continuing importance to him of the connections thus opened by his conversations with Bandelier. The benefits of their meeting were far from one-sided, however. Among other things that Bandelier learned from Cushing on this occasion was the identity of Zuni and its neighboring ruins with the long mysterious "cities of Cibola"—a discovery for which he himself would receive the credit, as the first to announce it in print.

Another congenial figure to emerge in this period (though his acquaintance with Cushing seems to have dated from the latter's visit to Thomas Keam's Hopi trading post in 1881 en route to Havasupai) was Keam's associate, Alexander Stephen. Though he had come to the Southwest with a degree in mineralogy and ambitions as a prospector, Stephen soon developed an interest in learning about the local Indians and their crafts and customs—a pursuit to which he would increasingly devote himself. One can see in the letter included below how his experience in Keam's trading post contributed to this transition from prospector to ethnographer. Given the enthusiasm of this and other letters he wrote to Cushing as a fellow worker in the field, one may also speculate on the role of Cushing's work in Zuni as a model for the important work Stephen himself would later do among the Hopis. Following Cushing's example, he too ultimately lived almost exclusively among the people he was studying.[3]

The Bandelier and Stephen letters aside, however, the surviving documents of this period have mostly to do with the trials and demands which were making Cushing's situation in Zuni increasingly precarious: ill health, tribal responsibilities, the threat to the Nutria farmlands, and attacks on his personal morals and professional credibility (attacks vigorously countered by several stalwart friends). Within the pueblo itself, as we learn from Bandelier's account, an opposition faction, led by Cushing's old enemy, Roman Luna, the Zuni Mormon, was cam-

paigning for Cushing's removal and the ouster of Palowahtiwa as Zuni governor. In the episode reported by Bandelier, this latter threat was, at least for the time being, turned aside ("owing to the fact that Mr. Cushing had all the old men on his side"), and a visitor the following month, while noting various other details of the Cushings' domestic life, made no mention of such unrest. Resentments continued to smoulder, however, aggravated in particular by the Nutria affair and what seems to have struck some of the Zunis at least as Cushing's unwillingness to act effectively on their behalf. Despite the efforts of his journalistic friends and the important appeal he finally sent under his own name in late March to the new Pueblo agent in Santa Fe, in the absence of results renewed hostility and apparently even the danger of actual violence lay ahead.

FHC TO POWELL

Zuni, February 3, 1883

Sir:

I have the honor to inform you that after many delays and accidents I have returned to Zuni to resume my legitimate work.

I am now engaged in preparing for Mr. Victor Mindeleff my report on the Oraibi Expedition, including catalogues of the Oraibi collection and of the ancient series gathered at Mui-shon-na-vi [Mushongnovi], Shi-pau-la-vi, and Sitch-om-na-vi [Sichomovi] with such notes as I was able to get relative not only to these collections but also to the customs, institutions and mythology of the people from whom they were gathered.[4]

I find, somewhat to my disconcertion, that neither my expenses of travel from Washington to Zuni last Summer nor my pay account for November, December and January have been settled. I hope you will see that the matter is attended to at once, as I am at present entirely without means.

The paper on Sociology relative to which I received a note from Mr. Pilling will necessarily be longer delayed on account of my protracted absence at Moqui. I will, however, produce it for you as soon as possible.

Very Respectfully,
Your Obedient Servant,
F.H. Cushing

FHC TO BAIRD

Zuni, February 2nd, 1883

My dear Professor Baird:

Delay in replying to your letter of December the 16th, 1882, and to the enclosure from Lieutenant Wotherspoon, dated December 14th, 1882, has been occasioned by absence on a collecting tour among the Moqui Pueblos.

I much regret that Lieutenant Wotherspoon (who was my kind friend, my generous host and constant defender during a visit to Prescott in the interim of my Hava Supai trip [and] whose acquaintance I remember always with mingled feelings of gratitude and pleasure) should have been compelled to such opinion of me as the tone of his letter seems to indicate he now entertains.

The mule in question was neither lost nor injured during my trip. After my return to Zuni, it was required, in latter November 1881, by Lieut J.G. Bourke (now Captain) of General Crook's staff, for the use of his driver in the recovery of some stray ambulance mules. By this driver, a private of the 15th Infantry, it was lost at Las Nutrias during the search. Lieutenant Bourke, immediately, if I rightly remembered, secured an affidavit from the driver and with characteristic kindness, assured me that such steps as he would take would relieve not only me but all persons concerned in the matter from responsibility. Nevertheless, I promptly wrote Lieutenant Wotherspoon, and have during nearly a year and half vainly awaited reply, not only to this but also to other letters (I think two) of a more personal nature; as well as acknowledgement of certain little compliments in the form of curios sent him and his friends and designed to show, to some extent at least, my appreciation of their many kindnesses.

As you are well aware, I mentioned to you in my letters from Prescott my indebtedness to Lieutenant Wotherspoon and General Wilcox, and more generally to the other officers of the Headquarters of the Department of Arizona; nor have I since ceased—when I could do so unobtrusively—to do the same on all possible occasions.

It is my misfortune that my letters and messages did not, perhaps, carry regularly, although it is difficult for me to imagine why they should not have

done so, as I always invested them with proper and explicit official address.

Not long previously to my departure for the East, I received, notwithstanding all these precautions, and Lieutenant Bourke's assurances, from Colonel Benjamin, Adjutant General of the Department of Arizona, a letter relative to the mule; and to him I wrote *full* particulars of the case, enclosing the name and statement of the private who made the loss. To this letter, as well as to a personal note acknowledging his courtesy, I received no answer, but was assured by the General, when I chanced to meet him in Washington last summer, that the affair was or would be righted and that pressure of duties had detained him from giving due polite attention to my communication.

The letter from Asst Surgeon H.J. Raymond addressed to me through you, I have no knowledge of.

From all this you will see that my seeming forgetfulness both of courtesy and duty was rather the result of accident than of deliberate neglect—with added ignorance, perhaps, of what should have been that duty, which I now see more clearly.

You are well enough acquainted with me to know that I never neglect acknowledgement in terms of gratitude of all kindnesses either official or personal; and even now, I must repeat to you that through the good offices of Dr. Washington Matthews I came to know in the person of Lieutenant Wotherspoon a very kind friend who, even beyond the claims of mere courtesy, was especially obliging to me, both in my private character and in my official capacity. I cannot do more than I have done to convince him and you of these things. I make haste to do this, promising you that as soon as the snow on the mountains will admit of the journey, I will go over to Fort Wingate and get a new affidavit from the driver mentioned.[5] I will also address a letter, this day, to my good friend Captain Bourke, asking him to sustain these statements.

I have the honor to be, dear Professor, Very Respectfully,

Your Obedient Servant,
F.H. Cushing

Alexander Stephen to FHC

Keam's Cañon
February 2, 1883

Dear Cushing:

Vic Mindeleff was kind enough to make the above drawing of a bowl I got t'other day from a Navajo. It is of the class we have been calling *transition*—you remember we talked of such a class—between Ancient & Modern. But I am of opinion that this bowl is of Zuni manufacture.[6] Will you be good enough to make some comparisons & see whether you can find a bowl with same ornamentation? If so, has it any symbolic or other significance? Is this ornamental design of modern date? I got this piece from a young Moqui who knew nothing of its history—

but, curiously enough, he got it from his mother, who lives away in the north from here.

I sent your traps by the wagon which went in to Holbrook from here on 28th—put everything in a box addressed to you c/o Dr. Matthews—Everything—barring a stick full of little gods! These were wrapped in a handkerchief—and stuck in an envelope just under the dark corner of the shelf. I just discovered them today. I don't think you attach any great value to them. I mean I fancy you can have no immediate use for them, so I don't send them. I have them here safe. If you need 'em, send for them and I shall dispatch by next courier.

Atkins also brought me back a pair of saddle bags he found. Navajo brought me in your darned old one-eyed pony today—sent him out with our herd.

Any other of your fragmentary *relicts* that may turn up will be embalmed.

10 O'clock O'Night

Stewart has just returned with buckboard. Our brace of Toms has gone to Washington and the other settlements. Stewart tells me they got off from Holbrook on evening of 30th. In mail I find February *Scribners*—have just glanced over the Zuni article II.[7] Will you row with me if I quote Bierce?[8] But if I were reviewer I would say sharper things than he did. What the devil do you mean by marring such a tantalizing-crippled-delightful-botched first paragraph?

The essence of (confound you, I was going to say something flattering, but I won't)—but just look at it—you verge on poetry—and you grovel in the bag of the newspaper reporter—"the narrow terrace-bounded streets" (surely you did not fail to recognize that here was picturesqueness—poetry). And what follows! oh wo! listen to the reporter!—"Your foot slips on melon rinds &—Tosh; you have ruined a beautiful picture. I have only read that first paragraph—but I have looked at all the pictures. Say to Metcalf that though I think Farny's sketches are wonderfully clever, they do not carry the satisfaction, however, to this critic as does "Women Grinding Corn."[9] That surely is capital with a great big "C." Don't forget that chapter we talked of. Think it up.

Yours,
A.M. Stephen

DRAFT: FHC TO HENRY KING

Zuni, February 2, 1883

Sir:

My friend Mr. Sylvester Baxter of the Boston *Herald* kindly sends me slips cut from your paper. They relate to me and need no further comment—indeed scarcely excuse my addressing you; only I am led to infer from Mr. Baxter's letter that he left you with the impression I would write you.

I regret not nearly so much that such statements relative to my character should have appeared in your paper as that you should have made or sanctioned them, or have had me so represented to you by those who, willing enough to do me courtesy in my presence, are quite industriously harming me of late while absent.

You are said to be, however, an advocate of truth; as much, even, I would infer from your pages, which seem sincere statements of your convictions. You are further said to be just; and again I would infer as much from Mr. Baxter's statement that you are disposed to "honestly do me justice." He adds that you are "willing to give me the names of the persons upon whose testimony your statements relating to the dance incident and the Havasupai trip rest."

These names I would like to know, not that I wish to, nor will I, enter into any newspaper controversy. I would rather ultimately vindicate my character by the works which in good time I shall publish for a scientific rather than a popular class of readers, which shall contain neither personalities nor fine writing and, above all, shall be printed in my own exact words, instead of misapprehended, abbreviated, and even headed with titles neither of my authorship nor least approval.[10] My object is simply to be able to judge of the motives of those who have been your informants—motives inimical to me certainly, as their spirit is conceived and born in falsehood.

Finally, candidly, I would ask you, unless your interests require otherwise, to read the *last* of my *Atlantic,* as well as *Century,* articles before pronouncing on them all and on me inferentially. I think you will find that even under editorial limitations I have imparted some information besides mere personal nonsense—nonsense to me as well as to you, but ordered, bought and paid for, as, doubtless, is a good deal of material in your own periodical.

I am, Sir, with apologies for having so lengthily addressed you,

Very Respectfully and Sincerely Yours,
F.H. Cushing

Capt. Henry King
Ed., Topeka Capital
Topeka, Kansas

Matthews in the Topeka Capital

THE ZUNI DISPUTE. An Army Officer's Defense of Mr. Cushing. To the Editor of the *Topeka Capital*.

Fort Wingate, February 3. I have just read an editorial article entitled "Reality vs. Romance" in the *Capital* of January 18th, which reflects so severely on the integrity of a gentleman whom I have long known and learned to trust that I feel called on to say a few words in his defense, knowing you will have the fairness to give the public the opinion of his friends, as you have given them those of his enemies.

What the exact language of Col. Rizer's criticisms of Mr. Cushing may be I know not, as I have not read the Colonel's correspondence, but the editorial referred to tells us that he met and studied the pueblos under all circumstances and with superior facilities for ascertaining the truth about them. Now these "superior facilities" consisted in two brief visits to Zuni, during which his actual presence in the pueblo did not extend over a period of more than four days, and during this time there was no interpreter in the village except, perhaps, Mr. Cushing himself. How Col. Rizer could have made such an exhaustive study of this people "under all circumstances" in this time I for one cannot imagine.

We are further told, concerning the Zunis, that there is no particular concealment, "so far as he (Rizer) was able to ascertain," about any of the tribal rites or superstitious observations; anybody is privileged to see them who desires to. Upon what ground such a sweeping declaration is made I cannot conceive. Col. R. is undoubtedly correct when he says "indeed it is not uncommon for things of that kind to be improvised without regard to dates, solely for the entertainment of visitors," but he has no right to infer from this that all their ceremonies are public property. Anyone who reads Mr. Cushing's article in the *Century* will see that he distinctly states that the Zunis had many public performances at which he was not only permitted but even encouraged by the Indians to take notes and sketches.

But he also tells us that there were other observances where the Zunis tolerated his presence with great reluctance and when they were much incensed with him for using his pencil. Where is the contradiction in these statements? The truth at the bottom of the mater is that the Zunis have various ceremonies of widely different characters—some are for worship, others merely for pastime. No doubt there were Christians a generation ago, and perhaps there are such today, who would object to a reporter writing or an artist sketching during divine service, while the same persons would see no harm in anyone taking notes or drawing pictures in a theater or ballroom. . . .

It is furthermore intimated that the story told in "My Adventures in Zuni" concerning a threatening demonstration made by the Zunis during the performance of a dance is necessarily untrue because these Indians are such a peaceable set. I cannot see that Mr. Cushing endeavored to persuade us that they are either brave or bloodthirsty. He says they treated him kindly and suffered for a long time patiently his objectionable endeavors to sketch their dances. He tells us too that to this day he does not know what the real intentions of the Indians were on the occasion in question. Mr. Cushing was a stranger in the country then and knew comparatively little about these Indians. How could he be assured that their intentions were pacific? Even the crushed worm turns on its enemy, and the history of Indian warfare abounds in instances of quiet and apparently subdued tribes who, pretending friendship to the last moment, suddenly broke out into the most relentless massacres. How could he tell that he was not to be the first victim of such an outbreak? My own opinion is that the Indians only wanted to intimidate him, or try his mettle; but there was no reason why he should have thought so at the time, and I consider that his coolness under the circumstances was very praiseworthy. But no matter what the intentions of the Indians were, I am satisfied that Mr. Cushing relates the incidents of that day exactly as they happened. Long before "My Adventures in Zuni" was written and long before Mr. Cushing had reason to think that the *Century* or any other magazine would ever want an article of his, I have repeatedly heard him tell this story and always in exactly the same way. He once brought into Fort Wingate a book of his dance sketches to show to interested friends. Among the pictures was the portrait of an Indian with very remarkable features (whose face was painted white in the dance). While we were commenting on the portrait, Mr. Cushing told us that it was the picture of one of the men who had been appointed to kill him at the dance of the great knife. Sometime afterwards I met this Indian and asked him in Spanish (a language spoken to some extent by many of the Zunis) concerning these statements of Mr. Cushing and he replied that they were true. . . .

The charge of falsehood is also raised against Mr. Cushing's article "The Nation of the Willows," which appeared in the *Atlantic*. It is said: "It is susceptible of proof by eye-witnesses that the leading incident . . . is a pure invention." What the "leading incident" is, I cannot conjecture, as many of the incidents related seem of about equal importance, and I am not informed of the names of "the eye witnesses"; therefore I cannot make a specific contradiction; but I can say that I have every reason to believe that his account of the journey to the Havasupai is substantially true. He made the trip during an unusually dry season and his sufferings from thirst and fatigue are, I am convinced, not in the least overdrawn. I happened to be in Zuni when he was preparing to depart, and I attended a council in which he brought up the subject for the consideration of the wise men of the pueblo. I remember that they all advised him against his proposed undertaking and that at the time he could not find a single man who would consent to accompany him. There was not one in the place who did not fear to cross the desert at that season. Anyone who thinks that his description of the wonders of Cataract Canyon are incorrect need only read *Ives' Expedition.*[11]

The Smithsonian Institution does not "owe it to itself," we think, to dispense with the services of this man; on the contrary, it "owes it to itself" not to be biased by every attack made upon the character of its servants. . . . I regret to say that Mr. Cushing has made many enemies in this country, not because there is anything in his amiable character which should engender hatred in the bosom of another, but because the champion of the oppressed is never in favor with the oppressors, and because there is nothing in the world more intolerant than self-satisfied ignorance.

W.M.

DRAFT: FHC TO SHERIFF THOMAS PEREZ

Zuni, February 14, 1883

[*The following responds to a letter from Perez announcing the capture, near the town of St. Johns, Arizona, of a pair of horse thieves and a band of Zuni horses they had stolen. "Have retained 6 horses of Zunis to satisfy costs in the sum of $99.00," Perez had written. "Horses must be sold unless costs are paid. Have no jurisdiction of case, hence must release prisoners or turn them over to you in N.M."*][12]

Sir:

I have your favor of the 13th inst., and have the honor to say that I shall try to come as you direct. I am, however, convalescent from a severe attack of influenza, which, in addition to weakness resulting from my kicked leg, has, during several days, confined me to my room and bed.

Although now considerably better, I am uncertain whether I can make the journey or not. I have ordered a team and shall start today. If powerless to reach your place, I shall either turn back or stop at Ojo Benado with my friend Mr. Daniel Dubois.

Your charges for legal proceedings of $99.00 (ninety-nine dollars) are not extravagant; but certainly should, I think, be covered by fewer than six horses. . . .

Regarding the prisoners, I would respectfully ask that in case I be unable to appear before you in person (which is probable), you turn them over to Mr. Daniel Dubois, at Ojo Benado, for delivery either to me or, in case of my absence from that place, to the Indians for delivery in turn to me. I would also particularly recommend that the Indians be instructed to do them no harm or violence *in transitu.* I will then see that they are turned over to the civil authorities at Fort Wingate, to await action by the latter or the decision of Dr. Thomas.

I am clearly aware that it is my duty to present myself at Saint Johns, but fear my illness may be as positive a hindrance as it is just now an inexorable evil. In the name of common justice, or the jeopardized interests of the Zunis, and of personal feeling, I am, honored señor, very respectfully and gratefully,

Your Obedient Serv't,
F.H. Cushing
1st War Chief of Zuni

Thomas Perez
Sheriff of Apache County
St. Johns, A.T.

Draft: FHC to Dr. B. M. Thomas

Zuni, February 15, 1883

[*Following up his letter to Sheriff Perez, Cushing wrote to the Pueblo agent, apprising him of the situation and the difficulties posed.*][13]

. . . .

Although unable to leave as I had intended yesterday, I am sure I shall be strong enough today to make at least part of the journey. I have secured a courier who leaves at once with this; and on my return will dispatch another with such information as I am able to obtain. Of course I shall secure the prisoners, and as humanely as possible take them to Wingate for incarceration by the Civil authorities, or in the absence of the latter, by the Military; there to await your directions relative to their disposition. I am luckily at present still the War Chief of the Zunis, which fact may insure the safety of the prisoners in my hands. But you know about how far a chief's authority extends with the Pueblos—Zunis in particular—and I cannot be certain what the result will be, as the Indians are not only greatly excited, but the ranchmen of this country are also by no means well disposed toward the culprits, since they are said by the ranchmen to be leading members of a band of horse thieves who have been operating in the region for 2 years. I thus inform you, in order that—should violence be done the prisoners while in my hands—you and others hold me innocent of such intentions from the beginning.

I have the honor to be, sir, very respectfully,

Your Ob't Servant,
F.H. Cushing
Ass't Eth.

Dr. B.M. Thomas
U.S. Indian Agent
Pueblo Indian Agency
Santa Fe, New Mexico

P.S. Mr. Willson's serious illness has detained him from taking any action in the matter, and will explain mine.

Henry King to FHC

The Capital
Topeka, Kansas, Feb. 16, 1883

Dear Sir:

In answer to your favor, permit me to say that I am in hearty sympathy with your work and disposed to forward rather than embarrass it, while personally I could of course have no wish to do you harm. My strictures were based upon what in the nature of things seemed to be good testimony; but had I known as much then as I have since learned about the subterranean contentions in your own camp, so to speak, I should have let the matter severely alone; and I am quite sure my friend Col. Rizer, who is a thorough gentleman and not at all inimical to you, would have done the same.

The names you ask for were given to me in confidence, but common fairness to myself as well as to you entitles you to them, I think. They are Prof. Stephenson [sic], Graham, the Zuni Storekeeper, and T.V. Keam of Holbrook, Arizona Ter.[14]

With sincere regret for any trouble I may have caused you, I am

Yours very respectfully,
Henry King

Baxter to FHC

Boston
February 19, 1883

My dear Tenatsali:

This morning's mail brought me three things of interest concerning you: a note from Prof. Baird saying he would "take great pleasure in informing Gen. Logan that Mr. Cushing has had nothing whatever to do with the article to which he took exception"; also a most cordial letter from your friend J. Stanley Brown, which I would enclose for you were it not marked "confidential," but I will quote: "I think you need give yourself no concern about any harm that may come to Cushing through Senator Logan. The blow would have to be struck through the Bureau of Ethnology and I should certainly know in advance before the stroke fell. I think the enemies of Frank have played their last trump while the 'faithful' still have a few in hand. You can rely upon my keeping my eyes open here and doing all I can to thwart any project looking to the defeat of Frank's prosperity. Major Powell told me a few days ago that he proposed to stand by Cushing. I have seen no demonstration from the threatening quarters." The third was sent me by Mr. White of the A.T. & S.F. in the shape of Dr. Matthews' noble vindication of yourself in the Topeka *Capital*. Mr. White was very indignant at the original attack & it was at his suggestion that I brought it to Dr. Matthews' attention. My dear boy, you have many true friends—more than you estimate. Trust them. Keep on your work and do not let slanders of the ignorant and malicious affect your scientific composure or trouble your mind. But be careful what you say and especially put on paper in criticism of others. It might be misused, if not misinterpreted. I have no fear for your future. Do not be blue, except as the sky, which is full of sunshine. That is the color and the mood of

your faithful friend,
Thli-a-kwa[15]

FHC TO BAIRD

Zuni, N.M., Feb. 20th, 1883

Dear Professor Baird:—

Your considerate, yet justly plain letter of January 29th, was received late yesterday, and I make haste to reply.

Of course, I sent acknowledgement and such explanations as I had to make immediately on receipt of your Wotherspoon enclosure, but permit me to repeat that through the carelessness of the Wingate Post Master, many of my letters were forwarded, during my absence in Moqui, not to the latter place but to Zuni. It was, indeed, by the merest accident that your communication relative to General Logan reached me any sooner than the other and antecedent one.

It is at present utterly impossible for me to do more than write, as I cannot get over to Fort Wingate until the snow is melted away from the mountains and a recent attack of lung trouble—from which I am even yet suffering—has passed over.

I have written you fully, not only in relation to the Lieutenant's matter but also relative to the Logan scandal and to my indebtedness to the Institution. To none of these writings have I received replies. It cannot be possible that they have missed you and thus thrown me into a false position, can it?

I sincerely hope not; but if so, I fortunately possess copies of all, and will copy and forward them, should my fears prove true.

I have the honor to be, Very Respectfully,

Your Obedient Servant
F.H. Cushing

MATTHEWS TO FHC

Fort Wingate, New Mex., Feb. 28, 1883

My dear Friend:

I got your letter some time ago, but from what your brother said, I thought you might come into Wingate almost any day, so I did not write. Don't be afraid. I haven't "gone back" on you.

Now I would like you to do me a little favor in a Scientific way. The bearer of this, Sergeant Barthelmess of the Band, goes to Zuni to take some negatives. I would like you to give him what assistance you can in taking two pictures for me, to illustrate my forthcoming article on Navajo weaving. I want a picture of a Zuni woman weaving a *belt,* the picture to show distinctly the arrangement of the wooden healds and the attachments of the warp at both ends (to *rafter* and to *woman*). I want this to illustrate the marked and interesting difference between the Navajo and Pueblo methods of accomplishing the very same results. I want also a picture of a loom used for diagonal or diamond weaving with the diagonal web on it. I do not necessarily want the whole loom taken in if Barthelmess's lens is too small. A small piece of the contrivance will do. I want *merely* to show the peculiar arrangement of the *multiple* sets of healds and rods, in which the loom for diagonal goods differs from the loom for simple goods (*Sabe Ud.?*). . . .[16]

I hope you got the Topeka *Capital* with my letter in it. Also the copy of the *Nation* where Mrs. Cushing and yourself were so favorably mentioned.[17]

Please come in soon. I have very much to say to you, both on business and science. I have got the Navajo Creation Myth at last. Am writing with a vilely stiff pen. Kind regards to Mrs. Cushing and all the rest of the family.

Your true friend,
W. Matthews

ADOLPH BANDELIER TO MRS. LEWIS HENRY MORGAN

[*Adolph Bandelier arrived in Zuni on the evening of February 21, after an all-day trek from the railroad stop at Navajo Springs, Arizona. As recorded in his diary, he arrived just in time to witness a dramatic episode in the still-continuing story of Cushing's (and the Zuni governor's) battle with the Zuni Mormon, Roman Luna. Accused by Luna of not doing his duty as war chief, Cushing had apparently resigned, and on the afternoon of February 22 a council of the pueblo at large was held in the big plaza. "Mr. Cushing's opponent, a thick, heavy-set man, with a Navajo headdress and a very wicked face showing clearly mixed breed {Luna, according to Bandelier, being half Navajo}, spoke long and with great vehemence. He has been head-chief in former times but they had to remove him. His elocution was great, and his manner forcible, passionate, pompous. He is a very impressive speaker. Cushing also spoke, but only very calmly." According to Bandelier's account, a canvass was later taken of those present, the result of which was "one against Mr. Cushing, 2 neutral, and the rest for him," whereupon he was begged "to withdraw his resignation and accept his situation as war chief again. . . . The fact that Mr. Cushing had all the old men on his side determined the result."*[18]

During the ensuing two weeks, Bandelier sat in on more council meetings, witnessed dances, inspected local ruins (including those on Dowa Yalanne Mesa), made paintings and drawings of what he saw, and had long talks with Cushing. On March 7, he and Cushing set out for Fort Wingate, driving behind a pair of mules so "cussed, mulish and stubborn" that Bandelier fell overboard from the wagon and was run over by it. Badly bruised, he stopped over in Nutria, while Cushing rode on to Wingate. The next day, Cushing sent his friend Metcalf back to Nutria with "a big 4 mule train loaded with choice provisions {including} beer and segars, also whiskey." Having gone "30 hours without a morsel," Bandelier "passed a most cheerful evening." He was then taken to the post hospital at Wingate, where Cushing and Metcalf remained with him for a week before returning to Zuni and leaving him to continue his travels. Here he reports to Mrs. Morgan on his stay with Cushing.][19]

Fort Wingate, N.M.
18 March 1883

. . . . At Bennett's Station [Navajo Springs] no horse could be obtained, so I walked over to Zuni (30 miles), where Mr. Cushing & his people received me with open arms. I spent 15 days in the most pleasant and most profitable manner imaginable. Cushing has with the utmost candor and frankness set before me all his material and given me every opportunity to judge for myself. My opinion of him is that he is the direct successor to Mr. Morgan in the study of Indian life, & that he has finally revealed the last secrets of their organization. His discoveries are marvelous and, what is stranger still, they are perfectly within the scope of our views. His secret societies, which form the basis of their worship and medicine, can exist (and I have convinced him of it) only with gentile society. Under any other form of government than the Indian democracy they would be impossible or else dangerous. These societies now embody all the inner life of the tribe, and they are only secret in as far as their ritual and ceremonies go, and this ritual, etc., reveals the creed, belief, the traditions, and the empirical knowledge of the people. . . . As far as Zuni is concerned and everything connected with it, Mr. Cushing is the source of information. We must be proud of this remarkable young man; he deserves our pride, our sincere attachment and support. How much our dear deceased one would have enjoyed to see his labours! I have become very intimate with Cushing, & he has often spoken to me of Mr. Morgan and of yourself.

Spontaneously, he mentioned the claim advanced by him to the discovery of two clans among the Iroquois and excused himself stating that it was done through ignorance.[20] He has few books to consult and therefore is not always "posted." I go out of New Mexico with a much lighter heart than I ever could hope, not only because I have secured so much information, but principally because I leave Cushing and his friend Dr. Washington Matthews behind, in whose hands the work to be done is better cared for than it would be in mine. . . .

BANDELIER TO FHC

Fort Wingate, 22 March 1883

My very dear friend Cushing!

A thousand thanks. I was here, waiting and waiting, using Christian terminology once [in] a while. Thanks again. It is as well as it is, after all, for the responsibilities in case of an accident on the trip would have been fearful.[21] Still, permit me to say that I do not give up the ship, for the simple reason that, after all I have learned since, the trip to Rito Quemado is, not an utter impossibility, but a barren fruitless affair. . . . I must therefore take the Zuni route again, in order to reach the South. Now this means in the first place, not another stay at your home, but only a day, in order to secure a companion as far as Camp Apache, and thus far I think Roman would go; perhaps a little further even! "*Puedo que si, puedo que no, quien sabe.*" Please therefore to keep the boy in sight without urging him, and wait for my arrival, which will be a week hence. I shall go tomorrow to Laguna, saddle up my horse and ride back to Fort Wingate, whence I expect to reach Zuni with all my traps. Gen. Bradley will manage the latter. His kindness to me is unbounded.

Let me arrive at Zuni like a bombshell, unexpected, and then go to work to find a companion. I don't say that I will succeed with Roman, but at all events I am very obstinate and have ended more than one long siege by a sudden dash. Therefore use your own discretion about it, and if the boy can be *confidentially* told of my coming, then tell him. If not, keep "mum" about it. I am reduced to this extremity by the fact that I have been unsuccessful in getting a Navajo who, as late as last night, had promised to go with me to Chihuahua if I could not get a Zuni. Neither at Acoma nor at Laguna could I obtain anyone farther than Zuni; the Rito Quemado is now out of the question, so I am compelled to knock at your door again, for go through I shall, God helping. I want to "fight it out" in the Arizona line; the more I hear of it, the more eager I become. If, then, Roman is utterly inaccessible, another one, who is footloose, may perhaps be secured. If everything fails, I will go alone, buying a burro at Zuni and leading it myself.

I am exceedingly sorry to fall upon you again in this manner, but I can't help myself. I hope Mrs. Cushing, to whom I have the honor of including a note, "con su permiso a Ud.," will not think too hard of this second intrusion.

Best regards to all.

Yours very affectionately,
Ad. F. Bandelier

[*Bandelier returned to Zuni on March 31 and stayed several days, in hopes that he could lure "Roman" into his service. Apparently failing in this endeavor, he left on April 5, accompanied at least as far as Hawikku and Ojo Venado by another boy (unnamed) and carrying with him the following letter of introduction to Dan Dubois, whose ranch would have been a stopping place en route. From there he proceeded on a four-month-long excursion through the deserts of southern Arizona surveying ruins.*]

FHC TO DUBOIS[22]

Dear Friend Dan:

I give this to the care of a jolly good friend of mine, a man of the highest cultivation, a student of the same branch of science which I am following, and at the same time far more profound and celebrated in it than I am.

His name, though celebrated—*Adolphus F. Bandelier*—you may not be acquainted with. Of course by reading it you will recognize a countryman, and one who can converse with you either in French, Spanish, or English. He is on his way to Chihuahua and the city of Mexico, but he will take time during his journey to examine all ancient ruins of interest he comes across. With this in view, I take the liberty of introducing him to you, with the hope that you or Joaquin may possibly show him some in your neighborhood. Kindly direct him on his way; and any other courtesy you may show him will be most highly appreciated by

Yours faithfully,
F.H. Cushing

Kindly present and take my regards and Mrs. Cushing's to your family and yourself. We send you a few newspapers.

Draft: FHC to J.H. Willson

Zuni, New Mexico
March 24, 1883

Sir:

I take pleasure in promptly furnishing you such information on the points touched upon in Dr. Thomas's letter as I am, without further investigation, able to give.

The most desirable location for the dam in question is at the passage of the Zuni stream ("river") through the wall of *Malpais* that bounds the valley five miles east and a little north of the Pueblo of Zuni.[23] This passage is narrow, very deep, and bounded on either side by *malpais* or lava rock. Rocks serviceable for the construction of a dam, also of *malpais,* may be found loose on or near the spot. Probably a dry dam would answer the purpose, although the pressure of water against it would, after a season, be very great. An engineer would positively be required to determine the proper height of the dam, and to run lines for the principal canal, which should pass along the northern edge of the valley, would need to be about nine miles in length—for the fullest practicable realization of benefit—and would pass no serious obstructions other than five or six arroyos, only three of which are of considerable depth. The Indians could dig only portions of this main canal, although the minor *acequias* they could of course easily manage. Sawed timbers would be required only in the construction of the water gate and perhaps in that of the passages of some or all of the arroyos. Other timbers, procurable in this region, would probably answer additional purposes.

By means of such a dam as the one thus described a large and nearly useless tract above the Black rocks, would be converted into a lake of considerable depth, fed constantly by eleven springs, and semi-annually by the waters from the Nutria region of the Zuni Mountains.

The practical benefits resulting from such a lake would be enormous and principally two-fold: first,

Nearly the whole of the immediate fertile valley of Zuni, both above and below the Pueblo, could be irrigated from it after the first or second year, thus rendering the cultivation of corn more secure and productive and of wheat, etc., possible.

Second, my Director, the Commissioner of Fish and Fisheries, has kindly promised assistance in the event of the building of such a dam, in stocking the lake with the vegetable eating German carp, and other food fishes, which, by recent experiment have been found to thrive in New Mexico and Arizona waters, thus furnishing an additional food resource and salable product to the Indians. The Mission and school buildings, as well as private farming places of the Zunis, could also be supplied with water by this means.

Permit me to suggest that Mr. Graham, who is expected daily to return from the East, be employed as the engineer; since in our frequent conversations and prospectings, he has manifested thorough conversance with and interest in the matter, is a most competent engineer, and is more readily accessible than others would be, in consequence of his residence in this place.

I have the Honor to be,

Very Respectfully Yours,
F H Cushing
Ass't Ethnologist

J.H. Wilson [sic]
U.S. Indian Teacher
Zuni, New Mexico

Draft: FHC to Dr. B. M. Thomas

Zuni, March 26, 1883

Dear Doctor Thomas:

Your acknowledgement of my letter and enclosures relative to the horse-thieves came by last mail, and I learn definitely by it of your rumored resignation. I had in view of this fact commenced a letter introducing myself to your successor, and addressing him on a matter of the utmost importance. I enclose the letter, which you may read if you choose, and which I wish you would hand to him, with such recommendations as your knowledge of me and of its contents may suggest or warrant.

I would appeal most strongly both to you and Colonel Chaves on this point, of vital importance to a hard-headed yet really deserving people.

Hoping that your departure for Tucson may not entirely sever our correspondence, or preclude the possibility of our occasionally meeting, I remain, very respectfully,

Yours Truly,
F.H. Cushing

Dr. Ben M. Thomas, U.S. Indian Agent
Pueblo Indian Agency
Santa Fe, New Mexico

DRAFTS: FHC TO COL. CHAVES[24]

Zuni, New Mexico
March 24 and 25, 1883

My dear sir:

Pardon me, please, for taking the liberty—a stranger—of addressing you, but as the matter relative to which I write you is more of a public than of a personal nature, and as I am perhaps to some extent to be regarded as one of your subjects, this license may not, I hope, meet with your disapproval.

You may be aware that during the past three years I have been connected with the Zuni Pueblo Indians, in the capacity first of an agent of the Smithsonian Institution and National Museum at Washington and later as Asst. Ethnologist of the Bureau of Ethnology, a branch of the same Institution and of the Department of the Interior. The purposes of my stay among these Indians have been to secure as much knowledge of their traditional history, mythology, sociologic organization, manners and customs (religious and secular), linguistics, arts, and industries as possible, not only as data for the reconstruction of the Spanish and aboriginal history of these parts but also as material for the better understanding of the Indian question, which the Government now deems of enough importance to require quite wide and special investigation. . . .

From this brief introduction you may infer that my desire is for their best advancement and for the protection, as far as they are deserving and as is possible, of their rights and interests; and this introduces us to the subject relative to which I write you:

I recently learn that for some time attempts have been pending for the removal of the Zunis from their principal farming pueblo of *Las Nutrias,* the land having been, it is said, purchased or applied for by certain Americans for the purpose of making of it a cattle ranch. The claim is now raised by these and other indirectly interested parties that the pueblos of *Las Nutrias* and *Ojo del Pescado* are "*at least six miles east of the Zuni Reservation limits.*"

The Executive Order of March 16th, 1877, bearing the signature of President R.B. Hayes [and relative to the Zuni Pueblo Reserve, reads: "It is hereby ordered that the following described tract of country in the Territory of New Mexico, viz: Beginning at the one hundred and thirty-sixth milestone on the western boundary line of the Territory of New Mexico, and running thence 61°45′ east 31 miles and eight tenths of a mile to the crest of the mountain a short distance above Las Nutrias Springs; thence due south twelve miles to a point in the hills a short distance southeast of the Ojo Pescado; thence south 61°45′ west to the one hundred and forty-eighth milestone on the western boundary line of said territory; thence north with said boundary line to the place of beginning, be, and the same hereby is, withdrawn from sale and set apart as a reservation for the use and occupancy of the Zuni Pueblo Indians."]

According to this, Nutria itself and Pescado, which are both below the springs designated, must be within Reservation limits. [Unfortunately, Dr. Thomas' efforts to get the desired tract of country surveyed have heretofore met with determined resistance, and people have decided to interpret the above-quoted lines according to their interests—consequently against those of the Indians. As I understand also, when Dr. Thomas requested the withdrawal of the Zuni Reservation from sale, he specifically worded his description in such a way that in all events the only three valuable possessions of the Zunis should be included in the boundary limits.

On the other hand, the Spanish conquistadores and Dominican monks of the Franciscan Order [sic] found the Indians, as early as 1560, in possession and occupation of *Las Nutrias, Ojo del Pescado,* and *Ojo Caliente,* which was then named and is often mentioned in their chronicles as Aguico (*Ha-wi-kuh* of the modern Zuni). Evidence attainable through a study of Zuni tradition, but of course not sufficient for use in legal contestation, exists that subsequently to the Pueblo rebellion of 1682 [sic], *Mercedes,* or grants of land were given for at least six of the then occupied pueblos of the Zunis.[25] I am hoping, during the summer, to be made the recipient, through friends in Mexico, of evidences of another and less easily disputable nature. Yet furthermore, it is now claimed that according to the Treaty of Guadaloupe all sedentary Indians of New Mexico to whom grants had been given are entitled to the rights of citizenship—on which grounds no disputation of their rights to the occupation of all their present farming and grazing lands under the "Homestead Act" can be adduced.[26]

Hoping that this matter shall claim your earliest and earnest consideration, and] [final salutation missing]

Colonel Chaves, U.S. Indian Agent
Pueblo Indian Agency
Santa Fe, New Mexico

FHC to Powell

Zuni, March 27, 1883

Dear Major Powell:

I am now engaged mostly on researches into the Zuni esoteric societies. Just how much of them is strictly aboriginal is of course difficult to ascertain. I wish to get at their primitive organizations and functions so far as possible before using them in their bearing on the paper which I am now trying to prepare for you. With the modern societies, there are, in each, offices (exerting more or less influence on the government) of priests, of various ranks, etc. Each priest according to his functions makes sacrifices of plumed prayer sticks peculiar to himself. In the caves and craters to the Southwest are well preserved sacrificial deposits antedating the earliest Spanish *conquistadores*. By an examination of these deposits and a careful comparison of their plumed contents with those of modern sacrificial deposits, I hope to be able to ascertain not only how many of the modern priestly offices existed originally but also much concerning the primitive populations of the region of the caves and craters.[27] Having made partial investigations of the kind already, I am convinced of their importance and even necessity to the completeness of my forthcoming paper.

Last autumn, Colonel Stevenson borrowed my rope ladder—which had been a year before sent me by him through Professor Baird—for use in exploring some of the Cochiti cliff villages. He promised to return it within two or three months.

I now write, as the time is passed, asking that you give him authority to send it back to me as immediately as possible. I shall positively require it in entering some of the deeper and more important of the caves and craters. I have also written Colonel Stevenson.

I have the honor to be, very respectfully,

Your Obedient Servant,
F.H. Cushing

General L.P. Bradley to FHC

Fort Wingate, March 28, 1883

Dear Sir:

Your letter of the 26th received. I am much obliged to you for talking to the Zuni chiefs and head men about grazing their sheep in the country north and east of Nutria and east of Pescado Springs. If I hear of them driving sheep into this country, I will send you word. The lands in the localities mentioned are now private property, at least the lands having water on them, and the Indians must keep off, whether they like or no.[28] Bandelier is now here and will take your freight to Zuni.

Yours truly,
L.P. Bradley

Baxter to FHC

Boston, March 30, 1883

My dear Tenatsali:

Prof. Horsford has just sent me a letter written by Mr. Bandelier to Mrs. Morgan, full of the most enthusiastic praise of yourself and written from a warm true heart. . . . [Baxter proceeds to quote from Bandelier's letter of March 18, 1883.]

My dear boy, look up! You have every reason to feel encouraged. All through the world you are gaining true friends in the very places you need them. If you could hear the warm praise of you that I so often hear, you would not be despondent. The more I live, the more occasion I have to see the noble disinterestedness of so many people the world over. There is, to be sure, enough base metal extant, but the pure gold of human nature outweighs it.

How about the *Century* paper No. III? Have you finished it yet?

Your faithful friend,
Sylvester Baxter

W.F. WHITE TO FHC

Atcheson, Topeka, & Santa Fe Railroad Co.
Topeka, Kansas
April 15, 1883

F.H. Cushing, Esq.
Zuni, Arizona Ty.
My dear Cushing:

I want to introduce the bearer, Mr. W.E. Curtis, Managing Editor of the *Chicago Inter-Ocean,* who will, in turn, introduce you to the ladies, and other gentlemen, in his party.

They all desire to become members of the Zuni Tribe, and, not being acquainted with any others, I am forced to call upon you to have them initiated.

Please put them through in good shape, and draw upon me for the amount of their initiation fees.

Yours very truly,
W.F. White
G. P. & T. A.

[The above note hardly requires comment as an example of popular conceptions in Cushing's time. The same sort of bluff, good natured, and entirely ethnocentric mentality that is evident in the note is also noticeable in the account of this visit Curtis later wrote in his book about Cushing and the Zunis: Children of the Sun *(Chicago: Inter-Ocean Publishing Co., 1883), some brief excerpts of which follow. How Curtis and his party were "put through" is not explained, but the visit was plainly a success. Curtis became one of the Zunis'—and Cushing's—most outspoken champions in their battle against that other Illinoisian, Senator Logan.*[29] *The passages quoted here were mainly selected for the glimpses they afford of the Cushing entourage in Zuni—and particularly of* Mrs. *Cushing—through the eyes of this guest.]*

WILLIAM E. CURTIS ON "MR. AND MRS. CUSHING AT HOME"

We were stretched around upon the soft sheepskins, listening with absorbed interest to the recital of Mr. Cushing's peculiar adventures, when the Governor, Pa-lo-wah-ti-wa, came in. By the brilliant light that came from the blazing branches of the piñon tree which flamed in the rude but picturesque corner fireplace, we could see a tall, gaunt man, with large, dark eyes, a sharp nose and a melancholy mouth—an Indian counterpart in countenance with Edwin Booth.[30]

"Here is the old Governor come to call upon you," said Mr. Cushing, and we arose and were introduced to him as "men who make meaning marks—friends of mine from Chicago". . . .

With Mr. Cushing as interpreter, we talked with him, and he expressed the admiration he felt for the greatness of Chicago. It was the first large city he saw on his Eastern trip, in the summer of 1882, and his recollections were amusing and interesting. . . . He was glad to see us as the friends of his brother, "Te-nah-tsa-li"—"Medicine Flower," as the Zunis have named Cushing, and, in his Oriental way, wished our visit "might be blessed with a multitude of pleasures". . . .

Pretty soon there was a timid rap at the door—a custom Mrs. Cushing has introduced. The Zunis enter the houses of each other without ceremony, at all times of day and night, not even asking as much as by your leave—but Mrs. Cushing has forbidden them to intrude into her apartments without permission, and since she has made frightful examples of some of them, they have adopted the civilized mode of knocking at the door and awaiting a welcome.

When Cushing cried out in Zuni "come in," the door slowly opened, and there appeared a fat little woman who stepped to the table and emptied from her blanket a large quantity of parched corn, explaining that she had prepared it for the friends of "Cushy-Cushy," as the scientist is more familiarly known. She intimated that some compensation would be acceptable, and was rewarded by the ladies of the party who offered her a few pieces of candy they had brought with them. To this Mrs. Cushing objected, as the knowledge that sweetmeats were in our possession would bring the whole community to the door; but the woman got her reward with an emphatic injunction that there was no more to be had. . . .

When [Cushing] first arrived at Zuni the Indians tried to drive him away. Now they are absurdly jealous in their regard for him, and observe the attentions he receives from visitors there with mingled gratification and dislike. They are particularly anxious for him to remain with them during his entire life; and in all cases of difficulty, the threat that he will go back to "the Land of Day" brings them to terms. . . .

Mrs. Cushing does not enjoy life in Zuni as her husband does. She does not and cannot share his fascination for the work in which he is engaged. She hates the uncouth women and the naked children, and despises their filthy ways, but she has made her mud hut a pretty little paradise and has developed the possibilities of comfort even in Zuni. . . .

She has a sister, Miss Magill, with her, who likes the Zunis better than Mrs. Cushing, and is talking of adopting their peculiar dress and joining the tribe.

"I would do it," said Miss Magill; "it would be so funny and romantic, but I don't like to cut my hair."

The family have a colored man for cook and "maid of all work"; and while their diet is confined to the slender resources of the Indian garden and the provisions of the commissary store at Fort Wingate, all who have visited them can testify to the hospitality, the wholesomeness, and the enjoyment of their table.

W.E. Curtis: Newspaper Story

[Tracked down from leads pursued in Santa Fe, Fort Wingate, and Zuni itself, this was the story the prospects of which must have been mainly responsible for Curtis' trip to the Southwest. As the headlines indicate, it is a thorough report of developments to the date of filing. The excerpts following, however, are confined to passages referring directly to Cushing.]

GENERAL LOGAN'S RANCH: A Charge That He Has Despoiled the Zuni Indians of Their Lands. His Son-in-Law and Friends Locate Upon the Indian Farms and Springs. Excitement and Anxiety Among the Indians. Logan's Attacks Upon Frank Cushing. A Mistake in the Description of the Reservation Gives Tucker and Company a Chance.
Santa Fe, N.M., April 21, 1883—

. . . .

The Indians became alarmed at the rumors of encroachment upon their reservation and pleaded with Mr. Cushing, with the officers at Fort Wingate, and with Mr. Graham, the trader who buys the limited supply of wool and cattle and produce they have for sale each year to protect them in the possession of their lands. These gentlemen were of course powerless to do anything and could only apply to the authorities of the Land Office in Santa Fe and to the Indian Agent there for information and relief. . . .

Mr. Cushing, who has become a member of the Zuni tribe, and naturally feels a lively interest in their welfare, immediately entered a vigorous protest, and was at once denounced as an imposter by the senior Senator from Illinois. The immediate adherents of General Logan at Washington and the military-official circle of which Major Tucker [Logan's son-in-law and one of the claimants to the Zuni lands] and Captain Lawton are members at Santa Fe began at once to echo the verdict of the distinguished Senator, and Mr. Cushing was flatly declared to be a fraud, his articles in the *Century Magazine* were declared to be groundless fiction, and the ceremonious journey of the Zunis to Boston last summer a deception and an imposition upon the public. . . .

The object of Mr. Cushing's work among the Zuni Indians was detected to be a morbid desire for notoriety, and that fact that he had been an office boy at the Smithsonian Institution several years ago, originally employed to dust the shelves and keep the specimens in order, was offered as evidence of his utter ignorance of the science of ethnology. The work did not stop here. An attempt was made to convince the officers of the Smithsonian Institution that Cushing was no better than he ought to be; rough stories were told of his debauchery and immorality, and it was asserted that his desire to live among the Zunis found its origin in a depraved and wicked lust.

It was a cruel and relentless war against a young man who could not know of the attacks that were being made upon him and had no means of making a defense of his private character or his professional reputation. . . .

The evidence advanced to show that he is an imposter and a writer of falsehoods in the name of science was based upon the investigation made by General Logan's party at Zuni during a two hours' visit during Mr. Cushing's absence. The General's friends relate with sober faces the fact that he asked an old Zuni if it was not true that Cushing was a fraud, and the Indian nodded his head in assent. The distinguished soldier and Senator then asked him if Cushing was not a worthless and wicked man, and if all the stories he had written about Zuni were not lies, and again the Indian nodded acquiescence. Somebody else asked why one old priest did not go to Boston with the other members of his tribe and help fill their sacred vessels with the water from the ocean, and he told them that the ceremony was all poppy-cock and he would have nothing to do with it, or words to that effect; and this convincing conversation was carried on with no interpreter but a lady who had visited Zuni but once before and understood little if any of their language, which it has required Cushing two years of constant study to master.[31]

And if any further evidence of Cushing's utter unreliability and worthlessness was needed, the people were invited to look at the blisters on his nose. [The article goes on to defend Cushing from the venereal insinuation by explaining the eruptions on his face as the result of the highly seasoned Zuni diet on which he had been obliged to live for several years.]

Is Cushing genuine? We asked everybody we saw around Wingate that question, and there was not one who had other than kind words for him and strong expressions of faith in the fidelity and accuracy of his work. . . .

Some of those with whom we talked do not, of course, enter into the spirit of Cushing's work nor appreciate its value. Some of them called him a crank and a fool, as they would consider anyone who would waste the best years of his life and suffer hardships and privations for the cause of science. Others thought he was an enthusiast who saw in the Indian legends and traditions more poetry and romance than sober, practical utility; but they all vouched for his genuineness. . . .

Chicago *Inter-Ocean,* 2 May 1883.

AGENT THOMAS TO U.S. INDIAN SERVICE COMMISSIONER

Santa Fe, New Mexico
April 12, [1883]

The Hon. H. Price, Commissioner
Washington, D.C.
Sir:

I have the honor to acknowledge the receipt of your letter of April 5 marked "L, 3,606, 1883," enclosing letters of the honorable Secretary of the Interior and Commission of the General Land Office in regard to entries recently made on the Zuni Reservation. The action taken, as shown by the enclosures, does not reach the real difficulty by any means. The difficulty lies in the manner of regarding the reservation, as shown on the maps, resulting in the contradiction of terms in the description of the boundaries of the reservation. "Beginning at the one hundred and thirty-sixth milestone on the western boundary line of the Territory of New Mexico and running thence north 61 deg., 45 min. east . . ." does not run that line (the northern) of the reservation "to the crest of the mountain, a short distance above Nutrias Spring," but leaves out that spring and the Nutrias farms which the Indians have cultivated from time immemorial and which are necessary to their support. The intention of the reservation was to secure to the Zunis three principal farming districts where they raise the means of subsistence, viz: Nutrias, Pescado and Ojo Caliente; but in making the original description of the boundaries I was misled by the surveyor who had surveyed the Territorial boundary line and who was with me at the time I located the reservation. He assured me that the angle "North 61 degrees 45 degrees East" would run the line so as to take in Nutrias; but it seems that it does not. The outrage of taking Nutrias from the Zunis *must not be consummated.* The thing to do is to follow the apparent intent of the description and run the north line to the crest of the mountain above Nutrias, regardless of the angle given, and then run the eastern line far enough south to take in Pescado Spring, which is still more important to the Indians than Nutria. I trust that you will secure an order to be issued to the Surveyor General of New Mexico to so lay off the reservation. The persons who have taken the preliminary steps to secure the land at Nutrias are mostly army officers, I understand, and one of them assured me today that if the land was subject to entry by any one they wanted it; but if it belonged to the Indians, and they (the Indians) were to have it, they would not press their claims as against the Indians, provided the money already paid were refunded to them, and their act would not exhaust their right to enter land.

Very respectfully, your obedient servant,
Ben M. Thomas
United States Indian Agent[32]

FHC TO POWELL

Zuni, N.M., April 19, 1883

Sir:

I have the honor to submit, for your rejection or acceptance, the request made known to me by last mail through the accompanying letter [a communication inviting Cushing to take part, with a company of Zuni headmen, in the Santa Fe "Tertio-Millenial" celebration coming up in July and evidently also raising the prospect that this visit could result in the formation at Zuni of a company of militia].

The Zunis are anxious to have me take them, and possibly they might reap benefit from the visit by having established among them a *militia* which, on account of their recent difficulties with horse thieves and Indian killers, they stand very badly in need of.

By this means, as I am still their war chief and would be made captain of their militia, my work might be considerably enhanced, but I certainly could not spare from my other occupations a full month.

I would be expected to deliver an address (I am indirectly informed) relative to the supposed condition of my Indians during the Spanish colonization. General Green writes me, I suppose, through suggestion of the Secretary of the Territory and gentlemen in the Surveyor General's office who are acquainted with me, on all of whose parts there is a strong wish for me to be present. As, however, I am neither independent of your authority in this or similar cases, and as I feel scarcely able to devote more than two, or at most three, weeks to the matter, I submit it to you.

I ask you to kindly give me answer according to your best judgment, without consulting my supposed wishes in the least, and I shall take pleasure in abiding by that judgment.

I am, sir, most respectfully,

Your Obedient Servant,
F.H. Cushing

FHC TO POWELL

Zuni, April 30, 1883

Sir:

I have the honor to state that I shall leave Zuni tomorrow for a trip of exploration toward the Southwest, probably to be absent from eight to fourteen days. I make this trip on account of ill health and by advice of my friend Dr. Matthews. Desirous of affecting at once benefit to myself and to the work in which I am engaged, I shall make a hasty reconnaissance of several ruins and localities mentioned in the Zuni traditions, etc., and for this purpose shall take with me one or two of the Zuni Indians.

I shall expect to bear wholly the expenses of this trip.

Hoping that this temporary absence will not meet with your disapproval and promising to promptly report results, I am, Sir, very respectfully,

Your Obedient Servant,
F.H. Cushing

9. *May–July 1883*

Politics, Illness, Travel

The first half of Cushing's fourth summer among the Zunis was punctuated at both ends by trips, each motivated in part by hopes of relief from the illness which had continued to afflict him since his return from Oraibi. The first was the field trip mentioned in the preceding letter. Accompanied by his artist friend Willard Metcalf and two Indians, he spent the first two weeks of May exploring ruins in an area of the mesa country to the southwest once occupied, according to tradition, by Zuni ancestors. Set forth in a long letter to Major Powell, his discoveries on this trip were, he wrote in his Annual Report for 1883, "the most important archaeologically he had yet made" (NAA). The second trip had to do with his other life, as a member and representative of the Zuni community. With a delegation of tribal brothers, he traveled to Santa Fe in late June to take part in that city's "Tertio-Millenial," celebrated in mid-July. Palowahtiwa had been invited to give a speech, with Cushing as interpreter, and Cushing himself, in his dual role as government representative and Zuni war chief, would be authorized by the territorial governor "to establish, on his return to the pueblo, a company of militia for the suppression of the frequent raids of horse thieves and for the resistance of the encroachments of settlers on the domains of the Indians" (Annual report on field work for year ending June 30, 1883, NAA).

With two exceptions, the papers dating from the period between these two trips concern matters relating to Cushing's life as a person of affairs in Zuni (or to his illness) rather than to his research. Most commanding of attention was of course the issue of the Nutria land claim, which was then coming to a head. According to the same Annual report, Cushing's powerlessness to resolve this matter on his own, compounded with his inability earlier in the year to exact punishment of the horse thieves who had been jailed in St. Johns, had "brought him into such disrepute with some of the Indians that an attempt was made during his absence {on the trip in May} to murder his family and indeed all the Americans at the pueblo." Fortunately, by the time he returned from this trip, the President had signed an Executive Order saving the disputed lands for the Zunis, and one of Cushing's first assignments back in Zuni was to translate a letter of gratitude composed by Naiiutchi.[1] (Thus in two of the documents we encounter individual Zuni leaders speaking through Cushing in his role of interpreter.) Several other letters reflect the euphoria generated by the President's action. The Nutria controversy persisted, however, and when Senator Logan took to the press with a counter-offensive later in May, Cushing was singled out with special venom. This attack in turn prompted a curious "interview," never published, in which Cushing presented his own brief (the first of at least two such efforts).

Another embroilment—that concerning the Navajo horses presumably shot by Cushing—does seem to have come to a satisfactory conclusion during this season. Judging by the extant correspondence, two successive Pueblo agents stood by Cushing in this difficulty and prevailed finally over the agents for the Navajos. On his side, as we see in other correspondence, Cushing served the agents—and others, such as the superintendent of the government training school for Indian children just established in the East—by acting as a conduit for communication with the Zunis and by keeping them in touch with developments in the pueblo. As these correspondents probably recognized, his "retrogression" in shooting the Navajo horses was less important than his function as a fellow implementer of government policy among the Indians, helping to open the pueblo to outside influences and promoting the education of Indian children in industrial skills and American cultural values. One surviving draft suggests that he even may have been willing to help hasten "progress" in the form of moves in the private sector to open the region to large-scale exploitation of its natural resources.

The documents of this period, then, illustrate the range of Cushing's roles and relationships and the variety of his voices. He wrote in turn as enthusiastic fieldworker and student of anthropology, dutiful employee, agent of the government, spokesman for the Zuni community, interpreter-amanuensis for his Zuni mentors, booster of industrial development, and publicist (at least in intent) in defense of his own exposed position as a white man living among the Indians. Framing the selection at the beginning and the end are his translations of the Naiiutchi letter and the Palowahtiwa speech, examples of statesmanship as practised by these two senior Zuni leaders in their effort to meet the complex challenges forced on them by the political, economic, and social realities of a world dominated by their new American masters.

NAIIUTCHI TO PRESIDENT CHESTER A. ARTHUR

nd

I speak to my father as though he were a Zuni and a visitor within my door.

Father, you have thrown the light of your favor upon a nation small and poor; yet, with the gratitude of a grander and wealthier nation, I speak the thanks of my children to you this day. My brothers and I had the sublime fortune to grasp your warm hand and breathe upon it and from it and to listen to your words and those of your chiefs in the great pueblo of Washington; and although today we do not hear those words or grasp that warm hand, yet, as if we heard them, they ring in our ears and rest in our hearts.

Father, ever since I visited you in your house of gold and white stone you have been with me and I have been with you as if we were in one house. Though far asunder, I have dwelt with you since that day. It has been said, and I have heard it, that our lands and waters would be taken from us, and, I said to myself, when [one] pueblo eats up the substance of another, whither will the inhabitants of the other go? Will they, who are men, become dogs and sit at the doorways of the other, owned and yet disowned, fed and yet hungry? I have heard the one pueblo is the nation of the Americans, the other is the nation of the Zunis. No, the father would not suffer his children to become as dogs at the doors of strangers. And we have a father.

Father, through your will we are this day happy, when but for your will we had been heavy with thoughts. Thank you, our father.

May the sun of all summers that number your years find you as happy as were your Zuni children when they listened to the words of you and your chiefs—words which sounded to their ears and to their hearts as beautiful as to the eyes look a vale of flowers. [dictated to and translated by FHC][2]

—from W. E. Curtis, *Children of the Sun,* p. 59

BAXTER TO FHC

Boston May 9, 1883

My dear Tenatsali:

Has all Zuni celebrated a day of thanksgiving? And does not Nai-iu-tchi think that Thliakwa [Baxter] is his loyal son? All of which refers to our triumph in the Nutria spring matter. I think there is a chance for you to make a strong point in increasing your influence; call a council and celebrate the matter, how it was done by your bringing their leading men East and the friends you have made for them; otherwise they would have been robbed of their land. The matter has made a deal of talk throughout the country, and the Senator is getting the dressing down he deserved for it. . . . You have many firm friends in Boston, upon whom you may depend for support in your labors. They will all stand by you devotedly. Cargill and I spent last evening with Prof. Horsford and we talked enthusiastically about you. Then there are Mr. Hale, Mrs. Hemenway, Prof. Putnam, Prof. Morse, Mrs. Goddard and many others.[3] Mr. Hale has been suddenly called to Europe on account of his daughter's illness, or I would see him. . . . I was much impressed by your letters, and I trust that things will be brighter for the poor Zunis, now that their lands are assured them. It will make them more friendly disposed towards the great mass of Americans, I think. I believe a better day is dawning for the Indians and we are gradually learning to understand them better, through just such labors as yours. . . .

Faithfully your friend,
Sylvester Baxter

CURTIS TO BAIRD

May 9, 1883

My dear Sir:

Permit me to call your attention to some copies of the [Chicago] *Inter-Ocean* I have taken the liberty to send you, containing letters descriptive of a recent visit to Zuni and a reference to the work Mr. Frank Cushing is doing there under your direction. I hear the complication in which Senator Logan is involved regarding the Zuni reservation may result in an attempt to prejudice yourself and the Regents of the Institution against Mr. Cushing; and I wish to place myself upon record to the effect that the facts contained in my letter relating to the Tucker Ranch were not obtained from Mr. Cushing but were gathered in the most part before I saw him, at the officers [clubroom] at Fort Wingate. Mr. Cushing was reluctant to discuss the matter, and urged me not to complicate [sic] him or involve him in the controversy lest it should impair his usefulness and injure his work. Anything that may be said to you regarding his desire to injure General Logan, or his effort to inspire newspaper attacks upon him, is, so far as I know, entirely false.

I desire to bear testimony to Mr. Cushing's honesty and accuracy in his work, and to repeat the expressions of confidence in him that were made to me by General Bradley and other officers at Fort Wingate.

With great respect,
Your obedient Servant
William E. Curtis
Managing Editor

Mumford to FHC

May 13, 1883

F.H. Cushing, Esq., Zuni
Dear Sir:

The bearer of this, Don Pedro Sanchez, is, as you may know, the new agent for the Pueblo Indians; he comes to see you in regard to the killing of 3 Navajo Indian ponies, which killing he informs me you admit. As complaint has been made to him in regard to this matter by the Navajo Indian Agent, his duty requires an investigation and he is anxious to have the matter settled as speedily as possible, and amicably; he says that steps were commenced in Albuquerque to bring an indictment against you before the Grand Jury, but he stopped this, feeling confident that he could obtain reparation from you for the wrong done without recourse to the Courts, which would possiby entail additional expenses to you together with personal inconvenience and perhaps undesirable and injurious notoriety, as your act was in violation of both State and Territorial Constitutional law.

I have assured Mr. Sanchez that he would have no trouble in arranging this matter satisfactorily with you; as he is the representative of the Zunis, he is in law your friend as opposed to the Navajos; his sole object is justice, and as your admission is in his possession, he is led to believe that the demand of the Navajos for about $100 or its equivalent, perhaps in ponies, is a just one.

Don Pedro Sanchez requested this letter of introduction; you will find him a gentleman of broad views, especially as to free school education.

Very Resp[ectfull]y,
T. S. Mumford
Regimental Quartermaster, 18th Inf., U.S. Army
Fort Wingate, N.M.

FHC to Powell

Zuni, May 17, 1883

Sir:

I have the honor to report my return to Zuni—after an absence of fourteen days—from the Southwest, with health considerably improved.

In addition to the accomplishment of the principal object of the journey, I was fortunate in the discovery, under the guidance of my Indians, of interesting ancient remains, a brief account of which may not prove uninteresting to you.

Most of our journey led us over the great elevated *malpais* plains which skirt the White Mountains and Sierra Escudia [Escudilla]. These plains are, at rare intervals, intersected by deep cañons, or, more properly, chasms, in which, at widely separated points, occur springs. Their rugged edges are capped by columnar basalt and in places, usually near the springs, cut up by tremendous fissures or vertical cracks—formed, doubtless, during the cooling of the lava, and so constant as to render the points at which they occur almost impassable.[4]

At such places as these I almost invariably came upon tremendous ruins, ingeniously built over the network of crevices, threaded by pathways and plazas of masonry and so constant in characteristic detail, both of architecture and site, as to make them a *type,* which I have named "the fissure type" or "fissure pueblos." I hasten to add, however, that this is rather a descriptive than an ethnographic type, albeit I regard the fissure pueblos as antedating, probably, the cliff and mesa ruins of the sand and limestone regions; or at least as possibly forming monuments of an era peculiar to themselves.

In extent, these ruins vary from a few hundred

4

2

refuse etc.

The accompanying plans, hastily sketched with sections, will serve to make the character of the fissure Pueblos more clear. (?)

Enclosures like corralls.
Ruined Pueblo
round booths
Basalt butte
Fissure Pueblo at El Valle Redondo on the Colorado Chiquito
Artificial foundations.
fissures.
refuse
granaries and places of refuge.
wall of masonry
raised bench for spectators
Sup. Estufa or Ki-Va.
Stair way.
Plan showing fissures booths, Pueblo estufas, etc.

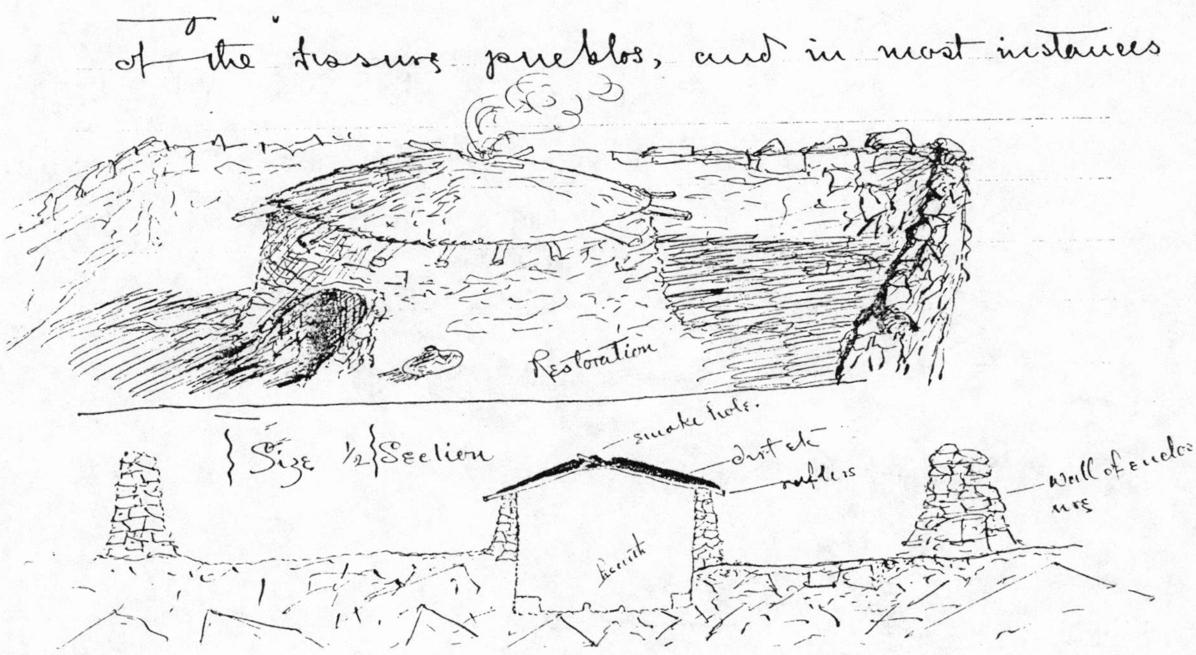

yards in length (by less in breadth) to *half a mile.* The largest one visited was traceable by its almost uninterrupted walls for more than the latter distance; the smallest contained only thirteen house sites. At first view, one of these pueblos would seem like a series of stone corrals connected by open passageways and containing roofless booths, also of stone, both *round* and square. Underneath them, the larger of the fissues formed granaries, places of refuge, worship and burial, depositories of sacrifices, implements and weapons, refuse, etc.

The accompanying plans, hastily sketched, with sections, will serve to make the character of the fissure pueblos more clear (?)[5]

The corral-like enclosures were formed in part by the clearing away of rock debris for the formation of house and plaza sites, in part as additional means of protection. The *round* foundations were *not* estufas, towers, or places of ceremonial, but actual dwellings, like Navajo *hogans,* save that they were of stone instead of wood and earth. Evidence exists that they were furnished with roofs, as indicated in the following sketch. They usually surrounded the main pueblo. They are *always* present in and about the enclosures of the fissure pueblos, and in most instances exceed them in extent and number—that is, exceed the number of dwellings at such places constructed on the usual square and terrace plan of pueblo dwellings. In fact, at two or more points the latter are absent and the round form only appears. Possibly these ruder forms antedate the others; but the pottery and other remains in and about them are the same. In fact, at two of the principal fissure pueblos I examined the pottery was of superior quality, the decoration being often of *glazed* paint burned into a plain, smooth surface.[6] The works about these pueblos, though rude on account of material, were tremendous, attesting, together with the debris deposited in the fissues below, extended occupancy and untiring labor of no mean degree of skill.

As illustrative of the latter, I will give one more example—that of the trails of dry masonry which enabled the inhabitants to pass over the honeycomb-like sites of their towns in safety and with ease. Wherever the fissure was wider at the top than immediately below, thus:

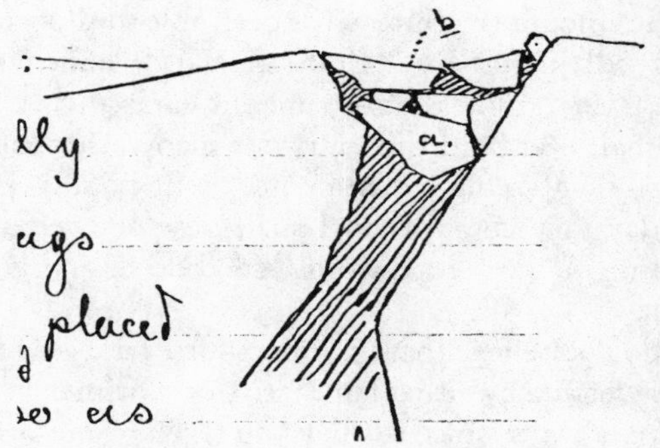

a large rock (a) was laid carefully in to support smaller, always angular ones, invariably placed with their flat surfaces upward, so as to make a smooth walking place. Where the fissues increased in width descending, various plans were adopted for bridging it over, the one illustrated below being most usually met with. That is, a notch (a) was pecked into one side or the other, an angular slab (b) laid across, being fitted into the notch at one end (a), while at the other it was weighted by other equally heavy slabs. So firm were these bridges that I led my horse over several without accident.

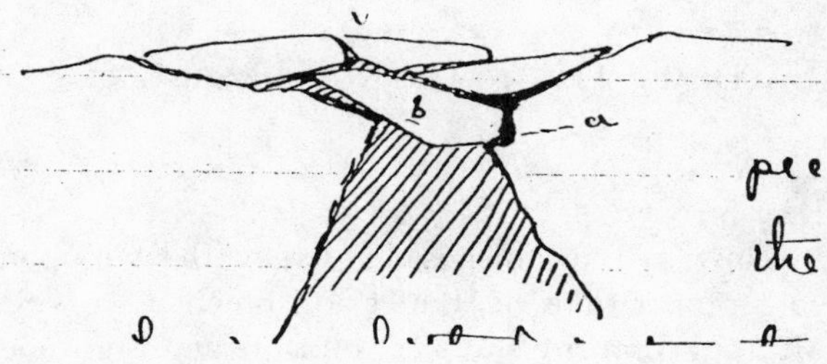

With reference to these curious remains, I have only to add that on account of the protected condition of the deposits underneath them in the fissure caverns, from the fact that the latter served as burial places, sacrificial altars, etc., their ultimate exploration will be productive of large material results, from which also the best knowledge of the arts, industries, and religious practices of the original occupants may be gleaned. For instance, at one of the ruins above referred to I penetrated more than fifty fissures from ten to sixty feet in depth (I should judge), many of them quite dark but all containing human remains. Had my transportation been less limited, I could have brought from this place alone, after a limited amount of excavation, hundreds of specimens consisting of bone and wood remains, stone articles, and pottery, much better preserved than is usually the case with those of other ruins. I brought with me on horseback two or three examples of the woodwork etc., which I shall take pleasure in forwarding at any time you may specify.

Leaving the region of the fissure pueblos to the South, I entered, in the valley of the Colorado Chiquito, the cave and crater section before referred to in letters addressed to yourself and Prof. Baird.[7] At one point, a particularly favorable ruin (of the ordinary kind) for excavation presented itself, where, with the crude appliances at hand I succeeded in excavating a hoard of stone age workmanship, a human skeleton, etc., and fragments of the matting in which the skeleton had been wrapped. Of the various specimens secured, only one or two could be brought away. The cranium, which was perfect, though frail, I was compelled to leave with a Mexican. The other remains were cached for future reference.

Between the mesa country surrounding Ojo Caliente in eastern Arizona and the *Malpais* belt bounding the Colorado Chiquito on the East, I found among the now forest-covered sand dunes many hundreds of graves, the fragmentary remains from which were scattered over many acres.[8] While these remains are apparently not as a whole sufficiently well preserved to be of service to collections, yet other cemeteries of a similar character exist, I am told by my Indians, west and south from Moqui, below the *Malpais* belt surrounding the plateaus of the Sierra San Francisco, in which the ceramic as well as osseous remains are wonderfully well preserved.

Each grave contained from one to three skulls, and before each skull had been evidently placed a handled pitcher, eating bowl containing invariably traces of a bone needle, etc., etc. Perhaps, had this locality been visited some years since, it would have been productive of large results in the way of collections. Its greatest importance dwells in the fact that it is what remains of a very ancient *Pueblo cemetery,* about which countless fragments indicate that it was a vast, very vast, depository of dead.[9] It may, however, serve me as the guide to other and more important fields. At any rate, the long sought-for "Pueblo graves" are now found.

I have to apologize to you—not for the length of this communication but for the haste with which it has been prepared and the consequent carelessness in terminology. My wish to be prompt in submitting to you its contents must serve as my excuse.

I have the Honor to be, Sir,

Your Obedient Servant,
F.H. Cushing
Ass't Ethnologist

FHC to Baird

Zuni, New Mexico, May 18th, 1883

My dear Professor Baird:

You will remember that during my preparations for departure from Washington last summer I applied to you for assistance. You kindly advanced to me the sum of two hundred and twenty five dollars, which I promised to pay from money I then expected to receive soon from the Century Company. . . .

I now have the pleasure of informing you that my Century pay has come, and although the amount of it is not quite as great as I had hoped it would be, I will do what I can to repay you for a loan without which I had been in great difficulty. Enclosed you will find a cheque (unendorsed) for my salary for April and an order on Mr. MacChesney for my May salary to be made over to you, together with the amount of the enclosed cheque, payable to your order. As soon as possible, I will send you the additional twenty five dollars; but as I shall not have the advantage of my May salary, this, at present, is impossible.

I have had, with the expenses of freightage, wood, etc., the constant crowd of visitors which the unfortunate popularity of Zuni has attracted, rather a hard time to pull through, this winter. In fact, had it not been for the returns for some little literary work I have been doing occasionally, I could not have lived on the amount the Bureau has been able to allow me. This will, I trust, dear Professor Baird, sufficiently excuse the tardiness of the present enclosure.

I shall ever hold this and your many other kindnesses in grateful remembrance, still hoping that the day may come when I shall be empowered to reward you with good words, good deeds and good gifts.

I do not believe that our intercourse has ever been characterized by either familiarity or sentiment; but I have, always, since the day you received me at the Smithsonian, kindly, yet with only brief words and few, and since the evening thereafter, when I found how well you had provided for me, thought of you affectionately, as a kind, though just, friend. I say always, for since my ever-to-be-regretted severance from you officially, I have continued to entertain the same feelings. I have deemed this a good time to give expression to my sentiments; if in doing so, I have taken unwarranted liberty with you, pardon me.

I am ever, dear Professor Baird, with regards from Mrs. Cushing to your daughter, Mrs. Baird and yourself,

Gratefully, and Very Respectfully Yours,
F H. Cushing

Draft: FHC to Unknown Recipient

Fort Wingate nd

Dear Sir:

I am very much disposed to look with favor upon your propositions for the establishment of a New Mexican company and with pleasure and gratitude upon your kindness in so favorably including my brother and myself in the arrangement.

I have, however, been detained from communicating with you earlier on account of being away on an exploration trip into Arizona at the time of the arrival of your long letters and the necessity of attention to official duties—which became the more urgent from my extended absence since that time.

The New Mexican field is a very rich one for our purposes. The Jernado [sic] Desert to the South and Southwest of Zuni—the Jernados del Muerte of

Spanish celebrity—are, I am informed by travelers, scouts, etc., very rich in auriferous sands, although inaccessible during most seasons of the year on account of the entire absence of water.[10] It is this circumstance which has at once hindered their working and thorough exploration. Hence they are new fields which, with all their richness, are open to dry process operations.

You may have seen, in a report of the early reconnaisances of this country by the government, mention of the discovery by Lt. Simpson of gold used among the Cremony Apaches as bullets and ornaments and which they willingly bartered for bullets of equal size in lead and for trinkets.[11] They also possessed gold dust which, with the nuggets, they claimed to have found in abundance in the dry streambeds of the mountains bord[er]ing the Gila country and the Great Jernado Deserts.

I am therefore encouraged to enter into this enterprise in case my principals concede to a proposition which I make by this mail for facilities and orders for explorations of ancient ruins in the neighborhood of the deserts and mountains mentioned. Otherwise it will be scarcely possible for me in consisting with my official duties to do much more than give the enterprise my hearty support, encouragement and assistance. My brother, however, being quite independent of such hindrances and any serious occupation here, would be entirely available for your use.

In regard to the locating of claims for sale by your company, would you not like to include not only gold and silver but copper and the precious [word missing]? I think I have knowledge of rich deposits of the two latter, so rich, indeed, that were I not engaged in scientific pursuits, I should attempt to establish and work or sell them on my own account.

I am in possession of some practical knowledge regarding the laws of New Mexico in reference to mining claims etc. and of the most recent and complete literature in the subject and will at an early day communicate more fully with you on the subject.

Believe me, Dear Sir,

Very Respectfully Yrs.,
[F. H. Cushing]

FHC to Putnam

Zuni, N.M., May 20, 1883

My dear Professor Putnam:

I hear of you occasionally, always to my advantage, since you are reported to me by various friends as saying very pleasant things of me, or more properly, of my work. I am thankful for this, dear Professor, and appreciate it. Nor have I ever ceased to remember the compliment you paid us Zunis on the occasion of our visit to your home in revered Cambridge. I hope, ere many months are passed, we will be investigating together—in the cause of collaboration—the wonderful sacred relics in one of your Peruvian cases. My Zunis put me on track of some most interesting comparisons while looking over the Peabody collections. I hope too that some means will present themselves rendering it possible for me, without lack of faith to my own Institution, to add, from the abundant archaeological stores of this great Southwest, to the collections in the museum under your charge.

If, in the interim, you find a few free moments some day, please let me know how you are getting along, both as my friend and as the Curator of the Peabody Museum. . . . I will yet see the day when I will be able to return your courtesy and sympathy.

I am, dear Professor Putnam,

Your Obliged and Faithful Friend,
F.H. Cushing

Present, please, my kind regards to Miss Putnam and your son.

Agent Sanchez to Commissioner Price

Pueblo Indian [Agency]
Santa Fe, May 22, 1883

Hon. H. Price
Commissioner
Washington, D.C.

Sir:

Referring to your letter of November 1st, 1882, no. 19570, I have the honor to inform you that I have recently returned from a trip to Zuni to which pueblo I went for the purpose of adjusting the difficulty which was reported to have been existing between Mr. Cushing and the Navajos on account of the former killing or wounding horses belonging to one of the latter.

I supposed from the correspondence between the parties that the claim [was] just and legal, and wrote Agent Riordan to that effect and requested that he meet me at Zuni on the 15th inst. with the view to a settlement, but he informed me the time of notice was too brief, but neither fixed nor suggested a day certain for a hearing.

Mr. Cushing says the Indian whose horses were reported to have been killed is one of his best friends and that he has lost but one horse and that died of influenza. Mr. Cushing absolutely refuses to pay the claim of $100 and earnestly reiterates the argument of his letter of Oct. 11, 1882 "B" 19570 Indian Office Enclos.

Very respectfully,
Your obdt. Serv't,
Pedro Sanchez
U.S. Indian Agent

Agent Sanchez to Agent Riordan

Pueblo Indian [Agency]
Santa Fe, May 28, 1883

D.M. Riordan
U.S. Indian Agt.
Fort Defiance, A.T.
Sir:

I am in receipt of a letter from F.H. Cushing, Esq., of Zuni in which he reports that the Navajo Indians of the region of Navajo Springs have stolen one of his finest horses. Also that a Navajo named *Telia-a-te-he-k'o* has stolen, or caused to be stolen, a gray horse purchased by a Zuni Indian named Juan Peria from an American. And further that there are constant annoyances by reasons of the Navajos trespassing on the Zuni lands.

As a means to preserve peace and harmony among the two tribes of Indians, as well as to teach them that they must be law abiding, I suggest that you take the necessary steps to bring them to speedy justice.

Very respectfully,
Pedro Sanchez
Indian Agt.[12]

News Item

"Gen. Logan and a Critic: A Vigorous Denial of Charges Recently Made" Chicago, May 28.— . . . [In a letter to the editor of the *Chicago Tribune* dated Santa Fe, N.M., May 22] Gen. John A. Logan replies in vigorous English to charges recently made against him by the [Chicago] *Inter Ocean*. That paper claimed that the Illinois Senator had been engaged in some disreputable land transactions by which the Zuni Indians had been despoiled of a valuable portion of their reservation. It was further charged that Gen. Logan and his son-in-law, Major Tucker, with Capt. Lawton, had conspired to defraud the Indians by "jumping their reservation," and that they could shut off the water supply from the Zuni country, starve out the tribe, and compel them to abandon the lands which Gen. Logan was credited with unlawfully coveting. The General's denial is a sweeping one. He says:

The truth is, I never located in any shape, manner, or form, either in my own name or in the name of any other person at or near the Zuni reservation, nor anywhere in the Territory of New Mexico, any lands whatever. Nor did I ever have any interest in any ranch with Major Tucker or Capt. Lawton at the place mentioned or elsewhere. Nor is it true that Major Tucker or Capt. Lawton, or either of them, have any ranch established there or at any other place. The facts are that Major Tucker and Capt. Lawton and their associates made a location last Fall at the head of the Neutria Valley, some 16 miles due south from Fort Wingate, including the Neutria Spring, some 30 miles to the north and east of the Zuni village, which is located in the valley of the Zuni River.

It is not true, however, as is attempted to be made to appear by this article, that it was on the Zuni land or any part of their reservation, but was from five to seven miles north and east of the line of the reservation. . . .[13]

The statement that the locations made by Capt. Lawton, Maj. Tucker, and their associates would deprive the Indians of their supply of water or grass is one of the most villainous falsehoods that could possibly be uttered. Any person who has passed over the ground that would make this statement is a debased slanderer and writes what he knows to be utterly false. . . . The Zuni River, fed from numerous little mountain springs and the Pescado and Savoyo Springs, becomes quite a large stream for that section near the Zuni villages, and affords a quantity of water sufficient for many times the number of inhabitants and much larger herds than now belong to the Zuni Indians. . . .[14]

Much is said in the article about my having made an attack on a person named Cushing, who seems to be a white Indian or to have joined the tribe and made himself one of the Zunis. All I have to say in answer to this is that any white man who will live in the midst of those Zuni Indians with his wife, disrobing himself of citizen's clothes, putting on leggings and moccasins, tying a handkerchief around his head, eating the vilest food ever known to a human being, and living in the midst of the most nauseating and offensive stench,[15] and signing himself officially "War Chief of the Zuni Indians," a tribe whom little Curtis [Logan's way of referring to the author of the *Inter Ocean* article] says are peaceful, never having killed anyone and never expecting to, and at the same time being known and published as the greatest liar who ever entered the Territory of New Mexico till little Curtis won away the blue ribbon, has my contempt, and I have not now nor heretofore had time to flatter or abuse such a subject. . . .

Take little Curtis' estimate of the number of Zuni Indians, 1600 men, women, and children, and you have 153 acres and a fraction for each man, woman, and child. This they had prior to the recent order issued by President Arthur, which adds 65,000 acres to the 240,000 acres they held before. . . . Will any man who believes in fair dealing with the Government as well as with the Indians say that these few indolent Indians, living in a little town or village, with but few cattle or horses, require any such amount of the public domain to the exclusion of all other citizens? . . .

If a civilized white man can now get only 160 acres of land as a homestead by paying for it, and an Indian can get over 1,000 acres without paying for it, had not the white man better adopt the Cushing plan and become one of the Zuni Indians? . . .[16]

SANCHEZ TO FHC

Pueblo Indian [Agency]
Santa Fe, June 3, 1883

F.H. Cushing, Esq.
Zuni, New Mexico
Sir:

I enclose herewith letters from the children at Carlisle, which, I am sure, you will take pleasure in translating to the parents.

I am glad to know that you have been so fortunate as to [recover] your horse which was stolen, and hope the other may soon be restored.

Very respectfully,
Pedro Sanchez
U.S. Indian Agent

MRS. CUSHING TO POWELL

June 5, 1883

Dear Sir:

Mr. Cushing wishes me to explain to you that soon after his return from the trip in the Southwest, his health, though temporarily benefited by the latter, began again to be impaired. He is now quite prostrated, although he trusts but for a short time. He regrets this for official reasons and hopes that it will serve not only to explain present delays but also his tardiness in producing work which he had hoped ere this to have nearly completed. He is under constant care of Dr. Matthews by correspondence, and will from time to time communicate with you as his hoped for improvement progresses.

Very Respectfully Yours,
Mrs. F.H. Cushing

TAYLOR F. EALY TO FHC

Indian-Training School
Carlisle, Pa., June 5th, 1883

My Dear Brother:

I have imaginray about you, and I hope you all very well and I am same here. I tell my father that I should not come to see you this Summer, I should go to see Dr. Ealy. I think I stay there about four months and I returned to Carlisle again. You said my people very angry because I did not come home.[17] You must tell them I don't want poor Chief unless I know all the white man way. I did not [know] enough yet that is reason I dont want to come home. They mustn't be so angry. All knowledge I get belong to my people not my pleasure and I learning all I can because education is the more necessary about the learning to read & write.

I want some more English language and I had learn some hard words in last year. That is reason I want to see Dr. Ealy. I have satisfied about the civilized way so I dont like to come back. Well I have so much interest about the what I have learning here. I would like to hear from you again and tell my [me?] what they [my people?] thinking about.

I am sorry my hand get tired & so I would not write much.

Good by.

I send my love to Mrs. Cushing.

From your Brother,
Taylor F. Ealy

CURTIS TO FHC

The Inter Ocean, Chicago
June 12th, 1883

My Dear Cushing:

Yours of the 5th is at hand, and I shall be very much pleased to read and forward to the President and print the speeches of my friend Plato [Naiiutchi] and others, and I am sure the President will be glad to receive the thanks in words and tokens of your people. I have tried to keep you posted on the Nutrias matter by sending you papers, but have little time to write.

Logan has determined upon a fight, and has written a furious letter to Washington because a decision was made without permitting him to be heard. The result will be that a special agent will be sent to Zuni to see whether the Indians use and need the land and springs. I am anxious to have Logan do his best, and promise you that he will hurt no one but himself. If you have read his letter which I sent you, you have seen that he makes it a personal fight on me, as well as yourself, and that is exactly where I want to get it. The newspapers of the country, east and west, are keeping up the agitation, particularly the religious papers, and the leading dailies, and as a sample of what they say, I enclose you a slip. The madder I can get him the worse it will be for his interest, and he is beginning to realize that his Presidential schemes are already knocked in the head.[18] He will be a very sick man before the Zuni question is settled. . . .

I am going to write a series of articles on Zuni and the other Pueblos from facts I have gained in reading everything relating to them, and propose in that way to keep up the agitation. My letters have been copied in almost every paper in the land, and I have the ears not only of our own subscribers but of those of a hundred other papers.

Send on your mss. as fast as you can, and I'll keep the interest up with that and other material I have.

Am sorry you have been ill and hope this will find you better. My regards, and those of Mrs. Curtis, to Mrs. Cushing and yourself.

Very Sincerely,
W.E. Curtis

PRATT TO FHC

United States Indian Service
Training School for Indian Youth
Carlisle Barracks
Carlisle, Pa.
June 13, 1883

My dear Mr. Cushing:

Yours in regard to Taylor Ealy and Mary Ealy received some time ago. The matter of a longer stay at this school before going home having been referred by the Department to the Agent for the Pueblos, I delayed reply that I might hear from the official source.

I perfectly agree with you that we must, all of us, keep faith in every way with our Indians. Taylor has made such good progress and is so promising a boy that it is most desirable his youth time should give him ample opportunity to get an education and hence I am reluctant to part with him if it can be arranged to the satisfaction of his friends that he remain. I see fully the delicate position occupied by you.[19] The Agent writes in the same strain with your letter and so, as the arrangement was that the children should go home at the end of three years, if a longer stay is not agreed to by parents and friends, I shall send Taylor and the Zuni girl Mary Ealy home soon after the beginning of the new fiscal year. Mary is not so desirable a pupil. We have often doubted her entire mental soundness. She is a good girl and works well. Both speak English well. Taylor is just now writing his friend Dr. Ealy near Bedford in the State.[20] There are about fifty children to return to their homes and when the time is definitely settled I will write to you again.

Truly your friend,
R.H. Pratt,
Capt. and Supt.

FHC TO POWELL

Zuni, June 17th, 1883

Sir:

It is with some regret that I write you of my still impaired health. Last week, Dr. Matthews, learning of my case, visited me here and remained with us two or three days. He pronounces me, chiefly on account of the water and of the debility resulting from my long continued dyspepsia, in a very bad, though not *serious* way, and has urged upon me the desirability of visiting Wingate if I do not speedily recover, for lengthy—more or less—treatment under him at the hospital. I have been looking forward to the proposed trip to Santa Fe with my Indians, as a hoped for means of raising both my energy and spirits, but the interference of outside parties, resulting from the present criticism (unmerited, I think) of me and my work bids possibly to indispose the Indians, if, indeed, I am, when the time comes, able to go.

I write to you relative to my condition, not in a spirit of complaint or in wish of sympathy—only that you may understand my idleness. Although besides the proper work in your cause, in my hands, many profitable, tempting and easy offers for my literary wares have been from time to time made me, I have to let them all go by—all save those endowed with superhuman patience. I have been unable during the past more than seven weeks to write consecutively even at dilatory correspondence.

It occurs to me that, as I am liable to be some time recovering, it would be well to improve that time by reading, which, with frequent rests, I am able to do with avidity.

I therefore have the honor to beg that you have forwarded to me such works on anthropology, particularly on sociologic and governmental subjects, as you deem good guides or knowledge indispensable to a student of my class. . . .

With best regards to the officers, I have the honor to be, very respectfully,

Your Obedient Servant,
F.H. Cushing

THE NUTRIA "INTERVIEW"

Among the Cushing papers in the Southwest Museum is a sheaf of some ten pages purporting to report an interview with Cushing obtained by an enterprising (though unidentified) resident in the Zuni locality. Since the handwriting and style are Cushing's own, it seems likely that the "interview" was a fiction invented by him as a way of getting certain things said which he could not otherwise gracefully (or safely) say. It also seems likely that nothing further came of this particular exercise in communication, the only known copy of the "interview" being the handwritten one found in Cushing's files. Among the points of historical interest is the story of the Palla family's three-century-old entitlement of land in the Nutria valley.

Ojo del Coyote
Valencia County, New Mexico
June 9, 1883

As there has been much discussion in the press of late relating to the Zuni farming pueblo of Las Nutrias, and as I have resided several years in the vicinity of that now famed place, it has occurred to me that it would be well to visit Zuni and interview Mr. Cushing, with whom I have been acquainted since he first came to Zuni.

I accordingly presented myself there an evening or two since and, without informing Mr. Cushing of the recent attack I had seen upon him and the Zunis by Senator Logan, asked him if he would tell me what he had been able to gather relative to Las Nutrias from traditional, historic, and ethnographic sources. With the enthusiasm he usually evinces on all subjects relative to his favorite topic, he without hesitation answered all my questions and gave me much added material which those questions suggested to him.

I need not explain my objects for this interview further than to state that, like nearly all other citizens of this section, I believe the Zuni Indians ought to have every inch of land granted them by the implied boundaries of the original Executive Order, as well as by the proclamation which President Arthur has recently issued; and I *know* Mr. Cushing to be sincere in his motives, honest in his assertions, and, in spite of his undeniable but voluntary and acknowledged "degradation," to have retained fully his moral character and his self respect and to have no other than purely unselfish and philanthropic motives in his sojourn with the Indians, as well as in all statements he makes relative to the Zuni lands. As will be shown further on, I sounded him regarding his feelings toward General Logan. His speeches in relation to the General were so free from animosity, so fair-minded and just, that it made me ashamed to hear one so abused by the latter speak in such generous, honorable terms of him.

Both for the sake of avoiding tediousness and for clearer presentation, I give the results of my interview connectedly. So far as I understand the subject, these results are correct. Certainly they are the products of careful, long-continued scientific investigation by a man morally and intellectually qualified—doubly so by his opportunities—to make them.

[*Several pages follow under a heading which reads, "'Las Nutrias: Traditional and Actual History, its Present Condition and its Relation to the Present and Future Interests of the Zuni Indians,' by F.H. Cushing." The "traditional" history is omitted here since it is essentially duplicated in Cushing's "Outlines of Zuni Creation Myths."*]

On the advent of Marcos Niza . . . in 1539, and of Coronado two years later, the Pueblos of Kia-ki-ma (Coquina), Shi-wo-na (Cibola), Ha-lo-na-wa (Alona), Ha-wi-kuh (Aguico) and other towns, including two pueblos at Pescado and one (the present) at Nutria, were all inhabited by the Cibola (*Shi-wo-na* or Zuni) Indians and were beyond peradventure, as proved by the Historic investigations of Bandelier and the Ethnologic researches I have had the honor to prosecute, the celebrated "Seven Cities of Cibola." Subsequently, during the Seventeenth Century, one of the Pescado villages was abandoned on account of Apache incursions and the failure of water. At the time of celebrated Pueblo Rebellion of 1680, *all* of the pueblos were abandoned, the strongholds of Thunder Mountain were rebuilt, and six towns erected inside of them (with a seventh for the Lagunans)—six towns, the grand ruins of which still stand. When Oñate overcame the Pueblos of the Rio Grande, a treaty was gained with the Cibola Indians [with the help of] the hostage priest of Zuni, who had escaped the general massacre through the good offices of a cacique named Francisco Palla; and by the recommendation of Oñate, a Royal grant was made by Carlos II of Spain to the said Francisco Palla of all the lands for a league from the center of Nutria Spring, in return for his services during the rebellion.[21]

Again the Indians descended from their mountain homes and rebuilt, in their order from the West, Aguico, Alona, Zuni, Coquina, Taya (Tā-äi-a or Nutria), and Pescado. During the succeeding decades, furnished with arms and horses, the Apache and Northern Apache (or Navajo) hordes, combined with the Utes and Pu-na-na (or Pawnees), gained such terrible advantages over the Pueblos that many of the minor tribes were entirely extinguished, nor did the outlying towns of Zuni suffer a kinder fate. Together with the mission of Guadaloupe and the Nutria, Pescado, Coquina and other pueblos, they were all frightfully depopulated—driven into the central Pueblo of Zuni. So essential were the farming lands of Las Nutrias and Pescado that three times they were occupied and abandoned by the Pallas and their kindred and destroyed by fire. During the last conflict of the Zunis with the Navajos at Nutria, whereby the Zunis were driven away, the grant of Francisco Palla (he himself being dead) was destroyed by fire. Holding only a precarious possession of Nutria thereafter, the Zunis nevertheless continued interruptedly to occupy their farms there and preserved their deference to the Palla claims in memory of the Spanish grant, until, after the final subjugation of the Navajos by Kendrick (aided valiantly by the Zunis themselves as attested by the latter), the nomads were removed to the Bosco [sic] Redondo.[22] Fearful that the absence of the grant mentioned would cause disputes to arise relative to the validity of their title, the Zunis made application to the commanding officer of Old Fort Wingate in 1868, and that gentleman, confident of their deserts, wrote for them the following certificate and notice of preëmption.

This remarkable paper, which the Zunis have fondly held to as their testimony of right, is still preserved by the aged great great grandchild of Francisco Palla, José Palla.[23]

During the past two years, seven of these men, with their families, have been compelled to abandon their farms at Pescado and through the water supply of Nutria, which is the most abundant in the Reservation, have been enabled to break up new patches below the old gardens and establish themselves there. Although the water supply of Nutria is, as I said before, more abundant than on any other portion of the Reservation, it is *all* required during three months of the year for irrigating the wheat fields of forty families. Indeed, it is too meager to permit of irrigating the whole in a single day, and hence you will observe that each chief of Nutria has a notched stick by which he regulates the equal distribution of the water to all the fields. The same is true of Pescado and Caliente. Even by this judicious management, the water supply is so barely sufficient to supply the present demands that the principal men of the pueblo refused the entrance of three families to the Nutrias this spring and issued the information that no others than those in possession would be permitted to enter. It is true the spring in former times, as shown by the document quoted above, supported a much larger population, but as the hoe and spud were then the only means of tillage, the size of the farms was limited.

Now, although Nutria is the *principal* farming Pueblo of the Zunis, and although it supports forty families and their immediate kindred, it might be spared, as none of its waters empty into the Zuni river save during the rainy or spring seasons. But had invalidity of the Indian title to these springs been shown, their only other springs of Pescado and Caliente would by the same fatal error have been counted out and open to the settlement of the whites. The risk, not very great with Caliente, would have been very great and imminent with Pescado, which indeed was already casually surveyed early in April for that purpose. The springs of Las Nutrias, Pescado and Caliente are positively the only ones which, without the expenditure by the government of thousands of dollars and involvement of skilled labor, could have been rendered fit for irrigation.

It is no exaggeration, therefore, that, had the Zunis lost Nutria, Pescado, the next important spring, would have followed, and they would have been rendered within two years practically paupers and dependents on the government. Even their boasted "river"—which at present flows past their doors with the depth of only two inches and a width of one foot in most places, and disappears beneath the sands the eighth of a mile below—has been twice absolutely dry since my sojourn in the pueblo and will probably not escape a similar fate this summer, should the drouth which is now scourging the valley continue three weeks longer.

With regard to the extent of their reservation, I earnestly prayed Secretary [of Interior, H.M.] Teller, during my recent visit to Washington in the spring, to enlarge its boundaries toward the South and East to nearly twice its present size, since, although extensive, two thirds of it [consists of] rock mesas, juniper jungles, and sand dunes, while the other third, although fine grassland, is all insufficient for even the limited number of herds the Zunis at present have. As an example of this, the Zunis lost last month by a slight snow squall which did not fall to the depth of three inches several hundred sheep, young cattle, and horses, on account of their poor condition, . . . while the Mexican ranchmen round about did not, according to their own brags, lose as many as a dozen animals.

The Zunis are most grateful to the President for his proclamation, which I have carefully translated and explained to them. In council, they begged me to write their eloquent and beautiful thanks to him and to send him one of their quaint embroidered cotton mantles of the sacred dance, which, after long deliberation, their old priest Nai-iu-tchi pronounced the "best hope their poor land gave bloom to." I frankly confess that I wrote these speeches out, but sickness, both physical and moral, detained me from sending them, for I naturally supposed that such a proceeding on my part would be regarded [as] officious, sensational, and scheming.[24] I say I naturally supposed so from the fact that, having overcome the obstacles of ignorance, superstition, illness, and almost death in the Zuni portion of my humble mission, I have been since assailed by an equal and exceeding ignorance and its unhappy consequences from my own people and, indeed (alas!), in some instances from my own kinsmen, whose names I have been endeavoring rather to exalt than degrade.

It is a great and noble action on the part of President Arthur and Secretary Teller, in the face of political criticism, against the tide of the relentless and century-swollen stream of injustice, to secure the titles of the Zunis to their all-important farming pueblos. It would be an act of infamy, after such proceeding and after being convinced of their errors, for the gentlemen who attempted the preëmption of Nutria to contest such noble wills. I therefore do not believe they will do it. Not even tempted by the whisperings of the two modern Furies, political and public animosity, do I think they will do this.

Las Nutrias are not valued by the Indians as [cattle] ranches but as the last resort for farming they have left besides the Ojo Caliente after the ravages of the grasshoppers at Pescado. The farms of Nutria, tilled with the hoe, like gardens, and watered with the cunning and patience of Chinese horticulturalists, give today support to forty Zuni families who, with their kindred, remain at Nutria to attend the corn and melon fields of that valley. The names of these, signed to and for a petition to the President, and before his humane proceeding was known in Zuni, are given below:

José Palla, Kwantonio, We-lo-tsai, Je-ni-li-saila-wa, Juan Peria, We-se-li-to, Uli-so-na, Lai-iu-ahtsai-lunkia, etc. etc.

Metcalf to FHC

Boston
July 3, 1883

My dear Frank:

. . . Do not mind the things which are said of you, . . . even by Eastern papers. . . . People whom I have met here loudly denounce the manner in which Logan assailed you, and all express the warmest and deepest sympathy for your position. . . .

While in Chicago (where I was treated handsomely), I did my best to offer my widow's mite to your cause—i.e., [I was] interviewed by "*The News*."[25] I only tell you this because you may have seen it. [While having no] desire to appear in print, I was still very glad to have an opportunity to express myself to or against those who have so scurvily blackguarded you, and if it helped you in the slightest degree I am happy. [But] don't I wish I was Baxter! I would make a little howl here. . . .

It is with the deepest regret that I hear and read what you say of your failing health. God grant you may recover, to be able to finish your crowning works. Do not let the world lose what you have accomplished: a work which can never be done again. What a wrong you do the world—and yourself—when you say you will never publish your report, should you have to leave Zuni. Change your mind before the resolution becomes too strong. . . .

Believe me ever

Your true friend,
Willard L. Metcalf

FHC to Pilling

Santa Fe, July 4, 1883

Sir:

I have the honor to acknowledge, with thanks, your letter relative to the establishment of a Post Office at Zuni.

As I found, before leaving Zuni, a decided lack of accommodativeness, I did not pursue the scheme very energetically. This lack of accommodativeness, I should have explained, was on the part of the missionary and trader elements. I shall, however, immediately on my return to Wingate, forward a petition signed by seventeen persons and, in case I can, the necessary papers, bonds, etc., for the creation of a Postmaster, to your care, for such action as may be deemed advisable by the Office.[26]

I most sincerely regret to say that I shall not be able to complete, in time for the forthcoming Annual, my much worked on paper relative to Zuni sociology. I have advisedly delayed replying to your numerous enquiries in relation to it, hoping from day to day, week to week, that I should be able to render a more favorable answer. Indeed, I might have produced a large paper in time for you, had not my condition of health been so wretched. I have never been in working condition since my return from Moqui last winter. Nevertheless, I could have handed you in a more simple paper than the one so urgently required, or the one in question even, had I not wished to produce for you as well as myself something creditable to the amount of investigation I have devoted to it.

I feel, more than ever, particularly since receiving from many parts of the world congratulatory and enquiring letters, that it is an essential duty for me to produce my best and completest in a work of such importance as that now in progress on the Zuni sociology etc. I have been much questioned as a student, on account of newspaper criticism, and I do not wish scientific or literary men to have an opportunity to verify that criticism in a perusal of my more serious works. I therefore earnestly beg that you shall wait patiently for my monograph, which, unless detained by my unfortunate illness, I shall be able to complete before next January—certainly in time for the Annual following the present. Now that I have a great deal of material on hand, I am anxious in working it over to have the advantage of some preliminary readings on the subject. On account of my isolation, I have, as you know, had very little training in this direction.

Pardon my incoherency and illegibility. The one is caused by my position in the midst of a "Howling Fourth" {of July}, the other by weakness resulting from my long suffering but now improving health. I have the honor to be, Sir, very respectfully,

Your Obt. Servant,
F.H. Cushing

BANDELIER TO MRS. LEWIS HENRY MORGAN

Highlands, Illinois, 18 July 1883

{Having stopped over in Santa Fe,} where nearly all my friends from New Mexico had congregated owing to the "Tertio Millenial," I succeeded in meeting Cushing and his folks again. He is well, somewhat exercised over the Logan affair, but otherwise pleased and hopeful. Of late he has made some very interesting finds and discoveries due south of Zuni, as well as at Zuni proper. If his hands were less tied up by the Smithsonian Institution and its strict rules of work, we should have the benefits of his labors at an earlier day. . . .[27]

PALOWAHTIWA'S SPEECH AT THE SANTA FE "TERTIO-MILLENIAL" EXPOSITION

In the "Tertio-Millenial" exposition of 1883, Santa Fe celebrated the three centuries of New Mexican history between the arrival of Coronado and the completion of the coast-to-coast railroad. It was evidently a grand affair, some ten thousand spectators gathering to watch the three-day series of elaborate parades, pageants, and "tableaux" commemorating the Spanish conquest and the opening of the area to Christian civilization. "Royal splendor and barbaric magnificence" were the order of the day. According to one news account of the principal parade, "the Thirteenth United States Infantry band, playing its most thrilling airs," was followed "in unique confusion" by "those splendid specimens of physical manhood, the Apache chiefs, warriors and hunters, with their gleaming spears and buckskin robes adorned with beads of many hues; the Oriental and innocent looking Zunis of the sixteenth century, with bows and arrows, . . . and {several companies of} richly robed knights, . . . a full quota of court officers, and a brilliant guard" (New Mexican Review, *July 19, 1883). The climactic event, in which Cushing's party of Zunis played a prominent part, was a reenactment of Coronado's attack on the chief of the "Cities of Cibola," ending with the surrender of the Indians.*[28] *Following this edifying spectacle came a series of speeches glorifying what the white speakers took to be* the *three centuries of New Mexico's history and* the *makers of that history. It was in this context that Palowahtiwa rose to give the speech he had been invited to make. Here again, through the medium of Cushing's translation, we hear the voice of a memorably individual Zuni leader—one gifted, as the speech demonstrates, not only with eloquence but with the realism of a practical politician.*

My friends and brothers:

In the days when the world was new there was given to the white man the gift of guessing, but to the fathers of the Zunis there was given only the medicines whereby they might cause the waters to fall and the evils of sorcery to waste away.

Thus it is, that the white man discovered how to

make marks with meaning, and with these marks he has preserved the words of his fathers. The Zuni is poor; but not for this do I say "Alas." For is not the tongue of the Zuni his writing stick, and are not the ears and hearts of his listeners his books? Therefore I speak straightly when I say that no less than our older brothers the white men, do we, their younger brothers, the dark men of earth, know the tales of times ancient!

Thus I have listened to the words of my leader in Council (Here the old chief referred to the oration in Spanish by Major J.D. Sena.) He has told you of the coming of the "bearded men" of the Land of Summer (the Spaniards). We too have been told of their coming, by our fathers, whose fathers told them as they themselves had heard it from their old ones.

Long after the last of strangers had met the Zunis in their wanderings toward the Land of Day (Eastward), there came the first white man our ancients ever saw. He was lean and his clothes were worn away; his hair and beard were long and tangled. Our fathers called him Nu-we (pronounced New Way). Now whenever he saw any food on the hearth, he took it and reached for more; so that the caciques and priests who were old and wise gathered the council and said to one another, "This man eats too much and demands more; therefore we must kill him." "No," said others; "Why kill him because he eats much?" "Because," it was answered, "no man ever lived who had not fathers and mothers, and many relatives. If this man stays here, his people will come to seek him, and what will the *A-shi-wi* then do for food; for the men of a nation are alike." When the sun rose one morning, Nu-we was gone, and when the people asked, "Where is he?" it was replied by the caciques and priests, "We have wrapped him in the magic matting of rush and he will awake in the Land of Everlasting Summer, where it is said others like him dwell." (Here Mr. Cushing explained that doubtless this tradition referred vaguely to the wanderings of Nunez Cabeza de la Vaca, who may have visited one of the then existing Zuni pueblos, and whose first name the Zunis evidently attempted to pronounce Nu-we.)[29]

Then there came from the Land of Summer which is now called So-no-li (Sonora) a man with many strange people, and our fathers called him the "Black Mexican with thick lips."

But when he entered our city of Kia-ki-ma, below Thunder Mountain, our grandfathers were frightened because he was black and bad tempered, and they killed him, with many of his companions.

At last there came from the Land of Everlasting Summer a man named Co-lo-na-lo (Coronado). This was nine, ten, eleven, even twelve generations ago, for the nation of Zuni has grown old and died twelve times since then, and each time it has grown smaller. Now our forefathers, thinking these strange people had come to avenge the death of the Black Mexican, they received him not gently, but with their poor weapons they greeted him; with their arrows and stones and clubs they met him. But when he opened his sticks that made thunder (so said our grandfathers), the war vanished as a rain storm does when it lightnings, and we found we were brothers.

My brother and your child (here he referred to Mr. Cushing) has told me that these who sit around me in council are dressed as were Coronado and his warriors. "If so," I say to myself, "Why did our grandfathers receive them with arrows and stones, instead of with warm hands and good breaths, for they are dressed as by magic."

I am told that this is a feast of my father in Washington, and that he wished it. Hence I have come with my children and speak here this day, for I know that my people are poor among men, and if they smile not on Washington and his children, then they will pass away, or like dogs, lie hungry at the doors of strangers.

My friends and brothers, we are children of one father, are we not? And that father is Washington, the Great Chief of the Land of Day. Therefore have I called you "brothers," and may we smile one upon the other, and be happy forever, and through all days.

Thus much have I spoken.

(The above speech was translated during the evening by Mr. Cushing and corrected by the old chief himself, who said it was well it should be marked for hearing if it would be going to the Land of Day.)[30]

10. August–December 1883

Settling In?

Having remained in Santa Fe through most of July in hopes of improving his health, Cushing was back in Zuni by the beginning of August. According to his Annual Report for 1884, he turned at once to the task of organizing the militia he had been authorized to establish. Called into action almost immediately by renewed raiding on Zuni stock, he led his warriors, "mostly unarmed," in an attack resulting in the death of two of the desperados (an American and a Mexican) and the suppression of outside difficulties for several months. {This success} reinstated him in the confidence of the tribe {and} influenced him to build a residence for his family in the outskirts of the village. Thus he still further secured the good will of the Indians {and induced them} at last to prepare for consummating his initiation, begun by the seaside at Boston in 1882, into their Kâ'-kâ or Sacred Dance Organization (NAA).

Extant papers from the summer and fall of 1883 help to fill in (or in some cases complicate) the picture thus sketched in Cushing's retrospective report. For instance, from several letters received by him we may infer that as well as fighting outlaws and working on his house, he was spending some of his time moonlighting as a private collector for the Berlin Museum (and others?), encouraged in this effort both by the enterprising Bandelier and by his other friends Alexander Stephen and the trader Tom Keam. It was also during this period that he began to produce the series of brilliant articles on "Zuni Breadstuff" commissioned by the Indianapolis Millstone*—a letter of December 7 from the publisher indicating that the first installment was that day received in his office.*[1] *In these extracurricular activities one may see signs not only of Cushing's expectation of a long-term stay in Zuni but of experiments in the direction of supporting himself independently of the Bureau. On the other hand, it is evident from the bulky reports submitted in November that he was also attending to his duties as Bureau ethnologist—at least in the period of relatively good health he enjoyed following his return from Santa Fe. Additional glimpses afforded in Cushing's own letters and in the account of a visitor to the pueblo suggest that from various standpoints this was a season of ups and downs. One source of encouragement must surely have been the warm solidarity expressed in the correspondence and notes of his still-growing circle of friends and supporters. Another was the mentioned promise of further initiation into the inner world of the Zunis. In the material world, however, the indications are that, to a greater degree than Cushing makes clear in his report, pueblo life—and therefore his own as well—continued to be disrupted and unsettled by encroachments on grazing land and raids on stock. About his health there is also some uncertainty, depending perhaps not only on when he was writing but to whom. While the report above and some of the letters suggest improvement, what he wrote to his Cambridge admirer, Professor E.N. Horsford, was sufficiently alarming to draw from the latter in mid-November an urgent plea to Powell which, along with an evidently coordinated appeal from another New England admirer, Reverend Edward Everett Hale, probably helped to bring about Cushing's recall from the field.*[2]

FHC to Putnam

Zuni, N.M., August 1, 1883

My dear Professor Putnam:

. . . .

Just what I need now is books. I have already read the works on Mythology and am now engaged in taking notes from them. Everything I read enhances to me the value and interest of my Zuni notes and observations. It is pleasant to live here face to face with a condition of the human mind of which such books treat in vaguely speculative lines—to breathe the very atmosphere, and sometimes, from sheer enthusiasm and sympathy in conversation and participation, to believe oneself almost converted to it. Thanks to the abundant folk-lore and more serious mythology of the Zunis, I shall be able to elucidate many problems in primitive conception and polytheism. At least, I shall be able to record such facts as shall enable philosophers to do this.

Write me some time about those Peruvian collections; and with sincere regards to Professor Horsford and other friends, should you see them, believe me

Very Sincerely Yours,
F.H. Cushing

Bandelier to FHC

Highland, Illinois
August 13, 1883

My very dear Frank,

Forgive me for not having written to you before. I must tell you that I had not even the intention of writing to you today, but I feel further delay would become unpardonable. Why, I shall soon tell you! But before everything and anything I must thank you for your kind letter and for its content. You were in a hurry with the draft. We must, in our exceptional situations, help each other as best we can and thus squeeze through this world of cuffs and elbowings.[3] More than for the draft, however, I thank you—we all thank you—and your little ladies for your kind and *so* comforting friendship. Joe sends her love and her photograph to "Miss Emma," as Father "No-mo-ho" calls Mrs. Cushing.[4] But she would like to be permitted to wish for a return. Would it be possible?

Now for that explanation. Shortly after my return, I received from the German Consul at St. Louis an exceedingly pleasant letter, enclosing an equally kind one from the director of the Royal Museum at Berlin.[5] They are well pleased with my collection and desire to continue. Of course there are the usual complaints about high prices, but they have cheerfully paid for the first lot, and I do not mind much the expressions of official penuriousness that follow. It's in the blood, and they would complain if you sent them gold nuggets for nothing. So I arranged for an interview with the consul here, and I have waited and waited as he deferred it from week to week, until it is at last final. My plan is the following: What they want is:

(1) idols ("*ma-i-ne*" and "*uan-a-me*"),[6]
(2) ornaments and ritual dresses (this is easier to get),
(3) genuine antiquities (the latter are very possible).

I want to tell the consul now that I can get these things, if the Museum pays for them. He has been recalled to a higher position in Germany ("Councilor of Legation" in reward for merit) and leaves in a week or two. I will tell him to arrange for payments to be made at St. Louis, and want to propose to you how to help me collect these things. Send me a list of objects with *your* prices on these pieces (not the cost of purchase but the price of sale, what *you* ask for them, packed, boxed, and delivered at Fort Wingate station ready for shipment. I want to charge a commission for myself and would like for you to suggest a percentage equitable to the Museum and just to me. Dr. Gerlich (the new consul) will see Dr. Bastian at Berlin and have him write to me at once so that I can get positive details before my return to Zuni in October. Should I be able to pick up things myself (for instance at Santa Fe), I will make my price and add to it the same commission for *you* (the same percentage) as I do give myself whatever you ship. If we can make it [agreeable to the people in] Berlin, then a snug little [bit] of revenue might result from this—perfectly legitimate—traffic.

It will have the advantage that, at the start, duplicates of what you have already sent to Washington is all that is required, so that you do not commit any breach of propriety. Later on we shall have to twist it into an irreproachable shape. For my part, I am not bound to any bureau [?] and can do just what I d— please, so that if the "negocio" goes under my own name, perhaps, nobody can utter a word.

The Bostonians treat me very shabbily. They have raised a plaintive wail for money ($500) wherewith to print my Mexican Report at last. This would look first rate, were it not for [the much greater expenditures on European archaeology]. . . .[7] I wish I had another Baxter who would look up matters for me at Boston and then, after he became thoroughly posted and satisfied, would write up that Institute of mine. I have written to Parkman (all the others have fled the "excessive heat" and the "absorbing labors"), but no reply has come. It is a shame and an outrage. And I gradually begin to suspect that my manuscripts are rather indiscreetly studied! But I have not a single friend East except Mrs. Morgan, and she cannot do anything of course.

Good-bye, my dear boy. God bless you and your little ladies. Give them all our best love, also to the folks at the Pueblo and to No-mo-ho. I wrote to the Doctor also. Reply as soon as possible.

Yours as usual,
Adolfo

Has Mr. Wilson ("hm! hm!") improved his Zuni? Give him my regards too if you feel like it.

Bartlett to FHC

Santa Fe, August 17th, 1883

F.H. Cushing, Esq.
Zuni, N.M.
Sir:

I was very glad to receive yours of 6th inst. this day and showed the same to His Excellency the Governor, who with me, was greatly pleased at the interest manifested by the Zunis in the proposed company of Militia and trusts that the same will continue until the company is fully organized and equipped. Please extend to them our earnest hope that they will persevere in their present efforts, and our assurance that we will assist them to that end in every direction in our power.

I think that upon proper application and through the right channels by the assistance of your army friends you could get them uniformed by the General Gov't, though an application of that sort made by me in behalf of the Lagunas was not granted. Yourself and friends would have more influence I am satisfied.

I have your Company already assigned to the New Cavalry Reg't which is being rapidly organized and which will have twelve full companies. And trust you will be ready to come into it.

I desire to repeat my offer of assistance to you in any manner that I may be useful—and remain, very respectfully,

Your Obedient Sv't,
Edward L. Bartlett
Adjutant General of New Mexico

FHC to Agent Sanchez

Zuni, New Mex., Aug. 17, 1883

Sir:

I have the honor to inform you that shortly after my return from Santa Fe, four Zuni horses were stolen from the Southern mesa—one of them my own; later, some two weeks, a large band were stolen from the same place, driven South toward the *Rito Quemado,* where many escaped and returned, only three of the best being taken away. . . . [There follows a description of the suspected thieves.]

Five days since, these men were seen at Jewett's ranch, but it was thought they would soon leave. They have now stolen horses from the Zunis two or three times. The result of these and other injustices the Indians are suffering at the hands of out-laws is—that they are becoming excited and quite unmanageable. I deeply regret to inform you that among those who try to subvert the authority of the chiefs in attempting to check their people from any promiscuous acts of violence is—as a leading spirit—*Ramon Luna.* I fear he is rapidly becoming violent again. I have had much difficulty in keeping the Indians from making a raid on travelers, to the Southward, and I am sorry to learn that in nobly assisting me the Governor has been encountered and publicly abused by Ramon. I heard Ramon councilling [sic] his followers, a few days since, to go into the Southern country and kill anyone who might be found off the roads. When I remonstrated with him, he desisted; but I am told by the Governor that he has resumed this course of argument again. His example has been promiscuous [sic] to the extent that we cannot well manage the people in any decisive action, and the Chiefs are thoroughly discouraged.[8]

They have heartily begged that I write you the above facts; hence I have taken the liberty of complying. . . .

There are many other minor subjects, yet important, which I would [like] to address to you; but as I am in haste for a mail which leaves at once, and as I have already, I fear, trespassed much upon your time, I must defer them to another letter, with entire confidence, Sir, in your judgement. I submit these facts to your criticism, merely awaiting such action as you may take, or such commands as you may deem proper to honor me with.

I have the honor to be, respected sir,

Your Obedient Servant,
F.H. Cushing
Ass't Ethnologist

The Honorable
Don Pedro Sanchez
U.S. Indian Agent

FHC TO POWELL

Zuni, August 20, 1883

Sir:

I have the honor to inform you that I am compelled at the approach of cold weather to abandon the better portion of the house I am now occupying. This becomes necessary for two reasons:

First, the Indians in possession of the portion referred to require it for their use during the coming year, on account of an increase in the number of their family and in consequence of the cold of winter, from which the rooms they are at present occupying afford but insufficient protection.

Secondly, during a professional visit to me in June, rendered urgent by my ill health, Dr. Matthews pronounced my malady as due to water poisoning and the unhealthfulness of my quarters.

These two considerations make it essential, very, that I build an addition to the small room which I purchased last autumn.

The total cost of this addition cannot be less than three hundred and twenty-five dollars nor more than four hundred dollars. None of the work is immediately pressing but the masonry which, including the making and hauling of the adobes, I am able to let out by contract at lowest and cheapest rate at two hundred dollars. Of this sum, I am totally unable to pay, on completion of the work in October, more than fifty dollars without throwing myself in debt and rendering the rest of the work a matter of indefinite postponement. I therefore appeal to you to aid me, if it be in any way possible, to the extent of one hundred and fifty dollars. The remaining expenditures, for roofing, doors, windows, etc., which may be made from time to time from October to the middle of December, I hope, by the exercise of strict economy, to be able to meet.

Permit me to inform you, in candor but not in a spirit of complaint, that but for the receipt of liberal payments for my *Century* and *Atlantic* articles and the aid of liberal and kind patrons in New England it had been impossible for me to support myself during the past year and carry on my work in Zuni. For this reason, while I have been almost niggardly in my economy, I have been unable to reserve sufficient means wherewith to meet this at once unexpected and unavoidable expense. By the construction of a suitable addition to the room I already possess, I shall be able in future to avoid an expense, by no means inconsiderable in the past, for rental etc.[9]

I have the honor to be, Sir, very respectfully,

Your Obedient Servant,
F. H. Cushing

P.S. Permit me to add that by means of the contract above referred to I am able to accomplish the work without the fraction of an interruption to my regular official duties.

Respectfully, F.H.C.

BANDELIER TO FHC

Highland, August 26, 1883

My dear Frank!

A few words in a hurry. Please send to D.W. Collet, Curator, Missouri Historical Society, the following articles:

One set of characteristic Zuni pottery of today. It should include one specimen of each kind of vessel used and be characteristic in shape and painting. I presume that 6 or 8 pieces would cover the case. Make the bill for the *full* amount as you proposed including my part of it—*without itemizing,* of course, and send it to Collet direct, with instruction to send you a New York or St. Louis check (as you choose).

He wants a *big flint-knife*! He just raves for it! I told him that it would be *impossible,* but that if, through some streak of luck, you could get one, that then he would have to "bleed" for it. So do as you think best, and for the balance, if you could manage to send one, do as above in regard to the bill.

I have told Collet that all articles would cost twice the price of purchase—*boxed and delivered at Fort Wingate.* Now *include* that item in your "cost" and add to it both commissions.

Tomorrow I shall write to Berlin and to *London*! The above is only a "feeler" thrown out by my St. Louis friends.

Joe sends her love to the ladies. As for me, you know what to say and to whom.

Yours,
Adolfo

I think there is not much danger of my being a coal-miner as yet. I shall rather throw away the whole coal mine. But I would seriously advise you to "enter" the localities of the main finds, when they can be entered. *Somebody* is in Arizona again.[10]

Herman ten Kate's Visit

On a stopover in Albuquerque, en route back to Zuni after the Tertio-Millenial Exposition, Cushing met a young university graduate from Holland who was initiating a career in anthropology through an extended tour of the American Indian country. This meeting with Herman Frederick Carel ten Kate (1858–1931) also initiated a lifelong friendship. The two were to meet again in the East in 1886, when ten Kate was on his way home to Holland from an anthropological trip through South America and the Cushings were living on the estate of Mary Hemenway near Boston. Cushing subsequently recalled ten Kate to America to join him on the Hemenway Expedition. One result of ten Kate's 1883 trip was a book on his travels: Reizen en Onderzoekingen in Noord-Amerika *(Leiden, 1885), one chapter of which is devoted to the visit he made to Zuni shortly after the Albuquerque encounter with Cushing. The days of that visit, he would recall in his obituary for Cushing, were "among the most interesting I spent during my long journey in the Southwest."[11] The following passages are excerpted from ten Kate's chapter on the first Zuni visit (translation by Curtis M. Hinsley, Jr.).*

Mr. Cushing lives in the lower floor of the house of Palowahtiwa, the governor of Zuni, which lies on the southeast corner of the pueblo. The small, dimly lit apartments present a strange jumble of Indian and Japanese artwork and Oscar Wilde's "aesthetics." The floor is covered and the walls are hung with colorful Navajo rugs, bear and puma skins, while above an Oriental divan Cushing's costume as a priest of the Order of the Bow is hanging. It's a pretty outfit, that colorful round shield bedecked with feathers and the graceful bow and quiver of puma hide. Here your eye falls upon rifles and revolvers, there on a book-rack; here on a chest with fine porcelain and Zuni pottery, over there on Japanese fans, peacock's feathers, sun flowers and multicolored Hopi baskets, which here and there decorate the walls. A soft light shines through the small rectangular windows and wraps the picturesque interior in shimmering halftones of richness and strength.

Before evening falls, I take a stroll with the two women [Emily Cushing and her sister Margaret Magill] through the pueblo, but rain showers and windstorms, long threatening, force us to turn quickly back; fortunately, the next day I have better opportunity to see the village. . . . (pp. 275–76)

The same afternoon that the *Kâkokshi* was in full swing Mr. Cushing returned. This time he was wearing a half-Indian, half-fantasy outfit. His long hair, falling to the shoulders, was held in a black headband. A short blouse of dark blue cloth, cut low at the neck, covered his upper body; a narrowly cut pair of pants, of the same material, decorated at the seams with rows of silver buttons reached to his knees; below this he wore brown leather leggins with beautifully woven red kneebands, and heavy moccasins. Around his neck, hanging midway down his chest, he wore valuable strings of worked shells and turquoise; around his right wrist an armband of small, fine oliva shells, the sign of his status as a Bow Priest.

The first tour that I took with him through the pueblo convinced me immediately that Mr. Cushing was completely at home here, and totally accepted as one of the people. Everywhere a friendly greeting, a nod of the head, or breathing on each other's hand—a means of greeting both graceful and symbolic. Exchanging a handshake, one brings, just for a moment, the other's hand to the mouth and breathes on it; it is the exchange of "the breath of life" (p. 280).

I have been able to observe Cushing and to get to know him in his work, among the people with whom he lives. Two things above all I have gained from this acquaintance: a deep admiration for a man who lives only on behalf of science and the conviction that his method of ethnology for studying a people is the only correct one (p. 282).

Metcalf to FHC

Paris, October 8, 1883

My dear Frank:

. . . My sojourn among the Zunis was well known

here among the artists and students (I *don't* mean the swell painters), and everyone has had a great [deal] to say and ask about "Cushing." And I tell you candidly, Frank, never have I met people who, being so far away, knew your work so well, and fully appreciated its value, as do the majority of the students I've met. What must it be among scientific men, whom I've *not* met and never shall. Frank, old boy, America is dearer to me than ever before, but I am aware of how very slow it is in certain questions. Why! if you were in France, you would be walking about the streets with a little red button on your coat lapel—and of course you know what that means—but it's a fact, men are awarded here for such work as yours. . . .[12] Great heavens! how I hope you will push your work through to a publication, and then you may go whither you will and be received as you should be, amongst scientists. I don't mean such people as Mr. and Mrs. Stevenson or any of their followers. . . .

Your true friend,
Willard L. Metcalf

FHC TO POWELL

Zuni, New Mexico, November 4, 1883

Sir:

As requested in your name by the Chief Clerk, Dr. J.C. Pilling, I have the honor to send you, under separate registered wrapper, by this mail, my Annual Report. This, in accordance with your instructions, I have written in the third person.

Although the Report has been prepared nearly two months (save that it was written in the first person), I have thus deferred sending it in the hopes of being able to forward with it an introduction to and Catalogue of the ancient series collected with other matter at Moqui.

The Report to Mr. Victor Mindeleff, on the Oraibi Expedition, I have already, in his absence, sent you. Together, these form the Annual Report (with the addition of my letter of May on the Fissure Pueblos etc., which please see) which I have divided, for convenience of segregation, into three parts, as follows:

Part I: Annual Report of Operations, etc., for 1882–1883,

Part II: Report of the Oraibi Expedition, 1882–1883,

Part III: Introduction to a Catalogue of the Ancient Series, Moqui Collections, made 1883. This includes a discussion of the origin and development of forms, symbolic decorations, etc., of the pottery of the Southwest, which I include for the sake of securing priority of statement if not of publication.[13]

The latter paper or essay has been, and must continue to be, delayed, for two reasons: It has (1st) assumed more importance and proportion than I had at first intended for it, and (2nd) my building operations, which although unavoidable, I had not sufficient means for carrying on, claimed and continue to claim considerable time from me, as I am compelled to do—as a measure of economy—much of the manual labor connected with them.

It gives me pleasure to find an interesting confirmation of my opinion relative to the former uses of the great, centrally pierced stone slabs of the Pueblo ruins (pp. 10 & 11 of the accompanying report) in the recent discoveries of Mr. Victor Mindeleff, at one of the ruins which I examined *en route* from Moqui to Zuni (see Report pp. 8 & 9).[14] He tells me that he found (at point *c* Plan III of Report) by excavation, one of these singular doorways, *vertically* in position, in the wall of a well preserved room. This goes to show that the mention of a "Stone close" (*al-athl-tinne*) in the reference in the tale I quote—and which I secured last May—is more trustworthy than I had at first supposed; for I had regarded these stones as the frames to sky-holes.

Hoping that you will find this Report—tho' hasty—in accord with your wishes, I have the Honor to be, Sir,

Very Respectfully,
Your Obedient Servant,
F.H. Cushing
Asst Ethnologist

E.N. HORSFORD TO POWELL[15]

Cambridge, November 19, 1883

My dear Major Powell:

I enclose to you a letter recently received from

Mr. Cushing [not found]. I am moved to this in part, and very largely, I may say, in the interest of your Department of Ethnology, in which I have from the outset, and indeed from the date of my early acquaintance with Lewis H. Morgan, permitted my sympathies to take very deep root.

From Bandelier I have learned, as well as from Cushing and from others, of the immense amount of material Cushing has accumulated. The value of it, properly digested and put into form for preservation, must be very great. In its present condition, if he were to turn it over to others, it could not fail to lose very greatly. It would be substantially a loss—and a loss that in all human probability could never be regained.

I am afraid we are in danger of losing it!

Cushing has repeatedly written me of his terrible suffering from dyspepsia. In this letter I see a little of the martyr spirit which alarms me.[16] We cannot afford to indulge in such sacrifice.

With this preliminary, I ask you to read his letter and judge whether it does not show that he is in a condition requiring his immediate call home—first to his home in the East for rest and then for systematic writing up [of] his work—and then, if later he feels like resuming it, you will promise whatever you deem wise.

If it be necessary for someone to advance a little aid for this purpose—assuming of course that you act on my suggestion, having seen with your other means of judging that I am justified with facts in making it—draw on me for $250 without hesitation. I do not care to be known in this matter to anyone—i.e., I have no scheme of notoriety at all.

I remember how Nicolai's vast accumulations were lost to science—*thirty years* of work among the Indians—simply because he put off the day of writing.[17] I know in my own case how great a mistake I made in delaying to write up my papers.

Now, if I have made a mistake in coming to you rather than to Dr. Baird, be kind enough to lay the matter before him.

I will thank you to return Mr. Cushing's letter when you have read it.

I am very truly yours,
E.N. Horsford

Powell to Hale [Marked "Personal"]

Washington, D.C., Nov. 24, 1883

My dear Doctor Hale:

I have read with care your letter of Nov'r. 21st, concerning Mr. Cushing, as well as the one from Professor Horsford, and fully appreciate the generous interest you take in his success.

For some time I have thought it much better that Mr. Cushing should come East and elaborate his material; or that he should at least spend a portion of each year in Washington for that purpose. He would thereby be enabled to obtain free access to valuable libraries, and by comparing his results with those of other investigators, guard himself against error. The adoption of this course would, I believe, result in physical as well as intellectual benefit. It would be better, however, for these suggestions to come from Mr. Cushing, for I fear that such an intimation on my part would be construed by him to mean a recall by reason of dissatisfaction with his work.

I appreciate with you Mr. Cushing's unfortunate temperament. He fancies he has enemies where none exist.

I should be very glad if, in your next letter to him, you would make suggestions in line with the views herein expressed.

Yours cordially,
J.W. Powell

Rev. Edwd. E. Hale, D.D.
Boston

ten Kate to FHC

Springfield, Mo., November 26, 1883

Dear Mr. Cushing:

I send you herewith my pistol, which I promised you when we separated at Fort Wingate in September last. It has been the faithful companion on all my lonely wanderings, and I should be happy if you would accept it as a token of my great esteem for you and keep it as a remembrance of your Holland friend.

Before I sail for the home of my fathers, I will write to you about my trips through Colorado and the Indian Territory.[18]

Remember me, please, kindly to your ladies, and believe me,

Very sincerely,
your friend,
H. ten Kate

BANDELIER TO FHC

Sante Fe, December 7, 1883

My dear Frank!

I write you, to your and almost to my own surprise, from this place. I had to return here from El Paso del Norte, on account of sickness! A severe cold coupled with fever caught me in the malarial Rio Grande bottoms of the South. When I reached here, it settled on the lungs and thus I am and have been coughing, mostly sleepless and sometimes speechless. I had formed the plan to go to Zuni from here, but physicians prohibit explicitly my exposure to cold and snow. They peremptorily send me south. So I shall start for Tucson Monday morning, if I am well enough, and thence go—wherever I can. Not all the roads are open today.

I must now write to you in detail about that order from Berlin:

The bill, including delivery at Fort Wingate, should not exceed $200 to $225—at most! This must include all commissions, etc. I cannot designate the objects beyond that they should include fetishes, dance-ornaments, idols (?) if possible, also medicine-bowls and wands. I think it would be politic, however, to make such a selection as would create the desire for more—thus nothing very extrafine for this time, so that they will have to send for more and for more important articles.

Please make out 2 bills, both for the same (total) amount, but only one of them specified. The unspecified one should read: "Royal Museum at Berlin, Germany, to A. F. B[astian]" (this is on [account] of the manner in which the order was given). If you have time, you may itemize this bill too, but it is not absolutely required. To me, however, care Dr. *J.B. Girard,* U.S. Army, *Fort Lowell, Arizona,* I wish you would send a very detailed list. That list I must translate into German, and send it to Dr. Bastian. But you must permit me to be perfectly frank with the latter and tell him through whom the articles were secured—in fact, refer him to you as my "alter ego" in case of future orders, as I may become unreachable for some time.

I enclose to you a draft on the German Consulate at St. Louis, Mo., for $150. I had to make it payable only after shipment by express. It will at least be a guarantee to you for your outlays, etc. etc. As soon as I have the full accounts, I shall settle the rest.

Has Collet paid? Please advise me. . . .

You see, my dear friend, that I am making arrangements for a long and doubtful journey. I want to penetrate into the Sierra Madre if possible.[19]

At El Paso del Norte (Mexico) I found a branch of the Pueblos which have never as yet been recognized as such. These are the "Mansos," now properly called "Lanos," and in their own idiom "*Tsha-iu-i-re-ue*" or men. These were living (in huts like the Pimas) at El Paso in the 16th century, but they reached there from the North (New Mexico) long previous to it. Their language is nearly lost; still I recovered a few expressions and personal names. They are divided into 6 clans whose names I have; they have the same officers as the Rio Grande villages. After a severe cross-examination I was at last admitted as one of their own and introduced to the Cacique, who went through all the formalities of reception with sacred flour and cigarettes—also at the leave-taking. The Mansos now live again in adobe houses, Mexican style, but they are an old Pueblo tribe from the North and, I predict it, not yet the most Southerly one that I shall find!

Besides the Mansos, I also visited the Piros.[20] These came there in 1681 by compulsion. They fomerly dwelt at Abó, Quivira, Socorro, San Marcial, and I suspect them to be—Queres![21] The Mansos claim to have relatives at Zuni!! But all these, and many other things should be talked over in that cosy little room at the Pueblo. Oh, if only God made it possible! But he sends me away, far away from my best friends—to go on an uncertain journey again quite alone. His will be done. But please do write to me again; it is so long since I have seen your writing.

Present to Mrs. Cushing and to Miss Margaret the expressions of most sincere regards, from my wife, from Papa, and myself of course. Greet the whole Pueblo—especially Roman and Nai-iu-tchi, and do not forget No-mo-ho! I have not forgotten Roman, but the trip which I undertake would be sure death to anyone, "renegade Apaches" excepted, and with these I intend to travel. I cannot give you any details until everything is perfected.

Good bye, my dear Frank. God bless you always. Do not forget your

faithful
Adolfo

Express the goods, of course not paying expressage.
Direct: "Imperial German Consulate"
St. Louis, Mo.

The conditions made by the Consulate were that the draft should be with express receipt attached! Please attach therefore.

STEPHEN TO FHC

Keam's Cañon
December 15, 1883

Dear Cushing,

> There was a piper had a cow;
> And he had nought to give her;
> He took his pipes and played a spring,
> And bade the cow consider.

And just a few paragraphs above I read "Keep thy heart resolute and still; look prudently out, take diligent advantage of what time and chance will offer, toil along and fear nothing." And can you not guess what I am reading? Thomas Carlyle to be sure; I pray you that if, in these days of twopenny editions, you have not Carlyle *in extenso,* by all means procure yourself the best edition you can afford—no healthier food ever found your stomach. Let not the carpings which of late, since the publication of the "Reminiscences," disturb you. On my soul, I can think of no study from which so enriching results can be obtained—especially by men situated as you and I. But I was led to make the quotation which heads this page while chewing over the closing paragraph of your letter to Tom Keam—which came to us yesterday by hand of our friend Tom Po-lak-akai.[22] I refer to the cache broached by the Philistines. May the mortified *manes* of the pre-Columbian potters haunt you and destroy your slumber for—until you come over here and reach absolution.

I like that term "pre-Columbian"—did you originate it? I ask not for idleness—but if I ever get my chaotic notes on the Keam's collection ready for the printer, I would like to use it.

In parenthesis, I have been trying to get some information from our friend "Jere"; he sent me yesterday his—what shall I call it—a manuscript.[23] I hope I am not betraying his confidence, but really I had, before I saw this—manuscript—an opinion that under his buffoonery there was some—brightness. But dear me, he sent me some terrible rubbish. Amongst [which] was an essay on "pottery"—I don't know whether or no it was the draft of something sent for publication (does he publish anything, or contribute to the Bureau?), but I think not. However, he advances, after a fashion, two ideas—1. Pottery decoration originated in dots and stripes of color laid on to conceal imperfections or flaws in [a] vessel. 2. The Spanish priests taught these people decoration in colors other than black. At least this is all I can gather from his drollery. And while I am on this subject (never say that I betrayed Jere's confidence!), let me ask you—In W.H.H. Davis' hotch potch history of the Conquest of New Mexico he quotes somebody (probably Melchior Dias) writing of the Province of Cibola: "They also manufactured a kind of pelisses of feathers. . . ." "The women . . . the hair was done up behind the ear in the shape of a wheel which resembles the handle of a cup." What have you discovered of aught of this? We have remains of the feather "pelisse"—Tom Keam found it in Cañon Se-gy (De Chelly). Anent the Spanish priest, I have been unable to discover aught that would lead me to fancy he ever influenced these people in any manner whatever. I forgot to say that Jere also points to certain Zuni decoration (cross etc.) as distinctly derived from priestly. Write to me about this—but what would be ten times better—come and talk it to me.

And this brings me back to what I had in mind when I began this letter (I have a Navajo friend a'squat & a'smoking on the hearth & he says who are you writing to? I say, "U-il-tcin-Hiluny" ["Many Buttons," Cushing's Navajo nickname].[24] Enquiry as to your whereabouts, etc. etc. These folks—Navajos—seem to have a very kindly memory for you too!) But *darn* it! Let us get back to our mutton—Of course we heard about the discovery per the "*Something Orion*" published at St. Johns—it was very funny—but at the same time, to tell you the truth, it was very mortifying. We laughed over the droll, rambling effusion in the paper, but you may rest assured we did not need your postscript to remind us that "the full particulars of the finding of the crockery-ware, beads, earrings, and other curiosities" had to us a still more vivid "head-line"—as this—"The Ravishment of Cushing's Cave," "The Vandals Raid on Cushing's Treasure," and many others.[25] Facetious readings occurred to us, and now you will please apply to yourself—after careful study—the Carlyle quotations with which I began the letter. But now, my dear Cushing, don't you misapply my promptings. Both Tom Keam and myself feel the pricking of the fleshly thorn as keenly as you can and assume to ourselves a larger blame for the mishap than pertains to you. But nevertheless we are thankful for it if it will only bring you and us in closer *rapport* in this matter.

Mr. Keam writes you a plain (confidential) business proposition; for the sake of your bank account don't allow anything to stand between yourself and us. For I feel well assured that from no other source can you reap half—no, not a tithe—of the benefit (substantially and financially) that you can in clinging fast to last winter's *talk* and working with us *stoutly* in this matter. Tom McElwell is coming in from our claims to spend Christmas and New Years. Mr. Fales who manages Mr. Keam's store at Fort Defiance (an old friend of ours—did you ever meet him?) is also coming to partake of our cheer. Do you also come and join in our festivities. Pray convey my most sincere compliments to Mrs. Cushing and Miss McGill [Magill]

Truly Yours,
A.M. Stephen

P.S. I break the envelope to add a post-script. May God pardon my forgetfulness in the common courtesies. I (including Keam) made invitation to *yourself* thinking of you a'horseback—but perhaps the good gods have sent you now wheeled transportation. Why could we not enjoy the happy gathering of yourself & wife and Miss McGill? Lord! Lord! What a happy cañon this would be! Since you were here we have transmuted the parson's dwelling . . . into a most delectable ter quaterque beatus—garlanded with purple and fine linen.[26] Just chaunt to your good wife and her charming sister the song of Amiens—for Tom and I—

> Come hither, come hither, come hither;
> Here shall they see no enemy
> But Winter and rough weather.[27]

KEAM TO FHC

Dec. 16th, 1883

Dear Mr. Cushing:

Your kind favor received by Pu-la-ka-kia; accept my thanks for the kind interest you took in the matter of writing me an explanation of his trade with the Zunis. Am rather surprised to think they were so foolish as to harbour the idea that I would attempt to trade wax for coral beads; at the same time it's difficult to estimate an Indian's judgement of a white man. They can rest assured, however; I have not, neither will I attempt to sell anything but the real coral.

I will take pleasure in getting you at cost the number of strings you mention when I go East; cannot give you the price at present, as the market changes.

I note what you say about the cave find and am sorry you have sustained this loss; which I consider you have. You write of two others on which I will make a suggestion; should you so desire and have the confidence in me, we will make it a matter of business *strictly private,* that you give me the following information: the exact spots where the other caches are, whether I can get there with a wagon, and what they consist of? If it's agreeable, will give you their value at reasonable figures when in my possession in coral beads and such payment as you desire.[28]

Would much rather, however, that you come here and talk the matter over with us; so if convenient come and spend New Years day with us, as I have lots here to interest you for several days, having made valuable additions to my collection, for which I am now negotiating across the water.

With kind regards and the compliments of the season to yourself and family.

Very truly yours,
Thomas Keam

P.S. Since writing the above, Stephen came in and talked the matter over. As our collection is catalogued etc., and consists of over 500 pieces, we will keep yours separate as an addition and pay you in ratio to the sum received for the whole. We leave this, however, entirely with you.

T.V.K.

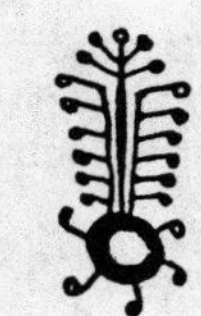

II. 1884

Last Months in Zuni

Two weeks after Cushing and his family moved into their new house on the edge of the pueblo, he received his orders to return to Washington. This development, as he remarked ruefully in his Annual Report for 1884, effectively "put a period to his fieldwork in Zuni," and, with a couple of exceptions, the papers dating from the next several months—including a feature article in the Boston Herald *perhaps authored by Cushing himself—all concern questions associated with his withdrawal from the pueblo. A somewhat different picture of what he was doing during these months (he didn't actually leave until the end of April) emerges in the retrospective Annual Report. According to this document, these were in fact months in which he accomplished a good deal in the field, carrying out "systematic explorations of the sacrificial grottoes and votive shrines of the Zunis in the main and tributary valleys of their pueblos." He reported having discovered and examined more than twenty such caves or rock-shelters in the vicinity of Zuni, Pescado, and Nutria and additional caves and ancient cemeteries some twenty or thirty miles to the south of the central Zuni valley. He also reported having witnessed, back in Zuni, one of the great quadrennially conducted ceremonies of initiation into the Kachina society—an initiation in which, but for his imminent departure, he would himself have taken part as one of the candidates. An occasion for the recitation (more than six hours long) of the epic ritual Cushing would expound in "Outlines of Zuni Creation Myths," the ceremony itself is briefly described in* Zuni Breadstuff*—a work also in progress during these last months in Zuni, though unmentioned in the papers to follow.*[1]

Pilling to FHC

January 19, 1884

My Dear Sir:

It is thought best that the valuable ethnologic material collected by you at the Pueblo of Zuni should be put in shape for publication at as early a day as practicable and that progress to this end would be facilitated by your presence, for a time, in the East. As soon, therefore, as you can settle your affairs in Zuni, and make the necessary arrangements—not later than Feb'y 15th, if possible—you will proceed to Washington and report to the Director.

Passes for three over the A. & P., and A. T. & SF. Railroads will be sent you at an early day, also Transportation orders from Kansas City to Washington, via St. Louis. Such shipments that you may have to make as will admit of delay, can be sent through the Quartermaster's Dep't. Your manuscripts, however, it is thought wise to trust to the custody of the express company.

By order of the Director, Yours with respect,
James C. Pilling

FHC to Powell

Zuni, New Mexico, January 29, 1884

Sir:

In reply to your orders of the 19th instant, transmitted through Mr. Pilling, permit me to state that it is my desire to comply with them. But also as somewhat affecting my power to do this immediately I would respectfully submit the following considerations.

You are duly informed that I have been engaged during the past four months in building a house adjoining the pueblo of Zuni [and] that the necessity of this measure existed not only in the comfort of my family but as a sanitary measure, as my health has been until recently steadily failing since my return from the East. Before I attempted this, however, I had the honor to submit the matter to you, asking your assistance or at least approval, in case you deemed my stay at Zuni would extend over the present winter. Although I did not hear directly from you, through your assistant I learned that you did not disapprove my plans, but that it might not be possible or convenient for the Office to aid me financially.

I therefore made contracts with the party [of] Malone & MacIntosh for the building. Of course, as is the case with all such undertakings, the expenses of this one came to far exceed my calculations. I was also, as a measure of economy, compelled, as duly reported to you, to do all the carpenter work etc. with my own hands.

I have now been two weeks settled in my new home.[2] My health and that of my family has improved, and I have been able to resume systematically my long deferred official duties. My house is commodious and comfortable, but it has cost me already the outlay in money and stock of six hundred and ninety-seven dollars, and I still have on account of the building for freightage seventy five dollars; for lumber, windows, doors, fittings, etc., two hundred and seventy five dollars; for day labor thirty seven dollars; and for paving stones thirty five dollars. In all, four hundred and twelve dollars of debt.

I cannot, from the nature of my obligation, leave Zuni before these debts are discharged. I therefore beg that you shall allow me from four to six months more in the field for the payment of them. I shall be able to make these payments much more expeditiously if—to the detriment of my paper work, it is true—I am allowed by you to enter into literary engagements, which heretofore I have, for considerations of honor, held in abeyance.

Relative to the progress of my work, it would be rather retarded than advanced by my *immediate* departure for the East. (1st) Thanks to the generosity of my Boston friends, I have received large and valuable additions to my special ethnologic library, including dozens of treatises on mythology and folklore as well as ancient Spanish publications relative to the Pueblos and their country. (2nd) So far as intercourse with Washington ethnologists is concerned, I care for the exchange of ideas with *not one* of them save with yourself and Mr. Holmes. No others could enhance my work at present in the slightest advantageous degree.

If, on the other hand, my return is a necessity or desirability for reasons which you have not deemed it wise to communicate to me (as I am to infer it is from the nature of information and letters received during December and the present month), please send me the money accounted for on signed vouchers forwarded to my friend Mr. Brown during Nov. last.[3] With this I solemnly promise to discharge the above mentioned debts and immediately return to Washington as per the letter of your orders. I should much prefer this to waiting, as I feel that my enforced want of alacrity in obeying your instructions—essentially so though it be—will not only annoy you but, if my information and inferences be correct—seriously interfere with more plans than one. If you find it expedient to aid me in this way, telegraph me at once, please, on receipt of this, in order that, awaiting the money and your further instructions, I may be engaged in preparations (they will be few) for the journey. I regret that by building (under the impression that I could *monograph* Zuni, and live to do it) I made a mistake. The error has, however, been committed and alas, I am consequently compelled to write you as I do.

If the above considerations seem either uncalled for or insubordinate, I beg earnestly you will forgive the liberty I have taken in submitting them, bear with and support me during the necessary preparations and correspondence accompanying my final withdrawal from the service of the government, and accept as heartfelt my profound gratitude for the many kindnesses and opportunities I have received at your hand.

On my return, which I trust will be speedy in either case, I shall bring with me the two blankets for which you still have credit with me.

I have the honor to be, dear and esteemed sir, very respectfully,

Your Obedient Servant,
F.H. Cushing
Ass't Ethnologist

Bandelier to FHC

Fort Lowell, A.T., February 6, 1884

My dear Frank!

Your two kind letters were forwarded here, where I arrived last Thursday, and I had so much to do since, that only today I am enabled to reply at least partly to their contents. Firstly, thanks for your friendship, and for the attachment of your dear ones at Zuni, whose symbolical card I have received too. Yes, let us never give up the ship! I have already looked forward in the future, and I hope for both of us. This topic will form the end of my letter. Now I must tell of something else:

The German Consul has written to me about the order. He is anxious; the draft has not been presented, and he fears we might have forgotten the whole thing. He will write to you, and I wish you would explain to him the difficulties of the task, give him a list of what you have already got together, and ship as soon as you can. The earlier the better. If we can satisfy him, it will be a good point for the future. At all events, write to me here immediately how matters stand, so that I can give him detailed information also. Those people want to be written to often.[4]

Now another thing. I am seriously contemplating a publication on my "own hook," and in Germany! But I would like for you to join in and make it a joint work. The language is no difficulty, as I should translate your part into German. One thing is certain: we can never realize anything out of our studies in this country, but I think that in Germany a subscription book would show well, *if it was profusely illustrated.* I have seen here a Natural History with color plates, magnificently done, by a first class artist, which has had, and still has, a splendid run, and the plates are sold separate from the text—in fact partially in advance of the latter. There are 170 plates, and they are sold here at $19—only! Now one could save the cost of the artist; my own collection will soon be composed of 300 sheets, and if you will take charge of the scenes of life and of the ritual part, including Zuni pottery, the Moquis, Hava-Supay, and such ruins as are within our reach, I think we can fill quite a respectable Atlas of chromo-lithographs.

My father is exceedingly taken with the idea of a joint publication. We could do good work, and on a much broader ethnological, archaeological and historical platform in this manner, and, if this be not too vain, fully eclipse the pompous folios of Washington in real value.[5] The landscapes I would suggest to put into the text. It is evident that, if the book has a good start in German, an English edition can soon be ready. Your original will be ready, and my German is quickly translated, [and] the plates are already done and in print.

Thus much for this part. Think over it and reply to me at once. My address will be at Tucson until I give you a different one, which will be when I leave for the "dark and bloody ground" in the South.

Meanwhile, excuse brevity. Tomorrow I go to Fort Grant with Chico, who is as good and bad as ever.[6]

By the way, have I told you that the Consul paid me $40 on . . . the order? I fear I forgot it. Make a memorandum of the amount. He wanted to give me the whole amount, but I could not take it. So that $190 is what is drawn.

Love to all. In haste,
Adolfo

FHC to Edward Everett Hale

Zuni, February 17th, 1884

Dear Doctor Hale:

Mrs. Cushing has received, this evening, your kind enclosure of novels. In my gratitude for her sake, may I be pardoned for thanking you first? I am mindful too of your recent letter, of the entertaining and thought-making book from your own hands—which we have all enjoyed—and of the beautiful, dearly treasured volumes which have been coming lately from you and Professor Horsford. I am ashamed that circumstances which would not have troubled me much two or three years ago now weigh me down woefully—so much so that I am sometimes physically ill from their effects, always intellectually deadened by them; hence, I may have been neglectful. I will not enlarge upon my new woes. I am ordered to Washington and it sickens me. My friends do not give me much sympathy, but consider rather the new turn of things a cause for congratulation. I suppose it is fancied I am tunneling too deep, may perhaps bury myself. The case is not understood as I see it, of course, and a great many things are inevitable!

I am always grateful for your helpful friendship to us all. I glory in it and shall many years hence when it becomes a beautiful memory woven with others of Boston. Please accept Mrs. Cushing's love.

I am always gratefully and devotedly yours,
Frank Hamilton Cushing

Rev. Dr. Edward Everett Hale
Roxbury Station
Boston, Massachusetts

I noticed the sweet remark you made one of your members of the palace make about the Zunis.

Draft: FHC to Miss Cushing

Zuni, March 16, 1884

Dear Miss Cushing:

As I do not think the possession of arms confers on anyone special superiority, only insofar as he or she may inherit and ennoble those virtues the exercise of which earned them for his or her ancestors; as, moreover, I do not deem a near degree of cousinship at all essential as an excuse for the asking of questions where there exists an interest such as yours seems to be in one's work, I am even now answering your pleasant long letter, which came with yesterday's mail.

You seem to make too great a distinction between the Massachusetts and New York Cushings, whereas that distinction is one only of three generations at most, and not of origin. Recurring to the arms, therefore, you are probably as much entitled to them as I am. The Fredonia Cushings and those of Wyoming and Madison County, New York, are, my father learned for me some five years ago, all derived from the old Hingham stock. As you belong to the first named, I to the last, of these branches, there remains no doubt of kindred—whether we be prepared to be proud of the fact or not![7]

A honey-bee cares little where he gets his honey. He may extract it from the downy bloom of colored clover fields or from the thorn encircled pollen-dusty flowers of thistles—it matters little to him. What matters more is that he gets the honey, for he must have it even in superabundance. While I would suffer industrially from the comparison, more than I would care to, this excepted it is with me as with the honey-bee. I have to have knowledge of savage life, and it matters less to me where I find it than it does in what measure I find it. Zuni, therefore, while I confess it to be a patch of thorns in the side of a civilized being, is attractive to me because of the satisfaction it gives to my craving after knowledge of savage lore and life. And now "what is the use of it all?" Of the many uses recognizable in ethnologic studies, two are sufficient to excuse any man for giving his life to them.

The first great use of studying savages is that, recognizing the truth of our own development from a barbarous unlettered condition very like that in which we find savages today—if not indeed identical with it—to our high state of civilization, we cannot understand this civilization of which we partake without understanding what it springs from and how. Therefore the ethnologist's function supplements the historian's—is able to restore thousands of his missing pages.[8]

The second greater use is suggested by what you say in telling me that "I have, like the majority of people, supposed until reading your papers on Zuni life, that the Indians were a very useless and at times a formidable burden on the government and that there was little in their daily life and likes to interest one."

I mean to say that by thoroughly studying and revealing the life and traits of the Indian, we cannot fail, if happy in our mission, of exciting interest in him where none existed before; cannot fail of showing him to be more human than we had supposed him, more capable of being made usefuller and better than it has been supposed possible—and will continue supposed until our knowledge of him is widened and *deepened* by the closest scrutiny and intimacy. That this increased knowledge and interest is sadly needed, you will not fail to grant when I tell you that the execution of the Streltsi by Peter the Great, the butchery of the French Revolution, bear no comparison with the cruelty, the sickening waste of life (both of white and Indian, but *more* of the latter) which, through a single century has resulted from our misunderstanding of the Indian.[9] Since I have become conversant with Indian character, not only from a singularly apt sympathy with it but from the employment of my best faculties in its study, I have learned that not *one* of our great Indian troubles but could have been averted, had we better understood the natures of the people we have so unwittedly and invariably made our enemies. During my long stay in Zuni I have witnessed numerous disputes—bitter word-broils—between whites and Indians which almost without exception I have been able to dispell instantly—simply because I understood the natures of both disputants. With less peaceful Indians I can readily imagine how those disputes arising from the simplest mutual misunderstanding could and *would,* without explanation, have resulted in war of the bloodiest and bitterest sort. [Further pages, if any, missing]

Pilling to FHC

March 20, 1884

Dear Mr. Cushing:

There will be sent you by today's mail U.S. drafts on St. Louis for the full amount of your vouchers and for your salary for the month of March, thus removing all obstacles to your speedy return to Washington.

There is sent you enclosed such transportation in the way of passes as we have been able to procure. A request has also been made by us on the Atlantic and Pacific Road, but unless the passes have been sent to you direct the request has not been honored. Upon receipt of this, please telegraph us if these (the A. & P.) passes have been received by you.

Keep a memorandum of your traveling expenses, the amount to be refunded to you by the Chief Disbursing Officer upon your arrival. Transportation orders from the Missouri River eastwards would be sent you, but this method has been abolished by order of the Secretary of the Interior.

In office letter of January 19th you will find instructions concerning the shipment of public property.

Please advise me of the receipt of the drafts and the probable time of your arrival here.

By order of the Director.

Yours, etc.
James C. Pilling
Chief Clerk

FHC to Powell

Zuni, March 30, 1884

Sir:

I have the honor to acknowledge with both pleasure and gratitude your orders of the 21st instant as also the receipt of sundry passes and draughts.

I beg leave to inform you that as these important letters and papers were not delivered to me until yesterday, it will be necessary for me to get the passes renewed, as those over the Atcheson Topeka and Santa Fe expire tomorrow, March 31st.

I therefore by this mail, ask in a letter to our good friend Mr. White, the General Passenger Agent, their renewal at earliest convenience.

The delay which this will entail is not to be deplored, because rendered necessary for two distinct reasons: First, my messenger found in the road between this place and Fort Wingate two wagons, one of [them] government [property], mired and abandoned. This results from the recent heavy snows on the mountains above Las Nutrias and the subsequent rain storms and floods. I therefore find it impossible to secure transportation for the present. A less serious difficulty—because temporary—is my present illness. Four days since, I was suddenly prostrated with an attack of pleurisy and I have not yet far enough recovered to leave my bed. I now have the benefit of Dr. Matthews' treatment and hope within a few days to recover. Meanwhile, under Mrs. Cushing's directions, preparations for our own departure from Zuni are being pressed forward.

I think I can safely assure you that we shall leave Fort Wingate station not later than the first of May, and I sincerely hope we may start much sooner. I have thus explained that you may understand my desire is to make avail of the facilities you have obligingly placed in my hands at the earliest practicable moment.

Passes for three over the A & P Railroad from Fort Wingate to Albuquerque N.M. arrived yesterday. I hope I do not commit wrong in acknowledging by this post General Smith's courtesy.

I do myself the honor to enclose under separate wrapper a recent issue of my authorship in the Indianapolis *Millstone.*[10] For this series, which has cost little time, I received extremely liberal aid toward the discharge of my debts.

Thanking you for the opportunity now afforded me for a visit and sojourn in the East, I have the honor to remain

Very Respectfully Yours,
F.H. Cushing

Newspaper Article

[*The following two-column story appeared in the Sunday* Boston Herald *of April 20, 1884 (p. 13), signed only with the initial "H." The author's identity is unknown; but given the nature of much of the information, as well as certain stylistic features (e.g., familiar involutions of syntax), Cushing's manifest concern for his public image,* and *the evidence of his authorship of the earlier so-called "interview" regarding the Nutria controversy, one might not be too far off the mark in guessing that here too is a case of self-service journalism and that the "H." stands for Hamilton, Cushing's own middle name. In any event, whoever wrote the piece, the major* source *was clearly*

Cushing—as it was in at least two earlier Herald *stories filed by his friend Sylvester Baxter.*]

INDIAN FOLK-LORE: Why Mr. Cushing Has to Stay So Long in Zuni. His Persecution by Senator Logan. Expected Results of His Self-Denying Mission. (From our Special Correspondent)

Santa Fe, N.M., April 16, 1884. Those who are conversant with American ethnology declare that the most exhaustive study ever made of any tribe of Indians is that which has been carried on through countless difficulties by Mr. Frank H. Cushing among the Zunis. The value of his researches has attracted the attention of foreign scientists, whose communications, both private and public, show that they are eagerly awaiting the completion of a task which, to bring convincing results, necessarily requires the devotion of several years. It is not strange that frontiersmen, who consider that "the only good Indian is a dead one," should misunderstand Mr. Cushing's work and misconstrue his motives. But it is almost incomprehensible that a man who calls himself a statesman and who aspires to be the President of the United States, should stoop to assail this self-sacrificing young scientist and endeavor not only to injure him socially here and in Washington but to procure his removal under a threat of withholding funds for the Smithsonian Institute. The *Herald* was the first to expose the selfish reasons for John A. Logan's bitter attacks upon Mr. Frank Cushing. Its readers will remember that Logan's son-in-law, Tucker, claimed the lands of the Zunis, including the Nutria and Pescado springs, which were essential to their support. Mr. Cushing naturally presented the side of the Zunis in temperate and dignified arguments, and at once Logan opened the floodgates of wrath upon him. President Arthur restored the lands to the Zunis, but Logan has demanded an official investigation of their claims, and, meantime, is doing his utmost to compel the Smithsonian to discard Mr. Cushing.

These facts are well known, but you are probably not aware that in February Mr. Cushing received an order to leave his work and come to Washington. It was the opinion here that Logan's threats and maneuvers had been successful. The order came at a peculiarly unfortunate time. After much labor and expense, Mr. Cushing had completed a house on Hallona hill, near the pueblo of Zuni, in which he, his wife, and sister-in-law, two Washington ladies, were comfortably settled. This work was done with the knowledge and sanction of the Washington officials, who were aware that Mr. Cushing required an extended stay for the thorough accomplishment of his researches. It is understood, however, that the order received by him, although stated to be for the benefit of his health and the hastening of the publication of his results, appeared to indicate a permanent separation from Zuni. Mr. Cushing was obliged to reply that he could not leave Zuni at once, as he must clear away obligations incurred for his house. For this he apologized and asked his director, if the delay seemed uncalled for, to bear with him during the arrangements necessary for his withdrawal from the service of the government. Mr. Cushing's manly submission of his resignation has become known only by accident.[11] It will be a surprise to his Boston friends to hear that his invaluable work has so nearly met with a final interruption. But fortunately the director of the Bureau of Ethnology met Mr. Cushing in an equally frank and generous spirit and gave him permission to remain. Whether the suggestion of Mr. Cushing's resignation had anything to do with this, I do not know. But he is still pursuing his work at Zuni. It is said that Logan's final and boldest attack upon the young man who maintained the rights of defenseless Indians against the son in-law of the all-powerful senator will soon be made. Mr. Cushing, officially, is an assistant ethnologist in [the] Bureau of Ethnology, whose director is Maj. J.W. Powell, also the director of the United States Geological Survey. This Bureau, like the National Museum, is under the Department of the Interior, but, while supported by annual appropriations, it is part of the Smithsonian Institute, its director being in some measure governed by and wholly accountable to the secretary of the Smithsonian, according to a relationship established in 1879. These appropriations are made in the sundry civil bill, usually the last to come up for discussion in Congress. When this bill reaches the Senate, it is stated that Logan will refuse to consent to the appropriation of any money for the Smithsonian so long as Mr. Cushing remains connected with it. The developments will be interesting. . . .

[*The article goes on to explain at length what Cushing was doing in Zuni, why it required his "self-sacrificing adoption of Indian life and his persevering devotion of years to the task," and some of what he had learned about Indian ways of thinking. This segment is omitted here as essentially duplicated by other Cushing expositions already in print.*]

[Though] he was abused and persecuted by men who can only understand self-sacrifice when it involves large acquisitions of the almighty dollar, Mr. Cushing's methods gave him such familiarity with Indian life as has never been attained before in his time, for no one had before adopted Indian life for his purposes. When he made statements as to his discoveries, he was charitably contradicted in some cases and in others accused of inventing marvels. This made him realize that it was necessary to surround himself with an army of invincible facts, and then assume an impregnable position. That is why he has wished a longer stay in Zuni. As he says, "Not that it takes years for me to get what I want for myself, but it takes many years to get what others will have to accept, whether they want to or not." And he adds, "I will not publish my results thus far, considerable though they be, unless I can make them invulnerable. I have been so misunderstood, so jealously discussed and so condemned that my final work must be my vindication." I happen to know that Mr. Cushing has always had in mind a possible result of ethnological researches in wearing away race barriers and benefitting the Indian. That is, to show what the Indian has been and may be and to prove that the blame of his doom rests not on natural causes altogether but on the selfishness, born of ignorance, and lack of sympathy, [on the part] of our race. I mention this only to show that Mr. Cushing has not been altogether a cold-blooded scientist. I have given only a few of the principles which he has discovered. To illustrate them by examples from the wealth of information regarding Indian folk lore, tradition and customs which Mr. Cushing has acquired would need more space than any daily journal could give. Mr. Cushing's own articles in the *Century, Harper's,* the *Atlantic* and other periodicals were published too early to more than foreshadow the results already reached and to come.[12] I have only tried to convey an idea of his objects in remaining at Zuni and to give some reasons for the length of time required to round off his great work with success.

H.

TELEGRAM: FHC TO POWELL

Albuquerque, New Mexico
April 26, 1884

Leave here at eleven thirty tonight. Will wire you from Chicago.

F.H. Cushing

Epilogue: Back in Washington

Cushing's severance from Zuni did not, of course, mean an end to his relationship with the Zunis; nor did it terminate his involvement with Zuni issues such as the Logan land claim. What follows is a kind of epilogue, consisting of a selection of letters written in the aftermath of Cushing's withdrawal—loose ends, strands of a conclusion which reads, "to be continued."

FHC to Matthews

June 5, 1884

Dear Doctor:

I hope you will forgive me for neglecting to send this yesterday. I had to go down to the Bureau, received news there which rather drove other things out of my mind—namely, relative to the arrival of our things, books, etc., from Wingate. Hence did not notice my omission until this morning.

If I can do anything more, let me know.

Where do the Philosophers hold their councils?

Always your friend,
FHC

FHC to Matthews

June 4, 1884

Dear Doctor:

Below you will find jotted hastily together some of the animal and other myths of observation commonly told during Winter by the Zuni in their recitals of Folk lore. I have added two or three examples from the Ha-va-su-pai, or Coçonino, and Oraibi Indians.

Zuni

Dogs

In the days of Creation there was a guilty pair of lovers. In those days, dogs talked. The girl was the daughter of a great priest. This priest owned a wise dog. The dog had the habit of lounging around everywhere; thus he discovered the guilt of the lovers and told the old priest. The priest did not believe him, so, possessed of magic power, as priests were then, he deprived the dog of speech. It happened that the dog discovered the guilt of the lovers again. He tried to speak, but could only bark. So he pointed to them with his ears and wagged his tail. The priest understood and punished the lovers, whereupon the latter, growing angry, cut off the dog's ears and tail; hence today, dogs, although cunning of thought, speak not, but bark and groan; yet they are always sneaking about, and in order that they shall not cause unnecessary trouble or suspicion in the world, we cut off their tails and ears.

The most casual visitor to Zuni will observe this peculiarity of the dogs there.

Crows

Crows were once beautiful. They had collars of white like shell necklaces about their throats, bright bands like embroidered scarfs on their shoulders, and their backs were glossy and blue like the wings of beetles. In those days the Maidens of Corn were lost. The priests called a council and decided to ask the crow's assistance in seeking them. When the crow entered, they gave him a cigarette of welcome. He greedily drew in such a big whiff of smoke that it strangled him and singed his feathers. Then they showed him an ear of corn and asked him to go seek the Maidens whose flesh it was. The crow snatched up the corn and flew away with it, laughing. Etc. etc.

This is why crows are black all over and cackle as they fly. Even now, as soon as they get into company (with other crows), they strangle and hawk—thinking they have just entered council! Moreover, they never see an ear of corn without thoughts of thieving.

Turtles

In ancient times the two little War Gods acknowledged many animals of "strong thoughts" as their grandparents; but as children nowadays—being nimble—play pranks on old people, so did the little War Gods delight in teasing their grandparents. One day as they were wandering down the Valley (of Zuni), they found their grandfather the turtle sprawled out on a slimy pool. Thinking to frighten him, they rushed up of a sudden and pelted him with arrows, so that his back was scratched and stained with slime—etc.

This is why the turtle's back is covered with marks and mottled with green and why also he dodges under the water the moment a man approaches.

Canes

The cane was the tallest plant of its size known, and the most rapid growing. So the Gods chose it to be the ladder on which men should climb out of the wombs of the Earth. Therefore canes now grow jointed, showing the notches made by the feet of the ancestors.

- - -

Rock Formations

In the days of Creation the world was too damp, and many great beings destructive to men and the creatures roamed abroad. So the "Two Little Ones" (prototypes of the Boy War Gods) shot their arrows of lightning out over the four regions of the Earth. The waters receded, the Earth was dried, the shells and monsters of the great waters, many ferocious beings and prey beasts were changed to stone or shriveled and hardened, the sand, earth and mud roasted and scorched or burned to lime and melted. Hence on the mountains, in ravines and valleys, among cliffs, we find strange forms of living beings in stone, and the rocks are red like baked clay, burned like scorched suet, white like ashes and lime, or melted like alum and salt turned to fluid in fire.

- - -

Ha-va-su-pai

Coyotes

When the first man died, the coyote said, "Burn him, and with his ashes you may dry the world"—for it was very damp. Forthwith, the coyote ran to fetch fire. The blue-bottle fly sitting on a dry twig said, "I will make fire." So rubbing his wing with his foot he struck off sparks which ignited the branch he sat on. The people began to burn the body with this fire, when the coyote saw the smoke from a long way off and ran back in rage. Before he could return, however, all of the body except the heart was consumed, but he rushed past the spectators and grabbing the heart from the fire raced away with it, eating half and burying the rest. Hence to this day the face and chin of the coyote is black where he singed it, and he always buries part of his food. Etc. etc.

- - -

Oraibi

A variant of this myth, even more ingenious but also more lengthy, occurs in Zuni; hence I produce the Oraibi form, which occurs in their Creation myth:

Locusts

"Go back," said the people to the locust. "I will not," replied the locust. In rage they ran him through and through with arrows so that his insides and blood flowed out over his body, which was white, turning it black and brown and causing it to shrink and the locust to die. Yet after a time the locust came to life again and ran about more nimbly than ever.

Therefore, locusts, when first born, are white and fat and live underground as did the first locust in the wombs of the world; but they die and after eight years or four, come to life again and are brown and black but slim and nimble.

- - -

Hoping you may find these mere extracts from long stories mostly, useful for your purpose, I am always

Yours Faithfully,
FHC

Bourke to FHC

Whipple Barracks
Prescott, Arizona
June 30, 1884

My dear Cushing:

I am afraid to say too much lest you doubt my sincerity, but in all truth I assert that to withdraw you from the field of labor among the Zunis will shortly prove to have been a grievous blunder and a great loss to ethnological science. Your "Zuni Fetiches" is an honor to the Smithsonian—by all odds the best pamphlet they have ever issued, to my knowledge.

The copy sent me was torn in unrolling; can you send me two others? I want one for myself and one to send to my wife's parents in Omaha, who have seen my torn copy and have learned much concerning you and your important labors. No matter what channel you may follow in the future, my best wishes will attend you. I hope that success may crown your efforts and that brilliant distinction may await you. Don't become downcast. If you have no other prospects of livelihood, let me suggest that you return to New Mexico, get the Zunis to point out to you some good cattle ranch outside their reservation but near enough so that you can have their protection and they your counsels. New York and Boston capitalists are now eager to back up just such men as you. You may, possibly, be taken up and encouraged by the Ethnological Bureau. I hardly expect that; your attainments are too solid and too varied. A congregation of penny-dips will not be disposed to let an electric light enter among them. You know well that I have always distrusted those people and that in our communications long ago we both concluded not to lean upon them too much. I believe that they were at the bottom of your failure to get a commission.

As I told you in a recent letter, I have done nothing of late except a little in regard to the gentile organization, marriage customs, religion and language of the Apaches; I haven't much in its way, but just enough to make me regret that I haven't more. I did think of sending the notes to Powell, but upon second thought have made up my mind to defer action, not wishing to wear myself out.

Good luck to you, old boy. If I can help you in any way, let me know. You'll find me ready. With the united regards of my wife and self to you and your wife,

Sincerely your friend,
John G. Bourke

Have you forgotten the meals we prepared conjointly at Zuni? And how the squaw took pity on my forlorn condition and made us bread?

Douglas D. Graham to FHC

Zuni Pueblo, June 5th, 1884

Dear Cushing:

Your letters, and packages for the Indians arrived safely, which I handed to each one. They were delighted with them and seemed as happy as a boy with his first pair of red-top boots.

I told the old Gov. about his packages at Wingate, he will go for them in a few days. When the packages arrived he wanted to take them all to his house, he said he would distribute them—but I thought best to follow directions which came out all right.

Should I decide to remain here another year, I should like to occupy your house, buy it, or rent it from you, as you see best. But I would much rather see you occupy it. I go over once in a while to take a look at it to see if everything is all right. As far as I can see, no one has been trying to break in. I heard they had stolen a window. I went over to see, but they are all there. I do hope you will come back, as I find it very lonesome since you went away. . . .

With kind remembrance to Mrs. Cushing, Miss Magill, and trusting you will favor me with more of your good letters, I remain

Yours,
Douglas D. Graham

Edwin A. Curley to FHC[1]

New York
July 18, 1884

Private

Dear Mr. Cushing:

Many thanks for your prompt response to my epistle. I received it this morning. I have since had a discussion on the subject with the *Herald.*

The idea is entertained of throwing its influence and its money into the breach and using any and all means to overthrow the despoilers.

If the *Herald* goes in on the plan that I have suggested, the conspiracy will be defeated without fail, but it will be several days before I get a decision and I very much fear that after all they will not think it worth while to undertake the task, which they know will not be a light one.

You know my view of the legal aspects of the case. You know also that what the law is is a matter of no possible consequence with Logan the despoiler [if there is] neither money nor influence on the other side.

I am a Republican, but my suffrage and my little influence is for Cleveland. Our mutual friend Curtis swallows Blaine and Logan, horns and all. He doesn't like the medicine but he dare not bolt the ticket.

You do right to be very careful in your circumstances. Of course I did not tell the *Herald* that I was in communication with you. It is *possible,* however, that the time may soon come when I can suggest to you the desirability of coming out squarely. If so, it will be because you can be entirely independent of your present *Lords and Masters*.

Queries:

1. What are Dr. Matthews' initials? 2. What is the name of the Zuni boy who was at Carlisle? 3. Can he read writing? 4. Could he translate a plain letter if I sent one to him for the Governor? 5. What is the Governor's name? 6. Could the boy probably be

trusted to report properly to the Governor the substance of a letter if I wrote him one? 7. Could he probably send me back intelligible answers to my questions?

I have no doubt that Dr. Matthews will respond to my enquiries but unfortunately I have forgotten his initials and I do not like to write without them.

Did I tell you that when I returned to Fort Wingate I made no secret of the nature of my report and that the direction of the sympathies of the officers was very evident?

They know that I used perfect discretion as to them, and I think that perhaps I might benefit by that fact if I should visit Wingate again.

I shall write again in a few days & in the meantime I shall do what I can. I confess that it is more than likely that I can do nothing effectual. But I shall nonetheless make every reasonable effort. I could use the press a little, but that alone would be worth nothing because insufficient in the present state of the case.

You are unfortunately so tied that you can do nothing (or very little, I should say), but if your hands were only free you could do more, much more than anybody else.

I shall be delighted to receive that book of yours.

I think that perhaps I could so call the attention of some of the most influential newspapers here that they would give you first rate notices, always supposing what I do not doubt is the fact, that it is well worthy of such attentions. I read some of your articles and they were clearly worthy of your very interesting subjects.

By the way, there is one thing that I am anxious about independently of those already mentioned. Could you, through some other person in whom you have confidence, get a rough tracing from the Gov. survey of Nutria and the neighborhood showing the subdivisions and the location of the village, the spring, stream ditch and if possible the cultivated fields. The sections numbered?

Also the sect. etc. of the filings thereon?

If so, what would it cost?

You will understand of course that I am far from wishing that you should get them personally, because I believe that course would be indiscreet.

Kindly excuse this long and hasty scrawl.

Doubtless Mrs. C[ushing] and Miss M[agill] enjoy their return to W[ashington], notwithstanding the disappointment which it involves and which they can but share. Please give them my kindest regards and believe me

Yours very truly,
Edwin A. Curley

Baxter to FHC

Boston, July 30, 1884

My dear Tenatsali:

. . . .

I have just forwarded to the *New York Sun* a statement of what I know concerning Logan's attempt on the Zuni land and his vindictive persecution of you. It can do you no harm, for Logan is bound to destroy you if he can, and it may contribute towards destroying him politically.

I have just had a letter from Bourke in which he denounces "the ticket," and Logan in particular for his persection of you, in his customary vigorous language.

I am in haste now, but shall write again soon. Meanwhile let me hear from you.

Your faithful friend,
Sylvester Baxter

Bourke to FHC

Whipple Barracks
Prescott, Arizona
September 13, 1884

My dear Cushing:

Mrs. Bourke wishes me to thank you most warmly for your congratulations upon the birth of our baby, and both she and I wish to add our reciprocations upon the brilliant success you have achieved at Montreal.[2] I don't want to suggest anything which may cause you to lose your cool judgment, but I cannot refrain from saying that you should strive for a *European* reputation. America offers no suitable field for you. Very few of our people care for the Indians, and nearly all of them manifest a suspicion of a man who presumes to consider their manners, customs and ideas worthy of note and preservation. Therefore, I say, cultivate such men as Tylor, Herbert Spencer, etc. You don't equal them yet in experience (literary) and attainments, but you have had a practical association with the Indians which has never been excelled and shall never again be excelled. In an article written about you some years since, I compared your practical note-taking to the work with which the Spanish missionaries have been credited. This difference must be indicated in your favor; you were a scientific ethnologist, which they were not. It will not be difficult for you to get ordered to London on some scientific work which will give the necessary facilities for cementing the pleasant relations begun in Canada. Don't worry about the illustrious (!) Senator.

My little book appeared in London last month. Scribner's have charge of its fate in this country.[3] Upon the arrival of the first invoice from England, a copy is to go to you, which please accept as a tribute from a warm friend and admirer. I will not ask you to say a word in its favor to anybody, as its defects will be detected by you at a glance. I have only to say that it was pressed to completion while I was under orders to go on the Sierra Madre campaign and that careful revision was impossible at that time and in this place.[4] My object was not to write a scientific book for scientific people, but a popular book to interest Americans in ethnology.

I have lately summed up the data accumulated in regard to the religion of the Apaches, giving their prayers to Snake, Sun, Earth, Winds, etc. etc. I am strong in the conviction that all Indian tribes have a common religion, or one based on [the] same general ideas. I have also some 1,200 odd words of an Apache vocabulary, with conjugations of some verbs, showing singular, dual and plural numbers, and a complete list of the clans of the different divisions of that family congregated at or near San Carlos (6,000 souls). I had intended sending those to Maj. Powell, but, upon reflection, prefer waiting until some future date when you may receive from the Smithsonian the prominence long withheld through jealousy of your talents and labors. In this case, I'll send to *your* Bureau. . . .[5]

A note came from Baxter last week; as usual, he mentioned you warmly. Kind remembrances to Mrs. Cushing.

Sincerely and truly yours,
John G. Bourke

Matthews to FHC

Fort Defiance Agency
November 4, 1884

My dear Frank:

Arrived here last night. Tomorrow I start for a place called "The Haystacks" to attend a *Yebitcai* dance; it will occupy five days. Yours of October 26th came to hand before I left Wingate, but I had not time to reply there. I will not have time to go to Zuni, but if the shells arrive, I will send them over to Palowahtiwa. Have just finished a ten days' visit to a *hockan* dance.[6] Got into the medicine lodge and saw things that I never dreamt of. Would you imagine that the rascals, who have neither ornamental robes, skins, or pottery, or carven idols, have nevertheless a complete system of pictographic mythic symbolism? They draw immense hieratic figures in powdered colors on the sanded floor of the medicine lodge, and when done, erase them and carry the very sand out of the lodge. Each day a separate design of really artistic appearance. Did you ever hear of such an art? A slight mention is made of something like this in Col. Dodge's last book; but elsewhere I have seen no mention of it. I will see more of their mythic designs at the *Yebitcai*. One who had never entered their medicine lodge could not dream that they had such an art. I have written to Powell about it; but I presume no notice will be taken of it. Think I will send a description of it to the "Peat Bog."[7]

There will, I think, be no necessity for your bringing in your Indians from Zuni or for your coming out here again. I saw Col. Stevenson at Wingate. He assured me that Mrs. Stevenson had learned to talk both Zuni and Spanish fluently and was obtaining no end of valuable information on all points from the Indians. From the way she is working, I think she will get all that is worth getting before long. The Indians are just unbosoming themselves to her. Col. S. too has explored a number of caves around Zuni and made wonderful discoveries. He has found images that apparently have beards. He is making a great collection of cave materials to be sent to Washington.

I plead guilty to tripping the "light fantastic" at Wingate. We had a delightful german of nine couples as a farewell to Mrs. Waterbury.

I find the new agent here just to my liking—a fine, free-hearted, hard-sense, strong-willed but unpretending Western man.[8] He is very kind and is doing everything he can to assist me.

Please tell me what you know about the "sand pictures."

With kindest regards to Mrs. Cushing and Miss Maggie,

Your sincere friend,
W. Matthews

FHC TO PALOWAHTIWA

Washington, D.C. [mid 1884]

My always Beloved Brother Palowahtiwa:

May you be happy! Yet again, through my reverenced friend, I speak to you. Grant me the kind favor that you treat him preciously; for this priest's influence and approval I long to win. Possibly he may wish to collect with wampum material and money a few utensils etc. of your people; in order to take them with him to the country of his nation, the English.[9] Help him; for as I have asked of you, so also I contemplate for you a favor, and shall soon send you, with our friend Dr. Matthews, much wampum material when he goes to Zuni. I tell you the exact truth in this; therefore wait patiently, though yearningly. Alas, alas, I all but accompanied the one who reads you this to your place, but my master chief withheld his encouragement. Never mind! Some time in the future our paths of life may join together. However I wish this might be, yet am I compelled to remain here. Still thinking always of you,

I remain Your Younger Brother,
Te-na-tsa-li

PALOWAHTIWA TO FHC

Zuni, New Mexico
nd

Thy Brother Palowahtiwa [speaks]:

How are you? Are you now no longer ill? Thy brother yearns toward you and would hurriedly wish you to join him.

And nothwithstanding letters day after day you write me, Tenatsali, quite what you say in them—there is no understanding; for Black-beard does not speak our language well.[10] It is *very* difficult! Very straight *you* speak—but!

How everything may be, make haste to speak; for the feast dance of the Priesthood of the Bow is to take place. Therefore thy brother wishes you. Now although he wishes you, should there be difficulty in the way of your coming, happily may you sit. Thy wife Em-a-li-a, happily may she sit; likewise thy younger sister Maggie, happily may she sit.

Make haste thou! finish me a letter—a long letter enclose to me.

Appendices

Appendix A

Account of Cushing's Search for the Tchalchihuitl Mines, December 1879

Mr. Graham, the trader, had returned, and it happened that a sort of wandering prospector and artisan named Williams was staying with him while engaged in building a derrick for a windmill down at the mission. He had rambled all over the Southwestern country. So one day when I told him that the Indians had, somewhere in the Sierra Madres to the Eastward, old mines of chalchihuitl, or green and blue stones, and that they had related a tradition of the place to me but had refused to reveal its location, he said that he thought he knew where it was. Years before, in prospecting, he had discovered ancient pits and shafts in the mountains, surrounded by stone ruins. He said he was going across the mountains again in a few days and that he would guide me there if I wished to go.

I determined to accompany him. On the evening of the last day of November I made hasty preparations for the journey. The Governor tried to disuade me, evidently suspecting my intentions, but he ultimately yielded and told me I must return within seven days or he would consider me lost and send a searching party. In order that I might be better protected from the cold, for winter had now fairly set in, [he] produced my corduroys and a flannel shirt. He would permit me, however, neither boots, coat nor hat, as he still insisted that I must have my "meat hardened."

Early next morning, joined by a passing traveler, we set out. A few miles beyond the pueblo of Pescado, one of the outlying farming towns of the Zunis, deserted during winter, we passed ruin after ruin, and in a little cañon through which our trail led, perched giddily up on the face of the precipice, were a number of ancient dwellings, of which the Zunis had told me, averring that they were the handiwork and strongholds of their ancestors.

It was long after dark when, nearly frozen, we reached the ranch of Cibollita, where we were entertained by some Mormons. The night was bitterly cold, as was the morning, when, long before sunrise, we resumed our journey. Early in the day we stopped at the little Mexican settlement of Tinaja, the last on our road; then struck out Northeastward across the plain and up a heavily timbered cañon into the pine-clad mountains.

Anticipating a solitary journey home, I observed closely every curious feature of the landscape, noting particularly a deserted little deer shelter and, further on, the black, burned trunk of an immense tree. Further into the mountains the snow became quite deep, impeding our progress; and as we climbed the great divide between the waters of the Atlantic and the Pacific and descended the other side into a grand, open, peak-bordered valley, I reached up to an overhanging branch of hemlock, snapped it, and jokingly exclaimed, "There, boys, lose me if you can."

We rode on for miles, passing by rude sheep corrals of felled trees, usually a deserted hut by the side of each, until, toward sunset, we arrived in sight of a great rugged, red rock wall, which apparently terminated the beautiful valley but which really changed its course abruptly to the Southeast. Suddenly, Williams, who had appeared rather anxious for some time, turned to me and said, "We are lost." He added, however, that we might strike a miners' camp, not far from the ancient ruins, by crossing directly over the mountains which bordered the Eastern side of the valley.

We climbed the cañon's broken, heavily timbered slopes until dark and continued on for some distance, until the cold became so intense and the darkness so black that we were compelled to halt and hobble our animals. We had little or no bedding and no food, as with the characteristic improvidence of the genus *prospectador,* Williams had said at the outset that it would be useless to load ourselves down with provisions. We built a great fire of pine logs and piñon boughs, scraped away a thin crust of snow from around it and, with our saddles for pillows and saddle blankets for beds, lay down to rest.

Before it was fairly light next morning, Williams arose and made a tour of observation, returning to camp just at dawn with the intelligence that he had satisfied himself of the way. We replenished the fire, warmed ourselves thoroughly, saddled up, and again set out.

We had not proceeded more than a mile before we came to a magnificent basin among the mountain heights. There was a snug little cabin at its end, whence a cañon led down the mountain and through which trickled a little stream fed by a spring as yet unfettered by the ice and snows of winter. As we rode up to the cabin there was no sign of life about, but a faint smoke curled up from the mud chimney.

We dismounted and yelled in concert. Presently a sleepy, good-natured looking youth unbarricaded and opened the rude door, supporting his hastily adjusted trowsers with one hand while with the other he held a double-barreled shotgun. "Oh!" said he, lowering the gun, "Come in, boys."

Williams entered first. Before we had finished unsaddling our animals, he had quietly helped himself to provisions and was already slicing bacon in preparation for a meal. Our sleepy and as yet silent host took a haunch of venison down from a peg between the logs and threw it before Williams with the remark that he guessed he would make us some bread, as we acted hungry. While engaged in this operation, he informed us that his name was Tyzack and that he was watching the claims of some copper miners, to whom the cabin belonged. He was by no means an ordinary camp boy, as shown by books and notes on a rude slab in one end of the room, among which I noticed a History of the United States, a work on natural philosophy, and a French grammar filled with exercises on brown wrapping paper. In answer to my queries, this lonely student enthusiastically replied that he had seen the ruins and pits I was in search of and had found rude digging sticks, wooden spades and chipped implements of flint about the place, some of which he showed me.

As soon as we had finished breakfast, we all went down to the spring and, before starting up the mountain, watered our animals. I tied my mule to a pine tree with a long, tough riata of buckskin. Our traveling friend soon grew tired of climbing and said he would go back and resume the trail and that Williams might join him further on.

At the top we found the ancient excavations, some of which were circular depressions many feet across and very deep, others mere pits. Near them, the Indians had erected, centuries before, great monuments of rock to mark the sites of their possessions, and over to one side, on a level piece of ground, they had built rude but substantial stone dwellings of many rooms, around the ruins of which were everywhere traces of their art. I became so interested in sketching these quaint ruins and traces of aboriginal work that I determined to remain on the mountain top until dinner time. Williams reluctantly said good-bye and departed. Tyzack enjoyed my enthusiasm immensely, and so engrossed did we become in a search for ancient remains that it was late ere we descended.

Under the pine tree in the place of my mule and riata was a broken rope which had belonged to our fellow traveler. He had stolen the riata and secured my mule with an old rope. The mule had escaped. While Tyzack prepared a meal, I searched in vain for traces of the missing animal. Late that night, by the moonlight, I discovered at some distance two or three of her footprints on the frozen snow-crust, followed by those of an Indian pony. She had been stolen by Navajos and was probably miles away.

Well, we went back to the cabin and built a big fire. Just as we were about to turn in for the night, the wind began to rise and within an hour the snow was falling as it does only among the mountains. Tyzack had but a few days' provisions left, and although the poor fellow offered to share with me, I accepted only a wheat cake and three or four sticks of bacon.

I slept heavily that night, and in the morning, as the snow still continued falling, I left letters describing my present situation in care of Tyzack, to be dispatched just in case I did not return within fourteen days. With a single blanket, note-books and carbine, I started across the mountains. During the afternoon I descended into the valley through which we had passed, which I recognized by one of the corrals. Entering the hut by the side of it, I built a fire with which to warm myself, ate part of the cake, then resumed the journey; but, with my utmost efforts, could only reach the dividing mountain. I built a great fire under some pine trees and rolled up in my single blanket beside it. As the night advanced, the snow fell more thickly than ever.

Toward morning I was awakened from a doze by the snap of a twig. Glaring at me from opposite the fire were two great round eyes. I hastily poked up the embers, shoved a cartridge into my gun, and saw by the increasing fire-light the form of a mountain lion. As I raised my gun, however, it retreated, doubtless more frightened by the fire than by my hostile demonstrations.

With the first break of day, I ascended the mountain. The snow was nearly two feet deep. All traces of our trail were covered. In vain I searched a maze of cañon depths stretched out in all directions from the base, and, as I had no compass I could not determine which one to take. Suddenly, I thought of the twig I had jokingly broken. I descended and by great luck discovered it.

I again climbed the mountain, surer of my direction, and went down into one of the cañons. It seemed the right one, for ere long I came to the blackened tree-trunk, further on, to the deserted deer shelter, and toward mid-day, in the face of a driving storm, came out on the plain and saw the still distant hovels of Tinaja.

During this foot journey, the soles of my moccasins had entirely worn away, and every step I took in the snow left a print of my bare foot. Trudging on, however, heedless of suffering in my anxiety to reach the distant ranch, I was unaware of the intensity of the cold until, at the doorway, I attempted to shake hands with the Señora in charge. My arms were paralyzed and my knees gave way. The hospitable Mexicans carried me inside, placed me by the side of a roaring little fire and, with a cup of hot coffee, some tortillas and wine, so revived me that I determined to resume the journey. They tried to dissuade me. They might have spared the effort, for, attempting to rise, I found myself utterly powerless. Before evening I was nearly delirious with fever and pain.

Early next morning, however, though still lame, I again started forward. I soon reached the Mormon settlement. On sitting down before the fire, I became so weak as to be for some time unable to move. I pleaded for a horse. They feared to trust me with one. So I again set out, but could proceed but slowly. Toward evening, as I was descending into the plain of Pescado, I heard, further behind, the sound of hoofs, and the clink of Indian bridles. Presently, three young Zunis overtook me.

"Well, if here isn't our poor little brother," said one of them.

"Here, give me that pack," said another. And the third, in spite of my remonstrances, hauled me up behind him. Away we galloped toward Zuni, but before we had reached the black hills, the Indian's pony began to flag and he reluctantly left me in the road again. It was late at night ere I rounded the western end of the pueblo— {ms. ends here.}

Appendix B

Note on the Scalp House—and Sacred Secrecy[1]

Deep in the store-rooms under the village lie buried the ancient treasures of Zuni. Alike the eyes of the hated Navajo, the despised Mexican, and the reverenced American never penetrate their obscurity; their hands never lift the latch string of their secrecy.

Out in the sandy plain near a little arroyo to the north of the town stands the ancient house of their slain enemies. Here, strung in spiral rows, hang the scalps and heads of centuries of their valor. Yet the eye of the passing stranger scarcely rests on the little mound and rude stone portal of this treasure house of the war chiefs of the Zuni. No ear save mine has listened to its strange and ghastly history, for it is a sacred secret on which the lips of all Zunians are as sealed and silent, save among their own, as are the stone portals which close it ever from the eyes of the curious foreigners.

But—inestimable advantage of being a Zuni—I have listened to this story. To *me* it is no sacred secret—for I tell it to my people.

When the moon with her two attendant stars sits low on the western hills, 'tis midnight and all Zuni sleeps. Then there silently steal down from the village five dark blanketed forms—the Cacique of the Sun, the War Captain, and his three Lieutenants. They bear the sacred meal—*wyavi* blue and red—and the sweet *he-pa-lo-kia* [corn cake], fresh from the lips of a virgin. The four warriors range themselves about the low house [correspondingly to the four world] quarters. The great *Pe-kwi-na* [sun priest] bends in prayer over the portal. The war song is chanted scarce louder than the sand-driving wind. The ancient prayer is uttered scarce louder than the wind-driven sand. The portal is lifted. The *Pe-kwi-na*'s fingers feel the long locks of hair. They are damp. "Thanks! It will rain." Or they are dry. "Alas, great father, when wilt thou give us rain?"

Appendix C

Sylvester Baxter: News Story (an Excerpt)

Logan's Land?

A Grievous Wrong Threaten[s]
the Zuni Indians.

The Illinois Senator Preëmpts
Their Nutria Fields.

The Citizenship Rights of
Southwestern Indians.

(From our Special Correspondent)[2]

Santa Fe, N.M., December 1, 1882.—The wagon road from Fort Wingate to Zuni and Camp Apache crosses the Zuni Mountains, descending abruptly into a charming pastoral valley at a point where the waters of a clear and abundant spring come out of a wild cañon, with walls of red sandstone towering perpendicularly on either side. This is the Nutria spring, and the valley which it waters is one of the loveliest in New Mexico. Springs are as precious as gold in this dry country, and now that the railroads have made the land accessible, they are as eagerly prospected for and preëmpted as mining claims are, for the rage for stock ranches is now almost as great as the mining fever. Without a spring, however, a stock ranch is impossible. The Nutria spring, though long known as of great value, has hitherto not been laid claim to by ranch men. The Zuni Indians have held undisputed possession of it for centuries. Their pueblo of Las Nutrias stands in the midst of the valley. It antedates the present great pueblo of Zuni, and had probably long been standing there when the Spanish conquerors came into the land. It is surrounded by fertile fields, irrigated by the waters of the spring. The Zunis have tilled these fields for ages, and they hold the land in severality under the laws of their nation—laws unwritten but handed down for ages by word of mouth and held as sacred as our own English common law. Their herds and their flocks have grazed in the valley for years. The land is theirs by virtue of possession reaching back into pre-Columbian times. In the case of Indians, however, it seems that possession is not nine [tenths] of the law.

The Nutria spring and the land round about it is now claimed by Senator Logan of Illinois. . . . Nutria spring had always been supposed to be on the Zuni reservation, but it seems that by some inadvertency the reservation lines have not included it, and recent surveys have shown the fact. This, however, was not publicly known, but Gen. Logan is said to have been informed from the surveyor's office that the Nutria spring was open to occupancy. Gen. Logan, therefore, in association with others, has taken the requisite steps to secure possession of the spring, together with a large tract of the surrounding land, for the establishment of a cattle ranch. It is difficult to believe that the Illinois senator could have been aware of the consequences of his action. It means nothing less than threatened famine to the Zunis. Their best wheat fields are at Las Nutrias. Zuni has three outlying agricultural pueblos—Las Nutrias, Pescado and Ojo Caliente. These are all probably much older than the present Zuni but are now only occupied as summer houses by those owning the irrigated fields round about. The Nutria valley is called the best of these, and its taking away would probably reduce the agricultural resources of the Zunis nearly one half. Sometimes it seems as if it were the deliberate policy of the government to do its best to discourage Indians in their efforts for improvement and to reduce self-supporting tribes to pauperism [and] vagrancy and to drive them into hostility.

I have never heard Senator Logan's personal integrity questioned. But is it fair to deprive a small and helpless people of what is morally and actually their right and thus to snatch the very bread from their mouths? . . . .

S.B.

Boston Herald, 11 December 1882.

Appendix D

From "The Discovery of Zuni, or the Ancient Province of Cibola and the Seven Cities"

Taken from the manuscript of a lecture delivered by Cushing before the American Geographical Society January 13, 1885, the excerpts below follow a lengthy review of early Spanish accounts of the discovery and conquest of "Nueva Mexico" and an account of his own discovery that the "cities" of Cibola had in fact been towns occupied by the Zunis.

I sincerely regret that the historical portion of this paper, without which the rest had been less significant, was unnecessarily so long that I have not space for several other equally quaint and interesting traditions. Perhaps the resemblances between the Zuni legend of the Black Mexican with thick lips and [Marcos de] Niça's narrative of Estevanico may appear in stronger light if I add that at the time when I jotted down the notes of [the former] I was wholly unmindful of [the latter]. . . .

As evidencing how far we may, within certain limitations, trust to the accuracy of at least *Zuni* Indian tradition, I venture one more glimpse of the Spanish from the viewpoint of the savage.

Once I happened to ask old Palowahtiwa, my adopted brother, whence came the mongrel dogs of Zuni.

"Dogs," said he. "*These* are not dogs! Or rather, dogs are not what they once were; for now they are mere village vermin, the beasts! It would have all been very well, had 'Nu-we' never come."

"Who was Nu-we?"

"Nu-we was the first *white* man our forefathers ever saw; and he kept saying 'Nu-we!' 'Nu-we!' So they named him 'Nu-we.' It was a long time ago. From the East he came to Ma-tsa-ki, followed by two lean mongrel dogs. He was haggard and bony. His long hair was grizzly and matted. His great beard fairly shadowed his shoulders, and his eye-balls glared out of their sockets. What with gray hair, beard, and eye-balls, he looked so much like the Storm Demon that our folks thought he must be a wizard and were frightened, but treated him gently because he had come from the Eastward. Wherever he went, he kept grabbing and touching everybody and every thing, muttering, "Give me this; give me that." He ate so much that the *A-shi-wa-ni* (or Priests) gathered at night in council and decided that they must get rid of him. For they thought "If we leave him alone, he will bring others of his race who, being equally hungry, will eat up all our people have to eat."

So when Nu-we was asleep they wrapped him in a magic circle and bag of yucca and sang a sacred incantation four times. Each time they chanted the song-name, the yucca-bag moved more and more, until the fourth time it flew off into space, Nu-we and all. When the people asked next morning what had become of that hungry creature, the *A-shi-wa-ni* replied that they had sent him to Summer-land by their own knowledge and power. But the dogs were left behind, and these beasts you see by the doorways are their descendants. It is said this is the reason why they are always so hungry and stare-eyed and jointy. Who knows?"

I need scarcely add that this story, divested of its magic and unessential Zuni hypotheses, instantly reminds one of the flight, with two dogs, of Andraez de Campo, of his habit of blessing the natives, and of his long hair and beard "tyed up in a lace."

[The story of this Portuguese servant who was left behind by the Coronado expedition far to the north and who made his way back to Mexico had been mentioned earlier by Cushing.]

It is not unlikely that the Portuguese [Andraez] had heard [from] Alvar Nuñez Cabeza de Vaca of the wonderful homage the Indians of the Southwestern country had paid him, and hence, hoping to secure their good will, had a habit of repeating the surname—Nuñez—of that first wanderer. At any rate, this would fairly explain the origin of the name "Nu-we" in the Zuni tradition.[3]

. . . .

Turning over the leaves of the old chronicles of early Spanish exploration and conquest, from the time of Nica and Estavanico in 1539 to the days of Vargas in 1689, not missing the unprinted records of the Franciscan missions of Our Lady of Guadalupe in the towns of the Zunis, we find the names of these towns variously stated by different authors; yet agreeing so far that we may readily, I think, identify any one from another. Let us, then, compare these names with the sounds which fall so fluently from the lips of the Indian raconteur.

According to this comparison, the name Cibola is a corruption of the Zuni phrase *Shi-wo-na,* from *Shiwi* = flesh, *wo-a* = to become, and *nau* or *na-wan* = within or at, and signifies "the place of nativity of the Zuni people," who call themselves "the Flesh."[4] The word *Shi-wi-na* means "the sitting place of the *A-shi-wi* or Zunis" and is applied to any permanent village or gathering of that people, by persons at a distance from it. Hence it is that Niça says the first town of the Province bears the name of Cibola; whereas Coronado, coming after, distinctly states that in this the Father Provincial lied; for every town had its particular name. "And none of them is called Cibola but all together they are called Cibola." Strangely enough, Coronado lied not less than the Father Provincial, yet both spoke the truth. Nica says that the white man of Cibola, whom he had met in the last valley, told him that the Lord of the Province dwelt in the principal city of the Seven, which he called "A-ha-cus with an aspiration." Espejo, in speaking of the same town, as the one at which certain of his soldiers remained while he was exploring the Province of Tusayan, names it Aguico, while later writers spell it Aquato and Agrico.

Casteñeda states that the city which Coronado and his army occupied was named Mazaque.

When Espejo returned from Tusayan, he picketed his horses near Aloma. This name is written in one of the manuscript deeds in my possession, granted by the Father Superior of Guadaloupe to a certain cacique—A'lona.

The same document mentions another town as Caquima, while elsewhere in older writings the word is given variously as Caguimo and Coguima.

Nowhere in these and other old writings am I able to find more than two additional names. The one is Aquinsa; the other, Canabi or Canabe.

Of the Seven Cities of Cibola, then, we have, variously spelled by different authorities, six names: Ca-qui-ma, Ma-za-qui, A-lo-na, A-quin-sa, Agui-co, and Ca-na-be.

Will my hearers kindly recall the formula with which a Zuni story teller normally begins one of his time-honored folk-tales of mid-Winter?

Bide we then with the ancients!
It is of the time
When Kia-ki-me was a village,
Ma-tsa-ki was a village,
When Ha-lo-na was a village,
A-pi-na-wan was a village,
When Ham-pas-sa-wan was a village,
Ha-wi-k'huh was a village,
When Kia-na-we was a village,
and in all directions where be now but old heaps of walls,
stood villages round about the homes of our Ancients. . . .

(1) Is not Caquima an evident corruption of Kia-ki-me—which means "the Home of the Eagles"?

(2) Is not Mazaque bad writing for Ma-tsa-ki, the "Place of Bitter Salt"?

(3) Alona of Ha-lo-na, the "Place of Sacred Favor"?

(4) Aquinsa of A-pi-na-wan, the "Town on the Trail of the Winds"?

(5) Aguico of Ha-wi-k'huh, the "Vale of the Fragrant Herbs," and

(6) Canabi of Kia-na-we, the "Place of the Moving Waters"?

(7) And thus, we have unaccounted for only Ham-pas-sa-wan, the "Town of the White-topped Bushes," which, in the North of the valley, standing alone and nearly abandoned at the time of the Conquest, escaped special mention by the Spaniards.[5]

Guided by these and other landmarks in language, it is easy for us to restore not only the boundaries of Ancient Cibola itself but also even those of the adjacent provinces.

At one time, long anterior to the Discovery of America, no fewer than nineteen of the towns, now ruins about the Borderlands and in the valleys of Zuni, were inhabited by the ancestry of that wasted tribe. When the Spaniards came, however, all save nine of these towns had been abandoned: two, and a few cliff villages in the more fertile cañons, were occupied annually, during the seasons of planting and gleaning; seven, as we already know, were the permanent abodes of the Cibolans. To the East was the Province which Niça's white man [a Zuni albino] called A-cus, which the later writers name A-cu-cu, a word derived from the Zuni *Ha-kuh* or *Ha-ku-kwe,* signifying the "People of Acoma," or the "Shriveled Leaf Country." To the South and East, stood the beautiful lava-stone towns of what Niça called Marata, the nearest he could get to Ma-k'iah-ta [Ma'k'yaya'a], meaning the "Region of the Southern Salinas." The people dwelling in those towns were the Kia-ma-kia-kwe or "Snail Tribes," subsequently subdued by and incorporated into the Zuni or Cibola nation, as were parts of their ritual, strange dances and language into the rites of its sacred priesthood.[6] To the West was Totonteac or Totenteal—from the Zuni "topa tea," which signifies simply "there also," and by which expression Niça's white man very probably referred to the people of the towns (now in ruins) so well described by Melchior Diaz.[7] This people were of the Zuni stock but were not, as Diaz seems to have imagined, politically a part of the nation of Cibola until after his day. Toward the North, and from Province to Province, wandered those restless traders and hunters, the Querechos—the predecessors and possibly the vanguard of the Navajos who dwell there today.

Secure in the midst of these surroundings, lay the country of the populous Cibolans, and today, with a sneer of impatience, a gesture of injured depreciation of the narrowness of his present possessions, any middle-aged Zuni will define minutely its boundaries.

These were: to the Eastward the plains at the foot of

the Gallo Mountains above Agua Fria; to the Northward, the trans-serranian valley of the Rio Puerco, from the longitude of Mount Taylor to the Colorado Chiquito; on the West, in Arizona, the latter river nearly to its sources; on the South, after the conquest of Marata, the valleys of the Salt Lake and the Rito Quemado, which lie along the bases of the Sierra Datila and the Sierra Ladrone. Thus the Cibolan dominion had, from West to East, an extent of one hundred and fifty miles; from North to South, of seventy-five or eighty.[8]

Nearer to the Northern and Western of these limits than to the Eastern and Southern, lay the "Seven Lost Cities." East from the present village three and a half miles stands the Great Mesa of Zuni. First to echo the storm-voices of the valley, first seen of all things in the morning, last kissed by the rays of the sunset—no wonder the nature worshiping Zunis have named it the "Mountain of Thunder," have scattered upon its broad summit the shrines of their most dreaded war gods, have hidden within its dark grottoes the sacrifices to their best beloved deities of the Wind, the Dew, and the Rain storm!

Sheer beneath the giant columns that sentinel its Southwestern border stand the walls of Kia-ki-me or Coquima. Half these walls, still in good preservation, are perched on a shelf of the precipice. The rest lie broken and scattered on a mound at the base of the mesa. This was the death place of Estevanico, the scene of the first siege of Coronado.

Over to the other side of the same end of the mesa, only two miles East of Zuni, is the ruin of Ma-tsa-ki or Mazaque. Today it is only a great mound of soil and chipped sandstone with bits of wall standing here and there along its sharpest slope-lines. In the center of its summit is a level space which was once its principal plaza. Here the Zunis still keep in rude repair the "Tower of the Sun." More than once have I cast into its ever open Eastern portal my sacrifice of prayer meal or "Sacred favor." Through a little notch in the Western side of this solar structure, the Zuni Sun priest makes the observations by which he determines the feast times and seasons. Often from this spot have I gazed Southward at the bolt crest of Nopon Mountain, whence Niça viewed a city, that very ruin, and on the brow of which still lies a "great heap of stones" that the Indians say they "builded not but found there."

Under the Northern center of Zuni, some of its rooms still in use but covered from sight by the larger superstructures of today, is a portion of the ancient A-lo-na or Ha'lona. The foundations of the outer half lie buried under the sand-mound and garden obliquely South over the river. West from this, on a long point of talus and red marl hills, loom up ever distinctly the ruins of A-pin-na-wa or Aquinsa. Although prominently seated and near the river, this town was never important, because too much exposed to the sand storms of Spring or late Winter, which so aptly gave it the name it still bears, of "Sown on the Trail of the Winds."

Below and across from there, on one of the low cedar-clad slopes which invade the North side of the valley, ten miles West of Zuni, is Ham-pas-sa-wan, once an important city as its long lines of straight walls can still prove.[9]

Twelve and a half miles due Southwest from Zuni, over many deep gorges and spurs of mesa-land, all hidden among the hills, is the Y-shaped fork of a broad but deep valley. Over the wide bottom of its confluent branches, course many clear streamlets, everywhere along the borders of which grow, bright green and heavy with fragrance, flowering grasses, tall rushes, and dense bushes. At the North side of the lesser vale stands the terminal promontory of a range of red sandstone hills. Upon the top, down the steep sides and under the base of this headland lie the tumbled walls of Aguico or Ha-wi-k'huh. The thousand and more little rooms still traceable throughout this splendid ruin testify to the truth of Niça's statement that it was the "Principall of the Seven."

Directly across to the Southward, just where the two little valleys join, is a low bluff of calcareous sandstone. White and sparkling as a mountain snow-drift is this bit of mesa in its setting of green, with its crystals of spar.

Below and around its sharp corner are three or four springs of warm water. Any morning in Autumn or Winter, albeit the valley is warm, you may see steam clouds rise up from these fountains. The Indians think that in the days of creation this steam shed its spray on the mesa and the gods turned the dew drops to crystal! But the Indians know less about this than they do [of the] days of their ancients. Well, I must not forget to say that on the top of this cliff of white sandstone tower, and totter, the gray walls of Kia-na-we, the last of the Seven Lost Cities.

Having traced out the extent of the Province of Cibola, having located by proofs akin to exact records the sites of its seven cities; having reached the inference that the Zuni Indians are the lineal descendants of its long lost people, but one further topic would demand our attention ere we might hope and expect to restore with like certainty of detail the history of that Province, those cities and those buildings. How far do the Shi-wis or Zunis of today differ from their Cibolan ancestors of three hundred and fifty years ago, or how little still remain unchanged?

Greatest of all the changes wrought on them has been the diminution of their population. A computation, based upon the number of rooms in the seven ruins above described, and allowing but four members to a family, would give a very considerable excess over seven thousand, the number claimed by Casteñeda; whereas today there are but sixteen hundred and twenty-three men, women and children in the tribe of Zuni. . . .

Coronado remarks that they "are of reasonable stature and wittie"; "well nurtured and condicioned"; and that one of their women was able to "grinde as much as foure women of Mexico." All this remains true in our time.

He writes of their food, "They eate the best cakes I ever sawe, and every body generally eateth of them." "They have most excellent salte in kernel which they fetch from a certaine lake a day's journey from hence." Casteñeda and Melchior Diaz state that this lake was distant two days to the South. Nowadays, the Zunis eat the best corn cakes *I* ever saw. And they still bring the "salte" from the lake two days' journey to the South. As they believe this salt is formed from the flesh of the Goddess who made it for them and who dwells in the lake, they use great care to avoid bruising or breaking the crystals in her presence.

In another place, Coronado says, "They have here certaine guinie cocks, but fewe. The Indians tell me in all these seven cities that they eate them not, but keepe them onely for their feathers. I believe them not, for they are excellent good." The Zunis still keep, exclusively for their feathers, not a few of these "guinie cocks" (which are turkeys), as also eagles, confined in rude walled cages of wood and adobe.

According to all these authorities, the Cibolans wore turquoises abundantly, in their earrings and necklaces. Thus the Zunis wear them still. Thus *I* have worn them until, as a Zuni would say, "my ears were tired."

Niça heard that they had garments with "sleeves as broad beneathe as above." They had, say Coronado and Casteñeda, long mantles of cotton, some painted or embroidered. Most of the men went ordinarily naked, but the entire middle of the body was covered with a garment which resembled a napkin, embroidered with tufts at the ends and fastened about the loins. They wore boots of tanned skin reaching to the ankles and sometimes painted. "The women wore a mantle over the shoulder fastened around the neck and passing under the right arm." Their hair was "divided on two sides and arranged so that the ears were exposed" or "done up behind the ear in the shape of a loop which resembles the handles of a cup." The Zunis exactly preserve all these and many other details of their attire, described by Spanish writers, in their ceremonial and dance costumes. . . .

[Among other] less tangible yet equally striking comparisons, the Cibolans married but once and but one wife, according to Casteñeda, and Coronado tells us that these "Indians loved their women more than themselves." The Zunis today are monogamists, and in case of the death of a wife often remain single the rest of their lives; but in case of divorce they marry again as soon as they recover from the discomfiture this mishap invariably throws them into. They do treat their women most fondly, and are the best husbands in America, but this happy state of things arises as much from their fear of divorce—which is in the hands of the women—as from sentiment, with [which] they are not, I have often thought, over-burdened. . . .

Espejo says that he found, among the various pueblos he visited, certain canopies and screens set up, gallantly trimmed with feathers and painted with figures of the Sun, the Moon and the stars. As he saw various sacrifices of food and meal placed before some of these, forthwith he inferred that they were erected in order that the Devil might take his siestas in them during his frequent journeys from province to province of these benighted heathen! I wish that my audience might see those set up in Zuni today. They are the often used altars of that most religious people and are not, I hardly need add, erected for the purpose Espejo assigned them. They are held by their strange builders as neutral between men and the gods; the border-land wherein the souls of men may approach the spirits of the gods they call the "makers of the trails of our lives," where too, in ancestral worship, the warm hand of mortal flesh which offers sacrifice antagonizes not the cold hand outstretched to receive it from beyond the dark dividing line of the paths of Life. The notions connected with them, however far from our own, are beautiful; and I have often found myself nigh unto all seriousness when compelled, in common with the priests who received me into their guild, to worship before them.

Espejo states that this people had idols and shrines. So have they today. . . . He tells us that while [he was] at one pueblo there was a solemn dance in which, however, were made "very wittie sports wherewith our men were exceedingly delighted." Summer and autumn ever since, such solemn dances have been held in Zuni, with "wittie" players to delight the audiences during the intervals of the more sacred ceremonials. And if these dances remain the same, why not the music?

Melchior Diaz says they played, where he went, on flutes of unequal size—five or six men together—and that these flutes had places marked on them for the finger. So, and with similar instruments, do the Zunis play today, but the marks on their flutes are simply the joints in the canes of which they are made. . . .

Thus lengthily, but after all leaving much unsaid, have I labored to locate the Seven Lost Cities of Cibola; to prove the truthfulness in almost everything they wrote (except in their accounts of mineral wealth) of the old Spanish writers; to prove the high value of Indian languages and traditions, to help restore, if closely and lovingly enough studied, the many lost passages in our old New World's history. . . .

So, today, we may study, point by point, the conditions encountered by those old Spanish soldiers. Once sure, as we happily now are, of the sites of their cities and province, we may restore its history, live over its scenes and incidents to the full and a thousand times; but alas not tonight, not tonight. The theme of the customs, laws, arts and religion, philosophy and mythology of Ancient Cibola, the description of its tragic decay, the story of the last Franciscan missionary of Ma-wi-k'huh and his romantic adoption of the Indian life—which made *my* experiment old, though I thought it new—all these things must serve a future occasion, or future books of many chapters, which books and which chapters will undoubtedly bear, somewhere in their lines, the little word *Zuni*.

Appendix E

Newspaper Interview.

Killing Sorcerers.

Remarkable Customs of the Zuni Indians in New Mexico.

Recent Reports Denied.

Frank Hamilton Cushing, of the Bureau of Ethnology, Gives Some Facts.[10]

"From personal investigation I can say there is no truth in the report that two female members of the Zuni tribe of Indians in New Mexico have been tortured to death for alleged witchcraft."

Mr. Frank Hamilton Cushing, of the Bureau of Ethnology, Geological Survey, made this remark to-day.

He was alluding to a dispatch published in a Sunday paper, to the effect that two Indian women had been killed for practicing sorcery.

Mr. Cushing related the history, laws and customs of the Zuni tribe in dealing with those practicing witchcraft. His story will undoubtedly be found interesting by the readers of The Evening News. Mr. Cushing being a member of the tribe by adoption, is able to impart accurate information. He said:

During the early part of 1880 I was first adopted into one of the families of the Zunis, and later into the clan Macawa, with fitting solemnities. That made me a member of the tribe, and as such eligible in time to membership in one of its thirteen secret assemblies, or sacred Cult societies. . . .

According as these societies are related to the seasons or elements and the regions they pertain to, they are supposed to be the possessors of secrets and medicines, generally of a magical nature, potent for use in the control of animals or their gods, or for the cure of various diseases, for the promotion of welfare, material and spiritual, and for the prevention and destruction of sorcery among men.

Peculiar to Winter.

For instance, the societies of the North represent the wind and cold. It is believed their medicines extend to the curing of diseases peculiar to winter and to the prevention of sorcery. The Society of Warriors or the Priesthood of the Bow pertains peculiarly to the North and West, and while its function is specifically to maintain the exercise and power of the medicines of war and protection against enemies, it is also the chief executive body of all the secret assemblies. As such it tries all cases of sorcery that may develop, and executes the sentence if the offender be found guilty. In the contention which is waged against sorcery or its effects, all of the secret societies in their respective places join, the extent to which they do this being determined by their relation to the West or the element of water and season of spring time; to the South or the element of fire and season of summertime, and to the East or the element of earth and the season of autumn. Further than this, in a brief article like the present, these societies and their functions cannot be explained.

Wizards or Sorcerers

I can speak intelligently of the so-called wizards or sorcerers, since I was initiated after several trials and ordeals into the particular society that deals exclusively with them, namely, the Priesthood of the Bow, and for more than three years I took part in all cases that came up for consideration before that body.

However absurd this may seem there is no question of the existence of a certain secret guild of at least would-be sorcerers or wizards among the Zuni Indians. Nor do they owe their reputation, either imputed or self-constituted powers, wholly to superstitious beliefs. In the first place, practically speaking, they possess, or apparently they have for ages, in common with the Indian tribes, a kind of hypnotic power, and, owing to the peculiar beliefs of these primitive people, the power of suggestion, or waking by means of it, is simply astounding, and can only be believed when seen.

Some slight explanation of this may be afforded by the fact that both the sorcerer himself and his victim believe firmly in occult powers founded on resemblances and analogies in nature. This may, perhaps, be made more clear by an illustration.

For instance, black is the color of night, because night is dark or black. Night is the time of sleeping and of evil as well. It is cold, and filled with dangers. Sleeping and cold are the two chief characteristics of death.

Consequently to the Indian mind black is the color of death and night the time when it is most imminent. A sorcerer intending to destroy an enemy will take a stick of the mountain laurel, the only shrub known to the Zunis which has no pith, and will then blacken it with soot and a sizing made of the juice of weeds gathered from the grave of some one who has died a violent death. Not only will he carefully observe all of these analogies but gather the materials at night when the god of sun is absent.

Symbolical.

That his incantation may be distinctly symbolized and wafted abroad he will take the plumes of the owl, the most distinctive bird of darkness he can find, and dipping the tips into yellow paint will attach them to the stick. In addition to this he will also bind to the stick either the spine of a cactus or a sharp splinter of obsidion winged with the feathers of the nighthawk, the swiftest and most silent bird of night. He will then either make a rude drawing of the totem or clan of the person whom he wishes to injure. In order that none but the one in question may be singled out he will form an effigy and call it also symbolically by the name of his intended victim.

Toward the heart or other part of the figure he points a mystic missile, accompanying each of these operations with archaic and malevolent formulae.

The work being finished, he will place this paraphernalia under the ladder or somewhere in the pathway of the person for whom it is intended. In the most roundabout way he will bring to the knowledge of his victim the fact that he is possessed, and this alone, without any further operations on the part of the sorcerer, so preys upon the mind of the victim, who most potently believes in the power of the possession, that his rest is disturbed and his physical condition lowered until he rapidly sinks under the spell. If he becomes feverish the operations of the shamans or priests of the Cult societies are called into play. Sometimes the medicines of the shamans are ineffectual, in which case an investigation, conducted with extraordinary vigilance and patience by members of the Priesthood of the Bow, is set on foot. When the charms which were used are found and traced to their owner, or the latter in some way is discovered, he is marked, but allowed perfect freedom until he is discovered operating on someone else.

In that event he is summoned to a strictly secret council of the Priesthood of the Bow, where he has a rigid and searching, but extraordinarily fair trial. Until a verdict is reached, no member of the society is permitted to absent himself on any pretext, nor is he allowed to smoke or partake of either food or drink during the progress of the trial.

If the sorcerer is proven to have meddled with occult matters, though he may be the brother or a near relative of some of the members of the society trying the case, he is exhorted to confess, and failing to do this, is taken out usually to one of the wide spaces of the pueblo, and suspended by his hands, not his thumbs, tied behind his back, and continually and solemnly requested to confess.

Simply Ostracised.

If a confession is obtained from him, unless the case be one of unparalleled atrocity, he is never executed, but simply ostracized or sent to live in a house outside of the pueblo. If he will not acknowledge his guilt further than to say he is a sorcerer, and defies them all, as I have personally heard these so-called wizards declare, they are sometimes sentenced to suffer the death penalty, but four days of grace are allowed, during which by some prescribed act they may show a willingness to forego following the black art. In the event of not desiring to stay the proceedings he is executed by the third chief of the Society of the Bow and three assistants, chosen by lot. The condemned man is executed by means of war clubs, there being no torture whatever.

Sorcery in Zuni does not depend wholly upon the superstitious beliefs of the members of the tribe. I have known several of these sorcerers. They are the anarchists of primitive life. It is their endeavor to overcome the sacred assemblies which have a general function in the social organization of the tribe. In pursuance of this object they resort not only to the operations which they regard as the most powerful and evil in the world, but sometimes to violence, and very frequently to actual poisoning. They never stop short of murder if they can compass it, and the sentences in almost all the cases are deservedly just.

Legal Methods.

In the state of society characterized by clans and groups of clans murders cannot be regarded as capital offenses, since the clan to which the murderer belongs may, by legal usage, compounded in money, slaves or by other means for the life of the man who has been killed free the murderer, and thus by a system of fines the crime may be wiped out. But if murder which has been committed is peculiarly atrocious and cannot be overlooked, the man or woman found guilty is by a sort of legal fiction regarded as a sorcerer, and is tried, condemned and executed as such. When I first witnessed the trial of a sorcerer, in a most foolhardy manner I attempted even by violent means to protect him. I did not understand the full intents and purposes of these so-called sorcerers at that time.

I have as a member of the Society of the Bow seen several trials in which it was proven that the defendants had committed murder by means of secret medicines, two only of which resulted disastrously to the ones tried. There were at least two cases in which I believed firmly in the innocence of those condemned, and contended, as indeed I almost always did, from humanitarian feelings, for acquittal. They were acquitted, and beyond the social ostracism of one of them, no harm resulted.

It is not wise to wholly condemn the Zuni, or any other similar people, for any action they may have taken in regard to punishing those found guilty of sorcery. The Zunis are all closely related, and they guard one another from enemies and injury with almost unequaled loyalty and patriotism. It is only in cases which are not amenable to any other laws of their government that trials for sorcery take place.

In conclusion, let me say that while the peculiar beliefs and principles of the Pueblo Indians in regard to sorcery have sometimes had most direful consequences, leading to divisions of the tribe and ultimate separation, yet throughout their entire history of gradual development in barbaric culture it can be seen that their only civil method of eliminating from the native population the undesirable element has been by trial, condemnation and execution.

Mr. Cushing fears that the Government has committed a grave error in sending troops to the Zuni Pueblo and that it should be remedied by their immediate recall.

Washington Evening News
27 December 1892

Appendix F

Extract from Catalogue of Prehistoric Zuni and Cave Remains[11]

Collected in the Spring of 1880 and later forwarded to Professor Spencer F. Baird in two lots, the first lot comprising a selected dozen objects sent by hand of Mr. Charles Kirchner, the second lot sent by freight in two 3 × 4 boxes, from Fort Wingate—catalog and descriptive letters accompanying—with various other ancient and a few choice modern specimens.

Cave Remains. Collection from the "Cave of Oblique Descent"—A-asselaie—*Introductory.*

This cave was situated near the little Mexican town of Las Tusas, in the midst of extensive ancient ruins which stand on both sides of the Colorado Chiquito above and below it in a wide basin some two or three miles in length. This deep basin or oval valley is surrounded by high and grim basaltic cliffs, many of which are as picturesquely columnar and regular as are those of the Giant's Causeway of Ireland. Throughout the little valley are some eight or nine conical hills, probably marking extinct volcanic springs and geysers—great bubbles of crystalline stone, some of them enormous, and all of them hollow or containing abysmal craters and fissures, the mouths of which vary in width from two feet to ten yards. In the depth of six of these I discovered traces of extensive shrines where paraphernalia and prayer-wand messages of the secret societies had been deposited centuries before by the dwellers in the ruins round about. As these ruins are alluded to by one of the chroniclers of Coronado's Expedition in 1539–40, as abandoned and desolate at that time, and as they are distinctly referred to as pertaining to the "Parrot and Seed clans of the ancestors" in the Zuni myths of creation, I had both historic and traditional warrant for regarding the sacrifices of these cave shrines as not only pre-Columbian but also very remote. The investigation of such of these places as were accessible to me—unaided and alone as I was—seemed of great importance, not withstanding the risk involved. Unfortunately, only this Cave of Oblique Descent and one other on the same or Eastern side of the little river were available to me under the circumstances.

By far the richest place of sacrifice occurred in the depths of the crater of a hill cone of mountainous proportions situated midway between these two caves, on the opposite or western side of the valley. By means of a long string I let a torch down into this twilit crater. On a broad, sloping shelf in the rim of its vast bell-shaped chamber two hundred and eighty feet below the narrow aperture, was a shrine surrounded by numberless tall, brilliantly painted, cane-like plume wands, undisturbed and untarnished in that dry and dimly lighted interior. By the prevailing color of these wands—though I could not reach them—I was able to determine that this was only one of a system of regional shrines, probably seven in all, though I located only six.

The Cave of Oblique Descent differed from the crater in question in that earth quakes had shattered and faulted it through the middle, so that all save a narrow section of it was closed by fallen rock walls and great masses or sheets of laminae from the interior of the still supported roof.

The fissure forming this open section threaded tortuously yet angularly [through] these titanic masses of debris, descending northwardly and at angles of 35° and 45° a little more than three hundred and seventy-four feet to a chamber of tiny proportions, the entrance to which was only a few inches wide and barbed, so to say, by sharp angles of rock. Throughout the entire passage, from the high vertical mouth of the cavern to this little chamber, pile on pile of elaborate ceremonial objects—masks, carved tablets, plumed sacred shields and mimic weapons—crumbled to cinders and ashes as I approached, for they had been burned by the fire lighted by some idle fun hunter in the rubbish at the entrance "to see the rats and cave bats scuttle."

A few of the more deeply buried of these things were, although scorched and broken, not entirely destroyed, but it was not until I reached the terminal chamber that I saw anything wholly unharmed by the fire. There, laid out on the narrow floor or leaning against the walls, were bows, arrows, bunches of cane cigarettes and quite elaborately painted "wand slats."[12] Stripping off my blanket-coat and dragging it behind me, I succeeded, by dint of a half hour's skin abrading work, in entering this chamber. The rich little collection catalogued below was my reward. But when I had rolled my treasures in the blanket coat and pushed them out before me, in form of a slender cigar shaped bundle, I found exit for myself apparently impossible. The jagged rocks all pointed toward me, like the fangs of serpents or the curved teeth of sharks, catching my clothes at every turn. Long before I escaped, my light burned out. I had entered the cave at eleven O'clock in the morning, fortunately trailing a cord behind me. Almost stripped of clothing, chilled and nearly exhausted with hunger and pain, and literally flayed alive, I emerged from that would-be tomb, after hours of twisting and turning, at between twelve and one O'clock that night—climbed forth, rolling my precious bundle before me, as a tumble bug does his ball, into the light of the stars, which seemed, in comparison to the ponderous darkness of the cavern depths, as the light of a clear dawning day.

It may be imagined that the dear-bought relics I brought up were precious to me, aside from their unique archaeologic valuation. But if precious then, they were rendered doubly so when, discovered by the Zunis, I was compelled to take them to their pueblo, lay them out to the east in a council chamber and undergo a trial as for sorcery by the tribunal of the entire secret priesthood of the tribe—saved only by the uninjured condition of the specimens—by the evidence therein of my "gentle and reverential handling" of them.

In the course of this trial, each particular object was minutely examined and commented upon in awed and low-toned converse by the two Priests of the Bow, the Master of the West [one of the chief rain priests], and the Elder of the Seed Clans before that grimly silent assemblage; and it was thus I learned, without the necessity of asking a single question, what each object had signified "in the days of creation." The object of this careful examination was the identification of such of the sacred objects as could on no account leave the custody of the priests. About a dozen of these objects were thus selected to serve as tribal relics, and were taken away from me, alas! The remainder, however, were ultimately yielded up to me in recognition less of my pleadings than in "token of the will of the Beloved (gods) as manifest in (my) escape alive from the "Hole of Descent" and in (my) loving care of the relics.

At a later date I explored a remarkable little lava grotto near some springs in the Valley of the Rio Concho, a tributary of the Colorado Chiquito, some thirty-five miles below the cave group already discovered, adding, as shown by entries in the following catalogue, considerably to the original collection.

. . .

I have entered thus fully into a sketchy narrative of the finding of these Collections and have commented thus on their nature [he had expatiated on the significance of the great age and the "protective" or "defensive" nature of the items collected in helping to solve "the problems connected with the very beginnings of decorative art as well as of their endings in iconomatic and hieroglyphic writing, so called"] in order to enlist speedy aid in a search for them through the stored material of the United States National Museum. For from the day when I dispatched these specimens from Fort Wingate to the present day, I have been able to find trace of only six or seven of them—of the lot forwarded by the hands of Mr. Kirchner to Professor Baird. . . .

Appendix G

FCH to Miss Faurote[13]

February 14, 1897

Dear Miss Faurote:

When your first note came, I was very desirous of writing you at once; for its receipt from my own old home among the Zunis gave me great pleasure. But I was extremely ill, as I am likely to be much of the time of late years, and therefore I could only send you the books.

I value very highly your kind offer to do me favors, and I am going to take immediate advantage of it; for I have not been able within the last four or five years to get one word to any of my old friends among the Zunis, so far as I can tell. I have sent them messages enough, but as you may be aware, nearly everyone who goes nowadays to Zuni, especially those who go to stay or investigate, seem to be unable to forgive me for having been the first man to live with them and learn their thoughts and ways and tell the world thereof.

I want to trouble you to read a long letter to my old brother Palowahtiwa and his kindred and friends, and I want you kindly to transfer to them some remembrances in the shape of gifts of shell and the like. I feel at last I can send them and know they will receive them. . . .

You will see that I speak freely on the hair cutting. Miss Disette does not know and apparently does not care to inform herself of the true meaning of the ways of wearing the hair among the Zunis. That their notions are wrong—but not morally more wrong than our own on the same subject—may be admitted; that their practices in this and in many other ways still more should be changed I agree as well. But the mode of changing them is not to forcefully alienate and ruthlessly *ruin* them and break their poor hearts and spirits; but to teach lovingly, teach them right ways of living, right ways of working; and without ever contemning or even referring to their present ways. Then the right ways of doing will follow and their old ways will fall away inevitably like dead leaves or worn-out garments—and a people noble in their olden faith and high ways of thinking according to their poor lights in years gone by will emerge enlightened according to our lights, transformed gladly (not unwillingly), made more noble with a still secure sense of dignity and freedom in place of the sense of wrong, of dishonor and of slavery, and the unavoidable degeneration which will follow such a sense.

I love the Zunis and would save them with my very life if I could. But instead of believing this, everyone seems to think I would keep them as they are for sentimental or scientific reasons. That belief is founded on pure and ignorant assumption—and it is an utterly unjust belief no matter on what ground entertained.

I opened the door of Zuni. Would that I never had, or would that some noble souled man or woman had entered the door I thus opened as I did—through the hearts of the people. Ere now they have been changed for the better, not the worse! [end of draft]

Appendix H

FHC to Palowahtiwa

Pálowahtiwa án-i

Hom pápa Pálowahtiwa, tem ta hom íyanikina témthla: Kóna ton téwanan áteaié? Élle tap ton i'-keetsana.

Téwanawe haw wéti; temta téwanawe haw lithl ton awen úlochnan tékwi yúasho ä'shsha. Ténat kʿyaki kowi ánaphoni'yunakʿyanawaná!

Imat ton awen Mé-Eläshtoki yam tsína-yánukʿyanakʿya Ékʿyätsiwe awa taia ámpinakya tséma! Tai-ö'ptschlinikʿya háiteshnan yäshsha! Yúhetaw! Kwa ósona Wássintona Mélikyanakwe awa háitoshnan téàmé. Tétakʿut kwa lésna hon awen léya téame. Yámante yáman tsémakwiwakʿya lukʿya Méwokʿya lésna yässha. Téyäthla tapte kwa ískon an pénan téame—kohóthl tapte; kwa ákʿya yúyanamme.

Hom leanakyap, hom ä'thnap, kwa haw keʿetsanammekʿyá, kwa hítianammekʿyá, akʿyap ton awa áwokya awen háitoshnawe ë'lle ta átehia! Wéwithlokʿya, wéwithlokʿya iyó hòm áhawi'! Ton awen yëllikʿyanakʿya haw lithl íkwanakyaná. Hànáhá! tapt kwa haw tsúmmamme. Lésnapte haw ámosi ta Péyenakwe yä'shuwakʿyana, óhsona tékwi.

Imat lukʿya, hom Pithlina ihtohkyanakwe, ta ton awen Mé-Tsita téuthlashi háw'i. Elle tap lésna.

Lewi, kési, ton awen haw lithl pénan ä'shsha. Kʿeétsinishi ton tínatú!

Ton áwen Sue,

[Washington, D.C., n.d.]

FHC to Palowahtiwa[14]

My brother Palowahtiwa, also all my relatives, how are you these many days? If things are going well, you are all happy [literally, your hearts make a tinkling sound].

Every day I am sick. Also, here I am always lonesome for your country. Perhaps soon we shall see each other.

It seems that your Anglo girl [Miss Disette] has already finished her letter about their [i.e., the young Zuni girls'] hair and demands to show it.

Listen, she asks that the hair of the young girls be cut. I do not believe that the men in Washington would listen to this. It is also not the way of the Zunis. On her own, the Anglo lady demands that the young girls be treated in this way. Also, she didn't ask anyone at Zuni about this. She is probably not a good [i.e., finished within herself] person.

When I heard this, I was not happy. She didn't listen to the traditional practice of your women. Harden the soles of your feet; be brave, my brother. I will work here for your protection. I am no longer strong. I will talk to my bosses, the ones who hold office in this land.

So, you who taught me the ritual of the Bow Priesthood, this is how it seems. Your American mother is also at home [probably a reference to Cushing's mother, at whose home in Albion, New York, Palowahtiwa had been a guest in 1886]. Well, that is the way it is.

This is all. Here I speak these words to you. May you be happy.

Your younger brother,
Tenatsali

Notes

Preface

1. The diaries belong to Anne E. Smullen, a grandniece of Cushing's wife. That the forty-nine in her possession are only a few of those accumulated in the years between Cushing's arrival in Zuni and his death in 1900 is strongly suggested by a number of considerations, not least of which is Mrs. Smullen's impression that many more of the same were among several boxes of family papers lost in a storage warehouse during World War II. Among those that have survived, moreover, there is a notably consistent regularity in making entries daily—one batch of thirty-one books, in fact, making up a consecutive journal covering the years 1892–1893. The latest entry (on a single loose slip of paper) is dated January 1, 1900. So much for the picture of Cushing later fostered by his brother-in-law Frederick Webb Hodge—as a prima donna who never took field notes and relied instead on his memory and intuition. It is now clear that Cushing did have the habit of scrupulously recording his activities and observations each day.

2. For a Zuni view of Cushing and some of the other anthropologists who had stayed with them, see Triloki Nath Pandey, "Anthropologists at Zuni," *Proceedings of the American Philosophical Society* 116 (1972): 321–37.

Introduction

1. Sylvester Baxter, "Father of the Pueblos," *Harper's* 65 (1882): 74. Baxter (1850–1927), who became a staunch friend and supporter of Cushing's, figures intermittently throughout this collection. A man with wide acquaintance among the intellectual and philanthropic circles of Boston society, he was instrumental in introducing Cushing into that world.

2. Alice Fletcher, quoted in a Cushing diary entry for August 30, 1893. Property of Anne E. Smullen.

3. Claude Levi-Strauss, *Structural Anthropology* (New York: Basic Books, 1963), p. 290.

4. In developing her notion of culture as the pattern of behavior typifying a given people, Benedict was of course building on the work of precursors more immediate than Cushing. For discussion of the line from Cushing to Benedict through Boas and Boas' earlier student H. K. Haeberlin, see Joan Mark, *Four Anthropologists: An American Science in its Early Years* (New York: Science History Publications, 1980), pp. 112–14. For discussion of Cushing's influence in Europe, by way of the work of his contemporaries Emile Durkheim, Marcel Mauss, and Lucien Levy-Bruhl, see Jesse Green, ed., *Zuni: Selected Writings of Frank Hamilton Cushing* (Lincoln: University of Nebraska Press, 1979), pp. 18–20 and 165–68.

5. In a piece on Zuni, the critic Edmund Wilson speaks of the recognition overdue to Cushing as an admirable writer who had something in common with Charles Montagu Doughty, author of *Travels in Arabia Deserta* (*Red, Black, Blond, and Olive: Studies in Four Cultures: Zuni, Haiti, Soviet Russia, Israel* [New York: Oxford University Press, 1956], p. 18). In addition to Wilson's journalistic treatment of Cushing, a number of more extended scholarly studies also should be mentioned here: Raymond Stewart Brandes, "Frank Hamilton Cushing: Pioneer Americanist" (Ph.D. dissertation, University of Arizona, 1965); C. Gregory Crampton, *The Zunis of Cibola* (Salt Lake City: University of Utah Press, 1977), pp. 127–37; Bernard L. Fontana, "Pioneers in Ideas: Three Early Southwestern Ethnologists" (*Journal of the Arizona Academy of Science* 2:124–29); Clarissa P. Fuller, "Frank Hamilton Cushing's Relations to Zuni and the Hemenway Southwestern Expedition" (Master's thesis, University of New Mexico, 1943); Marion Spjut Gilliland, *The Material Culture of Key Marco, Florida* (Gainesville: University of Florida Presses, 1975); Green, *Zuni*; Emil Haury, *The Excavations at Los Muertos and Neighboring Ruins in the Salt River Valley, Southern Arizona,* Harvard University, Papers of the Peabody Museum of American Archaeology and Ethnology, vol. 24, no. 1 (Cambridge: The Museum, 1945); Curtis M. Hinsley, Jr., *Savages and Scientists: The Smithsonian Institution and the Development of American Anthropology, 1846–1910* (Washington, D.C.: Smithsonian Institution Press, 1981), pp. 192–207, and "Ethnographic Charisma and Scientific Routine: Cushing and Fewkes in the American Southwest, 1878–1893" (in George W. Stocking, ed., *Observers Observed: Essays on Anthropological Fieldwork,* History of Anthropology Series vol. 1 [Madison: University of Wisconsin Press, 1983]); Joan Mark, *Four Anthropologists,* pp. 96–130; and Triloki Nath Pandey, "Anthropologists at Zuni."

6. Spencer F. Baird was Secretary of the Smithsonian Institution from 1878 to 1888. Friend of a Cushing neighbor, Baird had taken an early interest in Cushing, had supplied him with books, had solicited and published his first professional article, written at the age of sixteen (Frank H. Cushing, "Antiquities of Orleans County, N.Y.," *Annual Report of the Board of Regents of the Smithsonian Institution, 1874* [Washington, D.C., 1875], pp. 375–77), and had then appointed him at age nineteen to the Smithsonian staff. As Cushing's director and mentor at the Smithsonian, Baird was the recipient of a great many of the letters in this collection.

7. Frank H. Cushing, "My Adventures in Zuni" (*Cen-*

tury Illustrated Monthly Magazine 25 [1882]: 191) reprinted in Green, *Zuni,* p. 46. Citations of "My Adventures" hereafter will appear in the text in the abbreviated form: MAZ; page numbers as reprinted in *Zuni* are provided along with those of the original publication.

8. See Green, *Zuni,* pp. 41–42, for the dream.

9. *Report of the Secretary of the Interior on the Operations of the Department for the Fiscal Year Ended June 30, 1877,* vol. 1 (Washington, 1877), p. ix.

10. Quotation from William Culp Darrah, *Powell of the Colorado* (Princeton: Princeton University Press, 1951), p. 256. Hero of the Colorado River explorations and author of the revolutionary *Report on the Lands of the Arid Regions of the United States,* Powell was the master organizer in an era in which Washington became one of the great scientific centers of the world. In Wallace Stegner's words, Powell, as director for more than a decade of both the Bureau of Ethnology and the U.S. Geological Survey, "had in his control a good part of the Science of Man and Science of the Earth, and he conceived of both in the broadest possible terms" (*Beyond the Hundredth Meridian: The Exploration of the Grand Canyon and the Second Opening of the West* [Boston: Houghton Mifflin Co., 1954], p. 249).

11. More specifically, the "village Indians" of the Southwest, still living amid the ruins left by their pre-Columbian ancestors, seemed ideally suited for the purpose of verifying the theories of Lewis Henry Morgan, whose *Ancient Society,* published just two years earlier, was generally regarded in America as *the* handbook on social evolution.

12. A step in this direction had in fact been made by Powell, who, in the course of his Colorado River expedition, had camped for a month or so in the Ute country and spent considerable time among the Indian people learning what he could of their language and culture (see William Culp Darrah, *Powell of the Colorado,* pp. 175–76). In Zuni itself Cushing had been preceded by two other white men: a Franciscan monk who had put aside his habit and stayed on among his charges at the time of the great Pueblo Revolt of 1680 and a local mail carrier named Albert Franklin Banta, who had lived in the pueblo for several years in the 1860s. The point is that Cushing was the first to do what *he* did.

13. Anthony Forge, "The Lonely Anthropologist," in Solon T. Kimball and James B. Watson, eds., *Crossing Cultural Boundaries: The Anthropological Experience* (San Francisco: Chandler Publishing Co., 1972), p. 292. The earliest exposition in print of the practice to be known as participant observation has to be the following, reported by Sylvester Baxter in "The Father of the Pueblos" and probably spoken for Cushing by his friend Dr. Washington Matthews, the post surgeon at Fort Wingate and himself a pioneer student of Indian ethnology:

> "It is no streak of eccentricity that prompts him to dress that way. . . . He has an end in view and wisely adopts the means suited to its attainment. To make a success of his investigations, [he] cannot stand contemplating his subjects from the outside, like a spectator at a play. He must go on to the stage and take his own part in the performance. There are no people more distrustful of the motives of strangers than are the North American Indians. One can only learn anything trustworthy from them by gaining their confidence and sympathy; so Cushing has adopted the only sensible course. He has become one of the Zunis for the time being, has conformed to all their observances, and learned their language thoroughly . . ." (*Harper's* 65 [1882]: 74).

14. "Transactions of the Anthropological Society of Washington, February 10, 1879–January 17, 1882," p. 10, and "Abstracts of Papers," pp. 3 and 7, *Smithsonian Institution Miscellaneous Collections,* vol. 25 (Washington, D.C., 1883). The latter pages show a Cushing paper on "Relic Hunting" given at the Society's first meeting, in March 1879, and another on "Arrow-Head Making" given the following month.

15. The range of Cushing's reading in this period is suggested by a note among his papers in the National Anthropological Archives listing some twenty books from the Library of Congress which he wished to retain because of having "very frequent occasion to use" them. Among those listed are works by Edward Tylor, John Lubbock, Arthur Evans, Daniel Wilson, E. G. Squier, and Charles Pickering, as well as several books reporting exploring expeditions in both hemispheres, a book on cave writing, and a range of other books (both in English and French) on the ancient or primitive peoples of Central and South America, the South Pacific, the Far East, and Egypt. His acquaintance with the first four of these authors dates, in fact, from his fourteenth or fifteenth year, when he was befriended and lent books by the journalist and traveler, George Kennan (autobiographical fragments in the Hodge-Cushing papers at the Southwest Museum and Kennan's memoir of Cushing in the *Medina* [New York] *Tribune*).

16. George Kennan: "G. K.'s Column," *Medina* [New York] *Tribune,* December 6, 1923. The series of four columns written by this friend and neighbor in the hometown newspaper (on file in the National Anthropological Archives) comprises the only known firsthand memoir of Cushing's early years other than Cushing's own. An ardent Darwinist who loved discussing scientific and philo-

sophical issues, the elder Cushing, as pictured in Kennan's account, must surely have provided the younger with his earliest education in evolutionary thought, though the extreme rationalist bias attributed to the father is poles apart from the "peculiar fetichism" the son retrospectively associated with his own early bent for entering sympathetically into the mind of the "primitive." The young Frank's interest in Indians apparently received little explicit encouragement at home, particularly when it interfered with arithmetic assignments or resulted in filling the house with the objects he had unearthed. But the father's independence and unconventionality must have been an implicit encouragement—even when it came to resisting his expectation that Frank would follow him into the medical profession.

17. Frank H. Cushing, "The Arrow" (*American Anthropologist* 8 [1895]: 311); also, autobiographical sketch in Cushing Papers, Southwest Museum.

18. Cushing, "The Arrow," p. 313.

19. John Wesley Powell, "Remarks," in "In Memoriam: Frank Hamilton Cushing," Frederick Webb Hodge, ed., *American Anthropologist* n.s. 2 [1900]: 361. Cushing's "new method," Powell wrote, "laid the foundation of a system of investigation which has since proved of marvelous efficiency and which has been successfully developed by other laborers."

20. Personal communications from Professors Stuart Streuver of Northwestern University and Richard B. Woodbury of the University of Massachusetts.

21. Cushing, "The Arrow," 309–10.

22. Cushing Papers, Southwest Museum. Intended evidently for an encyclopaedia biography, the piece was composed by Cushing in the third person.

23. George Stocking, "Empathy and Antipathy in the Heart of Darkness," in Regna Darnell, ed. *Readings in the History of Anthropology* (New York: Harper and Row, 1974), p. 286. The Bronislaw Malinowski quotation is from the introduction to *Argonauts of the Western Pacific* (New York: E. P. Dutton & Co., 1961), p. 25.

24. Fletcher, "Remarks," in Hodge, "In Memoriam: Frank Hamilton Cushing," 367.

25. Sylvester Baxter, "Some Results of Mr. Cushing's Visit," *American Architect and Building News* 11 [1882]: 196. One "must share and appear to enjoy their ways of living and thinking; and must avoid giving the slightest occasion for allowing them to suppose that in any way he regards himself as socially above their level," Baxter continues, obviously paraphrasing Cushing himself.

26. Joan Mark, *Four Anthropologists,* p. 103. For a glimpse of Cushing the story-teller, as recorded by his friend John Bourke, see p. 183 above.

27. Actually, this was not the very earliest Cushing exposure or adjustment to Pueblos and their manners (see pp. 34–35); but it is typical.

28. This is essentially the course Malinowski later advised for the pidgin-English-speaking newcomer in his introduction to *Argonauts of the Western Pacific*—to "collect concrete data" (p. 5).

29. Born in 1840, James Stevenson had been involved in exploring and surveying enterprises in the West for almost the whole of his adult life. Before following Powell to the Bureau, he had been his chief of staff on the Geological Survey, and before that he had been on several western expeditions with Powell's predecessor, F. V. Hayden. With Hayden he had also already been over the ground in the Southwest territories, notably on a reconnaisance survey in 1869. The 1879 mission was his first for the Bureau. In the remaining nine years of his life he spent several months annually in the Southwest field, exploring and collecting for the Bureau and the National Museum. According to the *Dictionary of American Biography,* Stevenson was a "man of action, irked by writing, and gladly turned over most of his material to his wife." He died in 1888.

30. Hillers (1843–1925) had already accompanied Powell and/or Stevenson on several western trips, having served as photographer first on the Colorado River explorations and subsequently on several Geological Survey expeditions. He joined the Bureau of Ethnology in 1879. For his own account of the Colorado River ventures and a collection of his photographs of the Southwest, see *"Photographed All the Best Scenery": Jack Hiller's Diary of the Powell Expeditions, 1871–1875,* ed. Don D. Fowler (Salt Lake City: University of Utah Press, 1972).

31. Matilda Coxe Stevenson (1850–1915) is best known for her massive monograph, "The Zuni Indians: Their Mythology, Esoteric Fraternities, and Ceremonies" (*Twenty-third Annual Report of the Bureau of Ethnology, 1901–1902* [Washington, D.C., 1904]), and for her aggressive ways with Indians and whites alike. Born into a wealthy Washington family, she was clearly a person of strong character from the beginning. After a genteel education under governesses at home and in private schools, she took up the study of chemistry at the age of eighteen or nineteen, intending to become a mineralogist. Instead, she married James Stevenson in 1872 and began to develop an interest in ethnology. Regularly accompanying him on his field trips, she both aided in his work and became increasingly active as an ethnologist in her own right. By the time of his death in 1888, she had published several studies based on her visits to Zuni, including "The Religious Life of the Zuni Child"

(*Fifth Annual Report of the Bureau of Ethnology, 1883–1884* [Washington, D.C., 1887], pp. 539–55). In 1890, with an appointment as ethnologist on the Bureau staff, she returned alone to the Southwest to study the Pueblos. To this enterprise she devoted the remaining twenty-five years of her life, making a series of extended visits to Zia (see *Eleventh Annual Report of the Bureau of Ethnology, 1889–1890* [Washington, D.C., 1894], pp. 9–157), Zuni, and other Pueblo villages and finally settling on a small ranch near Taos, where she continued her research by means of the informants who came to visit her. What she thought of Cushing is conveyed succinctly in what she wrote on the back of a photograph of him:

> Frank Hamilton Cushing in his fantastic dress worn while among the Zuni Indians. This man was the biggest fool and charlatan I ever knew. He even put his hair up in curl papers every night [a detail, incidentally, noted by no one other than herself]. How could a man walk weighted down with so much toggery? (Cushing Papers, Southwest Museum).

While Mrs. Stevenson, like Cushing, spent considerable stretches of time among her subjects, and indeed formed fairly close relationships with a number of them, she was clearly not in sympathy with the idea of joining up with the Indians, as Cushing had done—an option which in any case would have posed even more difficulties for a female than for a male ethnologist, given the current attitudes about women on both sides of the cultural boundary. Her own method was more direct—and no doubt, in her view, justified not only by her superior cultural position but by the *need* for a woman to be aggressive if she were going to accomplish anything. In the way of information, sacred objects, or entry into forbidden places, what she couldn't obtain through respect or friendship she got by buying, demanding, or simply taking it, going where she pleased and observing what she wished, marching in on secret ceremonials without invitation and, on at least one occasion, threatening the Indians with the militia if they interfered with her. For all that, she was a remarkably perceptive, as well as meticulous, observer of ethnography, and her book holds a vast and invaluable treasury of Zuni lore. For a fuller account of her work, see Nancy O. Lurie, "Women in Early American Anthropology," in *Pioneers of American Anthropology,* ed. June Helm, American Ethnological Society Monograph 43 (Seattle: University of Washington Press, 1966), pp. 29–81, and Triloki Nath Pandey, "Anthropologists at Zuni," pp. 326–29. For more extended discussion of the professional rivalries in which Cushing was caught up, see Green, *Zuni,* pp. 28–31, and Hinsley, *Savages and Scientists,* pp. 196–99. This was not a unique case, of course. As James K. Flack remarks, "unrelenting antipathies were the rule, not the exception" in the pursuit of natural science in late nineteenth century America (*Desideratum in Washington: The Intellectual Community in the Capital City, 1870–1900* (Cambridge, Mass.: Albert Schenkman, 1975), p. 92.

32. Canyon de Chelly in Arizona, now a National Monument, is the site of a number of cliff pueblo ruins left by the Anasazi ancestors of the Zunis.

33. In fact, he was destitute—and remained so until sometime in January, when it finally registered at the Smithsonian that arrangements had not been completed for his salary to be sent to him.

34. "From Wife to Anthropologist," in Kimball and Watson, *Crossing Cultural Boundaries,* p. 22. This necessity had of course already been addressed, in much the same words, by Malinowski (*Argonauts of the Western Pacific,* p. 6). Cushing himself recognized the point in practical terms in an early letter to Baird: "The contrast between the present results of my labors and those which even exertion secured before the departure of our party is pronounced. Instead of being unfriendly and overbearing, as Col. Stevenson believed they would be in his absence, the Indians have become more communicative and unconstrained than ever." Things might of course have been otherwise but for the indigence that forced Cushing to submit, as he put it, to the Indians' "constant surveillance over my work and to their food" (Cushing to Powell, July 6, 1882, Southwest Museum Hodge-Cushing Collection, envelope 37). Such remarks suggest how much Cushing learned from involuntary circumstance.

35. Firth, "From Wife to Anthropologist," p. 23. Here again, it was Cushing (as reported in Baxter's initial *Boston Herald* story) who first articulated this point—in almost the same words that Firth used a century later. See p. 156 above.

36. According to Neil M. Judd (*The Bureau of American Ethnology: A Partial History* [Norman: University of Oklahoma Press, 1967], p. 59), Cushing acquired a reputation in the Bureau as a chronic complainer. Reading the correspondence, one can see why. Uncertain mails (hours spent writing an important letter only to have it lost in transit), difficulties and delays in obtaining needed supplies (after months of waiting, the shells sent for trading were the wrong kind), vagueness in Washington about conditions in the field, general incomprehension or worse regarding the probity of his relations with the Indians, conflicting demands on his time—there was much and frequent cause for Cushing's expres-

sions of impatience and frustration. If he was loquacious about the hardships, privations, and illnesses he suffered, that is no cause for inferring that they were any the less real or extreme. His need to talk about them in letters home was perhaps the greater for the silence about them he felt impelled to keep in the presence of the Indians. Complaint seems also to have served for Cushing as a way of fishing for the words of praise and approval he obviously needed both from his friends and from his "principals" in Washington. The "bad news" was in any case never more than part of the story. If he wrote on one page, "My life is simply horrible, unmentionable," he was sure to write on the next about some new discovery he had made or about what fine folk the Indians were after all.

37. Perhaps the best thing that can be said of Cushing's reported display of machismo on a number of occasions such as this one is that there is a distinct possibility of its having been exaggerated somewhat in the accounts written for publication. There is at least nothing in the letter to indicate that "braving all Zuni" meant pulling a knife.

38. Frank H. Cushing, "Primitive Motherhood," *Work and Words of the National Congress of Mothers: First Annual Session Held in the City of Washington, D.C., February 17–19, 1897* (New York: D. Appleton & Co., 1897), p. 35. One wonders in this connection how much Cushing was aided simply by his youth, as well as by a special touch he seems to have had in relating with his elders—something perhaps derived from the frailty that he spoke of as separating him as a child from his peers (autobiographical fragment, Cushing Papers, Southwest Museum). Nancy O. Lurie writes with great charm and perceptiveness about the importance of both these factors in her own first field experience in her esssay "Two Dollars" (Kimball and Watson, *Crossing Cultural Boundaries,* pp. 151–63).

39. Frank H. Cushing, *Zuni Breadstuff,* Indian Notes and Monographs, vol. 8 (New York: Museum of the American Indian, Heye Foundation, 1920), 598–600 (Green, *Zuni,* pp. 313–14). In citations of this work, page numbers are given as they appear in the Heye volume (cross-listed, where possible, with Green, *Zuni*) rather than as they appear in the original series of articles in the *Millstone* 9 (1884), nos. 1 and 2, and 10 (1885), nos. 1–4, since the latter are available only in a few libraries.

40. Cushing, "My Adventures in Zuni," p. 505 (Green, *Zuni,* p. 83). Again one may note a slight foreshortening: he had already been introduced into a sacred society in San Isidro months earlier, en route to Zuni.

41. I.e., on the condition that he participate, not merely look on. The imperative involved here differentiates Cushing's situation from that of Malinowski when he suggests that

> . . . it is good for the Ethnographer sometimes to put aside camera, note book and pencil, and to join in himself in what is going on. . . . Out of such plunges into the life of the natives . . . I have carried away a distinct feeling that their behavior, their manner of being, in all sorts of tribal transactions, became more transparent and easily understandable" (*Argonauts of the Western Pacific,* pp. 21–22).

For Malinowski such "plunges" were an option; for Cushing they were a requirement.

42. The ruin referred to here is actually in the area designated today as the Chaco National Monument, not in the Canyon de Chelly. Built by a people now called the Anasazi, Pueblo Bonito is the largest known remain dating from the era identified as Pueblo III (A.D. 1100–1300).

43. See Green, *Zuni,* pp. 172–75, for the story of this discovery, excerpted from the manuscript for a lecture given before the Geographical Society of Boston in 1885 under the title, "The Discovery of Zuni, or the Ancient Provinces of Cibola and the Seven Cities" (Cushing Papers, Southwest Museum). Cushing himself never developed this subject in print, but his friend Adolph Bandelier, who learned the story of the "Black Mexican" and other related details while visiting him in Zuni in 1883, credited him with proving "what I have only intimated, that Cibola represents the present country and tribe of Zuni" (*The Gilded Man . . .* [New York: D. Appleton, 1893], pp. 159–60). The line of research thus opened by Cushing was to be pursued in turn by Bandelier, Jesse Walter Fewkes, and Frederick Webb Hodge (Cushing's brother-in-law). The latter, in his detailed and elaborately documented *History of Hawikuh, New Mexico, One of the So-Called Cities of Cibola* (Los Angeles: Southwest Museum, 1937) summarizes the contributions of all his known predecessors—except for Cushing.

44. For a summary of this "mytho-sociologic" system, see Frank H. Cushing, "Outlines of Zuni Creation Myths," *Thirteenth Annual Report of the Bureau of Ethnology, 1891–1892* (Washington, D.C., 1896), pp. 368–73 (Green, *Zuni,* pp. 185–93).

45. Indeed, he still had a long way to go six years later, when he told a reporter:

> The seclusiveness and reserve of the Zunis is almost inexplicable, or perhaps I might better say inexpressible. . . . Although I have lived among them for years, have fasted in

their temples for consecutive days and nights, and have witnessed their secret religious rites, there are fetiches upon their altars which I have never been permitted to inspect closely, much less to touch, and at times I feel that I have hardly commenced to learn anything about the Zunis (*San Diego Daily Sun,* October 19, 1887).

46. Cushing's advice here is quite specific, the interview having been occasioned by an invasion of troops from Fort Wingate resulting in the arrest and jailing of a number of leading Bow Priests for their treatment of a suspected sorcerer—one of several such interferences which undermined the power of the Bow Priesthood and led ultimately to all kinds of changes in Zuni social organization. For analysis of these longer range developments, see Triloki Nath Pandey, "Factionalism in a Southwestern Pueblo," Ph.D. dissertation, University of Chicago, 1967.

47. *Second Annual Report of the Bureau of Ethnology, 1880–1881* (Washington, D.C., 1883), p. xxvi—the source for which is Cushing's summary of his activities from September 1879 through February 1882, addressed to Major Powell July 6, 1882 (Southwest Museum, Hodge-Cushing Collection, Envelope 37).

48. Sounding remarkably like Cushing, Malinowski even wrote at one point of the "delightful feeling that now I alone am the master of this village with my 'boys,'" though more often he seems to have used his diary to relieve feelings of annoyance—or worse, "general aversion"—for "the bloody niggers." "As for ethnology," he confessed in one entry, "I see the life of the native as utterly devoid of interest or importance, something as remote from me as the life of a dog" (*A Diary in the Strict Sense of the Word* [New York: Harcourt Brace Jovanovich, 1967], pp. 163, 167). In expressions like these Malinowski sounds remarkably *un*like Cushing. However aggressive the latter's behavior may sometimes have been, there is nothing in the record to suggest "aversion," and nowhere in his writing do we encounter pejoratives like "nigger" applied to Indians (or to Blacks either, for that matter, to say nothing of Melanesians).

49. The matter of titles generally is somewhat confusing. In his July 6, 1882, report to Powell, Cushing states that soon after his initiation into the Bow Priesthood he had been "elected assistant chief of the Governor or Head Chief of Zuni, which election was followed within a few months by nomination to and subsequent confirmation to the Head War Chieftaincy of the tribe" (Southwest Museum, Hodge-Cushing Collection, Envelope 37). As "second chief of the tribe" or assistant to the governor, we see him in a chapter of "Zuni Breadstuff" helping to preside over a "lawsuit" between rival claimants to a peach orchard. But it is difficult to see the difference between this office and that of "chief councilor" to which he was already referring in late 1880, nearly a year prior to his initiation to the Bow Priesthood. As to his war chieftaincy, the traditional title for the member of the Bow Priesthood who was charged with leading war parties was *I:Laknakva mossi,* or "war captain." Oddly enough, though Cushing was familiar with this title and though he took charge of war parties, it was not this but the other title of First or Head War Chief that he used in reference to himself. That Cushing possessed certain tribal functions and sanctions is not in doubt, but the inconsistencies in nomenclature suggest an improvisational aspect to his appointments, both from the Zuni standpoint and from his own. These too were something he was in *process* of learning about as he went along.

50. One wonders what his reaction would have been had he known of a note Cushing drafted at about this same time—probably to the U.S. agent in Santa Fe—reporting the governor himself, along with a number of other Zunis, for running whiskey!

51. In a later journal entry Cushing tells of a scene in which, after an exchange of jokes and pleasantries, he "took cane of office and ordered several men and women to sweep about their houses." Traditionally in Zuni, the authority of a secular official has been regarded as deriving from his "cane of office"—presented to him by the chief priests on his inauguration and returned to them on his departure from office. In the later history of Zuni there have been incidents, for example, in which governors have been removed from office by having the cane (in this case a silver-knobbed ebony cane presented to the Zunis by President Lincoln) taken away. See Triloki Nath Pandey, "Tribal Council Elections in a Southwestern Pueblo" (*Ethnology* 7 [1968]: 1) and "Images of Power in a Southwestern Pueblo" (in Raymond D. Fogelson and Richard N. Adams, eds., *Ethnographic Studies from Asia, Oceania, and the New World* [New York: Academic Press, 1977]), as well as his doctoral dissertation, "Factionalism in a Southwestern Pueblo." Cushing's cane, in other words, is confirmation that he did hold a genuine office in Zuni. It is important, however, to understand how strictly such authority may be defined and limited. In Cushing's case, to be specific, whatever his standing as "Chief Councilor" or "First War Chief," he was still very much the *younger* "brother" and subject to a good deal of supervision by his elders.

52. For history of the Anglo settlement of the Zuni area, particularly following the arrival of the railroad, see Crampton, *The Zunis of Cibola,* chapters 8–12; William S. Greever, *Arid Domain: The Santa Fe Railway and*

Its Western Land Grants (Stanford: Stanford University Press, 1954), chapter 4; and Irving Telling, "New Mexico Frontiers: a Social History of the Gallup Area, 1881–1901," Ph.D. dissertation, Harvard University, 1952, chapter 4. As Crampton points out, the slopes of the Zuni Mountains offered a great expanse of virgin grassland (much of it within the great swathe granted to the Santa Fe Railway to be sold off). The rapid influx of cattle ranchers into the region brought about both a displacement of Navajos from lands they had used freely for generations and encroachments on Zuni lands both by Navajos and by white and Mexican stockmen. In the range war which persisted all through the 1880s the Zunis were repeatedly subjected to raiding and rustling as well as poaching on their grasslands, and in defense of their territories they fought a number of pitched battles, in one instance losing as many as five Zunis to the bullets of the raiders (Edward H. Spicer, *Cycles of Conquest: The Impact of Spain, Mexico, and the United States on the Indians of the Southwest, 1533–1960* [Tucson: University of Arizona Press, 1962], p. 198). It was definitely a period fraught with threats to the survival of the Zuni community. For that matter, trespass did not soon cease to be a problem. A letter written to the Zunis four decades later expresses the hope that they "are no longer bothered by the Mexicans allowing their cattle to eat on the reservation . . ." (F. W. Hodge to "dear friends," February 6, 1918, Hodge Papers, Southwest Museum).

53. Hinsley, *Savages and Scientists,* p. 196.

54. But see his later explanation:

> Of course my experience is, in a certain sense, one-sided. I have a feeling of love and admiration for the Zunis, it is true, but in this I do not offer by any means a solitary example. Nearly everyone who has lived long and intimately with the Indians, no matter of what tribe, has learned to love them, and to have this feeling of particular admiration for the tribe he has best known, even as I have for the Zunis ("The Need of Studying the Indian in Order to Teach Him," *Twenty-eighth Annual Report of the Board of Indian Commissioners,* Washington, D.C., 1897, p. 111).

What Cushing exemplifies, rather than "detachment," is consciousness of the relativity of attachment.

55. Cushing's relationship with these two, and later with Naiiutchi, the elder chief Bow Priest, seems to have been a truly familial one. The gentle kindness and affectionate concern of the old father, Laiiuahtsailunkia, shines through every Cushing reference to him, and governor Palowahtiwa, as the reader will see, was indeed Cushing's inseparable companion, protector, and friend, though the relationship had its stormy intervals.

56. See, for example, his journal entry for December 8, 1881: "Was told by Tsai-lu-ai-ti-wa that I would probably have to go on the Navajo expedition tomorrow. In such matters I am chief indeed of the Zunis. They do nothing without my advice or action and always give me unending difficulty if I do not accede to their demands. . . ."

57. See in this connection Nancy Parezo, "Cushing as Part of the Team: The Collecting Activities of the Smithsonian Institution," in Triloki Nath Pandey, ed., *Essays on the Anthropological Career of Frank Hamilton Cushing.*

58. Letter to Sylvester Baxter, p. 181. Cushing refers in this same letter to the "tale of blood" he produced for the Zunis to account for his possession of the scalp. For a tale he produced for eastern listeners (almost certainly a fabrication), see Green, *Zuni,* pp. 153–156.

59. "Life in Zuni," a lecture given in Buffalo, New York, December 10, 1890 (Southwest Museum HC 214).

60. Fletcher, "Remarks," in Hodge, "In Memoriam," p. 369. In a letter written near the time of his initiation, Cushing himself expressed the view that winning membership in the Bow Priesthood was "the greatest achievement of my life perhaps."

61. For accounts of the trip, see Baxter, "An Aboriginal Pilgrimage"; Fred A. Ober, "How a White Man Became the War Chief of the Zunis" (*Wide Awake* [June 1882], 382–88); and stories in the *Boston Herald* (March 22, 23, 24, and 29, 1882); the *Boston Evening Transcript* (March 22, 23, 24, and 29, 1882); the *New York Times* (March 29 and April 2, 1882); *Frank Leslie's Illustrated Newspaper* (April 8, 1882); the *Washington Star* (April 8, 1882); and the *New York Tribune* (July 1, 1882), as well as Cushing's own *Zuni Breadstuff,* pp. 539–42 (*Zuni,* pp. 301–04).

62. Charles F. Lummis, "The White Indian," in *Land of Sunshine* 12 (1900): 11. For their part, Cushing's Zuni companions seem to have been gratified by their meeting with President Arthur and impressed by the grand scale of the American country and its lakes, cities, monuments, and powerful machines, though as much troubled by its cuisine as Cushing was by theirs.

63. See especially Sylvester Baxter, "An Aboriginal Pilgrimage," *Century Illustrated Monthly Magazine* 24 (1882): 534–36, and Fred Ober, "How a White Man Became War Chief of the Zunis," 386–88.

64. Another piece, "The Zuni Social, Mythic, and Religious Systems" (*Popular Science Monthly* [June 1882]: 186–92), based on the talk Cushing gave before the National Academy of Sciences, appeared while he was still in Washington. It was an early sketch of the theories

he would develop about the structural relationships underlying the Zuni social order.

65. Lummis, "The White Indian," p. 15.

66. William E. Curtis, *Children of the Sun* (Chicago: Inter-Ocean Publishing Co., 1883), pp. 40–41. According to a diary entry by Cushing on July 10, 1892, the marriage took place on July 10, 1882.

67. Both sisters figure intermittently in the materials collected here, and both also accompanied Cushing on the Hemenway Expedition to Arizona, taking active roles in the work involved. A gifted artist as well as a lively personality, Margaret Magill produced many sketches and drawings in the course of her visits in the Southwest. Some of these are preserved in the Southwest Museum. On the Hemenway Expedition she met her future husband, Frederick Webb Hodge, who was getting his first field experience as Cushing's secretary and general assistant. Both kept diaries; his are in the Hodge-Cushing Collection of the Southwest Museum, hers among other Hemenway materials in the Heye Foundation Library of the American Indian in New York.

68. Curtis, *Children of the Sun,* p. 17. Curtis' description of the Cushing household in Zuni is excerpted at greater length below.

69. For a glimpse of Cushing in action as "war chief" on this occasion, see his letter of October 3, 1882, to Baxter. The impression created here is one of leadership perhaps more imposed *by* him than *on* him—*viz.* the "forcible language" he reports using to win initially reluctant recruits for his company and the "lashing" he administered with his quirt to prevent one of the men from deserting.

70. The issue with Senator Logan was perhaps exacerbated by the timing—in the midst of maneuvering prior to the presidential campaign of 1884 (Logan ended up as Blaine's running mate on the Republican ticket). It is not unlikely that political as well as humanitarian motives inspired at least one partisan, William E. Curtis, editor of a rival Republican newspaper in Chicago, to make the most of Logan's unsavory role in the Nutria land scheme. On the other hand, if Curtis' report is to be believed, Logan and his associates had marked Cushing as a threat from the beginning and in an effort to neutralize him had begun as early as the fall of 1882 to spread rumors that he was a fraud, a libertine, an incompetent, etc., and that the trip east with the Zunis had been nothing but an elaborate hoax. There were even insinuations of a venereal infection, based on the facial blisters from which Cushing suffered in reaction to his Zuni diet. One is reminded by such scurrilities that it was the Blaine-Logan campaign which contributed to American folklore the famous "Rum, Romanism and Rebellion" slur against the Democrats as the party of lower class immigrants and Southerners.

71. On the question of widespread dislike of Cushing among the whites in the area, see Regna Diebold Darnell, "The Development of American Anthropology, 1879–1920: From the Bureau of American Ethnology to Frank Boas," Ph.D. dissertation, University of Pennsylvania, 1969, p. 113. On the other hand, as the reader of the present volume will notice, Cushing's journals are full of entries registering friendly contacts with his white neighbors. Until the arrival of his brother Enos, a dentist, some of them even depended on Cushing to pull teeth for them. In view of some of the accusations leveled against him, it is of interest to come across Cushing's own assessment of another man (Jeremiah Sullivan) who had actually married into the tribe he was studying:

> "The Moquis wanted me to live with them as I had among the Zunis, and a fellow has actually done it—the son of a former agent. He went into it with the avowed intention of studying the people, as I had done with the Zunis. He was a young fellow, quite bright, and a good physician, but he has degenerated into a 'squaw man.' That is dangerous to him, and dangerous to his purposes, and also to the people themselves . . ." (*San Francisco Examiner,* July 8, 1888).

72. Reviewing the book in 1921, Alfred Kroeber wrote: "There seems to be no other piece of writing that renders so complete and true and powerful an impression of Zuni as *Breadstuff*" (*American Anthropologist* 23 [1921]: 479).

73. For a study of Morgan's influence on Powell and the shaping of the Bureau's mission, see Hinsley, *Savages and Scientists,* chapter 5.

74. Lewis Henry Morgan, *Ancient Society, or Researches in the Lines of Human Progress from Savagery through Barbarism to Civilization* (New York: Henry Holt and Co, 1877), p. 6.

75. Edward B. Tylor, *Primitive Culture: Researches into the Development of Mythology, Philosophy, Religion, Languages, Art, and Customs* (London: J. Murray, 1871), p. 1.

76. There had also, of course, been Morgan's pioneering work among the Iroquois, beginning with his investigation of the Tonawanda in the 1840s. See Carl Resek, *Lewis Henry Morgan, American Scholar* (Chicago: University of Chicago Press, 1960), chapter 2.

77. Baxter, "Some Results of Mr. Cushing's Visit," p. 196.

78. Levi-Strauss, *Structural Anthropology,* p. 291. For Cushing expositions of this "model," see "Outlines of Zuni Creation Myths," pp. 367–77; "Zuni Fetiches,"

Second Annual Report of the Bureau of Ethnology, 1880–1881 (Washington, D.C., 1883), pp. 9–15, 30–31; "Discussion of J. Chester Morris' Address," *Proceedings of the American Philosophical Society* 36 (1897): 184–92; (Green, *Zuni,* pp. 185–218); and "Preliminary Notes on the Origin, Working Hypotheses and Primary Researches of the Hemenway Southwestern Archaeological Expedition," *Congres International des Americanistes, Berlin 1888* (Berlin, 1890), pp. 151–58.

79. Ortiz, "Ritual Drama and the Pueblo World View," in Alfonso Ortiz, ed., *New Perspectives on the Pueblos* (Albuquerque: University of New Mexico Press, 1972), pp. 135–36.

80. Ibid., p. 136.

81. The quotation regarding the "notion of the middle" comes from Cushing, "Outlines of Zuni Creation Myths," p. 373 (Green, *Zuni,* p. 192).

82. Robert Lowie, "Evolution in Cultural Anthropology" *American Anthropologist* 48 (1946): 225.

83. Mark, *Four Anthropologists,* pp. 110–12. That Cushing was getting this new plural notion of culture into circulation is evidenced by an interview published in the *Washington Star* of April 8, 1882, on the occasion of the visit of the anthropologist and his party to Boston. "The culture of Boston," the reporter writes, "communed with that strange culture which, for three centuries, has preserved its individuality and withstood the tides of civilization that have surged around [it]." In the course of the article the term "culture" is used at least five times—and in ways that make clear the necessity of its pluralizing:

> The vocabulary of the Zunis is rich, and though their language is unwritten, they have a grammar as regular and symmetrical as that of any tongue . . . [and an immense ritual epic handed down] from generation to generation, just as the Iliad of Homer is supposed to have been handed down and preserved in its primitive purity until it was committed to manuscript.

In short, as Cushing puts it, "*they have a culture of their own*" (italics added).

84. Untitled handwritten notes filed under "Notes on Myth and Folklore," pp. 3a–5a, Cushing Papers, Southwest Museum.

85. *Encyclopaedia of the Social Sciences* (1930 edition), vol. 4, p. 657.

86. Curiously enough, though Cushing himself seems not to have registered the connection, what it amounts to is an extension to the ethnologist's own researches of what he had learned from Tylor about how *savages* think. In a phrase more than once quoted by Cushing, Tylor characterizes the thinking of primitives as the product of a "confusion" arising, in Tylor's words, from the "tendency of the uneducated mind to give an outward reality to its own inward processes" (Edward B. Tylor, *Researches into the Early History of Mankind and the Development of Civilization* [London: J. Murray, 1865], pp. 100–104).

87. "Anthropologists and Historians as Historians of Anthropology," in George Stocking, ed., *Observers Observed: Essays on Anthropological Fieldwork* (Madison: University of Wisconsin Press, 1983), p. 385.

88. Sylvester Baxter, "F. H. Cushing at Zuni," *American Architect and Building News* 11 (1882): 56. See also the observation of Cushing's visitor at Zuni, John Bourke, on the subject of "throwing dust in the eyes" of the Zunis (p. 189 above). Of the publication of Zuni sacred legends and ritual practice and of the fieldwork procedures used to obtain such materials over the past century, Marc Simmons comments: "The pattern of Cushing's activity—overcoming suspicion, winning acceptance, assisting in solution of village problems, serving as an agent of acculturation, and eventually betraying this trust—was one repeated often by anthropologists and writers" (Ortiz, *Handbook of North American Indians,* vol. 9, p. 219). If by betrayal Simmons means Cushing's publication of sacred matters the Zunis wished to keep secret, there can be no argument. He did publish such matters—apparently considering that the secrecy was meaningful only *within* Zuni society and that it was no betrayal to tell Zuni secrets to his own people in the faraway East. This view is in essential agreement with that expressed by the Hopi Nanahe regarding his own obligations as he was about to divulge Hopi ceremonial secrets to Bourke and Cushing (see pp. 187–88). Cushing, however, does not seem to have confronted, as Matilda Stevenson and Washington Matthews had to confront, the possibility that his printed words would return to Zuni or to have worried, as Matthews did, over the "great breach of confidence" he had committed in publishing privileged information (see Robert Marshall Poor, "Washington Matthews: An Intellectual Biography," M.A. thesis, University of Nevada, 1975, p. 31).

89. Edmund Wilson, *Red, Black, Blond, and Olive,* p. 18. Red and white were in fact but two terms for a polarity of wider compass—as may be seen, for example, in a pair of entries in one of the diaries surviving from Cushing's later years. On one page, following several references to a psychic friend of his through whom he had been exploring (gingerly but sympathetically) the world and works of parapsychology, he reports a meeting with the spiritualist Annie Besant, who was in turn to intro-

duce him to the famous Madame Blavatsky. On the next page we are reminded that he also belonged to the quite *un*spiritual world of another contemporary, Thomas Edison. Like Edison, Cushing was an inventor of technology, and elsewhere in his papers we may read of the measures he developed for preserving artifacts, of his "device for and method of cooling journals and bearings," and of his design for a "flying bicycle"—as well as of his friendly interest in a scheme for a large-scale exploitation of the mineral deposits in southern New Mexico. The subject of this other diary entry is a Cushing invention for making rain through the use of carbonic acid gas. What, one wonders, would the Zuni priests have made of *that* method of summoning the precious fluid of life?

90. Hortense Powdermaker, *Stranger and Friend: The Way of an Anthropologist* (New York: W.W. Norton & Co., 1966), pp. 19–20.

91. In his book *No Place of Grace: Antimodernism and the Transformation of American Culture, 1880–1920* (New York: Pantheon Books, 1981), T. J. Jackson Lears summarizes the cultural critique of the antimodernists of Cushing's generation as stemming from "revulsion against the process of rationalization first described by Max Weber—the systematic organization of economic life for maximum productivity and of individual life for maximum personal achievement; the drive for efficient control of nature under the banner of improving human welfare; the reduction of the world to a disenchanted object to be manipulated by rational technique" (p. 7). To be sure, the general thesis of the book is that the antimodernists were only half revolted and were in fact instrumental in furthering the very progress to which they objected.

92. See Lears, *No Place of Grace,* pp. 144–49. The association of such ideals with the American Indian was not altogether new in the nineteenth century, of course. For example, speaking of a book written two centuries earlier by Thomas Morton (of Merrymount fame), Richard Slotkin points out that "in their primitive character [Morton's Indians] seem emblems of the innocent childhood of man. At the same time, they evoke primitive memories of an Heroic Age" (*Regeneration Through Violence: The Mythology of the American Frontier, 1660–1860* [Middletown: Wesleyan University Press, 1973], p. 59). Among Cushing's generation there were *scientific* questions at stake which mandated seeking out among the Indians (or other "primitives") those who were least touched by "civilization." But when Washington Matthews remarked in a letter to Cushing that the Acomas "don't compare to the Zunis (too much Americanized)," he was expressing—in common with Cushing, Bourke, Alexander Stephen, Matilda Stevenson, and perhaps anthropologists generally, then and still—a predilection not exclusively scientific in nature. It is the same attraction—*away* from "civilization"—as that which made amateur anthropologists of such writers as Herman Melville and Henry Adams.

93. Cushing, "The Need of Studying the Indian in Order to Teach Him," pp. 112–13.

94. Cushing, "Primitive Motherhood," pp. 43–44.

95. See, for example, the Zuni comments on the Americans during their later stay on Mrs. Hemenway's estate (Green, *Zuni,* pp. 409–25).

96. Cushing, "The Need of Studying the Indian in Order to Teach Him," p. 109. "To no man on earth," he writes elsewhere, "seems the future so gloomy and fateful as to the Indian; the past in such heroic, glorious contrast with it . . ." (*Zuni Breadstuff,* p. 55). The main aim of talks such as that to the Board of Indian Commissioners was to help mitigate, if not put off, that future. While acknowledging the Indian's need to be "fitted to survive among us and not be further degraded or utterly destroyed," he was pleading here against the *imposition* of such "help." In so many words, he was pleading for the Indian's right to his own culture as the necessary condition for the survival of his personal coherence—*and* as something valuable in itself. See Mark, *Four Anthropologists* (especially pp. 120–22) and Hinsley, *Savages and Scientists* (especially pp. 206–07) for perceptive and in some respects contrasting treatments of this theme in Cushing.

97. Emil W. Haury, *The Excavations at Los Muertos,* p. 3. Not only extensive architectural remains but an elaborate system of irrigation canals were unearthed and some five thousand specimens shipped back east during the fifteen months of excavation at this site. Further digs were conducted subsequently near Zuni. As Brandes has pointed out ("Frank Hamilton Cushing," p. 209), the Hemenway Expedition was important not only for the major discoveries involved but for the pioneer linkage established between archaeological and ethnological investigation. High expectations were nevertheless disappointed. Ill health forced Cushing to abandon the field in the winter of 1889, and he was subsequently replaced by Jesse Walter Fewkes, a Harvard-trained Ph.D. in zoology who was a friend of Mrs. Hemenway's son August. Several years of dispute and recrimination followed, and in the absence of a full report by Cushing it has been conventional over the years to label the venture a failure, though revision of this view seems now to be under way with several new studies in the works.

98. These were the famous cases of the painted shell

and the mosaic frog. The former involved an article in the collection brought back from Florida: a seashell with a painted line drawing of a man's figure on the inside—and a tiny barnacle, which Cushing claimed had grown *over* the drawing, thus evidencing its great age. When subsequent photographs seemed to show, on the contrary, that traces of paint overlay the barnacle, there were accusations by the photographer, Matilda Stevenson, J. W. Fewkes, and other adversaries within the Bureau that Cushing had painted the figure himself. It was in the midst of the furor over this accusation that another Bureau member, Frederick Webb Hodge, Cushing's secretary on the Hemenway Expedition and by now his somewhat estranged brother-in-law, came up with the other story—of a mosaic frog in the Hemenway collection which had *also* been the work of Cushing's own hand. In the latter case, though insisting on the authenticity of the frog, Cushing acknowledged having done a little touching up by way of restoration; in the former he stood his ground and was officially exonerated. A residue of disbelief lingered, however, and both shell and frog passed into the Cushing legend as hoaxes. It seems to have been in reference to this affair that Boas remarked that Cushing's "greatest enemy is his genius" (Boas to W. J. McGee, January 1, 1897, Unclassified BAE History file, National Anthropological Archives). For a full (and sympathetic) review of the painted shell case and texts of the major correspondence involved, see Gilliland, *The Material Culture of Key Marco,* pp. 179–84.

99. Robert Lowie, "Past Currents in Anthropology," *American Anthropologist* 58 (1956): 996.

100. Ibid. Despite current revaluations, the view expressed by Boas and various of his pupils is probably still the majority view. In a recent article on "Ethnographic Authority," James Clifford refers to Cushing as an "oddball," whose "intuitive, excessively personal understanding of the Zuni could not confer scientific authority" (*Representations* 1:2 [Spring 1983], 121, 123). There is perhaps some irony, however, in the fact that the main object of this essay is to point out the extent to which that "authority" in anthropology has been the product of rhetorical artifice and to delineate the growth in sophistication which has led to the "increasing visibility" in more recent anthropological writings of what Clifford calls "the creative (and in a broad sense, poetic) processes by which 'cultural' objects are invented and treated as meaningful" (130). One might say—to stretch a point—that it was not only his intuitive, personal way of understanding that made Cushing a misfit in his field but his premature recognition of that kind of understanding for what it was and his failure to pretend that it was something else. He was too gauche to be considered properly professional.

101. Hermann F. C. ten Kate, "Frank Hamilton Cushing," *American Anthropologist* 2 (1900): 769. Ten Kate's reference is to Cushing's "Commentary of a Zuni Familiar," in Edna Dean Proctor, *The Song of the Ancient People.*

102. Hermann F. C. ten Kate, *Reizen en Onderzoekingen in Noord-Amerika* (Leiden, 1885), p. 282 (quotation translated by Curtis M. Hinsley, Jr.).

1. August–December 1879

1. Powell's note placed Stevenson in charge of a "party organized to make ethnological and archaeological explorations in southwest New Mexico and contiguous territory" and, more particularly, "to make as careful a study as circumstances will permit of the Pueblo ruins and caves of that district of country." J.K. Hillers had been instructed to report to Stevenson as photographer, and Cushing was to "assist in making collections and in other ethnological work"—all to proceed "according to the general instructions" which Powell had already given orally to the three men (Powell to Stevenson, August 4, 1879, Stevenson Papers, National Anthropological Archives). Subsequent correspondence suggests that Cushing and the Stevensons differed somewhat in their understanding of those "general instructions."

2. The Pecos Mission Church and monastery were built after the arrival in 1598 of the first Spanish colonists in Pecos Pueblo.

3. One of the most populous pueblos at the time of the conquest, Pecos (about eighteen miles southeast of Santa Fe) was abandoned in 1838, its inhabitants moving mainly to neighboring Jemez. For a review of what is known about this and other Pueblo peoples, see Alfonso Ortiz, ed., *Handbook of North American Indians,* vol. 9, Southwest (Washington, D.C.: Smithsonian Institution, 1979).

4. *Alcalde:* Crier chief, who calls out the announcements and orders of the day.

5. Here Cushing's imagination seems to be compensating for what he does not yet know about Pueblo marital arrangements.

6. Tesuque Pueblo is the most southerly of the six remaining Tewa-speaking communities along the Rio Grande, and the one closest to Santa Fe. With a population of ninety-four in 1889, it has remained, according to Edelman and Ortiz, "the least known and most conservative of the Tewa villages, in spite of its proximity first to Spanish, then to Anglo-Saxon influence" ("Tesuque

Pueblo," *Handbook of North American Indians,* vol. 9, p. 330).

7. Alvar Nuñez Cabeza de Vaca: Author of one of the early Spanish chronicles of journey and discovery in New Spain. It was through Cabeza and his companions that word of the Pueblos first reached the Spanish rulers of Mexico in 1536. Sole survivors of a shipwreck on the Gulf Coast, Cabeza and three companions (one of them a North African slave named Estevanico) had spent eight years in a westward trek across the continent, turning up finally in the Spanish outpost of San Miguel Culiacan in the northwest corner of Mexico with stories they had heard of rich and populous cities (with "very large houses") to the north. Contrary to Cushing's impression at this point, however, they had not actually seen these "cities" themselves. Cabeza's "Relación" was later translated into English by Fanny Ritter Bandelier (*The Journey of Alvar Nuñez Cabeza de Vaca and his Companions from Florida to the Pacific, 1528–1536.* Introduction by Adolph F. Bandelier [New York: 1905]). For a thorough description of the enormous body of literature on the Spanish discovery, conquest, and occupation of the Southwest, see Henry R. Wagner, *The Spanish Southwest, 1542–1794: An Annotated Bibliography.* 2 vols. Los Angeles: Quivira Society, 1967.

8. Joseph Stanley-Brown, Powell's sometime secretary, now evidently "on loan" to the Land Commission. Stanley-Brown, who subsequently served as private secretary to President Garfield, would later return to the Bureau and, on Bureau business, would rejoin Cushing for a time in the Southwest.

9. Cochiti is a Keresan-speaking Pueblo community on the west bank of the Rio Grande about twenty-five miles southwest of Santa Fe. Population at the time of Cushing's visit would have been something under 300.

10. *Estufa:* Spanish for *kiva* (Hopi) or *kiwitsine* (Zuni). "Kiva" is the term now generally used to refer to the subterranean or semi-subterranean chambers found in all pueblos, modern or prehistoric. Built by ceremonial societies, clan groups, or individuals depending on which pueblo is involved, these rooms have traditionally been used for the performance of sacred rituals and as places for the member men to congregate socially or to pursue activities such as weaving or tool-making.

11. San Isidro is a small Mexican village located at the junction of what are now New Mexico state highways 4 and 44.

12. Keresan-speaking Zia (or Sia) is another of the group of Pueblo communities along the Rio Grande. Its population in 1890 was approximately one hundred. In the sixteenth century, however, Zia was described by one of the Spanish chroniclers (Espejo) as a large city with eight plazas, over a thousand several-storied houses, and a population of more than 4,000 adult males in addition to women and children.

13. The number of kivas in a pueblo varies according to their use. In some Pueblo communities there are two kivas, representing the ceremonial moieties into which the townspeople divide. In Zuni, on the other hand, where the kivas are used by the kachina society or order of the masked dance, there are six—in accordance with the sixfold division of that order (each kiva being identified with one of the six cardinal directions).

14. Cushing's observation here poses something of a mystery. While circular kivas (the Anasazi type) do seem to have been standard among Keresan pueblos since the time of Coronado, Zia, according to the reports of other early visitors, was at that time different. Hitherto regarded as the earliest of these visitors, Cushing's friend John Bourke wrote in 1881 of "the two Estufas of Zia" that one was rectangular (the Mogollon style), the other square (Lansing Bloom, ed., "Bourke on the Southwest," *New Mexico Historical Review* 13:2 (1938): 225. Perhaps this first structure shown to Cushing was no longer in use? Nevertheless, it suggests at least that the Zians of that period *had* had round kivas. For a summary of Zia's "remarkable and unusual history with respect to kivas," see Leslie A. White, "The Pueblo of Sia, New Mexico," Bureau of American Ethnology *Bulletin* no. 184 (Washington, 1962), pp. 50–52.

15. In historical terms the name Montezuma (Motecuzoma or other variants in Nahuatl) refers to the Aztec king conquered by Cortés and to an earlier king who expanded the Aztec empire and strengthened its island capital by building an aqueduct and dike. Montezuma is also a figure ubiquitous in Pueblo myth and legend. As Cushing was to discover, the name Montezuma was associated by the Zunis with that of the Pueblo culture hero Poseyemu (Poshaiyank'ia or Boshaiyanki in Zuni), who in turn has become associated with the figure of Jesus. For discussion of the Montezuma legends and the role of the Montezuma figure as a mediator between the Pueblo and Christian religions and between historic and mythic consciousness, see Richard J. Parmentier, "The Pueblo Mythological Triangle: Poseyemu, Montezuma, and Jesus in the Pueblos," in *Handbook of North American Indians,* vol. 9, pp. 609–22.

16. Bourke described very similarly the interiors of the kivas he saw in nearby Jemez Pueblo—in the first:

> walls covered with figures; of sun, moon, morning star, evening star, buffalo, pumpkin, corn, deer, horse, thunder,

clouds, lightning, snakes and sea-serpents. The second Estufa had pictures in large size and, like those in first, extremely well done, of turkeys, two eagles fighting, hares, morning star, moon, dipper of seven stars" (Bloom, "Bourke on the Southwest," p. 227).

The difficulty here is that the kivas viewed by Bourke in Zia were entered in the standard way, through the roof, rather than through a door. Cushing seems to have been introduced not into a kiva but into the secret chamber of one of the ceremonial societies.

17. *Cacique* (Spanish for chief, political boss): A term commonly used in reference to the chief priests in the traditional Pueblo theocracy. Judging from the titles, this cacique must have been the "Sun Watcher," responsible for observing the movements of that heavenly body and determining thereby the dates for the various ceremonials in the ritual calendar (E. Adamson Hoebel, "Zia Pueblo," *Handbook of North American Indians,* vol. 9, p. 112). This was the Zian counterpart of the sun priest known in Zuni as the *Pekwin* (*Bekwinne* in modern Zuni spelling)—a figure traditionally "supreme in national as well as in ecclesiastical office" (Cushing, "Zuni Social, Mythic, and Religious Systems," p. 187), though this office has not been filled in Zuni since the 1940s.

18. If there was a sequel to this truncated account, it has not turned up. What happened next must remain a mystery, though presumably the ceremony was in some sense one of adoption. The medicine water was probably an emetic, administered for purposes of purification.

19. Southwest Museum, Hodge-Cushing Collection, Envelope 37. Citation of items in this collection will appear hereafter in the abbreviated form: Southwest Museum HC (or SWM HC in notes) followed by the envelope number.

20. "Life in Zuni," a lecture given in Buffalo, New York, December 10, 1890 (SWM HC 214). For a survey of Zuni history and prehistory, see *Handbook of North American Indians,* vol. 9; C. Gregory Crampton, *The Zunis of Cibola*; and E. Richard Hart, ed., *Zuni History* (Tabloid [Sun Valley, Idaho: Institute of the American West, 1983]). For Cushing's own pioneer sketch of Zuni history during and prior to the Spanish era, see "Outlines of Zuni Creation Myths," pp. 326–67.

21. "Head chief" is—or at least was in Cushing's time—something of a misnomer for "governor," the officer in charge of the secular affairs of the tribe, including "international" relations. It was in the nature of the office that the man who occupied it should frequently be taken, by outsiders, for "head" chief, but he was, at least in those days, appointed by a council of priests and served at their pleasure.

22. Product of a thin batter, a hot baking stone, and a great deal of skill, *he-we,* the famous Zuni paper bread, is a subject about which more may be learned in Cushing, *Zuni Breadstuff,* pp. 317–43.

23. Daniel Leech was a clerk in the Smithsonian and a fellow member of the Anthropological Association of Washington.

24. "Clean and classical" were the terms Cushing used to describe this collection in another draft—meaning that it contained only purely Pueblo items. For discussion of this issue of "purity" vs. contamination by outside influences (an issue brought up several times in Cushing letters), see Nancy J. Parezo, "Cushing as Part of the Team: The Collecting Activities of the Smithsonian Institution," in Triloki Nath Pandey, ed., *Essays on the Anthropological Career of Frank Hamilton Cushing,* forthcoming from the University of New Mexico Press.

25. Cushing's underlining. The lady referred to was presumably Matilda Stevenson.

26. The Ute Indians had destroyed their agency and killed all the government employees. The "trouble" was to be short-lived, however, since the Indians surrendered almost immediately after the arrival of the troops.

27. This is the first extant version of an incident on which Cushing would elaborate in his next letter to Baird and again in *Zuni Breadstuff,* pp. 553–54.

28. *Homachi* is one of the traditional Zuni kachina figures, though not one about which much has been written. Ruth Bunzel includes the name in a list of "punitive and exorcizing katcinas" and provides a brief description of the costume ("Zuni Katcinas, An Analytical Study," in *Forty-Seventh Annual Report of the Bureau of American Ethnology, 1929–1930* [Washington, D.C., 1932], pp. 906, 1006). The name also appears in Elsie Clews Parsons' *Pueblo Indian Religion* in an illustrative quotation in which a Zuni mother cautions her children not to mock at the kachina, or "Blue Horn and Homachi will cut off your head" (2 vols. Chicago: University of Chicago Press, 1939, p. 52). In the account to follow, a group of twenty-six dancers are identified as *Homachis.* Whether the day-long ceremonial as a whole would have been thought of as a "*Homachi* Dance" is another question. It seems fairly likely that when he tried to ascertain the name of what was going on, Cushing was simply given the name of *one* of the dances or dance groups featured in the rite.

29. The association between harvest and war is perhaps explained by the fact that this was a time of particular threat by raiders attracted by the collected stores of food.

30. In one of her references to the *owinahaiye,* Parsons

mentions, along with the burlesque element, a "final exorcism by a Ne'wekwe" and also gives the impression that kachinas were involved in the ceremony—thus linking the name *owinhaiye,* used by Stevenson, with features of the ceremony described by Cushing (see Parsons, *Pueblo Indian Religion,* p. 621). In her 1917 study, "Notes on Zuni" (*Memoirs of the American Anthropological Association* 4 [Lancaster, Pa.], 1917], 243), Parsons refers to the *owinahaiye* as "an annual dance at harvest time [which] has not been held for eight or ten years," owing, according to her informants, to shooting accidents and to "the Americans'" objections to the dance with its show of firearms. In *Pueblo Indian Religion,* where she uses Stevenson's account as the source for her discussion (pp. 646–49), she states more specifically that the last performance she knew of had been in 1910 (p. 881). See also Bunzel, *Zuni Texts,* Publications of the American Ethnological Society 22 (1933), p. 73. While more recent observers have mentioned hearing about performances of this harvest dance (e.g., John J. Adair and Evon Z. Vogt, "Navajo and Zuni Veterans," *American Anthropologist* 51 [1949]: p. 548) or about the possibility of such performances (Triloki Nath Pandey, "Factionalism in a Southwestern Pueblo," Ph.D. dissertation, University of Chicago, 1967, p. 94), none seems to have been witnessed in the past several decades. Neither Cushing nor Stevenson makes any mention of firearms in describing the *harvest* war dance. This seems to have been a later innovation—one which, according to a recent Zuni informant's explanation, has taken a central position among the associations remaining attached to the *owinahaiye,* which this informant translated as referring merely to the boisterous celebration (shooting off guns and the like) at the close of *any* war dance when the serious part had been completed. Perhaps the shouting and shooting served as another form of exorcism?

31. In the original *Century* serial this episode is placed strategically (and in violation of the actual chronology) at the close of the first installment. Curtis Hinsley observes (personal communication) that the message thus conveyed—that it was because of his bravery that Cushing won his place in Zuni—was "precisely what the culture of his middle class readers demanded," though in fact his

entree to Zuni society lay rather in his patience and loving attention to the children and, through them—especially his treatment of their wounds and sicknesses (a common entree, by the way)—to the mothers. *Publicly* Cushing played up the warrior/male side of his life; ethnographically, the female relationships, as in *Zuni Breadstuff,* were equally, perhaps more, central to his knowledge.

32. Lupolita, a child mentioned here and there in Cushing's journals, is also the subject of a fragmentary note among the papers in the Southwest Museum. It appears to be one page from the draft of a letter written sometime early in his stay:

> Once the prejudice is overcome, one can find room in his heart to love these dark-skinned little creatures just as much as though they were of the same blood and hue as himself. I have a little favorite here named Lu-po-li-ta whom I became acquainted with through treating her for a diseased scalp. She has the most regular of features—the bright beautiful chestnut eyes of Indians, the olive rosy-cheeked complexion of Pueblos, and the shining dark . . . (Southwest Museum HC 45).

33. Cushing refers here to the then still unrestored ruin of the seventeenth-century Franciscan mission church of Our Lady of Guadalupe.

34. *Tcha-kwi-na:* Cushing's version of a name now usually given as Chakwena (Bunzell uses Tcakwena Oka). Chakwena or Chakwena Kachina Woman is a powerful female-masked deity, always impersonated by a male in Zuni ceremonial. A fertility figure (the *cha* in her name means "child, young of animals"), the special guardian of women in pregnancy and childbirth, and at the same time "Mother of Game" (Hamilton A. Tyler, *Pueblo Animals and Myths* [Norman: University of Oklahoma Press, 1975], p. 148), Chakwena is a prominent figure in various ceremonials (see Bunzel, "Zuni Katcinas," p. 935). On the darker side, as Cushing later learned, Chakwena figures in mythology as the Ancient Woman of the *Kyanakwe,* the terrible slayer of the Zuni ancients "who carried her heart in her rattle and was deathless of wounds in the body" ("Outlines of Zuni Creation Myths," pp. 424–25). See above, pp. 195–96 for the earliest recorded version of the story (also given in Stevenson, "The Zuni Indians," pp. 35–38, and Parsons, *Pueblo Indian Religion,* pp. 224–25) of how this dangerous enemy was finally killed by the twin war gods.

35. *Patu:* "Maori term for a kind of short club-like weapon of wood, stone or bone. It was originally long and adze-like and used to thrust and stab . . ." (Charles Winick, *Dictionary of Anthropology* [Totowa, N.J.: 1970], p. 405).

36. The sketchbook referred to here has not been found. However, the journal notebooks themselves contain a number of sketches, some of which are reproduced in the present volume.

37. These may have been clan signs for the *Tak'yakwe* (Toad people) and *Suskikwe* (Coyote people). The coyote

paw could also have signified membership in one of the brotherhoods of the hunt (see Green, *Zuni*, p. 190).

38. Literally, *awen:* great chief (or alternatively, *awan:* their); *tatchu:* father. In various prayers recorded by Bunzel, *awan tachu* is one of the forms for addressing the sun. The bowl would have contained sacred cornmeal used in the ceremonies.

39. The *Koyemoshis* (*Koyemci*): The famous "mudhead" kachinas, described in a Cushing note as "guardians of the 'Sacred Dance.'" The name derives, according to Jane Young, from *koko:* kachinas and *yemashi:* husband and doubtless has to do with their role as "husbands" or "caretakers" of the kachinas. In ceremonial performances, their business, as Cushing explains, is "to entertain the spectators, during the intervals of the dance, by rude buffoonery and jokes, in which comic speeches and puns play an important part. The office is sacred, and elective annually from among the priesthood of the nation ("My Adventures in Zuni," p. 195; Green, *Zuni*, p. 134). The offspring of an incestuous union between a brother and sister who had been sent in search of the middle of the world (Cushing, "Outlines of Zuni Creation Myths," p. 401), these sacred clowns, "privileged to mock at anything and to indulge in any obscenity, . . . are the most feared and the most beloved of all Zuni impersonations . . ." (Ruth Bunzel, "Introduction to Zuni Ceremonialism," *Forty-Seventh Annual Report of the Bureau of American Ethnology, 1929–1930* [Washington, D.C., 1932], p. 521). See also Louis A. Hieb, "Meaning and Mismeaning: Toward an Understanding of the Ritual Clown," in Ortiz, ed., *New Perspectives on the Pueblos*, pp. 163–95.

40. These were the *Newekwe* medicine society performers who would play such a leading role in the remainder of the proceedings. Of the *Newekwe* (a name for which no real translation has emerged), Cushing wrote in *Zuni Breadstuff*:

> Their medical skill is supposed to be very great—in many cases—and their traditional wisdom is counted even greater. Yet they are clowns whose grotesque and quick-witted remarks amuse most public assemblies of the Pueblo holiday. One of their customs is to speak the opposite of their meaning; hence too, their assumption of the clown's part at public ceremonials, when really their office and powers are to be reversed (p. 632; Green, *Zuni*, p. 363n).

For discussion of their relationship to the *Koyemci* see Alfred L. Kroeber, "Thoughts on Zuni Religion," in *Holmes Anniversary Volume: Anthropological Essays Presented to William Henry Holmes in Honor of His Seventieth Birthday* (Washington, D.C.: J. W. Bryan Press, 1916), p. 273; and Hieb, "Meaning and Mismeaning," in Ortiz, ed., *New Perspectives on the Pueblos*, pp. 163–95.

41. These new entrants to the performance were the *He-he-a*, figures described by Bunzel ("Zuni Katcinas," pp. 1077–78) in much the same way as they are here by Cushing. According to modern Zuni informants, the antics of the *He-he-a* are no longer to be seen.

42. This was Dr. Taylor F. Ealy, who served in Zuni as missionary, physician, and head teacher in the Presbyterian Mission School from 1877 to 1881. For an account of this figure, see Norman J. Bender, *Missionaries, Outlaws, and Indians: Taylor F. Ealy at Lincoln and Zuni, 1878–1881* (Albuquerque: University of New Mexico Press, 1984).

43. *We-we* or *We-wha:* A transvestite who would be Matilda Stevenson's principal Zuni informant. Note that Cushing refers, just as Stevenson would later, to *her*. According to one well-known story, Mrs. Stevenson did not discover We-wha's biological sex until after she had taken "her" to Washington and the latter had returned to Zuni with stories of all the important women "she" had encountered in the water closets. Jennie Hammaker was a teacher at the Presbyterian Mission School in Zuni from 1879 until her death from typhoid fever in 1881.

44. Of the illustrations made by Cushing at Zuni, the only survivors, apart from the sketches scattered through the extant notebooks, seem to be a few drawings in pen or pencil belonging to the Southwest Museum Hodge-Cushing Collection and another few in pencil, ink, and/or tempera in the National Anthropological Archives of the Smithsonian. Thirty large tempera drawings of dance figures made later (evidently for use in lectures) may also be found among the Cushing papers in the National Anthropological Archives. What happened to the rest is anyone's guess.

45. This announcement perhaps puts in question the earlier inference that Cushing had moved into the pueblo on September 27—before Stevenson's departure for the Hopi villages. On the other hand, it can also be read as Cushing's telling Stevenson that he—Cushing—is sticking to what he had started.

46. In fact, as Cushing soon learned, it was Fray Marcos de Niza himself who climbed the mesa and took back the first eyewitness report of a Pueblo settlement. With Cabeza's Moorish companion Estevanico as guide, Fray Marcos had been sent by the Viceroy of Mexico to reconnoiter the "cities" that had been reported. Arriving in the vicinity of one of the pueblos, Marcos discovered that Estevanico had been killed by the Indians and so contented himself with viewing the "city" from the distance—and claiming it for Spain. Having read about these events

as told by the early Spaniards, Cushing would later hear about them from the Zunis themselves—and be shown a stone-heap said to be the one on which Marcos had erected the cross marking his claim. "The mesa" referred to was of course the great Dowa Yallane, some three miles to the southeast, whose thousand-foot-high mass looms over the pueblo and figures so centrally in Zuni history and tradition. Its name translates equally as "Corn Mountain," "Thunder Mountain," or "Sacred Mountain," since the word *dowa* carries all three of those meanings.

47. By 1882, tracks for the Santa Fe Railroad had been completed through a settlement then called "Railtown"—now called Gallup—some forty miles northwest of Zuni. By the following year, connections had been completed through to the West Coast.

48. Evidently a fertility rite involving imitative magic, this "Blanket Dance" seems to have been named by Cushing for its principal character, Chakwena Kachina Woman.

49. As noted before, Cushing seems to have his ruin locations confused. Pueblo Bonito is not in the Canyon de Chelley but to the east, in Chaco Canyon.

50. Cushing here anticipates his discussion of Zuni *inote,* or "ancient sayings," and their role in preserving this sort of convention (see Cushing to Baird and Powell February 18–April 13, 1880).

51. A frequent feature in the Montezuma legends is the suggestion that the great hero will return to his people. In at least one version the Great Spirit sends the sacred eagle to assist him on his way. See Parmentier, "The Pueblo Mythological Triangle," p. 619.

52. *Pania* or *Paña:* Spanish name for the traditional Zuni headband.

53. This may be a unique moment in Cushing's correspondence. Here under the usual mattress of explanation there is actually a pea of admission that he himself had made a mistake.

54. According to the version of this episode that is presented later in "My Adventures," Cushing pulled a knife and threatened to slice up anyone who interfered with his note-taking (p. 15; Green, *Zuni,* pp. 69–70). The present account suggests that his actual behavior was somewhat more judicious. Referred to at various points to follow, the dances of the *Kokokshi* (sometimes spelled *Ka'kokshi*) or "Good Kachinas" are, according to Parsons, "the most sacred of the kachina dances and apparently the oldest" (*Pueblo Indian Religion,* p. 222). Featuring female figures impersonated by men, these dances play a prominent part in both the winter and summer solstice ceremonies, the dancers performing on several successive days on both occasions, in all four plazas and in the various kivas. See also Stevenson, "The Zuni Indians," pp. 145–47, and Parsons, *Pueblo Indian Religion,* pp. 409–10, 520–21, and 743–46.

55. Cushing seems to be referring here, though without much understanding as yet, to the shrines adjacent to the lake known as *Hatim Kaiakwi* (Lake of Whispering Waters), under whose surface, in the sacred village of *Kolhu/wala:wa* (a name meaning "village of the dance-gods"), dwell the spirits of the Zuni ancestors and their kachina gods. Located some eighty miles west of Zuni near the junction of the Little Colorado and Zuni rivers, this most revered of Zuni holy places is the object of a pilgrimage made once every four years at the summer solstice by a delegation from the Zuni kiva groups, who deposit votive offerings in the caves and bring the spirits and gods back to Zuni for their annual visit (in intervening years a spring at Ojo Caliente, fifteen miles southwest of Zuni, is used as a surrogate for the sacred lake). For full discussion of this sacred site, see E. Richard Hart, "The Zuni Indian Tribe and title to Kolhu/wala:wa (Kachina Village)," *Zuni Indian Tribe Lands Bill: Hearing Before the Select Committee on Indian Affairs, United States Senate.* Ninety-Eighth Congress, Second Session. S. Hrg. 98–892 on S. 2201 (April 9). Washington, D.C.: U.S. Government Printing Office, 1984.

56. Some months earlier a "Mr. J.R. Metcalfe of Silver City," had written to Baird proposing to sell to the Smithsonian the contents of a cave owned by him. Baird had subsequently written to Stevenson suggesting that Cushing be sent down to do the work of excavation and packing. The cave, a depository of Pueblo ceremonial sacrifices, is frequently mentioned in letters to come, but Cushing seems never to have managed the trip, owing, at least in part, to the intermittent Apache hostilities in that direction (to the south and east of Zuni).

57. *Po-shai-an-k'ia* (Poshayanki):

> God (Father) of the Medicine societies or sacred esoteric orders, of which there are twelve in Zuni, and others among the different pueblo tribes. He is supposed to have appeared in human form, poorly clad, and therefore reviled by men; to have taught the ancestors of the Zuni, Taos, Oraibi, and Coconino [Havasupai] Indians their agricultural and other arts, their systems of worship by means of plumed and painted prayer-sticks; to have organized their medicine societies; and then to have disappeared toward his home in *Shi-pa-pu-li-ma* (from *shi-pi-a* = mist, vapor; *u-lin* = surrounding; and *i-mona* = sitting place of—'The mist-enveloped city'), and to have vanished beneath the world, whence he is said to have departed for the home of the Sun. He is still the conscious auditor of the prayers of his children, the invisible ruler of

the spiritual *Shi-pa-pu-li-ma* [modern Zuni spelling: *Shiba:bulima*] and of the lesser gods of the medicine orders, the principal "Finisher of the Paths of our Lives" (Frank H. Cushing, "Zuni Fetiches," *Second Annual Report of the Bureau of Ethnology, 1880–1881* [Washington, D.C., 1883], p. 16).

58. Cushing refers here to the great annual year-end festival of the kachina advent or *Shalak'o* in November, when all the Zuni dead and all the kachinas return to be feasted—along with live Indians from all over the area and a host of interested outsiders as well. A many-faceted and several-week-long affair prepared for over the course of the whole preceding year, the festival is climaxed by the arrival, on the last night, of the six giant kachina war chiefs known as the *Shalak'o,* who come to consecrate the new rooms which have been prepared for this occasion in various of the pueblo households. An elaborate ceremonial feast follows, after which all the kachinas dance until daylight in the houses of their respective hosts. Cushing was to witness this subsequently famous ceremonial at least four times, and his accounts (in "My Adventures in Zuni," pp. 505–08, and *Zuni Breadstuff,* pp. 606–12 [Green, *Zuni,* pp. 83–89, 317–22]) are but the first of many by a succession of anthropological and literary visitors.

59. See Cushing, "Outlines of Zuni Creation Myths," p. 337 (Green, *Zuni,* p. 179) for an account of the Zunis' dismay and outrage at this desecration of their *missa k'yakwi.* Mrs. Stevenson's account is somewhat different:

> The church objects were in the custody of one Maritio, and in order to determine whether they might be removed a council of religious and civil officers was held. It was finally decided that it would be well to have these objects go with the other Zuni material to the "great house" (National Museum) in Washington, where they would be preserved (*The Zuni Indians,* p. 17).

This straight-faced statement might be more convincing were it not for Col. Stevenson's boast about stealing away with the articles in the dead of night.

60. In 1881 Matilda Stevenson published privately a pamphlet entitled "Zuni and the Zunians." If there were earlier publications, they have not been located.

61. E. Richard Hart, "Zuni Mining" (unpublished article), pp. 4–5.

62. The trader Douglas D. Graham opened his shop in Zuni (just to the south of the pueblo) in 1879. A familiar figure in the area through the next twenty years, Graham served also at different times as government schoolteacher in the pueblo, federal sub-agent, and government farmer.

63. "Account of Cushing's Search for Tchalchihuitl Mines" (see Appendix A).

64. This is the second of the recently unearthed diaries, labeled "Daily Journal, Zuni, VIII, November 30th–December 13th, 1879." Done in pencil, the writing is, in places, badly faded and barely (if at all) legible.

65. A Zuni farming village occupied in Cushing's day chiefly during the summer months, Ojo (del) Pescado (spring of fish or fish spring) derived its Spanish name from this item of local wildlife—a new variety, according to the explorer A.W. Whipple, who had passed that way in 1853 on his expedition to mark out a direct railroad route across the Southwest to California (Grant Foreman, ed., *A Pathfinder in the Southwest: The Itinerary of Lieutenant A.W. Whipple . . .* [Norman: University of Oklahoma Press, 1941], p. 137). The two ruins mentioned here are directly adjacent to what is now called Lower Pescado Springs, about a mile and a half upstream from the farming village to which Cushing refers. They are recorded by Leslie Spier ("An Outline for a Chronology of Zuni Ruins," *Anthropological Papers of the American Museum of Natural History,* vol. 18, pt. 3, p. 238) as ruins 84 and 85 and more recently by archaeologist Keith W. Kintigh as Lower Pescado and Pescado West (*Settlement, Subsistence, and Society in Late Zuni Prehistory.* Anthropological Papers of the University of Arizona 44. Tucson: University of Arizona Press, 1985, pp. 54–55). The village itself, now called Lower Pescado, is discussed (and illustrated) in Victor Mindeleff's classic "A Study of Pueblo Architecture in Tusayan and Cibola," *Eighth Annual Report of the Bureau of Ethnology, 1886–1887* (Washington, D.C., 1891), pp. 95–96.

66. This third set of ruins, identified by Spier as number 86 ("An Outline for a Chronology," p. 238) and by Kintigh (*Settlement, Subsistence, and Society,* pp. 49–50) as Upper Pescado, is about 3/8 of a mile east of the first two mentioned. According to Cushing's map, it was the locus of an ancient Zuni town named Heshota Tsina (or as it is now spelled, Heshoda Ts'in'a), mentioned in later communications. Associated nowadays with the farming village itself, the name (variously translated as "marked house" or "place of writing") is generally understood to refer to a nearby boulder which is covered with prehistoric petroglyphs. The area (briefly described as Site 5 in Jane Young and Nancy Bartman, *Rock Art of the Zuni-Cibola Region* [Zuni, 1981], p. 40) also features rock art on the mesa ledges above the valley floor.

67. "Route near the Thirty-fifth Parallel, under the Command of Lieut. A.W. Whipple, Topographical Engineers, in 1853 and 1854. Report upon the Indian Tribes, 1855," (vol. 3, part 3 of the 1856 U.S. War

Department *Reports of Explorations and Surveys to Ascertain the Most Practicable and Economical Route for a Railroad from the Mississippi River to the Pacific Ocean* [Washington, 1856]). The material on Zuni is in Chapters 8 and 9 (discussion of Pescado ruins in Part 1, p. 65).

68. These "small ruins" seem not to have been subsequently recorded. The large circular ruin is identified by Kintigh (personal communication) as the one he calls Lower Deracho Ruin (Kintigh, *Settlement, Subsistence, and Society,* pp. 30–31), recorded earlier by Spier as ruin 101 ("An Outline for a Chronology," p. 240). According to Kintigh, the long stone wall Cushing mentions must be part of Upper Deracho Ruin (see Kintigh, *Settlement, Subsistence, and Society,* pp. 26–27), recorded by Spier as ruin 102 ("An Outline for a Chronology," p. 240). Both these latter ruins were also recorded by Jesse Walter Fewkes ("Reconnoissance of Ruins in or Near the Zuni Reservation," *Journal of American Ethnology and Archaeology* 1 [1891]: 113–14).

69. Cushing was right about the prehistoric occupancy of these villages (according to later investigators, all had been abandoned by the time of the Spanish conquest). Dating on the basis of artifacts—particularly pottery types—has of course come a long way from this early surmise by Cushing, but he was on the right track regarding corrugated ware, a key trait identifying the periods now known as Pueblo I–IV (ca. A.D. 700–1600). For the latest and most thorough survey of Zuni ruins and the ceramic evidence of their dates of occupancy, see Kintigh, *Settlement, Subsistence, and Society.*

70. Kintigh (personal communication) identifies this ruin as Day Ranch Ruin (recorded in Kintigh, *Settlement, Subsistence, and Society,* p. 35; also in Spier, "An Outline for a Chronology," p. 242, as ruin 104). Noting the oddity of the "mud" pueblo reference here, since the construction is definitely sandstone (a fact registered by Cushing himself in the sentence following), Kintigh suggests that perhaps Cushing was referring to a surface of mud plaster.

71. Kintigh (personal communication) speculates that the cliff dwelling referred to here may be the one about three miles up Togeye Canyon from the Kay Chee Ruin (Kintigh, *Settlement, Subsistence, and Society,* pp. 28–29; recorded by Spier as ruin 110 ["An Outline for a Chronology," p. 242]), a ruin which seems to be registered on Cushing's map, south of those now called Deracho and Day Ranch. The cliff dwelling itself is marked on U.S. Geodetic Survey maps of the area. Cushing's route is not altogether clear. Kintigh thinks he probably went up Togeye Canyon past this cliff dwelling—but not necessarily.

72. Of this neighbor to the Zunis, Bourke wrote in his diary:

> Pedro [Pino] said, through Cushing, that about two years ago, Amantani [Ammon M. Tenney] the Mormon Bishop, came down to Isleta and from there accompanied a detachment from that Pueblo on its way to trade with the Moquis. He reached Pescado and there in the house of Ramon Luna spoke all night with a sweet tongue. He praised up the Mormons, said that in their own country they were very rich and had fine cattle, horses, and farms.
>
> They were not Americans and did not like the Americans; all this land west of and including Zuni belonged to the Mormons. . . . [the passage goes on to detail the bishop's boasts of Mormon power and his grandiose promises of what the Zunis would gain by joining the Mormon church] (Edwin V. Sutherland, "The Diaries of John Gregory Bourke: Their Anthropological and Folklore Content," Ph.D. dissertation, University of Pennsylvania, 1964, p. 914).

In any event, Tenney had settled and built a mission, which he called Savoia, a few miles north of where the Mormon village of Ramah would grow (Irving Telling, "Ramah, New Mexico, 1876–1900: An Historical Episode with Some Value Analysis," *Utah Historical Quarterly* 21 [1953]: 119). The name Savoia (or Savoita) evidently derived from *Cebollita* (wild onion), a place name also used by the locals—and by Cushing. As to Tenney's Zuni host, Ramon or Roman Luna, more will be heard of him in the pages to follow. He was one Zuni who did in fact take up Mormonism—a move which would lead to a complicated feud in which he was supported by the Presbyterian missionary against the Zuni caciques backed by Cushing and the Indian agent. A powerful (and, in Cushing's eyes, malign) figure, he would himself eventually serve for a time as Zuni governor. He was also to be one of Matilda Stevenson's chief informants.

73. They had in fact camped very close to their objective. In his later account Cushing writes that in the morning they "had not proceeded more than an hour before [they] came to a magnificent basin among the mountain heights," at the far end of which was the mining cabin. A century later, "following, as best as was possible, the route Cushing described, from Zuni to Pescado, then on to the Mormon settlement near the current site of Ramah, and from there to the tiny Hispanic community of Tinaja," Zuni historian E. Richard Hart "concluded that Cushing must have then taken a route up Ojo Bonito Canyon, over the Continental Divide and down the other side of the range, past the site of Copperton, to the Diener Canyon area. In that area (the northwest corner of Township 11 North, Range 12

West)," Hart, together with Zuni archaeologists T.J. Ferguson and Emily Garber, located in 1984 the site of what they take to have been the Zuni mine visited by Cushing ("Zuni Mining," pp. 38–39). Cañon del Cobre (Copper Canyon) was evidently a name bestowed by Cushing.

74. This was Herbert Tyzack, an employee of the copper miners who owned the cabin and the author, later on, of a letter to Mrs. Cushing which is printed below.

75. According to Cushing's later account, Tyzack had also "found rude digging sticks, wooden spades and chipped implements of flint about the place," and he himself found traces of Indian art everywhere around the ruins. The blue and green stones, of which Cushing speaks later at more length, were formed of an oxidized ore of copper containing malachite and azurite—chips of which Hart and Ferguson found still "strewn everywhere" in the area ("Zuni Mining," p. 39).

76. These are the "great monuments of rock" Cushing mentions in his later account as having been erected by the Indians "centuries before near the ancient excavations to mark the sites of their possessions." Until Ferguson and Hart reexamined the site in 1984, the ruins which Cushing had here been examining (once "crude but substantial stone dwellings of many rooms," as he later described them), were lost sight of from the archaeological standpoint. Meanwhile, as Hart points out, the area has been much disturbed by clearcutting, sheep and cattle grazing, and use by miners and railroad workers. Adequate archaeological investigation has yet to be pursued.

77. Cushing refers evidently to two sketchbooks, now lost.

78. Here may be a fairly accurate measure by which to calibrate the degree of Cushing's occasional exaggeration or embellishment when he wrote of his adventures for publication. In his later account the two bread cakes and half dozen strips of bacon are reduced to *one* "wheat cake and *three or four* sticks of bacon" (italics added).

79. The Mason (sometimes spelled Ma'son) ranch was in the little Mexican settlement of Tinaja, still shown on local maps a few miles northeast of El Morro National Monument. The name "Mason," though unusual for a Mexican family, reappears in a draft for a note Cushing wrote the following year naming several individuals involved in the illicit buying and selling of whiskey. The seller was one Jesús Mason, also reported for whiskey selling by missionary Ealy in an 1879 letter to Pueblo Agent Benjamin Thomas (Denver Federal Records Center, Records of the Bureau of Indian Affairs, Pueblo Indian Agency, Register of Letters Received).

80. This square ruin must be Pueblo de los Muertos (Kintigh, *Settlement, Subsistence, and Society,* pp. 50–51; Spier ruin 139 ["An Outline for a Chronology," p. 245]), which is next to a spring feeding Muerto Creek. According to Kintigh:

> Cushing's indication of circular and rectangular kivas at the ruin is interesting because use of circular kivas is a characteristic Anasazi trait, and use of rectangular kivas a Mogollon trait. A similar co-occurance of circular and rectangular kivas was found by Richard Woodbury in his excavations at Atsinna (A'ts'in'a), in El Morro National Monument. The presence of both types of kivas has been argued to indicate a mixture of these cultural traditions in the Zuni area (personal communication).

Excavations have been conducted at Pueblo de los Muertos under the direction of Washington University archaeologist Patty Jo Watson. A report of the findings, coauthored by Patty Jo Watson, Stephen A. LeBlanc, and Charles L. Redman, appeared in the *Journal of Field Archaeology* VII:2 (1980): 205–09.

81. Kintigh (personal communication) locates the Tenney ranch as probably having been about nine miles downstream from Pueblo de los Muertos, on the valley floor below the east end of Wild Sheep Mesa. As he points out, the USGS map (Ramah NM 7.5′) marks abandoned and occupied structures and a windmill on that site.

82. An early Jewish settler, longtime resident, and local entrepreneur, Solomon Barth was one of "the numerous, aggressive Barth clan, . . . known through the territory both as traders and as stockmen" (Frank McNitt, *The Indian Traders* [Norman: University of Oklahoma Press, 1962], p. 240). With his brother Si, he ran a trading enterprise in Zuni as well as supervising the delivery of mail on the route between Albuquerque and Prescott, raising oxen, and mining salt from the Zuni Salt Lake.

83. According to Kintigh (personal communication):

> The round and square pair of ruins is probably the Kluckhohn Ruin (Kintigh, *Settlement, Subsistence, and Society,* pp. 40–42; Spier ruin 138 ["An Outline for a Chronology," pp. 244–45]; Fewkes, "Reconnoisance of Ruins," pp. 114–16), named after the famous anthropologist Clyde Kluckhohn, who owned the ranch on which the ruin is located. If the location of the Tenney place has been identified correctly, the ruin would be about a mile southwest of it. This is a very large ruin with a rectangular section and a high circular section connected by what Fewkes called a "causeway." Cushing's sketch bears some resemblance to the actual ground plan of this ruin, although the rectangular section is actually to the southwest of the circular portion, not to the

southeast as shown in Cushing's sketch. Leslie Spier located this ruin at a place he called "Cebollita, in the pass between Josephina Canyon [Togeye Canyon] and the broad valley at the foot of the Zuni Mountains" ("An Outline for a Chronology," p. 244). I assume "Cebollita" is the "Savoita" of Cushing's journal. Spier notes that the two parts were connected by a ruin partly covered by sand or perhaps village debris. Another odd thing about Cushing's description is that I cannot imagine why the road would go between the two parts of the ruin, since the connecting mound between the two parts is even now quite high (perhaps eight feet), and it would be easy to get around the ruin altogether. Perhaps the ruin had substantially deteriorated between Cushing's and Spier's visits, forming a mound. Second, it is not inconceivable that someone might have intentionally done this to stop erosion or dam up water.

84. *Pueblos viejos,* or ancient pueblos: The ruins of the old abandoned towns.

85. The name Inscription Rock, in what is now El Morro National Monument, derives from the signatures carved on the rock face by passers by, from the time of the Spanish Conquerors on. However, according to Kintigh (personal communication), Cushing's geography here

doesn't make sense. Inscription Rock is seven and a half miles southeast of the Kluckhohn Ruin [i.e., to the south*east* of the Tenney ranch], whereas Cushing, approaching Pescado on his way back to Zuni, was some ten or twelve miles *west* of the Tenney ranch. I can only conclude that he misidentified his location and saw a mesa two miles south (left) that *looked* like Inscription Rock.

86. Cushing seems to be approximating the Zuni word *An-e,* a farewell salutation.

87. Maestro: The title conferred on the schoolmaster—in this case Dr. Ealy.

88. Governor Palowahtiwa was a silversmith, the forge part of his equipment.

89. These blue and green stones, ground up with water, formed a pigment used for painting prayer sticks and sacred masks and also for dyeing moccasins, belts, etc. (Bunzel, "Zuni Katcinas," p. 861).

90. This was presumably Roman (or Ramon) Luna, the Zuni Mormon, here still on good terms with Palowahtiwa.

91. Cushing seems to be approximating the name of Juan Septimo, which, spelled in this latter way, reappears in several other papers in this collection. Septimo is listed in John Bourke's Diary as one of the chief officers of the Zuni Order of Fire (Sutherland, "The Diaries of John Gregory Bourke," p. 943). He is also mentioned by Whipple in 1856 as one of the three Zuni guides who led his party on west into Arizona from Zuni (Foreman, *A Pathfinder in the Southwest,* p. 149).

92. To be discussed further below, the "little bows and arrows" mentioned here were votive offerings of a sort deposited periodically in certain sacred caves.

93. The terms "dance house" and "dance cave" refer to shrines where votive offerings are made to the kachinas—the dancing gods. According to Zuni archaeologist T.J. Ferguson (personal communication), the area referred to here is probably around Mt. Baldy in the White Mountains. This would be at or near Site #42 (Li'akwa k'yakwe'a), a turquoise source near a spring sacred to the Zunis (T.J. Ferguson and E. Richard Hart, *A Zuni Atlas* [Norman: University of Oklahoma Press, 1985], p. 127). As Ferguson adds, however, there are also turquoise gathering places near Clifton, Arizona, as well (see Site 225, ibid., p. 134).

94. What Cushing spells as "oblision" or "oblisia" is doubtless *oblación,* Spanish for oblation or offering. In a later reference an "oblisia" is sung.

95. Where Cushing got the name "Valle de los Argones" is not clear. In "My Adventures" he speaks of this trek as taking him to the "Valley of the Pines"—a name seemingly of his own coining. Possibly these two names, though seemingly unrelated, refer to the same place?

96. In his essay on "Primitive Copper Working," Cushing recounts how "in order to test [his] archaeological observations and some vague Zuni traditions regarding [their] method of reducing ore, [he] once gathered, while traveling through a portion of the Zuni Mountains, several stones showing traces of clear copper," which he then smelted by the method he had heard about (pp. 95–96). E. Richard Hart is doubtless correct in his surmise ("Zuni Mining," pp. 21–22) that this was the trip on which Cushing collected these "several stones."

97. The *he-po-lo-kia* spoken of here was a small cake made by mixing with water a quantity of a corn flour composed of the finely ground remains of dried wafer breads. Highly concentrated, it was a favorite food for travelers and hunters (see *Zuni Breadstuff,* pp. 38–40).

98. Rhynchonellid: a clam-like brachiopod with a highly fluted shell. Productus: another species of brachiopod.

99. Dumas Provencher, a settler in the Old Fort Wingate area, was also known to Bandelier, who followed this part of Cushing's route, riding his horse from Laguna to Wingate in March of 1883 (Lange and Riley, 1970, p. 64). By that time, he was riding along the railroad track.

100. A veteran of Col. Kit Carson's 1863 campaign against the Navajos," "Uncle Billy Crane" settled in the

valley east of Fort Wingate in the early 1870s. His ranch, which also served as a stage station for the Prescott coaches, supplied hay and beef to the fort. Selected in 1881 by the Atlantic and Pacific Railroad as the site of a construction camp, "Crane's Station" (subsequently named Coolidge) became for a time a "sprawling, brawling tent camp" in whose saloons the troops stationed at Fort Wingate, "mingling with Indians, ranchers, and cowboys, found their fun," (McNitt, *The Indian Traders,* pp. 231–32).

101. This letter from Herbert Tyzack, sent to Emily Cushing years later, was among the Cushing papers preserved, along with the diaries, by Emily's sister Eleanor and Eleanor's granddaughter, Anne E. Smullen.

102. Reference is to his note of December 6.

103. The "presence" Cushing had in mind was presumably Matilda Stevenson.

104. While time and officer turnover brought great improvement to Cushing's standing at Fort Wingate, and while he acquired many friends both in the army and among local residents, there were always those ("especially in the West," as he pointed out in one of his reports) who scorned the idea of living among "savages." This kind of "Western" contempt is perhaps typified by an article date lined from Fort Wingate, May 31, 1881: "Twenty-five miles south of Sheridan Station is Zuni Indian village. A young man named Cushing, a kind of sagamore, who was sent out by the Smithsonian Institution to study the history and habits of this tribe, is here in long hair and buckskin, and is an expert 'lug eater.' His mother had better send for him and take him home . . ." (*The Commonweal* [Topeka?], June 5, 1881; Wheelwright Museum, Washington Matthews Papers, Box XI, 2).

105. The mailed copy of this letter was received by Baird but lost in transit to Powell. Printed here is the later of two drafts kept by Cushing.

106. The officer referred to was Captain Frank Tracy Bennett, who also served twice as U.S. agent for the Navajos.

107. There are so many ruins in this area that it is not possible to identify which "chain" of them Cushing had in mind here.

108. Tusayan was the Spanish name for the Hopi country. A glance at the map will indicate how ambitious a travel plan Cushing was projecting: first south to Fort Bayard and Silver City (ten miles west of the fort), then north along the Rio Grande through the first set of pueblos mentioned, west to Zuni, southwest to the Arizona caves (in the Fort Apache area), back to Zuni, west to the Hopi towns, back east to Wingate and Albuquerque, and finally north again through the upper set of Rio Grande pueblos and on (still farther north) to the railroad terminal. His somewhat approximate placement of the various pueblos (Taos, for example, being northeast rather than northwest of Santa Fe) may be owing to the mentioned "want of detail" in the maps he had in hand.

109. The historian of Zuni ethnography and handcraft will appreciate the foreboding nature of this request for "any cheap imitation" of turquoise, and Baird's favorable response to it (see below, Baird to Cushing, May 15, 1880). Here is illustrated in sharp relief the irony involved in ethnological collecting. In his compulsion to make as large a collection as possible, Cushing was preparing for a trading practice whose effect would be to cheapen and corrupt one of the very crafts whose "purity" he was so anxious to have preserved in the products he was collecting. Fortunately, despite the infiltration of certain imported imitations, Zuni jewelry is still regarded as the finest of its kind.

110. This sentence seems to indicate that Cushing had still to receive his first paycheck as a member of the Bureau expedition. William Jones Rhees was Baird's clerk and the author of several works on the history of the Smithsonian. A collection of letters Cushing wrote to Rhees from Zuni (a few of which are included in this volume) may be found in the Huntington Library.

2. January–May 1880

1. The story to follow, an example of what Tylor termed "myths of observation," seems to have no clear bearing on the location of what Cushing here calls the principal Zuni source of turquoise. The mountain dwelling in the story is on the west side of the Rio Grande, whereas the latter reference is to a place east of the river—probably the great turquoise mines at Cerrillos, about twenty-six miles southwest of Santa Fe. The Cerrillos mines, and particularly Mount Chalchihuitl, contained "the most important deposits of turquoise in the United States," according to Joseph E. Pogue (*The Turquoise: A Study of its History, Mineralogy, Geology, Ethnology, Archaeology, Mythology, Folklore, and Technology* [Rio Grande Press: Glorieta, New Mexico, 1973], p. 52), and the Zunis were among the Pueblo tribes who worked these mines, though access was controlled during certain periods by other tribes. For further information on this subject, see E. Richard Hart, "Zuni Mining." As to the equally prized "peculiar black bead," Theodore R. Frisbie, who has also researched Zuni mineral sources, suggests that these were either obsidian tears or jet—and most likely jet, "because jet is equated, in the Zuni mind, with value equal to that of turquoise." Like turquoise,

according to Frisbie, jet was obtained from "a number of sources, including the Ramah area and trade with the Acomas" (personal communication).

2. There are caves a mile or two east of Zuni at Blackrock, where, according to Frisbie (personal communication), "legend claims salt originally was secured—until the people defiled the place. At this point [in the legend as he had heard it] both Old Salt Woman (Malokatsiki) and Turquoise Man departed south, Zuni Salt Lake becoming the new home and source." None of these local caves are known, however, for turquoise deposits. For a variant of the Salt Woman-Turquoise Man migration story, see Ruth Benedict, *Zuni Mythology.* Columbia University Contributions to Anthropology, no. 21 (New York: Columbia University Press, 1935), I, pp. 43–49.

3. The exposition of geography here leaves something to be desired; the Zuni Salt Lake is south of Zuni, not north.

4. These drilled beads, according to Frisbie (personal communication):

> . . . could well have been ceremonially deposited earlier in time (prehistory), either as bead offerings or attached to prayersticks by the old Cibola branch of the Mogollon peoples, many of whom were amalgamated with Zuni villagers. The fact that Cushing notes *both* turquoise and black beads came from the cave supports prehistoric deposition, since the two would not be found together naturally.

5. Cushing's reference is evidently to the cave just mentioned, a mile or two east of Zuni in the area of what is now called Black Rock.

6. Cushing is referring to the earlier mentioned cavern in the White Mountains, north of the San Carlos Apache reservation in Arizona.

7. Reference here is probably to a ranch owned by James W. Bennett, sometime partner of Douglas Graham, the Zuni trader. Navajo Springs is a little over three miles southeast of the town of Navajo, which, with the advent of the railway, became a stopping place known as Navajo Station (Will C. Barnes, *Arizona Place Names* [Tucson: University of Arizona Press, 1935], p. 297). It was also referred to as Bennett's Station.

8. Cushing refers again here to the ceremonial "burial" or "planting" of sacrifices performed during the winter solstice—specifically in this case sacrifices directed to the war gods (described at greater length in subsequent letters). The cigarettes are made of sections of cane which, like the plume-sticks, are decorated with paint and are then filled with wild tobacco, "supposed to have been planted by rain, hence sacred" (*Zuni Breadstuff,* p. 162). See Cushing to Baird and Powell, January 11, 1881, for similar finds later on in the valley of the upper Little Colorado.

9. The name "Ojo Pitchaiakwi" probably designates land originally owned by the Bikchi:kwe clan, the largest in the pueblo.

10. As a "vindicator" for the Zunis, Cushing stretches a point here; he is not known to have been employed by the Department of the Interior (except later on as a census collector), though he may have thought he was, as a subordinate to Major Powell, who was associated with the Interior through the Geological Survey.

11. E. Richard Hart observes (personal communication) that while the private ownership of land outside the reservation never became widespread, the practice being initiated, with Cushing's help, did turn out to have importance as one of the Zuni strategies to maintain, or regain, control of their tribal lands—much diminished by the lines drawn at the time their reservation was established. Over time, many of the lands thus acquired were absorbed into the reservation, though some were lost because of nonpayment of taxes. Some Zunis still have small private holdings outside the reservation.

12. Located near Atarque, which shows on local maps of the area, Kyama:kya (site 127 in Ferguson and Hart, *A Zuni Atlas*) figures importantly in Zuni origin stories as the home of the dread *Kyanakwe* kachinas and the locus of the twin war gods' victory over Chakwena Woman. It was also the place where the *Kyanakwe*—or, in one Cushing version, "the wonderful Snail people"—hid all the game animals in a canyon corral. In this version Cushing translates the name *Kyama:kya* as "Place of the Snails" ("Zuni Fetiches," p. 21). For comparison of variants of this story, see Benedict, *Zuni Mythology,* pp. 261–63.

13. In "My Adventures" Cushing suggests more explicitly that the initial cause of the pneumonia was a chill contracted on coming out into the cold morning air from an all-night initiation ceremony—meaning, perhaps, the January 17 ceremonial mentioned above.

14. Baird had been urging that Cushing get to Silver City to "overhaul" the Metcalfe cave there (letter of March 4, 1880, Baird Papers, Smithsonian Institution). Casa Grande, a large-scale ruin in the Gila Valley of Arizona, is now a National Monument, owing in some degree to Cushing's own lobbying efforts in 1889, when the bill was before Congress (brought up by Mary Hemenway's friends, the Massachusetts Senators Henry Cabot Lodge and George F. Hoar). Like the Los Muertos ruin Cushing's Hemenway crew was excavating at that time in the Salt River Valley, Casa Grande is a major site of the Hohokam Classic period (ca. A.D. 1200–1400).

15. New Mexico State Archives, Pueblo Land Grant

Papers, Case V: Zuni. Cushing's is one of two extant depositions pertaining to one of the first judicial inquiries into Zuni land rights following the establishment of the reservation in 1877 (the other, by Pedro Pino, essentially duplicates Cushing's). In question was a grant purportedly made in 1689 by one "Domingo Jironza Petroza de Cruzate, Governor and Captain General of the Province of New Mexico," deeding to the Zunis a two-league- (six-mile-) square area centered on Zuni Pueblo. This was one of a series of such grants said to have been issued by Cruzate to ten of the Pueblo peoples after a military tour through parts of his domain—at that time still empty of Spaniards, who were driven out during the Pueblo Revolt of 1680. As part of a general investigation by the New Mexico territorial government into the validity of these grants, the Surveyor General was at this time collecting testimony relating to the one applying to Zuni, an official English translation of which—but not the original—is among the papers filed with the depositions in the New Mexico State Records Center and Archives. The Surveyor General's satisfaction with the authenticity of the Zuni grant is attested in a fourth paper in the same file. Given that only one of the supposed ten documents has survived in the original and that at least one of the "copies" contains sentences plagiarized from a book published in 1832, however, the prevailing view is presently that some or all of the "Cruzate grants" were forgeries, made by a person or persons interested in *minimizing* the areas to which they entitled the Indians—the area occupied by the Zunis, like that occupied by various of the other Pueblo peoples concerned, being in fact much larger than was specified in the grant. E. Richard Hart (whose personal communication was the source of most of the information in this note) remarks that "much mystery surrounds the overall story of the Cruzate grants in general and the supposed original grant(s) to Zuni, now missing, in particular." No such suspicions seem to have existed in 1880, however, and the Zunis, like other Pueblos, were in any case anxious to secure official recognition of *whatever* papers they held giving them titles to their ancestral lands. Hence the depositions. The "old Pueblo of Zuni" referred to therein would have been the fortification on top of Dowa Yalanne which the Zunis had built following the great Revolt and which Cushing and Pedro Pino evidently assumed the people were occupying in 1689, the year named in the grant paper. Further information about the Cruzate grants can be found in Joe S. Sando, "Jemez Pueblo," *Handbook of North American Indians,* vol. 9, p. 422, and Florence Hawley Ellis, "Laguna Pueblo," same volume, p. 438.

16. The copy of this letter enclosed with that dated May 5 is not to be found in either the Smithsonian or NAA collections. Though received and responded to by Baird, it apparently never reached Powell. What is printed here is one of two draft copies (the clearer and apparently later one) kept by Cushing. While dated February 18, the text contains a reference to events occurring "three nights since (April 10)," indicating continued work on it through the period of Cushing's illness until at least April 13.

17. The two caves referred to here are presumably the Metcalfe cave in Silver City and the American-owned one in the Colorado Chiquito first mentioned in a letter written in November. Of the "American" we hear no further, but the "one" cave would turn out to be many.

18. Cushing may be referring to an observance which occurs on the fourth night after the winter solstice, when "the people of companion [kivas] often dance together, one [kiva] inviting the people of the other. . . . It is usual for the guests to prepare their own masks to suit the dance in which they are expected to join (Stevenson 1904, "The Zuni Indians," p. 142).

19. What Cushing's two phrases "admission into the sacred houses" and "initiation into the estufas" probably signify is that he was being allowed into meetings of the kachina society or cult of the masked rain gods. As mentioned above, membership in this society is divided among six kiva groups, identified respectively with the six directions, each male in the community being assigned, when he comes of age, to one or another kiva group, depending on which one the ceremonial father chosen for him belongs to. While Cushing did not *belong* to the kachina society, he was by now being allowed to witness at least some of their ceremonial proceedings inside the kiva.

20. There is a slip of the pen here. Cushing would have known by this time that the "burial" (which culminates the first half of the twenty-day winter solstice observances) is followed—not preceded—by a period of fasting and other constraints. On the other hand, his reference to the god A-hai-iu-ta as *the father* of the Zunis suggests that he may not yet have been familiar with the stories of the twin war gods Ahayu:da and Matsailema or have understood that when the Zunis spoke of "the god Ahayu:da" they really had both these gods in mind. The twins are prominent in the Zuni origin myths as the children and emissaries of the Sun Father who made the earth habitable, led the people out of their original dwelling place in the underworld into the light, and established the Zuni laws and curing societies. More to the point, as Cushing would discover, they are supposed

to have been the originators of the Zuni war society or Order of the Bow and the immediate ancestors of the two high priests of that order who are now their representatives and who have carried on from them "in one unbroken line . . . the breath of *Sawanik'ia* or the medicine of war" (Cushing, "The Zuni Social, Mythic, and Religious Systems," p. 190). The twins also appear in many of the Zuni folk tales, often as mischievous tricksters.

Later, when he became a Bow Priest himself, he learned that the god effigies and accompanying sacrifices were "buried" at each winter solstice in shrines on the mesa tops, "in front of their predecessors of centuries' accumulation," where they were believed "to guard from year to year, from sunrise to sunset, the vale and children of those [whom these twin gods] were first sent to redeem and guide" ("My Adventures in Zuni," p. 29; Green, *Zuni,* p. 98). According to Stevenson, such deposits are made alternately at shrines on ten different local mesas, one of which, at the winter solstice, is always Dowa Yalanne ("The Zuni Indians," pp. 606–07). For description of the "burial" procession, which he had witnessed in December 1879 and would witness several more times in subsequent Decembers, see Cushing, "My Adventures in Zuni," p. 29 (Green, *Zuni,* 97–98).

21. It is not clear from the context that Cushing was yet aware at this point of the specific meaning of *Pithlan* (bow) *Shiwani* (priest) as referring to the Zuni war society, the Priesthood of the Bow—an identity accounting for their warlike appearance if not for the outdatedness of their equipage. *Mosona* (or the suffix *mosi* or *mossi* [from Spanish *mozo,* servant?]) signifies the director or manager of the order—i.e., in this case, the elder or junior head Priest of the Bow.

22. *Nanakwe:* literally, spirits of the grandfathers.

23. Cushing must be referring here to the costume and mask of the "Jemez kachina" (*Hemishikwe*). The dance of the *Hemishikwe,* widespread among the Pueblos, features (almost uniquely among kachina dances) the use of a "musical rasp or notched rattle or fiddle" known as the "kachina gourd fiddle" (Parsons, *Pueblo Indian Religion,* p. 383).

24. *Quipu* (Quechua for knot): A device consisting of an arrangement of cords variously colored and knotted, used by the ancient Peruvians to keep accounts, record events, send messages, etc. The arrangement of wampum beads on a string or in a belt of strings was used for a similar mnemonic purpose by the Iroquois, but the shells used for wampum were conventionally only white or very dark purple. As to the use of such a contrivance in Zuni, while John Bourke was visiting the pueblo in the fall of 1881, Cushing translated for him a *Koyemci* prayer containing an allusion to a "Calendar of Strings"—an allusion regarded by Bourke as definitely implying "the former existence and employment among the Zunis of the Cord Calendar (or Quippu of the Peruvians)" (Sutherland, "The Diaries of John Gregory Bourke," p. 919).

25. Cushing's reference is evidently to the shrine in the ruin of Mats'a:kya, three miles east of Zuni near the northwestern base of Dowa Yallane—a shrine used by the Bekwinne in gauging the movement of the sun and determining the dates of the solstices. The citation regarding the Peruvian "Temples of the Sun" is to Ephraim G. Squier, *Peru: Incidents of Travel and Exploration in the Land of the Incas* (London, 1877), pp. 130, 360, and 438. This Peruvian connection is one that Cushing would explore with Frederic W. Putnam on his 1882 visit to Cambridge.

26. Exactly what Cushing was referring to in the story of Poshayanki is not clear. Possibly he had in mind the calendric associations of the Poshayanki story as a sun myth—associations he would have seen discussed in Tylor (cf. *Researches into the Early History of Mankind and the Development of Civilization,* pp. 129–31) in connection with the myth of Quetzalcoatl. Note also the pluralizing of the term "culture"—perhaps the earliest occurrence.

27. Cushing is speaking to an already strong interest on Powell's part, as evidenced in the Bureau's *First Annual Report,* which is given over to a massive compendium on the subject put together by Garrick Mallery.

28. Alexander von Humboldt, the German naturalist and explorer whose monumental *Carte General de Royaume de Nouvelle Espagne* (1811) was for years the basic scientific and cartographic text on the Southwest.

29. According to Morgan (Cushing's awareness of his work is apparent here), use of the term "brother" to refer to the son (or "sister" to refer to the daughter) of a parent's sibling signified a clan system of social organization (itself evolved from earlier, even less differentiated arrangements). Cushing's observation reveals, along with his sense of the importance of kinship nomenclature as a clue to social organization, a grasp of the fact that this nomenclature could be properly understood only in the context of its usage.

30. Strictly speaking, in the standard consanguineal usage of the day, the term *gens* (plural, *gentes*) should have referred to the familial extension on the father's side, as distinct from *clan* associations, which derive from *matrilineal* ties. Here—and usually—Cushing uses the term in the generic or general sense, interchangeably with "clan."

31. This whole section on the prehistory of Zuni is definitely "work in progress," subject to correction and

refinement by Cushing himself (for example in his "Preliminary Notes" on the Hemenway Expedition and "Outlines of Zuni Creation Myths") as well as by those who followed him in the field. However faulty some of the inferences may be, they nevertheless mark the opening of Cushing's inquiry into the "mytho-sociologic" organization of Zuni culture, as well as the beginning of that linkage between ethnological and archaeological inquiry which, as Raymond Brandes has observed (in connection with the Hemenway enterprise), "made possible some of the leading anthropological interpretations of the 20th century ("Frank Hamilton Cushing: Pioneer Americanist," pp. 209–10). It is also worth noting that the "two great divisions" here propounded represent the earliest recorded intimation of the Zunis' dual ancestry in the cultures now known as the Anasazi and the Mogollon. Centered during the period of their flourishing (about A.D. 1000–1300) in what is now southwestern Colorado and the adjoining parts of Utah, Arizona, and New Mexico, the former people were the builders of the great pueblos of Canyon de Chelly, Mesa Verde, Chaco Canyon, and others whose ruins were known to Cushing. Later they had migrated south into the valleys of the Little (Chiquito) Colorado and the Rio Grande and their respective tributaries, where they blended with the people who evidently already inhabited these areas. In the region of the Little Colorado this blend was with the Mogollon people, who are generally thought to have moved into the area from southern New Mexico and Arizona long before. Which of these two cultural ancestries was prior with respect to Zuni is not yet an entirely settled question, the chronology of the movements of these early peoples so far having been established only within broad general outlines. Recent findings seem to indicate, however, that it was the Anasazi (see, for example, John B. Rinaldo: "Notes on the Origins of Historic Zuni Culture" [*The Kiva,* vol. 29, no. 4, April 1964, pp. 86–98]). In any case, as the origin myths told, Zuni was indeed the "middle" at which these "wanderers" from the north and south found their common destination. Cushing's preliminary efforts to match the ruins with the migration myths (which he doubtless took too literally) obviously left much for later researchers to sort out. For a thorough review of and extensive bibliography on Pueblo prehistory, see Linda A. Cordell, *Prehistory of the Southwest* (New York: Academic Press, 1984); see also *Handbook of North American Indians,* vol. 9.

32. *Cos-nina* and *K'us-ni-ni:* Cushing's early approximations of the Hopi name for the Indians now generally called Havasupai. Without drawing any unduly naïve inferences from the notion of an origin "west of the west," one may note an expert's speculation that the Zuni language, long a conundrum to linguists, might be "perhaps distantly related to the California Penutian" (Fred Eggan: "Pueblo: Introduction," *Handbook of North American Indians,* vol. 9, p. 226).

33. Another version of the odyssey of this branch of the Zuni ancestry is given in Cushing, "Outlines of Zuni Creation Myths," pp. 426–27. Apart from Hawikku (no. 6) and Heshoda Ts'i'na (no. 16, adjacent to the farming village now known as Lower Pescado), few of the ruins mentioned here seem to have been reported in the archaeological literature—at least not under the names given by Cushing. Kintigh notes (personal communication) that from a map later drawn by Cushing "Kia'tsu-tama (no. 6) would appear to be the ruin of Ojo Bonito (Leslie Spier's ruin 168, "Notes on Some Little Colorado Ruins," *Anthropological Papers of the American Museum of Natural History,* vol. 18, pt. 4 [1919], p. 349), on Jaralosa Draw just south of the Zuni reservation and about one and a half miles west of the border. This is a large ruin with late ceramics that would indicate a 14th century occupation." Kyama:kya (no. 5), home of the *Kyana:kwe* kachinas, as already mentioned, appears as site 127 in Ferguson and Hart, *A Zuni Atlas.* Appearing on Cushing's map as several miles to the southeast of Kia'tsu-tama (Ojo Bonito), Kyama:kya was probably the large ruin in that location which Spier mentions having been unable to find (ruin 170, "Notes on Some Little Colorado Ruins," p. 350). Heshoda Yahlt'a (no. 11) also appears in Ferguson and Hart as site 39, located on top of El Morro. Finally, according to Kintigh, it seems clear that Heshoda im Koskwa (no. 14) is the Box S Site noted in his *Settlement, Subsistence, and Society in Late Zuni Prehistory* (pp. 33–34). This is a site also registered by Bandelier (*Final Report of Investigation Among the Indians of the Southwestern United States,* . . . Pt. 2, Papers of the Archaeological Institute of America, American Series, vol. 4, Cambridge, Mass.: John Wilson & Son, 1892, pp. 329, 340) and by Spier (Ruin 97, in "Notes on Some Little Colorado Ruins," p. 240). "But," says Kintigh, "much else remains speculative. Very little work has been done out in this area."

34. Actually, the term "*heshota*" or "*heshoda*" simply denotes (without differentiation) house, room, or town. (For the etymology of the term, see Frank H. Cushing, "A Study of Pueblo Pottery as Illustrative of Zuni Pueblo Growth," *Fourth Annual Report of the Bureau of Ethnology, 1882–1883* [Washington, D.C., 1886], p. 474.

35. *Hletonawe:* Literally, "all the clans together."

36. Shipapolima (Shiba:bulima) is the Zuni version of a name with various Pueblo pronunciations, referring to

the original underworld dwelling place in the east from which, in the origin myths, the people were led forth into the upper world by the twin war gods. The home of the "beast gods" or animal archetypes and other life-generating powers, it is visited each year by the Zuni kachinas after the close of the *Shalak'o* ceremonials. It is also a place to which at least some return after death: "In the Hopi and Zuni origin or Emergence myths, the first to die, little girls or boys, return . . . to the world below the place of Emergence" (Parsons, *Pueblo Indian Religion,* p. 217); and "The Zunis believe the entrance to Shipapolima to be on the summit of a mountain about 10 miles from the pueblo of Cochiti, N. Mex." (Stevenson, "The Zuni Indians," p. 407). The site, in what is now Bandelier National Monument, is known as Stone Lions Shrine, after the "two crouching lions, or cougars, of massive stone in bas-relief upon the solid formation of the mountain top [which] guard the sacred spot" (*ibid.*). According to Bandelier, Col. Stevenson had ambitions of removing these lions and transporting them, along with the rest of his hoard, to Washington—a plan which Bandelier called "very injudicious" (Lange and Riley, *Southwestern Journals of Adolph E. Bandelier* [1966], p. 244). Exactly what the name Shipapolima signified to Cushing at this point is not clear.

37. Upper Nutria Village is built on a prehistoric ruin, as noted by Victor Mindeleff ("A Study of Pueblo Architecture in Tusayan and Cibola," *Eighth Annual Report of the Bureau of Ethnology, 1886–1887* [Washington, D.C., 1891], pp. 94–95).

38. Here again, when noting Cushing's inaccuracies or oversimplifications, it is well to remember that he was the first to examine the evidence presented by these ruins. Actually, there is little to fault in the present inference; it is merely that we know more now than he did about the history of the two cultures represented by this "great division."

39. The name Pi-tchai-a-kwi would designate "land owned by the Bikchi:kwe clan." Reference is no doubt to a ruin.

40. "Capitan" Lotchi (or Lochi), a Cushing friend who appears intermittently in the following pages, was a great source of lore. He turns up again in *Zuni Breadstuff* as the teller of the marvelous yarn of "The Young Hunter" and his adventures when transformed into a mouse. Evidently a principal Priest of the Bow, he was killed in 1889 by white cattle rustlers (Arthur Woodward, "Frank Cushing—'First War Chief' of Zuni," *Masterkey* 13 [1939], p. 175n).

41. Cushing refers here to those ancient foes of the Zuni ancestors, the *Ky'anakwe,* who still require propitiation. Responsibility for this task was still in the same hands when Parsons observed several decades later that "the *Ky'anakwe* Rain chieftaincy, whose chief is chief of a nine-day ceremony, . . . is of the Corn clan; Corn clansmen and members of Chupawa kiva, the Corn clan kiva, impersonate the ancient *Ky'anakwe* enemies" (Parsons, *Pueblo Indian Religion,* p. 877).

42. In Zuni tradition, according to a composite of Cushing texts, the body which "governed, protected and cared for" the people of the pueblo was a council composed of the chief *A:shiwani* of the six cardinal directions plus a figure identified by Cushing as the *A-ta-a Shi-wan-na-o-k'ia* or All Seed Priestess and headed by the *Bekwinne* (who was chief Priest of the Zenith) and the Chief Priest of the North, known in this capacity as the *Kiakwe mosona* (*K'yakwe mossi* in modern Zuni), a title usually translated as "town chief." As chief priest of the Nadir, the elder chief Bow Priest was also a member of this council. In Cushing's phrase, these august figures were the "Masters of the Great House"—"house" in this context meaning literally their place of meeting (thought to be located directly over the center of the world) and in a more general sense the pueblo as a whole (Cushing, "Zuni Social, Mythic, and Religious Systems," pp. 187–88; "Preliminary Notes on the . . . Hemenway Expedition," pp. 153–54). Referred to by Cushing as "caciques of the pueblo," "caciques of the Temple," and "priests of the priesthood people," this body constituted, in his time at least, the highest order of authority in Zuni. Themselves removed from the world of secular work, warfare and day-to-day government (hence the need for "the good share"), it was they who named the officers who took practical charge of such affairs, including the governor and his lieutenant. Much has happened to Zuni government, of course, since Cushing's time, and much has also been written about it. For a review of the history of the Zuni council and of anthropological views about its composition and nature, see Triloki Nath Pandey, "Factionalism in a Southwestern Pueblo," pp. 78–91. For more general reviews of Zuni social and political organization and the history thereof, see the articles by Edmund Ladd and by Fred Eggan and T.N. Pandey in the *Handbook of North American Indians,* vol. 9, pp. 474–91.

43. This seems to have been the occasion on which Cushing first witnessed the great Zuni origin drama, whose performance is a regular feature of the quadrennial ceremonies of initiation into the Kachina Society. He would witness another enactment four years later, in the spring of 1884, just before his departure from the pueblo.

44. "The idea that the Anasazi were great and that the

Pueblos represent a decline from that greatness is a notion deriving from nineteenth-century romanticism—and one which has sometimes served in rationalizing exploitation of the latter Indians" (Hart, personal communication).

45. Tylor's term "myth of observation" refers to traditional stories supposed to have originated in actually observed events or phenomena, the usual pattern being etiological—stories "explaining" what had been observed (*Researches into the Early History of Mankind,* chapter 8). Examples in the present volume include the story accounting for the existence of turquoise (Cushing to Baird, January 11, 1880) and some tales Cushing later sent to his friend Washington Matthews (see Cushing to Matthews, June 4, 1884). Cushing's train of thought here with respect to the harmony of the Pueblo architecture with the natural terrain anticipates Vincent Scully's imaginative comparison of Pueblo art forms with those of ancient Greece (*Pueblo: Mountain, Village, Dance* [New York: Viking Press, 1975]).

46. Cushing's conviction that Pueblo culture and American Indian cultures generally were in all essentials the product of indigenous evolution, fostered by environment, rather than the product of influences imported from elsewhere was one in which he was encouraged, if not instructed, by Powell and Morgan. Later, this conviction would lead to arguments with Tylor, who put more stock in cultural diffusion.

47. Cushing translated the clan name *Pi-tchi-kwe* (*Bikchi:kwe*) as Parrot or Macaw, but "a more familiar acquaintance with the Zuni tongue" led Matilda Stevenson "to discover that the word comes from *pi'chiko,* dogwood" ("The Zuni Indians, p. 322n). Hence Dogwood People, a designation followed by all writers since Stevenson. As pointed out by both Stevenson and Alfred L. Kroeber ("Zuni Kin and Clan," *Anthropological Papers of the American Museum of Natural History,* no. 18, pt. 2, [1917], p. 100), the Parrot or Macaw people are a subdivision *within* the *Bikchi:kwe,* along with the Raven people. This division between Macaw and Raven was one Cushing himself noted in the Zuni origin stories, reflecting, as he saw it, an ancient organization of the tribe as a whole into two exogamous moieties ("Outlines of Zuni Creation Myths," pp. 386–87; also *Zuni Breadstuff,* pp. 189–91). Oddly enough, he seems to have missed this more immediate distinction within the *Bikchi:kwe.*

48. Indian games were later the subject of what was to have been a joint monograph by Cushing and his friend Stuart Culin. Overburdened with other unfinished projects, Cushing eventually withdrew from this partnership, and Culin completed the study by himself ("Games of the North American Indians," in the *Twenty-Fourth Annual Report of the Bureau of American Ethnology, 1902–1903* [Washington, D.C., 1907]), though he included various passages contributed by Cushing—including one on the origin of Indian games as exercises in divination (pp. 34–35).

49. Note that Cushing is still assuming a fairly imminent departure from Zuni. Here he is projecting a *return* visit.

50. If this particular report was continued in a subsequent letter, that letter has been lost. From later references to this single letter, however, it would seem to have stood as complete. It is interesting to compare this program of Cushing's with one which Powell sent to Baird in a letter of April 2, 1880. Powell listed eight general areas of American Indian ethnology being addressed by research in his Bureau: (1) somatology, (2) philology (study of Indian languages and classification of linguistic stocks), (3) mythology, (4) sociology ("relating to the organization of the family, clan, tribe, and confederacy among our North American Indians"), (5) habits and customs ("especially in relation to their mortuary observances and religious ceremonies"), (6) technology ("especially the pristine dwellings of the Indians, beginning in caves and lodges made of brush and bark and culminating in the Pueblo structure of the Southwestern portion of the United States"), (7) archaeology, and (8) history of Indian Affairs. While not identical, the two lists illustrate a fairly close community of view.

51. George Kennan, one of the older friends Cushing acquired as a teenager in Medina, New York, was the man responsible for introducing him to the works of Edward Tylor. See his memoir of Cushing's early years, "G.K.'s Column," *Medina Tribune,* December 1923–January 1924.

52. Cushing seems to be alluding to the manuscript titled "Ethnological Trip to Zuni," an excerpt from which appears at the beginning of this collection.

53. The similarity in date ("eight months" would put this fragment in May) and the "old boy" familiarity, along with the reference to "publicity," suggest the possibility that this fragment may belong to the letter above intended for Kennan, who worked for the Associated Press.

54. Cushing seems to be thinking of *Primitive Culture,* Chapter 7, on hand-numerals and etymology derived from counting on fingers and toes. He is here extending a method of inquiry he originally learned from Tylor. Archaic terms "surviving" in the Zuni language (or in the special jargon reserved for ceremonials) continued to be a major resource for gaining insight into Pueblo culture

and its "growth." Etymology is an important element, for example, in his argument for the derivation of Pueblo pottery-making from basketry ("Study of Pueblo Pottery as Illustrative of Zuni Cultural Growth") and also in his study of Zuni myth ("Outlines of Zuni Creation Myths"). By applying this "linguistic method" to the study of myths and folk tales, Powell wrote in 1885, Cushing was "able to trace the growth of mere ideas or of primitive conceptions of natural or biotic phenomena and of physical or animal function into the personae and incidents which go to make up myths, as well as to trace the influence of these growths on the worship of the Zuni" (*6th Annual Report of the Bureau of Ethnology,* p. xlvi). More specifically, this letter contains the germ of Cushing's later essay on "Manual Concepts" (original title: "Hand-Made Mind").

3. June–December 1880

1. "Empathy and Antipathy in the Heart of Darkness," in Regna Darnell, ed., *Readings in the History of Anthropology* (New York: Harper and Row, 1974), p. 284.

2. One of the most important orders of traditional Zuni society, the *A:shiwani* rain priesthood is a complex body composed of twelve separate groups (two for each of the cardinal directions), each group containing from two to six members (Bunzel, "Introduction to Zuni Ceremonialism," p. 513; see also Stevenson, "The Zuni Indians," pp. 163–80).

3. Cushing's note concerns observances followed in the summer solstice. Traditionally, at about this time in June, everyone would be involved in the making and planting of prayer sticks and preparations for the pilgrimage by selected kachina society members, including *Koyemci,* to fetch back the kachinas and spirits of the Zuni ancestors from their home in Kachina Town (Kolhu/wala:wa) under the sacred lake to the west. On the day before the departure of this group, "all *Shalak'o* impersonators, the chiefs of societies [and others] all make prayer-sticks for the kachina. *Koyemshi* come in unmasked, their hair falling over their face. Women drench them from the housetops. Called Tumichimchi from first word of their song" (Parsons, *Pueblo Indian Religion,* p. 527). Cushing's paraphrase of the song, if any, has not been found and translation has so far proved impossible.

4. Victorio, one of the last great Apache war chiefs, was leader of a band of Mescalero and Chiricahua Apaches involved in the raiding referred to here and elsewhere in the letters—hostilities occasioned in this instance by an American fiat eliminating their reservation. Hostilities continued in this part of the country—scene of the last major resistance to American rule—until Geronimo's surrender in 1886, two years after Cushing's departure from Zuni. Cushing's friend Bourke was involved in these campaigns and later wrote of them in two books: *On the Border with Crook* and *An Apache Campaign.* Alas, poor Metcalfe; he is never heard of again in these pages. Victorio himself was killed later in the same year that Cushing wrote this letter.

5. Along with Muma (for Mormon), Wamun, or Wamu, seems to have been one of the names of Roman Luna. According to Bandelier, Luna was part Navajo.

6. Reference here is to the removal of Galen Eastman as agent for the Navajos and his replacement, on June 12, 1880, by Captain Frank Tracy Bennett, who had served before in the same capacity (1868–1871). Eastman, ousted after little more than a year in his post on account of his ineptitude and unpopularity among the Navajos, was to be reinstated in June 1881 and reousted in January of 1883. More will be heard of him in correspondence to follow.

7. Given the date, these two dances relating to the sun were probably performances of the *Kok'okshi* or Good Kachina, following the summer solstice pilgrimage to the sacred lake of the dead, the ceremony described by Cushing at the close of "My Adventures in Zuni" (MAZ 44–47; Green, *Zuni,* 128–30) and also by Stevenson ("The Zuni Indians," pp. 151–62). In Cushing's account (which would have to have been based on a performance witnessed in this summer of 1880), the ancestors were brought back to the pueblo in the form of living turtles, which were then "returned" to their home in Kachina Town through ritual sacrifice. See also Parsons, *Pueblo Indian Religion,* pp. 736 and 985, on *Kok'okshi* turtle dances. Parson's calendar registers a series of performances of the *Kok'okshi* by four different kiva groups in the month of rain-summoning retreats following the solstice.

8. Cushing seems to be referring to the series of U.S. War Department *Reports of Explorations and Surveys to Ascertain the Most Practicable and Economical Route for a Railroad from the Mississippi River to the Pacific Ocean* (Washington, D.C., 1855–1861). The volume he had in hand was no doubt the same as that which contained the "Whipple Report" referred to earlier in his diary entry for November 30, 1879.

9. "John B. Brun, French ancestry, brother of Mrs. Dumas Provencher, . . . had charge of the churches and chapels of Cebolleta, Cubero, San Rafael, San Mateo, Laguna, Acoma, and Zuni" (Lange and Riley, *Southwestern Journals of Adolph Bandelier* [1966], p. 276n). The Zuni church of Our Lady of Guadalupe probably dates

from the arrival in Zuni of the Franciscan missionaries in 1629. Destroyed in the Pueblo Revolt of 1680, it was rebuilt between 1775 and 1780 ("Outlines of Zuni Creation Myths," p. 332). Long in ruins by the time of Cushing's stay in Zuni, it was eventually restored in the 1960s.

10. A.W. Whipple had in fact anticipated Cushing in recognizing the identity of Zuni with Cibola: "We have now passed through the ancient country of Cibola, described by Marco de Nica in 1539, and by Vasquez de Coronado in 1540." The descriptions written by these sixteenth-century Spaniards, he wrote, were "for the most part, applicable to the Zunian of the present day" (Grant Foreman, ed., *A Pathfinder in the Southwest,* . . . p. 140). Others, too, had considered Zuni as a probable candidate for the Cibola nomination. Without the kind of confirmation supplied by Cushing's knowledge of the Zuni story of the "Black Mexican" and of the Zuni town names here being reported to Baird, however, the linking of Zuni with Cibola had been suppositious. Though Bandelier was the only writer of his generation to acknowledge it, Cushing was the first to provide *proof,* and it is thus to him, as Bandelier wrote (Madeleine T. Rodack, ed., *Adolph F. Bandelier's The Discovery of New Mexico by the Franciscan Monk Friar Marcos de Niza in 1593* [Tucson: University of Arizona Press, 1981], p. 93), "that we owe the knowledge of the real name of the country and of the tribe of Zuni." As to *which* of the Zuni towns it was that Marcos described, some question remains (see p. 387 n. 44 below).

11. Cushing's reference is to Pedro de Casteñeda de Nacera, a private soldier in the Coronado expedition whose "Relación de la Jornada de Cibola" is probably the most authoritative of the surviving accounts of that journey in search of the "Seven Cities of Cibola." Excerpted in the Whipple volume, Casteñeda's "Relación" is quoted more extensively in another source to be requested by Cushing in this same letter—James Harvey Simpson's "Coronado's March in Search of the 'Seven Cities of Cibola' and Discussion of Their Probable Location," *Annual Report of the Smithsonian Institution, 1869* (Washington, D.C., 1872), pp. 309–40.

12. Cushing was evidently referring here to the list of ruins marking the migrations of the "southern division" of the Zunis' ancestors (Cushing to Baird and Powell, February 18–April 13, 1880). None of the names on that list clearly matches with those given here, however. Ma-kia-kwu-ta-hna (shortened to Ma-k'iah-ta) is translated in a later Cushing document as "Region of the Southern Salinas"—that is, the region of the Zuni Salt Lake (Ma'k'yaya is a modern spelling of this Zuni place name). Various later writers have had other ideas about the location of "the Kingdom of Marata." See p. 414 n. 6.

13. Richard Hakluyt (1553–1616) was famous for his collection of accounts by travelers and adventurers, *The Principal Navigations, Voyages, Traffics, and Discoveries of the English Nation, Made by Sea or over Land to the Remote and Farthest Distant Quarters of the Earth at Any Time within the Compass of These 1500 Years* (first edition, 1589). The work by Henri Ternaux-Compans (1807–1864) was *Voyages, relations et memoires originaux pour servir a l'histoire de la decouverte de l'Amerique* (Paris, 1837–1841), published in some twenty volumes, at least one of which contains accounts by Casteñeda and others of the Spanish discovery of Cibola. W.W.H. Davis was author of *The Spanish Conquest of New Mexico* (Doylestown, Pa., 1869). Captain Lorenzo Sitgreaves was one of the early American explorers of the Southwest seeking routes for transportation through to the coast. Cushing was requesting his *Report of an Expedition down the Zuni and* [*Little*] *Colorado Rivers* (1853), an expedition aimed at determining the "navigable properties"(!) of these rivers. The other requests were for the already mentioned Smithsonian *Annual Report* for 1869, an article by Oscar Loew (not found), and the first three volumes of Hubert Howe Bancroft's massive series on the Pacific states: *Wild Tribes, Civilized Nations,* and *Myths and Languages* (New York, 1874–1876).

14. Cushing was more correct in calling the church *one* of the earliest. It was not *the* earliest.

15. See Green, *Zuni,* pp. 157–60, for Cushing accounts of his trial for sorcery. For other accounts of such trials and the Zuni beliefs accounting for them, see Stevenson, "The Zuni Indians," pp. 392–406, and Watson Smith and John M. Roberts, *Zuni Law: A Field of Values,* Harvard University, Papers of the Peabody Museum of Archaeology and Ethnology, vol. 43, no. 1 (Cambridge, Mass.: The Museum, 1954). Cushing's contemporary in Zuni, the missionary Taylor Ealy, also reported on the torture and execution of suspected witches in Zuni (*Annual Report of the Commissioner of Indian Affairs for 1880* [Washington, D.C., 1881], pp. 135–36). As to Americans being considered free from the vice of sorcery, the Zunis had not yet paid their visit to Salem, Massachusetts.

16. "*Onawe*" [roads?] is a name used for the section of Zuni pueblo south of the mission church and also for one of the *A:shiwani* groups, the Priesthood of the South.

17. According to Stevenson:

> the drama of the *Hla'hewe,* which is enacted quadrennially in August [or July, in the case of 1880], when the corn is a foot

> high, is supposed to be a reproduction of the ceremonies held [according to the origin myth] at the time of the third appearance of the Corn maidens before the *A'shiwi* [the Zuni people], and is regarded as one of their most sacred festivals. Great preparations were made by the *A'shiwi* for the third coming of the Corn maidens, who were to dance that rains would come and water the earth, that the new corn might be made beautiful to look upon, and that the earth would furnish all food for nourishment. While the drama must be played once in four years, it may occur more often by order of the first body of the *A'shiwanni* [rain priests] ("The Zuni Indians," p. 180).

"One of the most beautiful of the native ceremonials," Cushing wrote in *Zuni Breadstuff,* this "dance of the Beautiful Corn Wands" (rendered there as *Thla-he-kwe*) was also

> one of the few sacred dances of the Zunis in which women assume the leading part. It is still performed with untiring zeal, usually during each summer, although accompanied by exhausting fasts and abstinences from sleep. Curiously enough, it was observed and admirably, though too briefly, described by Coronado . . . nearly three hundred and fifty years ago. It was with this ceremonial that the delighted nation welcomed the water which my party brought in 1882 from the "Ocean of Sunrise" (p. 631).

For a detailed account of *Hla'hewe* performances in 1890 and 1891, see Stevenson, "The Zuni Indians," pp. 180–204). According to Zuni informants in 1985, the dance hasn't been performed since 1946, since no one is left who knows how to perform the whole ritual correctly.

18. "While the drama is known as the *Hla'hewe,* the dancers and the choirs form into two parties, one side being called *Hla'hewe* [from hla'we, meaning "tender stems of a plant"], the other *Sho'ko'we* (singular *sho'kona,* flute), having reference to Pa'yatuma (god of music, flowers, and butterflies)" (Stevenson, "The Zuni Indians," p. 181). The young man is the "*yapota* (symbolizer of corn), who dances that the ears of corn may be perfect" (ibid., p. 182). The name *Hle-we-kwe* probably refers to dancers on the Sho'ko'we side, who, in addition to the ears of corn they carry, "have hle-we (tablets) ornamented with sun, moon, star, and cloud symbols, with white fluffy eagle plumes surmounting the tablets" (Stevenson, "The Zuni Indians," p. 186).

19. *Ale-kwe-uwe*: A drink made with the sacred corn flour.

20. See Cushing, "Outlines of Zuni Creation Myths," p. 429, for outline of the Zuni flood story. Other versions may be found in Stevenson, "The Zuni Indians," p. 61; Benedict, *Zuni Mythology,* vol. I, pp. 10–11, 206; and Parsons, *Pueblo Indian Religion,* p. 235.

21. Daniel Dubois, "a frontier character known to most of the residents in the area" (Brandes, "Frank Hamilton Cushing," p. 137), had a ranch in his later years at Ojo del Venado (Cushing was spelling by ear), about twenty-five miles southwest of Zuni next to the Rio Zuni. The letters and journal passages in which he figures suggest that he was a sometimes helpful, sometimes irascible neighbor who at any rate befriended Cushing. In fact he named his two daughters after Emily Cushing and her sister Maggie. Cushing later hired him as general utility man for the Hemenway Expedition camp (Brandes, "Frank Hamilton Cushing," p. 137; see also McNitt, *The Indian Traders,* pp. 242—44). The letter to follow suggests that at this point their relationship had not yet "matured."

22. The religious observance alluded to was the quadrennial pilgrimage to Kolhu/wala:wa spoken of above, and as Richard Hart points out (1984, p. 36), this letter records the earliest known instance of conflict between the Zunis and ranchers who took up—and fenced—land along the route to the shrines. In a memoir of "Old Dan Dubois," Cushing's brother-in-law and fellow Pueblo archaeologist, Frederick Webb Hodge, explains what happened:

> The Zuni Indians conduct periodically a ceremony that takes them to a sacred lake. Among the members of the pilgrimage is Shulawitsi, the Little Fire God, one of whose functions, during the return journey to Zuni, is to set afire anything that chanced to be in the way, not excepting ranch fences and the like. It happened that Dan's fence was along the trail of the Little Fire God . . . ("Old Dan Dubois," Los Angeles Westerners Corral Brand Book [Los Angeles: privately printed, 1950]).

Correspondence in the records of the BIA indicate that a similar "Zuni depradation" occurred in 1882 and that Cushing was again called upon to explain its nature (J.H. Willson to Agent Ben Thomas, November 13 and 29, 1882; National Archives, Denver Federal Center, Records of the Bureau of Indian Affairs, Pueblo Indian Agency).

23. One of the three principal outlying Zuni farming villages, Ojo Caliente is situated fifteen miles southwest of the main pueblo, near the ruins of Hawikku, largest of the Cibola settlements at the time of the conquest. In that earlier time, as in Cushing's own time, it was surrounded by fields and orchards made fertile by a system of irrigation fed by the warm springs from whence its Spanish name is taken (also its Zuni name—*K'yapkwayin'a,* or Place Where Hot Waters Flow). Unlike the houses in the main pueblo, which belonged to the women and passed

from mother to daughter, farm land, according to Cushing, belonged to him who first "raised the soil" and passed to members of his own clan unless otherwise specified (see *Zuni Breadstuff,* Chapter 3, particularly pp. 131–32, on "Land Law and Labor"). If Antonio was a large owner, it is likely that at least some of his land had been inherited from his mother's brother, who in turn may have increased the holdings inherited from *his* maternal uncle. Antonio must in any event have been a man of enterprise, for it will be recalled that he was one of the two Zunis assisted by Cushing in entering claims for private land outside the reservation.

24. Here again it seems likely that Cushing meant to refer not to the Sword Swallowers but to the group of *Hla he'we* dancers juxtaposed to the *Shoh k'o.* By "wand" Cushing evidently meant "prayer stick." His preparation of such a sacrifice had signified his "belonging."

25. Having already requested imitation turquoise for trading, Cushing is here asking for what his friend Washington Matthews was to call "fugitive" aniline dyes, as opposed to "the permanent native dyes formerly used." Use of these aniline dyes purchased from traders was to be responsible, as Matthews pointed out, for a deterioration in the traditional standards for woven products—the aniline dyes not only being inferior to the native dyes in respect to permanence but departing from tradition in their garish color prior to fading. Before blaming Cushing for this development in Zuni, however, one should note that he was writing this letter in 1880, and that Matthews (whom Cushing had not yet met) was himself requesting aniline dyes in 1882 (Matthews to Pilling, May 13, 1882, National Anthropological Archives). It was not until thirteen years later that he wrote of the deleterious results of their use (*Navajo Legends,* Memoirs of the American Folklore Society, no. 5, [Boston, 1897], p. 20). Perhaps by then Cushing too knew better.

26. The sacred caves referred to must be the local ones referred to above in Cushing to Baird, January 11, 1880, and Cushing to Baird-Powell, February 18–April 13, 1880.

27. The "capitan" would have been the Bow Priest Lotchi, already referred to. His companion was probably Jesús Eriacho, who would be Zuni governor in the 1890s. The Eriachos are still a leading family in Zuni.

28. Frank McNitt refers to William and John Burgess, who traded at Zuni in 1877 and again in 1880, as the first "nailed-down counter and shelf" traders in the area (1962, p. 240). Cushing's reference seems to indicate that only one of the two was there at this time.

29. This entry leaves much to be desired in the way of pronouns and other details. *Who* proposed killing the Navajo? And what was the "serious division" between the *Bekwinne* and the leader of the *Chuppawa* kiva? We are left in the dark.

30. This was the "Saint's Dance" (translated by Jane Young as "Doll Dance"), usually held in September according to Parsons, after the saint "has been laid down for four days, and set up for four days" (see *Pueblo Indian Religion,* pp. 528–29, for brief description, which is generally consistent with the Cushing notes that follow in his diary entries for September 6 and 7).

31. This was Ruth R. Ealy, who later wrote a memoir, *Water in a Thirsty Land* (Pittsburgh, 1955), about her father's life as a missionary.

32. Powell had evidently noted that the Hopi rain sign in the Bureau insignia, designed by W.H. Holmes in 1879, omitted the symbols of lightning to the left and right of the clouds.

33. One of the Zuni proverbs recorded by John Bourke during his stay with Cushing in November of 1881 was the following: "Son, do not get in the habit of sleeping too much. If you are asleep before the Three Stars (the Sword Belt of Orion) pass over you in the sky, they will drop lice upon you; but if you do not lie down until the stars of Morning pass, they will scatter blessings upon you" (Sutherland, "The Diaries of John Gregory Bourke," p. 908).

34. Unfortunately, Cushing did not record what these discoveries were, unless he did so in the undated draft printed on pp. 105–07 above—in which case that draft would better have been placed here.

35. *Wanuadina* is the generic Zuni word for spring or well. The site Cushing refers to by this name, known in white geography as Jacob's Well, is located a few miles southeast of Navajo Springs. Mentioned prominently in the reports of every military expedition that passed to the west of Zuni, it was an unusual spring at the bottom of a large hole shaped like an inverted cone (Hart, personal communication). By the 1930s, however, it was reported that the well was filled to within a few feet of the surface with windblown silt (Barnes, *Arizona Place Names,* p. 13).

36. Ho-Kwai-na-kwin seems to be Cushing's rendition of Ahok Kiana, the Zuni name for what is still on the map as Houck, Arizona. It is named for a mail carrier who set up a trading post there in 1877. The spring was called Houck's Tank (Barnes, *Arizona Place Names,* p. 13).

37. The sketchbook has not been found, nor is there any further information about the three men mentioned. They were evidently settlers in the area.

38. *Tona* is also the name of an Apache tribe dwelling

to the west in Tona Canyon, beyond Show Low, Arizona.

39. The Coyoteros: An Apache band assigned to the San Carlos reservation, adjacent to the Fort Apache reservation southwest of Zuni.

40. K'eshpahe had been Cushing's companion on his second trek to the mines in the Zuni Mountains the previous December.

41. For a description of the Zuni method of roasting corn in the field, see *Zuni Breadstuff,* pp. 204–08 (Green, *Zuni,* pp. 275–77).

42. According to T.J. Ferguson (personal communication), Cushing's Heshoktakwe was the same peach-orchard village to the northwest of Zuni identified in Spier, "An Outline for a Chronology of Zuni Ruins," as HeccotaLallo (ruin 42, p. 230; map on p. 220). Fewkes, who visited the site a few years after Cushing, rendered the name as Hesh-o-ta-thlu-al-la (Jesse Walter Fewkes, "Reconnoissance of Ruins In or Near the Zuni Reservation," *Journal of American Archaeology and Ethnology* 1: 111). Perhaps a place of refuge during the Pueblo Revolt period and later, the village had still been inhabited within the memory of some of the older Zunis encountered by Fewkes.

43. Kiau was Palowahtiwa's wife.

44. Matilda Stevenson noted a similar fissure on the side of Dowa Yalanne, into which hunters would shoot arrows to insure good hunting "The Zuni Indians," p. 439). Other "phallic shrines" on Dowa Yalanne are mentioned by Parsons (*Pueblo Indian Religion,* p. 574).

45. The *Atoshli* are the "old man and old woman kachina bogeys" who go around the pueblo late in January making house-to-house visits frightening and haranguing little children to reinforce discipline, respect, and obedience. "The old man carries a large knife, the old woman a basket to carry off a child to devour" (Parsons, *Pueblo Indian Religion,* pp. 51–53, 518).

46. Osh-te-k'ia-na is probably the place identified on nineteenth-century military maps as Arch Spring (Hart, personal communication).

47. *Ya-to:* Father of the Sun. The figures following are a series of dance deities. *Kia-kwe-nai* seems to be a variant spelling of *Chakwena Kachina Woman,* hero of the dread *Kia-na-kwe* (*Kyana:kwe*), also represented here. The "*Cha-la-k'o*" are of course the giant kachina warriors whose visit to the pueblo occasions the great November festival. *Sai-a-ta-sha* (Long Horn, a name corresponding to a prominent feature of the mask) is a priest kachina who plays a leading part in the *Shalak'o,* solstice, and other rites. *Shu-lu-wit-se,* traditionally impersonated by a young boy, is the god of fire, maize, and hunting, and is likewise a key figure in the *Shalak'o* as well as in the summer solstice pilgrimage and other ceremonies. *Ya-a-na* is one of the kachinas in Ruth Bunzel's list for the *Wo'temthla* or Mixed Dance ("Zuni Katcinas," p. 906).

48. The ritual here seems notably similar to that attached to the stone heaps known as *hermaia* which served as landmarks in ancient Greece and from which the god Hermes probably derived his name (see W.K.C. Guthrie, *The Greeks and their Gods* [Boston, 1955], pp. 88–89).

49. Cushing is referring to Kolhu/wala:wa (or as he renders it in "My Adventures in Zuni," Ka-thlu-el-lon), the dwelling place of the kachinas and the spirits of the Zuni ancestors, a place of whose existence he had learned the previous December and of which he had heard more on the occasion of the 1880 summer solstice pilgrimage there. The departure for and return from it are described in "My Adventures in Zuni" (pp. 45–47; *Green, Zuni,* pp. 128–32). Failing in the present circumstances to manage the visit to the lake, he would return in the coming December. Doubtless, the Zunis' lack of enthusiasm for this second trip and the offer to accompany him were prompted by the wish for him *not* to visit the lake shrines, forbidden to all save those delegated to make the quadrennial pilgrimage. For a study of the history and ethnology of this holy place, recently restored to Zuni control, see E. Richard Hart, "The Zuni Indian Tribe and Title to Kolhu/wala:wa (Kachina Village)."

50. Precisely this suggestion of Fazende's was what Cushing followed several years later as director of the Hemenway Southwestern Expedition, when he appointed Bandelier as historian for the project and sent him off to the archives of Mexico. Bandelier indeed devoted the rest of his life to the collecting of such records, and was in Spain doing so at the time of his death.

51. *Ham-pous:* Zuni term for watering place.

52. Cushing had been finding archaeological evidence in the field to support theories of the dual ancestry of the Zunis and their respective "migration tracks" which were propounded in his February 18–April 13, 1880, letter to Baird and Powell. The sun monument was a phallus-shaped erection used by the *Bekwinne* as a calendar.

53. In one of the not strictly ethnological assignments that Cushing was expected to undertake as an employee of the Museum, he had been asked by Baird to collect eggs of the Maximilian's jay (named for the German prince Alexander Philip Maximilian of Wied-Neuwied, who led a research team on a twelve-month journey up the Mississippi River in 1832).

54. Titskematske, a Cheyenne who had been through Hampton Institute in Virginia, had worked with Cushing in the summer of 1879 as an informant on Cheyenne

sign language (Cushing file cards in National Anthropological Archives). He was presently serving at the recently established Carlisle Indian Training School in Pennsylvania.

55. Cushing's Zuni really seems to mean something closer to "Town of the Boundary" (*Heshota:* dwelling place, *pahlto:* something indicating a boundary). Of the ruin described here, Kintigh writes:

> About 22 miles due north of Navajo Springs is Wide Ruin, illustrated by Mindeleff [*Eighth Annual Report of the Bureau of Ethnology*], and shown on standard road maps. There was, until a few years ago, an old trading post there (it burned down). I have seen Wide Ruin (also known as Kin Tiel), and the description fits very well, the ruin being divided by an arroyo. Note, however, that Mindeleff (who knew Cushing and whose map I trust) shows it as butterfly-shaped. Cushing's description serves to point out how much better preserved those ruins were then than they are today. Today there are no standing walls, although the rubble mound is quite impressive (personal communication).

56. Reference is to the already mentioned ranch belonging to James W. Bennett, sometime partner of Douglas Graham, the Zuni trader.

57. Cushing seems to have slipped a day here—in 1880 September 23 was on a Thursday.

58. There is no explanation as to why the governor should have been "shamed."

59. A letter from Baird to Cushing dated January 6, 1881, indicates that Mr. Rusby went on to make for the Museum the collection from the Silver City cave so often referred to by Cushing. It does not sound as though Cushing were encouraging that enterprise.

60. One of the chief rain priests (Cushing refers to him variously as head of the *Bikchi:kwe* clan and "Master Medicine man of the Order of Fire"), Laiiuaitsailunkia was Cushing's adoptive father. Described in "My Adventures" (pp. 27–29 [Green, *Zuni,* 90–94]), he figures intermittently in the pages to follow. One wonders what could have needed forgiving in this kind and gentle old man. In passages like this and another one later on in which he tells of reducing old Pedro Pino and his wife to tears, we see, if nothing else, the sheer power of Cushing's personality.

61. *Na-wa-lush-ni-kieu:* One of the summer dances, done five or six times.

62. Cushing was expecting the arrival of his older brother Enos, who would remain in the area for the next several years practicing dentistry and doing various odd jobs.

63. The *Shi'wanakwe:* One of the rain societies (and a medicine or curing society as well), accounted by Parsons to be the oldest of its kind in Zuni (*Pueblo Indian Religion,* p. 134).

64. Toi-akwe (Doya'a or Doya: Corn or Seed Place): The Zuni name for Las Nutrias or Nutria, the farming village in the northeast corner of the Zuni reservation which, with its springs and outlying lands, would be the focus of the famous controversy with Senator Logan.

65. John H. Sullivan, the Hopi agent, would be Cushing's host when the latter passed through the Hopi country the following June.

66. General Luther P. Bradley was the officer in command of Fort Wingate at this juncture.

67. August Lacombe was a local itinerant trader.

68. The works referred to are among those listed in Cushing's request of July 2, the first being the collection of excerpts from the old Spanish chronicles put together by James H. Simpson for the Smithsonian *Annual Report* for 1869. This seems to have been the occasion when Cushing learned the Zunis' own version of the killing of Estevanico, whom they called "the Black Mexican." For his account of this impressive "lesson in history" see Green, *Zuni,* pp. 172–75. As to the "Coll[ection]s of Myths and Traditions," various of Cushing's notes on myths and traditions survive in the Hodge-Cushing Collection, but not a discrete batch with this label.

69. Since Cushing himself omitted the closing quotation marks in this sentence, one can't know for certain which words were spoken and which merely thought. My choice gives him the benefit of *some* modesty.

70. Cushing was being ironic; having failed to appear on time to be met at Fort Wingate, his brother Enos would not arrive for another ten days.

71. Captain Bennett was the Navajo agent at this point.

72. For a detailed account of such a "trial," see Cushing, *Zuni Breadstuff,* pp. 134–51.

73. "Ki-se-wa" may have been an early approximation of the name of the Younger Brother chief of the Bow Priesthood, whose name is given later as Kiasi. In any event, no record seems to have survived of what this informant told Cushing.

74. Cushing's record of the responding speech by the Younger Brother Bow Chief (whose name is given hereafter as Kiasi) has not been found. Cushing seems to have been employed as a translator in a council the Indian agent (Benjamin Thomas) held with the Zunis—one of several during a three- or four-day visit to the pueblo. It is not entirely clear from this entry, but it seems probable that it was the *agent* who was speaking for the establishment of "obedience to officers" and "support of

the school." See the later comment by Cushing's friend Bourke on the "agreement" exacted from the Zunis by Agent Thomas for this support (diary entry for November 18, 1881). On the other hand, it was probably this visit that Cushing had in mind when he wrote to Baird later that he had been asked by the Pueblo agent "during the Autumn of '80 . . . to take charge of some matters for him, such as through my chieftaincy to aid the native chiefs and to insist upon both his own [i.e., the agent's] and my authority in vindicating and carrying through [the chiefs'] mandates." What Cushing seems to have got himself involved in was the familiar colonial strategy with natives of making certain some few persons were "in charge" so that the tribe could be dealt with through them. In this endeavor he would eventually find himself in conflict with that representative of higher civilization, the Presbyterian missionary schoolteacher, but his own role was less simply that of the defender of tribal conservatism than has sometimes been suggested. The centralization of governance he was promoting in alliance with the agent was distinctly counter to Zuni tradition; nor was this the only "progressive" project he initiated as "chief councilor."

75. Agent Thomas was staying at the home of the Presbyterian mission schoolteacher.

76. What Cushing meant by the "new work" of the governor and alcalde is not really clear. The context suggests that he may have been referring to their role in his adobe manufacturing project—in which case it is probably no wonder that they were feeling "very blue." But there are other possibilities, including one suggested by a combination of evidence advanced subsequently by Cushing himself and by two modern researchers, John Adair and Willard Walker. In his book *The Navajo and Pueblo Silversmiths,* Adair quotes an old Zuni silversmith's story of how he learned the craft from a Navajo and taught it in turn to a Zuni named Balawade, a close friend of Cushing's (Norman: University of Oklahoma Press, 1944, pp. 124–26). In his more recent piece of sleuthing, "Palowahtiwa and the Economic Redevelopment of Zuni Pueblo" (*Ethnohistory* 21 [1]), Walker, drawing on both Cushing and Adair, identifies Balawade as Palowahtiwa (the former version of the name is actually closer to Zuni pronunciation). In *Zuni Breadstuff* Cushing recounts Palowahtiwa's story of how "the punches and dies I pound out [silver] buttons with" were acquired—by murdering a Navajo silversmith (in revenge for the Navajo's earlier murder of Palowahtiwa's uncle) (pp. 533–34; Green, *Zuni,* p. 300). Walker might have mentioned, too, that Cushing also describes in "My Adventures" how he sat

> . . . day after day [watching Palowahtiwa], busy with his quaint forge and crude appliances, working Mexican coins over into bangles, girdles, ear-rings, buttons, and what not for savage adornment. Though his tools were wonderfully rude, the work he turned out by dint of combined patience and ingenuity was remarkably beautiful" (pp. 46–47; Green, *Zuni,* p. 128).

Both the tools and skill had been acquired before Cushing arrived on the scene, and it would be pleasant to think that in the passage above Cushing was encouraging the expansion of this craft rather than trying to steer his "elder brother" and the alcalde into some other occupation of his own invention. When he returned east, he did in fact, according to Adair's informant, send to Balawade or Palowahtiwa a new set of silver-working tools. That same informant reported that it was after "the white man, Cushing, came here to live" that Balawade or Palowahtiwa taught the craft to five other Zuni men (Adair, *Navajo and Pueblo Silversmiths,* p. 125). Could the alcalde have been one of those five men? At any rate, whatever work it was that Cushing was promoting, one may observe at the very least that he did not do as Matilda Stevenson was to do in the case of Adair's informant—bring about his *retirement* as a silversmith by buying his tools and sending them to the Museum in Washington! (ibid., p. 126).

77. Judging by a remark entered on the 25th, Tschushi may have been the son of one of the chief Bow Priests. The handcuffs, which Cushing probably would have ordered from Fort Wingate in order to carry out his mandate from the Pueblo agent in Santa Fe, are an eloquent symbol of the linkage between the Bureau of Ethnology and the other agencies of governmental control over the Indians.

78. At given times on the Zuni calendar, the respective orders of rain priests "go into the house," or undergo retreats, particularly during the summer, when they spend long periods in uninterrupted prayer and ceremonial observances. In this case, they are preparing for a ceremony of initiation, seemingly into one of the kiva groups of the kachina society (*upe:* kiva group). "This rite through which all boys pass between the ages of 5 and 9 [or perhaps later] is called *i'pu'anaka*—initiation, the same word that is used for initiation of adults into esoteric societies" (Bunzel, "Zuni Katcinas," p. 975). Like Christian baptism, this rite—which features whipping in the place of dousing—is essential for entry to heaven (Kolhu/wala:wa). A long and complex affair, the rite was not to be completed until late in November (unless the activities of a month later were for separate initiations). For a more detailed exposition, see Bunzel, "Zuni Kat-

cinas," pp. 975–1002, and Stevenson, "The Zuni Indians," pp. 102–04. The ceremonials described by Bunzel and Stevenson, however, occurred in the spring, around Eastertime, whereas the present initiation culminates at the time of the *Shalak'o* celebration.

79. Key words in this transcription from the Zuni language are evidently archaic; no translation was obtained. Cushing seems to be alluding not to the ceremony he was about to witness but to another initiation—evidently into the order of the *Sho'wekwe,* or fraternity of the Arrow-Reed or Arrow-Point people, an order originally organized, according to Stevenson, by the rain priests but "degenerated," in her opinion, "into a body of professional gamblers" ("The Zuni Indians," pp. 328–29). In any case, the initiation spoken of in this paragraph seems to have been an adult one.

80. It seems that this amazing remark must refer either to Kiasi or Naiiutchi, respectively the Younger and Older Brother Chiefs of the Bow Priesthood—both men of venerable and imposing authority. One of them was presumably the same man that Cushing had attacked several months earlier in his attempt to prevent an execution. Cushing was clearly in a very aggressive frame of mind during this period. Interestingly enough, despite his quite un-Zunian behavior, his position in the community continued to improve, and he would soon be a leading member of the very order on one of whose chiefs he was here speaking of using "force and violence."

81. The *mi-ile* is a perfect ear of white corn given as an offering—in this case in the ceremony of initiation and naming (Parsons, *Pueblo Indian Religion,* pp. 321–22).

82. The *Muluktakia:* Kachina figures, usually impersonated in dance by members of the Chuppawa kiva (Bunzel, "Zuni Katcinas," p. 887; Parsons, *Pueblo Indian Religion,* p. 530). According to Parsons, animal images made of dough also figure in rites associated with the winter solstice (*Pueblo Indian Religion,* p. 317).

83. *Yakto:* Hitting repeatedly; *Hani:* Younger brother. "The four exorcising *Sayathlia,*" or "Blue Horns," a name corresponding to the blue-horned turquoise-colored masks worn by their impersonators (Parsons, Pueblo Indian Religion, p. 575). These kachinas administer the final purifying whipping which is an essential part of the ritual of initiation into the Kachina society (Bunzel, "Introduction to Zuni Ceremonialism," p. 524). In this present phase of what appears to be an initiation into the kiva group of the *Bikchi:kwe* clan (i.e., of boys whose godfathers belong to that clan), it is the *Koyemci* who perform that function, in the presence of the *Sayathlia* (Cushing's *Sai-a-hle-an*) and the *Nalashi* (one of the *Koyemci* mudhead kachinas). Whipping by the *Sayathlia* would follow in two weeks.

84. The agent had written to Cushing on November 10 that Schedule No. 1 of the census *had* to be completed by December 1st. It is clear from a series of increasingly anxious follow-up letters that Cushing did not in fact complete this assignment until the following May (National Archives, Denver Federal Center, Records of the BIA, Pueblo Indian Agency).

85. *Tikia:* A generic term for medicine society; also sometimes used as a prefix denoting sacredness.

86. *He-he-a:* A clowning kachina group (featured also in the harvest dance described earlier by Cushing).

87. Usually translated as Mixed Kachina, the *Wo-temhla* or *Wa'temthla,* like the other kachina dances mentioned here by Cushing, belongs to a series of dances following the departure of the *Shalak'o* (among other times). As described by Matilda Stevenson (who called it All Herds), this dance was performed by seventeen kilted figures, seven of them boys ("The Zuni Indians," p. 266). Bunzel characterizes it as a dance made up of representatives of various groups of kachina impersonators ("Zuni Katcinas," pp. 906–07).

88. This feat belongs to a repertory of magic tricks through which the *Koyemci* demonstrate their supernatural powers.

89. *A-hla-shi:* "Old timers," a secular nickname for the *Koyemci* mudheads. It is not clear what distinction between the two Cushing meant to imply.

90. Cushing seems to be referring to a variant of the guessing game of *I'yanko lo'we,* or game of the hidden ball, described both in "My Adventures" (pp. 37–39; Green, *Zuni,* pp. 113–15) and in greater detail in a Cushing contribution to Stuart Culin, "Games of the North American Indians" (pp. 374–80). The "heaps" referred to would have been piles of goods contributed for prizes for making the correct guess. Large-scale betting by the onlookers would also have been the usual practice. As Cushing points out, the object of the game is divinatory—the particular prognostication aimed at varying according to the occasion (the pre-spring planting game, for instance, being intended to divine and to encourage the success of the crop). In the present case, the guessing seems to have involved not the whereabouts of a hidden ball but the identity of a hidden unknown object.

91. In this list of night kachina dances, the *Temtemshi,* along with *Homachi,* figures as one of the punitive and exorcizing kachinas—executioner of those who betray religious secrets (Bunzel, "Zuni Katcinas," pp. 906, 1006). *Tciltci* (*Tchi-tchil-tchi*) is listed by Bunzel among "supplementary and extra dances" ("Zuni Katcinas, p. 1065). The *Apatchu* (Zuni name for the Navajo) was another such dance.

92. Captain Richard Henry Pratt was superintendent

of the Carlisle Indian Training School in Pennsylvania.

93. L.H. Morgan, *Houses and Home Life of the American Aborigines* (Washington, 1881). The sketch provided by Cushing appears on p. 151 of that work.

94. Cushing's reference is to the ceremonials of the winter solstice, which he had just witnessed—and taken part in—for the second time. This is the time of year called by the Zunis *itiwana,* "the middle." Given the same name as that used in reference to the pueblo itself, *itiwana* "is the middle of the year, the point common to all the different cults, and is indeed the center of [the Zunis'] whole ceremonial life. . . . The [winter] solstice is the center of time, just as Zuni itself is the center of space" (Bunzel, "Introduction to Zuni Ceremonialism," p. 534). One of the two great ritual events to which Cushing alludes would have been the bow society procession up to the mesa tops to "plant" or "bury" the effigies of the twin war gods and to light the "Last Fire" (already alluded to). This event—which coincides with a general planting of plume sticks by all the various rain and medicine priesthoods—occurs at the midpoint of the twenty-day series of observances and is the culmination of several days and nights spent in preparation of the articles to be sacrificed. The ten days following this event are, for the various ceremonial societies, a time of retreats. For the pueblo at large they are a time when certain foods are taboo, trading is not done, and all fire, ashes, and refuse must be confined indoors. This second ten-day period culminates in the lighting of the "New Fire" and the arrival of Pautiwa, chief of the kachinas, to appoint those chosen for the various mask impersonations of the year to follow. On this day, when the New Fire has been kindled, all the accumulated ashes and refuse are taken into the fields and "planted" (so that the house may be as full of corn as it had been of ashes), food offerings are consigned to the flames, and there is general feasting and celebration of the New Year (*Zuni Breadstuff,* pp. 617–18 [Green, *Zuni,* pp. 322–23; Stevenson, "The Zuni Indians," pp. 115–41; Bunzel, "Introduction to Zuni Ceremonialism," pp. 534–35; Parsons, *Pueblo Indian Religion,* pp. 514–17).

95. L.W. Ledyard, who befriended Cushing when the latter was still a high-school boy in Medina, New York, was also the man who introduced him to Spencer Baird at the Smithsonian.

4. January–June 1881

1. According to Kintigh:

> The line of ruins referred to here, I would surmise, is in the Zuni River Valley between Hawikku and the point where the Zuni joins the Jaralosa. From there one might branch off from the river to go to St. Johns, through which runs the Little Colorado (Colorado Chiquito). Cushing's map seems to indicate that he followed this route to St. Johns (San Juan), an inference which seems consistent with the information given in the letter. This interpretation also fits with the archaeology; my recent work shows not only a whole series of ruins but also an incredible sequence of petroglyph panels, in the area of Ceadro Springs, that is nearly a mile long (personal communication).

2. E. Richard Hart, "The Zuni Indian Tribe and Title to Kolhu/wala:wa (Kachina Village)," p. 43. The second government representatives to visit the lake and the cave shrines, no doubt having learned of them from Cushing, were the Stevensons. See Matilda Stevenson, "The Zuni Indians," pp. 154–55, for an account of how they contrived to get there, using "extreme persuasion to induce [an old Zuni] to guide them" and ridiculing his conviction that this was a transgression punishable by death.

3. La Laguna del Colorado Chiquito was evidently Kolhu/wala:wa. Sor far as collecting was concerned, these two expeditions to the cave country of Arizona were ill-fated. According to Cushing's later account (see Appendix F), all but six or seven of the items sent to Washington disappeared, and, though a search in the National Museum was instigated a few years ago by T.J. Ferguson, they have still not been found. As to the cached articles, they seem to have been looted by treasure hunters (see Stephen to Cushing, December 15, 1883); at any rate, there is no indication of his having recovered any of these items.

4. In a letter of February 7, 1881, to Powell, Matthews wrote of Cushing, who had recently spent a week with him: "I was very much pleased with him. He seems to be a young man of keen observation and sound judgment . . ." (National Anthropological Archives). Matthews (1843–1905) was considerably Cushing's senior as a field ethnologist at the time of this meeting, having already published several works on the Hidatsa Indians of the Dakotas. On his new assignment in the Southwest, working as always in the interstices of his busy life as an army doctor, he set himself to learning the Navajo language and getting acquainted with the local Navajo community. By the time he met Cushing, he had witnessed part of a curing ceremonial, but for the first several years he concentrated mainly on material culture (see, for example, his articles on Navajo weaving and silverwork), and it was not until October 1884, after Cushing's return to Washington, that he was able to attend and record a full nine-day ceremonial performance (see pp. 327–28 for a letter to Cushing reporting some of his discoveries as the first anthropologist to witness such an event). The

result was Matthews' "Mountain Chant" (1887), a monograph which was to become, in the words of John Bierhorst, "a model for future investigators, establishing Matthews as the father of Navajo studies and one of the pioneer figures of American anthropology" (*Four Masterworks of American Indian Literature* [New York: Farrar, Straus and Giroux, 1974], p. 288). Over the next two decades, Matthews published some hundred or more scholarly pieces. His masterwork, the monumental *Night Chant* (1902), was, like "Mountain Chant," the product of studies commenced in 1884 with the witnessing of a full performance of this curing ceremonial.

In the years after Cushing's stay in Zuni, he and Matthews were associated once again when the latter served for a time on the Hemenway Expedition, caring for Cushing's health and studying the skeletons that were being excavated. They continued to exchange letters on into the years of Matthews' retirement in Washington. The bulk of the known remnants of this correspondence is in the Hodge-Cushing Collection at the Southwest Museum, though a few of the letters are preserved in the collection of Matthews papers at the Wheelwright Museum of the American Indian in Santa Fe. A microfilm edition of this collection, with accompanying Guide prepared by Dr. Katherine Spencer Halpern, has been published (1985) by the University of New Mexico Press. For a study of Matthews' professional life, with bibliography, see Robert Marshall Poor, "Washington Matthews: An Intellectual Biography." Earlier biographical sketches include M.S. Link, "From the Desk of Washington Matthews" (*Journal of American Folkore* 73:317–25); James Mooney, "In Memoriam: Washington Matthews" (*American Anthropologist* 7:514–23); and M.E. Schevill, "Dr. Washington Matthews" (*Kiva* 14:2–6).

5. Bourke (1846–1896) was also Cushing's senior, and, though newer to anthropology as a systematic pursuit, had already collected a considerable body of observation based on his contact with Indians, both Southwest and Plains, by the time he met Cushing. On assignment in Washington the year before, he had also met Powell and other figures in the Bureau of Ethnology. He presently was assigned to work fulltime at ethnological research for the army, and during his tour of the Southwest he visited Zuni twice—once in May while Cushing was away in Arizona and again in November, when he spent two weeks there as Cushing's guest. As the first eyewitness accounts of such affairs, his pamphlet on *The Urine Dance of the Zuni Indians of New Mexico* (1885) and the full-length *The Snake Dance of the Moquis of Arizona* (1884), both drawn from his diaries of the trip, attracted considerable attention both in America and in Europe and established Bourke's reputation in the scientific community.

A prodigious stream of other publications followed in the remaining decade of his life, divided between popular accounts of his experiences on the frontier as an Indian fighter (*An Apache Campaign in the Sierra Madre* [1886], *On the Border with Crook* [1891]) and ethnological studies. The latter studies include *The Scatological Rites of All Nations* (a lengthy compilation published in 1891 and later reissued in a German translation with foreword by Freud), "Medicine Men of the Apache" (*Ninth Annual Report of the Bureau of Ethnology, 1887–1888*), and several dozen articles which appeared in *American Anthropologist*, the *Journal of American Folklore,* and various other journals. The anthropological portions of Bourke's diaries have been assembled, with commentary, in several massive volumes of typescript by General Edwin V. Sutherland ("The Diaries of John Gregory Bourke: Their Anthropological and Folklore Content," Ph.D. dissertation, University of Pennsylvania, 1964; also on file, with the diaries themselves, in the library of the U.S. Military Academy at West Point). A two-part article by Sutherland, "John Gregory Bourke, USMA 1869: Soldier and Student of Indian Folklore," appeared in the USMA publication *Assembly* (23:3 [Fall 1964], 16–19, and 23:4 [Winter 1985], 16–17, 40–45). A more recent study is that of Joseph Charles Porter: "John Gregory Bourke, Victorian Soldier Scientist: The Western Apprenticeship, 1869–1896" (Ph.D. dissertation, University of Texas, 1980).

6. Baxter, who was also responsible for introducing Cushing to the culture circles of Boston, including the wealthy Mrs. Mary Hemenway, was later to serve as home secretary for the southwestern expedition she financed for Cushing. Over the next ten years, he also produced, in addition to his first two pieces on Cushing, some dozen additional articles and a book on his work.

7. The original of this letter has been lost. The text here has been taken from a typed copy apparently made for Powell.

8. The trail south to St. Johns seems to be the one also known as the Colorado River Valley (or Apache) Trail. *Kiatsutama* may be the Zuni name for Ojo Bonito, a ruin which shows on surveyors' maps as about four miles south of the Zuni River and one mile east of the state line.

9. Some of the "plans" (site maps, diagrams, sketches) Cushing mentions as having been enclosed are in the Hodge-Cushing Collection of the Southwest Museum. The itinerary map (printed on p. 141) is among the Cushing papers in the National Anthropological Archives.

10. Punatuma or Panatuma (the former is the Bureau typist's reading of the name given by Cushing, whose handwritten a's and u's are hard to distinguish) was fourth in the series of Pueblo ruins listed by Cushing in his long letter of February 18–April 13, 1880. It has not been identified by later researchers.

11. According to Kintigh:

> This first cave would appear to be in the area just north of modern Lyman Lake Dam. There is an abandoned settlement in this area marked as El Tule. This tends to agree with Spier (1918: 353), who says, "Ruins are said to lie at Tule, Tusas, and San Cosme ten miles above St. Johns in the gorge of the Little Colorado. These include pueblo ruins and caves. Bandelier says that the pottery from one of these is like that at the Showlow Ruin [ca. A.D. 1300]." There are conical hills in this area adjacent to the Little Colorado. However, Cushing would appear to have been six to nine miles almost due south of St. Johns, not southeast as he says. Several of the conical hills marked on the USGS map show a depression or crater (Salado AZ 7.5), but none show a depth of anything like 100 feet, although if the opening were small it would not show (personal communication).

In an entry for April 10, 1883, Bandelier mentions "passing the Tule [and reaching] the beautiful valley of San Jose, or 'Las Tusas,'" where he found a small, partly excavated, and occupied, pueblo. "Nearby there is Cushing's Cave, which contains many interesting things" (Lange and Riley, *The Southwestern Journals of Adolph F. Bandelier* [1970], pp. 76–77).

12. In his list of finds taken from this cave, Cushing mentions "miniature sacrificial bows belonging to the ceremonial of the *I'kwi-na-kya* or Face Blackening of the War Priesthood at New Year" (see Appendix F), a ceremonial perhaps related to the storied victory of the twin war gods over the *Kyana:kwe* and their hero, Chakwena Kachina Woman. In Cushing's version of this story ("Outlines of Zuni Creation Myths," pp. 424–25), the *Kyana:kwe* survivors, "blackened by the fumes of their own war-magic, yet comely and wiser than the common lot of men," were adopted by the Zunis and named *Kwinikwakwe* (Black people). The date of Cushing's descent into the cave would place the ceremonial in question on December 24 or 25. See above, p. 97, for an account of what was evidently this same event the year before (though on that occasion there were four priests instead of two). As to the designation "Priests of the Night," Cushing, in his early piece on "Zuni Social, Mythic, and Religious Systems," identified as "Priests of the Light or Day" the council composed of the chief *A:shiwani* of the six cardinal directions plus the "Priestess of Seed" and the elder brother and younger brother chiefs of the Bow Priesthood. The "Priests of the Night or Darkness," according to this account, were the "minor priests," belonging, like the others, to "those special clans which by heredity furnish the high priesthoods (mainly the Clan of the Parrots [Bikchi:kwe], itself considered consanguineally descended from the gods), and any one of [them] may be chosen [to succeed a deceased] priest of the light by the surviving companions (p. 187).

13. See below, Cushing to Powell, March 27, 1883, for a more specific statement of Cushing's deductions from this important find.

14. Zuni archaeologist T.J. Ferguson speculates that it may have been on account of his handling of these images of Ahayu:da that Cushing was initiated as a Bow Priest or War Chief. "Many Zuni people today believe that the only people who are supposed to touch the Ahayu:da are the War Chiefs or the Clan leaders who make them, and that if anyone else were to touch them, he would need to be initiated as a War Chief, as Cushing was" (personal communication).

15. "It is difficult to say where this second set of caves might be, although given the comment about the table lands 100 feet above, I would guess that they must be below (i.e., north of) Springerville, which is about 25 air miles from St. Johns, either somewhere on the east side of the Richville Valley or next to Lyman Lake in the canyon just above the Richville Valley" (Kintigh, personal communication).

16. *Hle:* board, *wekwe:* kachinas, *otiwa:* dance; hence "Tablet Dance," so called on account of the plaque topping the headdress worn by the female dancers.

17. This is the cave which Cushing in his later account calls the Cave of Oblique Descent. According to Keith Kintigh (personal communication), Cushing's map seems to imply that this cave may be in Scraper Knoll or the adjacent smaller knoll, about eight miles north of Springerville. If so, the very deep cave referred to earlier would be on the east side of Richville Valley.

18. See Appendix F for the more elaborate account of this adventure offered in the later "Extract from Catalogue of Prehistoric Zuni and Cave Remains."

19. What appears to be the map or sketch alluded to here has been preserved in the Southwest Museum Hodge-Cushing Collection, Envelope 205.

20. In one of the Zuni creation myths outlined by Cushing, the Sun Father takes the form of *K'yanas'tipe* (the water skate), extends his feet in all of the directions, and settles down—thus determining the center of the world ("Outlines of Zuni Creation Myths," pp. 428–29). *Wi-ile* is the Bureau typist's reading of Cushing's rendi-

tion, which was perhaps a shortened form of the Zuni word for lightning—given in "Zuni Fetiches" as *Wi-lo-lo-a-ne,* a word expressing the association of lightning with serpents since it derives from the latter's "most obvious trait, its gliding, zigzag motion" (p. 9).

21. These are the shrines adjacent to the sacred lake Kolhu/wala:wa, visited not annually but quadrennially at the time of the summer solstice. In "Zuni Fetiches," his first publication for the Bureau of Ethnology, Cushing describes the lake as:

> a marsh-bordered lagune situated on the eastern shore of the Colorado Chiquito, about fifteen miles north and west from the pueblo of San Juan [St. Johns], Arizona, and nearly opposite the mouth of the Rio Concho. This lagune is probably formed in the basin or crater of some extinct geyser or volcanic spring, as the two high and wonderfully similar mountains on either side are identical in formation with those in which occur the cave-craters farther south on the same river. It has, however, been largely filled in by the *debris* brought down by the Zuni River, which here joins the Colorado Chiquito (pp. 20–21).

22. This could be the cave he learned about from Palowahtiwa the previous December (diary entry for December 7, 1879) as the last stopping place for the turquoise urinator.

23. This was in fact but a beginning; the area is literally dotted with hundreds of caves. Cushing's reference here was to Dr. J. F. Bransford, J. G. Swan, and Paul Schumacker (see George Brown Goode, *The Smithsonian Institution: The History of its First Half-Century* [Washington, 1897], pp. 355–56).

24. Cushing seems to be referring to his efforts to follow the migration route of the Zuni ancestors by examining their "ruin trail."

25. The typescript reads *gradrometer*—probably a slip for *gradiometer,* an instrument used, according to *Webster's Third International Dictionary,* "for measuring the gradient of a physical quantity—as of temperature, the earth's magnetic field, a slope." In this case, what Cushing seems to have had in mind was an instrument for measuring the gradients of slopes, to be used in surveying ruins. Subsequent letters suggest that this and the other surveying instruments were procured and forwarded to Cushing.

26. The "House of the Sun" is the previously mentioned shrine just outside Zuni, used by the Zuni Bekwinne to determine important dates according to the sun's movement. The war god "temples" were probably among those already mentioned on several of the local mesas.

27. Lambert N. Hopkins was the post trader at Fort Wingate during Cushing's tenure in Zuni.

28. It is not clear what these "horrible adventures" may have been, since they are not mentioned in any of Cushing's own surviving letters.

29. Judging by the mention of the "great religious race" and the presence of Dr. Ealy, this note must have been written in the spring either of 1880 or of 1881 (by the time Cushing returned from the East, Ealy had left Zuni). Placement here is based on the possibility that the signing of names was connected with Cushing's census-taking.

30. Later versions of the origin story begun here may be found in Cushing, "Outlines of Zuni Creation Myths"; Stevenson, "The Zuni Indians," pp. 23–61; and Ruth Bunzel, "Zuni Origin Myths," *Forty-Seventh Annual Report of the Bureau of American Ethnology, 1929–1930* (Washington, D.C., 1932), pp. 584–602.

31. Among the Cushing papers in the National Anthropological Archives are the notes for this 1880 census taken by Cushing, an enterprise in which, anticipating Kroeber's study of "Zuni Kin and Clan" (*Anthropological Papers of the American Museum of Natural History,* no. 18, pt. 2 [New York: Trustees of the American Museum of Natural History, 1917]), he tallied some 1,600 individuals by name, clan, fraternity, kiva, civil or religious office, sex, age, farming village, occupation, and residential unit in Zuni itself. It *was* a monumental—and pioneering—enterprise, and, for all his complaining, one that he recognized to be full of significance for his investigation of Zuni social organization. Note the implication in a subsequent letter to Powell that it was his own idea to accompany Powell's census with "one of a gentile, phratral, religious, and architectural bearing." For analysis of this project, see Barbara Holmes, "The Cushing Census of Zuni" (unpublished paper, on file in American Philosophical Society Library). For Cushing enumerations of the Zuni clan and ceremonial organizations, see "My Adventures in Zuni," pp. 28–29 (Green, *Zuni,* pp. 96–97), *Zuni Breadstuff,* pp. 126–27, and "Outlines of Zuni Creation Myths," pp. 367–73 (Green, *Zuni,* pp. 185–93).

32. Here again Cushing uses the term *gentile* (from *gens*) to mean *clan.* The term *phratries,* used here in the standard sense, refers to tribal subdivisions composed of *groups* of associated clans—as, for example, the clan groupings Cushing would discover in Zuni based on the sevenfold directional division. He was here approaching that discovery. At the same time, as indicated by the additional religious and architectural "bearings," he was also coming to recognize a *multiple* scheme of organizational groupings—different *kinds* of phratries, as he would put it in a subsequent letter to Powell—and thus anticipating his various later expositions of the complex

"systems within systems" of Zuni social organization. In terms of its long-range ramifications, he was indeed correct in seeing this census as one of the most important works he had thus far accomplished in Zuni. Of course this branch of research has come a long way since Cushing, with the work of investigators such as A.L. Kroeber ("Zuni Kin and Clan") and others. The most authoritative modern study is still Fred Eggan's *Social Organization of the Western Pueblos* (Chicago and London: University of Chicago Press, 1950).

33. From Sutherland, "The Diaries of John Gregory Bourke," p. 258. Bourke was on his way east after the first of two lengthy tours of the Southwest in 1881.

34. Dr. Harry Crecy Yarrow was a member of the Anthropological Society of Washington and the Smithsonian's expert on exhumed bodies. He had informed Baird earlier of a request he had received from Cushing for a scalp "to be used for a certain ceremony" (May 9, 1881, Smithsonian Institution Archives).

35. Cushing writes here in the course of his second trip to the cave country in the valley of the Little Colorado River. "Camp Waterless" appears to have been a name coined by Cushing himself.

36. Harry Biddle was a young employee at the Smithsonian.

37. The "supernumerary" Cushing had in mind was of course Matilda Stevenson.

38. The ruins referred to appear to be those in the area of what is now Montezuma Castle National Monument and around Montezuma's Well. See Cosmos Mindeleff, "Aboriginal Remains in Verde Valley, Arizona," *Thirteenth Annual Report of the Bureau of American Ethnology, 1891–1892* (Washington, D.C., 1896), pp. 185–261, and Jesse Walter Fewkes, "Archaeological Expedition to Arizona in 1895," *Seventeenth Annual Report of the Bureau of American Ethnology, 1895–1896* (Washington, D.C., 1898), pp. 536–76, for surveys of this area in Cushing's own time.

39. From Sutherland, "Diaries of John Gregory Bourke," pp. 327–29.

40. Earlier in the month, while Cushing was away in Arizona, Bourke had spent several days in Zuni and had filled great stretches of his diary with observations (Sutherland, "Diaries of John Gregory Bourke," pp. 264–99). In the interim between that visit and this, he had been at Fort Defiance studying the Navajos. For a table showing Zuni clan lists made by Cushing, Stevenson, Hodge, and Kroeber, see Alfred Kroeber, "Zuni Kin and Clan," Table 2.

41. Bourke is approximating the Zunis' name for themselves and misapplying its singular form to the Havasupai.

42. Baxter's conflation of Zuni with Aztec seems to reflect an old-standing common notion that the Pueblos were descendants of the ancient Aztecs and that the ruins scattered through the region were the towns the latter people had left behind when they migrated south. Nothing in Cushing's own writings would indicate his responsibility for this journalistic oversimplification.

43. This somewhat extravagant passage prefigures the kind of spell Cushing and his Zunis would cast over the circle of spiritual Bostonians to which Baxter would introduce him (see Lea McChesney and Curtis M. Hinsley, Jr., "Anthropology as Cultural Exchange: The Shared Vision of Mary Hemenway and Frank Cushing" [in Triloki Nath Pandey, ed., *Essays on the Anthropological Career of Frank Hamilton Cushing*]).

44. Baxter is in error about Estevanico, who was killed prior to the Coronado expedition. It was Marcos de Niza whom he accompanied. As to which of the Zuni or Cibola towns it was in which the murder occurred and overlooking which Marcos planted his cross, there has been less agreement. Following Zuni tradition—and the eye-witness testimony of Pedro Pino regarding the cross—Cushing placed these events in Kyaki:ma, whose ruins lie a few miles to the southeast of the present Zuni on the slopes of Dowa Yalanne. Bandelier, who credited Cushing as "the source of all the facts related to the Zuni tribe, other than travel impressions or extracts from more or less ancient writers" (Madeleine T. Rodack, ed., *Adolph Bandelier's The Discovery of New Mexico,* p. 93), agreed with him in this choice of Kyaki:ma as the scene of the first Spanish sighting of "Cibola"—both in his 1886 articles on Friar Marcos and the "Discovery of New Mexico" (Rodack, *Adolph Bandelier's The Discovery of New Mexico,* p. 95) and in his book *The Gilded Man* (p. 159). In an 1895 article, however, and more extendedly in his *History of Hawikuh, New Mexico: One of the So-Called Cities of Cibola* (Los Angeles: Southwest Museum, 1937), Frederick Webb Hodge made a case for this latter pueblo, whose ruins are located to the south of Zuni, near the springs of Ojo Caliente. It is this latter pueblo which is usually named in the subsequent histories not only as the first to have been conquered by the Spanish (about that there is no disagreement) but also as the first pueblo to have been seen by them.

45. Dr. Elliot Coues (1842–1899) served as an army medical officer in the Southwest and later as surgeon and naturalist for the U.S. Geographical and Geological Survey of the Territories. A well-known contemporary of Powell's, and for a time on his staff, Coues was a man whose "enormous, encompassing, encyclopedic learning and crusty energy," made him, according to Wallace Stegner, one of the characteristic figures in the heyday of

Washington science (*Beyond the Hundredth Meridian: John Wesley Powell and the Second Opening of the West,* p. 117).

46. According to Kintigh:

> This mention of fortified and concealed pueblos affords support to the argument above (p. 385 n. 11) for locating Cushing's second series of conical caves next to Lyman Lake and in the canyon just above the Richville Valley. I visited a set of circular basalt ruins along the steep-sided canyon about 3 miles south of this general Lyman Lake area. At this site there were also major crevices that went down into the basalt in a way that may roughly correspond to Cushing's slanting cave idea, and it may be that Cushing is referring here to those round basalt structures, which are indeed unusual, associated with the crevices (personal communication).

Cushing returns to the subject of these lava forts in his discussion of Pueblo architecture in "Outlines of Zuni Creation Myths," p. 358.

47. Cushing's reference is not altogether clear. The *Wo'temthla* (Mixed Kachina Dance) is not an *annual* dance only; it has traditionally been performed at various seasons, as Cushing's own notes indicate.

48. Extracting this passage from Cushing's letter, Baird sent it over to Powell with the following message: "Permit me to call your attention to the enclosed. . . . If the relief he asks for can in any way be furnished, it will be not only of very great importance to the Indians but assist greatly in obtaining the information and materials desired by the National Museum and the Census of 1880" (June 20, 1881, National Anthropological Archives).

49. The obscurity in this reference to "the Navajo matter" seems to be cleared up by a passage in Irving Telling ("New Mexican Frontiers: A Social History of the Gallup Area, 1881–1901," Ph.D. dissertation, Harvard University, 1952). Telling quotes from the Fort Wingate record of "General and Special Orders," an order of June 12, 1881, directing Matthews and Lieut. James Fornance to visit Zuni. The former was to carry out the vaccination mentioned, the latter to consult with the Zuni governor "in relation to the intrusion by Whites and Navajo Indians on their reservation" (p. 119).

50. Cushing's foreboding doubtless stemmed from what might well have been taken by Palowahtiwa as an insult to his hospitality.

51. This last sentence and fragment appear to be Zuni remarks recorded by Cushing.

5. June–December 1881

1. Cushing's "series of notes," largely incorporated into his "Nation of the Willows," provided the first information of this kind available regarding this people. Among later studies, the classic work on the Havasupai is Leslie Spier's "Havasupai Ethnography," *Anthropological Papers of the American Museum of Natural History* 29, part 3 (New York, 1928), pp. 81–392. See also Douglas W. Schwartz, "Havasupai," (Alfonso Ortiz, ed., *Handbook of North American Indians,* vol. 10 (Washington, D.C.: Smithsonian Institution, 1983), pp. 13–24 (including bibliography).

2. Cushing's *Shoi'a* is probably a version of the Zuni place name *Shoya K'yaba'a,* site no. 89 in T.J. Ferguson and E. Richard Hart, *A Zuni Atlas.*

3. These are the villages of the Hopi "First" Mesa, so-called by Americans because on approach from the east it is the mesa first encountered. The village locations reflect social organization, the "mother" settlement, Walpi, being the least accessible and along with its offshoot, Sichomovi, buffered by the village of the immigrant Tewas. The acceptance of the guardian role by the latter was apparently the condition on which they were allowed to settle when they came here at the end of the seventeenth century as refugees of the great Pueblo Revolt. In the period of Cushing's visit, the Hopi villages are said to have had a collective population numbering between 2,100 and 2,500.

4. Pulakakai (some variant spellings: Pulakai, Pulakaia, Pulakaka) was to serve Cushing both on the present expedition and in his later collecting effort at Oraibi, and he is also mentioned (as Tom Pulakakia) in letters to Cushing from Alexander Stephen and Thomas Keam, the local trader. Later Pulakakai's own trading post on the mesa became a center for further settlement and eventually a separate village, named Polacca after its founder.

5. Cushing seems to be in error about the age of Awatovi, a town now generally taken to have been the first visited by the Spanish in the Hopi country. Converted to Christianity, Awatovi became a center for missionary activity. Because of the refusal of its people to renounce the foreign faith in the period following the great Pueblo Revolt of 1680, the village was destroyed by the Oraibians. See J.O. Brew, "Hopi Prehistory and History," *Handbook of North American Indians,* vol. 9, pp. 514–32.

6. Here again Cushing misses a day on the calendar (June 24 was on a Friday) and does not get back on schedule until the entry for Wednesday, July 6.

7. Of the elder Sullivan (John H.), Bourke observed: "the Agent was a very kind-hearted, superannuated gentleman, about seventy years old, honest and well-meaning, but not able to do much physical or mental labour, and, as goes without saying, entirely without

influence over the Indians who he was supposed to manage" (*Snake Dance of the Moquis,* p. 83). For an account of the politics leading to his removal as Agent in November 1881, see Stephen C. McCluskey, "Evangelists, Educators, Ethnographers, and the Establishment of the Hopi Reservation" (*Journal of Arizona History* 21 [1980], 363–90). According to McCluskey, the son, Jeremiah Sullivan, had been acting as agency physician, though without official permission. Staying on to live among the Hopis after the departure of his father, Jeremiah was later to be described by Cushing as a man who had emulated his own approach to ethnological study but who had "degenerated into a 'squaw man'" (*San Francisco Examiner,* July 8, 1888). No doubt it was suspicion of some such development which prompted an inspector in the U.S. Indian Service to complain in the same breath about Dr. Sullivan's conduct among the Hopis and Cushing's own "reputation for licentiousness" among the Zunis (see Howard to Powell, December 26, 1882). According to McCluskey, a principal motive for the establishment of a reservation for the Hopis in 1882 was to provide the government with a basis for ordering Sullivan out of it. Nevertheless, he seems to have held out until at least 1888, judging by McCluskey's assemblage of references to him by persons such as Elsie Clews Parsons, Herman ten Kate, and Alexander Stephen, who encountered him there.

8. The Indian Agency was located in Keam's Canyon, named for (or by) Thomas Keam, who had established his trading post there in 1875. Frank McNitt identifies a "Prof." Stevenson as the Bureau's Col. James Stevenson (*The Indian Traders,* pp. 172 and *passim*). Cushing's mention of "prospector fame," however, suggests that both he and McNitt's source were referring to someone else, whose name neither of them had quite caught—Keam's friend Alexander MacGregor Stephen. A Scot with a degree in mineralogy from the University of Edinburgh (hence "Prof."), Stephen (1850?–1894) had migrated to the Southwest in 1860 to pursue his fortune as a prospector—though his real calling, as it turned out, was to mine not in the ground but in the cultural life of the Indians.

9. Cushing says in "The Need of Studying the Indian in Order to Teach Him":

> If in place of the second or third rate men who too often receive appointment as Indian teachers we could select and send forth among the Indians only men of high ability and talent, men of true and strong feeling for humanity, and possessed of large understanding of human nature, . . . it would be well (pp. 109–10).

Judging by the cases reported in the present collection, Cushing's experience with missionary teachers seems to have been quite consistent.

10. Originally mistaken for a Mormon, Cushing was received more cordially when his true identity was established.

11. Passages like this one and several others to follow lend perspective to the story told in books with titles such as *Mormon Settlement in Arizona: A Record of Peaceful Conquest of the Desert* (by James H. McClintock). Each of the white groups who came to win the hearts and minds—and lands—of the Indians had its own style. Here, filtered through Cushing's hostility and that of the chiefs, we glimpse the Mormon style. Apparently, it was largely as a deterrent to Mormon (as well as Navajo) expansion that reservation boundaries for "the Hopis and other Indians" in the area were established in 1882. A number of later passages, however, reflect a somewhat more positive Oraibian view of the Mormons—as supporters of the Indians in opposition to the "Washington" Americans.

12. In response to a query as to whether "Mo-e-na-ka-ve" was Cushing's approximation for Moenkopi, the Hopi village in the valley west of Third Mesa, anthropology professor Emory Sekaquaptewa writes:

> If the place was Moenkopi, the sheepherder Cushing mentions in his account would have had to travel nearly fifty miles to visit and somehow carry the sheep over that distance. It seems more plausible to consider the route of the journey directly from the main villages (especially Oraibi) to the San Francisco Peaks, which would take the party through the sand dunes and the red sandstone cliffs and terraces that make up the terrain around the area now referred to as Sands Springs. The southern escarpment of Ward Terrace seems to be the area described in the account of the following day as the "sublime series of terraces" overlooking the painted desert and the Little Colorado River. The Dennibito Wash that cuts the valley on the west side of Third Mesa drains into the Little Colorado. Along this wash at the point of Sands Springs, the water springs from the floor of the channel and forms a small stream. This place is referred to by the Hopi as Munaqvi (place of the running water). I believe the term Mo-e-na-ka-ve in the account refers to this place, which is at most twelve miles from Oraibi and perhaps much less than that from a nearby Hopi sheep camp. This hypothesis is also supported by the placement of a spring encountered by Cushing in the same area. This spring, known as Vulva Spring, or Löwava (Hopi), is located on the southern escarpment of Ward Terrace and in the general area of Sands Springs (personal communication).

13. According to Emory Sekaquaptewa:

The name *Ka-winh-pe* appears phonetically similar to *Quawinpi,* which is the Hopi term referring to the area of present-day Gray Mountain. Gray Mountain falls in line with the route that I surmise was the travel route direct from Third Mesa to Havasupai. There are many oral accounts of trading journeys between the Hopi and Supai (the Hopi term for whom is *Koonina*), and these accounts talk about *Kooninyö* (Supai Trail). My guess is that Cushing's party was guided along this old established trail (personal communication).

14. *Malpais:* Spanish for "badland"; a term applied to mesas, lomas, or any more elevated plateau formed by igneous rock.

15. In his *Atlantic Monthly* account of this part of the journey, Cushing tells of having twice had to lay hand on his pistol to prevent his Indian companions from exhausting what water was left in the group canteen ("The Nation of the Willows," *Atlantic Monthly* 50 [1892]: 370–71). Given the absence of this detail in his journal and its incongruity with the personal relationships as reported there, it may be that this is another instance of a good story "improved" in being told for a popular audience. Oddly enough, the situation at this point seems considerably less desperate than on the trip ahead from Havasupai to Fort Whipple.

16. At various points in his Havasupai journal Cushing refers to this sketchbook and to "special notes" he was keeping. The former has not been found. What remains of the latter is in the Southwest Museum Hodge-Cushing Collection, envelope 213.

17. In "The Nation of the Willows," Cushing writes that, crossing a river and riding up the opposite bank on the way into the village, he and his friends

> were greeted by a waiting crowd of men, women, and children, who were gathered around two or three huts in front of a little sweat-house, closely covered with blankets. From out this primitive Turkish bath, heedless of the excited gestures of the presiding medicine men, issued in a cloud of steam a real American, red as a lobster, and half blinded by the steaming he had just passed through. . . . This exile proved to be a prospector named Harvey Sample . . . (p. 374).

18. In "The Nation of the Willows" this terse reference is amplified considerably. Pulakakai had traded, apparently to advantage, a "jade" (meaning, evidently, a worn-out horse rather than a precious stone), and his Havasupai counterpart wanted to cancel the exchange. Cushing, however, having "made a rule, in the first council, that any trade sealed by the customary handshake and '*a-ha-ni-ga,*' or 'thanks,' should be regarded as final," refused to permit this accommodation. The result, at least as he reported it in the *Atlantic,* was a confrontation in which he stood off a crowd of angry Indians, again making a show of his pistol (pp. 554–55).

19. Agasha: a settlement in the reservation of the Walapai, or Hualapai, Indians, a Yuman-speaking group with close cultural affinities to the Havasupai and Yavapai. Their population in 1882, following a period of war and epidemic, was counted at 667 (Thomas R. McGuire, "Walapai," *Handbook of North American Indians,* vol. 10, p. 25).

20. In the language of the Southwest, the word "tank," derived from the Spanish *tanque,* is used to denote a pool or spring.

21. The name is probably descriptive, referring to peach trees said to have sprung from some peach pits planted by a Mormon child sometime in the 1850s. Peach Springs is on the route followed not only by the Mormons but by Edward Beale and others and by the railroad line that resulted from their surveys.

22. In 1857–59 Lieut. Edward F. Beale laid out for the War Department a road from Albuquerque, via Zuni, to California. Beale's journal (1858) is also one of the early American sources on the Zuni country. The site here mentioned, which shows on old Land Office maps as "Collins Wells" or "Cullins Wells," northwest of Floyd's Butte (Mt. Floyd on current maps), was discovered by the Beale expedition in 1859 and named for F. C. Kerlin, Beale's clerk (Barnes 1960, p. 75). How Cushing could have arrived at this place by traveling *southwest* is not at all clear. If he did, he must have crossed, instead of following, Beale's Road and gone far out of his way, since Kerlin's Wells lay to the *northeast* of Peach Springs.

23. The location of Cushing's "Wickiup" is uncertain. It is not, however, the same as that shown on modern road maps.

24. According to Barnes (*Arizona Place Names,* pp. 84, 91), Charles Thomas Rogers had moved to this area from Maine in 1877 and established a ranch in what is now called Williams, after William Sherley Williams, a local mountain man. However, the Roger's Ranch referred to here was located not in Williams but due south of the present town of Seligman about half way between Kerlin's Wells and Prescott.

25. The name "Chino" derives from the Spanish word for curly hair. The valley was so named by Whipple for the abundant grama grass, called "de china" by local Mexicans (Barnes, p. 361). What Cushing called the Little Chino Valley shows on old maps simply as Chino Valley, slightly to the southwest of the town of Seligman. Passing along this valley in a southeasterly direction, he would enter the valley which shows on modern maps as

Big Chino Valley and thence into Williamson's Valley (referred to here as William's Valley).

26. Garfield had been shot on July 2, 1881, by a disappointed office-seeker. Powell's former employee and Cushing's friend Joseph Stanley-Brown had moved on to become Garfield's private secretary. Later he would return to Powell's service.

27. Camp Walapai was an army garrison assigned for supervision of the local Indians. Fort Verde, another military establishment in the locality, was vacated by the army and turned over to the Interior Department in 1884 (Barnes, *Arizona Place Names,* p. 361).

28. According to Barnes (*Arizona Place Names,* 1935, p. 62), a Paul Breon was postmaster in 1877 in a settlement called Mohave City, located on what is now the Fort Mohave Indian Reservation. Perhaps he had moved.

29. Thomas Moran (1837–1926) is chiefly known for his large panoramic paintings of the West—scenes such as "The Grand Canyon of the Yellowstone" and "The Chasm of the Colorado" (the latter bought by the government and hung in the Capitol building).

30. Reference is made later to "grave charges" made by Cushing "concerning the former missionary," without explanation of what these "grave charges" were (see Cushing to Baird, December 4, 1881). Despite various social calls and invitations to dinner, relations between Cushing and Ealy had always been uneven (beginning with the "misunderstanding" over the supplies left in Zuni by Col. Stevenson). In December 1880 and again in June 1881, Ealy had written to the Indian agent in Santa Fe complaining respectively "about Mr. Cushing & the Indians charging travelers for water" and about "F. Cushing interfering with school & certain other matters" (Pueblo Indian Agency Registry of Letters Received, Denver Federal Records Center). Now this.

31. Samuel A. Bentley was one of those "ignorant, bold and impudent missionaries" referred to later by Bourke as such parasites on the Indians; he would prove even more troublesome to Cushing than his predecessor.

32. "Probably the best known Thumb Butte in Arizona [of several landmarks with that name] is that which looms like a gigantic hand doubled into a fist, thumb slightly bent, behind the city of Prescott" (Barnes, *Arizona Place Names,* p. 172). In light of Cushing's identification of the symbols as Zuni, one may be reminded, as was Jane Young (personal communication), of the petroglyphs and painted images on the rocks above the ruins of the Village of the Great Kivas at Zuni. "Cushing's words remind me," she writes, "of two adjacent rock faces which contain the following: a crescent moon, a four-pointed star, a zigzag (Zunis identified as lightning), an owl, a corn plant, 2 spirals, a turtle, and a deer with oddly elongated antlers." A photograph of this site appears in her book *Signs from the Ancestors: Zuni Cultural Symbolism and Perceptions of Rock Art* (Albuquerque: University of New Mexico Press, 1988).

33. Cushing refers here to Galen Eastman, U.S. Agent for the Navajos, whose later (second) removal Baxter commended as "a good stroke of business, for more than once the Navajos have been on the verge of taking the war path in consequence of his swindling operations . . ." (*Boston Herald,* December 11, 1882). Bourke, too, came to know of Eastman on his visit to the Hopi country. "This Eastman," he wrote in his diary:

> had *on paper* a boarding school for Indian children, of which he wrote glorious accounts to the Sabbath-school papers and which I visited. It consisted of one miserable squalid dark and musty adobe dungeon, not much more capacious than the cubby hole of an oyster schooner; it was about 12 × 10 × 7 in height. No light ever penetrated, but one window let darkness out from this den and one small door gave exit to some of the mustiness; Eastman reported that he had accommodations for *sixty children,* but I saw only nine (9) cottonwood bunks, in which, if he had made them double up, eighteen little children could be made wretched" (Lansing B. Bloom, ed., "Bourke on the Southwest," *New Mexico Historical Review* 11 [1936], p. 85).

"This Eastman," whom Bourke also refers to as a "psalm-singing hypocrite" (ibid., p. 81), would later have much to say on the subject of Navajo horses shot by Cushing.

34. Prof. J. Howard Gore, a member of the Anthropological Society of Washington, was to make a presentation at the November 15, 1881, meeting of that organization on the "regulative system of the Zunis" ("Transactions, February 1879–January 1882," pp. 86–87, Smithsonian *Miscellaneous Collections,* Vol. 25 [Washington, 1883]). Evidently, he was on his way to collect the facts. Victor Mindeleff, a young member of the Bureau staff and future friend of Cushing's, had been assigned to assist Stevenson on his third collecting expedition in the Southwest.

35. This project, to be completed by Victor Mindeleff, was initiated by Powell as a preliminary to a series of studies aimed at tracing the development of architecture in relation to environment—that is, demonstrating the evolution of Pueblo architecture as an indigenous response to local resources and circumstances rather than as an import from the south. The model was built (it is still preserved in the Smithsonian), and five years later Victor Mindeleff completed similar surveys of the Hopi villages, preparatory for his "A Study of Pueblo Architecture:

Tusayan and Cibola" (*Eighth Annual Report of the Bureau of Ethnology, 1886–1887* [Washington, D.C., 1891], pp. 3–228).

36. The letter to which Matthews refers appeared in the July 28, 1881, issue of the *Nation.* Coues did have one good observation—that in pronunciation the final syllables of Havasupai words were often unvoiced. Hence "Havasu" or "Yavasu," from which it was only a step to "Agua su" or "Agua azul." So much for speculative inference.

37. Thomas Moran's "Mountain of the Holy Cross," based on studies made in the Colorado country in 1874, had been awarded a medal at the 1876 Centennial Exposition in Philadelphia. His younger brother Peter Moran (1841–1914), also a painter, accompanied Bourke on his tour of the Hopi country.

38. Cushing refers here to a piece in the Chicago *Times* of June 14, 1881, which carried an interview with Bourke. The latter had characterized Cushing as "not an outcast from his own race, but a gentleman in every sense of the word—a scholar of fine scientific acquirements, an artist of no insignificant merit, and possessed withal of youth, good looks, and refined manner"—and so on.

39. As reflected in the mythical account of their original appointment by the twin war gods, the Priests of the Bow were, in Kroeber's words: "the soldiers, as it were, who enforce[d] the decrees of the paramount theocracy" and guarded the public rituals ("Zuni," in James Hastings, ed., *Encyclopaedia of Religion and Ethics* [New York: Charles Scribner's Sons, 1922], vol. 12, p. 871). In earlier times, when the Zunis carried on warfare with various neighboring tribal groups, it was chiefly the Bow Priests who led the war parties—a function still needed in Cushing's day, though redirected to defense against horse thieves and poachers on Zuni pasturage. Traditionally, "membership in the Bow Priesthood was through killing an enemy, and it was mandatory for any warrior who had taken scalps to join the priesthood because it was the only escape from vengeance from the malevolent magic with which the enemy was supposedly endowed" (Triloki Nath Pandey, "Factionalism in a Southwestern Pueblo," p. 94). Beyond that, according to Ruth Bunzel, the initiation served to develop the dead enemy's capacities as a rainmaker, as well as to "celebrate fittingly with all manner of festivity" his destruction ("Introduction to Zuni Ceremonialism," p. 527). See also ibid., pp. 674–85; Parsons, *Pueblo Indian Religion,* pp. 622–44; and Stevenson, "The Zuni Indians," pp. 578–608, for descriptions of the scalp dance and initiation into the Bow Priesthood.

40. Prior to the establishment of the railway station at Holbrook there was a little community two miles to the east. In 1871 Juan Padilla established a saloon there, which, after a short time, was placed in the charge of one Barado Frayde. "Since Frayde used only his first name, the place soon came to be known as Berado's. . . . Berado's Station was the main crossing point for travelers to the south" (Barnes, *Arizona Place Names,* p. 240). The engagement reported from this stopping place seems to have been the windfall from which Cushing harvested his Apache scalp—details left unspecified.

41. In a later manuscript Cushing would write:

> My researches at Zuni relative to the thirteen secret or tabu societies of shamans or proto-priests, and my membership in the most privileged of them, that of war or the Bow, enables me to determine that they were not only associations of medicine men, but also that they were so systematically adjusted to the tribal sociologic organization as to constitute an essential part of it; and were so elaborately and consistently regulated according to the whole vast body of mythic lore, of which they were the chief repositories, that they constituted veritably the schools of philosophy and culture of this people; were, in other words, true cult societies. This confirmed the opinion of Major Powell regarding similar organizations among the ruder Shoshonean tribes of the Colorado and the recent researches of Mooney, Matthews, Bourke and Bandelier in the South and Southwest, of Dorsey, Miss Fletcher, and Hoffman in the North, and of Boas in the far Northwest—[and] established the fact that such cult societies of proto-priests as those of the Zunis are practically universal with tribes of primitive man occupying the same status as that of all North American Indians . . . ("Medicine Men or Cult Societies," Southwest Museum, HC 225).

42. No record survives of the expedition from Fort Whipple to the Mesa Verde "cliff ruins, graves, etc. etc." projected in Cushing's July 17 diary entry and, judging by this reference, accomplished before his return to Zuni—probably en route.

43. Given the timing of Cushing's return with the Apache scalp, the two festivals celebrated by the Bow Priesthood—the scalp ceremonial or initiation and the *Owinahaiye* harvest/war dance—may have been partially combined in this year.

44. Among the papers of the Bureau of Indian Affairs is a letter of August 8, 1881, to Pueblo agent Thomas from Dr. Ealy, the Presbyterian Missionary schoolmaster and sub-agent in Zuni reporting that Sol Barth—a man referred to by the agent himself in another letter as "a notorious rascal"—had bought some Zuni oxen but never paid for them (National Archives, Denver Federal Center, Records of the BIA, Pueblo Indian Agency). Perhaps the "Solomon Barth matter" had to do with this instance of rascality.

45. That is, to establish his Zuni identity (in principle) on the maternal side he was made a *Bikchi:kwe* (a clan name translated by Cushing as Parrot-Macaw), and on the paternal side he was designated (as would a young Zuni have been) as "child" of another clan, in his case that of the Eagles. The title "Junior Priest of the Bow" is not to be confused with that of Younger Brother Bow Chief, held by Kiasi; it indicates rather Cushing's status as a novice in the order.

46. Cushing somewhat underestimates here. Throughout the months in question, as Parsons' ceremonial calendar illustrates, there is considerable ritual activity, including a series of fraternity initiations, prayer-stick plantings, retreats—and much kachina dancing: "A few weeks after winter solstice ceremonial, during a period of five or six weeks, each of the six Zuni kivas presents a dance, . . . ," some of which might be done as night dances (Parsons, *Pueblo Indian Religion,* pp. 520–26, 737–43; see also Bunzel, "Introduction to Zuni Ceremonialism," pp. 534–40).

47. Cushing's title may be translated as "Great Chief of the Zunis."

48. This account has not turned up.

49. Baxter was working on "The Father of the Pueblos"—a title whose reference is to Zuni—the "parent," as he believed, of Pueblo culture.

50. For a version of this "tale of blood" (evidently a complete fabrication) and a later Cushing description of his initiation, see Green, *Zuni,* pp. 153–56.

51. *Kia-pin-a-ho-i:* Literally, "the raw beings," a term applied both to animals and to the supernaturals, as opposed to "cooked" or "finished" Zuni *people.* For Cushing's exposition of this differentiation and the "great system of all-conscious and interrelated life" to which it belonged—one of his clearest adumbrations of modern structuralist thinking—see his "Zuni Fetiches."

52. Martha LeBaron (Mrs. Francis Delano) Goddard was one of the wealthy "ladies of Boston" recruited by Baxter on Cushing's behalf.

53. "Head chief" refers to Palowahtiwa; the "high priest" was Naiiutchi, Elder Brother Chief of the Bow Priests. Despite whatever "force and violence" Cushing may earlier have visited on one of the chief priests of the Bow Society, Naiiutchi was to take a special interest in Cushing and his education as a member of this order. He would later also be a principal ally and informant of Matilda Stevenson's.

54. *Third Annual Report of the Bureau of Ethnology,* p. xx.

55. *Ibid,* p. xxi; Stevenson to Pilling, November 10, 1881 (National Anthropological Archives). According to the same reports, Stevenson collected another 3,000 items, amounting to 12,000 pounds, in the Hopi villages. Given the wagonloads hauled away during this and other Bureau collecting efforts, it is a wonder there was anything left for the Indians themselves, let alone "visitors and speculators."

56. Stevenson to Pilling, November 10, 1881, National Anthropological Archives. The illustrations themselves, many in full color and quite beautiful (particularly those of the pottery items), were among the first accurate ones ever published of Zuni artifacts.

57. Bourke had been in Zuni a few days the previous May while Cushing was at work in the cave country of eastern Arizona and again early in September following his witness of the Hopi Snake Dance. Since October 10, when Cushing had met him at Fort Wingate, Bourke had been completing his "round of the Pueblos of Arizona and New Mexico." Back at Fort Wingate on November 15, he had been given authority to spend the rest of the month in Zuni and to hire Pedro Pino for that period as his interpreter.

58. See Cushing's "Zuni Fetiches" for a pioneer exposition of the myths and beliefs associated with such "idols."

59. Interrogating Pedro Pino the following day, Bourke was told much the same thing, though assured that the practice was no longer observed.

60. Cushing several times wrote in concrete and specific terms about customs of this sort. The fact that he invariably did so in nonjudgmental terms is one of the characteristics differentiating him from most of his contemporaries, including Bourke.

61. In this group of Zuni headmen, no. 3 and no. 6 (the latter being Cushing's adoptive father) were members of the council of chief priests. No. 8, who later served a term as governor, was the teller of most of the stories translated by Cushing in *Zuni Folk Tales.* As principal figures on the Zuni scene, most of these men appear more than once in the present collection. Nos. 1, 2, 5, and 6 were to accompany Cushing on the trip east. Nos. 2, 4, and 5 were also to serve as informants to Stevenson ("The Zuni Indians," p. 20).

62. Bourke refers here to the agreement binding the United States and Zuni under the terms of the Treaty of Guadalupe Hidalgo ending the Mexican-American War. Among its stipulations is one guaranteeing that the Zunis would be "protected in the full management of all their rights of Private Property and Religion. By the authorities, civil and military, of New Mexico and the United States" (Articles of Convention, and Orders No. 41). Pedro Pino's copy of this agreement is preserved in

the Hodge-Cushing Collection of the Southwest Museum (envelope 2—one of several holding the Pino papers, spoken of by Bourke in this same passage as "of the utmost value and great interest"). Bourke was mistaken, however, about the name of the U.S. signatory. The name on the document is that of Lieut. Col. Henderson P. Boyakin.

63. The syntax here is unclear, but what Bourke has in mind as outside the law seems to be not the agent for the Pueblos collectively but the office of local or subagent for *Zuni* Pueblo, an office which seems to have been regularly assigned by the general Pueblo agent in Santa Fe to whoever was serving in Zuni as missionary schoolteacher.

64. Said to be no longer existent, the *Tulushtulu* were a group within the *Newekwe.* The rite mentioned here is reminiscent of that performed in the harvest war dance described earlier by Cushing. A number of "charters" for human sacrifice may be found in Zuni mythology, beginning with the story of the flood which rose near to the top of Dowa Yalanne and was stayed only by the sacrificing of a young boy and girl, who were tossed over the side. There was also what Parsons (*Pueblo Indian Religion,* p. 621) called a rite of "exorcism" and what Cushing called "the killing of a Navajo" (in the form of a dog) at the close of the harvest war dance (see his diary account above). Whatever the practices in Zuni may have been at the time Bourke was writing this note, Matilda Stevenson produced headlines thirty-two years later when she reported in 1913 that in Tewa women and children were still being sacrificed for rain.

65. This terse announcement seems to imply that Bourke had witnessed the execution. If so, Cushing must all the more certainly have done likewise as a member of the Bow Priesthood, the group which was charged with responsibility in such matters.

66. Though a Hopi, Nanahe was the husband of a Zuni woman and resided in Zuni.

67. In the printed version of this speech the speaker is identified as Nanahe himself, rather than, as would appear here, Naiiutchi (John Gregory Bourke, *Snake Dance of the Moquis,* pp. 183–84). Whoever the speaker, the statement—which seems to have provided a model for Cushing's own later line of reasoning on the question of secrecy—has been cited several times by subsequent writers (e.g., Byron Harvey, "An Overview of Pueblo Religion," in Ortiz, ed., *New Perspectives on the Pueblos,* p. 207) as characterizing what differentiates the medicine man from the witch in Pueblo thinking. "Motive is the key term," and unlike the secret order, which exists, as Nanahe says, for the benefit of everyone, "the witch benefits only himself" (ibid., p. 207).

68. Bourke had noted earlier in connection with the performance by the *Koyemcis* that

> the expression "make moccasins" [i.e., for the woman] refers back to the pristine Etiquette of this singular race, by which code, the acceptance of moccasins by a woman was the emphatic, even if silent, expression of her submission to the donor's carnal desires. These interpretations are not fanciful; the language of the first six speakers was vulgar to a degree, leaving nothing to be inferred or conjectured by the audience" (Edwin V. Sutherland, "The Diaries of John Gregory Bourke," pp. 919–20).

Other than in this last particular, the Zuni moccasin differs not much from the European slipper of Cinderella. If the shoe fits . . .

69. *Cobija:* Spanish for cover or blanket.

70. Bourke's assertion regarding Cushing's morality may have been prompted by the latter's own concern over rumors of scandalous behavior on his part—rumors of which he seems to have been the object from the beginning of his stay in Zuni until the end (e.g., see Cushing to Baird 14 December 1879, Howard to Powell 26 December 1882, and *Inter-Ocean* story of 2 May 1883). *Not* in question, of course, was the morality of "throwing dust in the eyes" of the natives. Had the deceptions practiced by Cushing upon his native brothers prompted any reflection on Bourke's part, he would doubtless have justified them, as did Baxter ("F. H. Cushing at Zuni," p. 56) and other spokesmen for ethnological progress in that period, on the grounds that they were harmless and in the interest of science.

71. The *Shalak'o* figures were departing from Zuni on their return journey to Kachina Village.

72. *Festina lente:* Make haste slowly; take it easy.

73. The subject of various communications over the next two years, the rebellion of Roman or Ramon Luna, later known as "Mormon" or "Muma," was an early instance of the dissension and factionalism notable in Zuni history down to the present (see Pandey, "Factionalism in a Southwestern Pueblo"). Luna would gain adherents, and in later years would himself serve a term as governor.

74. Note that Bourke's reasoning in his support of the authority of the established tribal leaders is the same as that of the Pueblo agent in his effort, mentioned earlier, to "establish obedience to officers." The point was not to promote "conservatives" over "progressives" but to support "Caciques who were (or were *supposed* to be) the Great Father's children"—that is, who were themselves committed to obedience.

75. *Inferno,* Canto 1, lines 22–27. The passages from Bourke's Diary, volumes 54–57, are excerpted from Suth-

erland, "The Diaries of John Gregory Bourke," pp. 874–1006.

76. This was the ruling council elsewhere identified by Cushing as the Priesthood of "the House" or "the Temple."

77. Bureau of Indian Affairs records show receipt of a letter of November 29, 1881, to Agent Thomas reporting the "arrest of Indian Roman Luna" (Register of Letters Received, 1881–1883, Denver Federal Center, Records of BIA, Pueblo Indian Agency). This was a matter in which Cushing, by *his* account (see letter of December 4 below) had a rather more active role than seems to be indicated in Bourke's account. Each narrator is the hero of his own tale.

78. Pablito seems to have been the Spanish name of Cushing's adoptive father, *Laiiuahtsailunkia.*

79. At the close of the *Shalak'o* festival, the *Koyemci,* along with the rest of the Kachinas, pay their annual visit to Shiba:bulima, the home of the beast gods and the place where the Zunis originally "emerged" into the world. Cushing refers here to preparations for the ceremonial associated with that ritual journey. This is also the ceremony marking the end of the *Koyemci* impersonators' year of service in that role; hence the communal gifts of meal and meat—the "tythes" mentioned in the entry following (see also Stevenson, "The Zuni Indians," pp. 273–77, and Parsons, *Pueblo Indian Religion,* pp. 755–56).

80. Chief of the masked kachina gods, *Pau'tiwa,* according to Bunzel, is

> one of the most impressive of Zuni impersonations. . . . In folk tales Pau'tiwa displays the most honored of Zuni virtues, dignity, kindliness and generosity, and also beauty. He has many love affairs with mortal maids, whom he rewards richly, and he is unfailingly generous to his mortal children. In tales it is always to Pau'tiwa that the Zunis appeal when in trouble" ("Introduction to Zuni Ceremonialism," pp. 521, 909).

One of the origin stories in which Pau'tiwa figures concerns the flight and return of the Corn Maidens, on whom the Zunis depended for their food, a story whose dramatic reenactment has a regular place in the Zuni ritual calendar. Each year on the last day of *Shalak'o,* when all the kachinas have gone east on their visit to Shiba:bulima, Pau'tiwa brings back to Zuni the Corn Maidens who had left them and run away to the village of the kachinas. He carries with him a gourd of water from the sacred lake, so that the Zunis "may have good luck with the summer rains" (ibid., p. 917). Accompanying him on this occasion as his *wo'we,* or attendant, is the original *Newekwe,* Bitsitsi ("Whistle," another name for Paiyatuma, the flute god). Hence Cushing's *he-we* in this paragraph is probably a slip of the pen for *wo-we.* For Cushing renditions of the Corn Maiden story (the hero of which in these versions is not Pau'tiwa but Paiyatuma), see *Zuni Breadstuff,* pp. 41–54 (Green, *Zuni,* pp. 356–62), and "Outlines of Zuni Creation Myths," pp. 431–47.

81. The *Wotem'thla* (Mixed Kachina) and *Muluktakya* dances are part of the traditional observances at this time. The "Apache Dance," in Zuni as in Hopi towns, is a purely social or secular dance, performed for entertainment.

82. According to Frank McNitt, Juan Lorenzo Hubbell was one of the two most powerful traders in the Southwest (along with Thomas Keam). By this time, he had posts for trade with the Navajos at Cornfields, Arizona (about ten miles southwest of Ganado), and at several other nearby locations in Arizona (McNitt, *The Indian Traders,* pp. 200–24, 282).

83. *Kâ'-kâ a-wi-a:* An abbreviation of *Kâ'-kâ a-we-kia,* "the coming of the Kachinas."

84. Unfortunately, the notes mentioned here have not turned up. Presumably, they would have given a fuller description of the ceremonies of the day, whose names, *Ko'ane* and *Molawia,* are translated by Parsons as "Kachina go" and "Melons come" (*Pueblo Indian Religion,* p. 531; see also Bunzel, "Zuni Katcinas," pp. 854–56)—the latter name deriving from the watermelons borne on the heads of the Corn Maiden figures on their "return" to Zuni. In this second rite, as in the myth associated with it, the *Newekwe* play a prominent role. In most versions of the myth of the Corn Maidens, it is Bitsitsi-Paiyatuma (original founder of the order) who tracks down the missing Maidens and, with Pau'tiwa, accompanies them back to Zuni (Stevenson, "The Zuni Indians," pp. 51–57; Bunzel, "Zuni Katcinas, pp. 914–19). See Stevenson, "The Zuni Indians," pp. 277–83, for a detailed account of the *Molawia,* among whose features, following the arrival of the Corn Maidens, is a sunset procession, led by the rhombus-whirling elder brother Bow Priest, to the shrine symbolizing the center of the world, where the jug brought by Pau'tiwa is emptied into one of the rain vases. The other features mentioned by Cushing likewise seem to have been standard—including the general merriment at the close of the ceremonies. The "*Cha-we*" referred to were evidently the same figures Cushing describes in *Zuni Breadstuff* as "strange mendicants disguised as saurian monsters" who go about collecting contributions of *hewe* and other food (pp. 624–26; Green, *Zuni,* pp. 325–26).

85. In accordance with the ubiquitous divisional system, there are six Ahayu:da figures, each of a color associated with one of the six directions.

86. The prayer anticipates a ceremonial to be con-

ducted by the Bow Priesthood several days hence. The work of the *A:shiwani* being to fast and pray, it used to be customary—and still was in Cushing's time—for corn and wood to be provided for them. This was the "good share" referred to in an earlier letter.

87. A later reference identifies Niesto as a "former high priest" (i.e., elder brother priest) of the Order of the Bow.

88. Hanthlibinkya, southwest of Witchwells, Arizona (site 10 in Ferguson and Hart, *A Zuni Atlas*), figures in Zuni tradition as the point of origin both of the twin war gods and of the Zuni division into clans (see Cushing, "Outlines of Zuni Creation Myths," pp. 415–27, and Stevenson, "The Zuni Indians," pp. 40–43). First stop in the renewed wanderings of the Zuni ancestors forth from Kolhu/wala:wa in search for the middle of the world, it was their base in the conflict with the *Kyana:kwe* kachinas (here called *Kia-kwe-na*) of nearby Kyama:kya. Niesto's story as here written down is the first version of this segment of the Zuni origin myth to be recorded. Later variants may be found in Stevenson, "The Zuni Indians" (pp. 34–38); Bunzel, "Zuni Origin Myths" (pp. 597–600); and Parsons, *Pueblo Indian Religion* (pp. 223–26); as well as in Cushing's own "Outlines of Zuni Creation Myths" (pp. 424–25).

89. Eleven years later, in a diary entry for November 23, 1892, Cushing recorded his rediscovery of this account, which he found so good that he determined to begin working his Zuni journals into a book. "I wonder at having forgotten so much and am delighted with the interest of these early writings and experience records. Shall do a little at them every day if I can." Unfortunately, other projects claimed priority.

90. For an account of a "lawsuit" evidently brought about by this act, see *Zuni Breadstuff,* pp. 134–51. It is not clear, however, when this lawsuit would have occurred amid the events as narrated here.

91. Cushing evidently refers here to his attempt, a year and half earlier, to interfere in the execution of an accused witch.

92. This is probably an overly ego-centered explanation. The ceremonial was that performed by the *Newekwe,* and as observed in Bourke's account, Bentley had left when the urine was brought in.

93. What these "grave charges" were is not known.

94. This is one of several cases in which old Pedro Pino seems to have been the source of negative allegations about Cushing (see, e.g., Sylvester Baxter, "The Tenacity of Indian Customs," p. 196). Perhaps the old man was prompted by the same resentment he apparently expressed to Bourke when the latter, whom Pino seems to have regarded as *his* friend, turned to anyone else for information (Sutherland, "The Diaries of John Gregory Bourke," p. 957). In the case of Cushing, Pedro Pino suffered altogether too much competition for his attention.

95. Cushing was referring here to the earlier mentioned agreement, signed by Pedro Pino and Lieut. Col. Boyakin, binding Zuni and the United States under the terms of the Treaty of Guadalupe Hidalgo. For a review of such formal agreements with the Zunis, see E. Richard Hart, "Boundaries of Zuni Land: With Emphasis on Details Relating to Incidents Occurring 1846–1946" (1980, *Zuni Indian Tribe v. United States,* Docket No. 161–79L, United States Court of Claims, written testimony submitted in behalf of the Zuni Indians, two vols.).

96. This is apparently the earlier mentioned letter written on his behalf by General Sherman in December 1879 at Professor Baird's request.

97. Probably a reference to Garrick Mallery, whose "Pictographs of the North American Indians," in the *Fourth Annual Report* of the Bureau of Ethnology, does draw on, and acknowledge, contributions from Cushing.

98. Charles Eliot Norton (1827–1908), Harvard professor, author, and one of the founders of *The Nation,* was also president of the Boston-based Archaeological Institute of America, which sponsored Adolph Bandelier's early researches in the Southwest. Eben Norton Horsford was another Harvard professor and financial supporter of the Archaeological Institute (he sent money to Bandelier and was at least to offer it in Cushing's behalf). Both were friends of Sylvester Baxter.

99. For Cushing expositions of the stick-race and the game of the hidden ball, see, respectively, *Zuni Breadstuff,* pp. 158–59 (Green, *Zuni,* pp. 251–52) and Stuart Culin, "Games of the North American Indians," pp. 375–80.

100. The *tethl'nawe* and *hla'we* are varieties of sacrificial plume-stick. According to Stevenson, the former are made of piñon and "measure from the bended knee to the heel," whereas the latter are "slender stems of a plant about 18 inches long, painted white, and adorned with delicate white duck feathers" ("The Zuni Indians," pp. 113, 186).

101. Of the stories mentioned here by Cushing, the only one represented in his own posthumously published collection, *Zuni Folk Tales,* is "The Maiden of Matsaki and Her Lovers," retitled "The Trial of Lovers; or, the Maiden of Matsaki and the Red Feather."

102. For the third time since his arrival in Zuni—and this time as a member of the Bow priesthood—

Cushing was to participate in the events of the winter solstice. This year, December 6 would have been the fourth or fifth day in the ceremonial sequence.

103. What Cushing seems to be describing is the collecting of the "good share" for the chief *A:shiwani.*

104. That is, these are the sections of the village designated for the collection. "The House" probably refers to the building housing the meeting place of the *Kyakwe mossi* and the council of town chiefs.

105. This day's "proceedings" seem to continue those of the previous day and follow the same route among the houses of the chief priests—the "good share" this time being of corn flour. For another Cushing description of this kind of event, performed for the governor's household and paid for with a feast, see the chapter on "Crooner Bands" in *Zuni Breadstuff* (pp. 382–90).

106. The reference is to the bracelet of shells denoting rank within the Bow Priesthood.

107. The *U-hu-hu-kwe* or Cottonwood-down People were a medicine society specializing, as the name suggests, in the curing of coughs and colds.

108. These "Stray Thoughts" were entered in a notebook now lost, but the "mention" referred to seems to correspond to the loose note of December 5, above.

109. *Shi-wan-o-kia:* The priestess member of the ruling council, designated elsewhere by Cushing as the "priestess of seed."

110. *Woina:* A variant of *wowe.* While meaning "literally servant or domesticated animal," Bunzel tells us, *Wowe* is "a word that defies translation" ("Introduction to Zuni Ceremonialism," p. 523). It is used to refer to a priest or one who plays the role of attendant in a kachina dance.

111. Rito Quemado: A ranching and vegetable-producing community some seventy-five miles south of Zuni.

112. Then and/or later, Thla-k'oa served as Zuni *Alcalde,* or Crier Chief. The import of his remark seems to be that—contrary to the views of Lucien Levy-Bruhl and others about "how natives think"—the participants in the ritual are not mere primitive "fundamentalists" but are quite conscious of the *symbolic* nature of their acts. This is likewise the import of a remark of Palowahtiwa's quoted by Cushing in his "Notes Made During a Visit of Palowahtiwa, Waihusiwa, and Heluta at Manchester-by-the-Sea, Massachusetts, 1886." "True it is," he says, speaking of the ceremonial paraphernalia:

> that these are only musty old plumes, broken beads and cornmeal and pitch tied up with rotten cords; yet when the gods gave these medicines and seeds of precious things to our ancients, they wrapped up in them the prayers and powers which are still there, that we might through them supplicate for all the surrounding cities of men, the seeds of earth for food, the water of life for drink" (Green, *Zuni,* p. 418).

113. Reference is to the ten-day winter solstice fast and fire restriction following the "burial" of the war-god effigies on the mesa tops and the lighting of the "last fire."

114. Bidding farewell to John Bourke after one of his visits to Zuni, Pedro Pino "called out at the top of his voice, *'Como sta? Mucho por Kenlique. Quiero mucho por Kenlique,'* meaning that he wished many kind messages to be conveyed to his old friend Professor [Henry Lane] Kendrick, of the U.S. Military Academy, formerly Major 3d Artillery and Commanding Officer of Old Fort Wingate" (Sutherland, "The Diaries of John Gregory Bourke," p. 770). According to Richard Hart:

> In the 1850s, while Fort Defiance was being constructed near the boundary between the Zunis and the Navajos, Kendrick and other army officers arranged for large purchases of corn from the Zunis. This trade in corn (thousands upon thousands of bushels were shipped to Fort Defiance) was extremely important to the Zunis, and Pino remembered Kendrick kindly. Col. J. Munroe was the superior of Henry L. Dodge, an excellent early agent to the Navajos and friend of the Zunis who also bought corn at the village (personal communication).

According to Myra Ellen Jenkens, Munroe was also the commander in whose presence in Santa Fe on August 7, 1850, Pedro Pino signed a treaty which obligated the United States "to adjust and settle in the most practicable manner, the boundaries of each Pueblo, which shall never be diminished, but may be enlarged whenever the Government of the United States shall deem it advisable" and stipulated that the Pueblos were to be governed by their own laws and customs ("Zuni History During the Early United States Period," in E. Richard Hart, ed., *Zuni History,* p. 22. Santiago Abreu was governor of New Mexico in 1832–1833 and was involved with the first American traders who came into New Mexico and onto Zuni territory. As Hart observes of this passage, it seems likely that Pino had been talking about trade and the importance of good ties with the U.S.

115. Cushing would refer a few weeks later to a new title granted him as "Warrior of the Cacique," a rank presumably received on the present occasion.

116. "F. H. Cushing at Zuni," p. 56. For commentary on Cushing's *Zuni Folk Tales* (New York: G. P.

Putnam's Sons, 1901; reissued, New York: Alfred A. Knopf, 1931), see Introductions by John Wesley Powell and Mary Austin respectively; also Green, *Zuni,* pp. 331–45; and Dennis Tedlock, "On the Translation of Style in Oral Narrative," *Journal of American Folkore 84* (1971): 116–17.

117. At daybreak on the morning after the ten-day winter solstice fast and fire restriction,

> . . . two nearly nude maskers of the dance may be seen in the twilight swiftly wending their way to a distant, lonely cañon, where the God of Fire is supposed to have once dwelt. There, with an ancient stick and shaft, they kindle tinder by drilling the two sticks together, and lighting a torch, hurry it back to the great central estufa, where matrons, maidens and young men anxiously await the gift of New Fire (*Zuni Breadstuff,* pp. 617–18 [Green, *Zuni,* 322–23]).

Cushing's kindlers of the New Fire are kachinas of the Big Firebrand society who regularly perform this function (Parsons, *Pueblo Indian Religion,* pp. 575–77). Balanced against the first ten-day period leading up to the burial of the war gods, this second ten-day period "belongs to Pau'tiwa." On this, the twentieth day, culminating all the ceremonies preceding, he comes into town to install the new kachina impersonators and to bring in, with the New Fire, the New Year.

118. Pilling had written to assure Cushing of Powell's and Baird's support, but with the advice that he try to avoid conflict with the missionary teacher so far as possible (December 17, 1881, National Anthropological Archives).

119. Cushing uses the terms "Cacique," "Priest of the House," and "Priest of the Temple" interchangeably in referring to the members of the supreme council made up of the heads of the various *A:shiwani* rain societies. The new title indicates that his position in the Bow society has given him a role *vis-à-vis* this ruling council.

6. January–August 1882

1. For discussion of the budgetary and political relationship between the Secretary of the Smithsonian and the Director of the Bureau of Ethnology (as revealed, among other places, in the correspondence between them preserved in the National Anthropological Archives), see Curtis M. Hinsley, Jr., *Savages and Scientists,* pp. 236–37. As head of the Smithsonian, Baird maneuvered to gain direct control over the budget allotted to the New Bureau which had been placed under the Smithsonian umbrella—particularly to insure that a portion of the Bureau appropriation be used for collecting materials for the Museum. Powell on his side was stiffly protective of the independence of this Bureau, for whose establishment he had been chiefly responsible, and of his primarily research oriented objectives. Cushing can be seen as one of the pieces in this organizational chess game.

2. Frederick Webb Hodge, ed., "In Memoriam: Frank Hamilton Cushing," p. 367. Powell and Cushing would of course have been acquainted prior to the Southwest expedition as fellow staff members at the Smithsonian, as fellow officers of the Anthropological Society of Washington (Powell was its first president, Cushing its first curator), and as fellow members of the Cosmos Club, the prestigious society of Washington scientists and intellectuals founded by Powell, Henry Adams, and others in 1879.

3. Captain Albert H. Pfeiffer served under Col. Kit Carson in the Navajo Wars. The only Pfeiffer correspondence surviving in Cushing's collection of Zuni papers is a letter to Pedro Pino giving him title to a rifle and twenty rounds of ammunition (Southwest Museum H-C 14). According to E. Richard Hart, Pfeiffer, who led various quasi-military forays against the Navajos, at some point made an agreement with Pedro Pino enlisting his aid in this warfare. The gun and ammunition given Pino were probably evidence of that agreement, though Pfeiffer may have told Pino he was writing something other than what he did write. Zunis rode with Pfeiffer during the Navajo Wars (personal communication). It is possible Cushing may have in mind the 1846 treaty negotiated by the United States jointly with the Zunis and the Navajos (see William Elsey Connelley, *Doniphan's Expedition* [Kansas City, Mo.: Bryant and Douglas Book and Stationary Co., 1907], pp. 193–94).

4. What this curious phrase means is not clear. Depressed as he sometimes could be, there is no evidence to suggest that he ever thought of suicide—or a Zuni marriage—as a recourse in case of failure to complete his Zuni monograph (which he ultimately did fail to complete).

5. Edward Everett Hale (1822–1900) was a popular preacher, author, and cultural spokesman of New England society. Among his best known writings were "The Man Without a Country" (1863), *East and West* (1892), *Franklin in France* (1887–88), and *A New England Boyhood* (1893).

6. Cushing had written earlier of this delegation, one member of which was a Zuni and "gentile brother" of his upon whom he hoped Baird would impress the truth of his, Cushing's, position in the Smithsonian.

7. In *Snake Dance of the Moquis* (p. 281), John Gregory Bourke mentions having encountered "Nahi vehma (the

Peace maker)." For his Hopi, however, Cushing instead chose Nanahe, who had indoctrinated him and Bourke in the mysteries of the Rattlesnake cult.

8. Among the social encounters during this stay in Washington was one recorded by Cushing's fellow pioneer fieldworker, Alice Cunningham Fletcher. Among her papers in the National Anthropological Archives are her "Notes on an evening spent with Frank Cushing and a Zuni friend [Naiiutchi], 5-10-82." A lifelong friend and admirer of Cushing's, she was the author of some of the more sensitive and perceptive remarks about him in the memorial meeting after his death (see Hodge, "In Memoriam: Frank Hamilton Cushing," pp. 367–70). For studies of Fletcher, see Nancy O. Lurie, "Women in Early American Anthropology" (in June Helm, ed., *Pioneers of American Anthropology,* pp. 43–54), and Joan Mark, *A Stranger in Her Native Land: Alice Fletcher and the American Indians* (Lincoln: University of Nebraska Press, 1988).

9. Four years later, this remarkable Zuni leader, who saw his people through a particularly critical period of adjustment, would go east again for a visit with his friend Cushing, who was then staying on the Hemenway estate on the Massachusetts coast. For a record of the conversations of Palowahtiwa and fellow Zunis on this second visit, see Green, *Zuni,* pp. 409–25.

10. Baxter, "An Aboriginal Pilgrimage," 527–28. The source for this account (and several more to come) was pretty obviously Cushing himself.

11. Baxter, "Aboriginal Pilgrimage," 528–29. For the Zunis, the question of cutting the hair was one not merely of taste but of religious belief. How serious a matter it was may be seen from the reactions to the enforced haircutting mentioned later. See Cushing to Faurote, February 14, 1897, in Appendix G.

12. According to a reprint of the *Tribune* article, Cushing and the Indians had taken a carriage to the outskirts of Washington (followed by a carriage-load of reporters) to plant sacrificial plumes—in a driving rain (*Pinal Drill,* July 1, 1882).

13. Even without Naiiutchi's or Kiasi's two daughters, whom Cushing had originally intended to include as "examples of young Zuni women" (FHC to Thomas, January 16, 1882, National Archives, Denver Federal Center, Records of BIA, Pueblo Indian Agency), one may note that the group Cushing selected to accompany him composed a nice microcosm of Zuni social organization with its intricate overlapping of clan, priestly, and kiva associations. Represented among these few travelers were at least three clans, five sacred fraternal orders, and presumably several kiva groups.

14. Baxter, "Aboriginal Pilgrimage," pp. 530–36. Here too, needless to say, Baxter must have depended on Cushing himself for most of his information, as well as for translation of remarks by the Zunis. An additional perspective on the enactment at the seaside is provided by an explanation Cushing subsequently gave to an interviewer:

> The Zunis believe that the ocean is the origin—or the embracing waters of the world, as they call them, are the birthplace—of the clouds. In their ceremonials at the summer solstice for securing the summer rain clouds, they use water from these oceans, [but] they have been unable for generations to secure any water from the eastern ocean, or the ocean of sunrise, [from which], according to the traditions handed down in a line of priests, . . . the first supply was obtained by Indians taken captive to Mexico 175 or 200 years ago. . . . They think that they will be able to cause clouds to follow this water to their own desert country. . . . They hold this water of the ocean as a hostage. They take infinite pains with it. In bringing it from Boston the chiefs carried it in their hands . . . (*Washington Star,* April 8, 1882).

15. "Aboriginal Pilgrimage," p. 536. Given his acceptance into the more exclusive and arcane Bow Priesthood, one might expect that initiation into the "*Kâ'-kâ*" or Kachina Society—an organization into which every male Zuni would normally have been initiated before the age of fifteen—would have been almost a matter of course. According to Cushing's account, however (see letters of June 11 and December 25, 1881, to Powell and Pilling respectively), the clan and family adoption on which initiation to the Kachina depended were themselves only provisional, pending his marriage within the tribe. To be fully recognized as a Zuni, he would have had to take a Zuni wife, had not his feat of conducting the headmen to the Ocean of Sunrise proved an acceptable alternative. Now admitted in principle, he had to await the next of the quadrennial Kachina festivals, due in the spring of 1884, for the full initiation ritual. Unfortunately, by that time he was under orders to return to Washington and so was able only to witness, not to participate in, the ceremonial.

16. Cushing is referring to the reception Putnam had hosted at his home—an honor that must have been particularly gratifying to the young fieldworker. Cushing's acquaintance with Putnam—who, along with Powell, was one of the chief early organizers of anthropological research in America—dated back to the 1876 Centennial Exposition in Philadelphia, where he himself, at age seventeen, had been assigned to his first job for the Smithsonian, as assistant in charge of the Smithsonian's

ethnological exhibit. Now he was meeting Putnam not as a lowly subordinate but as guest of honor.

17. The "Peruvian Mysteries" are explained by Sylvester Baxter:

> In visiting the Peabody Museum at Cambridge Mr. Cushing examined for the first time the splendid collection of Inca articles, which included certain things which have been the puzzle of archaeologists, and known as the "Peruvian mysteries." These he at once saw were the religious sacrificial paraphernalia of the Incas, and in essential characteristics substantially identical with those used by the Zunis. They were also identified by the Zunis as corresponding to their own. It is hoped that this important subject will be worked up by Mr. Cushing jointly with Professor Putnam . . . ("Some Results of Mr. Cushing's Visit," *The American Architect and Building News* 11:196).

Cushing never "worked up" this subject, but he did elaborate on the matter of Zuni-Inca parallels in "Preliminary Notes on . . . the Hemenway Southwestern Archaeological Expedition," pp. 191–94.

18. The request was granted for the duration of the Washington visit. Baird also endorsed a request by Cushing (not granted) to take the stenographer back with him to the Southwest.

19. It is not clear what printed matter Hale was alluding to. Logan and company had not yet gone to work on Cushing, but doubtless there were others ready to be scandalized by the notion of a white man taking up life among the savages.

20. Three days later Bourke wrote again, enclosing a note from Sheridan stating that he had done as requested and adding: "I sincerely hope [Cushing] will get his appointment; he will make a clever, nice young officer with plenty of ability and a specialty which will, with his industry, do credit to the service" (Southwest Museum HC 59).

21. Cushing refers here to Bourke's "Notes Upon the Pottery of the Pueblo Indians of New Mexico and Arizona, Prepared with Special Reference to the Small Private Cabinet of Lieut. General P.H. Sheridan" (privately printed, no date).

22. Another similar list of "Notes on Zuni Linguistics" may be found in the Hodge-Cushing Collection of the Southwest Museum, along with several batches of notecards indexing Cushing materials on the Zuni language and oral literature (envelope 182). Such of these materials as have survived are divided between this collection and that of the National Anthropological Archives.

23. "McCarty's (Valencia). Trading community on Acoma Indian Reservation on US 66, 13 mi SE of Grants. Named for the contractor whose camp was here when AT & SF RR was built through this section" (T.M. Pearce, *New Mexico Place Names: A Geographical Dictionary* [Albuquerque: University of New Mexico Press, 1965], p. 98).

24. Bandelier, whom Cushing had not yet met, was on his second tour of the American Southwest and had spent several weeks in the Acoma area in May.

25. Matthews is referring in his blunt way to the Bureau's practice of issuing under a single author's name works that included substantial contributions of others—for example, Garrick Mallery's giant monographs on pictographs and gesture language.

26. Cushing had evidently sent some of the photographs John Hillers had taken in Hopi during the Powell Colorado River expedition. Metcalf had used other Hillers photographs as the basis for his illustrations for "My Adventures in Zuni," some of which are mentioned later in the present letter.

27. *O'nok thli k'ia:* The Zuni name, meaning "The great dance plume," which Metcalf had been given by Naiiutchi during the visit to Boston.

28. It is evident from this letter that Powell intended to keep a tight control over Cushing's expenditures so that he would not again accumulate unauthorized debts. The effort was to be only partially successful.

7. September 1882–January 1883

1. According to Cushing's Annual Report:

> During the latter portion of October, complications arose in relation to a spring of water bordering on but outside the Southwestern portion of the Zuni reservation. The matter being referred in council to Mr. Cushing in his capacity as a native chief, he was compelled to visit the place, and attempted, by building there, to protect the spring from white encroachment" (Annual Report on field work for year ending June 30, 1883).

2. It is generally believed that Illinois Senator John A. Logan was responsible for the order recalling Cushing to Washington in early 1884, though the grounds for this belief are somewhat murky. Pandey ("Anthropologists at Zuni," p. 325) and others draw on a statement by Brandes to this effect ("Frank Hamilton Cushing," p. 104), but Brandes in turn had depended on an undocumented remark in E. DeGolyer's introduction to his edition of *My Adventures in Zuni* (Santa Fe: Peripatetic Press, 1941, p. 19). DeGolyer's source was almost certainly Cushing's

brother-in-law, Frederick Webb Hodge, who recapitulates in a letter to DeGolyer: "Cushing . . . returned to Washington not by reason of his health, but because Senator John A. Logan demanded his return under threat of 'killing' the Bureau of Ethnology's appropriation . . ." (Southwest Museum Cushing Papers). With Hodge's characteristically authoritative assertion we are getting somewhat nearer to a contemporary report, but this statement too was made long after the event, and the acts may not have been quite as simple as they seemed to Hodge. Cushing *was* ill, and there was serious concern about this in the East; witness, for example, the letter of November 19, 1883, from Professor E.N. Horsford, a Cushing admirer in Cambridge, urging Powell to recall the young martyr before it was too late. It may also be that the reason given in the Bureau's letter of recall was in fact the real one—namely, that it was time for Cushing to come home and write the monograph he had not been writing in Zuni. None of which, of course, is to rule out the Logan threat—which would have been quite in character and which did in fact get reported at the time in at least one news story (possibly authored by Cushing himself; see pp. 320–22).

3. According to Cushing's subsequent report to Powell on his visit to the Tonawanda reservation, the tribal "Grand Sachem" was a Mr. Abram. From the present entry it would appear that Mr. Abram had accompanied his new friends for a visit to Zuni.

4. This is not the El Rito shown on modern maps of New Mexico north of Santa Fe but another settlement, about seven miles north of Laguna.

5. Robert and Walter Marmon were traders at Laguna and Acoma pueblos (Frank McNitt, *The Indian Traders,* p. 118).

6. The plan to join the Army had by this time fallen through, and Cushing was thinking of alternatives—one of which was to enter into the ranching business.

7. The Stanley referred to was doubtless Cushing's friend Joseph Stanley-Brown, who, now back in Powell's service, was at Fort Wingate at this point on Bureau business.

8. What Cushing learned was that the Stevensons had been traveling with the Logan party and had gone with Logan to Zuni. According to a later account, Mrs. Stevenson, who also appears in a photograph taken at Zuni of the Logan party, served as the Senator's "interpreter" (Chicago *Inter-Ocean* 2 May 1883). As this later account makes clear, Logan also visited the Nutria Springs area which his group would shortly be attempting to liberate from the Zunis.

9. Professor A.H. Thompson was the newly appointed director of topographical work in the Southwest for the U.S. Geological Survey (Irving Telling, "New Mexican Frontiers," p. 274).

10. It is possible that "George" could have been either Cushing's friend George Kennan or his brother-in-law George Payne (married to Emma Cushing's sister Eleanor).

11. As part of the reception at Wingate, Matthews had recited a 104-line poem he had written, "The Pagan Martyrs," the text of which may be found in Sylvester Baxter, "The Tenacity of Indian Customs," p. 196.

12. It was on the Tonawanda reservation, several decades earlier, that Morgan, introduced by his young Tonawanda friend Ely Parker, had his first fieldwork experience as a serious student of ethnology (Carl Resek, *Lewis Henry Morgan, American Scholar* [Chicago: University of Chicago Press, 1960], pp. 36–40). Here Cushing is making a "correction" to Morgan's report for which he will later have to be excused by Morgan's protégé Adolph Bandelier.

13. Within the next several weeks, Metcalf and Emily Cushing's sister, Margaret Magill, would make the trip to Zuni together. Margaret would remain for the duration, Metcalf through the following June.

14. According to a footnote in *Zuni Breadstuff* (pp. 631–32), this was the dance of the *Thla-he-kwe* (or *Hlahewe,* translated by Cushing as "Beautiful Corn Wands"). See diary entries for July 21–31, 1880, for description of an earlier performance and rehearsals of this dance observed by Cushing.

15. *Akwe-le-alla-kwin* house: Literally, house of the red and south—one of the kivas.

16. Shasia, a Zuni, had been reported missing.

17. By "our" laws and regulations Cushing appears to mean not those of Zuni but those of the United States. He seems to have been resuming the project of adjusting the tribal government to bring it into accord with the Zunis' contemporary situation as wards of the United States.

18. A draft of Cushing's letter, describing the suspects and detailing the crime as deduced from the trail markings and other evidence, may be found in the Southwest Museum (HC 68). A letter from Graham to the sheriff and other correspondence relating to the murder are on file in the Denver Federal Center, Records of the BIA, Pueblo Indian Agency.

19. *Amole:* Mexican Spanish for the roots of any of various local plants used for making suds for cleansing—"soap plant."

20. One of the books Hale had sent was a copy of Casteñeda he had located in Paris. Onokthlikia was Cush-

ing's friend Willard Metcalf. Henry W. Henshaw served on the Bureau staff as a specialist in linguistics. Nell was Emma Cushing's other sister, Eleanor Magill Payne. The additional "Sister" was evidently the wife of Cushing's brother Enos, who had been living at Fort Wingate.

21. The last few pages of this notebook are taken up with rough sketches of the murder site.

22. The impression here may be one of leadership more imposed *by* Cushing than *on* him. To what extent his behavior on this occasion was in keeping with Zuni custom as well as with his own temperament and sense of exigencies is a question on which judgment will not be passed here. Some perspective on the authority of his office may be provided, however, by a statement made by Naiiutchi, Elder Priest of the Bow and Cushing's mentor in that order: "My position makes me a humble man; in time of peace I cannot raise my voice and must restrain my anger; in time of anger (war) I must say 'do so' and it is done, 'go there,' and my people go; and none then among my people have command over me" (quoted in Sutherland, "The Diaries of John Gregory Bourke," p. 958). Cushing's position was, of course, not quite the same as Naiiutchi's.

23. Eastman had written to Cushing on July 20 as follows:

> My Navajos complain to me that you did at two different times fire with a pistol into their horses, that in consequence thereof they found two horses dead and a third one they trailed by the blood a long ways and failed to find him, and not seeing him since believe him to be dead also. They desire me to present their claim and collect $100.00 as pay for the animals. I also respectfully request an explanation of the matter and the reasons why you did it.

That letter and the exchange to follow appear also in Arthur Woodward, "Frank Cushing—First War-Chief of Zuni." This correspondence, which Woodward found in the post letterbook at Fort Defiance, is now on file in the National Archives, along with several Agency letters on the same subject (Record Group 75, OIA Letters Received 1881–1907). Copies of most of the letters can also be found in the Denver Federal Center (Records of BIA, Pueblo Indian Agency). Whether Cushing paid the damages in the end is not known, but what appear to be the last two of the follow-up letters make it seem unlikely that he did (see Pueblo Agent Sanchez to Commissioner Price, May 22, 1883, and Sanchez to Navajo Agent Riordan, May 28, 1883, below. See also Cushing's diary entry for October 4, 1880).

24. It is not clear which "certain sources" Stanley-Brown had in mind, but judging by several Cushing remarks it appears that he was criticized not only from the "right," for degenerating into a savage, but from the "left" as well, for infiltrating himself among the Indians only to take advantage of them (see, for example, FHC to Miss Faurote, February 14, 1897, in Appendix). In the case of the Oraibi venture, there would have been some justice in criticism of the latter order.

25. James H. Willson, the new "U.S. Indian Teacher" in Zuni, arrived (according to Telling, "New Mexican Frontiers," p. 162) in October 1882 and remained about six years.

26. Like the rooms of the Stowe house in Hartford as described in Kathryn Kish Sklar's biography of Catharine Beecher, this pleasant room perhaps also

> . . . in one sense exemplifies the Victorian abhorrence for unfilled voids, the belief that for every space there is an object, for every question an answer, [while] in another sense exemplify[ing] a new set of social boundaries constructed and inhabited by nineteenth-century Americans [and defining] a new kind of space within which they forged their identities . . . (*Catharine Beecher: A Study in American Domesticity* [New York, 1976], p. xi).

Exotic here mingles with domestic, the strange with the comfortably familiar.

27. This letter is in the Denver Federal Center, Records of BIA, Pueblo Indian Agency.

28. Bourke had been visiting the Coyotero Apache reservation in southeastern Arizona. What he spent several years doing "among the Apaches," other than studying them, is told in his two books about Indian fighting with General George Crook. Currently he was at Fort Whipple awaiting the "inevitable eruption of the Chiricahua Apaches from their stronghold in the Sierra Madres" (*On the Border with Crook* [New York: Charles Scribner's Sons, 1891], p. 447)—the beginning of the last long campaign to subdue these holdouts against American rule.

29. Other than the "Urine Dance" pamphlet, nothing came of Bourke's idea of publishing a report on Zuni. Though he had collected almost as many notes on his Zuni visit as he had on his Hopi excursion, it was the latter he developed into the kind of book he was here projecting (i.e., *Snake Dance of the Moquis*). And instead of writing one popular catchall book on the Apache, he split his treatment between popularly written accounts of the fighting and more professional monographs and articles on the ethnology.

30. Thomas V. Keam, proprietor of a famous Indian

trading post in the Hopi country, had been Bourke's host and friend as well as Cushing's. What Bourke was about to say in this tantalizingly incomplete sentence may perhaps be guessed at on the basis of an offer Keam was to make later to Cushing himself—namely, that Stevenson was suspected of selling part of his Smithsonian collections for private profit. Keam himself was, of course, a businessman, willing to buy what he could sell to advantage. Who knows but that the collection of Hopi pottery he later sold to the Hemenways (from whom it went to the Peabody Museum in Cambridge) did contain items bought illicitly from Bureau collectors? For an annotated and beautifully illustrated catalog of this collection, see Edwin L. Wade and Lea S. McChesney, *America's Great Lost Expedition: The Thomas Keam Collection of Hopi Pottery from the Second Hemenway Expedition, 1890–1894* (Phoenix: The Heard Museum, 1980).

31. Cushing refers here to the ruin usually known as Kin-tiel, or Wide Ruin, which he had visited earlier (see diary entry for September 21, 1880), referring to it on that occasion as Heshota Pathl taie, a name which he translates variously as "Deserted City of Refuge" and (more accurately) "Town of the Boundary." What he seems to mean here is not that he has rediscovered the ruin as a whole but rather that he has made a new discovery in its outlying structure. This ruin was later excavated by Victor Mindeleff and is illustrated in his "A Study of Pueblo Architecture in Tusayan and Cibola," p. 92.

32. At various points in this report Cushing refers to drawings, none of which have turned up.

33. For the story of Um-thla-na and further description of the building in which he was killed, see Cushing, *Zuni Breadstuff,* pp. 197–202.

34. This same passage, credited to Cushing, is cited by Victor Mindeleff in his own discussion of the round-hole doorways of Kin-tiel and other ruins (Mindeleff, "A Study of Pueblo Architecture," pp. 192–93). Mindeleff came across these architectural novelties independently a year after Cushing's stop at Kin-tiel.

35. The selection here is taken in part from the copy of the annual report for fiscal year 1883 which Cushing sent to Washington and which is preserved among his papers in the National Anthropological Archives. In that copy, however, pp. 8–11 are missing. These are the pages which included most of the description of his two discoveries, taken here from the draft for this report which belongs to the Southwest Museum.

36. Powell's letter to Mindeleff, dated December 13, 1882, stated that the latter was to have Cushing's assistance in "the Scientific Department" of the expedition, the purpose of which, he wrote, was "to make as large an ethnological collection as possible at Oraibi and incidentally at the other villages of Tusayan" (Southwest Museum, Cushing Papers).

37. In this connection, see Nancy J. Parezo, "Cushing as Part of the Team: The Collecting Activities of the Smithsonian Institution."

38. Recalling what must have been a continuation of conversations in this same reflective mood, in the aftermath of the excitement at Oraibi, Metcalf wrote to Cushing following his own return to the East: "I understand some things in you, those things that I feel and try to be like to the bottom of my soul, for I realize fully—No! not half—what it has done for me to know you. I mean spiritually. My life shall be to follow those teachings that you so generously set forth to me in our quiet talks snowed up in Moqui—those talks which have become as sacred to me as the rituals of the Zunis . . ." (Southwest Museum HC 368). Unfortunately, Metcalf's journal does not record these later conversations, which might have provided further counterbalance to the pistol-waving image fostered by Cushing in his own published accounts.

39. Five days from the time of his arrival, according to Cushing's later report, "the wagons arrived and we bade farewell to foolish, bull-dozed Oraibi." Speaking of the present letter in that report, Cushing wrote, in a passage excised from the printed version:

> I regret that I cannot give this letter in full, as it was reported afterward that I wrote in great fright, begging Mr. Mindelef to come immediately or we should all be murdered, our goods stolen, etc. etc. of trash. Doubtless Mr. Mindeleff still preserves the letter; if so, it will speak for itself" (Annual report on field work for year ending June 30, 1883, National Anthropological Archives).

40. A ten-page "catalogue of collections made at Oraibi for the National Museum" was submitted to the Bureau as part of the annual report Cushing submitted for fiscal 1883 (National Anthropological Archives). He may not have "cleaned out" Oraibi, but his mission can hardly have been counted a failure.

41. According to E. Richard Hart:

> Senator Logan was involved in at least two schemes to pilfer lands from the government, the Zunis and others. As well as attempting to grab the Nutria springs through illegal desert entries, he was involved with a group which made fraudulent land entries to the south of Zuni, and evidently with the operations of the Cibola Cattle Company. [The latter, made up, like the Tucker group of Fort Wingate army officers,] brought cattle in on the rails and then ranged them on gov-

ernment land, reservation land and public domain, though they owned no land of their own. The method used in the fraudulent entries to the south of Zuni was to file on all the sources of water, so that the entire area could be controlled. In that area, legitimate homesteaders were murdered (personal communication).

Such seems to have been the pattern of land acquisition by ranchers generally. According to John A. Garrity, "they seldom hesitated to break the law when it suited their interests to do so. Perhaps as much as 95 per cent of the federal land occupied by ranchers under the Desert Act was obtained through fraud" (*The New Commonwealth, 1877–1890* [New York: Harper and Row, 1968], p. 12). See also Telling, "New Mexican Frontiers," pp. 235–37.

42. Having issued his Executive Order of May 1, 1883, correcting the Zuni boundaries to include Nutria within the reservation, President Arthur later reversed himself to allow for the ranchers' claim. Further protest by the Zunis and the Pueblo Indian Agency led to cancellation of the claims by the General Land Office. Further appeals followed, and the matter was not finally settled, in the Zunis' favor, until 1891, by which time Logan was dead and Cushing had long since left Zuni. For the official correspondence and presidential proclamations, see George E. Fay, ed., *Treaties, Land Cessions, and Other U.S. Congressional Documents Relative to American Indian Tribes. Zuni Indian Pueblo, New Mexico,* Part 1 (Greeley: University of Northern Colorado Press, 1971), pp. 1–48. For a contemporary account of the controversy and the text of principal documents, see William E. Curtis, *Children of the Sun* (Chicago: Inter-Ocean Publishing Co., 1883), pp. 43–59. Later accounts may be found in Clarissa P. Fuller, "Frank Hamilton Cushing's Relations to Zuni and the Hemenway Southwestern Expedition," Master's thesis, University of New Mexico, 1943, pp. 74–83; Brandes, "Frank Hamilton Cushing," pp. 96–107; Pandey, "Anthropologists at Zuni," pp. 325–26; and C. Gregory Crampton, *The Zunis of Cibola,* pp. 124–26.

43. Actually, the article was datelined Santa Fe, not Zuni. Was this merely a slip on Stevenson's part, or was he positively disinforming Baird in a way that would implicate Cushing? Bandelier, who had seen Stevenson a month earlier, reported him as "much incensed at Cushing" (Lange and Riley, *The Southwestern Journals of Adolph F. Bandelier* [1966], p. 366)—perhaps because he had got wind of what Cushing had written about him in "My Adventures," the first issue of which would appear in December. It is interesting to speculate on the role played by the Stevensons throughout the Nutria affair, beginning with their accompaniment of Logan the previous summer on his visit to Zuni and Mrs. Stevenson's services as "translator" (see pp. 240, 283). Col. Stevenson, Baird's informant in the present instance, may also have been one of the anonymous sources for an attack on Cushing which appeared the following month in the Topeka *Capital* (see pp. 265–66). Inasmuch as Cushing's removal from Zuni cleared the way for his replacement by Mrs. Stevenson, one cannot help noticing how much of the "instigating" was done by the Stevensons themselves.

44. Reference here is to the *hockan* or Mountain Chant, a nine-day healing rite performed as a rule "in the winter, the season when the thunder is silent and the rattlesnakes are hibernating" (Matthews, "The Mountain Chant," p. 386). Rizer had traveled to the dance site (some twenty miles from Keam's Canyon) in company with Cushing's friend Alexander Stephen (*Topeka Daily Capital,* January 14, 1883).

45. In this, as in various other instances, the press report of the Zunis' peaceful ways reveals American contempt for those who are not "fighters." It happens, however, that this popular American notion of the Zunis—a notion echoed in anthropological circles as well, following Ruth Benedict—was wrong, or at least a great oversimplification, as evidenced in the history of their long conflict with the Navajos. According to Willard Metcalf in a Chicago *Daily News* interview (June 15, 1883), the Zunis were outraged by the *Capital's* insinuation, and Naiiutchi, the senior war priest, was "excited to a relation of his youthful achievements. . . . He declaimed in impassioned manner about his campaigns and claimed seventeen Navajo scalps among his trophies."

8. February–April 1883

1. For letters Bandelier wrote criticizing Cushing's directorship of this enterprise (and offering to take over his job), see Leslie A. White, ed., *Pioneers in American Anthropology: The Bandelier-Morgan Letters, 1873–1883* (Albuquerque: University of New Mexico Press, 1940), vol. 1, p. 72n4; and Paul Radin, ed., *The Unpublished Letters of Adolph F. Bandelier Concerning the Writing and Publication of The Delight Makers* (El Paso: C. Hertzog, 1942), pp. 17–18 and 20–24.

2. Bernard L. Fontana, "Pioneers in Ideas: Three Early Southwestern Ethnologists," p. 125. Son of a Highland, Illinois, banker who had emigrated from Switzerland in 1848, Adolph Francis Alphonse Bandelier (1840–1914) brought to his studies a background quite different from Cushing's. Raised to speak and read several European

languages and educated at several European universities, he was, by the time he met Morgan in 1873, already familiar with many of the early chronicles of the Spanish conquest and such other literature on the Indians of Spanish America as he could track down in libraries. Libraries and archives continued to be central in Bandelier's research throughout a long career which included great stretches of time in the field, particularly during the dozen years between 1880 and 1892, when his studies focused on the Pueblo Indians of the Southwest and the relation of their ancestors to the pre-Columbian architects of Mexico. During this period he spent months at a time traveling about New Mexico, Arizona, and Mexico, often alone and on foot, examining ruins, observing the societies of extant Pueblos, and copying the records he found in the various local missions. Much more time went into copying documents in the greater repositories of Mexico City and Santa Fe.

"Undoubtedly the greatest ethnohistorian of the Southwest," according to Fontana, Bandelier was principally a historian rather than an archaeologist or ethnologist, but he was the first to survey the Pueblo ruins and settlements in a systematic way, and, like Cushing, he was, as Fontana points out, "ahead of his time in the recognition of archaeology as the lengthening arm of history and of ethnology . . ." (ibid). Author of more than eighty books and articles, including a novel on the Pueblos of prehistory, Bandelier is the subject of a number of studies, including Clarissa P. Fuller, "A Re-Examination of Bandelier's Studies of Ancient Mexico" (Ph.D. dissertation, University of New Mexico, 1950); Edgar F. Goad, "A Study of the Life of Adolph Francis Alphonse Bandelier, with an Appraisal of His Contribution to American Anthropology and Related Sciences" (Ph.D. dissertation, University of Southern California, 1939); and F.W. Hodge, "Biographical Sketch and Bibliography of Adolph Francis Alphonse Bandelier" (*New Mexico Historical Review* 7(4): 353–70). See also Lange, Riley, and Lange, eds., *The Southwestern Journals of Adolph F. Bandelier*; Madeleine T. Rodack, ed., *Adolph F. Bandelier's The Discovery of New Mexico by the Franciscan Monk Friar Marcos de Niza in 1593*; and Leslie A. White, ed., *Pioneers in American Anthropology.*

3. A small file of Stephen's letters to Cushing over the remaining decade of his life is preserved in the Southwest Museum Hodge-Cushing Collection (envelope 87). Stephen also collaborated with Jesse Walter Fewkes, later to succeed Cushing as director of the Hemenway Expedition. Fewkes, who concentrated his studies on the Hopis, depended heavily on Stephen for his knowledgeability and insight into Hopi life—sometimes acknowledging this indebtedness, sometimes not. During his later years, living on First Mesa, Stephen kept a journal, described by a later researcher as "astoundingly rich, profusely illustrated by eye-witness sketches and filled with minutely detailed descriptions of almost every event that he experienced" (Watson Smith, *Kiva Mural Decorations at Awatovi and Kawaika-a,* Papers of the Peabody Museum of Archaeology and Ethnology, vol. 37 [Cambridge, 1952], p. 99). Preserved by Keam, Stephen's notebooks were later published, in condensed form, by Elsie Clews Parsons (*Hopi Journal of Alexander M. Stephen* [2 vols.], New York, 1936).

4. Cushing's catalogue, incorporated in his annual report for 1883, is on file in the National Anthropological Archives.

5. Following through on this promise, Cushing found, on inquiring at Fort Wingate, that the driver in question was in a military prison. He wrote to the prison commandant, obtained the affidavit, and enclosed it in a letter to Baird dated April 6, 1883 (Smithsonian Institution Archives).

6. "Stephen's intuition was right. The bowl is Zuni, and most likely was of recent manufacture. Jonathan Batkin's *Pottery of the Pueblos of New Mexico, 1700–1940* (Colorado Springs: Taylor Museum, 1987) illustrates a bowl that has a very similar interior design, except that it includes bird motifs. He dates the bowl 1875–1880. As far as the Stephen bowl's design symbolism is concerned, I would interpret many of the elements, following Margaret Hardin, *Gifts of Mother Earth: Ceramics in the Zuni Tradition* (Phoenix: Heard Museum, 1983), p. 32, as feathers. Hardin follows Matilda C. Stevenson and Ruth Bunzel in generally interpreting pottery designs as prayers, most often for rain. I'm not sure, but I think the central design may represent the four cardinal directions." Lea S. McChesney, personal communication.

7. *Scribner's Monthly: An Illustrated Magazine for the People,* was a precursor to *Century Illustrated Monthly Magazine,* in which the Cushing pieces were appearing. Stephen was still calling the journal by its earlier name.

8. The American journalist and short story writer Ambrose Bierce (1842–1914) was, in fact, with Stephen Crane, one of the earliest American realist writers. He was writing in this period for two San Francisco papers, the *Wasp* and the *Argonaut,* and may have reviewed "My Adventures" in one of them.

9. Henry F. Farny (1847–1916): French-born artist who, with Metcalf, produced the illustrations for "My Adventures in Zuni." Later a well-known painter, Farny continued to do illustrations as well—for example, those in the popular McGuffy Readers, published in his adopt-

ed city of Cincinnati. "Women Grinding Corn" is one of the drawings contributed by Metcalf (MAZ 503; Green, *Zuni,* 80).

10. Cushing refers here to the title "My Adventures in Zuni," chosen for his *Century* series. He had proposed a number of duller titles but had also assured the editors that he did not consider the title they had chosen "too common." Objecting only to the "My," he gave them leave to select whatever title they liked "without fear of incurring either my criticism or displeasure" (Cushing to R.N. Johnson, August 18, 1882, Southwest Museum HC 55). Now, it seems, he had forgotten, or was regretting, that decision.

11. Reference is to the U.S. Army Corps of Topographical Engineers, *Report Upon the Colorado River of the West by Lt. Joseph C. Ives* (Washington, 1861).

12. The Perez letter is in the National Archives, Denver Federal Center, Records of the Bureau of Indian Affairs, Pueblo Indian Agency Register of Letters Received, 1881–1883 (Sheriff Thomas Perez to Cushing, Feb. 13, 1883; enclosed with Cushing to Agent B.M. Thomas, Feb. 15, 1883).

13. As noted in the Denver Federal Center Records of BIA, Pueblo Indian Agency Register of Letters Received, 1881–1883, Cushing enclosed with his letter to Thomas copies of the already reported letter from Sheriff Perez as well as his own reply, a letter to Dan Dubois, and three other letters concerning the affair and Cushing's efforts to have the prisoners brought safely to Zuni and to win a reduction in the legal fees the Zunis were being charged. Ultimately, as indicated in later correspondence in the same file, the prisoners were allowed to escape before they could be brought back to New Mexico, and the Zunis were charged four horses for expenses.

14. It would be interesting to know which testimonies came from which of these informants, at least two of whom seem generally to have been sympathetic to Cushing. As to the third, one cannot be absolutely certain whether the "professor" was James Stevenson or Alexander Stephen, though the former seems the likelier candidate.

15. Thliakwa (Blue Medicine Stone, or Turquoise): the name conferred on Baxter by Naiiutchi during the visit in Boston.

16. Accomplishment of this favor, typical of the kind of mutual support network operating within Cushing's circle of fellow ethnologists, is indicated by the appearance of both illustrations in Matthews' "Navajo Weaving."

17. Reference is to a passage in the "Notes" column of the January 25, 1883, issue of *The Nation.* In the context of an unfavorable review of Hubert H. Bancroft's recently published *History of Central America,* the editor mentions the "fabulous 'Seven Cities of Cibola' [which] have been plainly identified with the Zuni pueblos, whose mysteries and traditions we are in a fair way of penetrating through the self-sacrificing devotion to science of Mr. Cushing and his wife" (36: 87).

18. Lange and Riley, *Southwestern Journals of Adolph F. Bandelier* (1970), pp. 38–39. This account notwithstanding, Cushing himself labeled the "popular" notion of Indian democracy as erroneous so far as the Zunis were concerned ("The Zuni Social, Mythic, and Religious Systems," p. 188).

19. For Bandelier's full account of his visit to Zuni, see Lange and Riley, *Southwestern Journals of Adolph F. Bandelier* (1970), pp. 37–58. The letter following is from Leslie A. White, ed., *Pioneers in American Anthropology: The Bandelier-Morgan Letters, 1873–1883,* vol. II, pp. 248–51.

20. Cushing's claim of this discovery had appeared in Sylvester Baxter's "The Tenacity of Indian Customs," p. 196.

21. Bandelier had been waiting at Fort Wingate for a young Zuni named Roman, whom he wanted as guide. Unfortunately for Bandelier, Governor Palowahtiwa had objected to the arrangement, and Roman had failed to appear (Lange and Riley, *Southwestern Journals of Adolph F. Bandelier* (1970), pp. 61–63, 67). Cushing had evidently written to explain.

22. The letter to follow is from Frederick Webb Hodge, "Old Dan Dubois," Los Angeles Westerners' Corral *Brand Book* (Los Angeles, 1950); reprinted in Lange, Riley, and Lange, *Southwestern Journals of Adolph F. Bandelier* (1984), p. 353. For report of Bandelier's further travels, see Lange and Riley, *Southwestern Journals of Adolph F. Bandelier* (1970), pp. 67ff.

23. In another draft Cushing refers to this plan for "the dam in question" as his "original and best of all schemes" (Southwest Museum HC 74). Unfortunately, it did not turn out to be a good idea, though it was to be promoted by others less innocent in motivation than Cushing. Colonel Stevenson, who probably picked up the idea of the dam from Cushing, used it as an argument in favor of the Nutria land claims of his friend General Logan's group, since the dam would, he claimed, more than make up for any Zuni loss of water in the disputed area (letter to the Secretary of the Interior, April 1884, in Fay 1971, pp. 22–25). Similarly, when the dam was actually built, it was, according to E. Richard Hart, part of an effort "to try to force the Zunis to allot (and thus eventually also to open the rest of their reservation to non-

Zuni settlement)." Completed in 1908, the dam itself, Hart points out, "was a total failure. It was breached in 1909 and after being rebuilt, it silted in, destroying its original purpose, hurting the Zuni water supply and at the same time covering over very important farming lands and a sacred spring" (personal communication). So much for this particular, and originally well-intentioned, Cushing scheme.

24. The first half of what is printed here is taken from the later of two dated drafts kept by Cushing. The bracketed parts (including the Executive Order, which he didn't bother to recopy) are taken from the first draft.

25. Cushing slips on the dating here. The famous rebellion in question began on August 10, 1680. The Pueblos maintained their independence for the next dozen years, until the "Reconquest" initiated in 1692 by Diego de Vargas—the Zunis being ensconced through much of this period in their refuge on the top of the Dowa Yalanne Mesa. The grants referred to would have been the so-called Cruzate grants mentioned earlier. Though the Zunis' copy of their grant had been lost and was probably spurious anyway, Spanish law, according to E. Richard Hart (personal communication), had in any case guaranteed them and the other Pueblos the right to all the lands that they effectively planted and used.

26. Under the 1848 Treaty of Guadalupe Hidalgo which ended the Mexican-American War and brought New Mexico, Arizona, and California into the Union, the United States recognized some thirty-five land grants awarded by the Spanish (and confirmed by the Mexican republic) to various Pueblos, including the Zunis. Ironically, the very provision here adduced by Cushing—that the treaty guaranteed, with citizenship, the Pueblos' right to own property, thus distinguishing their status from that of "reservation" Indians—opened the way for acquisition of the "owned" property by non-Pueblos. Research following the reversal of that provision in 1913 revealed that approximately 3,000 non-Indians, representing families aggregating 12,000 persons, maintained claims within the boundaries of Pueblo grants (Mark Simmons, "History of the Pueblos Since 1821," *Handbook of North American Indians,* vol. 9, p. 215)—a complication that took decades to resolve. In any event, one cannot conclude from this one document that Cushing shared the enthusiasm of friends such as Alice Fletcher and Sylvester Baxter for conferring ownership of tribal lands upon individual Indians, in "severality." Possibly, in the present context, the implication of *private* ownership simply didn't occur to him.

27. Here is illustrated Cushing's recourse to archaeology and material culture as a means of pursuing his inquiry into the structure and functioning of social organization.

28. The lands referred to were not in the area involved in the Nutria controversy. In view of Bradley's official posture as commander of Fort Wingate and upholder of the laws, it is interesting to note that he too was involved in schemes to defraud the Indians of their land by entering illegal claims (Irving Telling, "New Mexican Frontiers," p. 234).

29. Indeed, it may have been the prospect of a feature story damaging to Logan's presidential aspirations that drew this newsman to Zuni in the first place. By the time of this trip west, William Elroy Curtis (1850–1911) was already a nationally known journalist, having for several years been chief of the *Inter-Ocean*'s Washington Bureau and before that having made a name through such coups as the interview he obtained with the James brothers during their war with the Pinkerton detectives in the 1870s, his reports on Custer's exploits during the Sioux campaign of 1874, and his investigative series on the activities of the Ku Klux Klan in the South. Apart from the chapter on the Nutria affair, much of what Curtis wrote of Cushing in *Children of the Sun* was drawn from the latter's own account in "My Adventures in Zuni" and from several of Baxter's articles, including "Father of the Pueblos" and "Aboriginal Pilgrimage."

30. Edwin Booth (1833–1893): Famous American Shakespearean actor.

31. Including this account in the book that came of his travels in the Southwest (*Children of the Sun*), Curtis corrected the "once" to "twice"—no doubt instructed by someone who wished for accuracy concerning the number of times Mrs. Stevenson had been to Zuni, if not how long she had stayed.

32. This letter appears both in Curtis, *Children of the Sun,* pp. 46–47, and in George E. Fay, ed., *Treaties, Land Cessions, and Other U.S. Congressional Documents Relative to American Indian Tribes. Zuni Indian Pueblo, New Mexico.* Part 1, pp. 8–9.

9. May–July 1883

1. For the President's order, see Fay, *Treaties, Land Cessions, and Other U.S. Congressional Documents . . . Zuni,* p. 2, or Curtis, *Children of the Sun,* p. 50.

2. A draft of this letter in Cushing's hand is in the Southwest Museum collection of Cushing Papers.

3. Edward Sylvester Morse (1838–1925), of Salem, Massachusetts, was professor of zoology at Harvard and author of books in the natural sciences and oriental studies.

4. "These are the canyons between Springerville and Lyman Lake, of which I think the two major ones on the Little Colorado are the one in Richville Valley and a smaller one between it and Springerville. I think there are others to the east" (Kintigh, personal communication).

5. Kintigh writes:

> I am aware of three sites to which Cushing's fissure pueblo type might apply. Two of these are associated with the Richville Valley already mentioned, and the other is Casa Malpais, a relatively well known site of the Pueblo IV period about two miles north of Springerville. This latter ruin was almost certainly the one whose ground plan was sketched by Cushing (compare with map in Edward Danson and Harold E. Molde, "Casa Malpais, A Fortified Pueblo Site at Springerville, Arizona," *Plateau* 22 [April 1950]: 61–67). None of these three ruins is as large as half a mile in length. However, Cushing apparently also explored the malpais area to the east of the Little Colorado, and there could well be more ruins of this sort out there. Local ranchers have told me that lots of artifacts have been removed from caves (which I suspect include Cushing's fissures) in the area between St. Johns and Springerville (personal communication).

6. Glazed paint would indicate a late occupation (i.e., post-A.D. 1275 or 1300).

7. "There is some good information here. Cushing says that leaving the region of fissure pueblos he entered the area of caves and craters. If he is going north along the Little Colorado, I think that he would be in the area of Lyman Lake" (Kintigh, personal communication).

8. Cushing's description is not very clear, but he evidently meant to designate the area under discussion in eastern Arizona as the country to the south of the mesas near Ojo Caliente and north of the upper Little Colorado badlands.

9. According to Keith Kintigh (personal communication), not much is known even now about these ancient burial grounds.

10. Cushing seems to be referring to a desert which lies southeast, rather than southwest, of Zuni. The Jornada del Muerto (journey of the dead man), "a waterless stretch of nearly 90 miles {which} lay on the caravan routes from Chihuahua to Santa Fe," seems to have been so named because of the many who perished in the crossing (T.M. Pearce, *New Mexico Place Names,* p. 77). Perhaps Cushing's spelling reflects local pronunciation.

11. Reference is to Lieut. James H. Simpson's "Journal of a Military Reconnaisance from Santa Fe, New Mexico, to the Navajo Country . . . in 1849" (U.S. 31st Cong., 1st Sess., Sen. Ex. Doc. 64 (Washington, 1850), pp. 55–168. By "Cremony Apaches" Cushing evidently meant the Indians treated of by John C. Cremony in his *Life Among the Apaches* (San Francisco, 1868). The story of the gold bullets, however, seems to have come neither from Cremony nor from Simpson but rather from one François X. Aubry. Traveling across the Apache country of Arizona in 1853, Aubrey reported:

> Met Indians today [from whom] we obtained over fifteen hundred dollars' worth of gold for a few old articles of clothing. The Indians use gold bullet for their guns. They are of different sizes and each Indian has a pouch of them. We saw an Indian load his gun with one large and two small gold bullets to shoot a rabbit (Ralph P. Bieder, ed., *Exploring South Western Trails, 1846–1854,* vol. 7 [Glendale, Calif., 1938], p. 370).

Whatever Cushing's private opinion of this claim may have been, one may note its possible strategic purpose in a letter which seems to have aimed at cultivating a potential source of support for his own archaeological work.

12. This letter, taken together with that of the previous week to Commissioner Price, suggests that Agent Sanchez had come around to Cushing's point of view regarding Navajos and horses. Writing to Cushing the following day, Sanchez reported that he had urged Riordan to "bring the guilty parties to speedy justice" and promised to keep Cushing informed. The Cushing letter referred to has not been found.

13. The righteous Senator is of course "interpreting" the boundaries as defined—mistakenly—in the executive order establishing the reservation.

14. Logan's claim is grossly exaggerated, of course. The Zuni River is one whose local depth, if any, is measured during most of the year in inches.

15. On the subject of stench, at least, Logan goes little farther than Bourke, who, on first visiting Zuni, wrote in his diary:

> The smell in Zuni is outrageous. Decayed meat, sheep and goats, pelts, excrement human and animal, unwashed dogs and Indians, fleas, lice, and bedbugs (the houses of the Zunis are full of these last)—garbage of every kind—it must be regarded as a standing certificate of the salubrity of this climate that a single Zuni is in existence today (Sutherland, "The Diaries of John Gregory Bourke," p. 282).

16. The selection here is composed of an amalgam of excerpts from the letter in the *Tribune* and the *New York Times* story reporting it.

17. Cushing had written to the school expressing

Zuni concern over its failure to send home this pupil (named after the former missionary teacher at Zuni) at the close of the agreed-upon period of his attendance.

18. Here perhaps Curtis betrays a motive independent of his interest in justice for the Indians. The primacy of Curtis' concern with Republican politics was to emerge later in his support (however reluctant) for the Blaine-Logan presidential ticket.

19. While Pratt appears here to appreciate Cushing's point about keeping faith with agreements, he elsewhere expressed dissatisfaction with the degree to which Bureau anthropologists generally cooperated in his endeavor at the Carlisle Indian Training School to separate the Indian children from "savagery" and "saw in the 'Bureau oligarchy' an insideous scheme to 'keep the Indians from the opportunities and environment of civilized life,' because Indian citizenship would render the Bureau obsolete" (Richard Henry Pratt, *Battlefield and Classroom: Four Decades with the American Indian, 1867–1904,* ed. Robert M. Utley [New Haven, Connecticut, 1964], p. 293).

20. A month later Cushing heard from Pratt that the boy had died—the third fatality among the four Zunis sent to Carlisle. "I had fondly hoped," he wrote, "that the development of character and capacity by Taylor would enable such good work among his people as would atone somewhat to them for the loss of [the other two who had died]. But alas, 'Man proposes but God disposes' " (Southwest Museum HC 56).

21. A Cushing version of the story of the hostage priest may be found in "Outlines of Zuni Creation Myths," pp. 330–32. However, it was not Governor Oñate, long dead, but Governor Cruzate who overcame some of the Rio Grande pueblos in 1689 and was believed to have afterwards issued grants of land to a number of them, including Zuni (see pp. 369–70 n. 15)—though it was not Cruzate but Diego de Vargas who regained Zuni and the other western pueblos, three years later.

22. Cushing seems to be thinking of Brevet Maj. Henry L. Kendrick, mentioned above in Bourke's diary. For a time he was commanding officer at Fort Defiance; he returned east, however, well before the Navajos were finally subdued (McNitt, *The Indian Traders,* pp. 258–61). His correspondence with Pedro Pino may be found in the Southwest Museum HC 3-10.

23. The paper mentioned here was not in fact quoted in the "interview" and was subsequently lost sight of. But what appears to be a copy of this 1868 document, typed in 1911 or 1912 by Zuni postmaster Robert Bauman or his wife, was found by E. Richard Hart in the Zuni Postmasters' file in the Denver Federal Records Center (Zuni Indian Agency, entry 157). It reads as follows:

> KNOW ALL MEN BY THESE PRESENTS:
> That Jose Balla, John Balla, Antonio Balla, Juan Berea Balla, Jose Gonzales Balla Naturales, of the Pueblo of Zuni, have with the consent of the Officers of the Pueblo of Zuni, they understand, taken possession of the ranch of the Nutries [sic]: this 10th day of January, 1868, One thousand eight hundred and sixty eight and has [sic] admitted One Hundred more persons of the Pueblo of Zuni; under the same right and possession as the above mentioned persons; which names are appended in Roll hereto and which Ranch has belonged to the Balla family for over one hundred years—given by the King of Spain to Jose Francisco Balla, Great Grandfather of the first mentioned undersigned and which Ranch has the following lines from the Nutria Spring 2 Two Miles East, West, North and South, which ranch lays within the Zuni pasture Grant, but conceded to the Balla family apart from the Tribe of Zuni on account of services rendered to the Spanish Kings during the Indian revulsion against the Spaniards and being inheritance of the first mentioned Jose Balla undersigned voluntarily agrees and takes in the persons mentioned in Role hereto in order to guarantee said persons a good right and possession as himself and his family for all time and duration.
>
> In witness whereof the undersigned Officers and Balla family sign their names this 10th day of January One Thousand Eighteen Hundred and Sixty Eight—1868.

Appended are the names of the Balla (or Palla) heirs plus those of Manuel McCavan (Cacique of Pueblo), Jose Lionicio Laitselsua [?] (First Capitan de Guerra), Jose Macketta (Captain of War), and Juan Septimo (Governor of Lajusia [?]).

24. Cushing may not have sent Naiiutchi's letter direct to the President, but he of course did send it to his journalist friend William E. Curtis (who published it in his *Children of the Sun* [p. 59]), with the request to have it delivered to the President.

25. The Metcalf interview appeared in the Chicago *Daily News* for June 15, 1883, under the heading "Logan and the Zunis. Some Disinterested Testimony. An Artist Showing the Disingenuineness of the Senator's 'Reply'—The Nutrias Spring Essential to the Zuni Nation." Of Logan's attack on Cushing in the *Chicago Tribune,* Metcalf said: "A man who would make such a narrow and bigoted statement as that I would not attempt to answer. It carries its own condemnation with it." The bulk of the interview is taken up with Nutria matter itself and Metcalf's refutation of the claim that the Zunis really did not need the spring in question.

26. In a previous letter (not included here) Cushing had requested his supervisors' response to a proposal that

a post office be established in Zuni with himself as postmaster. No such action seems to have been taken during his tenure in the pueblo.

27. From Leslie A. White, ed., *Pioneers in American Anthropology: The Bandelier-Morgan Letters, 1873–1883,* vol. II, pp. 252–53.

28. This exposition of 1883 seems to have been an early version of what became the annual Santa Fe Fiesta. Whereas the climactic pageant of the "Tertio-Millenial" was a reenactment of the original conquest by Coronado, however, the modern pageant features the *re*-conquest following the Pueblo Revolt of 1680. For a study of the modern fiesta, see Ronald Grimes, *Symbol and Conquest: Public Ritual and Drama in Santa Fe, New Mexico* (Ithaca: Cornell University Press, 1976).

29. Versions of this story of "Nu-we" were recorded by both Cushing ("Discovery of Zuni, or the Ancient Provinces of Cibola and the Seven Lost Cities" [see Appendix D]) and Bourke (Sutherland, "The Diaries of John Gregory Bourke," pp. 954–55). Ruling out what he took to be the former's proposal of Nuñez Cabeza de Vaca as the original of "Nu-we" on the grounds that this Spaniard never got to New Mexico, Bandelier argued instead that "Nu-we" and the "Black Mexican" were one and the same person: Cabeza's companion and Marcos' guide, Estevanico (Rodack, ed., *Adolph F. Bandelier's The Discovery of New Mexico,* p. 95). For a clearer statement of Cushing's own theory about "Nu-we," see Appendix D.

30. *New Mexican Review,* 19 July 1883. Cushing's manuscript copy of Palowahtiwa's speech is in the Southwest Museum (H-C 202).

10. August–December 1883

1. Southwest Museum HC 52.

2. Illness is probably to be included among the problematic subjects in Cushing's biography. No one doubts the reality of the ailments that recurrently disabled him, but there is sometimes room for speculation about the psychological or strategic dimensions of the timing. An aspect of Cushing's persona, in Curtis Hinsley's view, is that, "when under attack, he got ill. He did this all his life" (personal communication). *How* ill is not always equally easy to gauge either, as in instances where his own communications are the only witness and illness is the reason given for, say, missed deadlines or overdue letters. If he did dramatize the state of his health in writing to Horsford, it was a mistake, for the effect intended was surely *not* to get himself recalled to Washington.

3. In Bandelier, Cushing had a friend with as many money troubles as himself—and fewer scruples about exploiting his friends. Here, under the financial stress caused by the approaching failure of his father's bank in Highland, Illinois, he had solicited and received from Cushing a check for $100 (Lange and Riley, *The Southwestern Journals of Adolph F. Bandelier* [1970], p. 144). For a view of this pattern, including one plea spiced by dramatic hints of suicide unless the money was forthcoming, see Bandelier's correspondence with Charles Lummis (Lummis Papers, Southwest Museum).

4. Bandelier was speaking of his wife, Josephine Huegy. It is not clear who "Father No-mo-ho" was—evidently either a Zuni with problems pronouncing English or vice versa.

5. Adolph Bastian was director of the Berlin Museum and one of the major nineteenth-century European pioneers in anthropology.

6. "Our ancestors, the ones who have died—these are the rain. These become the *Uwanami,* the water spirits whose houses are the cumulus clouds" (quoted in Parsons, *Pueblo Indian Religion,* pp. 172–73). In Zuni tradition, it is on these cloud beings, who dwell respectively in the spirit worlds of the six directions (each represented by a priesthood), that the people must depend for rain, and on them a correspondingly high proportion of Zuni prayer and ritual is focused. *Ma-i-ne* (*ma:* piece of rock salt, *ne:* singular): possibly, according to Jane Young, a name for the Twin War Gods as dwellers in Zuni Salt Lake.

7. There follows an account of the Archaeological Institute's budget for the current and previous years.

8. By the end of the year, writing evidently in reference to subsequent developments in this same continuing dissension, the Pueblo agent in Santa Fe reported that "there are two antagonistic elements whose antagonism goes so far that it keeps this Pueblo, I believe, behind, superstitious and divided. They are fighting against each other. There is no peace there, but on the contrary they are machinating against each other all the time" (Pedro Sanchez to Commissioner H. Price, December 10, 1883, National Archives, Record Group 75, Office of Indian Affairs, Letters Received 1881–1907). For historical perspective, see Triloki Nath Pandey: "Factionalism in a Southwestern Pueblo." A brief survey of Zuni factionalism may also be found in E. Richard Hart, "Encroachment on Zuni Lands and Depredations Committed Against the People" (Senate hearing, February 21, 1975, *Congressional Record* 121(31): 2754–2763).

9. Apparently eliciting no positive response from the Bureau to this more modest initial proposal for building an annex to the house he was already living in, Cushing proceeded to build a house of his own.

10. Bandelier's diary indicates that he was at this point in financial difficulty relating to a jointly owned coal mine (Lange and Riley, *Southwestern Journals of Adolph F. Bandelier* [1970], p. 145). As to who "somebody" was, however, the diary gives no clue.

11. Herman F. C. ten Kate, "Frank Hamilton Cushing," *American Anthropologist* n.s.2: 769. For biographical information and bibliography of ten Kate's publications, see the obituary by Jac. Hayink and F. W. Hodge (*American Anthropologist* n.s.33: 415–17).

12. The red "button" signifies the French Legion of Honor. Metcalf, in Paris to continue his training as a painter, would remain in Europe until 1889.

13. Parts I (eighteen pages) and II (the fifty-two-page "Report on Oraibi" later published by Fewkes and Parsons) are on file in the National Anthropological Archives, together with a ten-page catalogue of the collections made in the Hopi country, five pen-and-ink drawings, and a watercolor sketch. Part III seems not to have reached the Bureau, but a ten page draft is among the Cushing papers in the Southwest Museum. Selected contents of Part I, like those of Cushing's other annual reports to the Bureau, are here printed piecemeal to maintain chronological order.

14. Cushing refers to the ruin of K'in-i-K'el or Kin Tiel, about twenty-two miles north of Navajo Springs, and to the section of Cushing's report which appears above, pp. 251–54.

15. Eban Norton Horsford (1818–93) was a former professor of chemistry at Harvard who pursued in later life an interest in archaeology and early American history. Among the subjects on which he wrote were Northmen settlements in America and American Indian languages.

16. Cushing's friend Metcalf voiced similar concern when interviewed in Chicago en route home from the Southwest. Cushing, he reported, "has nearly ruined his health, probably irrecoverably, in his self-sacrificing labors, but it goes for naught with him in case he be allowed to continue to the end, which he now thinks is approaching" (*Chicago Daily News,* June 15, 1883).

17. Horsford doubtless refers to the seventeenth-century French explorer, interpreter, and diplomat Jean Nicolet, the first European to make his way across Canada and down the Great Lakes to what is now Green Bay, Wisconsin. In the course of a two-decade career in the New World as agent for the French, Nicolet spent years living among the Indians—particularly the Algonquins and the Hurons—but drowned in a river accident before he could write his memoirs.

18. If such a letter was sent, it has not been found; but some twenty other affectionate letters from ten Kate to Cushing are preserved in the Southwest Museum Hodge-Cushing Collection.

19. Since his arrival in New Mexico on October 25, Bandelier had been investigating ruins and archives in the Santa Fe area and around El Paso. He would now head down the Rio Grande valley, west into Arizona, and then south into Mexico with the aim of tracing what he, like Humboldt and Prescott before him, believed to be the migration path of the ancient Pueblo ancestors of the Aztecs.

20. The Manso and Piro Indians live in the Las Cruces and El Paso area along the Rio Grande. Believed to have spoken originally a language in the Tiwa branch of the Kiowa-Tanoan family, both now use Spanish, with English as a second language.

21. The Gran Quivira ruins on the eastern slope of the Manzano Mountains in central New Mexico are now a National Monument. Queres: The Spanish original for Keres, from which the name Keresan was coined by Powell to denote a family of closely related Pueblo languages or dialects. The Rio Grande pueblos of Zia, Santa Ana, San Felipe, Santo Domingo, and Cochiti are all Keresan-speaking, as are the western Pueblos of Acoma and Laguna. The Pueblo communities Bandelier alludes to were among those in the more southerly part of New Mexico which were not involved in the Pueblo Revolt of 1680. They had retreated south with the Spanish and resettled along the Rio Grande near El Paso.

22. By the time Cushing came to know him (probably prior to visiting the Hopi country in 1881), Thomas Varker Keam (1846–1904) was already established as one of the premier Indian traders in the Southwest. He is remembered not only for the great collection of Southwest Indian craftwork he amassed but for his efforts on behalf of the Indians with whom he dealt and for his generous hospitality to all who visited his post in Keam's Canyon. A Cornishman who had gone to sea as a youngster to seek his fortune, Keam had made his way to the Southwest in 1865 by way of Australia and San Francisco. Licensed in 1875 to trade with the Hopis, Keam established his post just outside the eastern boundary of the Hopi reservation in the canyon which has since borne his name. Fluent in both Hopi and Navajo, Keam was "widely known to Indians in the Southwest as 'Tomas' and respected and loved by them" (Stuart Culin, "Thomas Varker Keam," *American Anthropologist* 7 [1905]: 172). "Po-lak-akai" was Stephen's version of the name of Cushing's guide from the Hopi villages to Havasupai and his companion on the more recent visit to Oraibi.

23. Stephen refers here to Jeremiah Sullivan, son of a former U.S. Agent, who had, after the departure of his

father, taken up residence in one of the Hopi villages and was attempting to assume an ethnological role. No doubt, had he seen Stephen's treatment of him here, he would have felt as abused as he did on reading Cushing's reference to him as a "squaw man" for whom the Hopis had "done everything they could," and from whom they had "put up with all kinds of things," because of their wish to keep up with the Zunis by having an adopted American of their own (see *San Francisco Examiner,* July 8, 1888, and an August 1888 letter of refutation from Sullivan to Cushing in the Southwest Museum collection, H-C 387).

24. According to anthropologist Jerrold E. Levy, the correct transcription of the Navajo, using the Robert Young alphabet, would be *yoo nilchini tlani* (*yoo* = beads; *nilchini* = strung out in a line, *tlani* = many).

25. It is not really clear from Stephen's letter whether the ravished cave was one in which Cushing had cached his finds from the Zuni shrines in the area or one of the shrines themselves.

26. "O terque quaterque beati" (O three and four times blessed), Aeneis cries in Book I, line 94, of the *Aeneid,* thinking of those who had died a dry death under the walls of Troy rather than drowning at sea, as he seems about to do. In spite of this rather grim context, the intent of Stephen's allusion seems to have been innocent of irony.

27. This last flower in Stephen's invitational bouquet is the closing verse of "Under the Greenwood Tree," sung by Amien, one of the lords attending on the banished Duke Senior, in Shakespeare's *As You Like It* (II.v.i).

28. Whether Cushing entered into this "strictly private" business with Keam is not known.

11. 1884

1. See *Zuni Breadstuff,* pp. 612–16 (Green, *Zuni,* pp. 320–22). In addition to discussing the creation epic and detailing his explorations, Cushing's fourteen-page Annual report for 1884 includes a summary of the results of his "linguistic, geographic, and traditional studies relative to the succession of architectural types in the Southwest," his studies of "the sociologic history of the Zuni Pueblos," and his studies "relating to the myths and folktales abundantly recorded by him. . . ." Slightly cut and edited by Powell, this report of Cushing's may be found in the *Fifth Annual Report of the Bureau of Ethnology,* pp. xxv–xxix.

2. This house of Cushing's, built on the site of Old Zuni, or Halona:wa, has had a history of its own—as well as contributing prominently to the wider architectural and demographic consequences of his residence in Zuni. Even before he built the house, Cushing had initiated a revolutionary break from the defensive Pueblo house design with its restricted ladder entry by inducing the governor to allow him to cut a ground-level doorway through the western wall of the pueblo into his room. The vermillion-colored door which he installed was much admired and widely imitated (Cushing, "The Need of Studying the Indian in Order to Teach Him," p. 112. The house too had an impact—one reason for which was simply its location, across the river from the main pueblo. Cushing was thus encouraging diffusion, or as C. Gregory Crampton puts it, a "trend to the suburbs" (*The Zunis of Cibola,* p. 141). When he returned to Zuni to undertake excavations as director of the Hemenway Expedition, Cushing had an additional room built on the house—a project which had unexpected archaeological significance, since in digging the foundations the workers uncovered buried parts of the old Halona. Still later, in 1916, Cushing's brother-in-law, Frederick Webb Hodge, would use the house as his headquarters in a major excavation of the old ruins. By this time Hodge had to deal with the bad feelings produced in Zuni by the American failure to live up to the promise Cushing had made to turn the house over to the Zunis when he was through using it (correspondence with Zuni Governor William J. Lewis, Hodge Collection, Southwest Museum).

3. Cushing's reference is presumably to the pressure he assumed was being applied on the Bureau by Senator Logan and his allies to have him removed from Zuni—and indeed dismissed from his job altogether. Cushing was putting a price on his immediate return, and judging by the March 21 letter from Pilling (see below), Powell seems eventually to have done what he could—short of actually paying the bills—to meet Cushing's terms. Cushing's return was delayed only three months instead of six.

4. According to a Bandelier letter of November 12, 1884 (Southwest Museum H-C 92), Cushing was paid $195 for the collections he ultimately sent to Germany.

5. Bandelier evidently refers here to the *Annual Reports* of the Bureau of Ethnology. Nothing came of this proposal for a joint publication with Cushing, though Bandelier was in Europe the following winter and must have investigated the prospects for such a venture.

6. Bandelier was writing from Fort Lowell, outside Tucson. Fort Grant, to the east of Tucson, was on his route, via Fort Huachuca, to the Mexican border. Chico was Bandelier's horse, which he had left at Fort Lowell the previous year and was now reclaiming.

7. Cushing shared with his father an interest in the family genealogy—and in fact is credited by James Stevenson Cushing, author of *The Genealogy of the Cushing Family: An Account of the Ancestors and Descendents of Matthew Cushing, Who Came to America in 1638* (Montreal: Perrault Printing Co., 1905), as the source of "much of our knowledge of the earlier history of the Cushings." He had traced the family origins back to the Vikings; so "Miss Cushing" knew to whom she was writing.

8. While firmly evolutionist, Cushing's credo, as expressed here, reflects a sense not only of the superiority of his own culture but of its *relatedness* to the lore and life of peoples living in a state of "savagery"—a position consistent with his aim not only to learn about Indians himself but to aid in "wearing away race barriers and benefiting the Indians" (see *Boston Herald* article of April 20, 1884, below).

9. The Streltsy ("musketeers") were a military corps established in Russia in the mid-sixteenth century. Involved in the succession struggle between Peter I and his half-brother Ivan, they were defeated by Ivan's forces, and over a thousand were said to have been executed and as many more mutilated.

10. The first installment of "Zuni Breadstuff" appeared in the January 1884 issue.

11. The reader of the letter in question (January 19, 1884) will note that it contains no statement of resignation. But this is the kind of privileged information (or misinformation) that suggests either Cushing's own authorship of the article or his close involvement in its composition.

12. Here the author is either misinformed (i.e., not Cushing) or slightly disingenuous. Cushing himself did not publish in *Harper's,* though he was the source of much of the information in an article published therein by Sylvester Baxter ("The Father of the Pueblos," *Harper's* 65:72–91).

Epilogue

1. Edwin A. Curley was travel editor of the Chicago publication *American Field* and author of several books on western and midwestern subjects. Before writing this letter to Cushing, Curley had written both to President Arthur and to Secretary of the Interior H. M. Teller appealing for justice for the Zunis and enclosing an article from the *American Field* of July 14, 1883, "written by myself as a result of a personal investigation of Senator Logan's Zuni land grab" (letters in George E. Fay, ed., *Treaties, Land Cessions and Other U.S. Congressional Documents . . . Zuni,* pp. 18–21). "I am confident," he wrote to Teller, "that my facts will bear thorough investigation. . . . I say confidently in addition that the general public opinion of New Mexico is in this case three to one in favor of justice, and all through the neighborhood of the Zunis where the particulars are best known it is practically unanimous . . ." (p. 21). The article, "The Land of the Zuni and Senator Logan," is a detailed refutation of Logan's May 22 letter in the *Chicago Tribune* (Cushing's name being carefully left unmentioned). Now, apparently, Curley was preparing to write a second article in defense of the Zunis.

2. Bourke's reference is to the Montreal meeting of the British Anthropological Association. Cushing had given a paper "On the Development of Industrial and Ornamental Art Among the Zunis," to appear later in the October 9, 1884, issue of the British publication *Nature.* In its completed form, it appeared in the *Fourth Annual Report of the Bureau of Ethnology* under the title "A Study of Pueblo Pottery as Illustrative of Zuni Cultural Growth."

3. Bourke here modestly refers to *The Snake Dance of the Moquis of Arizona: being a narrative of a journey from Santa Fe, New Mexico, to the villages of the Moqui Indians of Arizona, with a description of the manners and customs of this peculiar people and especially of the revolting religious rite, the snake dance; to which is added a brief dissertation upon serpent worship in general, with an account of the tablet dance of the pueblo of Santo Domingo, New Mexico, etc.* (London: Sampson, Low, Marston, Searl and Rivington, 1884, and New York: Charles Scribner's Sons, 1884).

4. Bourke's story of this campaign in 1883 against the Chiricahua Apaches is told in *An Apache Campaign in the Sierra Madre* (New York: Charles Scribner's Sons, 1886).

5. Bourke's "Medicine Men of the Apache" appeared in the Bureau's Ninth *Annual Report,* but that was the only one of his several dozen professional publications to appear under Bureau auspices.

6. Matthews had gone "to a place called Niqotilizi (Hard Earth), some twenty miles northwest from Fort Wingate . . . within the southern boundary of the Navajo Reservation" to witness this performance of the *hockan,* to be recorded in his "The Mountain Chant: A Navajo Ceremony" (*Fifth Annual Report of the Bureau of Ethnology* [Washington, D.C., 1887], pp. 379–467). The *Yebitcai* performance would introduce him to the subject of his later classic work, *The Night Chant: A Navajo Ceremony* (Memoirs of the American Museum of Natural History, vol. VI [New York, 1902]).

7. There was of course no periodical of that name.

8. Matthews is evidently speaking of Pedro Sanchez, who replaced Benjamin Thomas as Pueblo agent.

9. This would doubtless have been Edward B. Tylor, who visited Zuni in 1884. The Stevensons were there at the time, and later, at a meeting of the Anthropological Society of Washington, Tylor extolled their joint work, along with Cushing's. "One thing I particularly noticed," he said, "was that to get at the confidence of a tribe, the man of the house, though he can do a great deal, cannot do all. If his wife sympathizes with his work, and is able to it, really half of the work of investigation seems to me to fall to her, so much is to be learned through the women of the tribe which the men will not readily disclose. The experience seemed to me a lesson to anthropologists not to sound the 'bull-roarer,' and warn the ladies off from their proceedings, but rather to avail themselves thankfully of their help" ("How Problems of American Anthropology Strike the English," *Transactions of the Anthropological Society,* Vol. III, 1895: 93). A sound and foresightful point—but perhaps not quite what Cushing would have wished as the fruit of his efforts to win "this priest's influence and approval."

10. "Black-beard" was a Zuni nickname for the trader, Douglas Graham.

Appendices

1. There is no indication of when Cushing wrote this note—presumably intended for use in one of his lectures.

2. This was the piece by Sylvester Baxter which sounded the initial alarm on the Nutria land-steal scheme—and outraged Senator Logan. Accused of complicity, Cushing denied having anything to do with the piece, but, given the nature of some of Baxter's information, as well as the nature of the situation generally, the denial seems implausible. The article is long and detailed; due to space limitations, only a small portion is reprinted here.

3. Of this proposal regarding the name "Nu-we," Professor Madeleine T. Rodack remarks:

> It is most interesting and no more unlikely than any other idea that has been suggested. However, Andres del Campo was presumably accompanied by two Indians, Lucas and Sebastian (though Jaramillo calls them Negroes) when he escaped from Quivira. There are various references to dogs, but sometimes to only one dog who hunted food for them on the journey and accompanied them all the way back to Mexico. According to Casteñeda, however, the Indians stayed at Quivira to bury the priest [Andres' master] who had been killed and caught up with Andres later (but how much later?). Also there is the problem that most references to Andres say that he arrived from Panuco, which is in eastern Mexico, south of Texas, and imply that he traveled at first almost directly south. Anyway, the theory that he went to Zuni cannot be discarded in view of the conflicting reports on the whole thing (personal communication).

4. According to more recent linguistic studies, Cushing is in error here. The name *Shiwi* is *not* derived from the Zuni word for meat or flesh. It is unanalyzable and has no meaning except as a name (Fred Eggan and Triloki Nath Pandey, "Zuni History, 1850–1970," in *Handbook of North American Indians,* vol. 9, p. 480).

5. By his identification of Cibola with Zuni, Cushing answered a question long speculated on. Discussion at that point shifted to the question of how many "cities" of Cibola or Zuni were actually occupied at the time of the Conquest and which ones they were. Subsequent researchers have been in general agreement about five of the towns named by Cushing: Kia-ki-me (Kyaki:ma), Matsa-ki (Mats'a:kya), Ha-lo-na (Halona:wa), Ha-wi-kuh (Hawikku), and Canabi or Kian-na-we (more commonly known as Kechiba:wa). Beyond these five, consensus breaks down. Hodge, for example, in his *History of Hawikuh,* summing up research done after Cushing by Bandelier, Fewkes, and others, argued for a total of six rather than seven mid-sixteenth century Cibola towns and proposed—for the sixth one unmentioned by Cushing—Kwa'kin'a. See, however, the note below concerning Cushing's apparent confusion of Kwa'kin'a and Hambassa:wa. For a review of the question in 1917 in the light of pottery types found in the various ruins, see Leslie Spier, "An Outline for a Chronology of Zuni Ruins." According to Keith Kintigh:

> the archaeological evidence is still not adequate to provide clear answers. It does not contradict the inclusion of Kwa'kin'a as one of the six villages, and it seems to point to Chalo:wa [another village not on Cushing's list] as the seventh, if there was one. Chalo:wa appears to have a later *ceramic* assemblage than Binna:wa (Cushing's A-pi-na-wah). However, our samples from the two sites may not be representative of their occupation as a whole and could well be misleading. Hambassa:wa is a very small site with a variety of pottery on the surface that indicates use of this location for a very long time. In my view, evidence supporting the argument that there were only six rather than seven pueblos occupied at the time of Spanish contact is far from compelling. In short, beyond the five fairly well established candidates, the question remains open" (personal communication).

See T.J. Ferguson and E. Richard Hart, *A Zuni Atlas* for site locations. For modern analysis of Zuni town names, see *Handbook of North American Indians,* p. 481.

6. Actually, the "Region of the Southern Salinas"—if by that is signified the Zuni Salt Lake region—lies far-

ther to the south than the area of Kyama:kya, traditionally associated with the stories Cushing seems to have in mind here, of the *Kyana:kwe* who hid away all the game animals and fought with the Zuni ancestors. For a review of other theories about the location of the Marata of the Spanish chronicles and a brief history of the proprietary claims to the Zuni Salt Lake, now a part of the tribal reservation, see E. Richard Hart, "Damage to Zuni Trust Lands," Appendix VII.

7. This site is marked as "Topintea" on Cushing's sketched map of the region.

8. "At Santa Fe, Cushing told me that . . . the traditions of the Zuni reach as far south as the foothills of the Escudilla, and that the Zuni showed him an old historical painting on hide, which embodies their migrations. He made a facsimile of it" (Bandelier diary entry for July 22, 1883, Lange and Riley, *Southwestern Journals of Adolph F. Bandelier* [1970], p. 142).

9. In recollecting his ruins, Cushing seems to have two of them confused here. According to Kintigh:

> The site identified as Hambassawa by Spier and Mindeleff (who mapped the site) is in the middle of the valley, on the *south* bank of the river about 4.7 miles (as the crow flies) WSW of Zuni. It is not on a slope but on a low rise in the middle of a broad, flat floodplain next to the river, where cedars do not ordinarily grow. Furthermore, as Mindeleff's map shows, it is a small site with the longest stretch of straight wall extending only about 25 feet (1891: Figure 15). On the other hand, the description given by Cushing fits almost perfectly the site called Kwa'kin'a. Here cedar trees do grow up to the edge of the ruin, which is on a slope on the north side of the valley about 6.7 miles (as the crow flies) WSW of Zuni [see the map in Kintigh 1985: 22]. In 1979, walls about 400 feet long were traced [Kintigh 1985: 66]. In addition, the ceramics are consistent with a protohistoric date. Given all this, it seems clear that the site Cushing describes as Hampassawan (Hambassa:wa) is the one others have called Kwa'kin'a" (personal communication).

In short, Cushing seems to have been in consensus with later writers about the *locations* of six of the Cibolan towns but confused here about the *name* of one of them. Could he also have confused the names of the two towns in question in the list quoted from his memory of the storyteller's formula?

10. An entry for December 27, 1892, in Cushing's diary mentions the appearance of this interview but unfortunately does not explain its background. This was one of several occasions on which troops were sent to Zuni in connection with hangings of persons accused of witchcraft—at least one of which interventions led to the jailing of Cushing's and Stevenson's friend Naiiutchi, the elder chief Bow priest. A particularly famous—but hitherto rather vaguely dated—case was that of Nick Tumaka, or Dumahka, later governor of Zuni and a major collaborator both with Bunzel and with Benedict. Accused of sorcery and hung up by his wrists, Dumahka had sent his father into Gallup for help and had been rescued by a company of soldiers dispatched from Fort Wingate (Triloki Nath Pandey, "Factionalism in a Southwestern Pueblo," pp. 101 and 146; see also Edward S. Curtis, *The North American Indians* [Norwood, Mass., 1926], vol. 17, p. 111, and Alexander M. Stephen, *Hopi Journal of Alexander M. Stephen,* Elsie Crews Parsons, ed. Columbia University Contributions to Anthropology 23 [New York: Columbia University Press, 1936], p. 276). While the Cushing remark quoted at the beginning of the *Evening News* story would seem to suggest that two women had been the alleged victims on that occasion, a different possibility is suggested by another account of a sorcery-related military intervention in Zuni, also in late December, which appeared in the *New York Herald* of January 22, 1893. According to this story, the troops had been sent to make arrests on the complaint of a "medicine man" who had escaped to Gallup after being tortured for witchcraft because of his failure to produce rain. With allowances made for a normal measure of journalistic garbling and inventiveness, it seems likely that the incident behind both the *Herald* story and the Cushing interview was that involving Nich Dumahka.

11. Judging from a reference to his "Archaeological Explorations in Florida," Cushing wrote this "Extract" in the late 1890s.

12. Cushing evidently refers here to the slat-shaped effigies of the war gods "planted" each year by the Bow Priests in designated shrines.

13. Miss Faurote (or Ferrote) was a teacher in the government school at Zuni under the directorship of Mary E. Dissette (or DeSette), who also figures prominently in this letter. Miss Dissette, the last of the teachers who ran the school under the auspices of the Presbyterian mission, was in Zuni from 1888 to 1898. The haircutting campaign referred to in this letter, and in the letter to Palowahtiwa Cushing enclosed with it, was but one of her zealous efforts to civilize the Zunis. At another point, in order to stop the importation of liquor occasioned by the *Shalak'o* festival, she seems to have threatened to outlaw the festival itself, and she evidently requested help from the army to compel attendance at her school. It was she who, in 1897, called in the troops to arrest several Bow Priests—including, for the second time, Naiiutchi—for "dealing roughly with an elderly woman suspected of witchcraft" (Irving Telling, "New

Mexican Frontiers," p. 134). Following these arrests, troops were kept in the pueblo at her request for nearly a year, though there was no evidence of civil unrest and though the government dropped its case against the arrested men themselves after a few months and released them from prison (having meanwhile forcibly cut their hair). As a result of such interventions, the authority of the Bow Priests, and of the Zuni theocracy generally, was greatly undermined. As for Naiiutchi himself, the result of his prison experience was that "he got so sick inside that he could not live long," according to a later informant (Pandey, "Factionalism in a Southwestern Pueblo," p. 100). He died in 1904, attended by his friend Matilda Stevenson, who reported that no mask was buried with his body, as Naiiutchi "had never worn his mask or danced with the personators of anthropic gods since his hair had been cut while a prisoner. . . . His mask will go to a male member of his family and he will not dance in Ko'thluwala'wa [the village of the dead]" (Matilda Stevenson, "The Zuni Indians," p. 317). She had reason to know what was and was not buried with Naiiutchi, since she bribed his son to exhume the older man's sacred bundle for her—that is, for science (Stevenson to W.H. Holmes, August 30, 1904, Stevenson Papers, National Anthropological Archives).

14. The English translation, or interpretation, of Cushing's letter to Palowahtiwa represents the combined efforts of Wilfred Eriacho and Jane Young. Given the obscurities in Cushing's Zuni, some guesses had to be made as to the meaning intended—particularly in the first sentence of the penultimate paragraph.

Selected Bibliography

FRANK HAMILTON CUSHING

Unpublished Papers

1872–1900 Correspondence, MSS., and other papers. National Anthropological Archives, Smithsonian Institution, Washington, D.C.

1874–1900 Correspondence, MSS., and other papers. Southwest Museum, Los Angeles, California.

1886–1889 Papers relating to the Hemenway Southwestern Archaeological Expedition. Museum of the American Indian, Heye Foundation, New York.

1886–1959 Papers relating to the Hemenway Southwestern Archaeological Expedition. Archives, 1886–1894, and related papers in the "X" files, 1897–1959, MSS., Peabody Museum, Harvard University, Cambridge, Mass.

1896–1899 Correspondence relating to the Key Marco excavations in Florida and other subjects. University of Pennsylvania Library, Philadelphia, Pennsylvania.

1896–1898 Correspondence relating to the Key Marco excavations in Florida. American Philosophical Society Library, Philadelphia, Pennsylvania.

Publications

1875 "Antiquities of Orleans County, N.Y." In *Annual Report of the Board of Regents of the Smithsonian Institution, 1884,* pp. 375–77. Washington, D.C.

1880 "Ancient Cities in Arizona." *American Antiquarian* 10 (1880): 325–26.

1882a "The Zuni Social, Mythic, and Religious Systems." *Popular Science Monthly* (June): 186–92.

1882b "The Nation of the Willows." *Atlantic Monthly* 50: 362–74, 541–59. Reprinted in book form with introduction by Robert C. Euler, Flagstaff, Arizona: Northland Press, 1965.

1882–1883 "My Adventures in Zuni." *Century Illustrated Monthly Magazine* 25: 191–207, 500–11, and 26: 28–47. Edition in book form with Sylvester Baxter, "An Aboriginal Pilgrimage," and introduction by E. DeGolyer, Santa Fe: Peripatetic Press, 1941. Facsimile reprint in book form with introduction by Okah L. Jones, Jr., Palmer Lake, Colorado: Filter Press, 1967.

1883a "Zuni Fetiches." In *Second Annual Report of the Bureau of Ethnology, 1880–1881,* pp. 9–45. Washington, D.C. Facsimile reprint in book form with introduction by Tom Bahti, Flagstaff, Arizona: KC Publications, 1966. Reprinted, Las Vegas, Nevada: KC Publications, 1974.

1883b "Zuni Weather Proverbs." *Weather Proverbs,* pp. 124–27. Washington, D.C.

1884–1885 "Zuni Breadstuff." *Millstone* 9, nos. 1–12, and 10, nos. 1–4, 6–8. Edition in book form with introduction by John Wesley Powell, Indian Notes and Monographs, vol. 8, New York: Museum of the American Indian, Heye Foundation, 1920. Reprinted 1974.

1886 "A Study of Pueblo Pottery as Illustrative of Zuni Cultural Growth." In *Fourth Annual Report of the Bureau of Ethnology, 1882–1883,* pp. 467–521. Washington, D.C.

1890 "Preliminary Notes on the Origin, Working Hypothesis, and Primary Researches of the Hemenway Southwestern Archaeological Expedition." In *Contrès International des Américanistes, Berlin, 1888,* pp. 151–94. Berlin.

1892a "Manual Concepts: A Study of the Influence of Hand-Usage on Culture Growth." *American Anthropologist* 5: 289–317.

1892b "The Villard-Bandelier South American Expedition." *American Anthropologist* 5: 273–76.

1892c "A Zuni Folk Tale of the Underworld." *Journal of American Folklore* 5: 49–56.

1893a "The Giant Cloud-Swallower." *Archaeologist* 1: 241–44.

1893b "Commentary of a Zuni Familiar." In Edna Dean Proctor, *The Song of the Ancient People,* pp. 25–49. New York: Houghton Mifflin Co.

1894a "The Germ of Shore-Land Pottery: An Experimental Study." In *Memoirs of the International Congress of Anthropologists,* pp. 217–34. Chicago.

1894b "Keresan Indians." In *Johnson's Universal Cyclopaedia,* vol. 4. New York.

1894c "Primitive Copper Working: An Experimental Study." *American Anthropologist* 7: 93–117.

1895a "Pueblo Indians or Pueblos." In *Johnson's Universal Cyclopaedia,* vol. 6. New York.

1895b "Tañoan or Tanoan Indians." In *Johnson's Universal Cyclopaedia,* vol. 8. New York.

1895c "Zunian Indians." In *Johnson's Universal Cyclopaedia,* vol. 8. New York.

1895d Review of "As to Copper from the Mounds of the St. Johns River, Florida." *American Anthropologist* 8: 185–88.

1895e "A Preliminary Examination of Aboriginal Remains near Pine Island, Marco, West Florida." *American Naturalist* 29: 1132–35.

1895f "The Arrow." *American Anthropologist* 8: 307–49.

1896 "Outlines of Zuni Creation Myths." In *Thirteenth Annual Report of the Bureau of Ethnology, 1891–1892,* pp. 321–447. Washington, D.C.

1897a "Discussion of J. Cheston Morris' Address ['The Relation of the Pentagonal Do-decahedron found near Marietta, Ohio, to Shamanism'] and Remarks on Shamanism." *Proceedings of the American Philosophical Society* 36: 184–92.

1897b "Primitive Motherhood." In *Work and Words of the National Congress of Mothers: First Annual Session Held in the City of Washington, D.C., February 17–19, 1897,* pp. 21–47. New York: D. Appleton & Co.

1897c "Scarred Sculls from Florida." *American Anthropologist* 10: 17–18.

1897d "A Case of Primitive Surgery." *Science* n.s. 5: 977–81.

1897e "The Need of Studying the Indian in Order to Teach Him." In *Twenty-Eighth Annual Report of the Board of Indian Commissioners,* pp. 109–15. Washington, D.C. Reprinted, Albion, New York, 1897.

1897f *Tenatsali's Leaves.* N.p., n.d. (ca. 1897). A pamphlet of poems, 10 pp.

1897g "Exploration of Ancient Key Dwellers' Remains on the Gulf Coast of Florida," *Proceedings of the American Philosophical Society* 35: 329–448. Reprinted as *The Pepper-Hearst Expedition: A Preliminary Report on the Explorations of Ancient Key-Dweller's Remains on the Gulf Coast of Florida.* Philadelphia: MacCalla & Co. Reprinted, New York: AMS Press, 1977.

1898 "The Genesis of Implement Making." *Proceedings of the American Association for the Advancement of Science, 1897,* pp. 337–39. Salem, Mass.

1901 *Zuni Folk Tales.* Introduction by John Wesley Powell. New York: G.P. Putnam's Sons. Reissued with introduction by Mary Austin, New York: Alfred A. Knopf, 1931.

1907a "Observations Relative to the Origin of the Flyfot, or Swastika." *American Anthropologist* n.s. 9: 334–37.

1907b Contributions to Stuart Culin, "Games of the North American Indians." In *Twenty-Fourth Annual Report of the Bureau of American Ethnology, 1902–1903,* pp. 212–17, 221–22, 374–81, and passim. Washington, D.C.

1907–1910 Contributions to Frederick Webb Hodge, ed. *Handbook of Americans North of Mexico.* 2 vols. Bureau of American Ethnology Bulletin no. 30. Washington, D.C.

1923a "Oraibi in 1883." In Jesse Walter Fewkes and Elsie Clews Parsons, "Contributions to Hopi History." *American Anthropologist* 24: 253–68.

1923b "The Origin Myth from Oraibi." Edited by Elsie Clews Parsons. *Journal of American Folklore* 36: 163–70.

1949(?) *A Chant, A Myth, A Prayer: or, Pai-ya-ta-ma, God of Dew and the Dawn.* San Francisco: Grabhorn Press.

RELATED PUBLICATIONS

Works marked with an asterisk (*) include a bibliography related to Cushing or Zuni. See especially Brandes for a listing of unpublished Cushing material.

Adair, John J.

1944 *The Navajo and Pueblo Silversmiths.* Norman: University of Oklahoma Press.

Bailey, Lynn R.

1964 *The Long Walk: A History of the Navajo Wars, 1846–1868.* Los Angeles: Westernlore Press.

Bandelier, Adolph F.A.

1885 *The Romantic School in American Archaeology.* New York: Trow's Printing & Bookbinding Co.

1889 "An Outline of the Documentary History of the Zuni Tribe, 1680–1846." Chaps. 3–4. MS. for unpublished continuation of Bandelier 1892b. Peabody Museum Archives, Harvard University, Cambridge (another copy in History Library, Museum of New Mexico, Santa Fe).

1890a *Final Report of Investigations among the Indians of the Southwestern United States, Carried on*

Mainly in the Years from 1880 to 1885. Pt. 1. Papers of the Archaeological Institute of America, American Series, vol. 3. Cambridge, Mass.: John Wilson & Son.

1890b *Hemenway Southwestern Archaeological Expedition: Contributions to the History of the Southwestern Portion of the United States*. Papers of the Archaeological Institute of America, American Series, vol. 5. Cambridge, Mass.: John Wilson & Son.

1890c "The Historical Archives of the Hemenway Southwestern Archaeological Expedition." In *Congrès International des Américanistes: Compte-rendu de la Septième Session, Berlin, 1888*, pp. 449–59. Berlin: W. H. Kuhl.

1890d *The Delight Makers*. New York: Dodd, Mead & Co. (Reprinted, New York: Harcourt Brace Jovanovich, 1916, 1918, 1946, 1971).

1892a *Final Report of Investigations among the Indians of the Southwestern United States. Carried on Mainly in the Years from 1880 to 1885*. Pt. 2. Papers of the Archaeological Institute of America, American Series, vol. 4. Cambridge, Mass.: John Wilson & Son.

1892b "Hemenway Southwestern Archaeological Expedition. I, An Outline of the Documentary History of the Zuni Tribe." *Journal of American Ethnology and Archaeology* 3: 1–115.

1893 *The Gilded Man (El Dorado) and Other Pictures of the Spanish Occupancy of America*. New York: D. Appleton.

1966–1984 *The Southwestern Journals of Adolph F. Bandelier*. Charles H. Lange, Carroll L. Riley, and Elizabeth M. Lange, eds. 4 vols. Albuquerque: University of New Mexico Press. The School of American Research and Museum of New Mexico Press.

1981 *Adolph F. Bandelier's The Discovery of New Mexico by the Franciscan Monk Friar Marcos de Niza in 1593*. Madeleine T. Rodack, trans., ed. Tucson: University of Arizona Press.

Barnes, Will C.

1935 *Arizona Place Names*. Tucson: University of Arizona Press. Revised and enlarged by Byrd H. Granger, 1960.

Baxter, Sylvester

1882a "The Father of the Pueblos." *Harpers* 65: 72–91.

1882b "F.H. Cushing at Zuni." *The American Architect and Building News* 11: 56–57.

1882c "Some Results of Mr. Cushing's Visit." *American Architect and Building News* 11: 195–96.

1882d "An Aboriginal Pilgrimage." *Century Illustrated Monthly Magazine* 24: 526–36.

1882e "The Tenacity of Indian Customs." *American Architect and Building News* 12: 195–96.

1883 "Zuni Revisited." *American Architect and Building News* 13: 124–26.

1888 *The Old New World: An Account of the Explorations of the Hemenway Southwestern Archaeological Expedition in 1887–1888, Under the Direction of Frank Hamilton Cushing*. Salem, Mass.

1889 "Archaeological Camping in Arizona." *American Architect and Building News* 25: 8–10, 15–16, 32–34, 43–44; 26: 101–02, 120–22.

Bender, Norman J.

1984 *Missionaries, Outlaws, and Indians: Taylor F. Ealy at Lincoln and Zuni, 1878–1881*. Albuquerque: University of New Mexico Press.

Benedict, Ruth

1934 *Patterns of Culture*. Boston and New York: Houghton Mifflin.

1935 *Zuni Mythology*. Columbia University Contributions to Anthropology, no. 21. 2 vols. New York: Columbia University Press. Reprint, New York: AMS Press, 1969.

Bloom, Lansing B.

1933–1938 "Bourke on the Southwest," I–XIII. *New Mexico Historical Review* 8(1): 1–30, 9(1): 33–77, 9(2): 159–83, 9(3): 273–89, 9(4): 375–435, 10(1): 1–35, 10(4): 271–322, 11(1): 77–122, 11(2): 188–207, 11(3): 217–82, 12(1): 41–77, 12(4): 337–79, 13(2): 192–238.

Bourke, John Gregory

1872–1896 Diaries. U.S. Military Academy Library, West Point, New York.

1884 *The Snake Dance of the Moquis of Arizona - - - with an Account of the Tablet Dance of the Pueblo of Santo Domingo, New Mexico, etc*. London: Sampson, Low, Marston, Searl & Rivington. New York: Charles Scribner's Sons. Facsimile reprint, Glorieta, N.M.: Rio Grande Press, 1963.

1885 *The Urine Dance of the Zuni Indians of New Mexico* (pamphlet). Washington: U.S. War Department.

Brandes, Raymond Stewart

1965 "Frank Hamilton Cushing: Pioneer Americanist." Ph.D. dissertation, University of Arizona (available on microfilm, Ann Arbor, Michigan: University Microfilms).*

Bibliography

Bunzel, Ruth

1932a "Introduction to Zuni Ceremonialism." In *Forty-Seventh Annual Report of the Bureau of American Ethnology, 1929–1930*, pp. 467–544. Washington, D.C.

1932b "Zuni Origin Myths." In *Forty-Seventh Annual Report of the Bureau of American Ethnology, 1929–1930*, pp. 545–609. Washington, D.C.

1932c "Zuni Ritual Poetry." In *Forty-Seventh Annual Report of the Bureau of American Ethnology, 1929–1930*, pp. 611–835. Washington, D.C.

1932d "Zuni Katcinas, An Analytical Study." In *Forty-Seventh Annual Report of the Bureau of American Ethnology, 1929–1930*, pp. 837–1086. Washington, D.C. Facsimile reprint, Glorieta, N.M.: Rio Grande Press, 1984.

Cordell, Linda A.

1984 *Prehistory of the Southwest*. New York: Academic Press.*

Crampton, C. Gregory

1977 *The Zunis of Cibola*. Salt Lake City: University of Utah Press.*

Curtis, William E.

1883 *Children of the Sun*. Chicago: Inter-Ocean Publishing Co.

Darnell, Regna Diebold

1969 "The Development of American Anthropology, 1879–1920: From the Bureau of American Ethnology to Franz Boas." Ph.D. dissertation, University of Pennsylvania.

1974 *Readings in the History of Anthropology*. New York: Harper and Row.

Darrah, William Culp

1951 *Powell of the Colorado*. Princeton: Princeton University Press.

Durkheim, Emile, and Marcell Mauss

1901–1902 "De quelques Formes primitives de classification: Contribution à l'étude des representations collectives." *Année Sociologique*, VI.

Ealy, Ruth R.

1955 *Water in a Thirsty Land*. Pittsburgh.

Eggan, Fred

1950 *Social Organization of the Western Pueblos*. Chicago and London: University of Chicago Press.

Fay, George E., ed.

1971 *Treaties, Land Cessions, and Other U.S. Congressional Documents Relative to American Indian Tribes. Zuni Indian Pueblo, New Mexico*. Part 1: U.S. Congressional Documents, 1877–1967. University of Northern Colorado, Museum of Anthropology, Occasional Publications in Anthropology, Ethnology Series, no. 20. Greeley: University of Northern Colorado Press.

Ferguson, T.J.

1981 "The Emergence of Modern Zuni Culture and Society: A Summary of Zuni Tribal History, A.D. 1450–1700," in David R. Wilcox and W. Bruce Masse, eds., *The Protohistoric Period in the North American Southwest, A.D. 1450–1700*. Tempe: Arizona State University.*

Ferguson, T.J., and E. Richard Hart

1985 *A Zuni Atlas*. Norman: University of Oklahoma Press.*

Fewkes, Jesse Walter, ed.

1891a "A Few Summer Ceremonials at Zuni Pueblo," *Journal of American Ethnology and Archaeology*, 1: 1–62.

1891b "Reconnoissance of Ruins In or Near the Zuni Reservation." *Journal of American Ethnology and Archaeology* 1: 92–132.

1898 "Archaeological Expedition into Arizona in 1895." In *Seventeenth Annual Report of the Bureau of American Ethnology, 1895–1896*, pt. 2, pp. 519–742. Washington, D.C.

Flack, James K.

1975 *Desideratum in Washington: The Intellectual Community in the Capital City, 1870–1900*. Cambridge, Mass.: Albert Schenkman.

Fontana, Bernard L.

1963 "Pioneers in Ideas: Three Early Southwestern Ethnologists." *Journal of the Arizona Academy of Science* 2: 124–29.

Foreman, Grant, ed.

1941 *A Pathfinder in the Southwest: The Itinerary of Lieutenant A.W. Whipple During His Explorations for a Railway Route from Fort Smith to Los Angeles in the Years 1853 & 1854*. Norman: University of Oklahoma Press.

Fowler, Don D., ed.

1972 *"Photographed All the Best Scenery": Jack Hillers's Diary of the Powell Expeditions, 1871–1875*. Salt Lake City: University of Utah Press.

Fuller, Clarissa P.

1943 "Frank Hamilton Cushing's Relations to Zuni and the Hemenway Southwestern Expedition." Master's thesis, University of New Mexico.*

Garrity, John A.
1968 *The New Commonwealth, 1877–1890.* New York: Harper and Row.

Georges, Robert A., and Michael O. Jones
1980 *People Studying People: The Human Element in Field Work.* Berkeley: University of California Press.

Gilliland, Marion Spjut
1975 *The Material Culture of Key Marco, Florida.* Gainesville: University of Florida Presses.*

Goetzmann, William H.
1959 *Army Exploration in the American West, 1803–1863.* New Haven: Yale University Press.
1966 *Exploration and Empire: The Explorer and the Scientist in the Winning of the American West.* New York: Alfred A. Knopf.

Green, Jesse D.
1975 "The Man Who Became an Indian." *New York Review of Books* 22, no. 9 (May 29): 31–33.
1979 ed., *Zuni: Selected Writings of Frank Hamilton Cushing.* Lincoln: University of Nebraska Press.*

Greever, William S.
1954 *Arid Domain: The Santa Fe Railroad and Its Western Land Grant.* Stanford: Stanford University Press.

Hammond, George P., and Agapito Rey, eds. and trans.
1940 *Narratives of the Coronado Expedition, 1540–1542.* Albuquerque: University of New Mexico Press.

Hart, E. Richard
1980 "Boundaries of Zuni Land: With Emphasis on Details Relating to Incidents Occurring 1846–1946," Plaintiff's Exhibit 7000, submitted to the United States Court of Claims as evidence in the case *Zuni Tribe v. The United States of America,* Docket 161–79L. 2 vols.
1983 ed., *Zuni History.* Tabloid. Sun Valley, Idaho: Institute of the American West.
1984 "The Zuni Indian Tribe and Title to Kolhu/wala:wa (Kachina Village)." In *Zuni Indian Tribe Lands Bill: Hearing Before the Select Committee on Indian Affairs, United States Senate.* Ninety-Eighth Congress, Second Session. S. Hrg. 98–892 on S. 2201 (April 9). Washington, D.C.: U.S. Government Printing Office.
1985a "Damage to Zuni Trust Lands." Plaintiff's Exhibit 1000 submitted to the United States Court of Claims as evidence in the case *Zuni Tribe v. United States of America,* Docket 327–81L.
1985b with T.J. Ferguson, *A Zuni Atlas.* Norman: University of Oklahoma Press.
n d "Zuni Mining." Unpublished article.

Haury, Emil H.
1945 *The Excavation at Los Muertos and Neighboring Ruins in the Salt River Valley, Southern Arizona. Based on the work of the Hemenway Southwestern Archaeological Expedition of 1887–1888.* Harvard University, Papers of the Peabody Museum of American Archaeology and Ethnology, vol. 24, no. 1. Cambridge, Mass.: The Museum.*

Helm, June, ed.
1966 *Pioneers of American Anthropology: The Uses of Biography.* American Ethnological Society Monograph 43. Seattle: University of Washington Press.

Hinsley, Curtis M., Jr.
1981 *Savages and Scientists: The Smithsonian Institution and the Development of American Anthropology, 1846–1910.* Washington, D.C.: Smithsonian Institution Press.
1983 "Ethnographic Charisma and Scientific Routine: Cushing and Fewkes in the American Southwest, 1879–1893." In George W. Stocking, ed., *Observers Observed: Essays on Ethnographic Fieldwork.* History of Anthropology series, vol. 1. Madison: University of Wisconsin Press.

Hodge, Frederick Webb
1900 ed., "In Memoriam: Frank Hamilton Cushing" ("Remarks" by W.J. McGee, William H. Holmes, J.W. Powell, Alice C. Fletcher, Washington Matthews, Stuart Culin, and Joseph D. McGuire). *American Anthropologist* n.s. 2: 345–79.*
1907–1910 ed., *Handbook of Indians North of Mexico.* 2 vols. Bureau of American Ethnology Bulletin no. 30. Washington, D.C.
1920 *The Age of the Zuni Pueblo of Kechipauan.* Indian Notes and Monographs, vol. 3, no. 2. New York: Museum of the American Indian, Heye Foundation.
1926 "The Six Cities of Cibola, 1581–1680." *New Mexico Historical Review* 1: 478–88.
1932 "Biographical Sketch and Bibliography of Adolphe Francis Alphonse Bandelier." *New Mexico Historical Review* 7(4): 353–70.

1937 *The History of Hawikuh, New Mexico, One of the So-Called Cities of Cibola.* Los Angeles: Southwest Museum.

1951 "Old Dan Dubois." Los Angeles Westerners' Corral *Brand Book.* Los Angeles: privately printed, pp. 137–51.

Holmes, Barbara

1980 "The Cushing Census of Zuni." Unpublished paper, on file in American Philosophical Society Library, Philadelphia.

Judd, Neil M.

1967 *The Bureau of American Ethnology: A Partial History.* Norman: University of Oklahoma Press.

Kennan, George

1923–1924 "Frank Cushing." "G.K.'s Column," *Medina* (N.Y.) *Tribune,* December 6, 13, and 27, 1923, and January 3, 1924. Copies in Cushing file, National Anthropological Archives, Smithsonian Institution, Washington, D.C.

Kimball, Solon T., and James B. Watson, eds.

1972 *Crossing Cultural Boundaries: The Anthropological Experience.* San Francisco: Chandler Publishing Co.

Kintigh, Keith W.

1985 *Settlement, Subsistence, and Society in Late Zuni Prehistory.* Anthropological Papers of the University of Arizona 44. Tucson: University of Arizona Press.*

Kroeber, Alfred L.

1916a "Zuni Potsherds." *Anthropological Papers of the American Museum of Natural History,* no. 18, pt. 1, pp. 1–37.

1916b "Zuni Culture Sequences." *Proceedings of the National Academy of Sciences* 2: 42–45.

1916c "Thoughts on Zuni Religion," in *Holmes Anniversary Volume: Anthropological Essays Presented to William Henry Holmes in Honor of His Seventieth Birthday.* Washington, D.C.: J. W. Bryan Press.

1917 "Zuni Kin and Clan." *Anthropological Papers of the American Museum of Natural History,* no. 18, pt. 2, pp. 37–205. New York: Trustees of the American Museum of Natural History.

1921 Review of Cushing, *Zuni Breadstuff. American Anthropologist* n.s. 23: 479.

1930 "Frank Hamilton Cushing." In *Encyclopedia of the Social Sciences.* New York: Macmillan & Co.

Lange, Charles H., Carroll L. Riley, and Elizabeth M. Lange, eds.

1966–1984 *The Southwestern Journals of Adolph F. Bandelier.* 4 vols. Albuquerque: University of New Mexico Press. The School of American Research and Museum of New Mexico Press.

Leighton, Dorothea C., and John Adair

1966 *People of the Middle Place: A Study of the Zuni Indians.* Behavioral Science Monographs. New Haven: Human Relations Area Files.

Levi-Strauss, Claude

1963 *Structural Anthropology.* Translated by Claire Jacobson and Brooke Grundfest Schoepf. New York: Basic Books.

Levy-Bruhl, Lucien

1910 *Les Fonctions Mentales dans les Sociétés Inférieures.* Paris. English edition, *How Natives Think,* trans. Lilian A. Clare. London: George Allen & Unwin, 1926.

Lummis, Charles F.

1900a "Lost—A Man." *Land of Sunshine,* April, 159–61.

1900b "The White Indian." *Land of Sunshine,* June, 8–17.

McNitt, Frank

1962 *The Indian Traders.* Norman: University of Oklahoma Press.

1964 ed., *Navaho Expedition: Journal of a Military Reconnaissance from Santa Fe, New Mexico, to the Navaho Country Made in 1849 by Lieutenant James H. Simpson.* Norman: University of Oklahoma Press.

1972 *Navajo Wars: Military Campaigns, Slave Raids, and Reprisals.* Albuquerque: University of New Mexico Press.

Malinowski, Bronislaw

1967 *A Diary in the Strict Sense of the Word.* New York: Harcourt Brace Jovanovich.

Mark, Joan

1980 *Four Anthropologists: An American Science in Its Early Years.* New York: Science History Publications.*

Matthews, Washington

1887 "The Mountain Chant: A Navajo Ceremony." In *Fifth Annual Report of the Bureau of Ethnology, 1883–1884.* Washington, D.C.

1889 "The Inca Bone and Kindred Formations Among the Ancient Arizonans." *American Anthropologist* 2(4): 337–45.

1894 "Explorations in the Salado Valley." *The Archaeologist* 2(12): 351–66.

1900 "Cities of the Dead." *Land of Sunshine,* March, 213–21.

1902a *The Night Chant: A Navajo Ceremony.* Memoirs of the American Museum of Natural History. New York: Trustees of the American Museum of Natural History.

1902b Review of *Zuni Folk Tales. American Anthropologist* n.s. 4: 144.

Mindeleff, Victor

1891 "A Study of Pueblo Architecture in Tusayan and Cibola." In *Eighth Annual Report of the Bureau of American Ethnology, 1886–1887,* pp. 3–228. Washington, D.C.

Moorhead, Max L., ed.

1954 *Commerce of the Prairies* by Josiah Gregg. Norman: University of Oklahoma Press.

Morgan, Lewis Henry

1869 "The 'Seven Cities of Cibola.'" *North American Review* 108: 457–98.

1871 *Systems of Consanguinity and Affinity in the Human Family.* Smithsonian Contributions to Knowledge 17. Washington, D.C.

1877 *Ancient Society: or, Researches in the Lines of Human Progress from Savagery through Barbarism to Civilization.* New York: Henry Holt & Co.

1881 *Houses and House-Life of the American Aborigines.* U.S. Geographical and Geological Survey of the Rocky Mountain Region, Contributions to North American Ethnology, vol. 4. Washington, D.C.

Newman, Stanley

1958 *Zuni Dictionary.* Indiana University Research Center in Anthropology, Folklore, and Linguistics, no. 6. Bloomington: Indiana University.

Ober, Fred A.

1882 "How a White Man Became the War Chief of the Zunis." *Wide Awake,* June: 382–88.

Ortiz, Alfonso, ed.

1972 *New Perspectives on the Pueblos.* Albuquerque: University of New Mexico Press.

1979 *Handbook of North American Indians,* vol. 9, Southwest. Washington, D.C.: Smithsonian Institution.*

1983 *Handbook of North American Indians,* vol. 10, Southwest. Washington, D.C.: Smithsonian Institution.

Pandey, Triloki Nath

1967 "Factionalism in a Southwest Pueblo." Ph.D. dissertation, University of Chicago.

1968 "Tribal Council Elections in a Southwestern Pueblo." *Ethnology* 7 (1968): 71–85.

1972 "Anthropologists at Zuni." *Proceedings of the American Philosophical Society* 116: 321–37.

1977 "Images of Power in a Southwestern Pueblo." In Raymond D. Fogelson and Richard N. Adams, eds., *Ethnographic Studies from Asia, Oceania, and the New World.* New York: Academic Press, pp. 195–215.

Parsons, Elsie Clews

1916 "The Zuni A'Doshle and Suuke." *American Anthropologist* 18(3): 338–47.

1917 "Notes on Zuni." *Memoirs of the American Anthropological Association* 4(3-4), 151–327. Lancaster, Pa.

1923 "The Origin Myth of Zuni." *Journal of American Folklore* 36: 135–62.

1924 *The Scalp Ceremonial of Zuni.* Memoirs of the American Anthropological Association, no. 31.

1933 *Hopi and Zuni Ceremonialism.* Memoirs of the American Anthropological Association, no. 39. Lancaster, Pa.

1939 *Pueblo Indian Religion.* 2 vols. Chicago: University of Chicago Press.

Pearce, Roy Harvey

1953 *The Savages of America: A Study of the Indian and the Idea of Civilization.* Baltimore: Johns Hopkins Press. Reprinted 1965 under the title *Savagism and Civilization: A Study of the Indian and the American Mind.*

Pearce, T.M., ed.

1965 *New Mexico Place Names: A Geographical Dictionary.* Albuquerque: University of New Mexico Press.

Poor, Robert Marshall

1975 "Washington Matthews: An Intellectual Biography." M.A. thesis, University of Nevada.

Porter, Joseph Charles

1980 "John Gregory Bourke, Victorian Soldier Scientist: The Western Apprenticeship, 1869–1886." Ph.D. dissertation, University of Texas, Austin.

Powdermaker, Hortense

1966 *Stranger and Friend: The Way of an Anthropologist.* New York: W.W. Norton & Co.

Powell, John Wesley

1875 "The Ancient Province of Tusayan." *Scribner's Monthly* 11: 193–213. Facsimile reprint with introduction by Lollie W. Campbell. Palmer Lake, Colo.: Filter Press, 1972.

1881–1904 "Report of the Director." In Bureau of American Ethnology *Annual Reports,* vols. 1–21.

Pueblo of Zuni
1973a *A Glossary of Common Zuni Terms.* The Pueblo of Zuni.
1973b *The Zunis: Experiences and Descriptions.* The Pueblo of Zuni.

Quam, Alvina, trans.
1972 *The Zunis: Self-portrayals* by the Zuni People. Albuquerque: University of New Mexico Press.

Radin, Paul, ed.
1942 *The Unpublished Letters of Adolphe F. Bandelier Concerning the Writing and Publication of The Delight Makers.* El Paso, Texas: C. Hertzog.

Resek, Carl
1960 *Lewis Henry Morgan, American Scholar.* Chicago: University of Chicago Press.

Rinaldo, John B.
1964 "Notes on the Origins of Historic Zuni Culture." *Kiva* 29: 86–98.

Roberts, Frank H.H., Jr.
1932 *The Village of the Great Kivas on the Zuni Reservation in New Mexico.* Bureau of American Ethnology Bulletin 111. Washington, D.C.

Rodack, Madeleine Turrell
1981 ed., *Adolph F. Bandelier's The Discovery of New Mexico by the Franciscan Monk Friar Marcos de Niza in 1593.* Tucson: University of Arizona Press.*
1985 "Cibola Revisted." In Charles H. Lange, ed., *Southwestern Culture History: Collected Papers in Honor of Albert H. Schroeder.* The Archaeological Society of New Mexico, no. 10. Santa Fe: The Ancient City Press.*

Saxton, Russell S.
1981 "'The Truth About the Pueblo Indians': Bandelier's *Delight Makers.*" *New Mexico Historical Review* 56(3): 261–84.

Scully, Vincent
1975 *Pueblo: Mountain, Village, Dance.* New York: Viking Press.

Simpson, James Harvey
1850 "Journal of a Military Reconnaissance from Santa Fe, New Mexico, to the Navaho Country, Made with Troops under Command of Brevet Lieutenant Colonel John M. Washington, Chief of the Ninth Military Department and Governor of New Mexico, in 1849." U.S. 31st Cong., 1st Sess., Sen. Ex. Doc. 64, pp. 55–168. Washington, D.C.
1872 "Coronado's March in Search of the 'Seven Cities of Cibola' and Discussion of Their Probable Location." In *Annual Report of the Smithsonian Institution, 1869,* pp. 309–40. Washington, D.C.

Sitgreaves, L.
1853 *Report of an Expedition down the Zuni and Colorado Rivers.* U.S. 32nd Cong., 1st Sess., Sen. Doc. 59. Washington, D.C.

Smith, Watson, and John M. Roberts
1954 *Zuni Law: A Field of Values.* With an Appendix by Stanley Newman: "A Practical Zuni Orthography." Reports of the Rimrock Project, Values Series no. 4. Harvard University, Papers of the Peabody Museum of Archaeology and Ethnology, vol. 43, no. 1. Cambridge, Mass.: The Museum.*

Smith, Watson, Richard Woodbury, and Natalie F.S. Woodbury
1966 *The Excavation of Hawikuh by Frederick Webb Hodge: Report of the Hendricks-Hodge Expedition, 1917–1923.* Contribution from the Museum of the American Indian, Heye Foundation, vol. 20. New York: Museum of the American Indian, Heye Foundation.

Spicer, Edward H.
1962 *Cycles of Conquest: The Impact of Spain, Mexico, and the United States on the Indians of the Southwest, 1533–1960.* Tucson: University of Arizona Press.*

Spier, Leslie
1917a "An Outline for a Chronology of Zuni Ruins," *Anthropological Papers of the American Museum of Natural History,* vol. 18, pt. 3, pp. 205–331. New York.
1917b "Zuni Chronology." In *Proceedings of the National Academy of Sciences* 3: 280–83.
1918 "Notes on Some Little Colorado Ruins." In *Anthropological Papers of the American Museum of Natural History,* vol. 18, pt. 4, pp. 333–62.
1928 "Havasupai Ethnography." In *Anthropological Papers of the American Museum of Natural History,* vol. 29, pt. 3, pp. 81–392.

Stegner, Wallace
1954 *Beyond the Hundredth Meridian: John Wesley Powell and the Second Opening of the West.* Boston: Houghton Mifflin Co.

Stephen, Alexander M.
1936 *Hopi Journal of Alexander M. Stephen.* Elsie Clews Parsons, ed. 2 vols. Columbia University Contributions to Anthropology 23. New York: Columbia University Press.

Stevenson, James
1883 "Illustrated Catalogue of the Collections Obtained from the Indians of New Mexico and Arizona in 1879, [and] from the Indians of New Mexico in 1880." In *Second Annual Report of the Bureau of Ethnology, 1880–1881,* pp. 307–465. Washington, D.C.
1884 "Illustrated Catalogue of the Collections Obtained from the Pueblos of Zuni, New Mexico, and Wolpi, Arizona, in 1881." In *Third Annual Report of the Bureau of Ethnology, 1881–1882,* pp. 511–94. Washington, D.C.

Stevenson, Matilda
1881 *Zuni and the Zunians.* Washington, D.C.
1887 "The Religious Life of the Zuni Child." In *Fifth Annual Report of the Bureau of Ethnology, 1883–1884.* Washington, D.C.
1904 "The Zuni Indians: Their Mythology, Esoteric Fraternities, and Ceremonies." In *Twenty-Third Annual Report of the Bureau of American Ethnology, 1901–1902.* Washington, D.C.
1915 "Ethnobotany of the Zuni Indians." In *Thirtieth Annual Report of the Bureau of American Ethnology, 1908–1909.* Washington, D.C.

Stocking, George W., Jr.
1967 "Anthropologists and Historians as Historians of Anthropology: Critical Comments on Some Recently Published Work." *Journal of the History of the Behavioral Sciences* 3: 376–87.
1974 "Empathy and Antipathy in the Heart of Darkness." In Regna D. Darnell, ed., *Readings in the History of Anthropology.* New York: Harper and Row.

———, ed.
1983 *Observers Observed: Essays on Anthropological Fieldwork.* History of Anthropology Series, vol. 1. Madison: University of Wisconsin.

Sutherland, Edwin V.
1964 "The Diaries of John Gregory Bourke: Their Anthropological and Folklore Content." Ph.D. dissertation, University of Pennsylvania.
1964–1965 "John Gregory Bourke, USMA 1969, Soldier and Student of Indian Folklore." *Assembly,* Association of Graduates, U.S. Military Academy, 23(3): 16–19; 23(4): 16–17, 40–45.

Telling, Irving
1952 "New Mexican Frontiers: A Social History of the Gallup Area, 1881–1901." Ph.D. dissertation, Harvard University.
1953 "Ramah, New Mexico, 1876–1900: An Historical Episode with Some Value Analysis." *Utah Historical Quarterly* 21: 117–36.

tenKate, Herman F.C.
1885 *Reizen en Onderzoekingen in Noord-Amerika.* Leiden.
1900 "Frank Hamilton Cushing." *American Anthropologist* n.s. 2: 768–71.

Tylor, Edward B.
1865 *Researches into the Early History of Mankind and the Development of Civilization.* London: J. Murray. Abridged edition, ed. Paul Bohannan, Chicago: University of Chicago Press, 1964.
1871 *Primitive Culture: Researches into the Development of Mythology, Philosophy, Religion, Language, Art, and Custom.* 2 vols. London: J. Murray.

Wade, Edwin L., and Lea S. McChesney
1980 *America's Great Lost Expedition: The Thomas Keam Collection of Hopi Pottery from the Second Hemenway Expedition, 1890–1894.* Phoenix: The Heard Museum.

Wagner, Henry R.
1967 *The Spanish Southwest, 1542–1794: An Annotated Bibliography.* Los Angeles: Quivira Society. 2 vols.

Walker, Willard
1974 "Palowahtiwa and the Economic Redevelopment of Zuni Pueblo." *Ethnohistory* 21(1): 665–77.
1983 "Photographic Documentation in Zuni Ethnohistory" [study of photographs of Palowahtiwa]. *Masterkey* 57(1): 45–56.

Whipple, A.W.
1856 "Report of Explorations for a Railway Route, near the 35th Parallel of North Latitude, from the Mississippi River to the Pacific Ocean." In U.S. War Department, *Reports of Explorations and Surveys to Ascertain the Most Practicable and Economical Route for a*

Railroad from the Mississippi River to the Pacific Ocean 3: 1–136. Washington, D.C.

Whipple, A.W., Thomas Ewbank, and W.M. Turner
1856 "Route near the Thirty-Fifth Parallel, Under the Command of Lieut. A.W. Whipple, Topographical Engineers in 1853 and 1854. Report upon the Indian Tribes, 1855." In U.S. War Department, *Reports of Explorations and Surveys to Ascertain the Most Practicable and Economical Route for a Railroad from the Mississippi River to the Pacific Ocean* vol. 3, pt. 3. Washington, D.C.

White, Leslie A.
1940 *Pioneers in American Anthropology: The Bandelier-Morgan Letters, 1873–1883*. 2 vols. Albuquerque: University of New Mexico Press.

Wilson, Edmund
1956 *Red, Black, Blonde and Olive. Studies in Four Cultures: Zuni, Haiti, Soviet Russia, Israel*. New York: Oxford University Press.

Winship, George Parker
1896 "The Coronado Expedition, 1540–1542." In *Fourteenth Annual Report of the Bureau of American Ethnology, 1892–1893* 1: 329–613. Washington, D.C.

Woodbury, Richard B.
1956 "The Antecedents of Zuni Culture." *Transactions of the New York Academy of Sciences*, series 2, 18: 557–63.

Woodbury, Richard B., and Natalie F.S. Woodbury
1956 "Zuni Prehistory and El Morro National Monument." *Southwestern Lore* 21: 56–60.

Woodward, Arthur
1939 "Frank Cushing—'First War Chief' of Zuni." *Masterkey* 13: 172–79.

Young, Jane
1988 *Signs from the Ancestors: Zuni Cultural Symbolism and Perceptions of Rock Art*. Albuquerque: University of New Mexico Press.

List of Sources | Permissions

Each of the following items, hitherto unpublished, is printed with the permission of its holder, named in the same line.

1. An Ethnological Trip to Zuni. Cushing Papers, Southwest Museum, Los Angeles, California.
2. Reminiscence, from "Life in Zuni." Hodge-Cushing Collection (folder 214), Southwest Museum.
3. FHC: Two Notes. Hodge-Cushing Collection (34), Southwest Museum.
4. FHC to Thomas and Sarah Cushing (10/7/1879). Hodge-Cushing Collection (44), Southwest Museum.
5. FHC Diary Note (10/12/79). Hodge-Cushing Collection (51), Southwest Museum.
6. FHC to [Emily Magill?]. Hodge-Cushing Collection (44), Southwest Museum.
7. FHC to James Stevenson (10/15/79). Hodge-Cushing Collection (69), Southwest Museum.
8. FHC to Spencer Baird (10/15/79). Spencer F. Baird Papers, Smithsonian Institution Archives, Washington, D.C.
9. FHC to Spencer Baird (10/15/79 draft). Hodge-Cushing Collection (44), Southwest Museum.
10. FHC Note (10/17/79?). Hodge-Cushing Collection (69), Southwest Museum.
11. FHC Daily Journal (10/20–30/79). Papers of Anne E. Smullen.
12. Baird to FHC (10/25/79). Spencer F. Baird Papers, Smithsonian Institution Archives.
13. FHC to Stevenson (10/29/79). Hodge-Cushing Collection (69), Southwest Museum.
14. FHC to Baird (10/29/79). Spencer F. Baird Papers, Smithsonian Institution Archives.
15. FHC to Baird (11/7/79). Spencer F. Baird Papers, Smithsonian Institution Archives.
16. FHC to Baird (11/14/79). Spencer F. Baird Papers, Smithsonian Institution Archives.
17. Baird to Stevenson (11/18/79). National Anthropological Archives, Smithsonian Institution, Washington, D.C.
18. FHC to Baird (11/19/79). Spencer F. Baird Papers, Smithsonian Institution Archives.
19. Stevenson to James Pilling (11/21/79). National Anthropological Archives.
20. FHC to Baird (11/24/79). Spencer F. Baird Papers, Smithsonian Institution Archives.
21. FHC to Baird (11/27/79). Spencer F. Baird Papers, Smithsonian Institution Archives.
22. FHC Daily Journal (11/30/79–12/13/79). Papers of Anne E. Smullen.
23. FHC to Baird (12/3/79). Spencer F. Baird Papers, Smithsonian Institution Archives.
24. Herbert Tyzack to Emily Cushing (3/30/1911). Papers of Anne E. Smullen.
25. FHC to Baird (12/14/79). Spencer F. Baird Papers, Smithsonian Institution Archives.
26. FHC to Baird (12/24/79). Hodge-Cushing Collection (44), Southwest Museum.
27. Baird to Cushing (12/30/79). Spencer F. Baird Papers, Smithsonian Institution Archives.
28. FHC to Baird (1/11/80). Spencer F. Baird Papers, Smithsonian Institution Archives.
29. FHC to Baird (2/23/80). Spencer F. Baird Papers, Smithsonian Institution Archives.
30. FHC to William Jones Rhees (2/23/80). Huntington Library, San Marino, California (ref. RH 2986).
31. FHC to "Gentlemen" (4/7/80). Hodge-Cushing Collection (72), Southwest Museum.
32. FHC to "Whom it may concern" (4/1880). Hodge-Cushing Collection (72), Southwest Museum.
33. FHC to Baird (4/8/80). Spencer F. Baird Papers, Smithsonian Institution Archives.
34. FHC to Baird (5/5/80). Spencer F. Baird Papers, Smithsonian Institution Archives.
34a. FHC Testimony as to Boundaries. New Mexico State Archives. Pueblo Land Grant Papers, Case V: Zuni.
35. FHC to Baird and John Wesley Powell (2/18–4/13/80). Hodge-Cushing Collection (47), Southwest Museum.
36. Baird to FHC (5/15/80). Spencer F. Baird Papers, Smithsonian Institution Archives.
37. FHC to George Kennan (5/12/80). Hodge-Cushing Collection (62), Southwest Museum.
38. FHC to unknown addressee (nd). Hodge-Cushing Collection (204), Southwest Museum.
39. FHC Note (6/15/80). Cushing Papers, Southwest Museum.
40. FHC to Baird (6/20/80). Spencer F. Baird Papers, Smithsonian Institution and Hodge-Cushing Collection (45), Southwest Museum.
41. FHC to unknown addressee (6/27/80). Hodge-Cushing Collection (72), Southwest Museum.
42. FHC to Baird (7/2/80). Spencer F. Baird Papers, Smithsonian Institution Archives.
43. FHC to Baird (7/18/80). Spencer F. Baird Papers, Smithsonian Institution Archives.
44. FHC Daily Journal (7/21–7/31/80). Cushing Papers, Southwest Museum.
45. FHC to William Jones Rhees (7/24/80). Huntington Library, San Marino, California (Ref. 2987).

46. FHC to Daniel Dubois (7/25/80). Hodge-Cushing Collection (72), Southwest Museum.
47. FHC to Baird (8/2/80). Spencer F. Baird Papers, Smithsonian Institution Archives.
48. FHC Daily Journal (9/1/80–10/25/80). Papers of Anne E. Smullen.
49. FHC to Baird (9/18/80). Spencer F. Baird Papers, Smithsonian Institution Archives.
50. FHC to Baird (9/25/80). Spencer F. Baird Papers, Smithsonian Institution Archives.
51. FHC to [General Bradley?] (nd). Hodge-Cushing Collection (73), Southwest Museum.
52. FHC Daily Journal (11/12–28/80). Papers of Anne E. Smullen.
53. FHC to Powell (11/21/80). National Anthropological Archives.
54. FHC to Baird (11/28/80). Spencer F. Baird Papers, Smithsonian Institution Archives.
55. Pilling to FHC (11/30/80). National Anthropological Archives.
56. FHC to Baird (12/19/80). Spencer F. Baird Papers, Smithsonian Institution Archives.
57. FHC to L. W. Ledyard (nd). Hodge-Cushing Collection (66), Southwest Museum.
58. FHC to Baird and Powell (1/13/81). National Anthropological Archives.
59. FHC to L. N. Hopkins (nd). Hodge-Cushing Collection (66), Southwest Museum.
60. Washington Matthews to FHC (2/14/81). Hodge-Cushing Collection (284), Southwest Museum.
61. FHC to Rhees (2/16/81). Huntington Library, San Marino, California (Ref. RH 2993).
62. FHC note (nd). Cushing Papers, Southwest Museum.
63. FHC to Baird (3/12/81). Spencer F. Baird Papers, Smithsonian Institution Archives.
64. Baird to FHC (3/26/81). Spencer F. Baird Papers, Smithsonian Institution Archives.
65. FHC to Powell (3/26/81). National Anthropological Archives.
66. Powell to FHC (4/15/81). National Anthropological Archives.
67. FHC to Baird (4/15/81). Spencer F. Baird Papers, Smithsonian Institution Archives.
68. Edwin V. Sutherland, "The Diaries of John Bourke: Their Anthropological and Folklore Content." U.S. Military Academy Library, West Point, New York.
69. H.C. Yarrow to Baird (5/9/81). Spencer F. Baird Papers, Smithsonian Institution Archives.
70. FHC to Baird (5/12/81). Spencer F. Baird Papers, Smithsonian Institution Archives.
71. FHC to Baird (6/10/81). Spencer F. Baird Papers, Smithsonian Institution Archives.
72. FHC to Powell (6/11/81). National Anthropological Archives.
73. FHC Daily Journal (6/11/81–7/23/81). Papers of Anne E. Smullen.
74. FHC to Baird (6/24/81). Spencer F. Baird Papers, Smithsonian Institution Archives.
74. Matthews to FHC (7/21/81). Hodge-Cushing Collection (284), Southwest Museum.
76. Matthews to FHC (8/8/81). Hodge-Cushing Collection (284), Southwest Museum.
77. Daniel Dubois to FHC (8/9/81). Hodge-Cushing Collection (61), Southwest Museum.
78. FHC to John G. Bourke (8/13/81). Hodge-Cushing Collection (59), Southwest Museum.
79. FHC to General Bradley (9/12/81). Hodge-Cushing Collection (60), Southwest Museum.
80. FHC to Baird (9/24/81). Spencer F. Baird Papers, Smithsonian Institution Archives.
81. FHC to Matthews (9/30/81). Hodge-Cushing Collection (72), Southwest Museum.
82. FHC to Baird (10/12/81). Spencer F. Baird Papers, Smithsonian Institution Archives.
83. FHC to Rhees (10/15/81). Huntington Library, San Marino, California (Ref. RH 2994).
84. FHC to Sylvester Baxter (nd). Hodge-Cushing Collection (97), Southwest Museum.
85. Baird to Powell (10/27/81). National Anthropological Archives.
86. FHC Daily Journal (12/1–8/81). Papers of Anne E. Smullen.
87. FHC to Baird (12/4/81). Spencer F. Baird Papers, Smithsonian Institution Archives.
88. FHC note (nd). Cushing Papers, Southwest Museum.
89. FHC to [Bourke?] (12/12/81). Hodge-Cushing Collection (72), Southwest Museum.
90. Pilling to FHC (12/14/81). National Anthropological Archives.
91. FHC Daily Journal (12/22/81). Papers of Anne E. Smullen.
92. FHC to Pilling (12/24/81). National Anthropological Archives.
93. FHC to Baird (1/3/82). Spencer F. Baird Papers, Smithsonian Institution Archives.
94. Powell to Baird (1/14/82). National Anthropological Archives.

95. FHC to Pilling (12/25/81). National Anthropological Archives.
96. Baxter to FHC (1/23/82). Hodge-Cushing Collection (99), Southwest Museum.
97. Powell to Baird (1/23/83). National Anthropological Archives.
98. Baird to FHC (1/24/82). Spencer F. Baird Papers, Smithsonian Institution Archives.
99. Pilling to FHC (2/8/82). National Anthropological Archives.
100. FHC to Baird (2/10/82). Spencer F. Baird Papers, Smithsonian Institution Archives.
101. J. H. Klein to FHC (3/2/82). Hodge-Cushing Collection (363), Southwest Museum.
102. Telegram FHC to Baird and Powell (3/3/82). Spencer F. Baird Papers, Smithsonian Institution Archives.
103. Matthews to FHC (3/24/82). Hodge-Cushing Collection (284), Southwest Museum.
104. FHC to F.W. Putnam (3/26/82). Frederick Ward Putnam Papers, Harvard University Archives.
105. Baird to Putnam (4/8/82). Frederick Ward Putnam Papers, Harvard University Archives.
106. Francis Parkman to Powell (4/12/82). National Anthropological Archives.
107. Baird to Powell (4/25/82). National Anthropological Archives.
108. Edward Everett Hale to FHC (5/5/82). Hodge-Cushing Collection (276), Southwest Museum.
109. Bourke to FHC (6/7/82). Hodge-Cushing Collection (59), Southwest Museum.
110. FHC to Powell (7/6/82). National Anthropological Archives.
111. FHC to Bourke (7/7/82). Hodge-Cushing Collection (59), Southwest Museum.
112. FHC to Pilling (7/22/82). National Anthropological Archives.
113. Matthews to FHC (7/29/82). Hodge-Cushing Collection (284), Southwest Museum.
114. Baxter to FHC (8/16/82). Hodge-Cushing Collection (99), Southwest Museum.
115. Willard Metcalf to FHC (8/16/82). Hodge-Cushing Collection (84), Southwest Museum.
116. Powell to FHC (8/19/82). Hodge-Cushing Collection (50), Southwest Museum.
117. FHC to Powell (9/12/82). National Anthropological Archives.
118. FHC Daily Journal (9/18/82–10/2/82). Papers of Anne E. Smullen.
119. FHC to Powell (9/20/82). National Anthropological Archives.
120. Metcalf to FHC (9/21/82). Hodge-Cushing Collection (367), Southwest Museum.
121. FHC note (nd). Cushing Papers, Southwest Museum.
122. FHC to Baxter (10/3/82). Hodge-Cushing Collection (97), Southwest Museum.
123. FHC to Galen Eastman (10/11/82). National Archives, Record Group 75, Office of Indian Affairs, Letters Received 1881–1907, 1882–21402).
124. Eastman to FHC (10/21/82). National Archives, Record Group 75, OIA Letters Received 1882–1907, 1882–21402.
125. Eastman to Commissioner of Indian Affairs (10/23/82). National Archives, Record Group 75, OIA Letters Received 1882–1907. 1882–21402.
126. Joseph Stanley-Brown to FHC (10/30/82). Hodge-Cushing Collection (77), Southwest Museum.
127. Benjamin Thomas to Commissioner Price (11/22/82). National Archives, Record Group 75, OIA Letters Received 1882–1907, 1882–21402.
128. Bourke to FHC (11/25/82). Hodge-Cushing Collection (59), Southwest Museum.
129. FHC to Baird (12/1/82). Spencer F. Baird Papers, Smithsonian Institution Archives.
130. FHC Annual Report on field work for the year ending June 30, 1883. National Anthropological Archives.
131. FHC Annual Report on field work for the year ending June 30, 1883—draft copy of pages missing from item no. 130. Cushing Papers, Southwest Museum.
132. FHC Monthly Reports for October 1882–February 1883. National Anthropological Archives.
133. Willard Metcalf Journal. Willard L. Metcalf Papers, Thomas Gilcrease Institute of American History and Art, Tulsa, Oklahoma.
134. FHC to Victor Mindeleff (12/23/82). National Anthropological Archives.
135. W. Wotherspoon to Baird (12/14/82). Spencer F. Baird Papers, Smithsonian Institution Archives.
136. Sheldon Jackson to Baird (12/22/82). Spencer F. Baird Papers, Smithsonian Institution Archives.
137. James Stevenson to Baird (12/22/82). Spencer F. Baird Papers, Smithsonian Institution Archives.
138. Baird to FHC (12/23/82). Spencer F. Baird Papers, Smithsonian Institution Archives.
139. C.H. Howard to Powell (12/26/82). National Anthropological Archives.
140. FHC to Baird (1/3/83). Spencer F. Baird Papers, Smithsonian Institution Archives.
141. Baird to FHC (1/29/83). Spencer F. Baird Papers, Smithsonian Institution Archives.

142. Pilling to FHC (1/30/83). National Anthropological Archives.
143. FHC to Powell (2/3/83). National Anthropological Archives.
144. FHC to Baird (2/2/83). Spencer F. Baird Papers, Smithsonian Institution Archives.
145. Alexander Stephen to FHC (2/2/83). Hodge-Cushing Collection (87), Southwest Museum.
146. FHC to Henry King (2/2/83). Hodge-Cushing Collection (63), Southwest Museum.
147. FCH to Thomas Perez (2/14/83). Hodge-Cushing Collection (67), Southwest Museum.
148. FHC to B.M. Thomas (2/15/83). Hodge-Cushing Collection (70), Southwest Museum.
149. Henry King to FHC (2/16/83). Hodge-Cushing Collection (63), Southwest Museum.
150. Baxter to FHC (2/19/83). Hodge-Cushing Collection (99), Southwest Museum.
151. FHC to Baird (2/20/83). Spencer F. Baird Papers, Smithsonian Institution Archives.
152. Matthews to FHC (2/28/83). Hodge-Cushing Collection (284), Southwest Museum.
153. Adolph F. Bandelier to FHC (3/22/83). Hodge-Cushing Collection (92), Southwest Museum.
154. FHC to J.H. Willson (3/24/83). Hodge-Cushing Collection (71), Southwest Museum.
155. FHC to B.M. Thomas (3/26/83). Hodge-Cushing Collection (70), Southwest Museum.
156. FHC to Col. Chavez (3/24–25/83). Hodge-Cushing Collection (65), Southwest Museum.
157. FHC to Powell (3/27/83). National Anthropological Archives.
158. L. P. Bradley to FHC (3/28/83). Hodge-Cushing Collection (60), Southwest Museum.
159. Baxter to FHC (3/30/83). Hodge-Cushing Collection (99), Southwest Museum.
160. Telegram W.F. White to FHC (4/15/83). Hodge-Cushing Collection (88), Southwest Museum.
161. B.M. Thomas to H. Price (4/12/83). National Archives, Record Group 75, OIA Letters Received 1882–1907, 1883.
162. FHC to Powell (4/19/83). National Anthropological Archives.
163. FHC to Powell (4/30/83). National Anthropological Archives.
164. Baxter to FHC (5/9/83). Hodge-Cushing Collection (99), Southwest Museum.
165. William E. Curtis to Baird (5/9/83). Spencer F. Baird Papers, Smithsonian Institution Archives.
166. T.S. Mumford to FHC (5/13/83). Hodge-Cushing Collection (83), Southwest Museum.
167. FHC to Powell (5/17/83). National Anthropological Archives.
168. FHC to Baird (5/18/83). Spencer F. Baird Papers, Smithsonian Institution Archives.
169. FHC to unknown recipient (nd). Hodge-Cushing Collection (72), Southwest Museum.
170. FHC to F.W. Putnam (5/20/83). Frederick Ward Putnam Papers, Harvard University Archives.
171. Pedro Sanchez to H. Price (5/22/83). National Archives, Denver Federal Center, Records of Bureau of Indian Affairs, Pueblo Indian Agency.
172. Sanchez to D.M. Riordan (5/28/83). National Archives, Denver Federal Center, Records of BIA, Pueblo Indian Agency.
173. Sanchez to FHC (6/3/83). National Archives, Denver Federal Center, Records of BIA, Pueblo Indian Agency.
174. Emily Cushing to Powell (6/5/83). National Anthropological Archives.
175. Taylor F. Ealy (Zuni) to FHC (6/5/83). Hodge-Cushing Collection (57), Southwest Museum.
176. Curtis to FHC (6/12/83). Hodge-Cushing Collection (79), Southwest Museum.
177. R.H. Pratt to FHC (6/13/83). Hodge-Cushing Collection (56), Southwest Museum.
178. FHC to Powell (6/17/83). National Anthropological Archives.
179. FHC Nutria "Interview" (nd). Cushing Papers, Southwest Museum.
180. Metcalf to FHC (7/3/83). Hodge-Cushing Collection (368), Southwest Museum.
181. FHC to Pilling (7/4/83). National Anthropological Archives.
182. FHC to Putnam (8/1/83). Frederick Ward Putnam Papers, Harvard University Archives.
183. Bandelier to FHC (8/13/83). Hodge-Cushing Collection (92), Southwest Museum.
184. E.E. Bartlett to FHC (8/17/83). Hodge-Cushing Collection (75), Southwest Museum.
185. FHC to Sanchez (8/17/83). National Archives, Denver Federal Center, Records of BIA, Pueblo Indian Agency.
186. FHC to Powell (8/20/83). National Anthropological Archives.
187. Bandelier to FHC (8/26/83). Hodge-Cushing Collection (92), Southwest Museum.
188. Metcalf to FHC (10/8/83). Hodge-Cushing Collection (368), Southwest Museum.
189. FHC to Powell (11/4/83). National Anthropological Archives.

190. E.N. Horsford to Powell (11/19/83). National Anthropological Archives.
191. Powell to E.E. Hale (11/24/83). New York State Library.
192. Herman ten Kate to FHC (11/26/83). Hodge-Cushing Collection (140), Southwest Museum.
193. Bandelier to FHC (12/7/83). Hodge-Cushing Collection (92), Southwest Museum.
194. A.M. Stephen to FHC (12/15/83). Hodge-Cushing Collection (87), Southwest Museum.
195. Thomas Keam to FHC (12/16/83). Hodge-Cushing Collection (81), Southwest Museum.
196. Pilling to FHC (1/19/84). National Anthropological Archives.
197. FHC to Powell (1/29/84). National Anthropological Archives.
198. Bandelier to FHC (2/6/84). Hodge-Cushing Collection (92), Southwest Museum.
199. FHC to E.E. Hale (2/17/84). New York State Library.
200. FHC to Miss Cushing (3/16/84). Hodge-Cushing Collection (302), Southwest Museum.
201. Pilling to FHC (3/20/84). National Anthropological Archives.
202. FHC to Powell (3/30/84). National Anthropological Archives.
203. Telegram, FHC to Powell (4/26/84). National Anthropological Archives.
204. FHC to Matthews (6/4/84 and 6/5/84). Washington Matthews Papers, Wheelwright Museum of the American Indian.
205. Bourke to FHC (6/30/84). Hodge-Cushing Collection (59), Southwest Museum.
206. Douglas D. Graham to FHC (6/5/84). Hodge-Cushing Collection (111), Southwest Museum.
207. Edwin A. Curley to FHC (7/18/84). Hodge-Cushing Collection (78), Southwest Museum.
208. Baxter to FHC (7/30/84). Hodge-Cushing Collection (99), Southwest Museum.
209. Bourke to FHC (9/13/84). Hodge-Cushing Collection (264), Southwest Museum.
210. Matthews to FHC (11/4/84). Hodge-Cushing Collection (284), Southwest Museum.
211. FHC to Palowahtiwa (nd). Hodge-Cushing Collection (200), Southwest Museum.
212. Palowahtiwa to FHC (nd). Hodge-Cushing Collection (201), Southwest Museum.
213. FHC, "Search for the Tchalchihuitl Mines." Cushing Papers, Southwest Museum.
214. FHC Note (nd). Cushing Papers, Southwest Museum.
215. FHC, from "The Discovery of Zuni, or the Ancient Province of Cibola and the Seven Cities." Cushing Papers, Southwest Museum.
216. FHC, "Extract from Catalogue of Prehistoric Zuni and Cave Remains." Hodge-Cushing Collection (159), Southwest Museum.
217. FHC to Miss Faurote (2/14/97). Hodge-Cushing Collection (306), Southwest Museum.
218. FHC to Palowahtiwa (nd). Hodge-Cushing Collection (201), Southwest Museum.

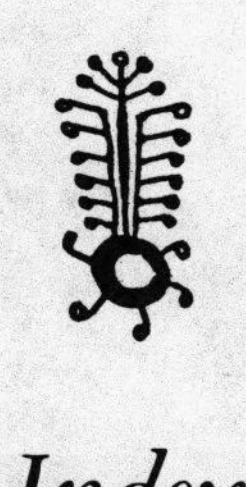

Index